INTERNATIONAL LAW AND HISTORY

This interdisciplinary exploration of the modern historiography of international law invites a diverse assessment of the indissoluble unity of the old and the new in the most global of all legal disciplines. The study of the history of international law does not only serve a better understanding of how international law has evolved to become what it is and what it is not. Its histories, which rethink the past in the present, also influence our perception of contemporary matters in international law and our understandings of how they may potentially unfold. This multi-perspectival enquiry into the dominant modes of international legal history and its fundamental debates may also help students of both international law and history to identify the historical approaches that best suit their international legal-historical perspectives and best address their historical and legal research questions.

IGNACIO DE LA RASILLA holds the Han Depei Chair in Public International Law and is a One Thousand Talents Plan Professor at the Wuhan University Institute of International Law in China. He is the author or editor of five books on international law and its histories including *Experiments in International Adjudication* (Cambridge University Press, 2019).

CAMBRIDGE STUDIES IN INTERNATIONAL AND
COMPARATIVE LAW: 152

Established in 1946, this series produces high quality, reflective and innovative scholarship in the field of public international law. It publishes works on international law that are of a theoretical, historical, cross-disciplinary or doctrinal nature. The series also welcomes books providing insights from private international law, comparative law and trans-national studies which inform international legal thought and practice more generally.

The series seeks to publish views from diverse legal traditions and perspectives, and of any geographical origin. In this respect it invites studies offering regional perspectives on core *problématiques* of international law, and in the same vein, it appreciates contrasts and debates between diverging approaches. Accordingly, books offering new or less orthodox perspectives are very much welcome. Works of a generalist character are greatly valued and the series is also open to studies on specific areas, institutions or problems. Translations of the most outstanding works published in other languages are also considered.

After seventy years, Cambridge Studies in International and Comparative Law sets the standard for international legal scholarship and will continue to define the discipline as it evolves in the years to come.

Series Editors
Larissa van den Herik
Professor of Public International Law, Grotius Centre for International Legal Studies, Leiden University
Jean d'Aspremont
Professor of International Law, University of Manchester and Sciences Po Law School

A list of books in the series can be found at the end of this volume.

INTERNATIONAL LAW AND HISTORY

Modern Interfaces

IGNACIO DE LA RASILLA

Wuhan University

CAMBRIDGE
UNIVERSITY PRESS

CAMBRIDGE
UNIVERSITY PRESS

Shaftesbury Road, Cambridge CB2 8EA, United Kingdom

One Liberty Plaza, 20th Floor, New York, NY 10006, USA

477 Williamstown Road, Port Melbourne, VIC 3207, Australia

314–321, 3rd Floor, Plot 3, Splendor Forum, Jasola District Centre, New Delhi – 110025, India

103 Penang Road, #05–06/07, Visioncrest Commercial, Singapore 238467

Cambridge University Press is part of Cambridge University Press & Assessment, a department of the University of Cambridge.

We share the University's mission to contribute to society through the pursuit of education, learning and research at the highest international levels of excellence.

www.cambridge.org
Information on this title: www.cambridge.org/9781108461481

DOI: 10.1017/9781108562003

First published 2021
First paperback edition 2023

A catalogue record for this publication is available from the British Library

ISBN   978-1-108-47340-8   Hardback
ISBN   978-1-108-46148-1   Paperback

To the *white angels* of Wuhan and elsewhere

For those who aim to find their intellectual standpoint in this world and who, accordingly, are used to viewing the world as historians

Wolfgang Preiser, 1984

CONTENTS

ACKNOWLEDGEMENTS

Every book begins somewhere. This multi-perspective historiographical enquiry into different contemporary modes of doing history in international law began in the ancient city of my ancestors. It was completed thousands and thousands of kilometres away from Seville in the equally millenarian city of Wuhan in China. Between these two geographically distant locations, the research for the book has accompanied me time and again on my travels between and across both Asia and Europe, and occasionally also to North America.

For their invitations during this period (even though, to my regret, I could not honour all of them) and for the time spent together, I am grateful to colleagues at the Pablo de Olavide University in Seville; the Max Planck Institute in Luxembourg; Brunel University London; the Lauterpacht Centre for International Law in Cambridge; Tilburg University; Manchester University International Law Centre; Hamburg University; CEU San Pablo University; the Catholic University of Lille; iCourts at the University of Copenhagen; the European Academy of Yuste; Hainan College of Economics and Business; the Institute for Global Law and Policy at Harvard Law School; the Max Planck Institute for Comparative Law and Public International Law in Heidelberg; the University of British Columbia; the Asian Law Institute at the Law School of the National University of Singapore; Complutense University of Madrid; the China-AALCO Training Program in Beijing; Harvard University Asia Center; the Beijing Institute of Technology; Xiamen University; the China International Import Export Legal Forum in Shanghai; Zhejiang University; Fudan University; EW Barker Centre for Law & Business, Law School of the National University of Singapore; and the Global Human Rights Campus in Venice.

Above all, I want to express my deepest gratitude to the Wuhan Law School and to the Wuhan University Institute of International Law. Its dean, Prof. Feng Guo, its director, Prof. Xiao Yongping, administrative director, Dr Deng Zhaohui, deputy director, Prof. Nie Jianqiang, and my esteemed colleagues Prof. Huang Deming and Prof. Huang Zhixiong, my assistants and students Shi Weimin, Dong Zhao, and Xiao Yang, and many more whom I cannot mention have made me feel extremely welcome in China. I will always be in their debt for their cheerful comradeship: 干杯! I am also grateful to David Kennedy, Philip Alston, Randall Lesaffer, Jorge Viñuales, Anne Peters, David Armitage, Frédéric Mégret, Andrea Bianchi, and Martti Koskenniemi, all of whom I hope may find some consolation in this book for the enduring patience, or lack thereof, they have shown towards my writings over the years. The editorial assistance of David Barnes to help me navigate the modern lingua franca is gratefully acknowledged, as is also Xiao Yang's editorial assistance with referencing and indexing and Dr Fiona Little's at the detailed copy-editing stage. My special thanks also go to two anonymous reviewers of the manuscript proposal for their careful and constructive comments and to a third one for his or her in-effect *nihil obstat*. Last but not least, I am sincerely appreciative of the work of the general co-editor of this series, Jean d'Aspremont, whose early support and advice were decisive in my embarking on this project. Finally, as always, it is a pleasure to acknowledge the professional support of Tom Randall and Finola O'Sullivan from Cambridge University Press.

Excerpts from my 'The Problem of Periodization in the History of International Law', *Law and History Review* 37 (2019) can be found in Chapter 11. Excerpts from my 'Concepción Arenal and the place of women in modern international law', *Tijdschrift voor Rechtsgeschiedenis* 88 (2020) can be found in Chapter 6 and, also, in Chapter 10. Revised excerpts from my 'The turn to the history of international adjudication' in Ignacio de la Rasilla and Jorge E. Viñuales (eds.), *Experiments in International Adjudication: Historical Accounts* (Cambridge University Press, 2019) can be found in Chapters 1 and 9.

This book was completed during the outbreak of the coronavirus that took the lives of so many and brought untold sorrow first to friends and fellow co-residents of the strong and resilient city of Wuhan and, then, to the world at large. It is dedicated to honour all those who strove together through this challenging period as well as to my wife, Dr Hao Yayezi, and to our daughter, Cristina Rya de la Rasilla Hao, who embodies, in my eyes, the quintessence of the perfect East-meets-West love story.

~

Introduction

International law is a result of the past and yet its history is being constantly reshaped in the image of contemporary times. This is so because all histories written about the past are invariably conditioned by the tendency, of which no historical work is absolutely free, to look at past events, actors, institutions, processes, and texts through the lenses of contemporary values, concepts, and circumstances. These new histories, which rethink the past in the present, influence our perception of contemporary matters in international law and also inform our understandings of how they may potentially unfold. However, while all historical research plays a performative narrative function, with a hidden potential to shape both contemporary and future events, this potential is particularly acute in international law, understood as the living legal system of a globally diverse international community of states and peoples. It is in this, albeit partial, sense that every epoch remakes the history of international law in its own image.

The contemporary state of the art in the history of international law mirrors the quantitative leap in academic production and in its wake the unparalleled thriving of theoretical and methodological diversity it has experienced over the last two decades. This development has often been referred to, somewhat ambiguously, as the 'turn to history in international law'. However, it should more properly be termed the 'turn to the history of international law', if only because it has encompassed contributions from several academic disciplines other than international law. Indeed, the history of international law has become a blossoming research area at the intersection of different disciplines and with a great diversity of methodological approaches over the last two decades. Inter-disciplinarity and, in its wake, much stricter attention to socio-historical contextualization have fostered the emergence of historiographical debates hitherto unheard of in this research field. As we shall see throughout the book, inter-disciplinarity and contextualization, together with the globalization of the history of international law in both time and space and the impact of new critical approaches to international legal scholarship are among the fundamental features of the turn to international legal history.

Over the last thirty years, the academic discipline of international law itself has also witnessed the rise of a sophisticated methodological diversity. As a general illustration of this trend, already two decades ago the *American Journal of International Law* offered in its pages a 'Symposium on Method in International Law', understood as 'the application of a conceptual apparatus or framework – a theory of international law – to the concrete problems faced in the international community'.[1] The methods selected by the authors included legal positivism; the New Haven School; international legal process; critical legal studies; international law and international relations; feminist jurisprudence; and law and economics, to which 'Third World Approaches to International Law'.[2] was later added. More recently, the volume *Research Methodologies in EU and International Law* (2011) offered a much wider list of 'theories, methodology [and] approaches', which its authors used 'to some extent . . . synonymously'.[3] This time, the list proposed included natural law; legal positivism; liberalism; cosmopolitanism; constitutionalism; new governance; idealism; Marxism; feminism; queer theory; postcolonial theory; critical theory; law and international relations/political science, within which were liberalism and constructivism; law and economics; law and sociology; law and history; law and geography; and law and literature.

More recently still, the *Oxford Handbook of the Theory of International Law* (2016)[4] presented a list of 'approaches' to international law with chapters on natural law in international legal theory; Marxist approaches to international law; realist approaches; constructivism and the politics of international law; international signs law; moral philosophy and international law; Yale's policy science and international law; international law and economics; liberal internationalism; feminist approaches to international law; cosmopolitanism and international law;

---

[1] Steven R. Ratner and Anne-Marie Slaughter, 'Appraising the methods of international law: a prospectus for readers' (1999) 93 *American Journal of International Law* 291–302 at 292.
[2] Steven R. Ratner and Anne-Marie Slaughter (eds.), *The Methods of International Law* (Washington, DC: American Society of International Law, 2004).
[3] Robert Cryer, Tamara Hervey, and Bal Sokhi-Bulley, *Research Methodologies in EU and International Law* (Oxford: Hart Publishing, 2011), p. 5.
[4] Anne Orford and Florian Hoffmann with Martin Clark (eds.), *The Oxford Handbook of the Theory of International Law* (Oxford: Oxford University Press, 2016).

global administrative law; and deliberative democracy. Another relevant recent reference is *International Law Theories: An Inquiry into Different Ways of Thinking* (2016),[5] in which the author analytically reviews the following 'international law theories': traditional approaches; constitutionalism; Marxism; the New Haven school and policy-oriented jurisprudence; international relations theory; social science methodology; critical legal studies; the Helsinki school; feminist approaches; 'Third World' approaches; legal pluralism; social idealism; law and economics; and law and literature. Last but not least, it is also worthwhile mentioning the second edition of *International Law and World Order* (2017). This examines the classical realist approach of Hans Morgenthau, the policy-oriented approach of Myres McDougal and Harold Lasswell, the world order model approach of Richard Falk, the feminist approach of Hilary Charlesworth and Christine Chinkin, and the 'new approaches' of David Kennedy and Martti Koskenniemi alongside the author's own 'Integrated Marxist Approach to International Law', which combines '*particular versions*' of Marxism, socialist feminism, and postcolonialism.[6]

However, the study of the history of international law is not merely influenced by international law theories, methods, and approaches that have impacted the disciplinary matrix of international law and other disciplines in recent decades. Even when the history of international law is written by academically trained and professional international law scholars, their studies are also influenced by a series of methods and approaches more generally associated with other academic traditions. When assessing the sheer background methodological diversity informing international legal history today, it is, however, often glossed over that when the history of international law is written by academics who have been trained and/or hold academic positions in other disciplines, their treatment brings a different set of methods, perspectives, and overall background disciplinary knowledge to its study. This usually encompasses an attachment to the conventions of their respective research fields and a tendency to organize historical inquiries around the demands of contemporary debates and the trends of thought within them.

[5] Andrea Bianchi, *International Law Theories: An Inquiry into Different Ways of Thinking* (Oxford: Oxford University Press, 2016).
[6] Bhupinder S. Chimni, *International Law and World Order: A Critique of Contemporary Approaches*, 2nd ed. (Cambridge, UK: Cambridge University Press, 2017), p. 2.

A good overview of the methodological diversity underlying fields adjacent to the history of international law, such as that of legal history, is offered by *The Oxford Handbook of Legal History* (2018).[7] Under the heading 'approaches and perspectives', one finds there law as social history; legal history as political history; the intellectual history of law; legal history as doctrinal history; historical method in the study of law and culture; legal history as economic history; legal history as the history of legal texts; archival legal history; quantitative legal history; Marxist legal history; structuralist and post-structuralist legal history; critical legal history; feminist historiography of law; and critical race theory and the political uses of legal history. As for the larger field of history itself, a widely used abridged introduction to the area, the volume *The Houses of History: A Critical Reader in Twentieth-Century History and Theory* (1999), lists what the authors characterize as the 'schools of historical thought which have had the greatest influence on the historical profession':[8] empiricists; Marxist historians; psychoanalysis and history; the Annales; historical sociology; quantitative history; anthropology and ethno-historians; the question of narrative; oral history; gender and history; post-colonial perspectives, public history, history of emotions; and the challenge of post-structuralism. Also illustrative of the methodological range of this field is the monumental *Companion to Historiography* (1997), which as part of its extensive coverage of a great array of topics and materials devotes the following chapters to 'approaches': the historical narrative; the Annales experiment; Marxist historiography; women, gender, and the fin de siècle; archives, the historian and the future; world history.[9] Adding to this methodological inter-disciplinary plurality converging into the history of international law as a research field, one should also refer to a list of research traditions in the field of international relations theory. One such list is provided in *Theories of International Relations* (2013): liberalism; realism; rationalism; the English School; Marxism; historical sociology; critical theory; post-structuralism; constructivism; feminism; green politics; international political theory.[10]

---

[7] Markus Dirk Dubber and Christopher L. Tomlins (eds.), *The Oxford Handbook of Legal History* (Oxford: Oxford University Press, 2018).

[8] Anna Green and Kathleen Troup, *The Houses of History: A Critical Reader in Twentieth-Century History and Theory*, 2nd ed. (Manchester: Manchester University Press, 2016), preface.

[9] Michael Bentley (ed.), *Companion to Historiography* (New York: Routledge, 1997).

[10] Scott Burchill and Andrew Linklater (eds.), *Theories of International Relations*, 5th ed. (London: Macmillan, 2013).

INTRODUCTION   5

The list of methods, theories, and approaches underlying the writing of
the history of international law might be extended, and yet, despite this
booming diversity of methodological backgrounds in contemporary
scholarship on the history of international law, the literature has
remained relatively silent on the question of how the methods,
approaches, and theories of international law are intersecting with other
disciplinary approaches and methods in the writing of international legal
history.[11] To put it somewhat differently, as of yet no attempt has been
made to analytically map the broad intellectual isthmus between the
methodological diversity in the background disciplines referred to, international law included, and the history of international law. While the
only two existing multi-authored general volumes on the history of
international law contain valuable reflections on method, they are not
structured around a list of methods or approaches to the history of
international law.[12]

For all these reasons, choices and judgement calls need to be made
regarding inclusions and exclusions in any minimally illustrative list of
contemporary approaches to the history of international law or, to
borrow from David Bederman, 'styles of international legal historiography'.[13] Indeed, the list of approaches offered in this book is invariably
arbitrary and, moreover, avowedly informed by the author's own relative
scholarly position as a generalist international law scholar. This mention
of the author's relative academic position in this context is not so much
included as a *captatio benevolentiae* addressed to my 'hypocrite lecteur, –
mon semblable, – mon frère!', to quote from Charles Baudelaire's preface
to his *Les fleurs du mal* (1857). Instead, it is included in order to indicate
that, by exclusion, the present selection has not been informed by the
author's relative scholarly position as a legal historian, historian of

---

[11] Valentina Vadi very briefly describes 'seven major methods and/or approaches to international legal historiography': (1) Structuralism; (2) Post-structuralism; (3)
Contextualism; (4) Textualism; (5) Critical Legal Studies; (6) Third World Approaches
to International Law; and (7) Law and Society. See Valentina Vadi, 'International law and
its histories: methodological risks and opportunities' (2017) 58 *Harvard International
Law Journal* 311–352 at 335–339.

[12] Alexander Orakhelashvili (ed.), *Research Handbook of the Theory and History of
International Law* (Cheltenham: Edward Elgar Publishing, 2011); Bardo Fassbender
and Anne Peters (eds.), *The Oxford Handbook of the History of International Law*
(Oxford: Oxford University Press, 2012).

[13] David J. Bederman, 'Foreign office international legal history', in Matthew Craven,
Malgosia Fitzmaurice, and Maria Vogiatzi (eds.), *Time, History and International Law*
(Leiden: Martinus Nijhoff/Brill, 2006), pp. 43–64 at 45.

international thought, or intellectual historian, or by any other relative scholarly position other authors may hold, like that of professional historians by training and craft. Moreover, other generalist international law scholars with a keen interest in the subject may well have structured an enquiry into the contemporary study of the history of international law and some of its fundamental debates around a different set of approaches (and hopefully willl do so!).

However, while the subjective selection of approaches offered in this book has, admittedly, been partly determined by the relative scholarly position of the author as a generalist international law scholar, it has also been informed by a series of underlying criteria. To begin with, these include the most prosaic need to address this multifaceted topic with a level of methodological coherence and manageability within the limited space reserved for each chapter and the book as a whole. Second, the approaches selected needed to account for the different uses and under-standings of history within contemporary international legal scholarship and thus to become a 'recognizable' and accessible, albeit necessarily partial, mirror of the literature in international legal history so as to enhance the book's capacity to structure the debate. Third, consideration has also been given to the aptitude of the selected approaches to reflect inclusive interdisciplinarity. Therefore, for instance, the selected approaches include some which mainly underlie particular theories of international law (e.g. 'normative approaches'), historical trends and/or historical methods (such as 'global approaches' and 'contextual approaches') or research traditions in international relations (e.g. 'histor-ical institutionalism').

Fourth, in selecting the approaches, their potential transdisciplinary appeal in the light of the present development of the research literature was also considered. As in the cases of 'critical/postmodern approaches', 'post-colonial approaches', and 'feminist and gender-centred approaches' to the history of international law, the selection assessed the extent to which single intellectual 'frames' may have had transdisciplinary impacts on international law, history, and international relations theories alike. However, their relative impact on the history of international law is examined mostly, although not exclusively, in each of these cases in the light of their cultivation by international law scholars writing on the history of international law. These remain, and for all the current inter-disciplinary appeal of the subject are bound to remain in the future too, the bulk of scholarly cultivators of this research field. Neighbouring fields will continue to nurture their own traditions of research into the history of international law and in doing so will greatly enrich this inter-disciplinary research area. However, the fact remains that the history of international law is cyclically handed to incoming generations of inter-national lawyers for them to become intellectually socialized within the tradition of the field and that the handing on of the tradition sets the ground for them to continue contributing to the development of the contemporary dimensions of the international legal order in the future of the theory and practice of the discipline. Without the mediation of a transformative event of the utmost magnitude, such as the one imaginatively described by the Chinese science-fiction writer Cixin Liu in his trilogy *The Remembrance of Earth's Past*, international law scholars are also bound to remain decisive for the relatively well-ordered and peaceful evolution of humankind on this planet, and perhaps beyond this planet too, in the foreseeable future.[14]

Fifth, like any, albeit necessarily partial, analytical stocktaking of an evolving research field, the selection of approaches has also been informed by the confidence that they may contribute to the development of a research agenda in new directions on the history and historiography of international law. And, last but not least, the approaches have been selected on account of their potential value to contribute to further exploring the relationship between the study of history and international law. This is why alongside several chapters devoted to the study of contemporary approaches to the history of international law, the scope of others is generally defined by their main theme or object of historical investigation.

The aforementioned criteria have also informed the loose analytical grid that is broadly applied to all the selected illustrative approaches in each of the chapters as a flexible underlying scaffolding rather than a fixed structural straitjacket. This broadly common analytical grid includes: a reference to the approach's intellectual and temporal origins, scholarly evolution, and relationship with other methods or approaches in the fields of international law, history, legal history, or international relations; a reference to the historiographical techniques, methods, foci, and topoi most commonly associated with the approach; attention to historiographical debates and methodological critiques in which the approach has been involved in its interaction with other approaches; and examples extracted from the contemporary literature. Part of this

---

[14] Cixin Liu, *The Remembrance of Earth's Past*, trans. Ken Liu and Joel Martinsen (London: Head of Zeus, 2017).

broad common analytical grid is also an examination of how each of the selected illustrative historical approaches contributes to knowledge creation processes within each of the non-discrete or ideal-type research areas that, in encompassing the study of the different facets of the relationship between history and international law, may be said to holistically configure what the object of study of the field of the history of international law consists of.

The application of this loose analytical grid is, moreover, oriented to ensure that the book remains faithful to its historiographical functional purpose in line with the author's own multi-perspective approach to the history of international law. Multi-perspectivity has been defined by Robert Stradling in the context of history education as 'a way of viewing, and a predisposition to view, historical events, personalities, developments, cultures, and societies from different perspectives through drawing on procedures and processes which are fundamental to history as a discipline'.[15] The ultimate purpose of a multi-perspective approach as understood here is to invite the reader to gaze at the history of international law through the lenses of the shifting kaleidoscope provided by different approaches, whether they are conceived in methodological terms, as reflecting a general orientation or, by reference to broad thematic areas as they explore the modern interfaces where history and international law meet and interact.

Inviting the reader to look at the history of international law from different and occasionally contrasting perspectives is not intended to instil a sense of historical relativism in the reader, although a healthy dose of it is recommendable. It is, instead, primarily premised on the understanding that all the approaches to the history of international law are functionally complementary insofar as they all contribute to the development of knowledge creation processes regarding the study of the history of international law as a whole. They do so across a broad spectrum of areas extending from the study of international normativity to the realm of contextually determined historical facts, or by helping to illuminate different historical times with reference to the life and works of some of the *dramatis personae* of international legal history. Furthermore, multi-perspectivity, as will be illustrated throughout the book, may help us to better come to terms with the underlying rationales, political-ideological uses (its descriptive analytical function), and relative

---

[15] Robert Stradling, *Multiperspectivity in History Teaching: A Guide for Teachers* (Strasbourg: Council of Europe Press, 2003), 14.

limitations (its critical function) of different contending approaches to the history of international law. In this sense, a multi-perspective analysis steers a middle course between, at one extreme, the pull of the *mainstream* which has long favoured a historiographical Eurocentric and normatively oriented progressive status quo in the international historical-legal field and, at the other extreme, the immanent and post-foundational radical critique that postmodern/critical historiography has subjected international legal history to.

Multi-perspectivity is also relevant in this research area because different approaches, methods, and styles in the history of international law are found combined and recombined through different historical narratives. This is because none of the approaches, even when they are solely considered as general intellectual orientations and, by definition, when they are considered in terms of both their methodological and/or thematic orientations, are mutually exclusive. In fact, they may reinforce each other and therefore often overlap in their historiographical narrative utility. On the other hand, contemporary international legal historians are instinctively aware that eclecticism in the service of a good story has become a convention within the discipline and they often interchangeably blend different approaches in different scales and degrees in their narratives. Yet the prevalence of certain historiographical techniques, methods, foci, and topoi which are generally characteristic of one approach may still be indicative of the methodological preferences and ideological significance an author attributes to some factors over others in his or her history of international law.[16] This, in turn, conveys useful information to the reader about the projection of each author's own personal circumstances and ideological preferences, or if preferred, of the projection of the author's subjective world view in her approach to the history of international law. This subjective world view may also go as far as colouring (on occasion disputably, that is, even beyond the generally accepted but invariably porous standards of professional historiography) the author's revisionist representation of particular episodes in the historical development of international law.

Finally, this book is above all a personal *carnet de voyage* of the modern historiography of international law and some of its fundamental debates and so, like any other travel journal into self-knowledge, an invitation to come to new realizations. While this exercise in learning

---

[16] Gary Y. Okihiro, *The Columbia Guide to Asian American History* (New York: Columbia University Press, 2001), p. 34.

offers an analysis of some the dominant modes in which the history of international law is currently being done in terms of the main historiographical trends and, thematically, in terms of some of its main objects of potential study, it is not prescriptive in the sense of offering a guide to doing the history of international law, and nor does it attempt to map the multiple modes in which this is, or might potentially be, written. Its aim is to provide a more critically structured perspective of the present historiographical and methodological variety in the history of international law in order to more fruitfully explore its research potential while arguing against the stagnation that may come from solidification along strict methodological and/or ideological lines of the present creative fluidity in this research area.

The ultimate ambition of the book lies in its potential usefulness as a compass for those who may find themselves interrogating the historical horizon of international law so that they might read more critically and reflect more functionally on their own historical projects. It is offered with a bow and trembling fingers to the minor altar of the historiography of international law to assist those approaching the field to identify the methods, approaches, or styles in historiography that may better suit their own research intuitions and international legal perspectives. In the understanding that historiography is not the master but merely the handmaiden of historical writing, it will hopefully be helpful to researchers so that they may become spokespersons for the causes that are truly their own, or for no cause at all, or for all the causes there may be, because even when our intellectual standpoint on this world may be different, the study of the history of international law is the common cause of all.

1

The Turn to the History of International Law

1.1 Introduction

The academically popular catchphrase 'the turn to history in international law'[1] is often used to broadly describe the expansion that the research scope in writing on international legal history and its theory has experienced since the turn of the twenty-first century. However, the expression may come across as a misnomer. This is so, first, because the academic phenomenon this byword purports to capture is not exclusive to international law as a disciplinary field alone but also encompasses several other disciplines, namely legal history, the history of international relations, the history of political thought, and history, which as a discipline has for some time now been engaged in its own 'international turn'.[2] Therefore to reflect the growingly interdisciplinary cultivation of the history of international law,[3] which partly accounts for some of its contemporary features, including a new set of historiographical and methodological debates and interdisciplinary dialogues, the recent expansion and diversification experienced by this research field may be more adequately described as a 'turn to the history of international law'.

Second, the idea of a 'turn to history in international law' may also be seen as a misnomer because international legal history cannot be

---

[1] Thomas Skouteris, 'The turn to history in international law', in *Oxford Bibliographies of International Law* (2017), www.oxford bibliographies.com/view/document/obo-9780199796953/obo-9780199796953-0154.xml.

[2] David Armitage, *Foundations of Modern International Thought* (Cambridge, UK: Cambridge University Press, 2013).

[3] The modern term 'international law' is used by default throughout the text. However, terms like *jus gentium, as-siyar,* 'inter-polity laws', *jus inter gentes, jus naturae et gentium, jus civitatum inter se,* 'law of nations', 'law of peoples', *jus publicum europaeum, droit public de l'Europe* and its translations in different languages, which like *Volkerrecht* may echo earlier historical terminology, may be found used throughout the book in particular historically situated contexts. The terms 'history of international law' and 'international legal history' are used synonymously throughout the book.

disentangled from international law as a historically embedded area of the social sciences. International legal history is, at all times, lurking behind, embedded in, intertwined with, and, overall, permeating everything international law has consisted or may be said to consist of. The intertwinedness of the past in international legal practice and the academic teachings of publicists results in a sheer impossibility of drawing a strict clear-cut disciplinary separation between international law and international legal history. In this sense, the field of international law has always been, both in its practical and academic dimensions, 'already turned' towards history; or, if preferred, international law is in both practice and in theory nothing but its own history 'turned' forward. With these caveats in mind, international legal scholarship has, nonetheless, long included a hitherto relatively marginal knowledge area commonly known as 'the history of international law' to which we will now turn our attention.

A standard definition of the scope of the history of international law characterizes it, according to Valentina Vadi, as 'the field of study that examines the evolution of public international law and investigates state practice, the development of legal concepts and theories, and the life and work of its makers'.[4] This standard definition, which is based on a selection of potential themes or objects of historical investigation, broadly corresponds to the tripartite classification of historical studies as 'the history of events, the history of concepts and the history of individual people'.[5] This standard definition of the research scope of international legal history is summarily indicative and may, therefore, be analytically useful in examining the contemporary state of research in the art of the history of international law across different areas today. However, it still constitutes only a partial delimitation of the scope of international legal history.

This is for two main types of reasons. First, this definition does not exhaust the potential objects of historical investigation falling within the scope of the history of international law as a research field. Indeed, the referred definition puts the accent on 'state practice' and does not explicitly refer to the role that international organizations and a large number of other non-state actors and transnational movements have played in

---

[4] Valentina Vadi, 'International law and its histories: methodological risks and opportunities' (2017) 58 *Harvard International Law Journal* 311–352.
[5] Bardo Fassbender and Anne Peters (eds.), *The Oxford Handbook of the History of International Law* (Oxford: Oxford University Press, 2012), p. 11.

the historical development of its body of international customs, norms, and principles. The expanding scope of the historical sociology of international law, an area which was traditionally neglected by earlier generations of international legal historians is, in fact, as we shall see in Chapters 8, 9, and 10, one of the characteristic features of the turn to the history of international law. Second, Vadi's standard definition does not explicitly refer to a meta-level of methodological and historiographical matters that should be seen as pertaining within the specific scope of the study of international legal history. This setting aside of questions of method and approaches obscures the important role that what one may refer to as the *animus historiandi* plays in the writing of the history of international law. This may be broadly understood as the main politico-epistemological purpose driving an international historical legal investigation.

Excluding the study of the *animus historiandi* from the scope of international legal history is tantamount to disregarding the political agenda underlying the knowledge creation process involved in any writing of the history of international law as something somewhat peripheral to the core of international legal history. By contrast, paying close attention to the political-epistemological purpose underlying a historical investigation allows us to appreciate that some contemporary approaches to the history of international law can themselves be framed as codas, when they are not part and parcel of 'scientific/intellectual movements' in international law scholarship or across other academic disciplines. 'Scientific/intellectual movements' are, according to Scott Frickel and Neil Gross's characterization, 'collective efforts to pursue research programs or projects for thought in the face of resistance from others in the scientific or intellectual community'.[6] Accordingly, paying attention to historiographical methods and approaches in international legal history helps us to better comprehend the conceptual intersections, thematic overlapping, and self-reinforcing linkages between different 'scientific/intellectual movements' in international legal history. This helps us understand better how some of them mutually corroborate each other's efforts to resonate more effectively with common disciplinary concerns,[7] but also how, on the other hand, as we shall also see, deep-seated methodological discrepancies may diminish the ability of certain

---

[6] Scott Frickel and Neil Gross, 'A general theory of scientific/intellectual movements' (2005) 70 *American Sociological Review* 204–232 at 205.
[7] Ibid.

'scientific/intellectual movements' to project sufficient discursive authority in international legal history. In fact, several of the methods and
approaches to the history of international law that have proliferated over
recent decades are intrinsically connected to 'scientific/intellectual movements' in international legal scholarship – including critical international
legal theory, Third World Approaches to International Law (TWAIL),
and feminist approaches as examined in Chapters 3, 4, and 6 – and, as
such, they are overtly informed by political discourses with potential
repercussions for the practice of international law.

In a nutshell, focusing on historiographical methods and approaches
in international legal history helps bring the politics of the history of
international law more squarely to the foreground of international legal
history as a research field.[8] This is relevant because the Janus-like relationship that international law entertains with its history, which has been
the paramount developmental force enabling the codification and progressive development of its norms, doctrines, and principles, distinguishes it from any other area of law. International law, traditionally
understood at its bare minimum as a normative body of voluntary law
based on the norm-creating fact of state consent, is conceived as one
operating within an international society of juxtaposed sovereign states
as the primary subjects of a legal order which is devoid of any international parliamentary legislative power, superior universal judge, or
effective enforcement mechanisms imposed through sanctions by an
acknowledged coercive body.[9] Set in this general context, the historical
experiences of different peoples with international law and/or the narrative constructed of such historical experiences play a significant role in
shaping the manner in which different states, peoples, and a myriad of
non-state actors engage with and constantly shape the international
legal order.

However, whereas the turn to the history of international law is, for the
reasons mentioned, not devoid of potential political effects in the
present, the expansion and diversification of this research field is also
extensively contributing to a growth in knowledge production processes
about the most disparate facets of the relationship between history and

---

[8] See Martti Koskenniemi, 'The politics of international law' (1990) 1 *European Journal of
International Law* 4–32. See also Martti Koskenniemi, 'The politics of international law –
20 years later' (2009) 20 *European Journal of International Law* 7–19.

[9] See, classically, Hans J. Morgenthau, *Politics among Nations: The Struggle for Power and
Peace* (New York: Alfred A. Knopf, 1948), p. 243.

international law. Surveying the modern interfaces between the two, that is, the points where they meet and interact in the light of the great boost known by contemporary scholarship in this area, is one of the purposes of this book.

Section 1.2 below introduces the question of what we talk about when we talk about 'the turn to the history of international law'. Section 1.3 provides an introductory overview of some of the earlier modes of engaging the history of international law while Section 1.4 points to some methodological and thematic differences between them and contemporary ones. Section 1.5 examines how historical writing about international law contributes to knowledge creation processes on the relationship between international law and history. Section 1.6 tackles the question of the uses of the history of international law and lists some of the different attitudes and purposes of those who find themselves interrogating the past of the 'law which Mirabeau tell us will one day rule the world'.[10]

1.2   Some Whats and Whys of the Turn to the History of International Law

The byword 'turn to the history of international law' can be employed to characterize the extension of the research scope, together with the methodological development both in the practice of history writing and regarding its theorization, experienced by the research area of international legal history since roughly the turn of the twenty-first century.[11] This academic development, which has stimulated the growth of historical narratives alternative to the erstwhile historically dominant Eurocentric narrative in this field, furthermore mirrors a new thematic expansion, specialization, and greater methodological awareness regarding international legal history among both international law scholars and scholars from adjacent disciplines.

This development has spurred a gradual process of institutionalization of international legal history as a specialized research area, and, for some

---

[10] James Brown Scott, 'Preface', in Richard Zouche, *Iuris et iudicii fecialis, sive, iuris inter gentes, et quaestionum de eodem explicatio*, ed. Thomas Erskine Holland Classics of International Law 1 (Washington, DC: Carnegie Institution, 1911), p. 2a.

[11] Ingo J. Hueck, 'The discipline of the history of international law: new trends and methods on the history of international law' (2001) 3 *Journal of the History of International Law* 194–217.

even, as an autonomous sub-discipline in its own right. The key characteristic features of the turn to the history of international law include,
other than the rise of critical historiography, the 'globalization' of the
history of international law in both time and space coupled with
interdisciplinarity and, in the wake of the latter, both a much stricter
attention to historical contextualization and a new methodological historiographical diversity. This, in turn, has fostered the appearance of
historiographical debates hitherto unheard of in this research field.

The turn to international legal history is primarily identifiable from
the critical mass of scholarship in the field since the early 2000s. This
post-2000 academic production, which is greatly diverse in both its
thematic and its geographical scope, has been in several languages.
However, with the sole exception of German, where there is a time-
honoured tradition of studying the *Geschichte des Völkerrechts*,[12] English
remains, for its wider greater scholarly accessibility as the contemporary
academic lingua franca, the main medium and epicentre of scholarly
debates within it. The new literature has included a new canon of
referential works,[13] a set of voluminous multi-authored research hand-
books,[14] the release of a number of specialized bibliographies,[15] and
numerous other contributions scattered in academic journals and edited
collections. This growth of a research field by academic retro-feeding is
aligned with well-known standard mechanisms for the production of
knowledge and, in particular, with what Michael Gibbons et al. termed
'Mode 1 of knowledge production'.[16] This presupposes 'a model of
intellectual history whereby increasingly specialized disciplines are seen
as the natural outgrowth of the knowledge production process, which is
envisaged as a kind of organism that develops functionally differentiated
parts (aka disciplines and sub-disciplines) over time as its investigations
become more deeply embedded in their fields of inquiry'.[17]

---

[12] See the extensive collection of studies published under the auspices of the Max Planck
Institute for European Legal History, Studien zur Geschichte des Völkerrechts, since
2001, www.rg.mpg.de/publikationen/geschichte_des_voelkerrechts?seite=3.
[13] Starting with Martti Koskenniemi, *The Gentle Civilizer of Nations: The Fall and Rise of
International Law 1870–1960* (Cambridge, UK: Cambridge University Press, 2001).
[14] See, e.g., Fassbender and Peters, *The Oxford Handbook of the History of International Law.*
[15] *Oxford Bibliographies of International Law*, www.oxfordbibliographies.com/page/inter
national-law.
[16] Michael Gibbons et al., *The New Production of Knowledge: The Dynamics of Science and
Research* (London: Sage Publications Ltd., 1994).
[17] Steve Fuller, 'Deviant Interdisciplinarity', in Robert Froedman (ed.), *The Oxford
Handbook of Interdisciplinarity* (2010), pp. 51–64 at 51.

This move towards specialization in international legal history has both triggered and been nurtured by the establishment of specialized academic journals,[18] the consecration of specialized symposia to the history of international law within generalist ones,[19] the launching of a series of book collections on the history of international law,[20] a more regular devotion of institutional resources to academic workshops about historical international legal subjects, and the formation of specialized research interest groups within the framework of transnational epistemological communities of international lawyers.[21] These factors have yet to become translated into the regular inclusion, some specific exceptions notwithstanding, of the history of international law as a teaching subject in international law, legal history, or history curricula in universities.[22] However, these developments, together with the exponential rise in the production of doctoral theses in the field, contribute to fostering a 'virtuous cycle' of communicating vessels that leads to a gradual consolidation of the field of studies as an academic sub-discipline. This recent evolution contrasts starkly with the previously generalized perception of the history of international law in Thomas Skouteris's characterization as a 'marginal professional occupation, relinquished to professional historians, and considered (at best) of peripheral significance to debates relating to the present'.[23]

Bhupinder S. Chimni has rightly pointed out that 'in each discipline, a certain approach to its study comes to be advanced at a particular historical juncture. Its origins and substance often becomes a subject of deep reflection. The reason is that the timing of the emergence of a particular theoretical approach has something to tell about the proposed approach, the discipline itself, and the times in which it is

---

[18] The *Journal of the History of International Law* since 2000; *Ius Gentium – Journal of International Legal History* since 2016.
[19] The European Tradition in International Law series at *European Journal of International Law* since 1990; the Periphery Series at *Leiden Journal of International Law* since 2006.
[20] Studies in the History of International Law series at Brill/Martinus Nijhoff since 2011; The History and Theory of International Law series at Oxford University Press since 2013; the thirteen volumes in preparation of *The Cambridge History of International Law*.
[21] The first one was the History of International Law Interest Group of the European Society of International Law established in 2014, esilhil.blogspot.com.
[22] Miloš Vec, 'National and transnational legal evolutions – teaching history of international law', in Kjell Å. Modéer and Per Nilsén (eds.), *How to Teach Comparative European History* (Lund: Jurisförlaget, 2011), pp. 25–38. Also William E. Butler, 'On teaching the history of international law' (2013) 53 *American Journal of Legal History* 457–461.
[23] Skouteris, 'The turn to history', p. 11.

advanced.'[24] Indeed, a series of causes may be seen as complementary in accounting for the expansion, diversification, and, as we shall later see, partial thematic fragmentation experienced by the cultivation of international legal history since the early 2000s. On the material plane, the turn to the history of international law has first and foremost been facilitated by new enabling conditions, and in particular by the so-called Third Industrial Revolution, that of the new technologies. The greatly increased online accessibility of digitalized international legal historical scholarly resources in the last two decades has enormously simplified recourse to both primary and secondary historical materials on international law. These were almost inaccessible for most in the early days of laborious research in dusty historical archives and were the least-visited shelves of highly specialized academic libraries often scattered in distant academic locations around the world. Although the new accessibility remains still relative, depending on factors such as geographical location and unequally distributed institutional resources, open-access policies have also largely contributed to extending and somehow popularizing the cultivation of the history of international law beyond the most elitist main access points to bibliographical and archival materials of not so long ago.

Furthermore, technologically driven material enabling conditions since the mid- to late 1990s have dynamically combined with a shifting doctrinal landscape marked by an unparalleled thriving of theoretical variety, methodological pluralism and interdisciplinarity in international legal scholarship.[25] This is what Emmanuelle Tourme-Jouannet and Anne Peters describe as the coincidence of the 'renaissance of historical studies' in international law with a 'certain decline' in 'the methodological primacy of technicism (doctrinalism) and pragmatism in international legal scholarship'.[26] A series of material enabling conditions and sociological transformations have in turn contributed to this background boom of intellectual diversity in international law. They have combined with a large internationalization of its academic poles in Western universities to contribute to an epistemic transformation which, albeit unevenly, later spread into some national epistemological communities

---

[24] Bhupinder S. Chimni, *International Law and World Order: A Critique of Contemporary Approaches*, 2nd ed. (Cambridge, UK: Cambridge University Press, 2017), p. 364.

[25] See, e.g., Andrea Bianchi, *International Law Theories: An Inquiry into Different Ways of Thinking* (Oxford: Oxford University Press, 2016).

[26] Emmanuelle Tourme-Jouannet and Anne Peters, 'The Journal of the History of International Law: a forum for new research' (2014) 16 *Journal of the History of International Law* 1–8.

of international lawyers, although not so much into others yet. Another important driver of the rise in the cultivation of international legal history is the tremendous growth in breadth and relevance of international law and international institutions for the management of global affairs over the last two decades. Likewise, globalization has also prompted an internationalization of the curriculum across all the fields of legal education. This development has particularly favoured the revamped engagement of legal historians with the history of international law as part and parcel of the so-called 'international turn of legal history'.[27] Equally a consequence of the effects of globalization on historical research to the detriment of the purview of 'methodological nationalism'[28] is how historians have also engaged with international legal history in the wake of the rise of 'global history' within their discipline. Similarly impacted by the new 'global' are other disciplinary traditions, such as the theory and history of international relations and the history of international political thought, which for as long as they have existed have shared a series of common foci and topoi with international legal history.

A final concomitant explanation of the causes behind the 'turn to the history of international law' is a renewed engagement on the part of international legal historians with Benedetto Croce's oft-quoted sentiment that 'every true history is contemporary history'.[29] This line of 'presentist' explanation has perhaps most famously been put forward by Martti Koskenniemi, for whom the 'increase of interest in international law's history' was linked to 'contemporary concerns' and in particular with a 'sense of increased political possibility connected with the end of the cold war'.[30] This was the context for the study of history of international law to be seen as either providing direction to a 'narrative of continuation with the past' back to the cosmopolitan interwar project interrupted by the Cold War or alternatively as marking a 'whole wholesale break towards the past' in the light of the new features of the post-Cold War period. Alongside these two trends respectively stressing continuity and discontinuity, Koskenniemi pointed out a corollary emphasizing the background influence of 'a postmodern outlook [which]

---

[27] Vadi, 'International law and its histories', p. 318.
[28] Daniel Chernilo, 'The critique of methodological nationalism: theory and history' (2011) 106 *Thesis Eleven* 98–117.
[29] Benedetto Croce, *Theory and History of Historiography*, trans. Douglas Ainslie (London: George G. Harrap & Company, 1921), p. 12.
[30] Martti Koskenniemi, 'Why history of international law today?' (2004) 4 *Rechtsgeschichte* 61–66 at 63.

does not subscribe to the "metanarratives" that provided coherence and direction to historical writing in the past[31] on the new study of international legal history.

1.3   Engaging with Earlier Histories of International Law

The 'turn' born from a cumulative array of factors has also been justified as a reaction to the incompleteness and flaws of earlier literature on the history of international law. Although international law and its history are practically indistinguishable from each other in both practical and academic terms, the history of international law has, nonetheless, a long history of its own as a somewhat separate research area within international legal scholarship. Telegraphically speaking, throughout the eighteenth century the field of the history of international law was sporadically cultivated alongside the history of natural law doctrines, including by José Marín y Mendoza, who published his *Historia del derecho natural y de gentes* in Madrid in 1776,[32] by Dietrich H. L. von Ompteda in 1785,[33] and by Georg Friedrich von Martens in 1795,[34] and already in the form of the 'first full-scale post-naturalist history of international law' by Robert Ward,[35] who stressed the European nature of the Christian law of nations from a historical perspective in 1795.[36] The academic study of the history of international law continued throughout the nineteenth century with contributions by Henry Wheaton,[37] Carl von Kaltenborn,[38] and François

---

[31] Ibid., p. 64.
[32] Joaquín Marín y Mendoza, *Historia del derecho natural y de gentes* (Madrid: Impr. Manuel Martín 1776); republished by Universidad Carlos III de Madrid (2015), e-archivo.uc3m.es/bitstream/handle/10016/22079/historia_marin_hd39_ 2015.pdf? sequence=4.
[33] Dietrich Heinrich Ludwig von Ompteda, *Literatur des gesammten sowol naturlichen als positiven Volkerrechts*, 2 vols. (Regensburg: Montags Regensburg, 1785).
[34] Georg Friedrich von Martens, *Summary of the Law of Nations*, trans. William Cobbett (Philadelphia: Thomas Bradford, 1795).
[35] Martti Koskenniemi, 'A history of international law histories', in Bardo Fassbender and Anne Peters (eds), *The Oxford Handbook of the History of International Law* (Oxford: Oxford University Press, 2012), pp. 943–971 at 951.
[36] Robert P. Ward, *An Inquiry into the Foundations and Origins of the Law of Nations from the Times of the Greeks and the Romans to the Age of Grotius*, 2 vols. (London: Butterworth, 1795).
[37] Henry Wheaton, *Histoire du progrès des droits de gens depuis la Paix de Westphalie jusqu'au Congrès de Vienne* (Leipzig: Brokhaus, 1841).
[38] Baron Carl Kaltenborn von Stachau, *Vorläufer des Hugo Grotius auf dem Gebiete des ius naturae et gentium* (Leipzig: G. Mayer, 1848).

Laurent.[39] It increased in importance during the last third of the nineteenth century, coinciding with a time when the study of both history and of law at the national level were tied to the European national state-building project and became professionalized as academic disciplines in universities across Europe and the Americas and, incipiently, in some Asian countries too.

The academic professionalization of international law, and by extension of the cultivation of the history of international law at this time, also responded to the transnational disciplinary galvanizing establishment of the first international law epistemological associations, the Institut de droit international (IDI) and the Association for the Reform and Codification of the Law of Nations (later renamed International Law Association) in Ghent and Brussels respectively in 1873. This is the context in which, as Jean d'Aspremont notes, 'providing a disciplinary history for international law proved a conscious way to confirm the maturity and respectability, identity, and scientificity of the field, entrench it in a tradition and make it universal'.[40] An important initial vector for the early development of the history of international law was, correspondingly, the search for the historical and intellectual origins of international law. An array of academic publications sought to investigate this during the 1880s, 1890s, and early twentieth century, including by authors such as Carlos Calvo[41] and Ernest Nys,[42] the latter of whom Martti Koskenniemi has considered the 'first professional historian of international law'.[43] This quest for the intellectual origins and historical foundations of the new discipline became, however, mostly conflated in practice with what would come to be known as the contest between the 'founding fathers' of international law.

Underlying the debate on the 'founding fathers' lay a consensus among late nineteenth-century international law scholars on the importance of investigating the forerunners of Grotius,[44] who until the third part of the

---

[39] François Laurent, *Histoire des droits des gens et relations internationales*, 18 vols. (Paris: Durand, 1951).

[40] Jean d'Aspremont, 'Critical histories of international law and the repression of disciplinary imagination' (2019) 7 *London Review of International Law* 89–115 at 98–99.

[41] Carlos Calvo, *Le droit international théorique et pratique précédé d'un exposé historique des progrès de la science du droit des gens*, 6 vols. (Paris: A. Rousseau, 1887–96).

[42] Ernest Nys, *Les origines de droit international* (Brussels: A. Castaigne, 1894).

[43] Koskenniemi, 'A history', p. 943.

[44] See further Ignacio de la Rasilla, 'Grotian revivals in the history and theory of international law', in Randall Lesaffer and Janne Nijman (eds.), *The Cambridge Companion to Hugo Grotius* (in press).

century had been widely regarded as, Peter Haggenmacher notes, 'the founder of the discipline and, in principle, its only founder'[45] on account of his three-volume treatise on the rights and duties of nations in times of war and its aftermath, *De iure pacis ac belli* of 1625. Grotius's unquestioned status as the 'father' of international law, which was buttressed by his central role in all discussions on the law of nations by successive authors and by his constant presence in all early historical accounts of the discipline, began to change with the discovery of the unpublished manuscript of *De jure praedae* in 1864. This *Law of Prize and Booty* was a brief that Grotius prepared at the behest of the Dutch East India Company (Vereenigde Oost-Indische Compagnie, VOC) to support its colonial competition with Portugal over spheres of commercial influence in east Asia in 1604–05. Its publication in Latin in 1868 made it apparent that Grotius's *Mare liberum*, an influential pamphlet on the freedom of navigation, fishing, and trade, which lay at the origin of what came to be known as the 'battle of the books'[46] over the dominion of the high seas in the seventeenth century, was not an independent essay, as it had been considered since its original release in 1609, but was originally a chapter – chapter 12 – of a larger work. The publication of *De jure praedae* also made evident, as Haggenmacher pointed out, 'the decisive influence of Spanish scholars, and especially of [Francisco de] Vitoria, on the thought of the Dutch jurist-consult'.[47] This contest among the putative fathers of the law of peoples gained further academic credentials when Thomas E. Holland (1835–1926) gave a lecture about Alberico Gentili (1552–1608) in Oxford in 1874 stressing that Alberico Gentili's *De jure belli libri tres* (1598) had been the model for *De jure belli ac pacis* and that, therefore, 'the first step toward making international law what it is was taken not by Grotius but by Gentili'.[48]

Underlying this investigation into the intellectual origins of international law lay a reconstruction of the historical origins of international law in a state-centric vein, retracing it to the Thirty Years War and with it to the central myth of Westphalia. This was coupled with forays into the

---

[45] Peter Haggenmacher, 'La place de Francisco de Vitoria parmi les fondateurs du droit international', in Antonio Truyol Serra et al. (eds.), *Actualité de la pensée juridique de Francisco de Vitoria* (Brussels: Bruylant, 1988), pp. 27–80 at 29.

[46] Monica Brito Vieira, 'Mare liberum vs. mare clausum: Grotius, Freitas and Selden's debate on dominion over the sea' (2003) 64 *Journal of the History of Ideas* 361–377.

[47] Haggenmacher, 'La place de Francisco de Vitoria', p. 29.

[48] Thomas Erskine Holland, 'Alberico Gentili', in *Studies in International Law* (Oxford: Clarendon Press, 1898), pp. 1–39. See further de la Rasilla, 'Grotian revivals'.

early modern age and the late Middle Ages in Europe in search of the origins of the sovereign nation-state. Earlier antecedents going back to Antiquity were also often examined both as a reassuring Western prologue and as a primitive counterpoint to this nineteenth-century Eurocentric narrative. This enabled scholars to bring to the foreground the quick-paced accomplishments of the present and the hopes for a future built on the basis of a positive law of nations premised on the doctrine of the legal equality and sovereignty of the Westphalia model and on the European experience, with the emergence of a society of nation-states that it evoked. This historical anchoring of the origins of international law on Westphalia, furthermore, projected a structural frame of reference into a new universal ordering of inter-state relationships led by Western civilization at a time of imperial competition for influence and territorial gains between European powers in Africa, the Middle East, and Asia, and similarly with the United States in the Pacific and the Caribbean.[49]

This late nineteenth-century carving out of the perspective of the arrow of time always pointing, in Koskenniemi's words, towards 'the transformation of humankind's collective experience into a redemptive future',[50] with Europe and later the Western world as its frame of reference, would remain a long-standing characteristic of most international legal historiography, with the exception of some limited interwar contributions that, as we shall see in Chapter 5, highlighted extra-European experiences, and later, as we shall see in Chapter 4, the emergence of the first post-colonial historiographies in the age of decolonization. Whether it is seen as an instance of a 'providential view of history' along the lines of a teleology inspired by Kantian Enlightenment world-project ideals,[51] or as a hegemonic epistemic framework which occluded, inter alia, other non-European, both past and contemporary, experiences with international law, or as both at the same time, this historiography generally relied on a Eurocentric and Vattelian statist world-view as its background structural framework of reference.

The study of the history of international law as a sub-field of scholarship among international lawyers and historians continued to extend through different waves throughout the twentieth century. One

---

[49] Gerrit W. Gong, *The Standard of Civilization in International Society* (Oxford: Clarendon Press, 1984).
[50] Koskenniemi, 'A history', p. 944.
[51] Ibid.

important driver during an early phase, which extended broadly until the end of the interwar period, was the continuation of late nineteenth-century debates on the intellectual origins of international law.[52] This is shown by the establishment of the collection *The Classics of International Law* under the auspices of the Carnegie Institution on the suggestion of James Brown Scott in 1906. Brown Scott, who also contributed decisively to the establishment of the American Society of International Law in that same year, built his request to the Carnegie Institution for financial support on the 'importance of making the works of the predecessors of Grotius, a proper edition of the masterpiece of Grotius himself, [and] the works of the chief successors of Grotius' broadly available to an American audience.[53] From 1911 to 1950, the project produced twenty-two titles published in forty volumes comprising the original Latin versions and English translations of classic works all written by European writers, except for the first English-language treatise on international law, which had been written by a United States citizen, Henry Wheaton, in 1836.

By the 1910s it was common to ascribe the historical evolution of the science of international law, as Amos S. Hershey did in 1912, as originating with Grotius, and some of his forerunners,[54] together with Westphalia as the product of the almost inseparable combination of 'certain theories or principles on the one hand, and international practice or custom on the other'.[55] This orientation resulted in the devotion of much attention to the works of writers reconstructing its evolution up to the time, which continued into the mid- to late interwar years with several courses by Camilo Barcia Trelles on the so-called Spanish classics of international law at The Hague Academy of International Law,[56] and Scott's own series of works on Francisco de Vitoria, Francisco Suarez, and what he termed the 'Catholic conception of international law',[57] both attempting to bring the foundational myth of the

---

[52] Antoine Pillet (ed.), *Les fondateurs du droit international* (Paris: V. Giard et E. Briere, 1904). See further Ignacio de la Rasilla, 'Grotian revivals'.

[53] James Brown Scott, 'The classics of international law' (1909) 3 *American Journal of International Law* 701–707 at 706.

[54] Amos S. Hershey, 'History of international law since the Peace of Westphalia' (1912) 6 *The American Journal of International Law* 30–69 at 67–69.

[55] Ibid., p. 30.

[56] Camilo Barcia Trelles, 'Francisco Suarez (1548–1617): les théologiens espagnols du XVIe siècle et l'école moderne du droit international' (1933) 43 Recueil des cours de l'Académie de droit international de La Haye 385–554.

[57] James Brown Scott, *The Catholic Conception of International Law: Francisco de Vitoria, Founder of the Modern Law of Nations; Francisco Suárez, Founder of the Modern*

origins of international law from Westphalia back to the discovery of America. Meanwhile, Dutch scholars had continued to sustain the reputation of Grotius by establishing in 1917 the Society for the Publication of Grotius, presided over by Cornelis Van Vollenhoven (1874–1933), who in 1918 published *De Drie Treden van het Volkenrecht* (*The Three Stages in the Evolution of the Law of Nations*).[58] Originally written in Dutch but rapidly translated into several other languages, Van Vollenhoven's book has been credited with having revitalized the engagement with the work of Grotius in the aftermath of World War I. On the basis of a selective reading of Grotius as much as through an instillation of his own moral ideas into Grotius's opus, Van Vollenhoven rendered an idealized portrayal of Grotius as an apostle of peace and the antithesis of Vattel, traditionally considered an early personification of the positivist method. The year 1925 provided a new occasion for the interwar 'Grotian' revival with the 300th anniversary of Grotius's widely celebrated masterpiece. The academic festivities surrounding the commemoration of this anniversary were accompanied by a great number of works on Grotius and his oeuvre in books and international law journals.[59]

This idealist intellectual historiography of international law with its focus on great writers was aligned, as Randall Lesaffer notes, with Friedrich Carl von Savigny's conception, which was influential at the time, of the role of the 'leading jurists acting on the interface between theoretical abstraction and practical application'.[60] The focus on the classics was also influenced by, and also in turn influenced, a revival of natural law doctrines applied to the intellectual upholding of the notion of the 'international community' and the justification of the binding nature of international law obligations in the shadow of the League of

Philosophy of Law in General and in Particular of the Law of Nations (Washington, DC: Georgetown University Press, 1934).

[58] Cornelis Van Vollenhoven, *The Three Stages in the Evolution of the Law of Nations* (The Hague: Martinus Nijhoff, 1919). See also Johanna K. Oudendijk, 'Van Vollenhoven's "The three stages in the evolution of the law of nations"': a case of wishful thinking' (1980) 48 *Tidschrift voor Rechtsgeschiedenis* 3–27.

[59] Arnoldus Lysen (ed.), *Hugo Grotius: Essays on His Life and Works Selected for the Occasion of the Tercentenary of His De jure belli ac pacis, 1625–1925* (Leiden: A. W. Sythoff's Publishing Co.,1925); Jesse Siddal Reeves, 'First edition of Grotius' *De jure belli ac pacis* 1625' (1925) 19 *American Journal of International Law* 12–22. Jesse Siddal Reeves, 'Grotius *De jure belli ac pacis*: a bibliographical account' (1925) 19 *American Journal of International Law* 251–262.

[60] Randall Lesaffer, 'The Cradle of International Law: Camilo Barcia Trelles on Francisco de Vitoria at The Hague (1927)' (2021) 32 *European Journal of International Law* (in press).

Nations during the interwar period. A parallel mode of more normative-oriented writing about the history of international law during the interwar period put the emphasis, as Koskenniemi highlights, on the 'application and development of great principles through successive periods'.[61] This had been already spurred by earlier efforts oriented to put the history of international law at the service of international codification.[62] Although there was some incipient and fundamentally speculative interest on a proto-global history of international law at the time, the great majority of historical oriented works produced during the interwar period, including, as Chapter 5 examines, those presented as courses at The Hague Academy of International Law, were predominantly Eurocentric in scope.

The aftermath of World War II saw another phase in the cultivation of the history of international law. To a certain extent this phase was freer from both investigation of the founders of international law and of international theoretical debates on its connection to natural law, with the development of more realist histories of international law. Examples include Carl Schmitt's *Der Nomos der Erde*,[63] the first edition (1944) of Wilhem Grewe's *The Epochs of* International Law,[64] and to a lesser extent Arthur Nussbaum's popular *Concise History of the Law of Nations*, in particular its first edition of 1947, where the bulk of the writing pertains to 'doctrinary and literary developments'. Nussbaum offered an abridged overview of the main historical stages in the development of international law from the practice of Mesopotamian cities in 3,100 BC to World War II, while still including within it a polemic on the founders of international law in support of Grotius,[65] whose relevance in the post-war era had already been stressed by Hersch Lauterpacht.[66] The most historiographically influential of these works was Grewe's book, which was first

---

[61] Koskenniemi, 'Why history of international law today?', p. 64, citing Robert Redslob, *Histoire des grands principes du droit des gens depuis l'Antiquité jusqu'à la veille de la grande guerre* (Paris: Rousseau, 1923).

[62] See e.g. Ernest Nys, 'The codification of international law' (1911) 5 *American Journal of International Law* 871–900.

[63] Carl Schmitt, *The Nomos of the Earth in the International Law of the* Jus Publicum Europaeum, trans. G. L. Ulmen (New York: Telos Press, 2003).

[64] Wilhelm G. Grewe, *The Epochs of International Law*, trans. Michael Byers (Berlin: De Gruyter, 2000), including the prefaces prepared by the author for the 2000, 1984, and 1944 editions.

[65] Arthur Nussbaum, *A Concise History of the Law of Nations* (New York: Macmillan, 1947); 2nd enlarged ed. (1954).

[66] Hersch Lauterpacht, 'The Grotian tradition in international law' (1946) 23 *British Yearbook of International Law* 1–53.

written in Germany in the last stages of World War II. In the successive editions of his book, Grewe conceptualized his own historical approach as a reaction to a mode of international legal history that had got lost in 'an abstract history of the theory' because it did not take enough account of the 'close connection between legal theory and state practice' nor of the 'concrete political and sociological background' to the theories of the most noted writers.[67] According to Grewe, this had obscured the real division of the history of international law as a superstructure, and it needed to be corrected by means of his influential periodization of successive epochs defined by the dominance of great hegemonic powers.[68] However, despite the now larger focus on state practice and legal developments, the intellectual stress on great scholarly figures and their doctrines continued to fill volumes on the history of international law during this period too.[69]

As the decolonization process and the parallel expansion of the notion of the 'international community' took root in international law, new historiographical trends began to emerge preoccupied with writing back into the history of international law what had previously been left out as a result of the earlier traditional stress on its state-centric and Eurocentric roots. As we shall see in more detail in Chapter 4, for post-colonial writers, such as Taslim O. Elias[70] and Charles H. Alexandrowicz,[71] the history of international law needed to come to terms with the existence of other systems and traditions in other regions and with their interactions with the European world before and throughout the historical impasse of European colonialism. Indeed, absent from the traditional historiography of a universal expansion of international law was what members of those extra-European communities often perceived as an 'unequal' imposition of international law as a foreign Western 'construct' on them. Over the course of the following decades, other international legal historians, such as Wolfgang Preiser,[72] would in turn, as Chapter 5 examines, contribute

---

[67] Grewe, *The Epochs*, p. 2.

[68] Ibid., p. 195.

[69] See, e.g., Albert de Geouffre de La Pradelle, *Maîtres et doctrines du droit des gens*, 2nd ed. (Paris: Les Éditions Internationales, 1950).

[70] Taslim Olawale Elias, *Africa and the Development of International Law* (New York: Oceana, 1972).

[71] Charles Henry Alexandrowicz, *The Law of Nations in Global History*, ed. David Armitage and Jennifer Pitts (Oxford: Oxford University Press, 2017).

[72] Wolfgang Preiser, *Frühe völkerrechtliche Ordnungen der aussereuropäischen Welt: Ein Beitrag zur Geschichte des Völkerrechts* (Wiesbaden: Steiner, 1976).

to setting international legal historiography on a course for ulterior historiographical developments, in particular the transcivilizational and the global historiography of international law. In parallel with these historiographical developments which set the ground for a set of contemporary historiographical approaches to international law, J. H. W. Verzijl began producing the eleven volumes of his *International Law in Historical Perspective*, giving a technical normative orientation to the history of the traditional branches of general international law.[73]

However, despite the precedents briefly described here and the existence of other multiple scholarly contributions to the history of international law, including in a 'critical/postmodern'-inspired mode since the mid- to late 1980s and, in particular, as Chapter 3 examines, through the 1990s in the form of monographs, journal articles, or book chapters that laid the groundwork for subsequent historiographical developments, the field of the history of international law has been described as 'the most neglected area of international law'[74] until the early 2000s. Against this background, the related stress on novelty and the rejuvenation of international legal history as a research field finds justification in the light of the sheer number of new works that have been contributed to it in recent years. This emphasis on novelty and rejuvenation is also justified by the extent to which the 'turn' to the history of international law has been presented both as an effort at stocktaking and a critical reaction to the orientation and/or deficiencies of previous literature on the history of international law.

Three general strands may be preliminarily mentioned as having structured this historiographical renovating effort. First, an element of the reaction against the predominant modes in which the earlier literature was written has involved attempts at re-organizing previous 'histories of international law'[75] into general categories. This has been done, for instance, with reference to the dichotomy between international legal theory and international legal practice. According to Koskenniemi, this allows distinguishing between the extremes of doctrinal or intellectual histories and realist histories.[76] In the first category, which is also

---

[73] Jan Hendrik Willem Verzijl, *International Law in Historical Perspective*, 11 vols. (Leiden: Martinus Sythoff, 1968–79).

[74] Randall Lesaffer, 'International law and its history: the story of an unrequited love', in Matthew Craven et al. (eds.), *Time, History and International Law* (Leiden: Martinus Nijhoff, 2007), pp. 27–41 at 28.

[75] Koskenniemi, 'A history', pp. 943–971.

[76] Martti Koskenniemi, 'Histories of international law: significance and problems for a critical view' (2013) 27 *Temple International Law and Comparative Law Journal* 215–240.

occasionally termed 'idealist histories', are those histories that focus on past learned writings on international law by writers, legal theorists, and philosophers and on their contribution to the development of the so-called science of international law over time. Their origin lies, as earlier mentioned, in the late nineteenth-century debates on the origins and the putative intellectual founding fathers of international law in Europe. By contrast, the second type contains histories with a larger focus on international legal practice and a more direct tie to diplomatic history. If the first category of histories presents linkages with the study of classic authors on the history of international political thought, the second one, while not devoid of an intellectual tradition of its own, is generally situated within the broader context of the history of international relations. Koskenniemi, in implicit reference to Wilhem Grewe's epochal history of international law, characterizes this latter type as histories 'that concentrate on State power and geopolitics and view international law's past in terms of the succession of apologies for State behaviour',[77] and one might add that they periodize accordingly. Needless to say, the interpretive entwinedness underlining this basic typological duality has resulted in many efforts at historiographical synthesis in historical writing in international law.[78]

A second strand involved in the critical revision of earlier literature on international legal history has often stressed its traditional responsiveness to an underlying progressive conception of history – this, as Chapter 7 examines, is the description of international legal history as a traditional companion of a grand narrative of progress[79] – rather than to a critically inspired reading and/or to the application of a strict historical contextualist method to the study of the intellectual and normative products of the past. Consequently, the turn to the history of international law has been partly justified as a reaction to earlier common methodological flaws or fallacies (anachronism, precursorism, hagiography, prolepsis, and a particular form of teleology of progress bordering with Whiggish historiography)[80] all in the name of an enhanced historical

---

[77] Martti Koskenniemi, 'Histories of international law: dealing with Eurocentrism' (2011) 19 *Rechtsgeschichte* 152–176 at 161.

[78] Anthony Carty, 'Doctrine versus state practice', in Bardo Fassbender and Anne Peters (eds.), *The Oxford Handbook of the History of International Law* (Oxford: Oxford University Press, 2012), pp. 972–997.

[79] Thomas Skouteris, *The Notion of Progress in International Law Discourse* (The Hague: T. M. C. Asser Press, 2010).

[80] Christopher R. Rossi, *Whiggish International Law: Elihu Root, the Monroe Doctrine, and International Law in the Americas* (Leiden: Brill/Nijhoff, 2019).

contextualization of the actual economic, social, cultural, religious, and political levers behind the historical evolution of the international *corpus iuris*, its intellectual landmarks, and interpretations thereof. Finally, a third important strand involved in a large-scale critical revision of all earlier literature presents itself as a reaction to the dominant Eurocentric and state-centric focuses and their related topoi (e.g. sovereignty, war, and peace), concepts, and institutions in earlier historical accounts of international law. Underlying this critique is an effort to unveil the geographical, temporal, and thematic historiographical blind spots that ensued from the previously dominant international legal historiographical paradigm, in a new critical, even radical, vein.

1.4 Stasis and Change in the History of International Law

The gradual establishment of a cognitive academic space of its own for the history of international law can be summarily illustrated by reference to several dimensions of topical expansion of the field, which, although incubated in the 1990s, have taken a more definite form since the early 2000s. First, this has involved a renewed treatment of traditional genres and research subjects in the history of international law. The 'general history of international law', or macro-history of international law, genre, which adopts a *longue durée* perspective on the evolution of international law in different places and periods until the present, has known a revival in various languages.[81] In addition, in the words of Koskenniemi, the 'well-established genre' of 'the writing of history as the history of doctrines (or of "the science of international law")'[82] has also expanded, although it is now cultivated in a far more stricter socio-contextualist vein. Moreover, the same methodological and theoretical plurality which characterizes the contemporary state of the art in international legal scholarship lurks behind the movement towards the 'historization' of different schools and traditions of international legal thought,[83] including some which are, historically

---

[81] See, e.g., Dominique Gaurier, *Histoire du droit international: de l'Antiquité à l'ONU* (Rennes: Presses Universitaires de Rennes, 2014).

[82] Koskenniemi, 'A History', p. 965.

[83] See, e.g., Anne Orford and Florian Hoffmann with Martin Clark (eds.), *The Oxford Handbook of the Theory of International Law* (Oxford: Oxford University Press, 2016); Mónica García-Salmones Rovira, *The Project of Positivism in International Law* (Oxford: Oxford University Press, 2013).

speaking, relatively recent.[84] Furthermore, the turn to the history of international law has also manifested itself in a rejuvenation of the intellectual biographical genre, which now includes a more historically contextualized attention to the lives, work, and times of international law scholars. Today, historians of international law make greater use of a 'biographical tone'[85] in examining the different historical contexts within which both international law practitioners and scholars have contributed to its study, codification, and progressive development over time. The turn to a contextual study of the life and works of individual people in the history of international law has developed in several directions, as will be examined in more detail in Chapter 10. However, despite this ongoing rejuvenation, as Chapter 6 shows, attention to the historical contribution of female international law scholars, or more broadly to women acting as agents of international legal change in the study and practice of international law, still remains fairly limited.

Second, the last twenty years or so have also witnessed a remarkable temporal and geographical expansion of the research scope of the history of international law. The classic debate on the 'origins' of the discipline has, on the one hand, been mostly relocated to the late nineteenth century, with a consequent upsurge of related literature on what it has to do with the professional, scientific, and disciplinary birth of international law in the modern sense.[86] However, on the other hand, as Chapter 5 examines in more detail, enquiry into the origins of international law as practice has transmuted into a large expansion of the temporal and geographical scope of historical research. Geographically, the scope of the history of international law has also extended into the study of inter-policy practices in regions traditionally neglected by international legal historians. Temporally, the now larger canvas of international legal history has stretched into Antiquity and the medieval era in a scale and degree of historical detail hitherto unheard of.[87] Historians

---

[84] Ignacio de la Rasilla, 'Notes for the history of new approaches to international legal studies: not a map but perhaps a compass', in José Maria Beneyto and David Kennedy (eds.), *New Approaches to International Law: The European and the American Experiences* (Hague: T. M. C. Asser Press), pp. 225–248.

[85] George Rodrigo Bandeira Galindo, 'Martti Koskenniemi and the historiographical turn in international law' (2005) 16 *European Journal of International Law* 539–559.

[86] Koskenniemi, *The Gentle Civilizer of Nations.*

[87] See, e.g., David J. Bederman, *International Law in Antiquity* (Cambridge, UK: Cambridge University Press, 2001).

have also delved in much greater depth into the modern era,[88] and in particular into the nineteenth and first half of the twentieth centuries. The commemoration of a number of centenaries, and in particular of World War I, has furthermore fostered an expansion of historical writing on early twentieth-century themes,[89] including on the League of Nations. Moreover, as we shall see in Chapters 4 and 5, in the wake of both the post-colonial historiographical challenge and the increasing application of global historical lenses to the history of international law, histories of international law have expanded their geographical scope, mushrooming into 'peripheral' and 'semi-peripheral' regions and nations[90] which were previously little studied. The background influence of a new set of perspectives and standpoints in international legal scholarship, such as those put forward in post-colonial approaches, has furthermore triggered detailed attention to historical 'events' traditionally neglected in international legal scholarship,[91] which are in turn becoming, as Chapter 11 examines, increasingly integrated in 'alternative periodizations' of the history of international law.

Third, the above-mentioned historiographical reaction against state-centrism and related topoi which were dominant in earlier accounts of international legal history has fostered an extension of the sociological dimension of the history of international law. Part and parcel of this sociological turn in the history of international law is greater attention to the history of multiple non-state actors, as will be seen in Chapter 8. This development, which penetrates into the traditional disciplinary domain of the history of international relations, has fostered the rise of histories of transnational movements, transnational private companies (e.g. the East India Company), and non-governmental organizations. Moreover, it has led to greater attention to the history of international organizations,[92]

[88] See, e.g., Randall Lesaffer (ed.), *Peace Treaties and International Law in European History: From the Late Middle Ages to World War One* (Cambridge, UK: Cambridge University Press, 2004).
[89] See, e.g., Susan Pedersen, *The Guardians: The League of Nations and the Crisis of Empire* (Oxford: Oxford University Press, 2015).
[90] See, e.g., Juan Pablo Scarfi, *The Hidden History of International Law in the Americas: Empire and Legal Networks* (Oxford: Oxford University Press, 2017); Stefan Kroll, *Normgenese durch Re-interpretation: China und das europäische Völkerrecht im 19. und 20. Jahrhundert* (Baden-Baden: Nomos, 2012).
[91] See, e.g. Nathaniel Berman, *Passion and Ambivalence: Nationalism, Colonialism and International Law* (Leiden and Boston: Martinus Nijhoff, 2012).
[92] Guy Fiti Sinclair, *To Reform the World: International Organizations and the Making of Modern States* (Oxford: Oxford University Press, 2017).

including among the latter international courts and tribunals, as Chapter 9 examines. However, new histories revolving around the nation-state remain an important component of the 'turn' to the history of international law to this day too.

Fourth, a remarkable thematic expansion of the research space covered has also resulted from the coincidence of the 'turn' to international legal history with what Pierre-Marie Dupuy dubbed the 'doctrinal debate par excellence of the globalization age'.[93] The academic fragmentation of the field of study of international law into niches of specialized international legal scholarship, which is a direct effect of the expansion and diversification experienced by international law over the last decades, has also been mirrored in a parallel thematic fragmentation of the history of international law where each sub-discipline has tended to generate its own sub-disciplinary historical narrative. This process of self-historicization results in a constant search, as will be examined though different chapters, for precedents and landmarks, which authors strive to fit into a genealogy of normative, sociological, and intellectual sub-disciplinary development in conjunction, on occasion, with the historical and intellectual development of their domestic legal counterparts. The topical expansion can be observed, with different degrees of intensity, across various sub-specialized areas of international law such as international criminal law,[94] international humanitarian law or the laws of war,[95] international investment law,[96] international environmental law,[97] and international human rights law,[98] to mention but a few. This increasing thematic fragmentation sometimes results in a series of academic sub-disciplinary international legal-historical tributaries generating their own historiographical debates that flow back into the general stream of the 'turn' to the history of international law.

---

[93] Pierre-Marie Dupuy, 'A doctrinal debate in the globalisation era: on the fragmentation of international law' (2007) 1 *European Journal of Legal Studies* 1–19.

[94] See, e.g., Frédéric Megret and Immi Tallgren (eds.), *The Dawn of a Discipline: International Criminal Justice and Its Early Exponents* (Cambridge, UK: Cambridge University Press, 2020).

[95] See, e.g., Stephen C. Neff, *War and the Law of Nations: A General History* (Cambridge, UK: Cambridge University Press, 2005).

[96] See, e.g., Kate Miles, *The Origins of International Investment Law: Empire, Environment, and the Safeguarding of Capital* (Cambridge, UK: Cambridge University Press, 2013).

[97] See, e.g., Peter H. Sand (ed.), *The History and Origin of International Environmental Law* (Cheltenham: Edward Elgar Publishing, 2015).

[98] See, e.g., Paul Gordon Lauren, *The Evolution of International Human Rights: Visions Seen* (Philadelphia: University of Pennsylvania Press, 1998).

Finally, alongside the quantitative expansion of the literature across the several dimensions indicated, the 'turn' to international legal history has brought in its wake a series of interdisciplinary methodological and historiographical debates on how to write international legal history. These new contributions to the literature have revolved around historiographical issues such as the place of contextualism and anachronism,[99] the role of periodization in international legal historical writing,[100] and the methodological impact of 'Eurocentrism'[101] in the writing of new histories of international law. Contributors to these theoretical debates, such as Anne Orford, have identified the characteristic feature of the 'turn' to history as a turn in international law's 'mode of writing history',[102] or more broadly an engagement with what Janne Nijman calls a *'Methodenstreit* – a debate on the methods of the field'.[103] Stress on the methodological impact of the 'turn' is also present in Thomas Skouteris's characterization of it as comprising 'six trends: a rereading of the history of international law that "provincializes" the present state of international law; a move away from grand Eurocentric narratives and toward global, micro, and subaltern histories; a renewed interest in sociohistorical accounts of the profession; a (re)turn to the archive; a reflection on epistemic questions; and a recognition of the significance of the field's historical consciousness for its legitimacy and vitality'.[104] Interpretations of the turn to history through reference to its methodological impact on

---

[99] Anne Orford, 'The past as law or history? The relevance of imperialism for modern international law', in Mark Toufayan, Emmanuelle Tourme-Jouannet, and Hélène Ruiz Fabri (eds.), *Droit international et nouvelles approches sur le tiers-monde: entre répétition et renouveau (International Law and New Approaches to the Third World: Between Repetition and Renewal)* (Paris: Société de Législation Comparée, 2013), pp. 97–118.

[100] Oliver Diggelmann, 'The periodization of the history of international law', in Bardo Fassbender and Anne Peters (eds.), *The Oxford Handbook of the History of International Law* (Oxford: Oxford University Press, 2012), pp. 997–1011.

[101] Koskenniemi, 'Histories of international law: dealing with Eurocentrism', pp. 152–176.

[102] Anne Orford, 'International Law and the Limits of History', in Wouter Werner, Marieke de Hoon, and Alexis Galán (eds.), *The Law of International Lawyers: Reading Martti Koskenniemi* (Cambridge, UK: Cambridge University Press, 2017), pp. 297–320 at 297.

[103] Janne E. Nijman, *Seeking Change by Doing History*, Oratiereeks, 591) (Amsterdam: Universiteit van Amsterdam, 2017), p. 7.

[104] Skouteris, 'The turn to history', p. 1. For a slightly different formulation where the author stresses a move 'towards sociological accounts of the international system, the profession, and its professional practices, as well as biographical accounts of its professionals or intellectuals', see Thomas Skouteris and Immi Tallgren, 'Editors' introduction', in Thomas Skouteris and Immi Tallgren (eds.), *New Histories of International Criminal Law* (Oxford: Oxford University Press, 2019), pp. 1–16 at 2.

traditional modes of writing history in international law – otherwise, the 'methodological innovations of the new form of engagement with history'[105] – are contributing to a self-reflective new genre of interdisciplinary historiographical literature in international legal scholarship.

1.5   The Contribution of Historical Writing to Knowledge Production Processes

The turn to the history of international law has undoubtedly opened new vistas of thematic and methodological knowledge in the field. In its wake, this has brought the politics of the history of international law to the forefront of scholarship in this area. Beyond this opening of the Pandora's box of the politics of the history of international law, which influences its historiographical debates, the 'turn' has also signified a quantum leap in terms of knowledge creation processes mediated by the deepening of the study of the relationship that international law and history entertain. Three main approaches to the interaction between law and history have been identified in a tripartite typology proposed by Mathew Craven[106] and elaborated upon by Randall Lesaffer.[107] According to the latter typology, which Chapter 2 introduces and Chapter 7 fleshes out in more detail, the interaction between history and international law may be examined under the categories of the 'history in international law', the 'history of international law', and 'international law in history', spanning a broad, shifting continuum.[108]

First, the category of 'history in international law', which largely corresponds to the uses of history in international law and is, as such, largely influenced by a form of juridical functional presentism, can be divided into four levels ranging from the uses of historical materials, normative and otherwise, to interpret, identify, and apply international law. Second, the category of 'history of international law' could in turn be deployed on both the micro and the macro levels with both sharing the

---

[105] Skouteris, 'The turn to history', p. 1.
[106] Matthew Craven, 'Introduction: international law and its histories', in Matthew Craven, Malgosia Fitzmaurice, and Maria Vogiatzi (eds.), *Time, History and International Law* (Leiden: Martinus Nijhoff/Brill, 2006), pp.1–25 at 7.
[107] Randall Lesaffer, 'Law between past and present', https://lirias.kuleuven.be/1856246. This essay also appears in Bart van Klink and Sanne Taekema (eds.), *Law and Method: Interdisciplinary Research into Law* (Tübingen: Mohr Siebeck, 2011), pp. 133–152.
[108] Ibid.

tendency to produce genealogies of doctrine from the present to the past which are often underlined by a progressive narrative of historical development. Indeed, historical writing about international law contributes to knowledge creation processes regarding the production of both macro and micro normative perspectives of the international legal order. From a macro viewpoint, historical writing about international law contributes to the study of the normative historical development of the international legal order both in a *longue durée* holistic perspective and in a fragmented sub-disciplinary sense. In the first case, this evolution is often found presented divided in a series of conventional historical periods build around a series of historical 'turning points' of the discipline which were hitherto generally accepted and are now increasingly questioned and supplemented by new alternative ones. In the second case, it can also be found studied in a fragmented manner through reference to the historical development of each and every one of the contemporary sub-disciplines of the field of international law in relation (or not) to the normative development of their counterparts in domestic legal systems. In both cases, the resulting knowledge is a valuable recipe against 'short-termism'[109] insofar as it contributes to unveiling deeper and, on occasion, repressed historical forces with the potential to re-explain the present and also determine future events. If instead one adopts a micro perspective on the international legal order, historical writing about international law contributes inter alia to the development of historical-normative studies of particular international doctrines, international legal principles, and norms in one or several sub-disciplines of international law both from a diachronic and a synchronic historical perspective. Moreover, historical writing about international law contributes to knowledge creation processes regarding the 'historical dimension of international legal theory'.[110] This hybrid form of conceptual history and the history of ideas, which relates inter alia to the study of international legal theories and doctrines in a historical perspective, explores, among other things, the ways in which they have developed historically 'within broader intellectual and political contexts'[111] both nationally and internationally

---

[109] David Armitage and Jo Guldi, *A History Manifesto* (Cambridge, UK: Cambridge University Press, 2014).

[110] Anne Orford and Florian Hoffmann, 'Introduction: theorizing international law', in Anne Orford and Florian Hoffmann with Martin Clark (eds.), *The Oxford Handbook of the Theory of International Law* (Oxford: Oxford University Press, 2016), pp. 1–20 at 10.

[111] Ibid.

and also how they have been refined and redefined in the service of different causes and purposes by different actors over time.

Finally, the third type, 'international law in history', which is considered to be the most 'historical' (or the only actually 'historical') of the three, is concerned with the contextual interaction of international law, or parts thereof, and society at a given place and time whether in the axis of synchronicity or in the axis of diachronicity. This means the relationship of mutual influence between international law and/or parts thereof with different national and international societal, ideological, intellectual, and professional historical contexts and particularly significant international 'events' over time.[112] Paying attention to 'international law in history' is a good recipe for scepticism about the ultimate irrelevance of international law. As James Crawford notes in the context of interwar England, this has for a long time provided 'part of the language in which international debates were conducted, the conduct of politicians criticized, proposals for settlement or change put forward and rejected or agreed'.[113] Moreover, historical writing about international law contributes to knowledge creation processes regarding the many dimensions of the 'historical sociology of international law'. These include but are not limited to the historical sociology of the academic international legal profession through the study of the life and works of international lawyers and other influential individuals as international norm entrepreneurs and their respective intellectual influence on particular historical junctures in the discipline or on its intellectual development both nationally and internationally. It also encompasses the history of transnational movements and social, cultural, and religious movements and the study of their influence on particular historical junctures in the discipline and on its intellectual shaping and development both nationally and internationally. Similarly, it extends to the history of other non-state actors including international organizations and, of course, to the study of minor and medium states and to the rise and fall of great state powers and the impact of their imperial architectures on international law.

To these three types, one may add a fourth general dimension based on the consideration that historical writing about international law contributes to knowledge creation processes regarding the study of the

---

[112] Lesaffer, 'Law between past and present', p. 7.
[113] See James Crawford, 'Public international law in 20th century England', in Jack Beatson and Reinhard Zimmermann (eds.), *Jurists Uprooted: German-Speaking Emigré Lawyers in Twentieth Century Britain* (Oxford: Oxford University Press 2004), pp. 681–693.

historiography of international law itself. This ongoing development, as David Bederman pointed out early on, is a reaction to the fact that 'the relationship between the domains of international law (as both an academic study and professional practice) and historiography remains cloudy and uncertain'.[114] This domain comprises questions about historical method and the self-reflective study of historiographical approaches to international law and, as we have seen, is one of the most characteristic features of the development known by international legal history in recent years. Finally, it should be stressed that all approaches to the history of international law are holistically complementary insofar as they contribute on different scales and degrees to knowledge creation processes across different dimensions of the existing interfaces between history and international law; in doing so, all of them inter alia contribute to the constant renewal of the periodization(s) of the history of international law.

1.6   Conclusion: The Uses of the History of International Law

The question of the uses (and misuses) of history as 'a discipline that seeks to reconstruct and remember the past' has extensively occupied historians.[115] However, beyond the great canonical discourses and the deeply nuanced historiographical reflections, in practice different people engage in the history of international law with different understandings of how international legal history may serve them personally, or what in general the history of international law ought to be all about. At one extreme, for the international legal practitioner or state foreign international legal advisor, international legal history may be merely instrumental to the achievement of the set of goals established by their paymasters or deemed to serve the 'national interest' of particular states. This is the foreign-office-like lawyerly use of international legal history to buttress a nationally apologist juridical argument or the use of international legal history by the international lawyer for hire who provides international legal services to some or other public or private entity. At the other extreme, a purely academic historian may approach the field

---

[114] David J. Bederman, 'Foreign office international legal history', in Matthew Craven, Malgosia Fitzmaurice, and Maria Vogiatzi (eds.), *Time, History and International Law* (Leiden: Martinus Nijhoff/Brill, 2006), pp. 43–64 at 43.

[115] See, e.g., Edward H. Carr, *What Is History?* (Cambridge, UK: Cambridge University Press, 1961).

animated by a non-instrumental investigative spirit which is aimed at the reconstruction of the historical record of an irretrievable past on the understanding that all pasts involving proto-forms of international law and the human species are important in the reconstruction of the *longue durée* perspective on the evolution of international law thorough different ages.

In between these two extremes, there are those who approach international legal history with a sense of moral duty towards those the history of international law has failed or left forgotten. This purpose may include uses of international legal history oriented to shed light on earlier injustices committed in its shadow so as to raise awareness about the plight of certain individuals, groups, or peoples, prevent the recurrence of similar behaviours, or even perhaps procure some sort of restorative justice for its alleged victims. Others may more generally approach the study of the history of international law with the aim of making this scholarly field a platform for highlighting present injustices, whether by extrapolation or by producing causal links between earlier abuses and the present circumstances of some of the most disadvantaged. Still other academics may, instead, be on a quest to question received wisdom on the study of a particular subject matter, whether by reference to specific new archival research or by unravelling alternative historical trajectories in the construction of a legal doctrine, norm, or institution. In some cases, they may even want through their historical work to make a larger use of the 'special powers' that historians have in 'destabilizing received knowledge',[116] and produce in its place a sense of paradox and opportunity for new causes and vocabularies which, in their view, carry a great emancipatory potential to emerge. However, in stark contrast to the latter 'social conflict perspective' on the history of international law, for others investigating international legal history may contribute to reinforcing the normative authority and legitimacy of well-established values and principles of the contemporary international legal order. Likewise, one may find those for whom the study of the history of international law is a vehicle to interrogate its future – in the guise of Winston Churchill, for whom 'the longer you can look back, the farther you can look forward' or to enable it to adapt to change and influence policy with the ability to shape its present. It is equally possible to find international law scholars for whom forays into history writing about international law

---

[116] Armitage and Guldi, *A History Manifesto*, p. 14.

are first and foremost an exercise in knowledge acquisition about the academic discipline they have made their lives' profession. This is history understood as the path towards a greater comprehension of the architecture of international law and therefore to the eventual possibility of competently mastering its vocabularies.

In conclusion, contrasting attitudes and purposes of those who find themselves interrogating the history of international law confirm that, as David Kennedy once pointed out with reference to international law, its history also 'means different things to different peoples in different places'[117] – and, one may add, at different times too. However, whether it is in the service of wealth, of power, of justice, of ideology, of humanity, of a better future, of a quest for a self-emancipatory mode of knowledge, or any set of different motivational combinations thereof, anyone engaging in the history of international law should be aware of stepping, as the following chapters will show, into a centuries-old living research tradition which, like all history, cyclically renews itself in the image of its time and age.

---

[117] David Kennedy, 'When renewal repeats: thinking against the box' (2000) 32 *New York Journal of International Law and Politics* 335–500 at 335.

2

Contextual Approaches to the History of International Law

2.1 Introduction

Since what has come to be known as the turn to the history of international law, international lawyers writing about international legal history have been partially freed from the pressing need to justify their research on the past of international law by referring to the present normative evolution of their field or its practical doctrinal utility in contemporary international legal debates. The gradual carving out of a sub-disciplinary and relatively self-contained academic space for international legal historical scholarship *proprio sensu* has been complemented by a closer attention to historical methods imported into the field by international lawyers or exported into it by scholars contributing from adjacent disciplines, namely legal historians and historians. The resulting interdisciplinarization of international legal history has prompted a series of methodological and historiographical debates around the distinction between two main ways of approaching it: those of historians and those of international lawyers. The first of these are allegedly concerned with guaranteeing a 'well-contextualised historical record of the past for its own sake', while the second have been described as being 'mostly interested in the international legal afterglow of past events'.[1]

Contextualism can be defined as an 'approach' in terms of the method it provides to investigate the different objects that may fall within the research scope of international legal history. According to Anne Orford, 'questions of method involve key decisions about what and how we read, the nature of the materials with which we engage, how we conduct our research, and how we understand the relation between critical thinking and its object'.[2] As David

---

[1] Valentina Vadi, 'International law and its histories: methodological risks and opportunities' (2017) 58 *Harvard International Law Journal* 311–352 at 311.

[2] Anne Orford, 'On international legal method' (2013) 1 *London Review of International Law* 166–197 at 167.

Armitage further notes, as a historical method contextualism relates to 'the most basic issues of historical methodology – of what problems we select, how we choose the boundaries of our topic, and what tools we put to solving our questions'.[3] The framing of the temporal and spatial contexts within which an historical investigation is to be carried out is the first of the contextualist demarcations through which boundary-setting in regard to a selected historical topic invariably proceeds. This first level of contextualist delineation is followed by further particular decisions on including or excluding each and every one of the manifold potential contexts which may be considered relevant to the investigation of the historical topic and, subsequently, by a still more specific demarcation of those contexts which have prima facie been deemed pertinent for inclusion. These contextualizing decisions and others regarding the relative scope and scale of the research involved are in turn conditioned by an array of factors. These include, but are not limited to, first, the author's degree of cultural and linguistic familiarity with the 'relevant' spatial-temporal historical context(s) under investigation; second, the gravitational pull of existing conventional period-izations – which are themselves often based on 'context-breaking events' – within the given field(s) of research involved; third, the author's field of academic specialization, and in its wake the specific baggage of disciplinary borders the respect for or transgression of which its main disciplinary interpretative community later subjects to critical assessment; fourth, the balancing exercise between, on the one hand, the claim for impartial scientific accuracy and historical objectivity that the author intends his or her historical narrative to convey and, on the other hand, the *animus historiandi* driving his or her historical investigation. The latter, in turn, may be largely influenced by the pull of specific historiographical trends in her field of academic specialization.

However, a more acute context-awareness in the task of the inter-national legal historian extends beyond its role in boundary-setting in inter alia temporal, spatial, disciplinary, or even authorial terms. It also brings about a series of limits to the scholarly treatment that any histor-ical subject may potentially receive. The first of these limits is the anti-anachronism function played by contextualism, with anachronism being generally understood as a 'wilful or inadvertent misunderstanding of the past by applying standards or interpretations from outside the immediate

---

[3] David Armitage and Jo Guldi, *A History Manifesto* (Cambridge, UK: Cambridge University Press, 2014), p. 118.

era, context or milieu under study'.[4] In the history of ideas, this includes the ascription to someone of 'beliefs and intentions that presuppose modes of presentation and types of description unavailable to a certain agent at a certain time'.[5] Or to put it differently using a terminology that performs a similar principled normative function among lawyers, the prohibition of anachronism works as a principle of non-retroactivity of sorts of legal, axiological, or otherwise contemporary categories to the study of the historical past.

Moreover, besides the red flag it attaches to anachronism, contextualism also works as a filtering time-net of sorts which catches other related historical fallacies common among non-contextualist-driven analyses. These include precursorism, with its elated reading of the present in the past by identifying antecedents – and even genealogies of antecedents – of present-day ideas, concepts, principles, or norms that were not yet in existence in earlier historical periods. They also include prolepsis, which is commonly described in the cinema as a 'flash-forward', otherwise'a moment in a narrative in which the chronological order of story events is disturbed and the narrator narrates future events out of turn',[6] and in history as the anachronistic representation of something as existing before its proper or historical time. More broadly, the application of historical contextualism also affects the orientation of the narrative itself. This is because it is widely considered a recipe against teleologically driven interpretations of historical development, including what Herbert Butterfield labelled the 'Whig interpretation of History' in order to criticize a 'British brand of national teleology' that is often applied pejoratively to histories that present the past as an inexorable march of progress towards enlightenment.[7]

However, contextualism's wariness of teleology and the intellectual apparatuses that have served as its scaffolding also includes in its purview the very counter-critical and alternative meta-historical narratives that

---

[4] David Armitage, 'In defense of presentism', in Darrin M. McMahon (ed.), *History and Human Flourishing* (in press), p. 3, https://scholar.harvard.edu/armitage/publications/defense-presentism.

[5] Carlos Spoerhase and Colin G. King, 'Historical fallacies of historians', in Aviezer Tucker (ed.), *A Companion to the Philosophy of History and Historiography* (London: Blackwell, 2009), pp. 274–284 at 275.

[6] Mark Currie, *About Time: Narrative Fiction and the Philosophy of Time* (Edinburgh: Edinburgh University Press, 2006), p. 29.

[7] Herbert Butterfield, *The Whig Interpretation of History* (Kensington: University of New South Wales Library, 1981).

may emerge to challenge previously dominant teleological paradigms. The fact that these critical counter-narratives may have found support in instances of contextualist re-reading of a hegemonic tradition which ratifies or normalizes the present does not preclude their disruptive presentist persuasiveness, or their deployment to 'describe an interpretation of history that is biased towards and coloured by present-day concerns, preoccupations and values',[8] being similarly affected by the constraints contextualism imposes on the treatment of historical subjects. The methodologically rigorous nature of contextualism has been at the heart of a debate on the degree of adaptation or departure from it that may or may not be required in order to be able to perform certain critical enquiries – in particular those in the axis of diachronicity – in international legal history.

Against this background, Section 2.2 below provides a general introduction to contextualism as an offspring of historicism and the main methodological tenets of the Cambridge School of intellectual history, before analysing the interaction between history and international law in the light of a tripartite typology that distinguishes between 'history in international law', the 'history of international law', and 'international law in history'. Section 2.3 provides some selected examples of the critical application of the 'contextual turn' in international legal history with regard to the development of the international legal profession and landmark historical events. Section 2.4 reviews the impact of contextualism on knowledge production processes regarding the relationship between international law and history. Section 2.5 presents a re-framed analysis of the methodological debate between contextualist and critical international legal historians on the question of anachronism in the light of a typology of presentisms. Finally, Section 2.6 considers the dynamics of confluence and divergence between historiographical trends and the performative narrative function of international legal history.

2.2   Themis and Clio, or the Radiography of an Inconstant Affair

It would appear to be common sense that one should place past events, concepts, and people relevant to international law (or to any other subject for that matter) in the historical context of their times, whether it is conceived as a political, economic, sociological, intellectual, legal, or

---

[8] Armitage, 'In defense of presentism', p. 3.

religious context or, as often occurs in the actual practice of historical writing, a combination to different degrees of some or all thereof with the emphasis being put on the context(s) that the author deems most relevant to the subject matter of the investigation. Indeed, contextualism as a historical method ultimately follows from the historicist principle that nothing can be detached from its time and remain equal to what it once was. This principle is, albeit with caveats, often foundationally retraced to the German historical school's conception of historical enquiry at the time of the emergence of the modern historical profession in Germany as *Geschichtswissenschaft* (historical science) in the mid- to late nineteenth century.[9] Having developed during the apex of the glorification of scientific methods struggling to free themselves from religious and metaphysical elements, this was understood as a science that followed a systematic or methodological procedure of enquiry as it sought to reconstruct the past, in the words of Leopold von Ranke (1795–1886), as 'how it actually [or essentially] was' ('wie es eigentlich gewesen ist').[10]

Historicism, with its 'recognition that all human ideas and values are historically conditioned and subject to change',[11] has been a 'term of art' in multiple philosophical discussions, as well as inter alia in historiographical ones in Germany, Italy, with Benedetto Croce's *storicismo assoluto*,[12] and elsewhere.[13] It is also a framing identifier of sorts for a scientific and methodological orientation in the study of history to which contextualism itself appertains. In terms of its contemporary influence, in particular among intellectual historians, one of the more sophisticated expressions of in-depth 'contextualisation as the historian's chief modus operandi'[14] is that proposed by the so-called Cambridge School. This is one of the main competing schools of interpretation of, or most influential methodological approaches to, the history of political thought, also

---

[9] Georg G. Iggers and Q. Edward Wang with Supriya Mukherjee, *A Global History of Modern Historiography* (New York: Routledge, 2013), pp. 117–132.

[10] Leopold von Ranke, 'Introduction', in *Histories of Latin and Germanic Nations 1494–1514* (London: G. Bell & Sons, 1887; first published 1824); cited in Iggers and Wang, *A Global History*, p. 122.

[11] Georg G. Iggers, 'Historicism: the history and meaning of the term' (1995) 56 *Journal of the History of Ideas* 129–152 at 133.

[12] Benedetto Croce, 'Il concetto della filosofia come storicismo assoluto' (1939) 37 *La critica: rivista di letteratura, storia e filosofia diretta da B. Croce* 253–268.

[13] Iggers, 'Historicism'.

[14] Martin Jay, 'Historical explanation and the event: reflections on the limits of contextualization' (2011) 42 *New Literary History* 557–571 at 558.

variously known as the history of political philosophy, the history of political theory,[15] or intellectual history in which 'reference is typically to one basic scholarly genre'.[16]

The emergence of the so-called Cambridge School is generally retraced to the publication of a series of theoretically influential articles in the late 1960s and early 1970s by Quentin Skinner, who, as Richard Bourke notes, co-opted 'a range of philosophical insights as a way of lending clarity and rigour to the common-sense historical view that past thought was best interpreted by contextualising its arguments'[17] and, therefore, as a recipe against anachronistic readings of it. Although, as Orford notes, 'Skinner's influence has seen a cultivated "sensitivity to anachronism"' among Anglophone historians of political thought, anachronism had already for long been the *mala maleficorum* among intellectual historians such as Lucien Febvre, the co-founder of the Annales school. Febvre in the late 1940s considered anachronism 'le péché des péchés – le péché entre tous irrémissible'[18] ('the worst of all sins, the sin that cannot be forgiven') in any attempt to 'restituer l'état d'esprit de nos aïeux' ('to restore the state of mind of our ancestors'), suggesting that careful attention should be paid to 'la série des précautions à prendre, des prescriptions à observer' ('the set of precautions to take, the prescriptions to observe') for avoiding it.

Sharing in this spirit, but notably influenced by the 'linguistic turn', Skinner proposed a methodology imbued with 'thoroughgoing historicism'[19] and revolving around the idea that the historian should 'approach the past in its own right, for its own sake and on its own terms',[20] and that to do that it was necessary to be wary of the various

---

[15] Terence Ball, 'The value of the history of political philosophy', in George Klosko (ed.), *The Oxford Handbook of the History of Political Philosophy* (Oxford: Oxford University Press, 2011), pp. 47–59 at 49.

[16] John G. Gunnell, 'History of political philosophy as a discipline', in George Klosko (ed.), *The Oxford Handbook of the History of Political Philosophy* (Oxford: Oxford University Press, 2011), pp. 60–74 at 60.

[17] Richard Bourke, 'The Cambridge School', www.qmul.ac.uk/history/media/ph/news/The-Cambridge-School.pdf, p. 2.

[18] Lucien Febvre, *Le problème de l'incroyance au XVIe siècle: la religion de Rabelais* (Paris: Albin Michel, 1947), p. 32.

[19] Mark Bevir, 'The contextual approach', in George Klosko (ed.), *The Oxford Handbook of the History of Political Philosophy* (Oxford: Oxford University Press, 2011), pp. 11–23; Bourke, 'The Cambridge School', p. 2.

[20] Quentin Skinner, 'Sir Geoffrey Elton and the practice of history' (1997) 7 *Transactions of the Royal Historical Society* 301–316; citing from Geoffrey Elton, *The Practice of History*, The Fontana Library (London: Collins, 1969), p. 86.

forms in which an inadequate 'mythology of doctrines' and also a 'mythology of coherence'[21] present themselves in works of historical exegesis in other methodologies and of the 'limitations of social context as a means of determining the meaning of the text'.[22] Focusing instead on the argumentative dimension of a historical text considered as an utterance in a search for its proper historical context, Skinner suggested borrowing from John L. Austin's 'speech-act' theory to distinguish between the 'locutionary meaning' of a text (extracted from the words in the text alone) and its illocutionary or performative force, in other words, the effects it was intended to or meant to have on the world independently of the extent to which it achieved what it set out to do – its perlocutionary effect.[23] Restoring a text to the historical context in which it was composed, and to the question(s) to which it was offered as an answer,[24] in turn brought Skinner to assert that 'to understand what any given writer may have been doing in using some particular concept or argument, we need first of all to grasp the nature and range of things that could recognisably have been done by using that particular concept, in the treatment of that particular theme, at that particular time'.[25]

The methodological insights contained in Skinner's influential writings, accompanied by those of John G. A. Pocock[26] and others, have since their earlier exposition been developed and, more importantly, applied by a large cohort of intellectual historians in their historical investigations. A subsequent large debate has developed over time about the limits of the methodology both in its importation to other disciplines and within the history of political thought itself.[27] Internally, some of the criticisms pointing to the limits of contextualism can be summarized, in Martin Jay's words, as 'in most cases' focusing

---

[21] Quentin Skinner, 'Meaning and understanding in the history of ideas' (1969) 8 *History and Theory* 3–53.

[22] Ibid., p. 48.

[23] Paraphrasing Jay, 'Historical explanation', p. 557.

[24] Ball, 'The value of the history', p. 57.

[25] Quentin Skinner, 'Motives, intentions and the interpretations of texts', in James Tully (ed.), *Meaning and Context: Quentin Skinner and His Critics* (Princeton, NJ: Princeton University Press, 1988), pp. 68–78 at 77.

[26] See generally John G. A. Pocock, 'Languages and their implications: the transformation of the study of political thought', in *Politics, Language, and Time: Essays on Political Thoughts and History* (New York: Atheneum, 1973), pp. 3–41.

[27] James Tully (ed.), *Meaning and Context: Quentin Skinner and His Critics* (Princeton, NJ: Princeton University Press, 1988).

on difficulties faced by the contemporary historian in gaining access to the past and reflecting on the evidence that exists in the present; how to establish contexts if their residues are themselves in texts that need to be stabilised and interpreted; how to decide which contexts are pertinent and provide plausible explanations; how to articulate the relationship among the sometimes incompatible contexts that might be adduced to explain a text; how to acknowledge the theoretical underpinnings, explicit or not, of our reconstruction of the past ... and so on.[28]

Meanwhile, externally, Skinner's assertion that 'any statement ... is inescapably the embodiment of a particular intention, on a particular occasion, addressed to the solution of a particular problem, and thus specific to its situation in a way that it can only be naive to try to transcend'[29] has placed it in sharp contrast in particular with those 'literary and philosophical ones that treat texts respectively as idealised aesthetic objects and contributions to timeless debates'.[30]

As in other disciplines, in international legal history too importing the contextualist methodology to bear on international law topics has led to a debate that revolves around the divide between the different modes of approaching the history of international law by historians, including intellectual historians, and international lawyers, with legal historians placed somewhat between the two. This debate is largely mediated by the disciplinary borders that distinguish law from history, which generally in the literature are explained as historians approaching the study of the past with the aim of reconstructing it as faithfully as is feasible and by international lawyers interrogating the past inspired by a form of 'functionalist presentism'.[31] However, because much historical writing by historians is also diversely inspired by the will to put historical knowledge either explicitly or implicitly at the service of a great variety of social purposes in the present, the idea of 'functionalist presentism' needs to be further connoted for it to specifically refer to an international juridical form of functional presentism in international legal history. To put it differently, the international lawyer's approach to the history of international law differs from that of the historian in that the latter's is never, or only on extremely rare occasions, principally addressed to putting

---

[28] Jay, 'Historical explanation', p. 562.
[29] Skinner, 'Meaning and understanding', p. 50.
[30] Bevir, 'The Contextual Approach', p. 11.
[31] Christopher Warren, 'Henry V, anachronism, and the history of international law', in Lorna Hutson (ed.), *The Oxford Handbook of English Law and Literature 1500–1700* (Oxford: Oxford University Press, 2017), pp. 709–727 at 714.

historical knowledge at the service of contemporary international juridical purposes.

This dimension of the disciplinary boundaries that exist between history and law can profitably be examined in relation to what has been termed by Matthew Craven the domain of 'history in international law', or that of the (legal-technical) 'uses of history for international law'.[32] The latter is a component of the general tripartite typology used to explain, as briefly seen in Chapter 1, the 'interaction between law and history'[33] among legal historians. As Randall Lesaffer explains, in fact, the three components in this typology 'span a broad continuum that gradually shifts from a true historical study of past law in its contemporary context ("law in history") to the historical study of law as a self-contained phenomenon ("history of law") to what is in fact historical jurisprudence or even the instrumental use of historical argument in jurisprudence or legal practice ("history in law")'.[34]

One may speak of two broad categories of 'history in international law'. One of them concerns the use of historical normative or legal materials *proprio sensu*: norms, principles, or legal doctrines in the form of invoking precedents. This is what Lesaffer describes as reference 'by lawyers, in whatever capacity ... to the past in order to argue the existence or the interpretation of a certain rule',[35] which he considers is a use that 'may be thus called instrumental'[36] insofar as it is informed by a quest to gain legal authority from history and clearly captures the above divide in terms of a juridical form of functional presentism in the international lawyer's approach to history. However, in further fleshing out Craven and Lesaffer's typology, one may argue that the use of history under the gravitational pull of juridical functional presentism also extends, as Chapter 7 examines in detail, beyond the normative realm *stricto sensu* so as to involve the appraisal of historical evidence under specific legal categories. In this case, which coincides with the domain of

---

[32] Matthew Craven, 'Introduction: international law and its histories', in Matthew Craven, Malgosia Fitzmaurice, and Maria Vogiatzi (eds.), *Time, History and International Law* (Leiden: Martinus Nijhoff/Brill, 2007), pp. 1–25 at 7.

[33] Randall Lesaffer, 'Law and history: law between past and present', https://lirias.kuleuven .be/1856246, p. 6. This essay also appears in Bart van Klink and Sanne Taekema (eds.), *Law and Method: Interdisciplinary Research into Law* (Tübingen: Mohr Siebeck, 2011), pp. 133–152.

[34] Ibid., p. 17.

[35] Ibid., p. 134.

[36] Ibid.

application of international law in international adjudicative settings, the analysis of the historical context is circumscribed to what is deemed to be legally relevant within the framework of established legal categories. Moreover, between these two, one should also situate an intermediate level that concerns how the outlines of a dispute and its eventual resolution are invariable conditioned by 'distinct temporal elements of particular rules',[37] including procedural and substantive limitations faced by international courts and tribunals in legally appraising past facts and conducts. Finally, one may also add yet another category to flesh out Craven and Lesaffer's treatment of the typology of the 'history in international law' encompassing the effects of the legal engagement by international law with history on historical research itself.

The second category in Craven and Lesaffer's tripartite classification is the 'history of international law' which, according to Lesaffer, holds 'a middle position in the continuum' between the domains of 'history in international law' and that of 'international law in history'.[38] The common denominator of this variant is that it 'extends to research which considers law a self-contained historical phenomenon'[39] worth studying separately or autonomously in a Kelsenian vein from the context provided by other disciplines. This is what legal historians also diversely term 'traditional legal history', defined as 'a historical analysis of law rather than a legal history' or 'a historical legal science [that] is written by lawyers for lawyers'.[40] This may be 'practised at both the micro and the macro level' as Chapter 7 examines with reference to contemporary international legal literature. At both levels, it is the 'gradual evolution from past to present'[41] of the law that interests the legal historian, and in this sense it is, as Craven describes it, 'a history mapped out in terms of its trajectory or teleology; a history written in narrative form that provides a story about its origins, development, progress or renewal'.[42] Indeed, the study of the 'history of international law' is often examined

---

[37] David J. Bederman, 'Foreign office international legal history', in Matthew Craven, Malgosia Fitzmaurice, and Maria Vogiatzi (eds.), *Time, History and International Law* (Leiden: Martinus Nijhoff/Brill, 2007), pp. 43–64 at 43.
[38] Lesaffer, 'Law between past and present', p. 7.
[39] Ibid.
[40] Dirk Heirbaut, 'A tale of two legal histories: some personal reflections on the methodology of legal history', in Dag Michalsen (ed.), *Reading Past Legal Texts* (Oslo: Unipax, 2006), pp. 91–112 at 91.
[41] Lesaffer, 'Law between past and present', p. 7.
[42] Craven, 'Introduction', p. 7.

diachronically in its internal evolution towards the present and that poses difficulties from an external or sociologically historically oriented contextual point of view. Lesaffer describes the historiographical dangers involved in 'this genealogical history from present to past' as one that leads to 'anachronistic interpretations of historical phenomena, clouds historical realities that bear no fruit in our own times and give no information about the historical context of the phenomenon one claims to recognise'.[43]

These just two preliminarily described domains of 'history in international law' and the 'history of international law' with their areas of overlap and interaction share, despite their differences, some common features. Included among the latter is that they both fall under the gravitational pull of the overarching positivist principle which prompts most international legal research (including historical research) to identify the 'law in vigour' and the related professional technical problem-solving-oriented expertise which is expected from lawyers, including international lawyers, in providing legally reasoned advice or solutions to legal problems on the basis of current legal materials.

Finally, completing Craven and Lesaffer's tripartite typology and less concerned with juridical functional presentism and more with the role of law in specifically contextualized past societies is the domain of 'international law in history', to which the term 'external legal history' could also be applied. This 'refers to the study of law within its broad social, economic, cultural and political context' and its 'object of study is the mutual interaction between law and society at a certain time and certain place in history'.[44] It cultivators are no longer lawyers writing for lawyers but more usually, as Dirk Heirbaut notes, 'social scientists for other social scientists, historians being the most prominent, though not the only ones, in this group'.[45] In this domain, where the concern is to 'identify international law's relationship to the wider world of politics, economics or sociology against which it is deployed, or within which it is inserted',[46] methodological contextualization, including that of the type preconized by the Cambridge School of intellectual history, is more readily

---

[43] Randall Lesaffer, 'International law and its history: the story of an unrequited love', in Matthew Craven et al. (eds.), *Time, History and International Law* (Leiden: Martinus Nijhoff/Brill, 2007), pp. 27–41 at 34.

[44] Lesaffer, 'Law between past and present', p. 7.

[45] Heirbaut, 'A tale of two legal histories', p. 94.

[46] Craven, 'Introduction', p. 7.

applicable in particular to its synchronic axis. It becomes more problematic when the historical contextualist methodology is stretched beyond
the synchronic axis, or beyond the study of 'law as a phenomenon within
the particular society the historian is interested in and not as a phase
within the evolution of the law',[47] and moved, instead, onto the
diachronic axis.

2.3   The Contextual Turn in the History of International Law

Contextualist historical methodology has been extensively applied in new
historical writing on international law. This greater attention to context is
bringing about a historical correction of earlier historical narratives and
perspectives. Indeed, in its application, contextualism is contributing to
dislodging events and concepts from the retrospective re-interpretations
and historical framing categories provided for them in the past.

In international legal history, the modern turn to context has often
been credited to the sizeable influence of Martti Koskenniemi's *The
Gentle Civilizer of Nations*[48] and the traces in it of the methodological
influence of the Cambridge School in the history of political ideas.[49]
Indeed, Koskenniemi implicitly relied on the insights of historical contextualism to provide a dynamic picture of the intellectual and normative
evolution of the international legal discipline as one informed by discontinuity and political agency with the professional international law
scholar at its heart. In moving to the 'external' context and thus beyond
the deconstruction of the 'internal' argumentative patterns in different
periods, which were tackled, as Chapter 3 examines, by David Kennedy
in the 1980 and 1990s, Koskenniemi was, however, similarly animated by
a will to disavow the canonical succession of authors anachronistically
reframed as synoptically fleshing out supportive illustrations of disciplinary discourse of international legal thought and their connected grand
narratives.

To do so, Koskenniemi relied on the insights of historical contextualism as a method for looking at 'people with projects' by placing international lawyers within particular traditions against the succession of

[47] Lesaffer, 'Law between past and present' p. 7.
[48] Martti Koskenniemi, *The Gentle Civilizer of Nations: The Fall and Rise of International
Law 1870–1960* (Cambridge, UK: Cambridge University Press, 2001).
[49] George Rodrigo Bandeira Galindo, 'Martti Koskenniemi and the historiographical turn in
international law' (2005) 16 *European Journal of International Law* 539–559.

specifically contextualized historical circumstances, and the related jur-idical debates within the discipline to which the 'doctrines of those men sought to provide response'.[50] This allowed him to bring 'international law down from universal narratives and conceptual abstractions' and to suggest instead that 'international law is made by individuals with their projects, interests and ambitions, rather than by abstract temporal concepts or ideas'.[51] In dislodging individuals and ideas from disciplinary discourses through contextual historicizing, which recalls Skinner's chastising of exegetical approaches focused on (in a favoured phrase) 'timeless elements' in the form of 'universal ideas', even a 'dateless wisdom' with 'universal application',[52] Koskenniemi aimed similarly to demythologize international law concepts and further unlock the closure effect of reconstructed trad-itions in order to foster a renewed critical potential in the contemporary engagement with international law's current political debates.[53]

This restoration of the works of international lawyers to their political/legal contexts, in other words to the situations in which they performed political/juridical tasks, is consonant with Koskenniemi's conceptualiza-tion of international law as ultimately no more than the 'language' used by international lawyers as they engage with international law as 'an argumentative practice' and his understanding that 'what passes for method' in international law 'has to do with what counts as persuasive in terms of "a good legal argument"'.[54] This 'legal realist' perspective is, as Chapter 3 further explores, one of the leitmotivs running through Koskenniemi's opus since his early structuralist works. When seen in the framework of his overall legal philosophy, contextualism served Koskenniemi to further anchor his perspective that international law, besides being a set of argumentative practices circularly oscillating between the confines of apology and utopia,[55] is an 'argumentative ...

---

[50] Koskenniemi, *The Gentle Civilizer of Nations*, p. 8.

[51] Ibid.

[52] Skinner, 'Meaning and understanding', p. 30.

[53] Eugeny Roshchin, 'The challenges of "contextualism"', in Andreas Gofas, Inanna Hamati-Ataya, and Nicholas Onuf (eds.), *The SAGE Handbook of the History, Philosophy and Sociology of International Relations* (Los Angeles: SAGE Reference, 2018), pp. 162–175 at 162–163.

[54] Martti Koskenniemi, 'Methodology of international law', in *Max Planck Encyclopedia of Public International Law* (2007), opil.ouplaw.com/view/10.1093/law:epil/9780199231690/law-9780199231690-e1440, pp. 2–9.

[55] Martti Koskenniemi, *From Apology to Utopia: The Structure of the International Legal Argument* (Helsinki: Lakimiesliiton Kustannus, 1989); reissued with a new epilogue (Cambridge: Cambridge University Press, 2005).

technique ... deployed in different contexts and for different purposes',
and also to show how 'legal vocabularies and institutions as open-ended
platforms on which contrasting meanings are projected at different
periods ... are each devised so as to react to some problem in the
surrounding world'.[56] Indeed, Koskenniemi has often emphasized in
his historical works the international lawyer's ad hoc responsiveness to
contingency. This in turn allows him to underscore discontinuities in
revisiting the works of some of the great European international lawyers
as 'men of their times' and, therefore, to downplay, in a critical fashion,
the traditional teleological perspective on progress in international law.

Ever since some of his early elaborated historiographical reflections,[57]
Koskenniemi has remained appreciative of contextualism as an 'important corrective to ways of doing international legal history'.[58] However,
there has also been a certain shift in perspective in Koskenniemi's own
methodological positions under the influence of the parallel emergence,
as Chapters 3 and 4 examine, of post-colonial approaches to the history
of international law.[59] In particular, some revisionist re-interpretations
performed by noted representatives of these approaches, namely Antony
Anghie in his work on Francisco de Vitoria, triggered what Orford terms
a 'policing of anachronism' by contextualist historians and legal historians 'in the response to critical histories of international law'.[60] It is partly
to lend methodological support, as we shall see in more detail below, to
post-colonial historiographical trends, and in particular to Anghie's
book, which was heralded as a landmark scholarly inflection point of
sorts in the rise of the critical international legal historiography associated with Third World Approaches to International Law (TWAIL), and
partly to justify certain methodological departures from contextualist
methodology in other works, that this retuning of methodological perspectives has emerged. This has brought in its wake a historiographical
debate on the problem of anachronism in international legal history
among international legal historians.

[56] Martti Koskenniemi, 'A History of International Law Histories', in Bardo Fassbender and
Anne Peters (eds), *The Oxford Handbook of the History of International Law* (Oxford:
Oxford University Press, 2012), pp. 943–971 at 969.
[57] Martti Koskenniemi, 'Why history of international law today?' (2004) 4 *Rechtsgeschichte*
61–66 at 64–65.
[58] Martti Koskenniemi, 'Vitoria and us: thoughts on critical histories of international law'
(2014) 22 *Rechtsgeschichte* 119–138 at 123.
[59] Ibid., p. 124.
[60] Orford, 'On international legal method', p. 172.

In Koskenniemi, the referred shift of perspective is also consonant with the attempt to capture the 'structural bias'[61] in international historical perspective with which he complemented his earlier structuralist analyses of the international legal argument in order to accrue the critical dimension of international legal historical work and its effects on the politics of the present. This strategic move consisted in astutely moving the emphasis from one extreme to the other in the same binary opposition in order to achieve a deconstructive demythologizing purpose of one teleological meta-narrative by stressing the uniqueness of the past as distinct from the present and yet then attempting to lend support to a reconstructive effort of the opposite one. He did so because in his view contextualism 'ends up suppressing or undermining efforts to find patterns in history that might account for today's experiences of domination and injustice'.[62] This purpose, which is explicit in his statement that 'I do not believe that to submit [Francisco de] Vitoria to a postcolonial critique is to commit the same mistake of which earlier hagiographic studies were guilty',[63] amounts, as will be shown below, to risk falling in the danger of abusing what one may term an otherwise historiographically assumed form of counter-teleological presentism for political ends.

Koskenniemi has reiteratively put stress on the importance of contextualizing the argumentative uses of international law by professional international lawyers and scholars, or, as Chapter 3 examines, of 'produc[ing] contextual readings of the works and lives of persons in the international law canon'.[64] In applying contextualist methods Koskenniemi has been particularly interested in the 'history of ideas' (*Ideengeschichte*) and its subfields, including in particular conceptual history (*Begriffsgeschichte*), which, as Chapter 7 further examines, is a particularly apposite receptacle for critical histories of international law. However, the contemporary use of contextualism has also particularly affected the 'history of events' (*Ereignisgeschichte*)[65] and has provided ample room for revision of the retrospective international legal

---

[61] Martti Koskenniemi, 'The politics of international law – 20 years later' (2009) 20 *European Journal of International Law* 7–19.
[62] Koskenniemi, 'Vitoria and us', p. 124.
[63] Ibid., p. 123.
[64] Ibid., p. 120.
[65] Bardo Fassbender and Anne Peters, 'Introduction: towards a global history of international law', in Bardo Fassbender and Anne Peters (eds.), *The Oxford Handbook of the History of International Law* (Oxford: Oxford University Press, 2012), pp. 1–26 at 11–14.

significance given to some of them,[66] beginning with those associated to international treaties. The early professional study of the history of international law in the late nineteenth century largely evolved from a basis provided by diplomatic history,[67] itself a handmaiden of the modern reorganization of the management of the foreign-policy realm that took the form of recollection and compilation of international treaties, whether they were peace treaties or treaties of alliance or commerce, in national chancelleries from the eighteenth and nineteenth centuries.[68] In this context, some of the most important treaties in diplomatic history, as epitomes of a realist history of international law based on state practice and its related companions (war, power, trade) over time,[69] were to become themselves symbolic events in the historical evolution of international law.

However, the modern larger attention to contextualization has contributed to making international treaties increasingly being understood on their own historical terms against the historical context of the times when they occurred, and dislodged from the retrospective 'mythical' reinterpretations provided of them in the past. The Peace of Westphalia is the most obvious example of this way of proceeding, which operates in the entangled areas of the study of the 'history of international law' and that of 'international law in history' and which extends but it is not limited to international historical treaties, including peace treaties, as part of a 'systematic and coordinated research effort into the history of international legal practice'.[70] International lawyers have indeed made much of Westphalia as a foundational myth for the discipline to explain its own genesis to itself, variously interpreting it as the moment of

---

[66] Fleur Johns, Richard Joyce, and Sundhya Pahuja(eds.), *Events: The Force of International Law* (New York: Routledge, 2011).

[67] David Atkinson, 'History of diplomacy', in David Armstrong et al. (eds.), *Oxford Bibliographies in International Relations* (2014), www.oxfordbibliographies.com/view/document/obo-9780199743292/obo-9780199743292-0013.xml.

[68] Jean Dumont, Jean Rousset de Missy, and Jean Barbeyrac, *Corps universel diplomatique du droit des gens: contenant un recueil des traitez d'alliance, de paix, de treve, de neutralité, de commerce, d'échange de neutralité, de commerce, d'échange, de protection & de garantie, de toutes les conventions, transactions, pactes, concordats & autres contrats, qui ont été faits en Europe, depuis le regne de l'empereur Charlemagne jusques à present* (Amsterdam: Brunel, 1726–39).

[69] Wilhelm G. Grewe, *The Epochs of International Law*, trans. Michael Byers (Berlin and New York: De Gruyter, 2000).

[70] Randall Lesaffer (ed.), *Peace Treaties and International Law in European History: From the Late Middle Ages to World War One* (Cambridge, UK: Cambridge University Press, 2004).

transition from empire to autonomous territorially delimited sovereign states in the European political order which inaugurated a new *jus publicum europaeum*; as a momentous sort of post-war multilateral treatment for the international system; as the stepping stone between theocracy and a secularist *cuius regio eius religio* informed by 'reason of state'; as a crystallizing moment for an intellectual transition from a natural-law-dominated world-view towards an increasing role for voluntary law, and towards the use of the language of law and legality to anchor the balance of power in interstate relations; as a converging point for the principle of equal sovereignty of European states in both their internal and external facets; and, all in all, 'as the spark that lit the fuse of the European sovereignty-based international society which would later spread through different colonization waves to the four corners of the earth'.[71] And yet, despite the traditional disciplinary emphasis on the centrality of Westphalia for understanding what international law is all about, recent contextual re-readings have shown that while the Westphalia Peace Treaties 'lay down the political and religious conditions for allowing the European powers to start building a new international legal order', they, as Lesaffer notes, 'did not lay down the basic principles of the modern law of nations'.[72] Efforts to re-contextualize other historical events with significance for international law similar to those carried out for Westphalia have also encompassed, as Chapters 7 and 9 further examine, many other events traditionally captured in a *histoire événementielle* of international law. This is a historical genre classically criticized by Fernand Braudel with reference to his description of events as 'surface disturbances, crests of foam that the tides of history carry on their strong backs'.[73]

2.4   The Contextualist Impact on Knowledge Production Processes

Contextualism, understood as a historical methodology increasingly being more attentively imported by international lawyers, or exported

---

[71] Ignacio de la Rasilla, 'History of international law 1550-1700', in *Oxford Bibliographies in International Law* (2013), www.oxfordbibliographies.com/view/document/obo-9780199796953/obo-9780199796953-0036.xml, pp. 1–20 at 7.

[72] Randall Lesaffer, 'Peace treaties from Lodi to Westphalia', in Randall Lesaffer (ed.), *Peace Treaties and International Law in European History: From the Late Middle Ages to World War One* (Cambridge, UK: Cambridge University Press, 2004), pp. 9–44 at 10.

[73] Fernand Braudel, *The Mediterranean and the Mediterranean World in the Age of Philip II* (New York: Harper & Row, 1972; first published 1949).

by historians to bear on the study of international legal history, has contributed to putting in question the 'historical' character of two of the dimensions of interaction of international law and history. Regarding 'history in international law' or the 'uses of history in international law', contextualism has contributed to casting a shadow on 'international legal office history', understood as the instrumental use of past normative materials in the form of legal precedents, the key attributes of which are, according to Bederman:

> (1) a lack of analytic rigour in historical investigations, (2) selective use of historical materials, (3) sloppy or strategic methodologies in the review of historical sources, (4) overt or implicit instrumentalism in the selection of historical data and/or the conclusions drawn from such material, and (5) an unwillingness or inability to reconcile conflicting sources, or an inability to accept ambiguity or incompleteness in the historical record.[74]

Contextualism has furthermore expanded the role of contextualist historical methodologies within the realm of analysis that pertains to the study of historical or factual context in the light of established legal categories as well as in relation to other aspects involved in the interaction of international law with history in this domain, as will be further seen in Chapter 7.

Regarding the 'history of international law', contextualism has contributed to dispelling teleologically inspired readings of the evolution of the international legal order, at both the micro and the macro levels, through a questioning of the traditional synoptic historical-legal-theoretical genealogy of the history of international law in normative-technical areas often dominated by rule-based historiographical approaches that tend to exclude extra-legal considerations from the lenses they apply to the study of the past. The tendency to over-dimension the normative realm over historical context is apparent in the inclination to reiteratively refer back to past doctrines, norms, and principles as legal magical formulae. Against the tendency to foster an extremely narrow view of international legal history as a repository of legal formulas abstracted from the historical process which travel in time almost like memory bullet points, a larger emphasis on historical contextualization has permitted modern historical writing to provide a broader view of a number of origins and evolutions of norms, doctrines, and principles, including how their rhetorical deployment in particular circumstances enabled them to be

[74] Bederman, 'Foreign office', p. 46.

further refined or even be transformed. This development has benefited from the contemporary expansion and sub-disciplinary fragmentation of the body of international law, which in turn favours, as Chapter 7 and 8 examine, historical enquiries oriented to providing each of the sub-disciplines with greater autonomy and therefore making them more attentive to historical contexts, and the role played by social actors in regard to the development of special international legal regimes.

Regarding the 'intellectual history of international law', contextualism, complemented, as Chapter 10 examines, with biographical approaches, has contributed to re-situating great and also lesser figures through a synchronically contextualist re-reading of them as 'men of their times',[75] and less as mere stages in a diachronic narrative informed by precursorism with its reading of the present (and the future) in the past by identifying antecedents of present-day ideas in earlier historical periods. It has furthermore made more apparent the intrinsic linkage that exists between internal normative history and the more interdisciplinarily oriented dimension of conceptual history in international law. Above all, the methodological toolkit of contextualism has in particular nurtured the study of 'international law in history'. This refers to the study of the relationship of mutual influence that international law and/or parts thereof have entertained with different national and international societal, ideological, economic, intellectual, and professional historical contexts and/or particularly significant events which have in turn become the object of thicker historical contextualizations. This is an area which also overlaps, as Chapter 8 examines, with the broad field made up of both the sociological history and the social history of international law. This has developed in many directions, including the giving of greater attention to the history of non-state actors in international law and the fostering of inter alia more investigations into different nationally contextualized histories of international law, an area of research that overlaps with intellectual history and that has so far mostly been limited to the history of the professional development of international law in certain 'great powers'.

The more attentive application of contextualist lenses in international legal history has also largely impacted the historiography of international law. One dimension of this impact has involved the rise of methodological debates on the possible adjustment and limits, as the next section shows, of a contextualist methodology in international legal history.

---

[75] See, e.g., Richard Tuck, *The Rights of War and Peace: Political Thought and International Order from Grotius to Kant* (Oxford: Oxford University Press, 1999).

This has prompted a strategic retuning of historiographical perspectives among critical international lawyers committed to maximizing the political uses of the history of international law in the present. Another notable dimension of the impact has had to do with the importing of historical methodologies, including both original archival research and primary source-based work, into a field of studies traditionally less prone to them up to the point that new 'archival research' is, as Thomas Skouteris notes, one of the 'morphological characteristic[s] of the historical turn'.[76] Connected to the greater use of archival resources, which is part of Lesaffer's specific advice to use primary sources as key for understanding and reconstruction, favouring the earliest possible engagement with them in any historical research endeavour, is a deepening or thickening of contextualization. Indeed, professional historians increasingly 'engaging with the subject as part of their turn to the international dimension of history',[77] like Lauren Benton and Lisa Ford, are mining long-neglected archival sources and applying a diverse array of socio-legal methods to produce more contextualized perspectives on the historical development of international law with reference to its role in the practice of law.[78] Another historiographical dimension where the impact of contextualism, in that it contributes to de-mythologizing a great variety of traditional historical landmarks, is apparent is, as Chapter 11 examines, the study of the periodization of the history of international law.

2.5 Historiographical Debates, Confluences, and Critiques

Contextualism à la Cambridge School in the history of ideas is generally understood as the idea that a historian should approach 'historical texts, characters and events in their context, asking what a text or author really meant to do or convey, in the light of the social and linguistic structures in place at the time',[79] because doing differently, as Skinner noted, risks

---

[76] Thomas Skouteris, 'The turn to history in international law', in *Oxford Bibliographies in International Law* (2017), www.oxford bibliographies.com/view/document/obo-9780199796953/obo-9780199796953-0154.xml, p. 20.

[77] David Armitage, *Foundations of Modern International Thought* (Cambridge, UK: Cambridge University Press, 2013).

[78] Lauren A. Benton and Lisa Ford, *Rage for Order: The British Empire and the Origins of International Law 1800–1850* (Cambridge, MA: Harvard University Press, 2016).

[79] Andrea Bianchi, *International Law Theories: An Inquiry into Different Ways of Thinking* (Oxford: Oxford University Press, 2016), p. 180.

mutating history into a mythology.[80] In recent years, a historiographical controversy has emerged around the question of what the proper contextualizing method for international legal history would be. The debate, as we shall see, has included contributions by contextualist historians who argue that 'the recent critiques of the contextual methodology of the Cambridge School's approach to the history of international law from within the discipline itself are based upon a misunderstanding of the contextual methodology and its own critique of anachronism'.[81]

The framework of the controversy is the continuum of interaction between history and international law. This can metaphorically (and also, well, ironically) be described by stating that while Themis and Clio do not dwell in the same lodgings, they share common premises and often pay visits to each other's houses to play a game of cards together. As we saw before in examining Craven and Lesaffer's tripartite typology, there is a methodological corrective role for contextualism to play with regard to the manner in which the dimensions of 'history in international law' and the 'history of international law' have traditionally been approached by international lawyers, even if this consists in questioning the 'historical' status of a large part of what passes as international legal history within their frame.

Several considerations are intermingled in the methodological rift between critical/postmodern historians of international law and contextualist intellectual historians on the limits of what Orford describes as the 'contextualist policing of anachronism'[82] poses for 'critical' histories of international law. On the one hand, as we saw before with reference to Koskenniemi's reliance on the contextualist method, this, by understanding international legal ideas not as ethereal entities but as enmeshed in argumentative practice, performs a task which resounds positively with critical international legal historians. Indeed, as Orford notes, 'Skinner's methodological manifestos played an important part in stressing the role of texts, including texts that made normative truth claims, as political interventions in particular social contexts and political power struggles.'[83] Highlighting the demonstration of the historically pervasive

---

[80] Skinner, 'Meaning and understanding', p. 10.
[81] Andrew Fitzmaurice, 'Context in the history of international law' (2018) 20 *Journal of the History of International Law* 5–30 at 16.
[82] Orford, 'On international legal method', p. 171.
[83] Ibid., p. 170. See also Anne Orford, 'International law and the limits of history', in Wouter Werner, Marieke de Hoon, and Alexis Galán (eds.), *The Law of International Lawyers: Reading Martti Koskenniemi* (Cambridge, UK: Cambridge University Press,

character through the ages of the 'politics of international law' is of essence of the ethos that inspires, as Chapter 3 examines, critical/post-modern approaches to the history of international law as it allows them to challenge the conventional historiography of international law as one that fosters a meta-narrative of historical progress which contributes to spreading the understanding of international law as being above all an 'instrument for some perennial human pursuit from a primitive past into an increasingly more enlightened future'.[84] However, if contextualism 'restores works of political philosophy to their political contexts – that is, the situations in which they performed political tasks',[85] a principle which applies generally, following Skinner's opinion that 'even the most abstract works of political theory are never above the battle; they are always part of the battle itself',[86] it does so at the expense of somewhat 'freezing' them in their own historical contexts and dislodging them from the present.

This tension has gained central stage in a series of contextualist criticisms of post-colonial re-readings,[87] namely of Francisco de Vitoria's significance in international law as a posited legitimizer of colonialism; these are surveyed in Chapter 4, together with other refutations addressed at Antony Anghie's revisionist work. It is explanatorily useful, relying on the categories previously examined, to classify the otherwise intermingled different arguments echoed during what Christopher Warren terms the debate on the 'problem of temporality at the interdisciplinary nexus' between history and international law (and in his view also literature)[88] alongside the axes of synchronicity and diachronicity and their mutual relationship with 'presentism'. Indeed,

2017), pp. 297–320; Anne Orford, 'The past as law or history? The relevance of imperialism for modern international law', in Hélène Ruiz-Fabri, Mark Toufayan, and Emmanuelle Tourme-Jouannet (eds.), *Droit international et nouvelles approches sur le tiers-monde: entre répétition et renouveau (International Law and New Approaches to the Third World: Between Repetition and Renewal)* (Paris: Société de Législation Comparée, 2013), pp. 97–118.

[84] Koskenniemi, 'Legal history as Begriffsgeschichte?', in Claudia Wiesner (ed.), *In Debate with Karl Palonen: Concepts, Politics, Histories* (Baden-Baden: Nomos, 2015), pp. 63–68 at 64.

[85] Ball, 'The value of the history', p. 57.

[86] Quentin Skinner, *Hobbes and the Republican Liberty* (Cambridge, UK: Cambridge University Press, 2008), p. xvi.

[87] Ian Hunter, 'The figure of man and the territorialisation of justice in "Enlightenment" natural law: Pufendorf and Vattel' (2013) 23 *Intellectual History Review* 289–307.

[88] Warren, 'Henry V, anachronism', p. 709.

as we saw before, contextualism in the axis of synchronicity within the category of the 'history of international law' can coincide with an internal approach to legal materials in a normative sense at one particular moment in time. It also broadly coincides within the category of 'international law in history' with the external contextual approach to events, concepts, and texts relevant to international legal history within a fixed historical temporal framework which cannot be distorted by anything ulterior to it. Koskenniemi summarizes this pristine ideal occasionally evoked in the literary quote that 'the past is a foreign country: they do things differently there',[89] in that historians 'honour the radical otherness of the past' by accepting that 'ideas do not have trans-historical meanings. They are part of vocabularies and systems of thought that emerge in particular periods, flourish and die. Their meaning is completely tied up with those systems and cannot be grasped separately from them.'[90]

The criticisms addressed to this view, therefore, revolve, as seen before in revising some of contentions that contextualism has generated, around the difficulties in ascertaining the 'relevant' context and the influence of the present in effectively determining the choices regarding it. This line of criticism has been used to argue that contextualism cannot claim any dogmatic methodological predominance over critical narratives of international legal history.[91] Indeed, a first line of critique against the so-called radical otherness of the past highlights the incommensurability of historical contexts. This is so because, according to Koskenniemi, the notion of historical context is ultimately boundless and subject to unavoidably subjective 'choices and evaluations'[92] that are, furthermore, irremissibly conditioned by the present. According to this view, all efforts at contextualization inevitably involve a number of decisions about scale and scope, and these decisions necessarily act as mechanisms of inclusion, and equally importantly exclusion, of particular contexts. For Koskenniemi, the indeterminacy of such decisions, in turn, shows that 'all history is contemporary history', paraphrasing Benedetto Croce's often-quoted aphorisim 'every true history is

---

[89] Leslie Poles Hartley, *The Go-Between* (London: Hamish Hamilton, 1953), p. 1.

[90] Martti Koskenniemi, 'Histories of international law: significance and problems for a critical view' (2013) 27 *Temple International Law and Comparative Law Journal* 215–240 at 227.

[91] See Koskenniemi, 'Vitoria and us'. See also Orford, 'On international legal method', pp. 170–174; and Koskenniemi, 'Histories of international law: significance and problems', pp. 229–232.

[92] Koskenniemi, 'Histories of international law: significance and problems', p. 230.

contemporary history',[93] and therefore 'all significant history is inspired by contemporary concerns and carried out through the lenses provided by the present'.[94]

Yet the type of presentism here evoked by Koskenniemi loosely coincides with what David Armitage calls 'idealist presentism', which Armitage further notes has long been 'assumed by historians from Leopold von Ranke via Croce and Collingwood to E. H. Carr and beyond'[95] as part of the historical craft. This type of presentism refers to the central interpretative role of the present in a historian's attitude regarding the (re)construction of the past, which depends on each interpreter's individual subjective predisposition towards particular choices. Other than by the present itself, this is, of course, also mediated by a series of personal features (nationality, language, race, gender, social class, etc.), positionality (e.g. geographical location), professional or ethical interests – which may be part of what has been termed 'motivational presentism'[96] – and the influence or pull of dominant historiographical trends. As was pointed out in the introduction to this chapter, all these are factors bearing on inclusion and exclusion choices per se, and, mediated by the *animus historiandi* and authorial or political intent, underlie any historical investigation. This is precisely the logic behind Edward H. Carr's often-quoted statement that 'the facts of history never come to us "pure", since they do not and cannot exist in a pure form: they are always refracted through the mind of the recorder. It follows that when we take a work of history, our first concern should be not with the facts which it contains but with the historian who wrote it.'[97]

However, this form of 'idealist presentism' is different, despite points of overlap, from the category of what Armitage calls 'analytical presentism'. This, otherwise known as 'present-centeredness', is 'the procedure of using current categories or imperatives not only to determine historical topics but then to interpret them in terms distant from, or unrecog-

---

[93] Benedetto Croce, *Theory and History of Historiography*, trans. Douglas Ainslie (London: George G. Harrap & Company, 1921), p. 12.

[94] Martti Koskenniemi, 'Imagining the rule of law: rereading the Grotian "tradition"' (2019) 30 *European Journal of International Law* 17–52 at 20.

[95] Armitage, 'In defense of presentism', p. 9.

[96] Ibid., pp. 17–18, citing Naomi Oreskes, 'Why I am a presentist' (2013) 26 *Science in Context* 595–609.

[97] Edward Hallet Carr, *What Is History?*, 2nd ed. (Cambridge, UK: Cambridge University Press, 1987), p. 22.

nisable to, the past itself.[98] But 'idealist presentism' is even more clearly different from 'teleological presentism', which can present itself not just in the form of 'Whig history' but also in the form of 'counter-teleological' presentism. This form of presentism, which is the reverse of a teleological hegemonic tradition which ratifies or normalizes the present, is particularly influential in shaping critical approaches to the history of international law like those methodologically defended, or espoused, by Koskenniemi and some of his methodological acolytes. However, this alone does not preclude their disruptive presentist persuasiveness. Their deployment to 'describe an interpretation of history that is biased towards and coloured by present-day concerns, preoccupations and values'[99] may, once its contextualist corrective function has been exhausted through instances of contextualist re-readings of the hegemonic tradition which ratifies or normalizes the present, also be similarly affected by the constraints contextualism imposes on the treatment of historical subjects. In the history of international law, it should, indeed, be remembered that 'presentism ... at worst becomes indoctrination' also by '[counter-]historical example'.[100]

Therefore, while the argument of the incommensurability of contexts brings us squarely to the author's own subjective approach as determined by a myriad subjective and positional factors, this fact alone does not necessarily warrant a letter of marque to the international legal historian for him or her to unreflectively embrace either 'analytical presentism' in its explicit interpretative dimension or the 'teleological' and/or 'counter-teleological' variant of presentism when confronted with his or her decisions to include, or equally importantly exclude, relevant contexts. These decisions are partly conditioned, as noted earlier, by the criterion of historical relevance or pertinence, which in turn is influenced by each author's ability to convincingly negotiate the necessary balance between the dispassionate portrayal of impartial objectivity (scientific ethos) and the *animus historiandi* (authorial or political intent). This balance, tenuous as it may be, nonetheless invariably insufflates all historical narratives with a particular interpretative edge. However, even if the interpretative edge is justifiable in terms of defensible criteria of relevance regarding the historical subject, these narratives can still be informed by a sense of

---

[98] Armitage, 'In defense of presentism', p. 8.
[99] Ibid., p. 3.
[100] Gordon S. Wood, *The Purpose of the Past: Reflections on the Use of History* (New York: Penguin Press, 2008), pp. 293–308, cited in Armitage, 'In defense of presentism', pp. 4–5.

equilibrium in pondering elements that speak for the two or more sides of the same (hi)story. This balancing of opposite perspectives, which is a skill that comes naturally to the trained legal mind, can be pushed even further to suggest giving consideration to multi-perspectivity as a historiographical compass assuring a balanced contextual assessment when confronted with 'the open-endedness of relevant contexts worthy of study'[101] in international legal history.

A second related criticism is that, according to Koskenniemi, 'the contextual view poses a real challenge for any effort to write critically about international law's past',[102] because it brings about a 'troubling, ultimately uncritical relativism' which derives from the fact that 'the meaning of a past text or event must be isolated in the context where it was written or where it took place'.[103] While, as we have just seen, the first part of Koskenniemi's critique, which is developed on an objective analytical basis, may be said to have long been assumed by contextualism, its second interrelated part presents a more defined normative character. Koskenniemi expresses this is in clear-cut critical manifesto-like terms, noting that 'the choices and evaluations which enable the historian to engage with the past ought to reflect an effort to attain a better understanding of the nature of the present, including the causes of today's domination and injustice, in order to contribute to their eradication'.[104]

Koskenniemi's latest remark brings us squarely back to the ambivalent relationship that exists between teleological and counter-teleological presentism, and more precisely to the methodological limits the latter may encounter. 'Counter-teleological presentism' is another name for what Armitage, following Loison, terms 'critical presentism' and calls the 'obverse of the Whig interpretation of history'.[105] This is defined as critical insofar as it seeks to 'dethrone the pretensions of the present' and 'dampens dogmatism', in particular 'in scholarly fields founded on assumptions about the progress and accumulation of knowledge'. In Armitage's description of it, this critical presentism appears as a sort of presentist anti-anachronism mechanism, the aim of which is 'to oppose presentism in its various teleological guises and also in its narrative

[101] Lauren Benton, 'Beyond anachronism: histories of international law and global legal politics' (2019) 21 *Journal of the History of International Law* 7–40 at 11.
[102] Koskenniemi, 'Vitoria and us', p. 122.
[103] Ibid., p. 127.
[104] Koskenniemi, 'Histories of international law: significance and problems', p. 230.
[105] Armitage, 'In defense of presentism', p. 17.

mode'.[106] Accordingly, it has been described as one that 'may thereby be more compatible than other forms of presentism with the practical work of researching and writing history'.[107] This form of corrective counter-teleological or critical presentism can be found in the types of contextualist readings influential in the history of international law credited by Martine Van Ittersum with having 'explored the "dark side of rights theories", and shown that the political thought of Grotius, Hobbes, and Locke form the building blocks of Western imperialism and colonialism'.[108]

It is clear that this form of corrective presentism falls short of Koskenniemi's all-encompassing programme for critical international legal history.[109] However, pointing out its existence allows understanding of Koskenniemi's critique as one that attempts to break the boundaries of his previously espoused form of critical presentism. It allows putting in perspective the argumentative basis of the criticisms that he addresses to contextualist historical methodology for being a methodology that 'under the guise of a methodological point' rejects 'open political engagement', which in his view makes it 'political through and through'.[110] One could also add that Koskenniemi's attack on contextualism for being politically conservative glosses over, as Bourke notes, the question of whether the 'Cambridge School's focus on the history of ideas risks reducing political thought to its historicity' (which he considers is a 'question-begging question: why should there be a problem with the historicity of thought, or even with the historicity of values?'). This has long been reflected on by Cambridge historians themselves, who 'have never been fully satisfied with justifying their relevance in terms of their simple historical interest' but have used their work as a means of 'moral exhortation'.[111] Even more specifically, Koskenniemi's insistence that the 'validity of our histories' lies not in their correspondence with context but in 'how they contribute

---

[106] Ibid.

[107] Ibid.

[108] Martine Julia Van Ittersum, *Profit and Principle: Hugo Grotius, Natural Rights Theories and the Rise of Dutch Power in the East Indies 1595–1615* (Leiden: Brill, 2006), p. xxxviii. For other examples from the literature, see Fiztmaurice, 'Context', pp. 14–15.

[109] Martti Koskenniemi, 'What should international legal history become?', in Stefan Kadelbach, Thomas Kleinlein, and David Roth-Isigkeit (eds.), *System, Order and International Law: The Early History of International Legal Thought from Machiavelli to Hegel* (Oxford: Oxford University Press, 2017), pp. 381–397.

[110] Koskenniemi, 'Vitoria and us', p. 129.

[111] Bourke, 'The Cambridge School', p. 5.

to emancipation today'[112] has been responded to by Andrew Fitzmaurice, according to whom 'one of the main points of the contextual approach to history has been to contest the political manipulation of the past for present political purposes', and who wonders, 'who is to judge which causes are emancipatory and, once such principles of historical practice are accepted, who is to restrict such practices to questions of emancipation?' Fitzmaurice continues, 'should historical debate be reduced to rhetorical arguments between contesting political positions? Should historians be uninterested in establishing criteria for contesting the truth of historical claims? Which position is relativistic?'[113]

Koskenniemi's critique, so far mainly examined in terms of the axis of synchronicity, is, nonetheless, connected to a partially overlapping set of problematics surrounding the application of contextualist methods in the axis of diachronicity. These revolve around the question of how to contextually treat the movement of concepts relevant to international law 'across time and space'.[114] There are two sides to the question of how to contextually interpret a text in relationship to the context that provides meaning to its illocutionary intention. One of these relates to the text in relation to its diachronic past while the other relates to the context in relationship to anything situated in its diachronic future. The first side, which involves analepsis, or a form of flashback to an earlier time, was considered by Skinner in noting that 'there is no implication that the relevant context need be an immediate one' and that, therefore, 'the problems to which writers see themselves as responding may have been posed in a remote period, even in a wholly different culture'.[115] It is the second side involving prolepsis, or flash-forward from the time of completion towards the present – or an evolutionary history reconstructed from the present to the past – which is, prima facie, more susceptible to committing the 'sin of anachronism'.[116]

It was against this background that Orford argued that other disciplines, 'such as law ... resist the contextualist prescription that present-day questions must not be allowed to distort our interpretation of past events, texts or concepts' and wondered, 'what kind of method is

---

[112] Koskenniemi, 'Vitoria and us', p. 129.
[113] Fitzmaurice, 'Context', p. 13.
[114] Orford, 'The past as law or history?'
[115] Quentin Skinner, *Visions of Politics:Regarding Method* (Cambridge, UK: Cambridge University Press, 2002), p. 116.
[116] Constantin Fasolt, *The Limits of History* (Chicago: University of Chicago Press, 2004), p. 6.

appropriate to a discipline in which judges, advocates, scholars and students all look to past texts precisely to discover the nature of present obligations?'[117] This in turn led her to suggest that the 'international legal method' is 'necessarily anachronistic',[118] because the 'operation of modern law is not governed solely by a chronological sense of time in which events and texts are confined to their proper place in a historical and linear progression from then to now'. The same line of argument led her furthermore to conclude that 'international law is inherently genealogical, depending as it does upon the transmission of concepts, languages and norms across time and space. The past, far from being gone, is constantly being retrieved as a source or rationalisation of present obligation.'[119]

However, on a closer look, the unavoidability of anachronism claimed by Orford does not spring out from the assumed types of presentism mentioned above but from the fact that she takes as her reference point in defending the unavoidability of anachronism in international legal history the argumentatively and instrumentally oriented use of normative materials from the history of international law – one of the components examined in the previously examined category of 'history in international law' – and that despite the criticisms addressed to it, as seen before, by Bederman and Lesaffer. Orford may have taken as her point of reference the 'evolutionary approach', which partly characterizes the different category of the 'history of international law' as one where, regarding a synoptic engagement of the diachronic axis inspired by an 'evolutionary' and teleologically suspicious approach, according to Lesaffer the historian of law will have to abstract a conception or rule throughout the different phases of its evolution as much as possible from its context, and regard it as an autonomous category.[120] However, in both cases the engagement is with the normative realm and therefore outside the realm of contextual history *proprio sensu*, which Fitzmaurice delimits as one marked by the 'time 'it ceases to represent some kind of account of the past which its inhabitants might recognise as a description of their own experience'.[121] Fitzmaurice furthermore highlights that for a 'contextual historian' . . . there is nothing wrong with being anachronistic in

---

[117] Orford, 'On international legal method', p. 171. See also Alexandra Kemmerer, '"We do not need to always look to Westphalia . . .": a conversation with Martti Koskenniemi and Anne Orford' (2015) 17 *Journal of the History of International Law* 1–14.
[118] Orford, 'On international legal method', p. 175.
[119] Ibid.
[120] Lesaffer, 'Law between past and present', p. 13.
[121] Fitzmaurice, 'Context', p. 12.

order to make a point of philosophy, political theory, law or economics',
but if it is not 'recognisable to historical subjects' one 'should not call it
history'.[122] In fact, as Koskenniemi readily admits, 'historians rarely
think nowadays' in terms of an approach that 'takes our present concepts
and institutions as its starting points and works backwards to sketch a
"tradition" operating as a conversation across generations over such
familiar topics as sovereignty, diplomacy, treaties, humanitarian limits
to warfare and so on, gradually gaining maturity in our present
institutions'.[123]

The question that ensues is whether there could be a proper 'international legal historical method' that would avoid the pitfalls of
anachronism. Orford herself points to it by signalling that John G. A.
Pocock has distinguished Skinner's strategy of focusing on 'the language
context existing at a particular time' from his own attempt to ask 'what
happens when a language of discourse persists and is redeployed in a
historical situation, or context, other than that in which it was deployed
previously'.[124] But, contrary to Orford's conclusions, this points to a
form of trans-historical serial contextualization. Indeed, if as noted by
Koskenniemi the reception of an author's writings 'by later generations
would put them in a number of different contexts – in a way that longue
durée studies would be necessary to grasp their meaning',[125] the appropriate method for going about this task would be to proceed through the
reconstruction of the different historical contexts of reception of an
intellectual work with due consideration to the 'historical presentisms'
involved in each reception and, as the investigation proceeds through
different contexts of reception, to the need to consider the effects of the
accumulation of these 'historical presentisms' and their relative effects
over time. A previous ascertainment of which are the proper contexts of
reception would go some way to assuaging what Fizmaurice calls the
extremely difficult task of writing 'serial contextualisation'.[126]

Although with some caveats, this perspective which prioritizes context
coincides with Lesaffer's recommendation of adopting a two-phase
method to approach the past for

---

[122] Ibid.
[123] Koskenniemi, 'Histories of international law', p. 227.
[124] Orford, 'On international legal method', p. 174.
[125] George R. B. Galindo, 'Splitting TWAIL?' (2016) 33 *Windsor Yearbook of Access to
Justice* 37–56 at 46.
[126] Fizmaurice, 'Context', p. 10.

scholars who want to use the past in order to understand or legitimate the present. First, they need to study the past in its own right and on its own terms. For this, the use of a sound historical methodology is mandatory. Second, they can use the understanding of past law to reconstruct the evolution of a certain rule, institution or doctrine, or to engage in comparative law through time.[127]

Lesaffer's view is that a 'true 'history of law' is impossible without engaging in 'law in history' first and evading the snare of a 'history in law' conception of the past'.[128] However, as Chapter 7 further examines, it would be naïve to consider that the strong gravitational pull of the juridical form of functional presentism that characterizes the field of international law and within it of international legal history can, merely, be disciplinarily dispelled by criteria transposed from other disciplinary traditions.

2.6 Conclusion

The interdisciplinarization of international legal history and in its wake the greater attention to questions of historiographical method, including historical contextualism, and its 'demythologizing' function of bringing, as Koskenniemi notes, 'legal principles down from the conceptual heaven and into a real world where agents make claims and counterclaims, advancing some agendas, opposing others',[129] has boosted a new methodological self-consciousness among international lawyers. In the wake of the academic space that the turn to the history of international law has opened for academic respectability and the marketability of historical enquiries in their discipline, international lawyers have been increasingly attracted to moonlighting as international legal historians or even as international legal historiographers of some repute. The latter is a much longed-for development in an area that the international legal 'professional elite has been scandalously negligent for too long in exploring'.[130]

In the wake of the increasing methodological self-awareness within the field has come a larger interpenetration of the hitherto separate 'structures of judgment and authority which are founded on a disciplinary

---

[127] Lesaffer, 'Law between past and present', p. 19.
[128] Ibid., p. 17.
[129] Koskenniemi, 'Vitoria and us', p. 123.
[130] Stephen C. Neff, *Justice among Nations: A History of International* Law (Cambridge, MA: Harvard University Press, 2014), p. 4.

division of labour'[131] (understood by Johan Heilbron as an 'institutional arrangement inseparably consisting of cognitive and social structures, that is, of fairly coherent sets of concepts, questions, references and methods, and a corresponding social order of acknowledged specialists')[132] between the fields of history, legal history, and international law. Because the methodological controversy previously examined between critical international legal historians and contextualist historians of political thought over the fact that the contextualist methodological knife may, unsatisfactorily for critical approaches, cut both ways, such an interpenetration is ultimately symptomatic of the new set of relationships based on confluence (corroboration to resonate more effectively) and divergence (reduction of the ability to project discursive authority) between the methodologies associated with different historiographical trends and the scientific and intellectual movements they represent.

While the open-ended nature of controversies about method in international legal history suggests paying attention to multi-perspectivity, the controversies similarly point to the question of the performative narrative function of all historical research, including international legal history in the present. Whether in an overtly intended or at least a declaratory manner, as in critical historiographies, or in a more nuanced and indirect way, all new writing in the history of international law, which revisits the past in the present, also affects our understanding of contemporary matters in international law and contributes to providing insights into their potential unfolding. This opens up the question of the uses to which new historical writing about international law is put, which is tantamount to hypothesizing, as Skinner originally suggested for historical texts, on what can be learnt from wondering about their 'illocutionary or performative force', in other words the effects that each author intends his or her new writing about the history of international law to have in the present world.

Similarly to the methodology propounded to gain a deeper contextual understanding of a historical text, this in turn relies on a deeper grasping of the context, understood as the contemporary conventions and usages of our own age to which historical writing about international law needs to relate in order to be effective. An enquiry like the one this book offers

---

[131] Johan Heilbron, 'A regime of disciplines: toward a historical sociology of disciplinary knowledge', in Charles Camic and Hans Joas (eds.), *The Dialogical Turn* (Lanham, MD: Rowman & Littlefield, 2004), pp. 23–42 at 23.
[132] Ibid.

into some of the contemporary modes of doing international legal history provides a radiography of the framework of dialogue that serves as the intellectual context for ascribing meaning to any new historical writing about international law. If, as Andrew Fitzmaurice notes, contextualism stipulates 'that the meaning of any particular text, or utterance, must be understood by placing the person who makes that utterance in her or his context' because 'each utterance is an act and to understand the nature of that act it is necessary to see what the author is doing in relation to a particular set of circumstances',[133] it also ensues that any new piece of historical writing about international law is also an 'utterance', or a 'speech act' and, as such, for the use of future historians of international law it also becomes historically contextualized in our present from the moment of its very inception.

However, while a deeper understanding of the historiography of international law helps provide a larger contextual understanding of the *animus historiandi* or the 'historian's motives in examining historical material', which, according to Hans-Georg Gadamer, should be a central part of any 'historical hermeneutics',[134] such a contextual understanding is also ultimately dependent on all contemporary international legal scholarship writ large. Indeed, it is within this broader context that the illocutionary impact – the intended purpose of the intellectual intervention – which in some of the historiographical trends examined in this volume is intended as a 'vehicle of political commentary, and even a mode of apology, for a wide range of contemporary normative concerns',[135] may take effect. However, as important as they may be for us to understand their meaning in context, the author's intentions may also instead become transformed in their perlocutionary effect into something rather different from what the author set out to do within the inextricable course of what, as Edward H. Carr reminds us, is the 'unending dialogue between the present and the past',[136] and more so particularly in such an instrumentally oriented discipline as international law.

The aforementioned clearly does not amount to suggesting forgetting the ironical intent of Lucien Febvre in paraphrasing the already ironical remark by Charles Peguy, according to whom 'il n'est pas bon que

---

[133] Fitzmaurice, 'Context', p. 7.
[134] Hans-Georg Gadamer, *Truth and Method* (London: Bloomsbury Academic, 2014), p. 334; cited in Warren, 'Henry V, anachronism', p. 714.
[135] Gunnell, 'History of political philosophy', p. 69.
[136] Carr, *What Is History?*, p. 24.

l'historien réfléchisse trop sur l'histoire. Du temps qu'il s'y occupe, il arrête son travail'[137] ('it is not good for the historian to think too much about history. Once he begins to do so, he stops working'). However, it may serve as an occasionally helpful reminder that contextualism, like any other historical method, should first and foremost be put at the service of a good international legal (his)story in the same way as in any true work of art the most refined technique serves to foreground the human spirit.

---

[137] Lucien Febvre, *Combats pour l'histoire* (Paris: Librairie Armand Colin, 1992; first published 1952), p. 418.

3

Critical/Postmodern Approaches to the History of International Law

3.1 Introduction

Different people write about the history of international law differently and for different reasons, inspired by the wish to put their international historical legal scholarship at the service of different causes. Some approach this study with a sense of moral duty to those whom the promise of international law has left betrayed or ignored and who are hopelessly wondering what international law's wrong turn or inaction has practically to do with their current dismal fate. On other occasions, international legal history is approached as part of an effort at international legal norm-entrepreneurship with a view to reforming a specific element in the international legal order with a statistically proven ability to save lives or reduce the likelihood of harm if they are faithfully complied with. In other cases, international legal history serves to trace parallelisms between past scenarios and present-day concerns in order to tailor, through trial and error, better policy choices than those delivered by the earlier adoption of a particular international legal course rather than other alternatives. At other times, thinking backwards and forwards in time may help one to see with greater acuity what particular style of scholarly treatment a subject deserves in order to render justice to the victims of past abuses, for impending crises to be timely deactivated, or for ongoing global threats to be handled in the most constructive and orderly possible manner. Sometimes, retrieving the historical memory of international law contributes to raising consciousness of the root causes underlying certain recurrent phenomena of international concern while catering for the intellectual and ethical betterment – although these two do not necessarily follow each other – of its contemporary protagonists in the light of less than edifying examples of some of their predecessors. While referring to different themes of historical investigation and making use of a diversity of historical methods, many of these and many other uses of historical research in international law perform a *critical* function. This is because by delving into the rich reservoir of accumulated – but never unequivocal – knowledge of international law that the past has bequeathed to us they intend to elicit, to different degrees and on different scales, a change or transformation in the present status quo inspired by an *esprit critique d'internationalité*.

While the label 'critical' is, therefore, not the property of any scholarly trend or any approach to the history of international law, the term 'critical international legal history' is used in this chapter in a narrower sense to characterize a series of historical and historiographical theoretical works by authors who see themselves as engaged in an overtly critical dialogue through the means of international legal history with the discipline writ large. In doing so, they also see themselves as 'people with projects' who contribute to the academic production of a contemporary 'intellectual/scientific movement' understood as a 'collective effort to pursue research programmes or projects for thought in the face of resistance from others in the scientific or intellectual community'[1] in international legal scholarship. This effort, the origins, development, and impact of which on the study of the history of international law are the subject of this chapter, can be described as being loosely united by its commitment, to echo Robert W. Gordon's definition of 'critical legal history', to an

> approach to the past that produces disturbances in the field – that inverts or scrambles familiar narratives of stasis, recovery or progress; anything that advances rival perspectives (such as those of the losers rather than the winners) for surveying developments, or that posits alternative trajectories that might have produced a very different present – in short any approach that unsettles the familiar strategies that we use to tame the past in order to normalize the present.[2]

'Critical history' has a long tradition in historical and historical legal studies under the inspiration of background political ideologies such as, classically, Marxism, with its central tenet that history must be primordially understood in materialist terms and that, accordingly, throughout its development '[i]t is not the consciousness of men that determines their being, but, on the contrary, their social being that determines their

---

[1] Scott Frickel and Neil Gross, 'A general theory of scientific/intellectual movements' (2005) 70 *American Sociological Review* 204–232 at 205.
[2] Robert W. Gordon, 'The arrival of critical historicism' (1997) 49 *Stanford Law Review* 1023–1030 at 1024.

consciousness'.[3] However, in international legal scholarship a more specifically defined 'critical' historiographical modern orientation grew only
as part and parcel of a particularly situated academic matrix.[4] This has
been known, among other labels, as 'newstream',[5] New Approaches to
International Law (NAIL),[6] the international legal branch of Critical
Legal Studies (CLS),[7] 'new thinking in international law',[8] critical
approaches to international law,[9] or merely the work of 'crits'.[10] These
can be generally framed as critical/postmodern approaches to the history
of international law, and they emerged in the mid- to late 1980s, evolved
during the 1990s, and coalesced with the turn to the history of international law in the early 2000s, in the development of which they have
remained an important vector. In their evolution they have borrowed
from and engaged in critical dialogue with historical methodologies,
namely, as was seen in Chapter 2, historical contextualism in the history
of ideas, and have overlapped and closely integrated with other
approaches. These are namely post-colonial and critical feminist ones,
which are also characterized by their militant will to 're-emphasize the
potential of the use of history for political ends'[11] or, to echo an otherwise

---

[3] Karl Marx, 'Preface to a critique of political economy', reprinted in *Karl Marx: Selected Writings*, ed. D. McLellan, 2nd ed. (Oxford: Oxford University Press, 2000), pp. 424–428 at 425, quoted in Susan Marks, 'Introduction', in Susan Marks (ed.), *International Law on the Left: Re-examining Marxist Legacies* (Cambridge, UK: Cambridge University Press, 2008), pp. 1–29 at 2.

[4] David Kennedy, 'A new stream of international law scholarship' (1998) 7 *Wisconsin International Law Journal* 1–49.

[5] Deborah Cass, 'Navigating the newstream: recent critical scholarship in international law' (1996) 65 *Nordic Journal of International Law* 341–383.

[6] David Kennedy and Christopher Tennant, 'New Approaches to International Law: a bibliography' (1994) 35 *Harvard International Law Journal* 417–460; Thomas Skouteris, 'New Approaches to International Law', in *Oxford Bibliographies in International Law* (2011), www.oxfordbibliographies.com/view/document/obo-9780199796953/obo-9780199796953-0012.xml, p. 1.

[7] Nigel Purvis, 'Critical Legal Studies in public international law' (1991) 32 *Harvard International Law Journal* 81–127.

[8] David Kennedy, 'My talk at the ASIL: what is new thinking in international law?' (2000) 94 *Proceedings of the American Society of International Law* 104–125.

[9] Jean Pierre-Cot, 'Tableau de la pensée juridique américaine' (2006) 110 *Révue générale de droit international public* 537–596 at 587–589.

[10] Outi Korhonen, 'New international law: silence, defence of deliverance?' (1996) 7 *European Journal of International Law* 1–28.

[11] Henry Jones, 'The radical use of history in the study of international law' (2012–13) 23 *Finnish Yearbook of International Law* 309–350 at 309.

intrinsically ambivalent term which is often used in critical international legal historiography, to produce 'human emancipation'.[12]

The series of methods, foci, topoi, and historiographical queries most commonly associated with the critical/postmodern historiography of international law are, as we shall see, very diverse. However, they share a particular *animus historiandi*, that of generating a comprehensive critique of the liberal narrative of cosmopolitan progress underlying international law through the deployment of a more granular, nuanced, and politically contingent picture of its historical evolution. Their revisionist reading of the historical evolution of international law can serve various purposes, including, but not only, that of illustrating the entwinedness of international law with structures of domination, in particular imperialism, and the recurrent reproduction of these same structures up to the present. Critical/postmodern approaches have played a central role among the factors underlying the 'turn to the history of international law' and the debates it has spawned. They have also contributed largely to problematizing and, up to a point, to transforming the traditional international lawyers' *habitus* understood by Pierre Bourdieu as a 'subjective but not individual system of internalized structures, schemes of perception, conception and action common to all members of the same group or class'.[13]

This chapter gives a flavour of the historiographical contribution of critical/postmodernist approaches to the history of international law. Section 3.2 provides a summary characterization of their background origins, their scholarly evolution, their relationship with earlier approaches, and their main intellectual features. With reference to the work of 'critical' international law scholars from different overlapping generations, Section 3.3 then analyses the historiographical themes, techniques, methods, foci, and topoi most commonly associated with this historiography, while Section 3.4 examines their impact on knowledge production processes related to the study of the relationship between international law and history. Section 3.5 provides a tenfold list of their main scholarly features, and analyses their role in contemporary historiographical debates in the field and some of the critiques addressed to

---

[12] Martti Koskenniemi, 'Histories of international law: significance and problems for a critical view' (2013) 27 *Temple International and Comparative Law Journal* 215–240 at 231.

[13] Pierre Bourdieu, *Outline of a Theory of Practice*, trans. Richard Nice (Cambridge, UK: Cambridge University Press, 1977), p. 86.

them. Finally, Section 3.6 summarizes the main lines of historiographical evolution experienced by critical/postmodern approaches to international legal history since the mid-1980s.

3.2 The Critical Revamping of International Legal Scholarship

Under the generic label of 'critical approaches' to international law, cryptically identified by Martti Koskenniemi as a 'new critical sensitivity consciously self-reflective',[14] one can refer to the formation of an 'epistemic community' loosely united, according to David Kennedy, by its will to escape 'the neo-liberal triumphalism of the post-Cold War discipline'.[15] Developing from the mid- to late 1980s, this was to become composed of a large body of critical and intellectually heterodox scholarly works by an interdisciplinary and heterogeneous group of inter alia international lawyers, philosophers, legal theorists, legal historians, comparative lawyers, legal anthropologists, sociologists, and so on.[16] For ease of reference, their intellectual production can be framed within what Duncan Kennedy calls 'mpm/left' ('modernism/postmodernism and leftism').[17] According to Kennedy, who was one of the founders of CLS in the mid- to late 1970s,[18] there are two main strands of CLS: the first strand focuses on left-wing political action ('changing the existing system of social hierarchy'); the second strand focuses on the 'modernist/post-modernist' cultural rebellion ('achieving transcendent aesthetic/emotional/intellectual experiences at the margins, or in the interstices of a disrupted rational grid').[19]

In international legal scholarship, there is an echo of the referred typology in the fact that the 'critical' international legal epistemic community follows a generic trend in legal thought that combines or follows a critical left-wing orientation in methodology and approach, and/or applies and/or is influenced by the postmodernist turn in

---

[14] Martti Koskenniemi, 'Preface' (1996) 65 Nordic Journal of International Law 337–340 at 337.

[15] David Kennedy, 'When renewal repeats: thinking against the box' (1999–2000) 32 New York Journal of International Law and Politics 335–500 at 491.

[16] Kennedy and Tennant, 'Bibliography'.

[17] Duncan Kennedy, A Critique of Adjudication: Fin de Siècle (Cambridge, MA: Harvard University Press, 1997), p. 7.

[18] Roberto M. Unger, The Critical Legal Studies Movement: Another Time, a Greater Task (London: Verso, 2015).

[19] Duncan Kennedy, A Critique of Adjudication, pp. 6–7.

philosophy in its study of the international legal system. For generally descriptive purposes, this corpus of critical international legal scholarship may be divided into two main strands, termed, following Andreas Paulus, 'internal' or 'epistemological' critique and 'external' or 'normative' critique. The first branch of the critical project in international law is aimed at unveiling 'the internal inconsistency of mainstream international law', while the second one, which is generally defined by its external or normative features, 'points towards the ideological and political bias of supposedly 'neutral' legal rules'.[20] Whereas the second strand possesses its own scholarly roots, it can also be approached as one that has evolved from or that has both methodologically and historically benefited from the ground-setting work of the first and more theoretical and philosophically oriented variety of 'critical/post-modern' scholarship in international law.This division, although admittedly reductive of the sheer diversity of critical approaches in international legal scholarship, partially coincides with their first and second overlapping generations and as such can help to impressionistically 'historicize' the internal development of critical/postmodern approaches to the history of international law as they 'radically challenged the dominant strain in which the history of international law had been written'.[21]

An overview of the 'internal' or 'epistemological critique' should begin with David Kennedy,[22] whose book *International Legal Structures*[23] and a number of his journal articles written in the early 1980s[24] pioneered the application of the structuralist critique in international legal scholarship.[25] In his own words, Kennedy's aim was to 'reformulate the relationship between law and politics in rhetorical terms'[26] by looking at

[20] Andreas L. Paulus, 'International law after postmodernism: towards renewal or decline of international law?' (2001) 14 *Leiden Journal of International Law* 727–755 at 731.
[21] Jennifer Pitts, 'International relations and the critical history of international law' (2017) 31 *International Relations* 282–298 at 284.
[22] For an earlier treatment, see Ignacio de la Rasilla del Moral, 'Notes for the history of new approaches to international legal studies: not a map but perhaps a compass', in José M. Beneyto and David Kennedy (eds.), *New Approaches to International Law* (The Hague: T. M. C. Asser Press, 2012), pp. 225–248.
[23] David Kennedy, *International Legal Structures* (Baden-Baden: Nomos Verlagsgesellschaft, 1987).
[24] David Kennedy, 'Theses about international law discourse' (1980) 23 *German Yearbook of International Law* 353–391.
[25] Anthony Carty, 'Critical international law: recent trends in the theory of international law' (1991) 2 *European Journal of International Law* 1–26.
[26] David Kennedy, 'A new stream', p. 7.

'public international law from the inside'[27] in order to unravel 'the relationships among doctrines and arguments and upon their recurring rhetorical structure'.[28] In seeking 'to unify the historical, theoretical, doctrinal and institutional projects of the discipline' through 'a methodological reformulation',[29] Kennedy furthermore declared that he was aiming at dislodging the 'discipline of international law from its stagnation'[30] in 'the tragic voice of post-war public law liberalism'.[31] He described this iconoclastically as 'one in which no one seemed to think international legal theory could offer more than an easy patois of lazy justification and arrogance for a discipline that has lost its way and kept its jobs'.[32] Indeed, following in the footsteps of CLS, Kennedy criticized the United States' mainstream approach to international law both internally and externally in his early works: internally 'for failing to complete its own anti-formalist project, for continuing ambivalence about the state, about legal sovereignty, and so forth'[33] in order to identify the blinds spots, overstatements, or elisions which are part of the discipline's normal doctrinal or institutional practices;[34] and externally by seeking 'to link the mainstream to an ideological bias' and to thus come up with a 'situated historical and strategic' project that investigates 'how one or another mainstream blend of rule and policy may function as a cover or polemic for particular interests'.[35]

Kennedy shared with the first generation of CLS a will to pursue the anti-formalist lineage of American legal realism in the 1920s and 1930s to its limits.[36] Duncan Kennedy defined this endeavour as 'resurrecting the

---

[27] Ibid., p. 11.
[28] Ibid., p. 10.
[29] Ibid., p. 11.
[30] Ibid., p. 6.
[31] Ibid., p. 2.
[32] Ibid. This is a clear homage to the CLS manifesto by Roberto Unger, and in particular to the well-known phrase 'when we came, they [the law professors] were like a priesthood that had lost their faith and kept their jobs. They stood in tedious embarrassment before cold altars. But we turned away from those altars and found the mind's opportunity in the heart's revenge.' See Unger, *Legal Studies Movement*, p. 119.
[33] David Kennedy, 'The disciplines of international law and policy' (1999) 12 *Leiden Journal of International Law* 9–133 at 34.
[34] Ibid., p. 35.
[35] Ibid.
[36] Richard W. Bauman, *Critical Legal Studies: A Guide to the Literature* (Boulder, CO: Westview, 1996); George Edward White, 'Round and round the bramble bush: from legal realism to critical legal scholarship' (1984) 95 *Harvard Law Review* 1669–1690; Joseph W. Singer, 'Legal realism now' (1988) 76 *California Law Review* 465–544 at 476.

critical strands in pre-World War I legal progressive thought and legal realism, so that we could claim a tradition for our highly controversial positions in the domestic legal debate while at the same time finding a place in the larger development'.[37] Indeed, features of 'legal realism' borrowed by CLS include, to name but a few, the realist objection to the formalism of previous legal and social thought, its emphasis on the interplay of external factors or biases in the development of legal doctrine, the fear of reification of legal concepts, and the 'adoption of the realists' twin orientations toward an iconoclastic historiography and a rigorous analytic jurisprudence'.[38] These along with other legal realist insights were developed on a more radical transformative political basis under the influx of a general epochal mood of 'expanding eclecticism'[39] among critical-oriented United States academics in their re-appraisal of the methods of legal scholarship.

For what regards the discipline of international law, the international legal-critical zeitgeist of the mid- to late 1980s included to various degrees 'the intellectual legacies of the [CLS] school', and therefore what was already by then a sophisticated CLS ongoing 'trashing' of United States domestic liberal legalism,[40] but it also extended them, as David Kennedy notes, 'beyond legal realism [to] include *inter alia* Marxism, new left anarchism, Sartrean existentialism, structuralism, neo-progressive historiography, liberal sociology, radical social theory, empirical social science'.[41] Critical approaches to international law would, in particular, be influenced by the deep 'methodological turn' that took place in legal sciences in the 1970s and 1980s and also benefited from the influence of 'critical theory' following the Frankfurt School and from new structuralist lenses provided by anthropological and psychoanalytical cognitive insights.

Although diverse in their location of the core of a binary 'deeper level' (whether ideology/false consciousness or *langue*) that 'reproduces or structures both doctrines and theory'[42] at the surface level or *parole*, the common aim of these two critical traditions to displace the

---

[37] Duncan Kennedy, 'The paradox of American legal realism' (1997) 3 *European Law Journal* 359–377 at 366.
[38] White, 'Bramble bush', p. 1677.
[39] David Kennedy, 'Critical theory, structuralism and contemporary legal scholarship' (1985–86) 21 *New England Law Review* 209–289 at 210.
[40] Roberto M. Unger, *Knowledge and Politics* (New York: Free Press, 1976).
[41] David Kennedy, 'Critical theory', p. 210.
[42] Ibid., p. 271.

'relationship between theory and practice with which legal scholars are familiar'[43] was key for CLS to come to grips with the 'fundamental contradiction' between self and other or individuality and community. The implicit underlying 'foundationalism' (understood as the pretension to have found the 'true, essential' structure of legal doctrine)[44] of this structuralist insight would in time be challenged by deconstruction. This is a post-structuralist technique of analysis built on what is perceived as 'Derrida's most enduring philosophical legacy today' (in other words, 'the theory that all binary oppositions are essentially unstable'[45] – or différance). It is this post-structuralist challenge, understood in Kennedy's words as a 'response to the difficulties encountered by the synchronic of the structuralist tradition and the dialectics of critical theory',[46] that determines the otherwise admittedly blurred line separating the first and second generations of CLS scholarship.[47]

The structuralist/post-structuralist divide within CLS would also exert its influence over the internal (or epistemological) and the external (or normative) branches of the critical movement in international legal scholarship. The radical methodological eclecticism and the interdisciplinary ambition of the critical legal movement found in the use of post-structuralism a methodological justification for its ambition to confront the sempiternal distinction between theory and practice which, according to David Kennedy, neither the critical theory of the Frankfurt School's application of it to the science of international law nor structuralism was able to transcend.[48] The use of post-structuralism and in particular of Derridean deconstructionism and Michel Foucault's studies on power would become increasingly influential within the internal or epistemological trend which led to a post-structuralist internal CLS debate between the 'possibility of coexistence of hypercritical post-modernist attitudes with the programmatic aspirations of the

---

[43] Ibid.
[44] Duncan Kennedy, 'The structure of Blackstone's commentaries' (1979) 28 *Buffalo Law Review* 205–382 at 213.
[45] Akbar Rasulov, 'International law and the poststructuralist challenge' (2000) 19 *Leiden Journal of International Law* 799–827 at 800.
[46] David Kennedy, 'Critical theory', p. 276.
[47] Ibid.
[48] Ibid.; Günter Frankenberg, 'Critical theory', in *Max Planck Encyclopedia of Public International Law* (2010), opil.ouplaw.com/view/10.1093/law:epil/9780199231690/law-9780199231690-e693?prd=EPIL.

multicultural activists'.[49] These aspirations would be widely applied to the history of international law and to its doctrine, as we shall later see, in a series of 'external' or 'normative' critical narratives that saw their mission to be to rethink from the 'thousands of politics of identity' the pervasive notion of disciplinary progress within the jus-internationalist tradition.

However, before entering that phase in its evolution, the idea of a 'fundamental contradiction', which was originally examined in the legal field by Duncan Kennedy,[50] was to lie at the core of the analysis of the structure of the international legal argument developed by Martti Koskenniemi in his landmark book *From Apology to Utopia*.[51] Analytically inspired by David Kennedy's effort to deconstruct 'public international law from the inside'[52] and the last of three book-length 'critical' contributions to international law published in the 1980s,[53] Koskenniemi's work greatly contributed to the reception of what was by then a decade-long, ground-setting work on critical perspectives in international law. By outlining, as Kennedy notes, what 'it could mean to integrate the field around a recurring problem rather than as progress toward a cosmopolitan solution',[54] *From Apology to Utopia* not only helped pierce the 'consciousness of the establishment'[55] but also awoke it, as Bruno Simma notes, from its 'theoretical dormancy'.[56]

Koskenniemi's treatise was deeply influenced by the CLS reformulation of the classic themes of leftist legal thought. As Roberto Unger notes,

---

[49] Duncan Kennedy, 'Nota sobre la historia de CLS en los Estados Unidos' (1992) 11 *Doxa* 283–293 at 287.

[50] Duncan Kennedy, 'Form and substance in private law adjudication' (1976) 89 *Harvard Law Review* 1685–1778.

[51] Martti Koskenniemi, *From Apology to Utopia: The Structure of the International Legal Argument* (Helsinki: Lakimiesliiton Kustannus, 1989); reissued with a new epilogue (Cambridge: Cambridge University Press, 2005). See, for an earlier treatment, Ignacio de la Rasilla del Moral, 'Martti Koskenniemi and the spirit of the beehive in international law' (2010) 10 *Global Jurist* 1–53.

[52] Bhupinder S. Chimni, *International Law and World Order: A Critique of Contemporary Approaches*, 2nd ed. (Cambridge, UK: Cambridge University Press, 2017), p. 253.

[53] The other two seminal works are Anthony Carty, *The Decay of International Law: A Reappraisal of the Limits of Legal Imagination in International Affairs* (Manchester: Manchester University Press, 1986); and, as already seen, David Kennedy, *International Legal Structures*.

[54] David Kennedy, 'The last treatise: project and person (Reflections on Martti Koskenniemi's *From Apology to Utopia*)' (2006) 7 *German Law Journal* 982–992 at 992.

[55] Ibid.

[56] Bruno Simma, 'Editorial' (1992) 3 *European Journal of International Law* 215–218 at 215.

this consisted in 'a criticism of formalism and objectivism' and a 'purely instrumental use of legal practice and doctrine to advance leftist aims'.[57] For Koskenniemi, building on David Kennedy's deconstructive work, this was translated into a critical 'internal' analysis of the structure of the international legal argument in the mode of 'immanent critique', otherwise a 'mode of critical theoretic analysis' used to detect 'the societal contradictions which offer the most determinate possibilities for emancipatory social change'.[58] Koskenniemi's key early contribution to the internal or epistemological strand of the critical project in international law was to apply the 'indeterminacy critique' to the international legal argument – one that as a result came to be described as being eternally damned to oscillate between its apologetic ascending search for concreteness and its utopian descending claim of normativity. This 'totemic' dancing mirrors the self-reproducing tensional relationship between sovereign freedom and world order, which in turn constitutes a reflection of the tension between individual freedom and social or communal order at the domestic level.[59] This tension had been previously described, as noted earlier in this chapter, as the 'fundamental contradiction' of liberal theory by Duncan Kennedy, for whom 'the more sophisticated a person's legal thinking, regardless of her political stance, the more likely she is to believe that all issues within a doctrinal field reduce to a single dilemma of the degree of collective as opposed to individual self-determination that is appropriate'.[60]

For Koskenniemi, international law's indeterminacy is intrinsically linked to the reproduction of 'the paradoxes and ambivalences of a liberal theory of politics'[61] and especially to the ruling exigencies of the principle of the primacy of the rule of law, understood as the liberal answer to the subjective indeterminacy of values. This subjective indeterminacy of values is inherent in the epistemology of a liberal theory which is by definition impermeable to any theory of justice on which to ground a universal morality, including the principle of liberty, because even this is in conflict with liberalism's horizontal approach to values. All the argumentative positions to which international legal discourse can give rise are, according to Koskenniemi, trapped in this structure. These positions are

---

[57] Unger, *Legal Studies Movement*, p. 1.
[58] Robert J. Antonio, 'Immanent critique as the core of critical theory: its origins and developments in Hegel, Marx and contemporary thought' (1981) 32 *The British Journal of Sociology* 330–345 at 332.
[59] Martti Koskenniemi, 'A response' (2006) 7 *German Law Journal* 1103–1108.
[60] Duncan Kennedy, 'The structure of Blackstone's commentaries', p. 213.
[61] Koskenniemi, *From Apology to Utopia*, p. xiii.

explicitly concretized by the author as the 'rule approach, the teleological approach, scepticism and idealism' and their cross-bred combinations.[62]

Once opened to an internal critique of its logic, the analysis of the liberal theory of politics that frames international law's evolution becomes a critique of international law's ethos which relies on a recurring antinomy in doctrinal argument. This antinomy is a contradiction founded on the bipolarity of composite conceptual differentiations that – while they are dependent upon each other – cannot but lead to the irremediably indeterminate nature of international law. This conse- quently appears portrayed as a pattern of rhetorical legitimation of a politically limited series of choices between apparently juridical pre- ordained outcomes. This tension becomes 'an indeterminacy that is a central aspect of international law's acceptability' and leads the author to conclude 'that there is no space in international law that would be free from decisionism, no aspect of the legal craft that would not involve a choice – that would not be, in this sense, a politics of international law'.[63] In the tradition of immanent critique, Koskenniemi's work was, as we have seen, oriented to show that international law fails dialectically in its own terms and therefore should be politically questioned and subverted for it to better live up to its emancipatory potential. Koskenniemi went on to explain his 'structural method' in a similar vein several decades later by noting that

> instead of guiding the researcher to produce solutions to problems given from the outside, it examines the way some things emerge as 'problems' worthy of the time of researchers and the resources of legal and academic institutions. Instead of merely teaching students to produce new rules and policies within the field's well-established discourses and biases (though it does this, too), it is interested in the field itself as part of the problem.[64]

The argument 'that the structure of international law understood synchronically as a normative framework without foundation must swing aimlessly between the non-law of state power and the non-law of foundation-less normative standards'[65] came as a disciplinary cold

---

[62] Martti Koskenniemi, 'The politics of international law' (1990) 1 *European Journal of International Law* 4–32.

[63] Koskenniemi, *From Apology to Utopia*, p. 596.

[64] Martti Koskenniemi, 'What is critical research in international law? Celebrating structur- alism' (2016) 29 *Leiden Journal of International Law* 727–735 at 734.

[65] Anthony Carty, 'International legal personality and the end of the subject: natural law and phenomenological responses to New Approaches to International Law' (2005) 6 *Melbourne Journal of International Law* 534–552 at 549.

shower at the time of *From Apology to Utopia*'s original publication in 1989. This doctrinal reaction is explained by the fact that the search for an objective non-political authority has traditionally been a lodestar in a discipline historically forced to continually restate its relevance against the perils stemming from the competition and struggle between national sovereign powers prone to provoke international anarchy and all types of military conflicts. The relentless assessment of this ensuing Sisyphus-like flight from politics through technicality in the continual effort by international lawyers to formally restate, in the image of its domestic counterparts but without the closure provided in terms of a central authority that characterizes the state's legal order, the relevance of international law vis-à-vis the realm of international politics is one of the fundamental key-interpretative lenses that in diverse guises and in multiple contexts traverse the whole of Koskenniemi's examination of the ethos of international law.[66]

It is indeed in the will to escape from the repetition of conflict through history that the two premises of liberal internationalism, that is to say, a sovereign-centric conception of world order and the principle of subjective value have been traditionally theorized. This theorization allows the identity of international law to be grounded beyond normative and descriptive accounts of politics in its departure from a posited original Hobbesian state of nature in the light of the domestic analogy. This anchorage would empower international law to ideally tame, in a gentle civilizing fashion, the discretionary ruling acts of the single normatively empowered units in the international system. However, as already explained, Koskenniemi shows that international law's *fuite en avant* is grounded on the staging of a reiterative and overlapping display of a normative and a descriptive account of politics, damned to reach for but never attain each other. According to the author it is this 'generative grammar' that accounts for both 'the simultaneous sense of rigorous formalism and substantive or political open-endedness of argument about international law'.[67] This simultaneity can be found in all argumentative positions to which the international legal discourse structurally associated with the liberal theory of politics can give rise, and as a result, he argues, all we are left with is a sense of pragmatic eclecticism in the ever-shifting pendulum of mainstream scholarship.

---

[66] Martti Koskenniemi, 'The fate of public international law: between technique and politics' (2007) 70 *The Modern Law Review* 1–30 at 1–2.
[67] Koskenniemi, *From Apology to Utopia*, p. 562.

Therefore, as Koskenniemi notes, 'the main target of *From Apology to Utopia* is a culture of pragmatic instrumentalism as transmitted through the language of international law'[68] resulting in the merging of 'sovereignty and sources into and yet remaining in tension with each other, their relationship thus ensuring the endless generation of international legal speech – and with it, the continuity of a profession no longer seeking a transcendental foundation from philosophical or sociological theories'.[69] This same confrontational stance towards pragmatism and the technocratic and managerialist culture that goes hand in hand with it and muffles, according to the author, the emancipatory potential of international law, also explains how, in its author's view, 'from the perspective of *From Apology to Utopia* ... the offer of policy-relevance by engaging in institution-building was a poisoned chalice'.[70] In a nutshell, Koskenniemi's ultimate aim was to provide the profession with a cause for engagement against what he has repeatedly considered to be 'one of the problems with modern international law ... its routinization, the absence of reflection by the profession on its embedded preferences'.[71] Indeed, writing on the occasion of the twentieth anniversary of the first article published in the *European Journal of International Law*, Koskenniemi insisted that '20 years ago it seemed intellectually necessary and politically useful to demonstrate the indeterminacy'[72] and as a result 'the inevitability of politics in the profession of public international law'.[73]

Koskenniemi's work, here briefly summarized, did wonders for the intellectual respectability of NAIL. It would also inform the task of a new generation of critical-oriented international lawyers who, more attentive to the dark sides and limitations of their disciplinary vernacular, now felt elevated to the rank of social engineers in their approach to the international *ars boni et aequi*. Furthermore, as an emblem of the critical international legal project of scientific re-conceptualization it opened a Pandora's box in a discipline that was previously firmly rooted in an orthodoxy that had traditionally conceptualized its history in terms of cosmopolitan progress in the pursuit of liberal values, and that was

[68] Ibid., p. 604.
[69] Ibid., p. 575.
[70] Ibid., p. 603.
[71] Koskenniemi, 'A response', p. 1007.
[72] Martti Koskenniemi, 'The politics of international law – 20 years later' (2009) 20 *European Journal of International Law* 7–19 at 11.
[73] Ibid., p. 7.

trained to present the art of its *officium* in terms of professional objectivity and technical neutrality. Instead, following from the indeterminacy thesis comes, as we have seen, a critique of any pretension of dominance, or, if preferred, of legal authority of any legal position vis-à-vis any other and, in its wake, a new focus on the critical preoccupation with revealing the relations of power undergirding both the present and pasts of international law. This stress on the indeterminate nature of the duality of concretion and normativity by which the expansive ideal of the rule of law is inspired would, in opening a crack in the intellectual system-supportive apparatus of international law, foster a degree of epistemic destabilization from which would ensue a turn to an international legal scholarly political combat more acutely sensitive to the injustices lurking behind the contemporary international reality and to the constitutive role of international law – both present and past – in relation to them.

The academic success of the 'indeterminacy thesis' and the aura of intellectual prestige among the cognoscenti that it would accord to its expounder and his fellow travellers would set the ground for the development of ulterior radically subjectivist critical approaches to international law. Commenting on the influence of *From Apology to Utopia*, Sahib Singh has correctly noted that in international law 'critical thought has, in part, founded its success upon its relentless willingness to intertwine epistemological concerns with ethical ones'.[74] Indeed, Koskenniemi's contribution to the first 'internal' or epistemological critical trend, which like that of other critical authors in the earlier generation attempted to re-conceptualize the idea of international law through a triple 'conceptual, methodological and strategic challenge',[75] opened the door for the ethical/political-oriented struggles which are overtly present in the second, otherwise the 'external' or 'normative' strand of NAIL. As it corresponds to the internalization of postmodernists' insights and their definition of international law as both an intellectual discipline and a professional culture open to social critique, this strand would go on to denounce international law's historical, and also contemporary, complicity with, among other things, the structures of

---

[74] Sahib Singh, 'The critic(-al subject)', in Wouter Werner, Alexis Galán, and Marieke de Hoon (eds.), *The Law of International Layers: Reading Martti Koskenniemi* (Cambridge, UK: Cambridge University Press, 2017), pp. 197–224 at 197.

[75] James Boyle, 'Ideals and things: international legal scholarship and the prison-house of language' (1985) 26 *Harvard International Law Journal* 327–359 at 328; Cass, 'Navigating the newstream'.

male-chauvinist and patriarchal dominance (feminism), racism (critical race theory), or as we shall see in more detail in Chapter 4, Eurocentrism, imperialism, and the perpetuation of economic and development inequalities between centre and periphery (TWAIL) on a global scale.

This critical 'external' development found fertile ground in the integrative academic platform developed by David Kennedy under the label of 'New Approaches to International Law' (NAIL).[76] Specifically used in 1988 with reference to Kennedy's own work,[77] NAIL gradually became constituted around a series of conferences and academic events that integrated a number of other projects and intellectual sensitivities in a bric-a-brac fashion. During the 1990s these projects included Third World Approaches to International Law, 'international legal feminism', the 'feminism, law sexuality and culture project' (FLASC), 'the new approaches to comparative law project', the 'postcolonialism and sexuality project',[78] and others such as international legal history, critical international economic law and regulatory policy, critical race theory, critical human rights law, new social movements, a resurgent interest in Marxist perspectives on international law, law and development, postcolonial studies, Lacanian studies, et cetera.[79]

While the heterogeneity of the critical movement excludes any fixed categories or methodological and disciplinary boundaries, it has been the object of several studies and even a number of annotated bibliographies that trace multiple intellectual connections and common influences among its members.[80] In practice, under the influence of a new type of postmodern 'identity politics',[81] different scholarly sensitivities have grown into different branches and subgroups with ramifications in the academic study of international law that the internal epistemological critique presented as 'ethically incoherent, intellectually constrained, logically indeterminate and self-validated in terms of its own authority'.[82]

---

[76] The term has been used before in Richard A. Falk, 'New approaches to the study of international law' (1967) 61 *American Journal of International Law* 477–495.

[77] David Kennedy, 'A new stream', p. 7.

[78] See, with corresponding bibliography, David Kennedy, 'The disciplines', p. 15.

[79] Ibid.

[80] See e.g. Jason Becket, 'Critical international legal theory', in *Oxford Bibliographies in International Law* (2012, rev. 2017), www.oxfordbibliographies.com/view/document/obo-9780199796953/obo-9780199796953-0007.xml.

[81] Nathaniel Berman, *Passion and Ambivalence: Nationalism, Colonialism and International Law* (Leiden and Boston: Martinus Nijhoff, 2012), p. 85.

[82] Purvis, 'Critical Legal Studies', p. 81.

From this followed a call for a greater situationality among critical voices in international law, such as that of Nathaniel Berman in favour of an understanding of 'the identity of internationalism as a whole, not as that of a system with a fixed ideology, but as a work-in-progress, subject to constant revision through situational engagement'.[83] It is largely against this critical theoretical background that 'critical/post-modern approaches' to the history of international law and their interconnected tributaries have developed over, roughly, the last thirty years in international legal scholarship.

3.3   Critical Histories of International Law

Historical writing about international law prominently figures in the scholarly curriculum of authors affiliated with the original NAIL, following in the footsteps of the transposition to international law of the legal historiographical orientation of the works of the original founders of the CLS movement like Duncan Kennedy, whose early work on the rise and fall of classical legal thought in the United States between 1850 and 1940[84] set the ground for a continual interest by CLS authors in both American and comparative legal history.[85] This interest on history parallels complex theoretical developments in CLS scholarship regarding critical legal history such as, to mention just one, Robert Gordon's highly influential analysis in what he termed the 'pocket guide to the common and exotic varieties of the social/legal histories of North America', which went on to serve as a 'guidebook' for a generation of critically oriented legal historians in the United States from the mid-1980s.[86]

Indeed, much of the critical terminology and many of the conceptual constructs that were to be transposed, or merely filtered, into international legal history by critical legal scholars in subsequent years may

---

[83] Berman, *Passion and Ambivalence*, p. 85.
[84] Duncan Kennedy, 'The rise and fall of classical legal thought', unpublished manuscript, 1975; reformatted 1998; published with a new preface by the author, 'Thirty years later', as *The Rise and Fall of Classical Legal Thought* (Washington, DC: Beard Books, 2006).
[85] Duncan Kennedy, 'Three globalizations of law and legal thought: 1850–2000', in David Trubek and Alvaro Santos (eds.), *The New Law and Economic Development: A Critical Appraisal* (Cambridge, UK: Cambridge University Press, 2006), pp. 19–73.
[86] Robert W. Gordon, 'Critical legal histories' (1984) 36 *Stanford Law Review* 57–125 at 58. See, further, Robert Gordon, *Taming the Past: Essays on Law in History and History in Law.* (Cambridge, UK: Cambridge University Press, 2017).

be identified in the bluntly political and methodologically polarized academic debates which were diversely inspired by the 'linguistic turn' across both law and history and transformations within the 'Law & Society' movement in United States academia in the 1970s and 1980s and beyond.[87] Within this broad and heterogeneous body of scholarship, there are echoes of academic historiographical debates in international legal history such as, for instance, the recent methodological rift, as seen in Chapter 2, between critical and contextualist approaches about the problem of presentism and anachronism in international legal history. Indeed, as Howard Schonberger highlighted back in the mid-1970s, 'presentism is a fighting word within the historical profession. For over fifty years the battle has raged between the presentists who argue for a "usable, value-laden" history and those historians who defend a "disinterested, neutral, scientific and objective" scholarship . . . In the war over presentism, there are few neutrals.'[88]

However, during the early phase of the historical work of international critical/postmodern legal scholars their perspectives on the past of the discipline were more directly informed by methodological perspectives with marked postmodernist pedigree such as structuralism, poststructuralism, and deconstructionism. This early historiographical orientation is exemplified by David Kennedy, who in a series of his works spanning from the mid-1980s to the mid-1990s excluded 'a history of the development of legal doctrines [and] a social history'[89] from the scope of his approach and applied instead an analysis at the level of 'description of texts' following a method of 'deconstruction of the "inside" of international law of scholarship in particular phases of history'.[90] Kennedy's particular line of historical enquiry began with the internal argumentative structure of international law's classic texts provided, in his description, with a 'distinctive lexicon with its own textual characteristics and assumptions',[91] including those of Francisco de Vitoria, Alberico Gentili, and Hugo Grotius during the phase of

---

[87] Catherine L. Fisk, '&: law _ society in historical legal research', in Markus Dirk Dubber and Christopher L Tomlins (eds.), *The Oxford Handbook of Legal History* (Oxford: Oxford University Press, 2018), pp. 479–496.

[88] Howard Schonberger, 'Purposes and ends in history: presentism and the new left' (1974) 7 *The History Teacher* 448–458 at 448.

[89] David Kennedy, 'Primitive legal scholarship' (1986) 27 *Harvard International Law Journal* 1–98 at 13.

[90] Chimni, *International Law*, p. 265.

[91] David Kennedy, 'Primitive legal scholarship', p. 3.

'primitive international legal scholarship'.[92] It continued by moving from 1648 to another landmark in the history of international law, 1919, the birthdate of the League of Nations, with Kennedy deploying his critical discourse analysis to 'some narratives told by the discipline of international institutions about its origin and practice'.[93] Highlighting that the 'discipline of public international law has a keenly developed sense of history [and that] indeed much of the field's theoretical and doctrinal debate is conducted as a debate about history',[94] Kennedy's historiographical emphasis was on how historical arguments and international lawyers' relationship with the past of the discipline at different times in its history shaped their discourses as they set out their proposals for reform and renewal in relation to them through reference to past rhetorical patterns.

This early strongly deconstructionist approach to history, which according to Bhupinder S. Chimni produces a 'historical writing that it is ahistorical by design'[95] in the sense that it focuses on 'revealing internal contradictions that mark the disciplinary discourse on international institutions and is not intended to look at the external realities in the matrix of which their creation is undertaken',[96] continued in Kennedy's works against the background of the early post-Cold War period in the early and mid-1990s. Indeed, Kennedy could come back to the deconstruction of the rhetorical patterns of internationalist discourse by focusing on the 'ex-post reconstruction of a classic doctrinal system' in the interwar period to show that 'the nineteenth century may teach us the modernist pragmatism and progressivism of today's international law is more rhetorical effect and polemical claim than historical achievement, and more part of the internal dynamic of the field's development than an artefact of a distant era'.[97] However, in comparison to the analytical deconstructive techniques employed in his earlier historical works, in this and other works by Kennedy in the 1990s,[98] with their focus on the analytical examination of the discursive structures historically used by

---

[92] Ibid., pp. 1–98.
[93] David Kennedy, 'The move to institutions' (1987) 8 *Cardozo Law Review* 841–998 at 849.
[94] David Kennedy, 'A new stream', p. 12.
[95] Chimni, *International Law*, p. 271.
[96] Ibid., pp. 269–270.
[97] David Kennedy, 'International law and the nineteenth century: history of an illusion' (1997) 17 *Quinnipiac Law Review* 99–136 at 104.
[98] David Kennedy, 'The international style in postwar law and policy' (1994) 1 *Utah Law Review* 7–103; David Kennedy, 'When renewal repeats', pp. 335–389.

international lawyers to produce a sense of disciplinary progress and professional legitimization of their intellectual projects there is a greater effort to nurture re-descriptions and draw parallelisms between the interwar and post-Cold War eras.

This veiled presentist shift from an ahistorical internal perspective towards a greater engagement with the external historical context becomes particularly apparent in the parallel work of Nathaniel Berman, who adopted a more historical specific focus on the relationship of the phenomenon of nationalism with international law by engaging the 'international legal modernism' of the interwar period.[99] Berman engaged in a genealogical approach to the history of international law of Foucauldian inspiration,[100] which he described as an examination of 'the appropriation and re-appropriation of law by the heterogeneous forms of power as well as the constitution and reconstitution of power by the heterogeneous forms of law'.[101] Also influenced by post-colonial critical literary theory and cultural studies, Berman's work places marked emphasis on the deep-rooted influence of cultural trends and the politically explosive tensions engendered by the formation of collective identities.[102] Indeed, Berman's study of several episodes of internationalist intervention to tame the 'crater filled with flames and smoke' – as Robert Redslob defined nationalism[103] – in the interwar period was linked to a critical examination of 'an ever-advancing dialectic of renewal and restatement'[104] as international law engaged with the rise of ethno-nationalism-driven conflicts and the debates on the 'conditions for the deployment of legitim-ate international power'[105] with regard to them during the 1990s.[106] In this

---

[99] Emmanuelle Jouannet, 'A critical introduction', trans. Euan Macdonald, in Nathaniel Berman, *Passion and Ambivalence: Nationalism, Colonialism and International Law* (Leiden and Boston: Martinus Nijhoff, 2012), pp. 1–38 at 34.

[100] See, e.g., Michel Foucault, 'Nietzsche, Genealogy, History', in *Language, Counter-memory, Practice: Selected Essays and Interviews*, ed. Donald F. Bouchard (Ithaca, NY: Cornell University Press, 1977), pp. 139–164 at 139. See also Ben Golder, 'Foucault and the incompletion of law' (2008) 21 *Leiden Journal of International Law* 747–763.

[101] Berman, *Passion and Ambivalence*, p. 76.

[102] Ignacio de la Rasilla, 'International law in the historical present tense' (2009) 22 *Leiden Journal of International Law* 629–649.

[103] Robert Redslob, *Le principe des nationalités les origines, les fondements psychologiques, les forces adverses, les solutions possibles* (Paris: Recueil Sirey, 1930), p. 38, trans. in Berman, *Passion and Ambivalence*, p. 140.

[104] Berman, *Passion and Ambivalence*, p. 44.

[105] Ibid., p. 446.

[106] See e.g. Nathaniel Berman, 'A perilous ambivalence: nationalist desire, legal autonomy, and the limits of the interwar framework' (1992) 33 *Harvard International Law Journal*

line of works there is an apparent effort to abscond from the internal and more analytical abstract epistemological critique in the historical investigation of international law and, instead, situate the international lawyers' work against a background of external historical realities drawing, furthermore, genealogical parallels between two distinct historical periods.

Critical/postmodern international legal historical production in the 1990s lies at the origins of a series of critical historiographical scholarly trends that would gain further momentum in the 2000s. Included among these are earlier works by Antony Anghie on the colonial origins of international law,[107] and some earlier intellectual portraits of international lawyers, a genre that would later develop, as will be seen in Chapter 10, with a more definite bio-intellectual contextual orientation in the wake of the 'turn' to the history of international law years later.[108] Indeed, while the latter is generally given, as Chapter 1 showed, the conventional birthdate of the turn of the millennium, a critically revisionist international legal historiographical tradition was already well developed by then. As Deborah Cass noted, in describing the central role history played in the 'theory battle'[109] in which newstream and mainstream were, in her description, engaged by the mid-1990s, 'the Newstream scholarship maintains that Mainstream international legal history is self-servingly repetitive, excessively linear in focus, unstable and that it conceals interests other than the purely legal'.[110] In the wake of this 'theory battle' a series of already fairly sophisticated reflections were penned in the by then emerging critical/postmodern line of works on the role of history in international law. One example among many is provided by Philip Allott's elaborate cogitations on how 'after five centuries of the intrinsic and extrinsic history of international law, five centuries of the negotiating of an idea of itself and an idea of its place within international society, there is still no effective functional integration of a theory of international law

---

353–380; Nathaniel Berman, '"But the alternative is despair": European nationalism and the modernist renewal of international law' (1993) 106 *Harvard Law Review* 1792–1903.

[107] For example, Antony Anghie, 'Francisco de Vitoria and the colonial origins of international law' (1996) 5 *Social and Legal Studies* 321–336.

[108] Carl Landauer, 'J. L. Brierly and the modernization of the law' (1992–93) 5 *Vanderbilt Journal of Transnational Law* 881–917.

[109] Cass, 'Navigating the newstream', p. 341.

[110] Ibid., p. 354.

within a theory of international society'.[111] Another one is that of Outi
Korhonen's efforts at raising awareness of a need for a critical agenda
for international legal historians by stressing 'several characteristics of
History' that make it a 'means of totalization in that they produce
manipulated appearances of reality while, in fact, alienating the observer and simplifying the links between motives, causes, stakes and
outcomes'.[112]

However, two major intellectual developments were, broadly speaking,
to signal a more specific historical and historiographical orientation in
the works of critical international lawyers and, also, a far larger reception
of their works in the field as a whole from the early 2000s, when
international legal history was considered, according to Thomas
Skouteris, to 'still be a blue-sky affair, trending yet marginal'.[113] One of
them was that the incipient historiographical critique and the critical
technologies refined by the early and more philosophically-oriented work
of NAILers contributed largely to nurture a post-colonial historiographical orientation from the mid- to late 1990s which culminated in Antony
Anghie's celebrated *Imperialism, Sovereignty and International Law* in
the early to mid-2000s.[114] This orientation has not only led to the
emergence of a distinctive TWAIL/post-colonial historiography with an
insistence on retelling 'history from the vantage point of peoples who
were subjugated to international law',[115] as Chapter 4 examines, but
also has developed a relationship of mutually reinforcing influence with
the tenets of 'critical' historiography of international law writ large.
Indeed, the two had entertained a relationship of contribution and
borrowing from their main foci and topoi, inter alia including 'imperialism', 'periphery', and the 'standard of civilization' as both strands

---

[111] Philip Allott, 'International law and the idea of history' (1999) 1 *Journal of the History of International Law* 1–21 at 2.

[112] Outi Korhonen, 'The role of history in international law' (2000) 94 *Proceedings of the Annual Meeting (American Society of International Law)* 45–46 at 46.

[113] Thomas Skouteris, 'The turn to history in international law', in *Oxford Bibliographies in International Law* (2017), www.oxfordbibliographies.com/view/document/obo-9780199796953/obo-9780199796953-0154.xml, p. 2.

[114] See Antony Anghie, *Imperialism, Sovereignty and the Making of International Law* (Cambridge, UK: Cambridge University Press, 2005).

[115] Ibid., p. 6. See also as relevant in the critical international legal historiography of the early 2000s, Gerry Simpson, *Great Powers and Outlaw States: Unequal Sovereigns in the International Legal Order* (Cambridge, UK: Cambridge University Press, 2004). See Upendra Baxi, 'New approaches to the history of international law' (2006) 19 *Leiden Journal of International Law* 555–566 at 555.

collaboratively weaponize 'the history of international law, a history of universalism and hierarchy intertwined'[116] into their critical and presentist historiographical orientations.

Similarly stimulated by the ground-setting critical historiographical work of the internal or epistemological critical approach, and culminating an early interest among critically oriented international lawyers 'in the history of the self-understanding and sensibility of international lawyers, and the relation of the profession to a broader range of political, social and cultural developments in the late nineteenth and early twentieth centuries',[117] was the publication of Martti Koskenniemi's *The Gentle Civilizer of Nations* in 2001. Twelve years after *From Apology to Utopia*, Koskenniemi presented his new book as a shift from his structuralist method into 'a kind of experimentation in the writing about the disciplinary past in which the constraints of any rigorous method have been set aside in an effort to create intuitively plausible and politically engaged narratives about the emergence and gradual transformation of a profession that plays with the reader's empathy'.[118]

Koskenniemi's opus, which, as seen in Chapter 2, was largely inspired by inter alia historical 'contextualist' insights in his exploration of the evolution of the international legal profession across different national European traditions, has gone to serve as the intellectual backbone for the production of many intellectual historical studies in the discipline in Europe (and elsewhere) ever since. It also to a large extent inspired, as Chapter 10 shows, a refurbished (re)turn to international intellectual legal biography in context. More broadly, Koskenniemi's widely discussed seminal 'narrative of the mainstream as a story about its cosmopolitan sensibilities and political projects'[119] was to become central to what Thomas Skouteris calls 'the turn to history debate'. Developed since the early 2000s, this debate aims at providing 'justification for the

---

[116] Pitts, 'International relations', p. 292.

[117] Anne Orford, 'International law and the limits of history', in Wouter Werner, Marieke de Hoon, and Alexis Galán (eds.), *The Law of International Lawyers: Reading Martti Koskenniemi* (Cambridge, UK: Cambridge University Press, 2017), pp. 297–320 at 298.

[118] Martti Koskenniemi, *The Gentle Civilizer of Nations: The Rise and Fall of International Law 1870–1960* (Cambridge, UK: Cambridge University Press, 2001), pp. 9–10.

[119] Koskenniemi, *The Gentle Civilizer of Nations*, p. 9. See, e.g., Wouter Werner, Marieke de Hoon, and Alexis Galán (eds.), *The Law of International Lawyers: Reading Martti Koskenniemi* (Cambridge, UK: Cambridge University Press, 2017); see also Chimni, *International Law*, pp. 246–357.

reinstatement of international legal history as a valid academic specialization and as a vernacular with critical potential'.[120]

The Gentle Civilizer of Nations placed Koskenniemi in the avant-garde of the 'historiographical turn in international law'.[121] He has since then prolifically produced several dozen other contributions to the intellectual history (*Ideengeschichte*) of international law and has remained a constant participant, as was seen in Chapter 2, in its main related historiographical debates.[122] Particularly noticeable in his intellectual production are his commentaries and reinterpretations to the works of individual scholars. The list is very extensive, including, at different reprises, Hersch Lauterpacht,[123] but also Carl Schmitt,[124] Georg Friedrich von Martens,[125] Immanuel Kant,[126] the Spanish Seconda Scholastica[127] (with a particular

---

[120] Skouteris, 'The turn to history', p. 2; 'it provides the field with its own disciplinary historical consciousness; it performs a genealogy of modes of speaking about the past; it presents reasons that might have led to today's renewed interest; and it distinguishes between new forms of engagement from older ones'.

[121] George Rodrigo Bandeira Galindo, 'Martti Koskenniemi and the historiographical turn in international law' (2005) 16 *European Journal of International Law* 539–559.

[122] Koskenniemi, 'Histories of international law: significance and problems', pp. 215–240; Martti Koskenniemi, 'A history of international law histories', in Bardo Fassbender and Anne Peters (eds.), *The Oxford Handbook of the History of International Law* (Oxford: Oxford University Press, 2012), pp. 943–971.

[123] Martti Koskenniemi, 'Lauterpacht: the Victorian tradition in international law' (1997) 8 *European Journal of International Law* 215–263; Martti Koskenniemi, 'Hersch Lauterpacht and the development of international criminal law' (2004) 2 *Journal of International Criminal Justice* 810–825; Martti Koskenniemi, 'Hersch Lauterpacht 1897-1960', in Jack Beatson and Reihard Zimmermann (eds.), *Jurists Uprooted: German-Speaking Emigré Lawyers in Twentieth-Century Britain* (Oxford: Oxford University Press, 2004), pp. 601–662; Martti Koskenniemi, 'The function of law in the international community: 75 years after' (2008) 79 *British Yearbook of International Law* 353–366.

[124] Martti Koskenniemi, 'International law as political theology: how to read the *Nomos der Erde*' (2004) 11 *Constellations* 492–511; Martti Koskenniemi, 'Carl Schmitt and international law', in Jens Meierhenrich and Oliver Simons (eds.), *The Oxford Handbook of Carl Schmitt* (New York: Oxford University Press, 2016), pp. 592–611.

[125] Martti Koskenniemi, 'Georg Friedrich von Martens (1756–1821) and the origins of modern international law', in Christian Calliess, Georg Nolte, and Peter-Tobias Stoll (eds.), *Von der Diplomatie zum kodifizierten Völkerrecht: 75 Jahre Institut für Völkerrecht der Universität Göttingen (1930-2005)* (Cologne: Heymanns, 2006), pp. 13–30.

[126] Martti Koskenniemi, 'Constitutionalism as mindset: reflections on Kantian themes about international law and globalization' (2007) 8 *Theoretical Inquiries in Law* 9–36.

[127] Martti Koskenniemi, 'Empire and international law: the real Spanish contribution' (2011) 61 *University of Toronto Law Journal* 1–36.

emphasis on Francisco de Vitoria),[128] Hugo Grotius,[129] Samuel Pufendorf,[130] James Lorimer,[131] and, moving beyond the canon of international lawyers, others like inter alia Karl Marx[132] and Adam Smith.[133] During the last decade or so this attention to reinterpreting the significance of noted historical contributors to the intellectual history of international law has revolved around the correlation between sovereignty and property, which in a structuralist fashion Koskenniemi calls 'the yin and yang of international law'[134] because both, in his depiction, 'have always operated together so as to create the structure of power that is, at any moment, the real government of the world'.[135]

More specifically, Koskenniemi's interest in 'the relationship of law and political economy in historical terms'[136] has already translated, inter alia, into critical re-readings of the intellectual opus of the School of Salamanca. Indeed, according to Koskenniemi the 'Spanish theologians and jurists of the sixteenth and seventeenth centuries appear not so much as reluctant advocates of a formal Spanish lordship over distant peoples but as articulators and ideologists of a global structure of horizontal relationships between holders of the subjective rights of dominium – a structure of human relationships that we have been

---

[128] Martti Koskenniemi, 'Vitoria and us: thoughts on critical histories of international law' (2014) 22 *Rechtsgeschichte: Zeitschrift des Max-Planck-Instituts für europäische Rechtsgeschichte* 119–139.

[129] Martti Koskenniemi, 'Imagining the rule of law: rereading the Grotian "tradition"' (2019) 30 *European Journal of International Law* 17–52.

[130] Martti Koskenniemi, 'Miserable comforters: international relations as new natural law' (2009) 15 *European Journal of International Relations* 395–422.

[131] Martti Koskenniemi, 'Race, hierarchy and international law: Lorimer's legal science' (2016) 27 *European Journal of International Law* 415–429.

[132] Martti Koskenniemi, 'What should international lawyers learn from Karl Marx?' (2004) 17 *Leiden Journal of International Law* 229–246.

[133] Martti Koskenniemi, 'International law and the emergence of mercantile capitalism: Grotius to Smith', in Pierre-Marie Dupuy and Vincent Chetail (eds.), *The Roots of International Law/Les fondements du droit international: Liber Amicorum Peter Haggenmacher* (Leiden: Martinus Nijhoff, 2013), pp. 3–37.

[134] 'Interview to Martti Koskenniemi: dovereignty, property, and the locus of power', *The Blog of the Journal of the History of Ideas*, jhiblog.org/2018/10/17/sovereignty-property-and-the-locus-of-power-anne-schult-interviews-martti-koskenniemi-on-the-conceptual-history-of-international-law/.

[135] Martti Koskenniemi, 'Sovereignty, property and empire: early modern English contexts' (2017) 18 *Theoretical Inquiries in Law* 357–389 at 389.

[136] Chimni, *International Law*, p. 256.

accustomed to label "capitalism"'.[137] Koskenniemi attributes to them the understanding that 'economics and not politics could provide the language of the universal' and that therefore 'international law had to be transformed into "[the] law of a universal commercial society"'.[138] This re-reading is an illustration of the interpretative matrix running through different episodes of Koskenniemi's long-in-the-making new monograph on the uses of 'different legal vocabularies by ambitious European legal and political thinkers in the period c. 1300–1800 in order to defend, explain and organize the exercise of power outside the domestic commonwealth'.[139]

Twenty years since the publication of *The Gentle Civilizer of Nations* and in the wake of Koskenniemi's other works and many other contributors, the field of international legal history has blossomed, along some of the lines already examined in Chapter 1 and further explored in other chapters, as an interdisciplinary and relatively self-contained research area in international legal scholarship. This development has indeed contributed to both greatly enlarging and transforming the perception of the 'disciplinary history' of international law. This, as Jean d'Aspremont correctly notes, is 'instrumental in the self-awareness of those actors constituting the discipline that they are agents of a disciplinary project'.[140] It is in relation to the larger problematization of the conventional understanding and the subsequent reinterpretation of the ultimate nature, scope, and character of the 'disciplinary project' of international law where the political intervention in the present of critical/postmodern approaches to the history of international law ultimately aspires to lie.

3.4   The Critical Impact on Knowledge Production Processes

All historical writing about international law contributes to knowledge creation processes regarding various dimensions of the relationship

---

[137] Martti Koskenniemi, 'Empire and international law', p. 32. See also this move in Matt Craven, 'On Foucault and Wolff or from law to political economy' (2012) 25 *Leiden Journal of International Law* 627–645.

[138] Koskenniemi, 'Empire and international law', p. 32.

[139] Koskenniemi, 'Sovereignty, property and empire', p. 357. The monograph is titled *To the Uttermost Parts of the Earth: Legal Imagination and International Power c. 1300–1800* (in press).

[140] Jean d'Aspremont, 'The critical attitude and the history of international law' (2018) 1 *International Legal Theory and Practice* 1–60 at 1.

between history and international law. Critical/postmodern approaches, which like postmodernism are 'congeries of method',[141] have variously contributed to the fleshing out of these epistemic interfaces where international law and history meet and interact. Many of these contributions partially overlap with those produced by critical-oriented historiographies like TWAIL and post-colonial approaches, which should be seen to a large extent, as will be examined in Chapter 4, as complementary to them, in particular since the mid-2000s.

Critical historiography, which in international law scholarship originally presented a markedly theoretical-philosophical bent, has heavily impacted the study of the 'historical dimension of international legal theory'.[142] First, a great body of literature spurred by Koskenniemi's works has contributed extensively to the intellectual history of international law and produced an alternative doctrinal reconstruction of sorts of the main strands in international legal thought and its most representative figures in a critical socio-historical vein.[143] Second, critical revisionist readings cast a different light on central concepts and notions in international law which, as we shall see in more detail in Chapter 7, underlie normative constructs such as that of the 'international community',[144] thus contributing to *Begriffsgeschichte* or conceptual history as they seek to retrace their genealogical formation in order to inter alia cast light on their uses over time and in the present. Third, critical scholars have contributed largely to the historization of their own movement[145] and its intellectual tributaries in general and to the retrospective analytical re-examination of the works of their main intellectual figures,

---

[141] Joshua Foa Dienstag, 'Postmodern approaches to the history of political thought', in George Klosko (ed.), *The Oxford Handbook of the History of Political Philosophy* (Oxford: Oxford University Press, 2013), pp. 36–46 at 46.

[142] Anne Orford and Florian Hoffmann, 'Introduction: theorizing international law', in Anne Orford and Florian Hoffmann with Martin Clark (eds.), *The Oxford Handbook of the Theory of International Law* (Oxford: Oxford University Press, 2016), pp. 1–20 at 9.

[143] Mónica Garcia-Salmones Rovira, *The Project of Positivism in International Law* (Oxford: Oxford University Press, 2013).

[144] 'Martti Koskenniemi, "International Community" from Dante to Vattel', in Vincent Chetail and Peter Haggenmacher (eds.), *Vattel's International Law from a XXIst Century Perspective* (Leiden: Brill, 2011), pp. 49–74.

[145] See Akbar Rasulov, 'New Approaches to International Law: images of a genealogy', in José Maria Beneyto and David Kennedy (eds.), *New Approaches to International Law: The European and the American Experiences* (The Hague: T. M. C. Asser Press, 2013), pp. 151–191.

in particular Koskenniemi's intellectual contributions and also, albeit to a lesser degree, those of David Kennedy and other figures.[146]

Fourth, historical writing about international law also contributes to knowledge creation processes regarding the production of both macro and micro normative perspectives on the international legal order. Indeed, as Chapter 7 examines, as international legal history has progressed in parallel with the phenomenon of fragmentation of international law, so have new histories of sub-disciplinary normative compounds mushroomed. In this context, and considering the central ideological-methodological lines which are oriented to questioning the tenets of liberal theory that are inspiring critical/postmodern perspectives and also, as is examined in Chapter 4, post-colonial approaches, it is not surprising that one of the historiographically dominant foci of critical approaches has been a critical re-reading of the history of international human rights law. This, which in part arises from questioning the prominence human rights acquired in the post-Cold War era, as David Kennedy notes, as 'a universal ideology, an international standard of legitimacy for sovereign power, a common vernacular of justice for a global civil society and as a vocabulary of the centre against the periphery',[147] has partly revolved around a historiographical contest for the genealogy of human rights.[148] A similar critical historiographical questioning of mainstream histories has surrounded, as Skouteris remarks, the triumphalist narrative that has accompanied the rise of international criminal law and related tribunals in the post-Cold War period,[149] whether in terms of their origins, both remote and modern,[150] or the factors underlying their historical evolution. Another related line of critical historiography has also developed with regard to the ability of international criminal tribunals to provide an accurate historical record

---

[146] De la Rasilla del Moral, 'Notes for the history', pp. 225–248; see, e.g., Jouannet, 'A critical introduction'.

[147] David Kennedy, 'The international human rights regime: still part of the problem', in Rob Dickinson et al.(eds.), *Examining Critical Perspectives on Human Rights* (Cambridge, UK: Cambridge University Press, 2013), pp. 19–34 at 20 and 25–26. See also, earlier, David Kennedy, 'The international human rights movement: part of the problem?' (2002) 14 *Harvard Human Rights Journal* 101–126 at 101.

[148] Samuel Moyn,*The Last Utopia: Human Rights in History* (Cambridge, MA: Harvard University Press, 2012).

[149] Immi Tallgren and Thomas Skouteris (eds.), *The New Histories of International Criminal Law: Retrials* (Oxford: Oxford University Press, 2017).

[150] Mark Lewis, *The Birth of the New Justice: The Internationalization of Crime and Punishment 1919–1950* (Oxford: Oxford University Press, 2014).

of past atrocities and render justice to their victims,[151] and also regarding the legal-historical narratives that emerge from their being internationally adjudicated.[152]

The contribution of critical historiography to the study of the legal-technical 'uses of history for international law'[153] has also made more apparent the extent to which legal and historical discursive arguments are intertwined in the practice of international law. Indeed, what has been described as the highly intellectualized 'battleground between different interpretive communities'[154] of international legal history is also relevant to the practice of international law, or, as Skouteris notes, 'understanding the precise role of the past, of history, of historiography and of historical narrative in the structure and authority of legal argument would cast light on the practices of international law'.[155] However, beyond this realization and its stress on the cyclical repetition of rhetorical patterns of internationalist discourse to provide a sense of progressive motion to the historical development of the discipline, the specific impact of critical/postmodern scholarship on the study of history for the purposes of international law-making, international law argumentative practice and international adjudication have remained overall diffuse.[156]

Another area where historical writing about international law contributes to knowledge creation processes is that of the study of 'international law in history'.[157] By providing alternative explanations and by unravelling hitherto unexplored connections relevant to the historical understanding of different episodes and the effects they trigger or the historical patterns within which they may themselves be structurally re-integrated, critical approaches enrich the study of the mutually constitutive relationship of influence between international law and/or parts thereof across different national and international societal, ideological, intellectual, and professional historical contexts. They also illuminate different blind spots in the study of significant

---

[151] Costas Douzinas, 'History trials: can law decide history?' (2012) 8 *Annual Review of Law and Social Science* 273–289.

[152] Skouteris, 'The turn to history', pp. 16–18.

[153] Matthew Craven, 'Introduction: international law and its histories', in Matthew Craven, Malgosia Fitzmaurice, and Maria Vogiatzi (eds.), *Time, History and International Law* (Leiden: Martinus Nijhoff/Brill, 2006), pp.1–25 at 7.

[154] Valentina Vadi, 'Perspective and Scale in the Architecture of international legal history' (2019) 30 *European Journal of International Law* 53–72 at 59.

[155] Skouteris, 'The turn to history', p. 5.

[156] Fouad Zarbiyev, *Le discours interprétatif en droit international contemporain: un essai critique* (Brussels: Bruylant, 2015).

[157] Ibid.

international 'events'[158] over time and thus provide reinterpretations of what was the previous traditionally accepted interpretation of their significance for international law. Furthermore, they have drawn attention to other 'events' as well as to the systemic implications of other social phenomena in the historical development of the discipline and the ways of conceiving it. Similarly, critical historical writing about international law contributes to knowledge creation processes regarding the many dimensions of the 'historical sociology of international law' in particular by a marked cultivation of the conceptual history of underlying concepts such as empire, colonization, civilization, etc. It also contributes, as examined in Chapter 8, to the history of social actors in the history of international law by revealing the influence of previously little-studied transnational companies in colonial enterprises, by stressing the role of social and cultural movements, and also by combating an excessive Eurocentric perspective to the exclusion of hitherto neglected groups and voices in the construction of narratives about the history of international law.

Another important effect of critical/postmodernist approaches has been in fostering epistemic debates relevant to the study of the historiography of international law. These have contributed to importing postmodern historiography that, as Joshua F. Dienstag notes, 'points toward a form of textual analysis that will attempt to uncover or at least be sensitive to the past exercises of power that shape our contemporary vocabulary and the vocabulary of whatever text we examine'[159] into international legal history. In its wake, many fundamental tenets and historiographical battlegrounds animated by postmodernists have been filtered into international legal historiographical works and reflections. Among these is the central targeting of the 'narrative of progress' underlying international law, which postmodern historiography has made a constant object of critique. Starting, as we have seen, with David Kennedy's internal deconstructive efforts, on the bandwagon of this incredulity regarding grand narratives has in particular come a critical historical approach arguing 'against the traction of paradigmatic progress narratives (for example, about perpetual peace, humanitarianism, civilization, liberty, democracy and so on)'[160] among critical historians of international law.

---

[158] Fleur Johns, Richard Joyce, and Sundhya Pahuja (eds.), *Events: The Force of International Law* (New York: Routledge, 2011).

[159] Dienstag, 'Postmodern approaches', p. 39.

[160] Thomas Skouteris, 'What is progress in international law?', in Anne Orford and Florian Hoffmann with Martin Clark (eds.), *The Oxford Handbook of the Theory of International Law* (Oxford: Oxford University Press, 2016), pp. 939–953 at 940.

As an overtly militant historiography which considers that all history writing constitutes an intervention in the present and conceives of history, in the words of George R. B. Galindo, as a 'force field; of often conflicting impulses, pulling it in one way or another',[161] critical/postmodernist approaches are almost ontologically pitched to invariably politicize and provide alternative visions and historical accounts. The latter critically antagonizing attitude has magnified their presence in methodological debates on the history of international law, as was illustrated in Chapter 2. Furthermore, critical attention to the 'others' of international law has nurtured the field with a series of 'expanding histories of international law'[162] and the replacing of conventional interpretations of history with critically oriented historical meta-narratives of international historical evolution. According to Alan Megill's categorization, these '[draw] upon some particular cosmology or metaphysical foundation'[163] in order to foster alternative ideological reinterpretations of the history of the discipline that then become translated into the creation of a scholarly space, as will be examined in more detail in Chapter 11, for a continual fleshing out through new critical contributions of new alternative periodizations in international legal history.

3.5 Historiographical Debates, Confluences, and Critiques

The overall impact of critical/postmodern approaches and their interconnected tributaries on historiographical debates has been ample. One may recapitulate in non-exhaustive terms some of the traits that have characterized the scholarly contribution of New Approaches to International Law, in particular regarding the study of its history as being, first, a profound distrust of historical 'grand narratives' and in its wake of ever-progressive linear conceptions of the role of international law in history as a tool for enlightened progress.[164] Second, there is a

---

[161] George Rodrigo Bandeira Galindo, 'Force field: on history and theory of international law (2012) 20 *Rechtsgeschichte – Legal History* 86–103 at 86.

[162] Anne Orford (ed.), *International Law and Its Others* (Cambridge, UK: Cambridge University Press, 2006); Martti Koskenniemi, 'Expanding histories of international law' (2016) 56 *American Journal of Legal History* 104–112.

[163] Alan Megill, '"Grand narrative" and the discipline of history', in F. Ankersmit and H. Kellner (eds.) *A New Philosophy of History* (Chicago: University of Chicago Press, 1995) pp. 151–173 at 152.

[164] Thomas Skouteris, *The Notion of Progress in International Law Discourse* (The Hague: T. M. C. Asser Press, 2010).

similar misgiving about proclamations of abstract and universal concepts and principles that characterize modernist thinking, which are instead often re-examined as intellectual smoke and mirrors for the concealment of particular interests. To put it differently, critical/postmodern approaches rely on a 'hermeneutics of suspicion', understood by Andrew F. Sunter as 'an interpretive account that reads against the grain, attempting to expose hidden meaning from the person making the expression and not the expression itself.[165] This, in turn, translates into a study of the impact of entrenched and hidden interests in the re-reading of international law's historical evolution or episodes thereof.

Third, attention is devoted to tracing intellectual parallelisms across periods and to unveiling the distributive consequences triggered by the rhetorical renewal of repeated patterns of self-legitimizing international legal discourse over an inherently discontinuous conception of time. Fourth, these approaches have a marked leaning towards deconstruction and a tendency to delve into the paradoxes and ambivalences that surface from the unstitching of the creases in the history of international legal thought. Fifth, critical/postmodern approaches focus on place, gender, origin, and other situational and identity-related factors in approaching historical relations of domination in fruitful combination with a keen awareness of the legacy of the imperial, colonial, racist, and patriarchal heritage inserted into international law structures over time. Sixth, in a critical theory vein they insist on a consciousness of international law's ultimate indeterminacy and structure-related biases combined with an attempt to deflate pretensions of dominant approaches to project authority through their formal interpretations and to recast scholarly enquiry in a more overtly political key. Seventh, they stress discontinuities, which results in an ontological questioning of conventional historical periodizations and in the historization of alternatives paths not taken or transformative trajectories and visions of global justice not fulfilled. This aligns with critical theory's general orientation, which, as Robert Cox highlights,

> stands apart from the prevailing order of the world and asks how that order came about. Critical theory, unlike problem-solving theory, does not take institutions and social and power relations for granted but calls them into question by concerning itself with their origins and how and whether they might be in the process of changing. It is directed towards

---

[165] Andrew F. Sunter, 'TWAIL as naturalized epistemological inquiry' 20 *Canadian Journal of Law & Jurisprudence* (2007) 475–507 at 498.

an appraisal of the very framework for action, or problematic, which problem-solving theory accepts as its parameters.[166]

Eighth, they issue an ethical-oriented awakening call to hone one's self-reflective mastering of the study of the theory and history of international law in a critical vein against doctrinal, technocratic, and legal managerialist practice so as combat the mainstream leaning towards the depersonalization of international legal thinking. Ninth, they call on one to assume, instead, the political character of one's international legal expertise in order to curb the often non-assumed complicit character of individual scholarly work in oppressive and conservative international legal structures. And, tenth, they provide for a regeneration of history and (of the stories) of the discipline as open fields of reflective contestation of 'regimes of truth' that are bound up with 'systems of power', all while remaining in keen awareness of the role of contingency, and therefore of agency, in history in order to contribute to emancipatory knowledge through the means of international legal historical scholarship.

This militant intellectual background helps make better sense of the methodological debate between contextualists and critical international law historians regarding the diverse roles that each of them, for instance, ascribes to presentism and anachronism in international legal history. As has already been examined in detail in Chapter 2, this revolves around the question of knowing whether contextualism as a method of historiographical enquiry can (or cannot) claim any dogmatic or disciplining methodological predominance over critical narratives of international legal history.[167] Underlying this debate, the very existence of which points to an increasing interpenetration between the history of international law traditionally cultivated by international law scholars and, professional legal history and historians, lies a certain degree of anxiety on the part of critical/postmodern approaches about the risk of becoming methodologically disciplined themselves by the far more developed professional standards of modern historiography or of seeing their hard-fought historiographical critical space increasingly colonized by new overly 'disciplinary' professional histories of international law.

While some critical/postmodern scholars have countered-argued along the lines described in Chapter 2 by, inter alia, pointing to the limits of

---

[166] Robert Cox, 'Social forces, states and world orders: beyond international relations theory' (1981) 10 *Millennium: A Journal of International Studies* 126–155 at 128–129.
[167] See Koskenniemi, 'Vitoria and us'.

contextualist methodology in international legal history, they have also pushed back by bringing the methodological battleground back to the domain of professional historiography, where they may inter alia find comfort in the challenges posed by postmodernism in history. As Georg G. Iggers and Q. Edward Wang describe, this involves an 'increasing scepticism regarding the possibility of objective knowledge in historical and social studies and erode[s] the strict border which the traditional social sciences had maintained between fact and fiction, historical study and imaginative literature. In its most radical postmodernist form, it denies the very possibility of historical knowledge, which it demotes to pure ideology and myth'.[168] This perspective is apparent in Hayden White, who criticized 'the reluctance to consider historical narratives as what they most manifestly are: verbal fictions the contents of which are more invented than found and the forms of which have more in common with their counterparts in literature than they have with those sciences'.[169]

Not surprisingly, this linkage to rhetorical history has in turn led to a call for engagement in 'a trilateral discussion among historians, international lawyers, and literary scholars' like that proposed by Christopher Warren and a suggestion that 'disputants over anachronism in international legal history can learn from literary texts and literary studies, which house an extensive and growing toolkit for transmitting meaning in and through time'.[170] Whereas the postmodernist critique has generated a large literature it has, needless to say, been countered by a defence of 'professional historical scholarship', which, as Jerry H. Bentley notes, 'in the absence of any alternative approach capable of achieving absolute objectivity or yielding perfect knowledge', is held to remain 'in spite of its problems, ... the most reliable, most responsible, and most constructive mode of dealing with the past'.[171] This is so because in contrast to 'other alternative ways of accessing and dealing with the past' it 'approaches the

---

[168] Georg G. Iggers and Q. Edward Wang with Supriya Mukherjee, A Global History of Modern Historiography (New York: Routledge, 2013), p. 392.

[169] Hayden White, Tropics of Discourse: Essays in Cultural Criticism (Baltimore: Johns Hopkins University Press, 1982), p. 82. See, e.g., Hayden White, 'The question of narrative in contemporary historical theory' (1984) 23 History and Theory 1–33.

[170] Christopher N. Warren, 'History, literature, and authority in international law', in Maksymilian Del Mar, Bernadette Meyler, and Simon Stern (eds.), The Oxford Handbook of Law and Humanities (in press), pp. 565–582 at 570.

[171] Jerry H. Bentley, 'The task of world history', in Jerry H. Bentley (ed.), The Oxford Handbook of World History (New York: Oxford University Press, 2013), pp. 1–22 at 1.

past through systematic exploration, rigorous examination of evidence, and highly disciplined reasoning'.[172]

This polemic is, thus, an extension of the controversies surrounding the reception of critical/postmodern approaches in international legal scholarship. Indeed, the fact that some of these trends are grounded on an anti-foundationalist critique,[173] the difficulty in appraising the complex 'ethics of post-modernism' with its irreverent tone and dismissive 'trashing' of other perspectives alongside the radical causes that it has embraced through its denial of disciplinary progress, and its questioning of the central tenets of liberal internationalism have long variously led to accusations of nihilism, cynicism, mere irresponsibility, or of being 'overly theoretical or willfully obtuse'.[174] As Koskenniemi noted with regard to the reception of his *From Apology to Utopia* and David Kennedy's earlier *International Legal Stuctures*, 'no doubt, some regarded them as wholly irresponsible specimens of academic intellectualism, a kind of wordplay, unconcerned about the reality of the world's problems and the pressing need to devote the diminishing funds for academic research to their resolution'.[175]

However, despite its being an offspring of them, in general the reception of the historiographical variant of critical/postmodern approaches has been less controversial among international lawyers (some exceptions notwithstanding like, for instance, d'Aspremont's recent internal charging critical scholarship with being too 'complacent with the accepted markers, periodization and causal sequencing of the existing historical narratives about international law')[176] than its structural and deconstructionist theoretical variants. This may have to do with the fact that the critical edge and emancipatory potential of highly sophisticated and erudite intellectualized re-readings of the past with reference to events and intellectual constructions sometimes dating back centuries in the profoundly sociologically, politically, and technologically transformed conditions of the present day remain, for all their declared 'critical' intentions, objectively debatable for those international lawyers who are outside the closely networked circle of cognoscenti.

---

[172] Ibid.
[173] Euan MacDonald, *International Law and Ethics after the Critical Challenge: Framing the Legal within the Post-foundational* (Leiden: Brill/Nijhoff, 2011).
[174] See, e.g., Cass, 'Navigating the newstream', p. 342.
[175] Koskenniemi, 'What is critical research in international law?', p. 729.
[176] D'Aspremont, 'The critical attitude', p. 6.

The relatively unproblematic reception of critical/postmodern histories in international law circles – albeit less so, as seen in Chapter 2,
among intellectual historians – may also be partly due to the generalized
perception *à tort ou à raison* in the mainstream of a disconnection or
ultimate irrelevance of critical historical research to the modes of scholarship they predominantly resort to as they remain functionally divided
in highly technical and specialized clusters of research with a particular
focus on present and ongoing developments. It may also be connected to
the perception that historical writing about international law serves,
whatever its orientation, a didactic disciplinary purpose insofar as it
contributes to the intellectual socialization of new generations of international law scholars and to the formation of what is otherwise perceived
as a reassuring tradition of historical knowledge formation in the field.

This noted, worries have nonetheless been expressed, in particular by
professional historians and international lawyers alike, about how the
proliferation of historical radical international law discourses and
unbridled calls for politically inspired methodological experimentation
which abandon 'some standards of historiographical analysis'[177] in the
field may be a double-edged sword insofar as they can inter alia foster
revisionist and conflict-prone historical narratives and discourses which
may, on occasion, have effectively illiberal consequences in a newly
transformed international political scenario. A continuation of this line
of critique is the realization, long ago remarked by Karl Popper and
Bertrand Russell, of critical 'epistemological relativism' being in a 'close
relationship with authoritarian and totalitarian beliefs'[178] or in some
manner contributing to their development. This line of critique has
grown in parallel with the rise of ethno-nationalism and anti-
internationalist tendencies fostered by (alt and far) right-wing policies
around the globe.[179] In the age of post-truth and diffidence about expert
knowledge, nationalist, xenophobic, and anti-globalist populist political
trends, albeit with opposite declared intentions, also build their critiques –
and in their case reactionary proposals and initiatives – by appealing in a

[177] Pablo Zapatero, 'Legal imagination in Vitoria: the power of ideas' (2009) 11 *Journal of the History of International Law* 221–271 at 221, 268, and 271; cited in Orford, 'International law and the limits of history', p. 321.
[178] Referred in Anna Green and Kathleen Troup, *The Houses of History: A Critical Reader in Twentieth-Century History and Theory* (Manchester: Manchester University Press, 1999), p. 8.
[179] Martti Koskenniemi, *International Law and the Far Right: Reflections on Law and Cynicism* (The Hague: T. M. C. Asser Press, 2019).

critical fashion to discontent and perceived grievances, contemporary and historical, against the 'global' and the 'international', and by exten-sion against the spread of liberal cosmopolitan values and the inter-national institutions and mechanisms that stand for them and from which an epiphenomenal international law derives its strength and power of persuasion. As Anne Peters notes in this regard, 'these politicians and their think-tanks have hijacked and twisted the insights generated by postmodernism, social constructivism and cultural studies, and are now applying these insights and concepts for political ends which run counter to the critical camps' emancipatory aspirations. The merry moral, cultural and epistemic relativism propagated by postmodernists has paved the way to the "post-truth age" or "post-factual age"'[180] That there are, indeed, points of critical correlation, as has always been the case regarding the 'anti-establishment' extremes of the ideological and political chessboard, between critical/postmodern (alt and far) left-wing and (alt and far) right-wing ideologies seems to confirm the old saying that politics make strange bed-fellows. It is also a reminder of what Friedrich Nietzsche, generally appraised as the great-grandfather of critical/postmodern scholarship,[181] warned: that one should 'beware that, when fighting monsters, you yourself do not become a monster ... for when you gaze long into the abyss, the abyss gazes also into you'.[182]

Another, albeit less often remarked, blind spot in the critical apprais-ing of critical/postmodern approaches to international law relates to the pitfalls in 'market commodification' of critical international legal schol-arship and their related historizations. More than three decades since its first articulation, the term 'critical' in international legal scholarship and by reflection in the study of the history of international law, has long become 'commodified' in the professional market of international law ideas. Admittedly, from its origins the critical movement was nurtured by the initiatives of David Kennedy, who, as Bhupinder S. Chimni notes, early on learnt 'the lesson that innovators in the discipline had to actively recruit adherents and build an audience if their work had to become

---

[180] Anne Peters, 'Multiperspectivism in and on international law', in *Völkerrechtsblog* (15 January 2019), voelkerrechts blog.org/multiperspectivism-in-and-on-international-law/, p. 2.
[181] Dienstag, 'Postmodern approaches', pp. 36–46.
[182] Friedrich W. Nietzsche, *Beyond Good and Evil*, trans. Helen Zimmern (Miami, FL: Oregan France, 2020), p. 15.

influential'[183] and consequently set out to make a 'self-conscious effort to build a collective international project of disciplinary criticism and renewal'.[184] This notwithstanding, in the early days, academic pigeon-holing itself was often challenged by critical international law scholars.[185] This resistance to scholarly labelling was perhaps best exemplified by Martti Koskenniemi's *disputatio* in the late 1990s of the liberal underpinnings of what he termed the 'shopping-mall approach' of a symposium organized by the editors of the *American Journal of International Law* on the 'methods of international law'[186] while stressing the 'dangers, discontinuities and mechanics of exclusion'[187] inherent in a classifying methodology that 'flattens out difference and neutralizes critique'.[188] However, as time went on most critical-oriented scholars, including Koskenniemi, would increasingly find comfort in identifying themselves as professional 'crits' and in seeing their work as contributing to a larger collective 'critical' effort, including by penning manifesto-like contributions oriented towards popularizing and programmatically introducing the main features of 'critical thinking' in international law to a broader readership.[189]

All 'epistemic communities', understood, as Bianchi notes, as 'fairly heterogeneous social groups that perform functions related to the formation of knowledge in the field of international law', the 'ultimate stake' of

---

[183] Chimni, *International Law*, p. 248. See Institute of Global Law and Policy at Harvard Law School, iglp.law.harvard.edu/about/.

[184] David Kennedy, 'When renewal repeats', p. 489.

[185] Thomas Skouteris, 'FIN de NAIL: New Approaches to International Law and its impact on contemporary international legal scholarship' (1997) 10 *Leiden Journal of International Law* 415–420 at 417.

[186] Martti Koskenniemi, 'The style as method: letter to the editors of the symposium' (1999) 93 *American Journal of International Law* 351–361 at 352; Steven R. Ratner and Anne-Marie Slaughter, 'Appraising the methods of international law: a prospectus for readers' (1999) 93 *American Journal of International Law* 291–302.

[187] Martti Koskenniemi, 'Le style comme méthode: lettres aux organisateurs du symposium', in *La politique du droit international* (Paris: Pédone, 2007), pp. 391–408 at 407.

[188] Ibid., p. 393.

[189] Bhupinder S. Chimni, 'Third World Approaches to International Law: a manifesto' (2006) 8 *International Community Law Review* 3–27; Koskenniemi, 'What international lawyers should learn from Karl Marx'; Martti Koskenniemi, 'Why history of international law today?' (2004) 4 *Rechtsgeschichte* 61–66; Martti Koskenniemi, 'What should international legal history become?', in Stefan Kadelbach, Thomas Kleinlein, and David Roth-Isigkeit (eds.), *System, Order and International Law: The Early History of International Legal Thought from Machiavelli to Hegel* (Oxford: Oxford University Press, 2017), pp. 381–397.

which is 'to acquire and maintain control of a scientific or social field by imposing its own vision of the field as the most authoritative',[190] are united by certain affiliation criteria – whether thematic expertise, national identity, methodological orientation, ideological affinity, or others – and, as result, all of them seek to replicate and perpetuate their orientation in terms of branding through the exercise of control over the message they convey to different degrees and on different scales. This in itself fosters a phenomenon of intellectual market 'commodification', in the wake of which comes an increasing self-containment of a closely linked 'scientific/intellectual community' with its own gatekeepers and their control of access to institutional resources, academic appointments, elite networks, prestigious publishing venues, and other academic benefits. Usually, intellectual market 'commodification' coincides with an overlapping of an original 'creative' generation in any 'epistemic community' with a subsequent generation of 'doctrinal systematization' which follows in the footsteps of its predecessors and buttresses the former's attempt to control what Harold M. Collins called the 'intellectual attention space'.[191] This move, in turn, may solidify the central axioms and produce a radicalization of the ideational or knowledge core positions as a distinguishable 'branding' feature of the scholarly identity of its group members. These, engaged in a competition for power, attention, and control of the discourse within the field and of its scarce available resources, may adopt a sectarian 'friend/enemy-like' Schmittian approach towards members of 'other' 'scientific/academic communities' or even against those who engage or are perceived to engage in internal contention within the group, who may consequently find themselves ostracized.

However, as pre-fabricated methodological slogans increasingly guide enquiry and fixed recognizable attitudes replace due safeguarding that one's intellectual horizons do not become impoverished, or even crippled by gregarious adherence to the established parameters, themes, and terminology within the 'epistemic group', there is also an increasingly perceivable degree of replication of common foci and topoi within it. Alongside this increasing intellectual self-referentiality, there may also be an excess of intellectual artificiality indulged in as style or posing as

---

[190] Andrea Bianchi, 'Epistemic communities', in Jean d'Aspremont and Sahib Singh (eds.), *Concepts for International Law: Contributions to Disciplinary Thought* (Northampton, MA: Edward Elgar Publishing, 2019), pp. 251–266 at 251.
[191] Harold M. Collins, 'The TEA-set: tacit knowledge and scientific networks' (1974) 4 *Social Studies of Science* 165–184; cited in Frickel and Gross, 'A general theory', p. 207.

creative critical reflectiveness alongside a reiterative and reverential appraisal by the rank and file of the 'authoritative' work of their intellectual leaders, some of whom may well end up becoming the object of a small industry of academic commentary as they near the end of their academic life cycles. These considerations, which go some way to highlighting the dynamics and some of the consequences of the intellectual 'market commodification' of international legal scholarship in general and of critical approaches to international law and its histories in particular, also underline the significance of being attentive to the shifting lenses of multi-perspectivity, as Chapter 11 examines, in functionally appraising the relative merits of different approaches to the history of international law.

3.6   Conclusion

The criticisms addressed by the CLS-inspired new trend in international legal thinking to what Emmanuelle Jouannet calls the 'empty, lifeless, soulless pragmatism of international law'[192] and the related effort to unbalance what, in the critical theory tradition, one may call an internal false state of reconciliation in the discipline have, since the mid- to late 1980s as they progressed through different trends in legal thought and academic persuasions, had a major impact – one which has even been portrayed as a 'Copernican revolution'[193] – on international legal scholarship and also on its historiography.

Broadly described, they have evolved from the application of a deconstructive structural method focused on the 'internal' structure of internationalist discourses to a more attentive and nuanced attention to the evolving intellectual history of the international law profession and its dramatis personae in an uncountable number of shifting political, cultural, sociological, and intellectual contexts. This move to the contextual perspective was greatly impacted by the influence of post-colonial historiography, and gradually in its wake by a turn to the historical study of the entwinedness of international law and international political economy in critical approaches to international legal history. This orientation

---

[192] Jouannet, 'A critical introduction', p. 7.
[193] Andrea Bianchi, *International Law Theories: An Inquiry into Different Ways of Thinking* (Oxford: Oxford University Press, 2016), p. 161 and pp. 150–162 (reflecting on the 'new stream scholarly legacy').

has been complemented by an increasingly abstract and historiographical scenario of debates about the methodology of international legal history where critical-oriented international legal historians often borrow from kindred critical historiographical trends in the field of history or resort to both traditional and novel critical legal historiographical lines of argumentation and analysis to sustain their choices against the different criticisms addressed to them.

The arsenal of 'critical' historiographical technologies with its promise to recast international law as an arena of social struggle has made a remarkable contribution in opening a scholarly space for creativity and new voices in international law against the traditional anti-intellectualist penchant common among legal practitioners and the consequent 'void created by pragmatism, namely the void that resulted from ignoring the most recent developments in philosophy, anthropology, social sciences or even historiography'.[194] They have also contributed to fostering many a scholarly polemic from which much contemporary international legal historical literature regularly springs. However, some celebrated exceptions notwithstanding, the truth remains that critical historiographical technologies have often become methodologically diluted into the writing of critical histories. Despite being methodologically branded and carefully wrapped up as 'critical work' in their introductions, these have often remained overall attached to fairly conventional historical modes. This is because it remains one thing to engage in conceptual complex polemics about international law and history writing – increasingly a genre in its own terms – and another one to actually write 'critical' international legal histories with scholarly acumen and historical finesse. For all the contributions to self-reflexivity of critical/postmodern historiographies, the contemporary literature still shows a perceivable gap between the effort to conceptually push the field to new scholarly agonistic confines with great interdisciplinary theoretical sophistication and the proper application of historical methods in appraising facts, consulting archival resources, properly contextualizing events and processes, peoples, and intellectual constructions, and then, in a bricolage-like fashion, composing with the resulting fabrics sufficiently engaging historical critical narratives. This *decalage* between 'high' critical theory and actual history writing is also a consequence of new realizations that the attentive

---

[194] Galindo, 'Martti Koskenniemi', p. 548.

study of 'history' inevitably brings in its wake and that can only be fully experienced by doing history instead of merely theorizing about it. Indeed, doing history brings in its wake an all-embracing rethinking of all preconceptions and dogmas, a keener intellectual discernment of the role that time plays in constantly shaping realities in the present, and also an acuter perception of where each one is positioned in relation to them.

4

TWAIL/Post-colonial Approaches to the History
of International Law

4.1 Introduction

One may agree with Martti Koskenniemi that 'much of the recent surge of interest in the history of international law has been fed by postcolonial attitudes in the legal academy'.[1] The rise of post-colonial international legal historiography ensued logically from the fact that between the end of World War II and the fall of the Berlin Wall alone eighty-nine colonies reached sovereign independence: eleven in the first five years after the end of World War II; eight in the 1950s; forty-four in the 1960s; twenty-four in the 1970s; and two in the 1980s. Originally spurred by decolonization,[2] in recent years this historiographical trend has been further favoured by globalization and the shift towards a multipolar world.

Post-colonial approaches to the history of international law can be broadly identified by their main object of historical investigation, namely the study of the history of international law in, and with regard to, non-Western societies with a common history of subjection in different forms and degrees to Western empires and colonialism. Their common foci include study of the historical role played by international law in justifying and effectively legally scaffolding colonialism and the accompanying plunder and exploitation of natural and other resources – such as cheap labour, including through the so-called peculiar institution of slavery[3] – in the outer-European colonized areas that came in its wake. This is translated into the post-colonial historiographical recurrent recourse to

---

[1] Martti Koskenniemi, 'Expanding histories of international law' (2016) 56 *American Journal of Legal History* 104–112 at 104.

[2] Mai Taha, 'Decolonization in international law', in *Oxford Bibliographies in International Law* (2019), www.oxford bibliographies.com/view/document/obo-9780199796953/obo-9780199796953-0195.xml.

[3] Frederic Megret, 'Droit international et esclavage: pour une réévaluation' (2013) 18 *African Yearbook of International Law* 121–183.

common topoi such as 'Eurocentrism',[4] 'civilizing mission',[5] 'standard of civilization',[6] 'imperialism',[7] 'unequal treaties',[8] 'periphery',[9] and other related terminology associated with what are appositely called 'technologies of empire'.[10]

Post-colonial approaches also share a particular *animus historiandi* consisting in 'decentring' and challenging a conventionally celebratory Western history of international law infused with a narrative of progress for the sake of the whole of humanity. In its place, they aim to trace the historically constitutive connections between different specialized areas of international law and its doctrines and Western colonial and imperial enterprises. As Bhupinder S. Chimni has noted, this approach 'proceeds on the assumption that a reliable history of international law cannot be written without taking into account the narratives emanating from nations that were the objects of colonial oppression'[11] – and, one might add, as will be seen in Chapter 5, the pre-colonial history of international law or autochthonous forms thereof (e.g. inter-polity laws) in these regions.

However, the historical interpretative reconstruction of what post-colonial perspectives assess as the unforgettable (or, in some accounts, merely unforgivable) complicity of the 'Western construct' of international law with past structures and doctrines as tools for the domination and subjugation of non-European peoples in the colonial past is not

---

[4] Arnulf Becker Lorca, 'Eurocentrism in the history of international law', in Bardo Fassbender and Anne Peters (eds.), *The Oxford Handbook of the History of International Law* (Oxford: Oxford University Press, 2012), pp. 1034–1057.

[5] Liliana Obregón, 'The civilized and the uncivilized', in Bardo Fassbender and Anne Peters (eds.), *The Oxford Handbook of the History of International Law* (Oxford: Oxford University Press, 2012), pp. 917–943.

[6] Gerrit W. Gong, *The Standard of 'Civilization' in International Society* (Oxford: Clarendon Press, 1984).

[7] Martti Koskenniemi, Walter Rech, and Manuel Jiménez Fonseca (eds.), *International Law and Empire – Historical Explorations* (Oxford: Oxford University Press, 2017).

[8] Anne Peters, 'Treaties, unequal', in *Max Planck Encyclopedia of Public International Law* (2018), opil.ouplaw.com/view/10.1093/law:epil/9780199231690/law-9780199231690-e1495?rskey=jQDTL7&result=1&prd=OPIL, pp. 1–14.

[9] See Fleur Johns, Thomas Skouteris, and Wouter Werner, 'Editors' introduction: Alejandro Álvarez and the launch of the Periphery Series' (2006) 19 *Leiden Journal of International Law* 875–1040 at 875–877.

[10] Sundhya Pahuja, 'Technologies of empire: IMF conditionality and the reinscription of the north/south divide' (2000) 13 *Leiden Journal of International Law* 749–813.

[11] Bhupinder S. Chimni, *International Law and World Order: A Critique of Contemporary Approaches*, 2nd ed. (Cambridge, UK: Cambridge University Press, 2017), p. 16.

only for the historical record in their historical narratives. Indeed, underlying contemporary post-colonial historiography and, in particular, the scholarly production associated with what has come to be termed TWAIL (Third World Approaches to International Law), there is an attempt to trace the 'legacies of imperial formations in contemporary legal concepts, practices and institutions'[12] up to the present time in a double and mutually reinforcing sense. First, it is in order to highlight their lasting influence in the perpetuation of inequalities, understood in terms of underdevelopment and social disparities across great parts of the post-colonial 'periphery', a terminology inspired by 'world-system theory' in the field of international political economy.[13] Second, it is to denounce the fact that international law's historical imperialism remains 'ingrained in international law as we know it today'[14] and that it therefore continues to serve as a transmission belt for new forms of 'neo-colonialism' in the contemporary age.

To put it differently, the corollary of the post-colonial historiographical argument is that 'colonial international law' has been transmuted into contemporary structures, institutions, and legal concepts through revamped versions of colonial doctrines such as the 'standard of civilization',[15] which justified unequal treatment of some non-Western polities during the 'age of imperialism', or what Partha Chatterjee terms the operation of 'the imperial privilege (which) still exists in a world without colonies'.[16] This politically 'presentist' orientation in TWAIL/post-colonial approaches to international legal history in their arguing for the 'decolonization' of the international order – one that is written in

---

[12] Anne Orford, 'The past as law or history? The relevance of imperialism for modern international law', in Mark Toufayan, Emmanuelle Tourme-Jouannet, and Hélène Ruiz-Fabri (eds.), Droit international et nouvelles approches sur le tiers-monde (International Law and New Approaches to the Third World: Between Repetition and Renewal) (Paris: Société de Législation Comparée, 2013), pp. 97–118 at 98.

[13] The seminal account is Immanuel Wallerstein, The Modern World-System: Capitalist Agriculture and the Origins of the European World-Economy in the Sixteenth Century (New York: Academic Press, 1976).

[14] James Thuo Gathii, 'Neoliberalism, colonialism and international governance: decentering the international law of governmental legitimacy' (2000) 98 Michigan Law Review 1996–2020.

[15] George Schwarzenberger, 'The standard of civilization in international law' (1955) 8 Current Legal Problems 212–234 at 215.

[16] Partha Chatterjee, 'The legacy of Bandung', in Luis Eslava, Michael Fakhri, and Vasuki Nesiah (eds.), Bandung, Global History, and International Law: Critical Pasts and Pending Futures (Cambridge, UK: Cambridge University Press, 2017), pp. 657–674 at 674.

the language of international law but is ultimately epiphenomenally dependent on other extra-juridical and super-structural factors – works as a shortcut to project their historical analyses as political 'interventions' in contemporary debates on the unequal dynamics of globalization. Analogously, this underlying understanding that '[t]he end of formal colonialism, while extremely significant, did not result in the end of colonial relations'[17] colours reinterpretations of events, individual people, concepts, and also the operation of international organizations in the history of international law. Furthermore, the ongoing 'TWAILing' of international legal history, has prompted, as seen in Chapter 2, historiographical debates on the proper role of 'contextualism' in regard to 'anachronism' and to different forms of presentism that were previously unheard of in international legal history.

Against this background, Section 4.2 below revisits the now commonplace distinction between a 'first' and a 'second' generation of postcolonial approaches to international law and its histories and examines their main features and contributions. Particular attention is then paid in Section 4.3 to the role of history among self-identified representatives of the scholarly movement known as TWAIL and its intellectual roots and central features. Section 4.4 examines how the TWAILing of the history of international law by a late 1990s and twenty-first-century generation of 'global south' international academic lawyers has proceeded, partly because of an 'anxiety of influence' in confronting their 'predecessors' from the decolonization decades, with reference to a set of historical studies on particular peoples, events, and legal concepts. Section 4.5 examines the influence of post-colonial historiography on knowledge creation processes on the relationship between international law and history with attention *in fine* to the construction of an alternative meta-periodization of the history of international law premised on post-colonial landmarks. In Section 4.6, first TWAIL as such and then more specifically its tackling of international law histories are confronted by their critics. The conclusion takes stock of the overall influence and large contribution of TWAIL/post-colonial approaches to the 'renewal' of the history of international law while reflecting on the extent to which they may risk soon becoming out of touch with contemporary historiographical dynamics in an increasingly interdisciplinary field.

---

[17] Antony Anghie, 'The evolution of international law: colonial and postcolonial realities' (2006) 27 *Third World Quarterly* 739–753 at 748–749.

4.2 Post-colonial Generations of Historical Writing about International Law

The study of the history of international law in colonial territories and the history of international law as seen from the perspective of the 'colonized' was, some exceptions notwithstanding, generally disregarded under the deep-seated influence of an overarching Eurocentric historiographical framework, as Chapter 1 and, in particular, Chapter 5 show, until the onset of the decolonization decades. The role of history in post-colonial international legal scholarship mainly developed from the 1950s and 1960s in contributions by what has been retrospectively termed the 'first generation' of TWAIL (TWAIL I). Indeed, as the decolonization process across Africa and Asia unfolded, so did the attention of Asian and African authors to international law, and by extension to the history of international law. Often cited among the representative international law scholars of this generation are the Indian scholars Ram Prakash Anand (1933–2011), Nagendra Singh,[18] S. P. Sinha,[19] and J. J. G. Syatauw,[20] the Nigerian author Taslim O. Elias,[21] the Egyptian Georges Abi-Saab,[22] the Algerian Mohammed Bedjaoui,[23] and the Sri Lankan Christopher Gregory Weeramantry,[24] together with several others, occasionally including schlolars of European origin but working and living in Asia, such as the Polish but then nationalized British scholar Charles H. Alexandrowicz.[25] Many of these 'peripheral' scholars had

---

[18] Carl Landauer, 'Passage from India: Nagendra Singh's India and international law' (2016) 56 *India Journal of International Law* 265–305.

[19] Prakash S. Sinha, 'Perspective of the newly independent states on the binding quality of international law' (1965) 14 *International and Comparative Law Quarterly* 121–131.

[20] J. J. G. Syatauw, *Some Newly Established Asian States and the Development of International Law* (The Hague: Martinus Nijhoff, 1961).

[21] See recently Carl Landauer, 'Taslim Olawale Elias: from British colonial law to modern international law', in Jochen von Bernstorff and Philipp Dann (eds.), *The Battle for International Law: South–North Perspectives on the Decolonization Era* (Oxford: Oxford University Press, 2019), pp. 318–340.

[22] Georges Abi-Saab, 'The newly independent states and the rules of international law: an outline' (1926) 8 *Howard Law Journal* 95–121.

[23] See, e.g., Mohammed Bedjaoui, 'Problèmes récents de succession d'états dans les états nouveaux' (1970) 130 *Collected Courses of The Hague Academy of International Law* 455–586; Mohammed Bedjaoui, 'Non-alignement et droit international' (1976) 151 *Collected Courses of The Hague Academy of International Law* 337–456.

[24] Christopher Gregory Weeramantry, *Islamic Jurisprudence: An International Perspective* (London: Macmillan, 1988).

[25] Charles H. Alexandrowicz, *An Introduction to the Law of Nations in the East Indies* (Oxford: Clarendon Press, 1967).

earned an elite Western legal education and went on to become highly respected and rewarded members of the international law 'establishment' within which they successfully integrated. They often taught and lived outside their countries of origin and engaged in diplomatic, legal advisory and international judicial endeavours,[26] including service on the bench of the International Court of Justice (ICJ), over which three of them went on to preside,[27] in the Appellate Body of the World Trade Organization (WTO) and sometimes the International Criminal Tribunal for the former Yugoslavia (ICTY) or the International Criminal Tribunal for Rwanda (ICTR).[28]

The immediate political context of their scholarly work was coincidental with the processes through which numerous new sovereign nations were becoming members of the quickly growing international community of states as former European empires disintegrated. This accounts for the centrality in their work of reassertions of the post-colonial states' 'hard-won prize of sovereignty'[29] through their defence of certain international legal doctrines. These included the principle of 'self-determination of peoples', the 'right to development', the 'prohibition of racial discrimination', 'sovereign control over natural resources', and discussions on the principle of *uti possidetis iuris*. They also comprised legal proposals oriented to setting up limits to special protections for foreign investors inherited from customary international law, and to requesting special treatment in international trade relations and others inter alia addressed at altering the dynamics of 'international law-making processes' so as to maximize the new majorities held by developing countries at the UN General Assembly.[30] Despite apparent differences in the cultures and historical experiences among newly independent countries both within and across continents, their sharing, according to Georges Abi-Saab, of 'the same grievances and claims: the grievance of

---

[26] See by its own recollection, Georges Abi-Saab, 'The Third World intellectual in praxis: confrontation, participation, or operation behind enemy lines?' (2016) 37 *Third World Quarterly* 1957–1971.

[27] Judges Singh (1985–88), Elias (1982–85), and Bedjaoui (1994–97) served as presidents of the ICJ and Judge Weeramantry as its vice-president (1997–2000): www.icj-cij.org/en/all-members.

[28] Judge Abi-Saab (1933) served on the Appeals Chamber of the ICTY and for Rwanda, and on the WTO's Appellate Body (2000–08), including as its president: www.wto.org/english/tratop_e/dispu_e/popup_gm_abisaab_e.htm.

[29] Abi-Saab, 'The newly independent states', pp. 95–121.

[30] Andrea Bianchi, *International Law Theories: An Inquiry into Different Ways of Thinking* (Oxford: Oxford University Press, 2016), p. 214.

colonial past and exploitation, and of actual marginalization; and a claim for greater equality and equity, as well as for effective participation in global decision-making[31] was to be projected as part of semi-concerted political strategies in what has later been historiographically periodized as the 'battle for international law' (1955–75).[32] The latter is how the semi-concerted foreign-policy strategies that new sovereign nations were to develop against the background of the Cold War have come to be known. These are often retraced to the Bandung Conference (1955), before evolving through the 1960s in the 'Non-Aligned Movement' (1961) and the establishment of the 'Group of 77', reaching their apex with the Declaration on the Establishment of a New Economic Order (1974)[33] and later culminating in the Declaration on the Right to Development (1986).[34]

Despite their underlying 'reformist' academic production, which was concerned, according to Matthew Craven, with 'put[ting] at centre-stage the concerns and interests of the non-European world in conditions under which it had effectively been written out of the discipline's own history',[35] the specific contribution of this generation to international legal history was, however, in most cases relatively sporadic. While being a reaction to the traditional historiographical Eurocentrism of inter-national legal history, their work was complementarily informed by a double national /cosmopolitan 'contributionist' perspective.[36] Through this they aimed first to 'contribute' to the retrieval of their own national and/or regional histories in which colonialism was deemed, in some

---

[31] Georges Abi-Saab, 'Foreword', in Luis Eslava, Michael Fakhri, and Vasuki Nesiah (eds.), *Bandung, the Global South, and International Law: Critical Pasts and Pending Futures* (Cambridge, UK: Cambridge University Press, 2017), pp. xxix–xxx at xxix.

[32] Jochen von Bernstorff and Philipp Dann (eds.), *The Battle for International Law: South–North Perspectives on the Decolonization Era* (Oxford: Oxford University Press, 2019).

[33] UN General Assembly, Res. A/3201 (S-VI). Mohammed Bedjaoui, *Towards A New International Economic Order* (Paris and New York: Holmes & Meier, 1979). See Ingo Venzke, 'Possibilities of the past: histories of the NIEO and the travails of critique' (2018) 20 *Journal of the History of International Law* 263–302; Nils Gilman, 'The new inter-national economic order: a reintroduction' (2015) 6 *Humanity: An International Journal of Human Rights, Humanitarianism, and Development* 1–16.

[34] UN General Assembly, Res. 41/128, 4 December 1986.

[35] Matthew Craven, 'Theorizing the turn to history in international law', in Anne Orford and Florian Hoffmann with Martin Clark (eds.), *The Oxford Handbook of the Theory of International Law* (Oxford: Oxford University Press, 2016), pp. 21–37 at 32.

[36] James T. Gathii, 'Africa', in Bardo Fassbender and Anne Peters (eds.), *The Oxford Handbook of the History of International Law* (Oxford: Oxford University Press, 2012), pp. 407–429 at 407.

cases, to have been 'an interlude only',[37] and secondly to claim their national and/or regional cultural share of the 'global' reservoir of historical practices and ideas of the cosmopolitan discipline they had made their lives' profession.

In this context, India, one of the first countries to become independent (1947), was and has remained an important pole for the production of non-European autochthonous histories of international law. Although the pre-colonial history of international law in India had precedents in writings by Indian scholars on the history of international law in the interwar period,[38] an influential source for its post-independence development was Charles H. Alexandrowicz (1902–75), whom David Armitage and Jennifer Pitts have considered 'the forgotten founder of the current critical movement to historicize international law'.[39] In 1951 Alexandrowicz took a professorship of international law in Madras, from where he was to foster attention to the history of international law through his own academic production – namely with his work on the East Indies, in which he highlighted that the South Asian region had had a system comparable to the European law of nations for longer than Europe[40] – and through his founding of the *Indian Yearbook of International Affairs* (1952)[41] and the Grotian Society in India (1960). The latter, the purpose of which was to 'promote the revival of the much-neglected history of the law of nations',[42] included a programme of publications in the form of a homonymous series of books and a sequence of supplements to the *Indian Yearbook of International Affairs* devoted to the study of historical topics in international law. A generation of Indian international lawyers, including H. Chatterjee,[43]

---

[37] David Armitage and Jennifer Pitts, '"This modern Grotius": an introduction to the life and thought of C. H. Alexandrowicz', in Charles H. Alexandrowicz, *The Law of Nations in Global History*, ed David Armitage and Jennifer Pitts (Oxford: Oxford University Press, 2017), pp. 1–34 at 18.

[38] See Pramathanath Bandyopadhyay, *International Law and Custom in Ancient India* (Calcutta: University of Calcutta Press, 1920); S. V. Viswanatha, *International Law in Ancient India* (London and New York: Longmans, Green and Co., 1925), cited in Landauer, 'Passage from India', pp. 271 and 272.

[39] Armitage and Pitts, '"This modern Grotius"', p. 15.

[40] Ibid., p. 18.

[41] Landauer, 'Passage from India', p. 272.

[42] Charles H. Alexandrowicz, 'The Grotian Society' (1967) 61 *American Journal of International Law* 1058.

[43] Hiralal Chatterjee, *International Law and Inter-state Relations in Ancient India* (Calcutta: Mukhopadhyay, 1958), pp. 79–80.

M. K. Nawaz,[44] and N. Singh, followed suit. For instance, N. Singh's *India and International Law* (1969) sought to establish the precedents of the modern fundamental concepts and institutions in international law with reference to ancient and medieval Indian traditions,[45] claiming that they contained a more 'universal' conception than 'Western international law', which was laden with standards informed by Christian dogma and had excluded others not belonging to its same 'civilization'.[46] Another particularly influential author in this historiographical orientation was R. P. Anand,[47] mainly through his *New States and International Law* (1972)[48] and his *Origin and Development of the Law of the Sea: History of International Law Revisited* (1983)[49] and later through his collected works on the topic.[50] Meanwhile in Africa, influenced by the common trend in historiography in Asia of bridging the new nations with the Western centres of knowledge, albeit with their own particularities,[51] other examples include works by another president of the ICJ, Taslim O. Elias, such as the collection of essays and articles in his *Africa and the Development of International Law*.[52] This is considered one of 'the most significant scholarly works of this period that makes the best case for rejecting and, therefore, redefining categories such as '"backward",

---

[44] M. K. Nawaz, 'The law of nations in ancient India' (1957) 6 *Indian Yearbook of International Affairs* 172–188, cited in Landauer, 'Passage from India', p. 271.

[45] Nagendra Singh, *India and International Law* (Delhi: S. Chand, 1969).

[46] Cited in Landauer, 'Passage from India', p. 271.

[47] Liliana Obregón, 'Martti Koskenniemi´s critique of Eurocentrism in International Law', in Wouter Werner, Marieka de Hoon, and Alexis Galán (eds.), *The Law of International Lawyers: Reading Martti Koskenniemi* (Cambridge, UK: Cambridge University Press, 2017), pp. 360–392 at 370–371; Prabhakar Singh, 'Reading RP Anand in the post-colony: between resistance and appropriation', in Jochen von Bernstorff and Philipp Dann (eds.), *The Battle for International Law: South–North Perspectives on the Decolonization Era* (Oxford: Oxford University Press, 2019), pp. 297–318.

[48] Ram P. Anand, *New States and International Law* (Delhi: Vikas Publishing House, 1972).

[49] Ram P. Anand, *Origin and Development of the Law of the Sea: History of International Law Revisited* (Leiden: Martinus Nijhoff, 1983).

[50] Ram P. Anand, *Studies in International Law and History: An Asian Perspective* (Leiden: Martinus Nijhoff, 2004).

[51] See recently Jakob Zollmann, 'African international legal histories—international law in Africa: perspectives and possibilities' (2018) 31 *Leiden Journal of International Law* 897–914.

[52] Taslim Olawale Elias, *Africa and the Development of International Law* (Leiden: A. W. Sijthoff, and Dobbs Ferry, NY: Oceana, 1972); Mark Toufayan, 'When British justice (in African colonies) points two ways: on dualism, hybridity, and the genealogy of juridical negritude in Taslim Olawale Elias', in Oche Onazi (ed.), *African Legal Theory and Contemporary Problems* (Dordrecht: Springer, 2014), pp. 31–70.

"uncivilized", and "barbaric", assigned to African communities in international legal history'.[53]

Chronologically, the work of the first post-colonial generation coincided with that of European scholars, particularly from Germany, which was informed by the backdrop of decolonization and inspired by the tenets of 'world history'. These scholars produced significant works retrospectively deemed to be significant in the post-colonial historiography of international law.[54] As Chapter 5 shows, the contribution by Wolfgang Preiser was to become particularly influential. From the 1960s, Preiser led efforts to retrace the emergence of the nation-state before Westphalia in the Western world back to the 1300s, while on the other hand contributing to extending the history of international law both temporally and spatially far beyond the geographical boundaries of the European world.[55] This historiographical frame has recently regained momentum, as Chapter 5 examines, under the impulse of both 'trans-civilizational' historical perspectives and 'global history' approaches to international law.

4.3   The TWAIL Generation – Moving to the 1990s

Often identified with the TWAIL movement, the 'second generation' of post-colonial approaches to international law has much in common with other critical/postmodern schools of international legal thought under, as we saw in Chapter 3, the general umbrella, particularly auspicated by David Kennedy since the late 1980s,[56] of 'New Approaches to International Law' (NAIL).[57] An offspring of sorts of this, TWAIL also originated in the same 'elite' academic setting of the doctoral programme of Harvard Law School in the late 1990s,[58] under the intellectual patronage of members of the Critical Legal Studies (CLS)

---

[53] Gathii, 'Africa', p. 409.

[54] Jörg Fish, *Die europäische Expansion und das Völkerrecht* (Stuttgart: Steiner, 1984).

[55] Wolfgang Preiser, *Frühe völkerrechtliche Ordnungen der aussereuropäischen Welt: Ein Beitrag zur Geschichte des Völkerrechts* (Wiesbaden: Steiner, 1976).

[56] David Kennedy, 'A new stream of international law scholarship' (1988) 7 *Wisconsin International Law Journal* 1–49.

[57] Thomas Skouteris, 'New Approaches to International Law', in *Oxford Bibliographies in International Law* (2011), www.oxfordbibliographies.com/view/document/obo-97801997 96953/obo-9780199796953-0012.xml.

[58] From which several of its best-noted representatives – or kindred figures – graduated or were to do so: B. Rajagopal, A. Anghie, J. T. Gatthi, V. Nesiah, L. Obregón, A. Becker Lorca, etc.

movement.[59] In particular, according to Kennedy, 'TWAIL arose at a moment – among a generation of scholars in rebellion against two traditions: against the tradition of third world engagement with the international legal order associated with decolonization, the UN and the politics of the nineteen sixties and seventies. But also against the tradition of third world professional assimilation and intellectual invisibility associated with the eighties and nineties.'[60]

Originating as an international legal scholarly trend aimed at contesting, like its NAIL counterparts, the 'politics of knowledge in international law'[61] through the advancement of a critique 'using a range of social and political theories that include liberal, Marxist, feminist, postcolonial and postmodern theories',[62] TWAIL is understood by its members as a transnational epistemological community that takes the form of a 'decentralised network'[63] or, according to Bhupinder S. Chimni, a 'loose network of third-world scholars who articulate a critique of the history, structure and process of contemporary international law from the standpoint of third world peoples, in particular its marginal and oppressed groups'.[64] It has spread in a militant activist-like fashion, producing a large body of scholarly literature,[65] and also expanding in different languages,[66] since its first foundational statement in 1997.[67] According to this, TWAIL was

> grounded in the united recognition that we need democratization of international legal scholarship in at least two senses: (i) first, we need to context[ualize] international law's privileging of European and North

---

[59] More recently through the Institute of Global Law and Policy (established in 2009); see iglp.law.harvard.edu.

[60] David Kennedy, 'The TWAIL Conference: keynote address, Albany, New York, April 2007' (2007) 9 *International Community Law Review* 333–344 at 334.

[61] George R. B. Galindo, 'Splitting TWAIL?' (2016) 33 *Windsor Yearbook of Access to Justice* 37–56 at 44.

[62] Chimni, *International Law*, p. 15.

[63] James T. Gathii, 'TWAIL: a brief history of its origins, its decentralized network, and a tentative bibliography' (2011) 3 *Trade Law and Development* 26–32 at 26.

[64] Chimni, *International Law*, p. 15.

[65] See the journal *Third World Quarterly*, 37 (2016), issue 11, *Third World Approaches to International Law (TWAIL)*.

[66] See, e.g., in French, Mark Toufayan, Emmanuelle Jouannet, and Hélène Ruiz-Fabri (eds.), *Droit international et nouvelles approches sur le tiers-monde: entre répétition et renouveau* (Paris: Société de Législation Comparée, 2013), or, in Italian, Luigi Nuzzo, *Origini di una scienza: diritto internazionale e colonialismo nel XIX secolo* (Frankfurt am Main: Klostermann, 2012).

[67] Gathii, 'TWAIL: a brief history', pp. 26–32.

American voices by providing institutional and imaginative opportunities for participation from the third world; and (ii) second, we need to formulate a substantive critique of the politics and scholarship of mainstream international law to the extent that it has helped reproduce structures that marginalize and dominate third world peoples.[68]

Central to this self-definition of TWAIL is its location of the 'Third World', today more commonly known as the 'developing world' or the 'global south', as a 'central epistemological category' which, according to Balakrishnan Rajagopal, 'should be re-imagined as a counter-hegemonic discursive tool that allows us to interrogate and contest the various ways in which power is used'.[69] Against criticisms addressed, as we shall later see, to TWAIL's appropriation of the 'Third World' label and terminology, TWAILers such as Makau Mutua have stressed that the 'Third World' remains a necessary epistemological category because it is 'more truly a stream of similar historical experiences across virtually all non-European societies that has given rise to a particular voice, a form of intellectual and political consciousness'[70] and therefore it is in this sense 'a political reality'.[71] Variously defined as 'a discipline in transition, expansion, definition and internal contestation about the varied agendas of its scholars, all at the same time'[72] in its 'counter-hegemonic orientation against prevailing neo-liberal forms of governance in the third world',[73] TWAIL has amply applied deconstructionist techniques to the 'ensemble of methods, practices and understandings in relation to the identification, interpretation and enforcement of international law'.[74]

One particularly noted object of TWAIL critique has been the centrality of human rights and the so-called right to democratic governance[75]

---

[68] Karin Mickelson, 'Taking stock of TWAIL histories' (2008) 10 *International Community Law Review* 355–362 at 357–358.

[69] Balakrishnan Rajagopal, 'Locating the Third World in cultural geography' (1998–99) 98 *Third World Legal Studies* 1–20 at 1–2.

[70] Makua Mutua, 'What is TWAIL?' (2000) 94 *American Society of International Law Proceedings* 31–38 at 35.

[71] Ibid.

[72] Gathii, 'TWAIL: a brief history', p. 34.

[73] Ibid.

[74] See Bhupinder S. Chimni, 'An outline for a Marxist course on public international law' (2004) 17 *Leiden Journal of International Law* 1–30 at 1.

[75] Makau Mutua, 'The ideology of human rights' (1995) 36 *Virginia Journal of International Law* 589–657; Opeoluwa Adetoro Badaru, 'Examining the utility of Third World Approaches to International Law for international human rights law' (2008) 10 *International Community Law Review* 379–387; Luis Eslava and Sundhya Pahuja, 'Between resistance and reform: TWAIL and the universality of international law'

in what TWAILers appraise as the 'neoliberal agenda' of the so-called Washington Consensus, within which framework in their view they perform a Trojan horse-like function in regard to 'the threat of recolonization that is haunting the Third World'.[76] Indeed, TWAIL authors have often highlighted that 'the Third World, in all its complexity, needs to internalize the uncomfortable fact that human rights discourse is part of the problem of global hegemony and the absence of global justice'.[77] TWAIL has been particularly influenced by the Marxist/CLS 'critique of rights' in its application to the international human rights movement.[78] This is one of the vectors of the critical targeting of the so-called discourse of the right to democratic governance and international human rights law which gained momentum among critical-oriented international law scholars at a time of liberal triumphalism and end-of-history narratives in the early post-Cold War era.[79] As was seen in Chapter 3, this critical counter-narrative has later been translated into the project of rewriting the 'progressive' history of international human rights in a critical and revisionist vein.[80] The critical idea that 'substantive rights established by the rules exist in order to protect certain interests'[81] has been taken up by TWAILers, for whom 'the Third World, in all its complexity, needs to internalize the uncomfortable fact that human rights discourse is part of the problem of global hegemony and the

(2011) 3 *Trade Law and Development* 103–130; Thomas M. Franck, 'The emerging right to democratic governance' (1992) 86 *American Journal of International Law* 46–91 at 47.

[76] Bhupinder S. Chimni, 'Third World Approaches to International Law: a manifesto' (2006) 8 *International Community Law Review* 3–27 at 3.

[77] Rémi Bachand, 'Critical approaches and the Third World', report presented in the framework of the colloquium 'Evaluating Critical Approaches to International Law', University of Paris I, 12 December 2009 (on file with the author).

[78] See, for example, Duncan Kennedy, 'The critique of rights in Critical Legal Studies', in Wendy Brown and Janet E. Halley (eds.), *Left Legalism/Left Critique* (Durham, NC: Duke University Press, 2002), pp. 178–228; David Kennedy, *The Dark Sides of Virtue: Reassessing International Humanitarism* (Princeton, NJ: Princeton University Press, 2004); Martti Koskenniemi, 'Human rights mainstreaming as a strategy for institutional power' (2010) 1 *Humanity: An International Journal of Human Rights, Humanitarianism, and Development* 47–58.

[79] Susan Marks, *The Riddle of All Constitutions, International Law, Democracy, and the Critique of Ideology* (Oxford: Oxford University Press, 2000), p. 121.

[80] See, e.g., Samuel Moyn, *The Last Utopia: Human Rights in History* (Cambridge, MA: Harvard University Press, 2012) and Samuel Moyn, *Human Rights and the Uses of History* (London: Verso, 2017).

[81] Rémi Bachand, 'Le droit international et l'idéologie "droits-de-l'hommiste" au fondement de l'hégémonie occidentale' (special issue, 2014) *Revue Québécoise de droit international* 70–97 at 82.

absence of global justice'.[82] This questioning of international human rights discourse is associated with an understanding that one of the 'fundamental functions of international law and the human rights' ideology' has been that of legitimating military interventions and coercive measures, or to put it in Gramscian terms, that the legitimacy that international law and human rights' discourse offer is 'central to the constitution of spontaneous consent', which in turn serves as the cornerstone of the reproduction of a Western hegemonic international legal system.[83]

The critical contesting of the overarching ideology of international human rights law is attuned to TWAIL's main focus, which has been that of highlighting the maintenance of historical Western economic and ideological hegemony through international law understood as a superstructure, both epiphenomenal and reconstitutive of conditions that perpetuate Western-dominated centre–periphery relations in a world order marked by global asymmetries of power mirrored, as seen in Chapter 9, in the architecture of international institutions. The Marxist international law scholar Bhupinder S. Chimni, who had previously described international institutions as a 'global imperial state in the making' dominated by Western powers and managed by 'transnational capitalist classes',[84] has more recently suggested that 'the most significant feature' of what he terms 'global imperialism, that is, imperialism in the era of globalization' is 'that universalizing capitalism penetrates and integrates national economies more deeply, imposing serious constraints on the possibility of a Third World state pursuing an independent path of development.'[85] These critical features have in turn translated into a particularly militantist historiographical orientation whereby the 'turn to history' in international law developing since the early to mid-2000s

---

[82] Balakrishnan Rajagopal, 'Counter-hegemonic international law: rethinking human rights and development as a Third World strategy' (2006) 27 *Third World Quarterly* 767–783 at 768.

[83] Bachand, 'Le droit international', p. 82. See also Frédéric Mégret, 'Where does the critique of international human rights stand? An exploration in 18 vignettes', in David Kennedy and José Maria Beneyto (eds.), *New Approaches to International Law: The European and American Experiences* (The Hague: T. M. C. Asser Press, 2013), pp. 3–40.

[84] Bhupinder S. Chimni, 'International institutions today: an imperial global state in the making' (2004) 15 *European Journal of International Law* 1–37 at 1.

[85] Bhupinder S. Chimni, 'Anti-imperialism then and now', in Luis Eslava, Michael Fakhri, and Vasuki Nesiah (eds.), *Bandung, the Global South, and International Law: Critical Pasts and Pending Futures* (Cambridge, UK: Cambridge University Press, 2017), pp. 35–48 at 36.

has been interpreted as a 'site of struggle and of promised emancipation' that is 'here to stay'.[86]

One of TWAIL's identifying features is its ambivalence towards the scholarly work and the international legal historiography produced by those who they ex post-facto identify as TWAIL I. In an example of what, *mutatis mutandis*, Harold Bloom famously defined as the 'anxiety of influence' in the field of poetry, which is popularly understood as 'the psychological struggle of aspiring authors to overcome the anxiety posed by the influence of their literary antecedents',[87] TWAILers have examined their predecessors' work in terms of continuities but also differences or discontinuities.[88] On the one hand, there is acknowledgement of the important contribution made by earlier 'Third World' scholars in the light of their 'historical critique in the early post-colonial period, whether to challenge the parochial and celebratory history of international law or its complicity with colonialism'.[89] However, according to subsequent readings, the historiographical effort made by the earlier generation was 'integrationist' or 'contributionist' in scope because in highlighting that non-Western peoples had also developed rules regarding the central institutions of international law, like treaty-making, laws of war, including humanitarian aspects, and immunities for foreign envoys that 'pre-existed colonial rule and interacted with it',[90] they ended up subsuming 'the non-European periphery into an essentially European narrative of progress'.[91] Thus, considering that the early post-colonial critique 'was not undertaken simply to repudiate international law [but that] it was part of an effort to produce *universal* international law'[92] and therefore 'reinforced the status quo',[93] TWAILers distance themselves from this 'early scholarship [that] tended to treat the colonial encounter as marginal to the story of international law' and also, according to Chimni,

---

[86] Bhupinder S. Chimni, 'The past, present and future of international law: a critical Third World approach' (2007) 8 *Melbourne Journal of International Law* 499–515 at 513.
[87] See further Harold Bloom, *The Anxiety of Influence: A Theory of Poetry* (New York: Oxford University Press, 1973).
[88] Antony Anghie and Bhupinder S. Chimni, 'Third World Approaches to International Law and individual responsibility in internal conflicts' (2003) 2 *Chinese Journal of International Law* 77–103 at 79–84.
[89] Chimni, 'The past, present and future', p. 499.
[90] Craven, 'Theorizing the turn to history', p. 32.
[91] Ibid., p. 33.
[92] Chimni, 'The past, present and future', p. 501.
[93] Liliana Obregón, 'Peripheral histories of international law' (2019) 15 *Annual Review of Law and Social Science* 437–451 at 443.

'failed to stress the class and gender divides within it' and proved themselves unable 'to grasp the growing collaborative character of the third world élite'.[94] The consequence of TWAIL's critical detachment, as Martti Koskenniemi notes, 'from older histories of the field that were either more neutral in conception or associated the growth of international law with peace and enlightenment',[95] is a dynamic of mutually reinforcing influence of TWAIL with the critical/postmodern approaches examined in Chapter 3 and thus a much more radically analytical distrust in the liberal underpinnings of international law and the social-reformist cosmopolitan promise held by international institutions.

4.4   TWAILing the History of International Law: Peoples, Events, and Concepts

TWAIL's meta-historiographical orientation foundationally rests on an assessment that Western international law as we know it was *ad condita* fundamentally shaped by the 'great encounter'. This historiographical retracing of the origins of international law to this foundationally 'colonial matrix' is corroborated by David Kennedy, for whom 'TWAIL ... was forged in Anghie's encounter with the history of international law.'[96] This connection has prompted, as seen in Chapter 2, a historiographical debate on the critical merits and methodological demerits of Anghie's work from the perspective of methodological contextualists and critical international historians. Furthermore, it has greatly contributed to the interrelated historization of individual peoples, events of international legal significance, and international legal concepts in the light of an overarching interpretative post-colonial meta-perspective in the TWAIL/post-colonial literature.

First, post-colonial attention to individual people has played an important role, as will be seen in Chapter 10, in the (re)turn of international law biography in context in international legal historical works. Three main categories of this post-colonial focus can be distinguished. The first one revolves, as we have seen, around the historization of the contribution by a series of international law scholars originating in particular from Asia and Africa who began to write their academic contributions during the decolonization age. While contemporary TWAILers appraise the work of their 'predecessors' ambivalently, they

---

[94] Chimni, 'The past, present and future', p. 503.
[95] Koskenniemi, 'Expanding histories', p. 104.
[96] David Kennedy, 'The TWAIL Conference'.

do continue to devote much attention to their intellectual biographies and to analysis of how they 'acted in and thought about the international legal scenario'[97] in their own time.[98] Second, the post-colonial biographical interest has also extended to earlier generations of peripheral writers, in particular from Latin America but also from other regions including Japan and China, who embodied strategies of 'appropriation' of the language of international law informed by 'particularistic universalism'[99] in peripheral countries, and to studying the modification and transformation of international law as a result of these processes. In particular, Liliana Obregón, who coined the term 'criollo (or creole) international law',[100] and Arnulf Becker Lorca, coiner of the term 'mestizo international law',[101] have both devoted the bulk of their scholarship to bringing 'to light the critical contribution of scholars from the periphery in appropriating and reformulating key features of the discipline'[102] since the independence of the Latin American republics and also across other geographies. Inspired by, and often working in collaboration with TWAIL approaches, but also influenced by 'global history', this trend includes, as Martti Koskenniemi summarizes, 'narratives that emphasize the way "semiperipheral" actors from Latin America, Japan, Turkey, and China have, from the late 19th century onwards, adopted and adapted international law of European origin so as to further domestic agendas, constrain Europeans, and to transform European legal categories'.[103] The fact that original TWAILers such as Balakrishnan Rajagopal have corroborated this historiographical move by situating the beginning of TWAIL I around the turn of the twentieth century, when the articulation

---

[97] Galindo, 'Splitting TWAIL?', p. 53. See Sundhya Pahuja, *Decolonising International Law: Development, Economic Growth and the Politics of Universality* (Cambridge, UK: Cambridge University Press, 2011).

[98] The bibliography is very large; see, e.g., Umut Ozsu, '"In the interests of mankind as a whole": Mohammed Bedjaoui's New International Economic Order' (2015) 6 *Humanity: An International Journal of Human Rights, Humanitarianism, and Development* 129–143.

[99] Arnulf Becker Lorca, 'Universal international law: nineteenth-century histories of imposition and appropriation' (2010) 51 *Harvard International Law Journal* 475–552.

[100] Liliana Obregón, 'Noted for dissent: the international life of Alejandro Alvarez' (2006) 19 *Leiden Journal of International Law* 983–1016.

[101] Arnulf Becker Lorca, *Mestizo International Law: A Global Intellectual History 1842–1933* (Cambridge, UK: Cambridge University Press, 2015).

[102] Craven, 'Theorizing the turn to history', p. 33.

[103] Martti Koskenniemi, 'A history of international law histories', in Bardo Fassbender and Anne Peters (eds.), *The Oxford Handbook of the History of International Law* (Oxford: Oxford University Press, 2012), pp. 943–971 at 963.

of the Calvo and Drago doctrines, the critique of imperialism, debates on universalism, particularism or the role of regionalism,[104] and the creation of international control for the administration of colonies emerged,[105] bears witness of the historiographical vector role that the cultivation of contextualized international legal biography plays in the development of 'alternative' histories in the field.

While two of the categories of post-colonial biographical attention referred focus on the retrieval and historical contextualization of the work of peripheral or semi-peripheral writers and actors, the third one revolves, by contrast, around Western writers, and can be divided into two main categories. On the one hand, there is study of early classic European writers – in particular, Francisco de Vitoria and Hugo Grotius, but also others – whose works are re-depicted as apologist for imperialism. The most noted example of this revisionist trend, which, as seen in Chapter 2, has largely profited from the work and insights of methodological contextualists in the history of ideas, has been Francisco de Vitoria's works at the time of the Spanish discovery and conquest of America. Indeed, as will be examined in more detail below, according to Antony Anghie, Vitoria's opus should 'be read as a particularly insidious justification of conquest precisely because it is presented in the language of liberality and even equality'.[106] The second main category of dramatis personae in the history of international law who have attracted the attention of post-colonial historiography consists of nineteenth-century and early twentieth-century international lawyers who were imbued with the epochal mindset of Western civilizational superiority, such as James Lorimer[107] and Johann Caspar Bluntschli.[108] The post-colonial attention to these writers since the early 2000s has in turn largely benefited from

---

[104] Alejandro Alvarez, *Le droit international américain: son fondement, sa nature; d'après l'histoire diplomatique des états du nouveau monde et leur vie politique et économique* (Paris: Pédone, 1910).

[105] Balakrishnan Rajagopal, 'International law and its discontents: rethinking the global south' (2012) *106 Proceedings of the Annual Meeting of the American Society of International Law* 176–181.

[106] See Antony Anghie, *Imperialism, Sovereignty and the Making of International Law* (Cambridge, UK: Cambridge University Press, 2005), p. 28.

[107] James Lorimer, *The Institutes of the Law of Nations: A Treatise of the Jural Relations of Separate Political Communities* (London and Edinburgh: W. Blackwood & Sons, 1883–84).

[108] Johann Caspar Bluntschli, *Das moderne Völkerrecht der civilisierten Staten, als Rechtsbuch dargestellt* (Nördlingen: Beck, 1868).

Martti Koskenniemi's ground-breaking work on the modern 'professional' origins of international law in the late nineteenth century, as was seen in Chapter 2.[109] A second interrelated focus of TWAIL/post-colonial scholarship in a historical perspective is on events of significance from the perspective of the non-Western 'other', whether singled out as samples of 'imposition' by international law schemes of Western 'dominance' or as sites of 'resistance' to it. This list of events and processes would non-exhaustedly inter alia include the discovery and conquest of America, European trade relations in East Asia since the sixteenth century, the Opium Wars (1839(42), the Berlin Conference (1885),[110] the establishment of the 'mandates system' during the League of Nations,[111] the Bandung Conference (1955),[112] the founding of the 'Non-Aligned Movement' (1961), the Declaration on the Establishment of a New Economic Order (1974),[113] and the UN Declaration on the Right to Development (1986),[114] with some extending the list up to the present period so as to also include 'the oil and debt crises of the 1970s; the eruption of neoliberalism in the 1980s and 1990s, and the long "war on terror"'.[115]

A third interrelated focus that post-colonial approaches to international law have stressed in their scholarship in order to 'reinscribe the periphery within an account of mainstream legal thought and practice'[116] is that of a particular version of *Begriffsgeschichte*, or the history of concepts which, according to Koskenniemi, seems 'eminently suited for studying the operation and transformation of legal institutions and

---

[109] Martti Koskenniemi, *The Gentle Civilizer of Nations: The Rise and Fall of International Law 1870–1960* (Cambridge, UK: Cambridge University Press, 2001).

[110] Matthew Craven, 'Between law and history: the Berlin Conference of 1884–85 and the logic of free trade' (2015) 1 *London Review of International Law* 31–59.

[111] Antony Anghie, 'Colonialism and the birth of international institutions: sovereignty, economy, and the mandate system of the League of Nations' (2002) 34 *New York University Journal of International Law and Politics* 513–563.

[112] Luis Eslava, Michael Fakhri, and Vasuki Nesiah (eds.), *Bandung, the Global South, and International Law: Critical Pasts and Pending Futures* (Cambridge, UK: Cambridge University Press, 2017).

[113] UN General Assembly, Res. A/3201 (S-VI); von Bernstorff and Dann (eds.), *The Battle for International Law.*

[114] UN General Assembly, Res. 41/128, 4 December 1986.

[115] Luis Eslava, 'TWAIL coordinates', in *Critical Legal Thinking* (2019), criticallegalthinking.com/2019/04/02/twail-coordina tes/#fn-27281-3.

[116] Craven, 'Theorizing the turn to history', p. 33.

vocabularies'.[117] The classic example in the TWAIL literature, with its purpose of 'identifying the periphery as the "unspoken referent" of doctrinal argument'[118] in the history of international law, is the concept of 'sovereignty'. This is exemplified in the work of Anghie on the premodern period of the history of international law, building on debates on the Western 'origins' of international law in the work of Francisco de Vitoria, who presided over the sixteenth-century School of Salamanca, in order to retrace the constitutive role of imperialism in the formation of state 'sovereignty',[119] understood by the principal judicial organ of the UN as the cornerstone of the international legal order.[120]

4.5   The Post-colonial Impact on Knowledge Production Processes

The impact of post-colonial approaches to the history of international law, which have the underlying aim, in Dipesh Chakrabarty's oft-quoted expression, to 'provincialize Europe' and thus to 'find out how and in what sense European ideas that were universal were also, at one and the same time, drawn from very particular intellectual and historical traditions that could not claim any universal validity',[121] is, as we have seen, informed by a strong 'revisionist' goal. It is scattered in its impact on knowledge creation processes on international law and history across different areas.

The contribution of post-colonial approaches to the historical dimension of international legal theory[122] and to the study of the normative development of the international legal order has been particularly extensive. This has included, to mention but a few examples, study of the role of the 'colonial encounter' in the conceptual construction of sovereignty; the nineteenth century's crystallization of a state-centric international legal positivism as Western countries engaged in nation-building

---

[117] Martti Koskenniemi, 'Legal history as Begriffsgeschichte?', in Claudia Wiesner (ed.), *In Debate with Karl Palonen: Concepts, Politics, Histories* (Baden-Baden: Nomos, 2015), pp. 63–68.

[118] Craven, 'Theorizing the turn to history', p. 33.

[119] Anghie, 'The evolution of international law', p. 753.

[120] Military and Paramilitary Activities (Nicaragua v. United States of America), Merits [1986] ICJ Rep 14, para. 263.

[121] Dipesh Chakrabarty, *Provincializing Europe: Postcolonial Thought and Historical Difference* (Princeton, NJ: Princeton University Press, 2000), p. xiii.

[122] Anne Orford and Florian Hoffmann with Martin Clark (eds.), *The Oxford Handbook of the Theory of International Law* (Oxford: Oxford University Press, 2016), p. 10.

projects, and its role in the setting up of new parameters informing the relations between the 'centre', the 'semi-periphery', and the 'periphery'; or the international legal scaffolding of the mandate system in the interwar period. It has also contributed to further illuminating projects of international reform involving international norm-entrepreneurship (e.g. the right to development) and alternative visions of world order and of global solidarity underlying a revamped conception of the 'international community' and some of the fundamental principles of international law contained in UN General Assembly Resolution 2625 on the Friendly Relations Declaration.[123]

Many of these legal theoretical and normative investigations have been produced in a broadly contextualist and, as will be seen in Chapter 7, an 'external normative' perspective on both general international law and some of its specialized international legal regimes, thus contributing to illuminating the study of international law in history. In this sense, the shift in perspective to the non-European viewpoint has expanded the attention of international legal history to other dimensions of national and international societal, ideological, intellectual, and professional historical contexts. This has nurtured another way of looking at the significance of a number of traditionally held central historical events in international law, including the 'turning points' of World War I and World War II and also other events and processes that were hitherto little studied across different regions. The inclusion of the absent viewpoint of 'the other' has also contributed to revisiting widely held views on decision-making processes built around a set of international legal concepts (e.g. humanitarian intervention) in a different light and with reference to previously less explored historical materials.

Many of these historical efforts have been made in the shadow of the post-colonial project of unveiling its own historical tradition of 'reform and resistance',[124] which as a historiographical driver accounts for their remarkable contribution to the area of 'sociological history of international law'. Indeed, as previously noted, those who started to write in the late 1990s and successive generations contributed to the historization of what they retrospectively deem the work of their predecessors, in

---

[123] See, e.g., Samuel Moyn and Umut Özsu, 'The historical origins and setting of the Friendly Relations Declaration', in Jorge E. Viñuales (ed.), *The UN Friendly Relations Declaration at 50: An Assessment of the Fundamental Principles of International Law after Half a Century* (in press).

[124] Eslava and Pahuja, 'Between resistance and reform', p. 103.

particular by producing intellectual biographical accounts of their oeuvre and other diplomatic and judicial activities of Asian and African international lawyers and earlier ones from Latin America. This biographical intellectual attention has also extended, as is examined in Chapter 10, to many a revisionist post-colonial reading of the works of canonical Western scholars from the 'great encounter' onwards. Similarly expanded through the historiographical contribution of post-colonial approaches has been the history of non-state actors, including early transnational corporations like the Vereenigde Oost-Indische Compagnie, the Compagnie Française des Indes Orientales, and the British East India Company, and their influence in setting up informal imperial compounds across vast territories, as well as social and grass-roots movements.[125] However, the contribution to international law-making and international adjudicative processes of the second generation, which is characterized as more 'academic' in orientation and less 'professional' and policy-oriented than that of its predecessors,[126] has generally been less accentuated regarding the domain of 'history in international law' that regards the uses of history for international law, including the study of history for the purposes of technical international law-making, international legal argumentative practice, and international adjudication.

Finally, the TWAIL/post-colonial contribution to historiography is apparent in its attempt to dent in a postmodernist vein the progressive teleology underlying the 'grand narrative' of international law: the conviction that 'there is progress in international law and that international law contributes to progress in a general sense'.[127] Animated by this counter-narrative effort, it has furthered investigation of historical methods and a self-reflective study of historiographical approaches to international law. This has included filtering 'analytical tools' such as 'dialectics, dyads, or opposites' which, as Andrea Bianchi notes, are often used by TWAIL's scholars in international legal historiography. These discursive strategies in which 'the South is almost invariably opposed to the North, both literally and metaphorically, the "colonizer" inevitably presupposes the existence of the "colonized", just as "subjugation" is

---

[125] Balakrishnan Rajagopal, *International Law from Below: Development, Social Movements and Third World Resistance* (Cambridge, UK: Cambridge University Press, 2003).

[126] Bianchi, *International Law Theories*.

[127] Tilmann Altwicker and Oliver Diggelmann, 'How is progress constructed in international legal scholarship?' (2014) 25 *European Journal of International Law* 425–444 at 425.

contrasted to "domination", the "centre" to the "periphery", the "political" to the "economic", the "global" to the "local", and the "particular" to the "universal"[128] also deeply permeate TWAIL historical works. Alongside this post-colonial set of binary oppositions, TWAIL/post-colonial scholarship has also interdisciplinarily fleshed out, as already noted, many historiographical 'concepts for international law'[129] (civilization, empire, periphery, etc.) and gone some way to coining new terminology (e.g. 'particularistic universalism', understood by Arnulf Becker Lorca as a 'semi-peripheral form of classical legal consciousness'),[130] all of which is central to its historiographical epistemology. TWAIL work has also impinged on the study of often elusive areas of historiography such as that of periodization. In this sense, as we shall see in more detail in Chapter 11, perhaps the ultimate and longer-lasting outcome of TWAIL's semi-concerted scholarly efforts in macro-historiographical terms has been its contribution to the gradual emergence of a meta-narrative of the history of international law with its own underlying post-colonial alternative 'grand periodization'. The bones of this alternative grand periodization – according to which, 'if Westphalia serves as the creation myth of international law, the myth of Bandung is its counterpoint'[131] – are continually being fleshed out by new writings on the historical development of international law from a post-colonial perspective.

4.6 Historiographical Debates, Confluences, and Critiques

TWAIL, described by George Galindo as a 'scientific-intellectual movement'[132] which is understood as a 'collective effort to pursue research programs or projects for thought in the face of resistance from others in the scientific or intellectual community',[133] has confluences and thematic

---

[128] Bianchi, *International Law Theories*, p. 208.
[129] Jean d'Aspremont and Sahib Singh (eds.), *Concepts for International Law: Contributions to Disciplinary Thought* (Northampton, MA: Edward Elgar Publishing, 2019).
[130] Becker Lorca, 'Universal international law', pp. 475–552.
[131] Luis Eslava, Michael Fakhri, and Vasuki Nesiah, 'The spirit of Bandung', in Luis Eslava, Michael Fakhri, and Vasuki Nesiah (eds.), *Bandung, the Global South, and International Law: Critical Pasts and Pending Futures* (Cambridge, UK: Cambridge University Press, 2017), pp. 3–32 at 16.
[132] Galindo, 'Splitting TWAIL?', p. 52, citing Scott Frickel and Neil Gross, 'A general theory of scientific/intellectual movements' (2005) 70 *American Sociological Review* 204–232.
[133] Frickel and Gross, 'A general theory', p. 205.

intersections with other approaches to international law and its histories. One of these, as Chapter 5 will examine, is that of 'global history'. Another important confluence is, as seen in Chapter 2 with contextual methodologies, although this is one mediated by TWAIL's even closer affinity with critical/postmodern approaches to the history of international law, as was examined in Chapter 3. In particular, the association of a critique from the Third World with the epistemological relativism of critical/postmodern approaches has fostered radically defiant anti-liberal and anti-globalization perspectives that question and problematize the role of what they portray as both a historically and contemporarily West-centric and structurally biased international legal order that perpetuates global inequality.

The proselytizing political virulence of some TWAIL scholarship in its purported construction of a 'counter-hegemonic international law'[134] has in turn fostered a critical scrutiny of its tenets, which earlier 'Third World' international lawyers who find it difficult to self-identify with TWAIL, like Mohammed Bedjaoui, have considered amount to 'a too-pessimistic approach that opens no or only a scarce possibility for the building of a different international order through international law'.[135] Similarly in 'two minds about the label TWAIL' are other early Third World international lawyers like Georges Abi-Saab, who prefers to engage in 'constructive criticism' through reform proposals rather than in radical critique.[136] Often highlighted in this regard is the very centrality of the 'Third World' as one that many would see as an 'anachronistic or terribly imprecise'[137] epistemological category. Some would go on to argue that it has lost the relevance and legitimacy it once had as a signifier of the 'political affinity or contingent coalition binding some countries together'[138] during the Cold War in a new post-9/11 scenario where a series of nationalist and often illiberal non-Western emerging powers are increasingly calling the shots in an emerging multipolar international legal order. This is characterized by regional projects of economic and political integration, and an overall diffusion of power and

---

[134] Eslava, 'TWAIL coordinates'.

[135] Mohammed Bedjaoui, 'Observations sur le texte d'Antony Anghie', in Mark Toufayan, Emmanuelle Jouannet, and Hélène Ruiz-Fabri (eds.), *Droit international et nouvelles approches sur le tiers-monde: entre répétition et renouveau* (Paris: Société de Législation Comparée, 2013), pp. 81–92 at 83.

[136] Abi-Saab, 'The Third World intellectual in praxis', p. 1958.

[137] Bianchi, *International Law Theories*, p. 205.

[138] Ibid.

competition for leverage of unbundled capital flows on a global stage. According to this critique, the intellectual manipulation by TWAIL of the dubious relevance of the nostalgic category of the 'Third World' – with many sympathetic voices highlighting that there is, in fact, a so-called First World in the 'Third World' and a 'Third World' in the 'First World'[139] – would make the 'emancipatory knowledge' about international law that post-colonial approaches proclaim to be projecting through lofty 'global justice' manifestos in the name of the 'wretched of the Earth' suspicious.[140] Instead, by supporting a form of post-colonial exceptionalism and diffidence towards universal values – including the narratives of democracy and human rights – and associated international legal regimes,[141] TWAILers may risk becoming some may argue, the intellectual butterflies of paternalistic and illiberal authoritarian regimes at home.[142] This critical consideration is compounded by the fact that as an intellectual-scientific movement TWAIL has also often been criticized for its 'elite configuration' in the light of the fact that it originated at Harvard Law School, and many – if admittedly not all – of its leading representatives are members of an academic 'diaspora' living and working outside the Third World or global south who have benefited from the support of elite law schools, as a source of both prestige and material support for the development of TWAIL.[143] Set in this context, TWAIL has also been criticized by Olivier Corten as an exercise in 'academic marketing'[144] which some would argue has artfully hijacked the voice of the 'oppressed' and 'appropriated' it in its articulation of a highly intellectualized and academically sophisticated discourse addressed at other fringe elitist minorities, thus usurping the space of

---

[139] David Kennedy, 'The political economy of centers and peripheries' (2012) 25 *Leiden Journal of International Law* 7–48.

[140] Muthucumaraswamy Sornarajah, 'On fighting for global justice: the role of a Third World international lawyer' (2016) 37 *Third World Quarterly* 1972–1989 at 1974.

[141] See e.g. John Reynolds and Sujith Xavier, '"The dark corners of the world": TWAIL and international criminal justice' (2016) 14 *International Criminal Justice* 959–983.

[142] Philip Alston, 'Remarks on Professor B. S. Chimni's *A Just World under Law: A View from the South*' (2007) 22 *American University International Law Review* 221–236 at 224.

[143] Bianchi, *International Law Theories*, p. 206.

[144] Olivier Corten, 'Les TWAIL: approche scientifique originale ou nouveau label fédérateur?', in Mark Toufayan, Emmanuelle Tourme-Jouannet, and Hélène Ruiz-Fabri (eds.), *Droit international et nouvelles approches sur le tiers-monde: entre répétition et renouveau (International Law and New Approaches to the Third World: Between Repetition and Renewal)* (Paris: Société de Législation Comparée, 2013), pp. 359–366.

other academic approaches and studies which are more constructive and conducive to influencing 'decision-making processes at the international level'[145] for the benefit of the needs and poverty-alleviation requirements of hundreds of millions living in developing countries.

These general critiques are partially filtered in the appraisal of the historiographical contribution of post-colonial approaches. First, one general line of criticism addressed at TWAIL is that having made 'the common history of subjection to colonialism and neo-colonialism'[146] its overarching framework, it homogenizes what is otherwise a non-homogeneous history among different peoples and regions. Second, a related line of critique is that TWAIL has a reductive and often confrontational coloured perspective on the history of the Western world and a generalization of its interpretative framework – e.g. imperialism and eurocentrism – which does not distinguish between Western national histories of international law, such as e.g. eastern, Nordic, and some southern European, that themselves suffered waves of imperial policies. Third, TWAIL's historiographical contribution has also been questioned for its historical reductionism and either explicit or 'hidden' Eurocentrism[147] in developing a 'counter-narrative' that in fact 'perpetuates what it seeks to condemn'[148] and also detracting attention from imperial trends in different regions in both the past and the present. This shift in focus is important for the appreciation of other non-European contrasting world-views in shaping the history of non-European people such as Islam-centrism, Sino-centrism, and others.

Fourth, the continual focus of TWAIL on the legacy of colonialism risks generating a complacency over countries' own responsibility for unsuccessful nation-building projects whose post-colonial development has been more than occasionally marked by the rule of regressive, ethno-nationalist, autocratic, and kleptocratic domestic elites. This is connected to a tendency to romanticize both past episodes and authors and foster

[145] Bianchi, *International Law Theories*, p. 209.
[146] Chimni, 'The past, present and future', p. 499.
[147] Anne Orford, *Reading Humanitarian Intervention: Human Rights and the Use of Force in International Law* (Cambridge, UK: Cambridge University Press, 2003), p. 39.
[148] Bardo Fassbender and Anne Peters, 'Introduction: towards a global history of international law', in Bardo Fassbender and Anne Peters (eds.), *The Oxford Handbook of the History of International Law* (Oxford: Oxford University Press, 2012), pp. 1–26 at 3–4, citing Emmanuelle Jouannet, 'Des origines coloniales du droit international: à propos du droit des gens moderne au XVIIème siècle', in Vincent Chetail and Pierre-Marie Dupuy (eds.), *Mélanges Peter Haggenmacher* (Leiden: Brill, 2012).

what some may appraise as an excessive nostalgia in retrospective myth-making of earlier activist projects in order to foster re-emerging militant scholarly attitudes. In this connection, TWAIL has also been criticized from within its own lines because of its approach to TWAIL I, which, according to Galindo, can fall into what is described as 'the historical fallacy of historical teleology', in which 'the precursor concept provided not only retrospective continuity; it may also furnish legitimacy, much like the practice of reading one's own views into a sacred text so one can read them back out endowed with authority'.[149] Fifth, as will be examined in Chapter 6, another area where TWAIL's historical approach is open to critique is from the perspective of women's history of international law, which TWAIL has broadly disregarded, despite having some feminist Third World scholars in its camp.[150] Finally, it should be remembered that, in the same manner as, according to Karen Mickelson, TWAIL is 'an intellectual movement inserted into an intellectual tradition',[151] by which she means that it is 'a part of a Third World tradition of international law scholarship rather than the overarching framework into which all Third World scholarship can be fitted',[152] TWAIL approaches to the history of international law are not the overarching framework into which all colonial history of international law, as many examples in the recent literature suggest, can be fitted either.[153]

Alongside these critiques, which question the emancipatory political drive of TWAIL approaches to the history of international law, central as it is to their self-understanding, is, as was seen in Chapter 2, the debate based on the contextualist critique and claims of anachronism addressed to post-colonial historiographical readings of the pasts of international law by historians and legal historians trained in the formal methods of historiography.[154] In the light of its seminal centrality in the meta-

---

[149] Galindo, 'Splitting TWAIL?', p. 44, citing Carlos Spoerhase and Colin G King, 'Historical fallacies of historians', in Aviezer Tucker (ed.), *A Companion to the Philosophy of History and Historiography* (London: Blackwell, 2009), pp. 274–284 at 275.

[150] Vauki Nesiah, 'The ground beneath her feet: Third World "feminisms"' (2003) 4 *Journal of International Women's Studies* 30–38.

[151] See Galindo, 'Splitting TWAIL?', p. 56.

[152] See Mickelson, 'TWAIL histories', p. 357.

[153] Mamadou Hebié, *Souveraineté territoriale par traité: une étude des accords entre puissances coloniales et entités politiques locales* (Paris: Presses Universitaires de France/The Graduate Institute, 2015); Mieke van der Linden, *The Acquisition of Africa (1870-1914): The Nature of Nineteenth-Century International Law* (Leiden: Brill/Nijhoff, 2017).

[154] See also Galindo, 'Splitting TWAIL?', pp. 47–48.

historical narrative developed by post-colonial historiography and also, as Chapter 11 examines, its corresponding emerging alternative periodization, much scholarly attention has been given to the post-colonial revisionist reading by Antony Anghie of the Dominican friar and Prima Professor of Sacred Theology at the University of Salamanca, Francisco de Vitoria (c. 1483 –1546), who presided over the Spanish neo-Thomist school of moral and legal theologians of the sixteenth and early seventeenth centuries known as the Salamanca School.[155]

This reinterpretation took its cue from the long-standing debate on the so-called founding fathers of international law dating back, as was seen in Chapter 1, to the late nineteenth century, when the history of international law began to be professionalized. This gained new credentials with the interwar effort by inter alia James Brown Scott to replace the intertwined aetiological myths of Hugo Grotius's *De iure belli and pacis* (1625) and the Peace of Westphalia (1648) as the birthdate of the law of peoples with Vitoria's *Relectiones*, in particular *De indis noviter inventis* and *De indis relectio posterior, sive, de iure belli hispanorum in barbaros*, both from 1532, and the 'great encounter'.[156] Set in this context, the revisionist reinterpretation of Vitoria's significance in the history of international law is deployed as a critical counterpoint to the humanitarianly teleological and ever-upgraded universalist blueprint for international law that some have identified in the 'Vitorian tradition' of international law.[157] Indeed, as Martti Koskenniemi notes, 'it is perhaps above all the person of Francisco Vitoria, a Dominican scholar from Salamanca in the first part of the 16th century, whose role and significance for the history of international law has been the object of the greatest recent interest'[158] among international legal historians.[159]

---

[155] See, originally, Antony Anghie, 'Francisco de Vitoria and the colonial origins of international law' (1996) 5 *Social and Legal Studies* 321–336; later developed in Anghie, *Imperialism*.

[156] Paolo Amorosa, *Rewriting the History of the Law of Nations: How James Brown Scott Made Francisco de Vitoria the Founder of International Law* (Oxford: Oxford University Press, 2019).

[157] Ibid.

[158] Martti Koskenniemi, 'Vitoria and us: thoughts on critical histories of international law' (2014) 22 *Rechtsgeschichte* 119–138 at 121.

[159] The following excerpts build on Ignacio de la Rasilla, 'The three revivals of Francisco de Vitoria in the history of international law', in José Maria Beneyto (ed.), *Peace or Just War? The Influence of Francisco de Vitoria and Erasmus on Charles V and the Law of Nations* (in press).

Although similar reinterpretations had previously been put forward by Tzvetan Todorov in 1982[160] and Robert A. Williams in 1990,[161] the Sri Lankan Antony Anghie is the author of the most oft-quoted post-colonial re-reading of Vitoria's work.[162] The basis for Anghie's reinterpretation are Vitoria's two most famous *relectiones*, *De indis noviter inventis* and *De indis relectio posterior; sive, de iure belli hispanorum in barbaros*,[163] where respectively he organizes the legitimate and illegitimate claims for the Spanish title to American lands and discusses just and unjust wars. In doing so, Vitoria relies – as David Kennedy, Anghie's doctoral supervisor at Harvard Law School, had noted in his study of 'primitive legal scholarship' many years earlier – 'on a notion of absolute rights and wrongs which determine the capacities of sovereigns and justify exercises of sovereign will'.[164] In his *De indis*, Vitoria's analysis of the seven *tituli non idonei nec legitimi* and the same number of *tituli idonei ac legitimi* makes for a dual intertwined mode of *pars destruens* followed by one of *pars construens* in the manner of scholastic argumentation.[165]

However, Anghie turns upside down this uniform pattern, which, as Ursula Vollerthun states, sets out 'the question, the proposed answer, the argument and the counter-argument, making much of distinctions and qualifications'[166] in order to substitute the established late nineteenth-century classical portrayal of Vitoria as a critic of empire with a new depiction of him as legitimizer of the Spanish *conquista*. This characterization serves Anghie to depict Vitoria as an early precursor of a juridical mode of discourse subsequently pursued by imperialist projects up to the present day. This is because, according to Anghie, Vitoria's work may 'be read as a particularly insidious justification of conquest precisely because

---

[160] Tzvetan Todorov, *La conquête de l'Amérique: la question de l'autre* (Paris: Seuil, 1982).
[161] Robert A. Williams, Jr, *The American Indian in Western Legal Thought: The Discourse of Conquest* (New York: Oxford University Press, 1990).
[162] Anghie, *Imperialism*.
[163] Francisco de Victoria, *De indis et de iure belli relectiones* (Washington, DC: The Carnegie Institution of Washington, 1917).
[164] David Kennedy, 'Primitive legal scholarship' (1986) 27 *Harvard International Law Journal* 1–98 at 20.
[165] Simona Langella, 'The sovereignty of law in the works of Francisco de Vitoria', in José Maria Beneyto and Justo Corti Varela (eds.), *At the Origins of Modernity: Francisco de Vitoria and the Discovery of International Law* (Cham: Springer, 2017), pp. 45–61 at 57.
[166] Ursula Vollerthun, *The Idea of International Society: Erasmus, Vitoria, Gentili and Grotius*, ed. James L. Richardson (Cambridge, UK: Cambridge University Press, 2017), p. 72.

it is presented in the language of liberality and even equality'.[167] Indeed, for Anghie, 'international law was created out of the unique issues generated by the encounter between the Spanish and the Indians'[168] as they are reflected in Vitoria's tackling of these issues, insofar as the sovereignty doctrine, which is a central concept in the international legal discipline, 'emerges through his attempts to address the problem of cultural difference'.[169] In other words, Anghie attempts to portray Vitoria's tackling of the issues arising out of the great encounter as what we may call an international-law original sin of sorts, which has somewhat irremediably conditioned its ulterior development. This interpretation provides an interpretative lens through which, according to Anghie, we can 'understand the difficulties colonized peoples have encountered in entering the realm of sovereignty, the compromises they have made for the purposes of doing so and the limitations from which they suffer in attempting to pursue their interests and aspirations through a "universal" language of international law which, arguably, was devised specifically to ensure their disempowerment and disenfranchisement'.[170]

Anghie's critique has received numerous qualifications and refutations. In general terms, some authors, like Ursula Vollerthun, have attributed the scholastic method followed by Vitoria in which 'the overall import may not be clear – seemingly more a debate than a conclusive argument'[171] as going 'some way towards explaining why [Vitorian writings] are open to such radically different readings'.[172] Others, like Andrew Fitzmaurice, have also tried to account for the divergent interpretations of Vitoria's texts on the basis that the post-colonial critiques 'focus . . . on the discussions of the rights of communication and guardianship' and thus 'present Vitoria as an apologist for empire', while others focus on Vitoria's examination of 'the Spanish claims to dominium' and consequently present him as a 'critic of empire'.[173] Nonetheless, for Fitzmaurice Anghie fails to acknowledge that 'many of the legal

---

[167] Anghie, *Imperialism*, p. 28.
[168] Ibid., p. 15.
[169] Ibid., p. 17.
[170] Ibid., p. 31.
[171] Vollerthun, *The Idea of Iternational Society*, p. 72.
[172] Ibid.
[173] Andrew Fitzmaurice, 'The problem of Eurocentrism in the thought of Francisco de Vitoria', in José Maria Beneyto and Justo Corti Varela (eds.), *At the Origins of Modernity: Francisco de Vitoria and the Discovery of International Law* (Cham: Springer, 2017), pp. 77–93 at 84.

arguments employed by Vitoria' were 'employed by non-Europeans to oppose European empire'[174] and that, therefore, Anghie's totalizing perspective underscores the 'malleability of political ideas' by treating 'concepts as in some way the hostages of the contexts in which they are created'.[175] This, Fitzmaurice implies, is the Achilles heel of the post-colonial criticism of Vitoria's writings alongside the fact that it is ana-chronistic to judge authors for having 'failed to conform to principles of equality and universality that were themselves products of a post-Kantian European intellectual world whose resources were not available to most of the early modern subjects who had failed to conform to them'.[176] This builds on Ian Hunter's previous highlighting that 'scholars engaged in the advocacy of present political positions (often postcolonial) have attrib-uted modern doctrines (generally incriminating) to early modern polit-ical jurists: as if the truth and impeccability of modern "progressive" scholarship might be demonstrated by inculpating the error and venality of its intellectual ancestors'.[177]

In the same sense of pointing to anachronistic post-colonial reinter-pretations of classic writers, Georg Cavallar has criticized Anghie for making 'fanciful connections between the sixteenth-century theologian Vitoria and the secularized discipline of nineteenth-century international law – when the key concepts and approaches were civilization, race, sovereignty, state will and legal positivism, all of them rather alien to Vitoria's natural-law thinking'.[178] This is in line with other criticisms that stress the 'essentialist' presentist reinterpretations of past doctrines and highlight that 'International is not and was neither "good" nor "bad". It can be used for different and contradictory ends: for oppression and hegemony, but also for emancipation and stability' by different actors in different contexts.[179] Others academics like Pablo Zapatero Miguel have produced more biographical-based refutations of Anghie's by stressing inter alia the historical context and the personal biography of a black friar who devoted his life to his teaching in Salamanca and was subjected to

---

[174] Ibid., pp. 85, 86.
[175] Ibid., p. 85.
[176] Andrew Fitzmaurice, 'Context in the history of international law' (2018) 20 *Journal of the History of International Law* 5–30 at 8.
[177] Ian Hunter, 'The figure of man and the territorialisation of justice in "Enlightenment" natural law: Pufendorf and Vattel' (2013) 23 *Intellectual History Review* 289–307 at 289.
[178] Georg Cavallar, *Imperfect Cosmopolis: Studies in the History of International Legal Theory and Cosmopolitan Ideas* (Chicago: University of Chicago Press, 2011), p. 36.
[179] Fassbender and Peters, 'Introduction', p. 4.

great pressure for maintaining views opposing the interests of the mighti-
est monarch of the times.[180] In the same critical vein, Anthony Pagden
also highlights that the post-colonial interpretation 'attributes to Vitoria
things which he did not say, could not have said, and which none of his
subsequent readers from the sixteenth to the twentieth centuries supposed him to have said'.[181] Finally, others like Vincent Chetail place
Vitoria in his proper historical context by noting that by 'the time of his
lecture "On the American Indians", colonization of the New World was
already a *fait accompli* and his great ambition was not to legitimate it but,
instead, to constrain and regulate this reality within a general system
based on moral and legal precepts'.[182]

Francisco de Vitoria, together with other canonical Western pace-
setters of *ius gentium* like Hugo Grotius, continues to be discussed in
academic articles penned by historians of international law engaged in
a debate, between representatives of the contextualist methodology of
the so-called Cambridge School of the history of political thought and
the provocative questioning to which their rigorous contextual
approach is made the object by the critical historiographical branch
of historians of international law, some of whom, as was seen in
Chapter 2, have gone as far as defending 'anachronism' as part of a
valid 'international legal method'.[183] The insightful sophistication of
these methodological debates is a further proof of the extent to which
post-colonial approaches to the history of international law, once
marginal, have gained centre stage in discussions about the history
of international law.

---

[180] Pablo Zapatero Miguel, 'Francisco de Vitoria and the postmodern grand critique of
international law', in José Maria Beneyto and Justo Corti Varela (eds.), *At the Origins of
Modernity: Francisco de Vitoria and the Discovery of International Law* (Cham: Springer,
2017), pp. 177–196.

[181] Anthony Pagden, 'Legislating for the "whole world that is, in a sense, a commonwealth":
conquest, occupation, and "the defence of the innocent"', in Anthony Carty and Janne
Elisabeth Nijman (eds.), *Morality and Responsibility of Rulers: European and Chinese
Origins of a Rule of Law as Justice for World Order* (Oxford: Oxford University Press,
2018), pp. 132–148 at 134.

[182] Vincent Chetail, 'Sovereignty and migration in the doctrine of the law of nations: an
intellectual history of hospitality from Vitoria to Vattel' (2016) 27 *European Journal of
International Law* 901–922 at 906.

[183] Anne Orford, 'On international legal method' (2013) 1 *London Review of International
Law* 166–197.

4.7 Conclusion

In the same manner as, as William A. Green noted, 'historical epochs should exhibit important long-term continuities, and moments of transition between epochs should involve the dissolution of old continuities and the forging of new ones',[184] decolonization can be seen as a long-drawn-out, epoch-turning moment of transition in historiographical terms. Recently favoured by the structural dynamics, including the boost known by the sheer rise in mobility of both academics and students brought about by globalization, fostering, as was seen in Chapter 1, the turn to the history of international law, the rise of post-colonial approaches to international law is historically speaking a perfectly logical historiographical development for international legal history to have been experiencing for some time now. This is apparent when one considers, as Douglas M. Johnston recalls in his monumental *oeuvre* that 'by 1905, almost two-thirds of the territories outside Europe were dominated – and more or less directly ruled – by colonial regimes designed to extract imperial advantage from the resources made available to them'.[185] It also becomes obvious when the rise of post-colonial historiography is seen in the light of the more recent increase known by the membership of the UN from its 51 original members, of which twenty were Latin American, in 1945, and when, furthermore, 'some 750 million people, nearly a third of the world's population, lived in territories that were dependent on colonial powers',[186] to its current 193 sovereign member states, out 195) at present.

One may agree with (or by contrast maintain a healthy dose of realistic scepticism towards) TWAIL's maximalist defiance or markedly adversarial view of contemporary international law and institutions as inherently complicit – and thus 'part of the problem' – in the unequal global distribution of power and welfare or with its related argumentative 'presentist' discursive weaponization of the history of international law. One may alternatively (or otherwise) see, in what does not exactly amount to the same thing, a strategic balancing value in the existence of a scholarly international legal academic discourse that critically

---

[184] William A. Green, 'History and theory' (1995) 34 *World Historians and Their Critics* 99–111 at 101.

[185] Douglas M. Johnston, *The Historical Foundations of World Order: The Tower and the Arena* (Leiden: Martinus Nijhoff, 2008), p. 549.

[186] 'Decolonization', www.un.org/en/sections/issues-depth/decolonization/index.html.

engages with the historical foundations and development of international law so as to 'unhinge' it from its Eurocentric framework and thus make cognitive space for (radical) reform and change through the medium of international legal scholarship. However, whatever one's own perspective on these issues is, what is beyond question is that TWAIL has to a large extent succeeded in its foundational aim of 'penetrating into the international legal mainstream discourse'[187] and challenging what 'epistemic and systemic colonialism'[188] in international legal scholarship may serve in its appraisal. In this sense, TWAIL, like other critical militant scholarly trends, has contributed to questioning 'the impression that international law is essentially a technical business designed to enable a professional elite to maintain the existing worldwide order of state bureaucracies, rather than a morally significant effort to progress toward a single world legal culture committed to social and individual welfare'.[189] This, in Johnston's view, is precisely a legacy of the 'traditional conception of international law – reflecting the influence of compatible European legal cultures'.[190]

With its politically charged academic agenda, TWAIL, like other critical trends examined in Chapter 3, has admittedly gone some way to de-romanticizing international law and international institutions and undermining, as Martti Koskenniemi would put it, international lawyers' enchantment with its tools.[191] By insisting on the need to remember international law's irredeemable colonial past,[192] it has also contributed to awakening the hitherto bland area of international legal history from its relative intellectual dormancy. Indeed, post-colonial approaches have fostered the retrieval of many 'untold stories' of international law and the unearthing of many new interesting historical materials. They have also fleshed out many historiographical 'concepts for international law'[193] and

---

[187] Galindo, 'Splitting TWAIL?', p. 41.

[188] Henrique Weil Afonso and José Luiz Quadros de Magalhães, 'The Third World, history and international law' (2013) 8 *Anuário brasileiro de direito internacional* 107–125 at 122.

[189] Johnston, *The Historical Foundations*, p. 107.

[190] Ibid.

[191] Martti Koskenniemi, 'Enchanted by the tools? An enlightenment perspective' (2019) 113 *Proceedings of the ASIL's Annual Meeting* 3–19.

[192] Nathaniel Berman, *Passion and Ambivalence: Nationalism, Colonialism and International Law*, with an introduction by Emmanuelle Jouannet (Leiden and Boston: Martinus Nijhoff, 2012).

[193] D'Aspremont and Singh (eds.), *Concepts for International Law*.

promoted new historiographical debates among international law historians. Moreover, by contributing to providing international law with a
deeper and more diverse plural historical pedigree, post-colonial histories
of international law also, in a sense, contribute to restoring a more
realistically informed hope for the discipline to contribute to the realization of more enlightened futures.

TWAIL, as an 'epistemic community' or, as Bianchi notes, as one of
the 'fairly heterogeneous social groups that perform functions related to
the formation of knowledge in the field of international law', the 'ultimate
stake' of which is 'to acquire and maintain control of a scientific or social
field by imposing its own vision of the field as the most authoritative',[194]
has undoubtedly contributed to the formation of new vistas of knowledge in the field of international legal history. However, it may be
short-sighted to consider that the historiographical dynamics
unleashed by the tectonic shift of decolonization are bound to remain
active in historiographical terms for the indeterminate foreseeable
future. Post-colonial approaches to the history of international law
have themselves been 'colonized' by (mostly radical) leftist and 'alternative' political agendas, which hammer insistently on the contemporary implications of what others, nonetheless, appraise as the
already fairly passé historical hiatus of Western colonialism in the
deeply internationally transformed scenario of the 2020s. With
the 'founding' TWAIL generation and also other 'founding' critical
fellow travellers already nearing the end of their academic life cycles,
they may therefore risk being soon out of touch with the potentially
positive influence of new interdisciplinary historiographical dynamics
in international legal history including contextualist, socio-historical,
feminist, historical institutionalist, and global history approaches. The
latter, as we shall see in Chapter 5, although they share many points in
common with post-colonial perspectives, either considerably connote
some of the post-colonial historically agonistic and presentistically
confrontationist narratives in a more contextualized and detachedly
'neutral' account of the past of international law or increasingly seek
to transcend that particular phase in the history of international law
from a *longue durée* perspective.

---

[194] Andrea Bianchi, 'Epistemic Communities', in Jean d'Aspremont and Sahib Singh (eds.),
Concepts for International Law: Contributions to Disciplinary Thought (Northampton,
MA: Edward Elgar Publishing, 2019), pp. 251–266 at 251.

5

Global Approaches to the History
of International Law

5.1 Introduction

In its post-2000s expansion, the history of international law has more openly embraced the interdisciplinary pollination of a research field that blends international relations theory and its historical discourse, legal history, the history of ideas and political thought, and history writ large with the history of international legal practice and theory. It is being currently cultivated by a heterogeneous group of scholars made up of international lawyers occasionally transmuted into amateur historians; legal historians sporadically struggling to present themselves as savvy international lawyers; historians of international political thought sometimes posing as all the aforementioned; and, occasionally too, professional historians, who, as Andrew Fitzmaurice notes, are increasingly 'engaging with the subject as part of their turn to the international dimension of history'.[1] The disciplinary boundaries of international legal history have correspondingly become more fruitfully porous to a number of adjacent academic disciplines which, like international law itself, have also been significantly impacted by globalization and, in its wake, by the decrease in the intellectual leverage of 'methodological nationalism'[2] which the professional birth of the academic disciplines of both law and history were born tied to in the late nineteenth century.

The rise of 'global history' is a long-incubated reaction against the blind spots, according to Sebastian Conrad, 'affecting interactions and connections that have made the modern world' which resulted from the traditional 'compartmentalization of historical reality' into the ruling

---

[1] Andrew Fitzmaurice, 'Context in the history of international law' (2018) 20 *Journal of the History of International Law* 5–30 at 6.

[2] See, e.g., Daniel Chernilo, 'The critique of methodological nationalism: theory and history' (2011) 106 *Thesis Eleven* 98–117.

'container-based paradigm' of 'national history'.[3] Under the new framework of global history, which been dubbed the 'fastest-growing field
within the discipline',[4] new terms, such as 'connections', which is 'the
keyword most immediately associated with the term "global"', and
'a whole cascade of related terms' such as 'exchange', 'intercourse', 'links',
'entanglements', 'networks', and 'flows' have become commonplace in
the literature.[5] The new historiographical centrality gained by the terminology of historical contacts, nodal points, interfaces, interactions,
circulations, and transformations, and other similar ones pointing to
the idea of a multiplicity of mutually constitutive 'encounters' over time,
is a logical corollary of one of the 'two key modes' of global history as an
'approach to the past'.[6] This is what Richard Drayton and David Motadel
call the 'connective approach', which seeks to elucidate 'how history is
made through the interactions of geographically (or temporally) separate
historical communities'.[7] The other parallel key mode of global history is
'the comparative approach', which 'seeks to understand events in one
place through examining their similarities with and differences from how
things happened somewhere else'.[8]

Both global historical approaches, which for ease of reference we may
call the global 'encounters-based' approach to the history of international
law and global comparative international legal history, have been filtered
to different degrees and on different scales into the study of the multiple
pasts of international law. There, they have met a previously established
research tradition similarly oriented towards 'world history' which had
been seeking to decentre the history of international law from the
traditional Eurocentric framework that had dominated its study since it
began to be 'professionally' cultivated as a research field in the late
nineteenth century. In particular, since the decolonization decades, international legal historians cultivating this universalizing historical
approach have sought to provide the history of international law, as

[3] Sebastian Conrad, *What Is Global History?* (Princeton, NJ: Princeton University Press, 2017), p. 5.
[4] Ibid..
[5] Ibid., p. 64.
[6] Richard Drayton and David Motadel, 'Discussion: the futures of global history' (2018) 13 *Journal of Global History* 1–21 at 3.
[7] Ibid.
[8] Ibid.

Otfried Nippold speculatively suggested back in 1924, with a *sub specie aeternitas* orientation.[9]

Indeed, it is difficult to imagine any other legal field more global and inherently relational than international law when it is understood in classical normativist positivist terms as the body of legal rules governing interactions between sovereign states (*civitas superiorem non recognoscens*) as they have emerged over time from those very same interactions. However, it was this very historical identification of international law with the law governing the relationship between sovereign states (initially between European sovereign states and only later between Western and non-Western states and then between non-Western states too) which limited the global scope of the study of the history of international law until relatively recent times.

Indeed, the traditional Eurocentrism of the history of international law was born alongside the academic study of international law, and by extension of its history, by European and also American scholars (with the latter paying more attention to American regional developments and specificities, albeit without questioning the historical Eurocentric pedigree of the field) in the nineteenth century. Although the interwar period saw some efforts to enlarge the historical geographical scope of international law beyond European history and its own accompanying geographically specific 'turning points' and major intellectual household names, it was during the decolonization process, as we saw in Chapter 4, that international legal history began to be considered in practical research terms, although still timidly, a truly global affair. The contemporary acceleration of the globalizing of the history of international law beyond the conceptual straitjacket informing its scope that the positivist international legal framework initially bequeathed to its study in the late nineteenth century is one of the defining features of the turn to the history of international law. Part and parcel of this globalizing and sociologically inclusive process is inter alia the greater attention being currently devoted, as Chapters 8, 9, and 10 examine, to different individual dramatis personae and other non-state actors in the history of international law in different periods and regions.

Against this background, Section 5.2 below examines some precedents, and the methodological moves involved, in the extension of the historiographical gaze beyond the purview of the traditional Eurocentric 'double

---

[9] Otfried Nippold, 'Le développement historique du droit international depuis le Congrès de Vienne' (1924) 2 *Recueil des cours de l'Académie de droit international de La Haye* 5–124.

temporal and spatial exclusionary bias'[10] informing the scope of the history of international law. Section 5.3 examines how the 'global history of international law' has become fashionable in recent years and the array of factors and intellectual trends that have contributed to this historio-graphical development. Section 5.4 examines the contribution of the global turn in the history of international law to knowledge creation processes on the relationship between international law and history, and Section 5.5 critically looks into some of the historiographical debates that have emerged in its wake, with particular attention to the historiograph-ical demarcation between post-colonial and global approaches to inter-national legal history. Section 5.6 points to the importance of zooming out to a *longue durée* historical perspective to better appraise the signifi-cance of contemporary global historiographical developments in inter-national law while cautioning about not taking them for granted in a period of reviving ethno-nationalism.

5.2   From a Eurocentric to a Global History of International Law

Despite the existence of treatises infused with historical materials written in Europe since the late Middle Ages, and the existence of some works from the late eighteenth century with the purported aim of retracing historical theoretical developments and the repertoire of international legal practice in the field, the professional academic study of the history of international law emerged in Europe in the mid -to late nineteenth century. This study, which was originally premised as an effort to provide the new 'science of international law' with historical foundations, was initially animated by a quest to unearth the intellectual origins of the discipline in Europe. This historiographical quest would soon become transmogrified, as we saw in Chapter 1, into a historiographical contest about the putative founding fathers of international law. The underlying dominant historiographical perspective behind early research was based on an understanding that international law was a relatively recent off-spring of what was by far the world's most advanced civilization – the Christian European one – and that any possible primitive precedents in ancient times were unworthy of being considered comparable to *le droit public de l'Europe*.

---

[10] I originally used this term in Ignacio de la Rasilla, 'The shifting origins of international law' (2015) 28 *Leiden Journal of International Law* 419–440.

For nineteenth-century and early twentieth-century Western international lawyers, it was consequently the retrospective intellectual reconstruction of the coming into being of the *jus publicum europaeum* with its generally considered Grotian intellectual pedigree and Westphalian geopolitical origins that was generally deemed to constitute the proper scope of the study of the history of international law. This was conceived as 'essentially a product of Christian civilization'[11] and was to become, subject to an operationalization of the 'standard of civilization',[12] gradually universalized as a complete legal system between 'civilized' states deemed able to follow its rules and abide by the duties it imposed on them. As an illustration of this way of thinking, back in 1883, soon after the foundation of the Institut de droit international, one of its founding members, James Lorimer, mirroring the impact of the apogee of the 'standard of civilization' at the height of the imperial age, proposed a differentiation of peoples for the purpose of recognizing them as members of the international legal system and subjects of international law. According to his influential classification, 'humanity is divided into three zones or concentric zones: civilized humanity, barbarous humanity, and savage humanity'. The first sphere included Europe and its colonies (or former colonies) in America, including the United States and the Latin American republics. This civilized sphere was accorded plenary recognition. The second sphere was composed of Turkey, Persia, China, Siam, and Japan, which were granted partial recognition of their barbarian identity as independent political communities. The remaining sphere comprised 'the rest of humanity', to whom, being savages, mere human recognition was available.[13]

International law and its history were generally thought of in this context as a self-evident corollary of what global historians would later term the 'Western meta-narrative' of the 'rise of the West' and the 'Westernization of the rest'.[14] Regarding the globalizing spatial and temporal scope of international legal history, it was in the interwar period

---

[11] Lassa Oppenheim, *International Law: A Treatise*, 2 vols. (London: Longmans, Green and Company, 1905), pp. 3–4.

[12] Gerrit W. Gong, *The Standard of 'Civilization' in International Society* (Oxford: Clarendon Press, 1984).

[13] James Lorimer, *The Institutes of the Law of Nations: A Treatise of the Jural Relations of Separate Political Communities* (London and Edinburgh: William Blackwood & Sons, 1883–84).

[14] William Gervase Clarence-Smith, Kenneth Pomeranz, and Peer Vries, 'Editorial' (2006) 1 *Journal of Global History* 1–2 at 1.

that, despite some earlier precedents,[15] some efforts were made to extend the historical scope of international law beyond its hitherto mainly Eurocentric confines. Beginning in 1923, the annual expert 'rendez-vous' at The Hague Academy of International Law's courses largely contributed to the mainstreaming of international law as a legal discipline by providing a forum for leading authorities to contribute to the development of international law with doctrinal materials and analytical interpretations, giving a sense of direction to its contemporary extension, and also contributing as a ricochet to the investigation of its evolution in a historical perspective.

Of the approximately 300 courses devoted to different aspects of international law taught at The Hague from 1923 to 1939, around 25 had an explicit historical focus in their titles, and most of them to different degrees and on different scales delved into historical materials, in some instances to examine legal questions involving the interaction of European powers with outer European communities.[16] A representative sample of the courses most apparently historical in their scope may be classified into six minor loose categories. First, several courses provided a general perspective on the historical evolution of international law in either its public or private dimensions.[17] A second series of courses focused on the development of international law in Eastern Europe and also on the influence of Byzantium on the development of Western

---

[15] See Mauritius Müller-Jochmus, *Geschichte des Völkerrechts im Altertum* (Leipzig, 1848; reprint Berlin: Kessinger, 2010), which according to Stephane Verosta was the first to include special chapters on China, Israel, India, Persia, and Islam in a history of the Law of Nations. See Stephan Verosta, 'International law in Europe and western Asia between 100 and 650 A.D.' (1964) 113 *Recueil des cours de l'Académie de droit international de La Haye* 485–620 at 492.

[16] See, e.g., Baron Alphonse Heyking, 'L'exterritorialité et ses applications en Extrême-Orient' (1925) 7 *Recueil des cours de l'Académie de droit international de La Haye* 241–335.

[17] Baron Serge A. Korff, 'Introduction à l'histoire du droit international' (1923) 1 *Recueil des cours de l'Académie de droit international de La Haye* 1–23; Nippold, 'Le developpement historique'; Max Gutzwiller, 'Le développement historique du droit international privé' (1929) 29 *Recueil des cours de l'Académie de droit international de La Haye* 291–400; Louis-Erasme Le Fur, 'Le développement historique du droit international: de l'anarchie internationale à une communauté internationale organisée' (1932) 41 *Recueil des cours de l'Académie de droit international de La Haye* 501–601; René Dupuis, 'Aperçu des relations internationales en Europe de Charlemagne à nos jours' (1939) 68 *Recueil des cours de l'Académie de droit international de La Haye* 1–94.

European international law.[18] A third group focused on the Spanish classics of international law – in particular, Francisco de Vitoria, Francisco Suarez and Fernando Vazquez de Menchaca – and Spanish natural law thinkers in an effort to draw comparisons between their doctrines and 'modern' international law.[19] Keeping up with this classical orientation, a fourth group was of courses devoted to 'great' European thinkers, namely Hugo Grotius, Niccolò Machiavelli, and Jean Bodin, and also to the nineteenth-century Italian 'masters' of international law and four great British jurists.[20] Fifth, several courses were devoted to retracing the historical development of specific legal institutions and doctrines like arbitration and the peace doctrine to the Middle Ages and Antiquity in Europe.[21] Finally, a sixth group included a couple of

---

[18] Baron Michel de Taube, 'Études sur le développement historique du droit international dans l'Europe orientale' (1926) 11 *Recueil des cours de l'Académie de droit international de La Haye* 341–536; Boris Mirkine-Guetzèvitch, 'L'influence de la Révolution française sur le développement du droit international dans l'Europe orientale' (1928) 22 *Recueil des cours de l'Académie de droit international de La Haye* 295–458; Baron Michel de Taube, 'L'apport de Byzance au développement du droit international occidental' (1939) 67 *Recueil des cours de l'Académie de droit international de La Haye* 233–340.

[19] See Camilo Barcia Trelles, 'Francisco de Vitoria et l'école moderne du droit international' (1927) 17 *Recueil des cours de l'Académie de droit international de La Haye* 109–342 at 133; Louis-Erasme Le Fur, 'La théorie du droit naturel depuis le XVII siècle et la doctrine moderne' (1927) 18 *Recueil des cours de l'Académie de droit international de La Haye* 259–442; Camilo Barcia Trelles, 'Francisco Suarez (1548–1617): les théologiens espagnols du xvie siècle et l'école moderne du droit international' (1933) 43 *Recueil des cours de l'Académie de droit international de La Haye* 385–554 at 385; Camilo Barcia Trelles, 'Fernando Vazquez de Menchaca (1512–1569): l'école espagnole du droit international du XVIe siècle' (1939) 67 *Recueil des cours de l'Académie de droit international de La Haye* 429–534 at 430.

[20] Charles Benoist, 'L'influence des idées de Machiavel' (1925) 9 *Recueil des cours de l'Académie de droit international de La Haye* 127–306; Willem van der Vlugt, 'L'œuvre de Grotius et son influence sur le développement du droit international' (1925) 7 *Recueil des cours de l'Académie de droit international de La Haye* 395–510; Enrico Catellani, 'Les maîtres de l'école italienne du droit international au XIXe siècle' (1933) 46 *Recueil des cours de l'Académie de droit international de La Haye* 705–826; André Gardot, 'Jean Bodin: sa place parmi les fondateurs du droit international' (1934) 50 *Recueil des cours de l'Académie de droit international de La Haye* 545–748; Alexander Pearce Higgins, 'La contribution de quatre grands juristes britanniques au droit international (Lorimer, Westlake, Hall et Holland)' (1932) 40 *Recueil des cours de l'Académie de droit international de La Haye* 1–86.

[21] Ludwig Quidde, 'Histoire de la paix publique en Allemagne au Moyen Âge' (1929) 28 *Recueil des cours de l'Académie de droit international de la Haye* 449–598; Baron Michel de Taube, 'Les origines de l'arbitrage international: Antiquité et Moyen Âge' (1932) 42 *Recueil des cours de l'Académie de droit international de La Haye* 1–116; Michel Zimmermann, 'La crise de l'organisation internationale à la fin du Moyen Âge' (1933)

courses devoted to examining the influence of the Catholic Church and the Reformation on the evolution of international law in a historical perspective.[22]

The overarching orientation of these early historical courses delivered at The Hague was to identify the history of international law with European experiences. In this, the courses of The Hague Academy were not too dissimilar from some of the most often referenced history-oriented works from the period, such as Paul Vinogradoff's historical typology of international law, despite the fact that this work extended its gaze back before the 'birth of the sovereign state in early-modern Europe'.[23] Indeed, leaving aside a course devoted exceptionally, as we shall later see, to the Islamic history of international law at The Hague in 1935, the most remarkable exceptions to this geographically limited coverage were a couple of courses revolving around the history of international law in America and inter-American relations.[24] Although the American continent was widely seen as pertaining to the European and Christian sphere of historical civilization, these courses were walking, as Liliana Obregón has explained, in the footsteps of earlier

44 *Recueil des cours de l'Académie de droit international de La Haye* 315–438; Christian L. Lange, 'Histoire de la doctrine pacifique et de son influence sur le développement du droit international' (1927) 13 *Recueil des cours de l'Académie de droit international de La Haye* 171–426; Charles Dupuis, 'Les antécédents de la Société des Nations' (1937) 60 *Recueil des cours de l'Académie de droit international de La Haye* 1–110; Eduard-Maurits Meijers, 'L'histoire des principes fondamentaux du droit international privé à partir du Moyen Âge spécialement dans l'Europe occidentale' (1934) 49 *Recueil des cours de l'Académie de droit international de La Haye* 543–686.

22 George Goyau, 'L'église catholique et le droit des gens' (1925) 6 *Recueil des cours de l'Académie de droit international de La Haye* 123–240; Marc Boegner, 'L'influence de la Réforme sur le développement du droit international' (1925) 6 *Recueil des cours de l'Académie de droit international de La Haye* 241–324.

23 Paul Vinogradoff, 'Historical types of international law' (1923) 1 *Bibliotheca Visseriana* 1–70. See Randall Lesaffer, 'The classical Law of Nations (1500–1800)', in Alexander Orakhelashvili (ed.), *Research Handbook on the Theory and History of International Law* (Cheltenham: Edward Elgar Publishing, 2011), pp. 408–440 at 410.

24 Jesus Maria Yepes, 'La contribution de l'Amérique latine au développement du droit international public et privé' (1928) 32 *Recueil des cours de l'Académie de droit international de La Haye* 691–800; Camilo Barcia Trelles, 'La doctrine de Monroe dans son développement historique particulièrement en ce qui concerne les relations interaméricaines' (1930) 32 *Recueil des cours de l'Académie de droit international de La Haye* 391–606 at 391; Edmund A. Walsh, 'L'évolution de la diplomatie aux États-Unis' (1939) 69 *Recueil des cours de l'Académie de droit international de La Haye* 149–236.

'peripheral histories of international law'.[25] These emerged in the nineteenth century in the wake of the independence of the United States and the Latin American republics – particularly in works by Henry Wheaton[26] and Carlos Calvo[27] – and underwent a new historiographical development spurred by Alejandro Alvarez's Latin American regionalist project in the early twentieth century.[28] Also indirectly contributing to the integration of the Americas in the history of international law was James Brown Scott's campaign in the mid-1920s to replace the intertwined aetiological myths that Hugo Grotius's *De iure belli and pacis'*(1625) and the Peace of Westphalia (1648) had given birth to international law with Vitoria's *Relectiones*, in particular *De indis noviter inventis* and *De indis sive de iure belli hispanorum in barbaros*, both from 1532, and the European discovery and conquest of the American continent. Scott's Spanish origin narrative'[29] was itself a historiographical coda to earlier debates on the European 'founding fathers' of the discipline animated by Ernest Nys,[30] which had in turn crystallized into the canon of the classics of international legal history that Scott had established, as we examined in Chapter 1, with the support of the Carnegie Endowment for International Peace. Moreover, while Scott's 'Spanish origin campaign'[31] did not question, and indeed only buttressed, the Eurocentric pedigree of international legal history, it nonetheless provided what was still mainly approached as a purely intra-European historicized development with a powerful interactive outer European historical connection. Bearing witness to the remarkable role historiographical genealogies play within the field is how Scott's campaign was to become

---

[25] Liliana Obregón, 'Peripheral histories of international law' (2019) 15 *Annual Review of Law and Social Science* 437–451.

[26] Henry Wheaton, *History of the Law of Nations in Europe and America: From the Earliest Times to the Treaty of Washington* (New York: Gould, Banks & Co., 1842).

[27] Carlos Calvo, *Una página de derecho internacional: la América del Sur ante la ciencia del derecho de gentes moderno* (Paris: A. Durand, 1864).

[28] Alejandro Álvarez, *Le droit international américain: son fondement, sa nature; d'après l'histoire diplomatique des états du nouveau monde et leur vie politique et économique* (Paris: A. Pédone, 1910). See also Alejandro Alvarez, 'Latin America and international law' (1909) 3 *American Journal of International Law* 269–353.

[29] Paolo Amorosa, *Rewriting the History of the Law of Nations: How James Brown Scott Made Francisco de Vitoria the Founder of International Law* (Oxford: Oxford University Press, 2019), p. 312.

[30] Ernest Nys, 'Les publicistes espagnols du XVI siècle et les droits des indiens' (1889) 21 *Révue de droit international et de législation comparée* 532–560; Ernest Nys, *Les origines du droit international* (Brussels: Alfred Castaigne, 1894).

[31] Amorosa, *Rewriting the History of the Law of Nations*, p. 183.

the launching pad, as it was seen in Chapters 2 and 4, for ulterior counter-reinterpretations of the origins of international law in a post-colonial vein.

Although the scope of the research covered by the courses of The Hague Academy revolved almost completely around European materials, there was, nonetheless, an incipient universal historiographical awareness of sorts in the works of certain authors. One of these was Baron Serge Korff, who highlighted the mistake that the nineteenth-century masters of international law had made regarding the non-existence of systems of international law in the past, which he attributed to a lack of development of the corresponding branch of historical research.[32] Instead, he stressed that 'the ancient world ... knew very well the sense of international relations and used a system of very developed and firmly established institutions'.[33] A similar conception is also mentioned in the work of the Swiss diplomat and scholar Otfried Nippold. Nippold, who taught in Tokyo throughout his career and inter alia cited Takahashi's 'Le droit international dans l'histoire du Japon',[34] explicitly noted that 'in the same way that there is no limitation to the study of international law from the perspective of time, there is no limitation of international law from the perspective of space'[35] in historical terms. This led him to assert that 'in fact, international law needs to be studied "*sub specie aeternitas*"' because 'it is a law that has existed for ever and within all civilizations. It is therefore neither an acquisition of our times nor of our culture.'[36] However, these occasional invocations of the trans-cultural and trans-civilizational origins of international law were not actually translated into deep analyses of outer European historical research material by their authors, whose work mainly remained within the European frame of reference.

It was, as Wolfgang Preiser notes, 'from the beginning of the 1930s, following in the footsteps of historical and archaeological research, [that] the history of international law finally began to explore the wider world beyond Europe'. This coincided with the early rise of world–history-

---

[32] Korff, 'Introduction', p. 6.

[33] Ibid., p. 5.

[34] Susumu Takahashi, 'Le droit international dans l'histoire du Japon' (1901) 3 *Revue de droit international et de la législation comparée* 188–201. See the historical portrait of Takahashi in Arnulf Becker Lorca, *Mestizo International Law: A Global Intellectual History 1842–1933* (Cambridge, UK: Cambridge University Press, 2015).

[35] Korff, 'Introduction', p. 6.

[36] Nippold, 'Le développement historique', p. 5.

oriented historical works as shown by the popularity gained by Oswald
Spengler's *The Decline of the West*[37] and the first instalments of Arnold
Toynbee's twelve-volume *A Study of History* on the rise and fall of
twenty-six human civilizations.[38] Following in the footsteps of this
broader historical canvas, according to Preiser, 'first of all the history of
international law turned to the ancient Near East – which also includes
Egypt – and to later international legal developments in the region; in
particular, those brought into being from the sixth decade of the seventh
century onwards by the formation and spread of Islam'.[39] It was Ahmed
Rechid who provided the most apparent instance of this historical orientation at The Hague Academy with his course devoted to proving that
'Muslim authors had written in this area long before the Christians had
published their first books on topics more or less connected to the law of
peoples.'[40] Although some of these references can be found scattered in
general works and books that address other subjects, such as the Qur'an,
its exegesis the Hadith, and its commentaries and books of jurisprudence,
Rechid pointed to a large number of volumes on a proto-form of
international law produced between the ninth and the thirteenth to
fourteenth centuries, starting with the Siyar-i-Kebir. Divided into two
volumes and written by bin-Hassan-el-Shaybani (804–952), this is considered a true treatise on the law of nations *avant la lettre*.[41] This
orientation was reaffirmed during the decolonization decades in the
aftermath of World War II when the geographical and temporal scope
of the study of the history of international law began to be amply
extended beyond its Eurocentric confines. Underlying early post-colonial
efforts to extend the geographical and temporal scope of the history of
international law was, as we saw in Chapter 4, a cosmopolitan/nationalist

[37] Oswald Spengler, *Der Untergang des Abendlandes: Umrisse einer Morphologie der Weltgeschichte* (Munich: H. Beck, 1923).

[38] Arnold Toynbee, *A Study of History*, 12 vols. (Oxford: Oxford University Press, 1934–61).

[39] Wolfgang Preiser, 'History of international law: basic questions and principles', in *Max Planck Encyclopedia of Public International Law* (2007), opil.ouplaw.com/view/10.1093/law:epil/9780199231690/law-9780199231690-e717, p. 3.

[40] Ahmed Rechid, 'L'Islam et le droit des gens' (1937) 60 *Recueil des cours de l'Académie de droit international de La Haye* 371–506 at 385.

[41] Ibid., p. 386. Also from the same year, see Choucri Cardahi, 'La conception et la pratique du droit international privé dans l'Islam (étude juridique et historique)' (1937) 60 *Recueil des cours de l'Académie de droit international de La Haye* 507–650. The next course devoted to Islam was published by Louis Milliot as 'La conception de l'état et de l'ordre légal dans l'Islam' (1949) 75 *Recueil des cours de l'Académie de droit international de La Haye* 591–688.

urge on the part of elite scholars belonging to the new sovereign nations to repossess their own history, and by extension their countries' cultural contributions to the history of the international legal universe against long-standing conceptions of Western cultural superiority.

Beyond the contributions by early post-colonial writers examined in Chapter 4, the precursors of the contemporary 'globalist' change of historiographical tide in international law also includes a number of earlier intradisciplinary developments that set the ground for the twenty-first century's expansion of the history of international law both in space, by extending the geographical boundaries of the field beyond Europe, and also in time, by extending the classically depicted geopolitical origin of a modern (or classical) law of nations back before Westphalia or alternatively the discovery and conquest of America. The fundamental question was, as many have asked ever since, whether international law is 'a concept fairly unique to the European society of states in pre-modern or modern times or whether the concept of international law or the law of nations is truly ubiquitous throughout the world and throughout history'.[42] If only the former were true, as the *Encyclopaedia Britannica*, after dismissing all non-European earlier history as irrelevant, stated until not long ago – 'international law is the product of a threefold process initiated in the Western world: the disintegration of the medieval European community into a European society, the expansion of this European society, and concentration of power in a developing world society in the hands of a rapidly declining number of major world powers'[43] – then the study of pre-modern extra-European practices would be merely an exercise in international legal antiquarianism. This was also the position of the Dutch international legal historian J. H. W. Verzijl, who, as Arnulf Becker notes, ridiculed the alternative by claiming that international law was 'essentially the product of the European mind' and that in consequence it had been received ... lock, stock and barrel by American and Asian states'.[44] However, if by contrast the second preposition was the better view, then far more historical

---

[42] Masaharu Yanagihara, 'Significance of the history of the law of nations in Europe and East Asia' (2014) *Recueil des cours de l'Académie de droit international de La Haye* 273–435 at 287.

[43] MIT Western Hemisphere Project, 'International Law: Encyclopaedia Britannica', web .mit.edu/esg-conscience/www/resr/ilaw.pdf.

[44] Jan Hendrik Willem Verzijl, 'Western European influence on the foundations of international law' in Jan Hendrik Willem Verzijl (ed.), *International law in Historical Perspective* (Leiden: A. W. Sijthoff, 1968), p. 442, quoted in Becker Lorca, *Mestizo*

research was warranted on the subject than historians of international law had so far offered.

Wolfgang Preiser (1903–97), the leading German international law historian in the 1960s and 1970s, understood well that chronology and geography – or more broadly time and space – do play key roles in the periodical demarcation, or subdivisions, of the history of international law and that the crux of the matter therefore lay in the underlying definition of international law itself. On this basis, Preiser's methodological historiographical reconsideration of the origins of international law developed in two directions. The first of these involved extending the geographical reach of the history of international law by expanding its definition beyond the positivistic conceptualization of it as the 'law governing relations between sovereign states', which until then had generally undergirded the mainstream periodization, to the socio-legal understanding that *ubi societas inter potestates, ibi ius gentium*. The second and parallel element of the new orientation was to extend the temporal focus to before Westphalia and the writings of Francisco de Vitoria in the age of discovery or the 'great encounter' in order to highlight 'continuity' in the history of international law. For Preiser, it was 'evident from a comparatively early point that the basic requirements for an international legal order were fully present in the European society of States not just at the beginning of the modern era, but, at the latest, by the end of the 13th century' and moreover that 'the concepts of law and legal validity underlying European international law ... all went back to the early era of the ancient Greek polis'.[45] In tracing this continuity, Preiser sought continuity not at the normative level – that is, not at the level of substantive rules of law – but instead at the deeper and more abstract level of 'non-normative elements such as structures, principles and ideas',[46] which in his view informed the inner development of the international legal order.

International Law, p. 31. See also, citing other examples from European authors, ibid., pp. 31–33.

[45] Preiser, 'History of international law', p. 4. See also, earlier in time, Wolfgang Preiser, 'Über die Ursprünge des modernen Völkerrechts', in Erich Bruel (ed.), *Internationalrechtliche und staatsrechtliche Abhandlungen: Festschrift für Walter Schatzel zum 70. Geburtstag* (Düsseldorf: Hermes, 1960), pp. 373–387.

[46] Heinhard Steiger, 'Universality and continuity in international public law', in Thilo Marauhn and Heinhard Steiger (eds.), *Universality and Continuity in International Law* (The Hague: Eleven International Publishing, 2011), pp. 13–43 at 35.

Preiser's historiographical agenda, which is reminiscent of Nippold's older call for a study *sub specie aeternitas* of international law, could be summarized in his statement that 'general legal history is, for good reasons, concerned with all legal developments of the past regardless both of where they appeared and also of whether or not they prevailed over the longer term. The history of international law has no reason for proceeding otherwise.'[47] Among other pioneering historiographical works since the early 1960s, Preiser's somewhat globalist *avant la lettre* research programme was translated into his seminal volume published in 1976 on the international law of ancient extra-European cultures, including pre-Colombian America, the Polynesian Islands, sub-Saharan Africa, the Indian subcontinent, China, and adjacent regions.[48] These historiographical developments would find an echo in some of the courses taught at The Hague Academy, which had been interrupted because of World War II until 1947. However, it would not be until 1958 that an Asian country became the object of a new course, which followed the pattern of the 'contributionist' perspective that, as we saw in Chapter 4, characterized early post-colonial international legal scholarship,[49] while, in 1959 Antonio Truyol y Serra, the first Spanish professor to hold a chair in international relations, devoted a course to the history of international law from the perspective of the sociology of international law and the theory of international relations.[50] It was in the 1960s that courses of The Hague Academy beyond the Westphalian paradigm began to take root with German historians of international law, such as Stephane Verosta,[51] on the relationship between the Roman and Persian empires, laying the historiographical foundations for the new research extending from

---

[47] Preiser, 'History of international law', p. 4.

[48] Wolfgang Preiser, *Frühe völkerrechtliche Ordnungen der aussereuropäischen Welt: Ein Beitrag zur Geschichte des Völkerrechts* (Wiesbaden: Steiner, 1976). See an updated and extended version in French, Robert Kolb, *Esquisse d'un droit international public des anciennes cultures extra-européennes: Amérique precolombienne, Iles Polynésiennes, Afrique Noire, Sous-continent indien, Chine et régions limitrophes* (Paris: Pédone, 2010).

[49] Chirakaikaran Joseph Chacko, 'India's contribution to the field of international law concepts' (1958) 93 *Recueil des cours de l'Académie de droit international de La Haye* 121–221.

[50] Antonio Truyol y Serra, 'Genèse et structure de la société international' (1959) 96 *Recueil des cours de l'Académie de droit international de La Haye* 553–642.

[51] Verosta, 'International law', pp. 491–615. See Stephan Verosta, 'Regionen und Perioden der Geschichte des Volkerrechts' (1979) 30 *Österreichische Zeitschrift für öffentliches Recht und Volkerrecht* 1–21.

ancient civilizations that developed decades later.[52] The geographical lenses were also extended, as we saw in Chapter 4 in the work of Charles Alexandrowicz,[53] and in other courses examining, for instance, the cultural-religious roots of international law in Asia.[54]

Building on older historiographical research dynamics in the field, these new research efforts influenced by decolonization were to become confluent with the movement and related tenets of 'world history'. This, as a modern historiographical trend, is generally retraced to a celebrated monograph by William Mcneill in 1963,[55] which, according to Patrick Manning, 'made it possible for historians to consider world history as academically feasible, and not simply philosophically speculative'.[56] Over the next years, the new historiographical trend became institutionalized with the founding of the World History Association (1982) and the launch of the *Journal of World History* (1990), devoted to historical studies from a global point of view.[57] Contemporary with these historiographical developments was, in international legal history, the trans-civilizational approach to the history of international law most notoriously associated with the Japanese scholar Onuma Yasuaki.[58] Onuma, whose early works in the 1980s included contributions to the history of international law in Japan since the nineteenth century,[59] built on 'world

---

[52] David J. Bederman, *International Law in Antiquity* (Cambridge, UK: Cambridge University Press, 2001). See also Amnon Altman, *Tracing the Earliest Recorded Concepts of International Law: The Ancient Near East (2500–330 BCE)* (Leiden: Martinus Nijhoff, 2012).

[53] Charles H. Alexandrowicz, 'The Afro-Asian world and the law of nations (historical aspects)' (1968) 123 *Recueil des cours de l'Académie de droit international de La Haye* 117–214 at 121.

[54] Kulatissa N. Jayatilleke, 'The principles of international law in Buddhist doctrine' (1967) 120 *Recueil des cours de l'Académie de droit international de La Haye* 441–568.

[55] William H. Mcneill, *The Rise of the West: A History of the Human Community* (Chicago: University of Chicago Press, 1963).

[56] Katja Naumann, 'Long-term and decentred trajectories of doing history from a global perspective: institutionalization, postcolonial critique, and empiricist approaches, before and after the 1970s' (2019) 14 *Journal of Global History* 335–354 at 337, citing Patrick Manning, 'William H. Mcneill: Lucretius and Moses in world history' (2007) 46 *History and Theory* 428–445 at 428–429.

[57] Jerry H. Bentley, 'A new forum for global history' (1990) 1 *Journal of World History* iii–v.

[58] Onuma Yasuaki, *A Transcivilizational Perspective on International Law: Questioning Prevalent Cognitive Frameworks in the Emerging Multi-polar and Multi-civilizational World of the Twenty-First Century* (Leiden and Boston: Martinus Nijhoff, 2010).

[59] Onuma Yasuaki, '"Japanese international law" in the prewar period: perspectives on the teaching and research of international law in prewar Japan' (1986) 29 *Japanese Annual of International Law* 23–47. See also Onuma Yasuaki, '"Japanese international law" in the

history' historiographical developments and some of the early post-colonial contributions in order to put in perspective the history of international law in non-European regions before the globalization of European international law in the nineteenth century.

Onuma's trans-civilizational approach to the history of international law sought to displace the centrality of the West-centric perspective by insisting on the European regional character of international law, that is, by considering modern European international law as just one historical type of international law among others and by emphasizing the distinctiveness of other non-European views and civilizations against the predominantly Eurocentric narratives,[60] which, as we have seen, had defined the study of the historical development of international law. In this context, he suggested, that the aim of a trans-civilization perspective or reappraisal of the history of international law was to 'review the history of international law with a keener and more sensitive concern for the global (including trans-cultural, trans-religious, and trans-civilizational) legitimacy of international law'.[61] This, in Onuma's view, involved, for instance, a careful attention to the retrospective projection to the past of central concepts of contemporary international law such as the notions of 'treaty, State and international law',[62] which in his view could be done only with 'full awareness of the different assumptions in today's world and in the worlds we seek to explore'.[63] In particular, Onuma argued that instead of the concept of 'international' the 'concept of inter-cultural, inter-religious, trans-cultural, trans-religious, or trans-civilizational may be more appropriate to express the relations between the politico-religious entities under the rule of politico-military-religious leaders in pre-modern days'.[64] Underlying these trans-civilizational historical enquiries is an attempt to put forward a trans-civilizational' perspective, understood as an alternative cognitive framework for understanding, interpreting, and assessing international law in a way that gives recognition to the plurality of civilizations and cultures in the present.[65] In this

---

postwar period: perspectives on the teaching and research of international law in postwar Japan' (1990) 33 *Japanese Annual of International Law* 25–53.

[60] Onuma Yasuaki, 'When was the law of international society born?' (2000) 2 *Journal of the History of International Law* 1–64.

[61] Onuma, *A Transcivilizational Perspective on International Law*, p. 268.

[62] Ibid., pp. 270–274.

[63] Ibid., p. 274.

[64] Ibid.

[65] Ibid., p. 81.

context, historical knowledge is seen as a heuristic for international law to be able to better adjust and be seen as more functionally legitimate in the emerging 'multi-polar and multi-civilizational global society'[66] of the twenty-first century.

5.3   Globalizing the History of International Law

An increasingly 'globalized' world in the early stages of an unprecedented technological revolution which is fostering unparalleled forms of inter-connectivity and cultural exchange across the globe has naturally fostered in its wake new global lenses through which to study the history of international law. In the image of the contemporary world these new lenses paradigmatically transpose the centrality of 'connections' to the multiple pasts of international legal history. Likewise, a growingly multi-polar world engaged in previously unimaginable processes of regional and global economic, political, social, and cultural integration fosters new academic efforts addressed to providing a *longue durée* perspective on the historical development of international law across different regions and times in order to better understand how it came about and also, perhaps, to discern the historical patterns of its future unfolding.

This historiographical development is nurtured by contributions from different disciplines. Underlying this move among historians is the influ-ence of the 'international turn in the writing of history',[67] which is, according to David Armitage, 'perhaps, the most transformative historio-graphical movement since the rise of social history in the 1960s and the linguistic turn in the 1970s'.[68] This movement was animated by a series of landmark books published in the early 2000s,[69] and by the launch of the *Journal of Global History* in 2006, followed by other notable contri-butions.[70] This led to new synergetic forms of communication between historians of international law and transnational historians, comparative historians, and global historians as they tackled the question of 'how

---

[66] See Onuma, 'When was the law of international society born?', p. 61, 11.

[67] Ibid., p. 18.

[68] David Armitage, Foundations of Modern International Thought (Cambridge, UK: Cambridge University Press, 2013), p. 18.

[69] See, e.g., Kenneth Pomeranz, *The Great Divergence* (Princeton, NJ: Princeton University Press, 2000). See also Christopher A. Bayly, *The Birth of the Modern World 1780–1914: Global Connections and Comparisons* (Malden, MA: Blackwell, 2004).

[70] See, e.g., Jürgen Osterhammel, *The Transformation of the World: A Global History of the Nineteenth Century* (Princeton, NJ: Princeton University Press, 2014).

[contemporary historians should] approach the challenge of writing global histories for a self-consciously global age'.[71]

Among international lawyers, the cultivation of the global history of international law, albeit with several precursors and precedents as we have seen in this and previous chapters, has only recently become terminologically 'mainstreamed' as the object of an extensive research programme. Representative of this orientation is a recent multi-authored volume including contributions from several disciplines but predominantly written by international lawyers, which, according to its editors, 'represents a first step towards a global history of international law' with the aim of leaving the 'well-worn paths' of the 'Eurocentric story of international law'.[72] Indeed, echoing the tenets of global history and thus adopting a non-Eurocentric and a sociological-oriented non-statist standpoint on historical writing about international law, Bardo Fassbender and Anne Peters engaged in the historical restorative pro-gramme already preconized by Preiser by highlighting the need to bring back the 'too many other experiences and forms of legal relations between autonomous communities developed in the course of history'.[73] The contributors to this voluminous edited volume touched on most of the foci and topoi that have come to be readily associated with both post-colonial and global history such as Eurocentrism,[74] colonialism,[75] the terminology of 'encounters', the dichotomy between 'interaction and imposition', and the standard of civilization.[76] The global orientation also underlined the book's focus on regions in geographical terms (e.g. the Americas and the Caribbean)[77] and within them attention to

---

[71] Armitage, *Foundations of Modern International Thought*, p. 18.

[72] Bardo Fassbender and Anne Peters, 'Introduction: towards a global history of international law', in Bardo Fassbender and Anne Peters (eds.), *The Oxford Handbook of the History of International Law* (Oxford: Oxford University Press, 2012), pp. 1–26 at 2.

[73] Ibid.

[74] Arnulf Becker Lorca, 'Eurocentrism in the history of international law', in Bardo Fassbender and Anne Peters (eds.), *The Oxford Handbook of the History of International Law* (Oxford: Oxford University Press, 2012), pp. 1034–1057.

[75] Matthew Craven, 'Colonialism and domination', in Bardo Fassbender and Anne Peters (eds.), *The Oxford Handbook of the History of International Law* (Oxford: Oxford University Press, 2012), pp. 862–889.

[76] Liliana Obregón, 'The civilized and the uncivilized', in Bardo Fassbender and Anne Peters (eds.), *The Oxford Handbook of the History of International Law* (Oxford: Oxford University Press, 2012), pp. 917–943.

[77] Antony Anghie, 'Identifying regions and sub-regions in the history of international law', in Bardo Fassbender and Anne Peters (eds.), *The Oxford Handbook of the History of International Law* (Oxford: Oxford University Press, 2012), pp. 1058–1080.

cultural-religious factors (such as Islam for some regions), and on the international legal history of particularly prominent extra-European nations (like China, India, Japan, and the Ottoman Empire). Furthermore, the volume relied on strands of research developed in regional studies on international law in a historical perspective, the literature on which has continued expanding exponentially since its publication, for instance in the form of exchanges of intellectual ideas among geographically situated traditions,[78] and even, by referring to global compilations of relevant primary sources, on 'internationalist ideas',[79] thus showing a willingness to overcome 'the traditional reluctance of many scholars to examine international law's reception by and transformation in the extra-European world'.[80]

However, while the book was welcomed as a valuable contribution to the history of international law,[81] including its historiographical domain,[82] it was also fairly criticized for remaining Eurocentric in the overall scope of the research it covered and its design.[83] One fairly glaring example was that, leaving aside two North American authors, it included only a single extra-European one among the twenty-one biographed 'people in portrait' in its concluding section (and also only one woman!). Commentators also highlighted that the volume had many other gaps in its historical coverage,[84] among these the fact that it did not include

[78] See, e.g., Anthony Carty and Janne Nijman (eds.), *Morality and Responsibility of Rulers European and Chinese Origins of a Rule of Law as Justice for World Order* (Oxford: Oxford University Press, 2018).
[79] Emmanuelle Tourme-Jouannet, Dominique Gaurier, and Alix Toublanc (eds.), *Histoire globale des idées internationalists: recueil de textes* (2017), globalhistoryofinternationallaw.wordpress.com.
[80] See Umut Özsu and Thomas Skouteris, 'International legal histories of the Ottoman Empire: an introduction to the symposium' (2016) 19 *Journal of the History of International Law* 1–4 at 1.
[81] It was a winner of one of the American Society of International Law's annual prizes in 2014.
[82] In particular, Oliver Diggelmann, 'The periodization of the history of international law', in Bardo Fassbender and Anne Peters (eds.), *The Oxford Handbook of the History of International Law* (Oxford: Oxford University Press, 2012), pp. 997–1011; and Martti Koskenniemi, 'A history of international law histories', in Bardo Fassbender and Anne Peters (eds.), *The Oxford Handbook of the History of International Law* (Oxford: Oxford University Press, 2012), pp. 943–971.
[83] See e.g., Anne-Charlotte Martineau, 'Overcoming Eurocentrism? Global history and *The Oxford Handbook of the History of International Law*' (2014) 25 *European Journal of International Law* 329–336.
[84] Among the commentaries, Alexandra Kemmerer, 'Towards a global history of international law? Editor's note' (2014) 25 *European Journal of International Law* 287–295.

encounters among non-European peoples. Instead, despite relying on 'global-history'-related terminology like that of 'encounters', this volume remained focused on European encounters with the 'rest', whether they were great non-European powers (China, Japan, India, and Russia) or North American indigenous peoples. Another area which was not covered – in this case not inadvertently but by design – was the global history of international law since decolonization. As we saw in Chapter 4, this tends to revolve around the new post-colonial historiography produced from that period onwards and the life and works of its main actors in context. It has more recently also included the recapitulation of the semi-concerted international action carried out by certain developing countries in what has retrospectively been called the 'battle for international law',[85] including historical episodes like the Bandung Conference in 1955[86] and attention to the impact of decolonization during the Cold War.[87]

Another, and even larger research project, *The Cambridge History of International Law*, which is currently *in nuce* or in its early stages of preparation, embodies a more ambitious research project in a globalist direction with a large interdisciplinary aspiration. Taking its cue from Preiser's historiographical agenda and ulterior post-colonial and global historiographical developments, the research project of this multi-authored work in thirteen programmed volumes explicitly 'builds on the recent turn to a global, pluralist and inclusive history of international law' and 'breaks with the traditional reductionist approach to the history of international law of constructing a narrative about the direct antecedents and the emergence of the modern international law of the 19–20th centuries'.[88] The large-scale design of the project, which 'aspires to encompass any historically significant tradition or system of the legal organization of inter- and trans-polity relations',[89] is bound to have a profound historiographical impact in tune with Preiser's ultimate

---

[85] Jochen von Bernstorff and Philipp Dann, *The Battle for International Law: South–North Perspectives on the Decolonization Era* (Oxford: Oxford University Press, 2019).

[86] Luis Eslava, Michael Fakhri, and Vasuki Nesiah (eds.), *Bandung, Global History, and International Law: Critical Pasts and Pending Futures* (Cambridge, UK: Cambridge University Press, 2017).

[87] Matthew Craven et al. (eds.), *Cold War and International Law* (Cambridge, UK: Cambridge University Press, 2019).

[88] Randall Lesaffer (series editor), *The Cambridge History of International Law* (in press), general outline of series proposal (on file with the author), p. 1.

[89] Ibid., p. 6.

ambition that 'the last and not least gain that may be expected from an unrestrictive inclusion of all that ever came into being as international law on the earth is the new possibility of a comparative legal history on a grand scale'.[90] The design of the series encompasses inter alia the study of premodern forms of inter-power or inter-polity laws before Western colonization in Asia and Africa in the nineteenth century, and in the American continent before the age of its discovery and conquest by Europeans from the late fifteenth century onwards. It also progresses through its different volumes to the modern contemporary period, including the study of global international law after the Cold War. Furthermore, the series also foresees the first multi-authored volume exclusively devoted to the historiography of international law from different regional viewpoints,[91] thus holding the promise of laying deeper foundations for both comparative international legal history and its historiographies.

Finally, just as despite its areas of overlap the global history of international law is not synonymous with post-colonial history, it is worth noting that the global expansion of the reach of international legal history has also coincided with the local and national expansion of international legal history. Similar to historiographical developments affecting other regions, global lenses have been influencing the study of the Western European history of international law too. For Thomas Duve, who has tackled the trend from the perspective of the development of a new European legal history, this 'means to envision a legal history that is able to establish new perspectives, either through opening for different analytical concepts or by fusing them with [their own traditions], by tracing worldwide entanglements or by designing comparative frameworks which can shed light on unexpected parallel historical evolutions'.[92] An illustration is the renaissance experienced by critical well-contextualized new accounts of national histories of international law in Europe,[93] and also incipiently in other geographical locations as Chapter 8 examines.

---

[90] Preiser, 'History of international law', p. 5.
[91] Randall Lesaffer and Anne Peters (eds.), *The Cambridge History of International Law*, vol. 1: *Historiography* (in press).
[92] Thomas Duve, 'European legal history – global perspectives', working paper for the colloquium 'European normativity – global historical perspectives', Max Planck Institute for European Legal History, Frankfurt, 2–4 September 2013, ssrn.com/abstract =2292666.
[93] See, e.g., Giulio Bartolini (ed.), *A History of International Law in Italy* (Oxford: Oxford University Press, 2020).

The multiple *terrae incognitae* in the comparative history of international law in Europe (and elsewhere) are bound to find fertile ground in this and all the aforementioned ongoing historiographical developments in the rapidly maturing field of international legal history.

5.4   The Globalist Impact on Knowledge Production Processes

The potential impact of global approaches to the history of international law on the study of the relationship between history and international law is very ample. More intensive attention to global history fostering a historical development of international law beyond its Eurocentric matrix will naturally be translated into a more extensive consideration of non-Western practices, both ancient and modern, in the customary formation of international law. It will similarly contribute to greater study and greater acceptability of historical materials to establish the 'historical record' whenever international tribunals are asked to adjudicate historical claims. In the domain of 'history in international law' or the uses of history for international law, Western materials – which have themselves been the object of more attentive and scholarly comments and recording, and generally also of more attentive preservation – have been more prone to be used as authoritative and referential in international law-making and for international adjudication purposes over time. The increasing cultivation of the global history of non-Western practices is bound to reduce this material bias, which is partly an offspring of a traditional epistemic Eurocentrism not devoid of practical normative effects.

Another area where global history is showing a large potential impact is 'international law in history'.[94] The larger the geographical coverage of the study of the mutual influence between international law and/or parts thereof and both regional and national contexts across the world becomes, the more inclusive and socio-historically nuanced the picture of its evolution and the factors underlying it over time is bound to be. Furthermore, the comparative international legal dimension of global history is bound to gain in importance the closer to the present the historical investigation is set. Similarly, global historical lenses contribute to re-conceptualizations and new understandings of the 'historical

---

[94] Ibid.

dimension of international legal theory',[95] understood as a form of intellectual history. The geographical and temporal extension of this naturally becomes transmuted into a larger consideration of the 'broad intellectual and political contexts'[96] in which ideas have developed both nationally and internationally, and also as a result of different trans-civilizational encounters. This allows the often historically silent 'other',[97] or even the 'other's other',[98] to be brought back into the genealogical study of the conceptual evolution of international legal theories and doctrines, thus casting new light on the instrumental uses to which they have been put over time.

Moreover, global history can also unearth and re-engage the genealogies of neglected or cast-aside historical legal concepts and doctrines, or even other systems of inter-polity law based on different premises from those of Western state-centric sovereignty. Another area in which globally oriented historical writing about international law contributes to knowledge-creation processes is across the many dimensions of the 'historical sociology of international law.' As Chapter 10 examines in detail, these dimensions include a more inclusive approach to the sociology of the international legal profession through the study of the lives and the contexts in which they developed their works of non-Western international thinkers, law scholars, and other individuals who have influenced the development of international law, the law of nations, the law of peoples, *siyar*, *ius gentium*, etc. over time and space. Particularly promising is the role of global history in unravelling, as will be examined in Chapter 8, the historical influence on international law of several types of private non-state actors, transnational movements, and social, cultural, and religious movements with their own particularities outside the Western epistemological frame. However, a truly global history of international law would not only examine their interactions with their Western counterparts but would also extend the focus to the constitutive

---

[95] Anne Orford and Florian Hoffmann, 'Introduction: theorizing international law', in Anne Orford and Florian Hoffmann with Martin Clark (eds.), *The Oxford Handbook of the Theory of International Law* (Oxford: Oxford University Press, 2016), pp. 1–20 at 10.

[96] Ibid.

[97] Anne Orford (ed.), *International Law and Its Others* (Cambridge, UK: Cambridge University Press, 2006).

[98] Pierre-Alexandre Cardinal and Frédéric Mégret, 'The other "other": moors, international law and the origin of the colonial matrix', in Ignacio de la Rasilla and Ayesha Shahid (eds.), *International Law and Islam: Historical Explorations* (The Hague: Martinus Nijhoff, 2018), pp. 165–197.

nature of a multiplicity of other non-Western-to-non-Western encounters. This has the potential not only to extend the cultural analytical
awareness of international lawyers but also to enrich the historical
understanding of the evolution of each and every one of the contemporary sub-disciplines of the field of international law both in international
terms and in relation to the normative development of their counterparts
in domestic legal systems.

The impact of global history on the historiography of international law
is, as we have seen, highly influential in methodological terms, including
through 'encounters-based' research and comparative international legal
history. Particularly interesting is also the promise held by the new
comparative study of international legal historiography itself.
Comparative international legal historiography may be defined as the
field of study that examines the differences and similarities in terms of
perspectives, methods, techniques, themes, foci, and topoi existing alongside different national, regional, or otherwise culturally and linguistically
akin traditions of doing the history of international law and thinking
about the methods and purposes of international legal historical enquiry.
However, the mere existence of such a field hinges on the precondition
that enough distinctive features might be identified across different
national, regional or alternatively culturally and linguistically akin communities of international legal historians over a sufficiently extended
period of time. Only then could one speak of a series of historiographical
traditions which might be worth examining in comparative terms in
order to shed light on often intuited yet little systematically explored
historiographical themes.[99]

Finally, a key area of historiographical impact of global approaches has
been the periodization of international law, which has been turned upside
down in terms of both time and geography when seen from a *longue
durée* perspective. This influence becomes translated into a questioning
of the conventional Eurocentric historical periods built around a series of
historical 'turning points' in the discipline which have been generally
accepted as standard subdivisions of the historical development of international law, as they have come to be replaced or supplemented by new
alternative ones in accordance with a multi-perspectival approach.
Moreover, and perhaps more importantly, by zooming out to a larger

---

[99] See further David Armitage and Ignacio de la Rasilla, 'The most neglected province:
British historiography of international law', in Anne Peters and Randall Lesaffer (eds.),
The Cambridge History of International Law, vol. 1: *Historiography* (in press).

historical frame, global histories allow us to gaze beyond the contemporary horizon and so to perceive the contours of the historical hiatus that
Western international law may well represent in the historical development of the ordering of the relationship between members of the human
species loosely organized in historically fluid and shifting political
communities.

5.5 Historiographical Debates, Confluences, and Critiques

The consolidation of the globalization of the history of international law
in both time and space is taking place along with interdisciplinarity and
in its wake methodological historiographical diversity and a much
stricter attention to historical contextualization. As we have seen, the
history of international law's embracing its own description as a global
historical process is to a large extent premised on its ability to overcome
the Eurocentrism and state-centrism that have been bequeathed to its
study since the late nineteenth century. In this sense, international legal
history follows the familiar patterns of the 'older paradigm of world
histories' with Europe at its centre. In these 'world histories', civilizational
'dynamics were primarily depicted as generated from within' and then
increasingly diffused 'from centres of power to the periphery', typically
assuming the form of a transfer from the West to 'the rest'.[100]
    The effort to transcend through modern 'globalist historical' lenses the
classical Eurocentric perspective on the historical evolution of international law as an offspring of the gradual emergence of the European
nation-state and on its transposition to the rest of the world through
different waves of conquest and colonization is part and parcel of the
project of 'provincializing Europe'.[101] But is it possible to put the genie of
'the conceptual toolbox of the social sciences and humanities [which]
abstracted European history to create a model of universal development'[102] back into the bottle? Can the influence of the Western tradition
shaping the historical evolution, the epistemic categories, and the fundamental concepts of international law be brushed completely aside? How

---

[100] Conrad, *What Is Global History?*, p. 63.
[101] See, e.g., Ignacio de la Rasilla, 'Medieval international law', in *Oxford Bibliographies in
International Law* (2014), www.oxfordbibliographies.com/view/document/obo-
9780199796953/obo-9780199796953-0112.xml; Dipesh Chakrabarty, *Provincializing
Europe: Postcolonial Thought and Historical Difference*, 2nd ed. (Princeton, NJ:
Princeton University Press, 2007).
[102] Conrad, *What Is Global History?*, p. 4.

can the new history of international law unpack its 'global history' from the historically predominant Western perspective?

One approach to this dilemma is that of revisiting the history of international law's record as it has been historically experienced by the non-Western world. This is the approach cultivated by a post-colonial trend in international legal scholarship known, as we saw in Chapter 4, by its acronym TWAIL. The resulting picture offers a far less idealized and rosy depiction of the levers and dynamics informing the evolution of the Eurocentric system of international law, thus serving as a counter-point to the 'uniformity of the previous grand discourse'[103] of the Western 'universalist' mission rooted back in the European Enlightenment which provides international law with a liberally progressive *raison d'être*. Instead, this historical perspective highlights the historical complicity of international law with the legitimation of experiences of Western oppression that resounds, according to the TWAILers, far beyond the historical temporal canvas of European colonialism. The centrality of the colonial experience in post-colonial scholarship is apparent in Anghie and Chimni's characterization of post-colonial historiography as one oriented to:

> understand[ing] the extent to which the doctrines of international law had been created through the colonial encounter. It was principally through colonial expansion that international law achieved one of its defining characteristics: universality. Thus, the doctrines used for the purpose of assimilating the non-European world into this 'universal' system, the fundamental concept of sovereignty and even the concept of law itself, were inevitably shaped by the relationships of power and subordination inherent in the colonial relationship.[104]

However, as examined in Chapter 4, while there is historical truth in this perspective, it does not contain all historical truth. Moreover, attempts by TWAIL to politically instrumentalize colonial history in the present lead, as we saw in Chapter 4, to a number of historiographical blind spots. These include, first, a neglect of the history of non-Western forms of imperialism in those regions temporarily subjected to European

---

[103] Emmanuelle Tourme-Jouannet and Anne Peters, 'The Journal of the History of International Law: a forum for new research' (2014) 16 *Journal of the History of International Law* 1–8.

[104] Antony Anghie and Bhupinder S. Chimni, 'Third World Approaches to International Law and individual responsibility in internal conflicts' (2003) 2 *Chinese Journal of International Law* 77–103 at 84.

empires and the related difficulty in coping with forms of non-Western hegemony in them at present; second, a historical glossing-over of the comparative cultural hybridness and resulting enriching influences that have characterized all regional historical experiences, beginning with Europe itself as a historical crossroads and melting-pot of the most varied ones over the ages; and third, in the most radical versions, a romanticized vision of the local past that glosses over the many 'forms of oppression involving class, gender, religion, and violence'[105] present at the time of the 'European encounter' – a romanticized version which may then be deployed to buttress illiberal, nationalistic, and human rights relativistic exclusionary agendas in those very same places in the present age.[106]

In a nutshell, whereas post-colonial approaches contribute to an inclusive globalization of historical knowledge about international law, their historiographical virtue is not without dark sides. Moreover, by its very scope, in focusing on the role of international law with regard to the experiences of non-Western peoples under colonial rule, TWAIL is invariably pitched to always remain bound to a form of 'hidden Eurocentrism' as the gravitational core around which by definition all post-colonial historiographical attitudes revolve. In other words, the very post-colonial historiographies that decry Eurocentrism ultimately depend on making Europe's rules 'the silent referent of historical knowledge'[107] for the perpetuation of its own rhetorically entrenched arguments.

In the light of this, the question remains whether the post-colonial gaps and biases may be bridged by 'global approaches' to the history of international law animated by *animus historiandi* which could transcend the constant hammering of the 'post-colonial' critique of international law as the leitmotiv of post-colonial historiography. Indeed, global approaches should have the potential to present a less passive and also less somewhat 'victimized' image of the non-Western world through, for instance, a more nuanced genealogy of appropriations and transformations of the very international legal discourse in anti-hegemonic terms.[108] The more culturally fragmented and ethnically diverse history of international law that emerges from these perspectives is one that offers a larger historical depiction of previously unwritten histories and

---

[105] Martineau, 'Overcoming Eurocentrism?', p. 336.
[106] Heinhard Steiger, *Die Ordnung der Welt: Eine Völkerrechtsgeschichte des Karolingischen Zeitalters (741 bis 840)* (Cologne: Böhlau Verlag, 2010).
[107] Chakrabarty, *Provincializing Europe*, p. 28.
[108] Becker Lorca, *Mestizo International Law*, p. 31.

forgotten traditions and may, therefore, offer a more precise picture of how the peculiar historical circumstances in which the encounter or different regions and nations with Western international law took place went on to fashion its reception and both mould their own experiences and to subsequently reshape certain elements of the international system as a whole.

A more detailed account of the ideas, concepts, and framing categories which have shaped the history of international law multiplies its ability to provide a more nuanced understanding of its multiple political, social, economic, and cultural genealogies and the ramifications for all peoples of its constitutive 'cross-cultural interactions'.[109] This variant of the move to restore the history of international law from what Jack Goody called *The Theft of History*[110] is also one that makes the history of international law become more permeable to constructive trans-civilizational perspectives in its constant unfolding. These have sought to displace the centrality of Eurocentric narratives of the history of international law as a cultural by-product of the Western world,[111] by emphasizing the distinctiveness of other non-European views and civilizations and their contributions to the global genealogy of the discipline. Moreover, the more one adopts a canvas that encompasses events and processes – including regional institutional ones and, as of late, a return to traditional 'sovereignist' conceptions spurred by right-wing populist movements in the West and embodied by the metaphor of 'Eastphalia' in the East – that are closer in time to the present and therefore more distanced from the dissolution of former Western empires, the more it becomes apparent that the global historical perspective is increasingly relevant and that it is bound to remain so in the future.

The impact of post-colonial critiques and more nuanced, integrative, and forward-looking trans-civilizational and global perspectives can be perceived in the development of new historiographical methodological lenses and in the geographical and temporal expansion of the research scope of international legal history beyond the historical 'double temporal and spatial exclusionary bias'[112] bequeathed to historians of international law by the traditional Western state-positivist historiographical

---

[109] Jerry H. Bentley, 'Cross-cultural interaction and periodization in world history' (1996) 101 *American Historical Review* 749–770.
[110] Jack Goody, *The Theft of History* (Cambridge, UK: Cambridge University Press, 2006).
[111] Onuma, *A Transcivilizational Perspective on International Law*.
[112] De la Rasilla, 'The shifting origins', p. 419.

paradigm. However, whereas the shaking up and decentring of the Westphalian tradition is fostering an extension of the temporal research scope of the history of international law, its actual historiographical impact should not be overblown or inflated. The ongoing temporal expansion of the global scope of international legal history must still convincingly show that it is able to transcend the temporal axes within which the history of international law has traditionally remained 'contained' and the related reiterative and overlapping historical accounts of a series of Western events and Western intellectual figures, the study of which has, in fact, been revitalized by revisionist post-colonial reinterpretations. Approaches in this direction may also foster what is still the rare combination of a temporal expansion with a spatial expansion of the research scope into remote episodes of the history of international law.[113] Still equally rare in the literature is a combination of the temporal and spatial expansion of the research scope of the history of international law in order to investigate interactions between non-Western peoples over time. Therefore it is from this perspective of mutually interactive, multipolar, and trans-cultural world history evolving towards the present, which is defined not only by the relation of the 'rest' with the 'West' but also by acknowledgement of the constitutive relationship of everyone who is Western and non-Western with everyone else in the *longue durée*, that 'global approaches' to the history of international law hold the promise of offering their more distinctive and lasting contribution to international legal history.

5.6   Conclusion

Decolonization and later globalization and in their wake post-colonial historiographies and the rise of 'world' and then 'global' history, with the subtle differences between them being largely semantic, although relevant regarding innovation in methodological terms,[114] largely account for the contemporary tendency among international law historians to write histories of international law about non-European peoples and from non-European perspectives. This new globalist historiographical

---

[113] Altman, *Tracing the Earliest Recorded Concepts.*

[114] See Drayton and Motadel, 'Discussion', p. 6, referring to the foundation of the *Journal of Global History* in 2006 and noting that 'No consensus emerged, then or since, however, about the utility of this distinction between "world" and "global" history, and in practice these flags sheltered very similar initiatives'.

orientation is, arguably, succeeding in re-including a more nuanced account of the constitutive interactions between the Western world and traditionally excluded groups – among which were peoples from non-Western countries across Asia, Africa, and the Middle East and also to a large extent Latin America who were previously considered peoples without a history of international law[115] – in the study of the writing and practice of international law in a historical perspective.[116] Moving beyond the Eurocentric framework has, furthermore, contributed, as Bardo Fassbender and Anne Peters note, to unearthing a historical record 'of violence, ruthlessness and arrogance which accompanied the dissemination of Western rules, and the destruction of other legal cultures in which that dissemination resulted'.[117]

While this new stream of global and, as seen in Chapter 4, post-colonial, histories makes possible the unearthing of forgotten, suppressed, or untold disciplinary pasts, the development of historical investigation is, moreover, also allowing appreciation with greater acuity of the neither silent nor passive contribution of non-European peoples to the historical development and contours of modern international law over time. Furthermore, as global approaches seek a voice emancipated from post-colonial approaches and their leitmotiv regarding the 'tainted' past (and for the most militant also the 'tainted' present) of international law forged in the colonial matrix, they may allow international legal historians to glance deeper through the looking-glass of a more inclusive engagement with the past, present, and future of the most global of all legal disciplines.

However, while greater engagement with the global history in international law is a cause for historiographical celebration for what it represents in terms of inclusiveness and the nurturing of larger doses of multi-perspectivity in historical enquiries about international law, there are shadows on its future horizon at a time of a backlash against globalization and of renascent ethno-nationalism. This may foster a retreat from the 'global' with its promise of inclusiveness and sense of responsibility that derives from being empowered as an actor in the larger scheme of things. However, the backlash against

---

[115] To paraphrase a classic title: Eric R. Wolf, *Europe and the People without History* (Los Angeles and Berkeley: University of California Press, 1982).

[116] See, e.g., Bardo Fassbender and Anne Peters (eds.), *The Oxford Handbook of the History of International Law* (Oxford: Oxford University Press, 2012).

[117] Fassbender and Peters, 'Introduction', p. 2.

the 'global'[118] also signals a very present danger concerning the original cosmopolitan ethos of global historiography. In this scenario, global international legal historiography or, by the same token and to a larger degree, post-colonial historiography itself may well end up being recaptured by the 'container-based paradigm' of 'national history' or even by more localized and fragmented container-based paradigms. After all, it is the 'national' perspective on international law that still functionally dominates scholarship in many nations at a time when the contours of what an 'authoritarian international law'[119] may look like in the twenty-first century are already being envisaged. In their wake, following a cyclical occurrence in historical patterns occasionally termed the 'revenge of the local',[120] backward and regressive international legal concepts and ideologies risk returning to haunt, in a Tower-of-Babel vein, the perhaps too gratified, privileged, and detached international legal historiographical aspiration of building a global cosmopolitan society on the basis of a common past and a shared future.

---

[118] Martti Koskenniemi, *International Law and the Far Right: Reflections on Law and Cynicism* (The Hague: T. M. C. Asser Press, 2019).

[119] Tom Ginsburg, 'Authoritarian international law?' (2020) 114 *American Journal of International Law* 221–260.

[120] Clarence-Smith, Pomeranz, and Vries, 'Editorial', p. 1.

6

Feminist Approaches to the History
of International Law

6.1 Introduction

Feminist or gender-centred approaches to the history of international law can be very broadly identified by their object of historical investigation, namely the study of the impact of international law on the status and treatment of women across different historical periods and regions, the role played by women, both as individuals and as a group, as agents of international legal change, and their intellectual contribution to international legal scholarship over time. They can also be broadly identified by their common *animus historiandi*. The chief purpose driving a historical investigation into women's histories in international law is that of redressing the 'invisibility of women' in the history of international law. This finds its justification in a primary need to bridge gaps that exist in the historical record of international law so as to make international legal history as complete, inclusive, and accurate as possible. It is also premised on the acknowledgement that, as the historian Gerda Lerner noted, 'the fact that women were denied knowledge of the existence of women's history decisively and negatively affected their intellectual development as a group'.[1] The *animus historiandi* of feminist or gender-centred approaches to the history of international law may also involve contributing to the theoretical exemplification of the purported 'patriarchal basis' and 'male-gendered nature of international law and its doctrines' in a historical perspective, in particular when the analysis is informed by critical feminist perspectives. This is part of a broader use, according to Christine Chinkin, of 'feminist theory as a basis for critical analysis, that is to show how the structures, processes, and methodologies of international law marginalize women by failing to take account of

---

[1] Gerda Lerner, *The Creation of Feminist Consciousness: From the Middle Ages to Eighteen-Seventy* (Oxford: Oxford University Press, 1993), p. 12.

their lives or experiences[2] today, as they have also largely done throughout history.

Women's histories and feminist or gender-centred historical studies – with 'gender' being understood as a cultural and social construction that influences both gender behaviour and social relations of power – remain, however, latecomers in the turn to the history of international law. Indeed, despite the ongoing rejuvenation of the field of international legal history, historical attention to the contribution of female international law scholars to the study and practice of international law, or more broadly to women in international legal processes, still remains very limited.[3]

Section 6.2 below briefly examines the emergence of what are often referred to as 'feminist approaches to international law' in the early 1990s, noting that in spite of their subsequent growth and 'mainstreaming' in international legal scholarship there is still a notable lack of a systematic stream of literature oriented to unearthing neglected episodes and figures in the history of women in international law, and that consequently women's historiography of international law still remains in its infancy. Sections 6.3, 6.4, and 6.5 illustrate this wanting state of historiographical affairs by providing an overview of women in international law and its histories until World War I, during that war, and in the interwar years, and also by paying attention to subsequent developments in the aftermath of World War II and during the Cold War. Section 6.6 examines the potential of the still-to-be-fully-realized contribution of gender and the history of international law to knowledge production processes on the relationship between international law and history. Section 6.7 looks into a number of related historiographical debates and confluences of women's histories with other contemporary historiographical trends in international law. Finally, Section 6.8 highlights the historiographical importance of readdressing the invisibility of women's engagement with international law in a historical perspective.

---

[2] Christine Chinkin, 'Feminism, approach to international law', in *Max Planck Encyclopedia of Public International Law* (2010), opil.ouplaw.com/view/10.1093/law:epil/9780199231690/law-9780199231690-e701, p. 1.

[3] A token of the lacuna that still exists regarding women writers in the literature on the history of international law are the twenty-one bio-intellectual portraits contained in *The Oxford Handbook of the History of International Law*: the greats of the discipline, extending from Muhammad Al-Shaybānī (749/50–805) to Hersch Lauterpacht (1897–1960), all are men except for Bertha von Suttner (1843–1914). See Simone Peter, 'Bertha von Suttner (1843–1914)', in Bardo Fassbender and Anne Peters (eds.), *The Oxford Handbook of the History of International Law* (Oxford: Oxford University Press, 2012), pp. 1145–1149.

6.2 The History of Women in International Law: Neglected, Forgotten, or Lost?

Multiple studies by international lawyers and international legal historians have been devoted to the so-called founding fathers of international
law and other 'classic' writers on international law up to the present day.
Moreover, the large body of academic work which now offers a diverse
series of interpretations and reinterpretations of the significance of different classic authors' landmark contributions to the law of peoples has
even revitalized the study of the lives, times, and works of those responsible for their modern fame in international law.[4] In recent times, the
traditionally reiterative attention to the (white male) European 'classics
of international law'[5] and their epigones by international lawyers has
been supplemented with a more geographically and racially inclusive
cultivation of intellectual international biography in context. While, as
Chapter 10 examines, this has largely contributed to revamping the
'who's who' of the history of international law, the study of women's
contribution to international law remains dramatically understudied
among international legal historians.[6]

The general neglect of women, some exceptions notwithstanding, in
the history of international law results in the study of this field still being
dominated by intellectual constructions predominantly attributable to
men, and in men (in their different professional roles as legal advisors,
diplomats, or judges) being portrayed, with few exceptions, as the main
or most often the only relevant characters in historical events of international legal significance. This relative lack of attention by international
lawyers to the history of women in their discipline is in stark contrast
with developments in the field of history since the 1960s women's

---

[4] See, e.g., Georg Cavallar, 'Vitoria, Grotius, Pufendorf, Wolff and Vattel: accomplices of
European colonialism and exploitation or true cosmopolitans?' (2008) 10 *Journal of the
History of International Law* 181–209; John T. Parry, 'What is the Grotian tradition in
international law?' (2014) 35 *University of Pennsylvania Journal of International Law*
299–377. See also, e.g., Joshua Smeltzer, 'On the use and abuse of Francisco de Vitoria:
James Brown Scott and Carl Schmitt' (2018) 20 *Journal of the History of International Law*
345–372.

[5] James B. Scott (ed.), *The Classics of International Law*, 22 vols. (Washington, DC: Carnegie
Endowment for International Peace, 1911–50).

[6] No specific references to historical female writers can be found in the collection of
bibliographical works devoted to the history of international law in *Oxford
Bibliographies in International Law*, ed. Anthony Carty www.oxfordbibliographies.com/
page/international-law.

liberation movement, when 'women began actively working to redress the absence of their lives and experiences from most historical writing'.[7]

Instead, international law scholars took several more decades to come to grips with how feminist theory could be brought to theoretically bear on the study of their discipline. Although with certain precedents,[8] the emergence of what are often referred to as 'feminist approaches to international law' as a distinct modern school of international legal thought is generally traced back to the publication of a prize-winning academic article in the early 1990s.[9] The scholarly credentials of this early feminist critical analysis of international law and institutions were further boosted by the gradual building up of a substantial debate and a growing feminist international law literature during the subsequent decade.[10] Roughly the same academics who had 'seminally' deployed an amalgamated critical feminist view which presented various epistemological connections and affinities with the critical and postmodern trends in international legal thought seen in Chapter 3 went on to denounce a male-dominated international law system and its related scholarship and to further elaborate the theoretical premises of feminist approaches in a new prize-winning book published at the turn of the millennium.[11] Amply reviewed, and influential in putting feminism on the theoretical map of international law,[12] *The Boundaries of International Law* built eclectically on several trends in feminist thinking,[13] understood as 'a variety of analytic strategies',[14] to propose the central argument that international law was deeply 'gendered'.

---

[7] Anna Green and Kathleen Troup, *The Houses of History: A Critical Reader in Twentieth-Century History and Theory* (Manchester: Manchester University Press, 1999), p. 253.

[8] Kate Ogg and Susan Harris Rimmer, 'Introduction to the *Research Handbook on Feminist Engagement with International Law*', in Kate Ogg and Susan Harris Rimmer (eds.), *Research Handbook on Feminist Engagement with International Law* (Cheltenham: Edward Elgar Publishing, 2019), pp. 1–16 at 5.

[9] Hilary Charlesworth, Christine Chinkin, and Shelley Wright, 'Feminist approaches to international law' (1991) 85 *American Journal of International Law* 613–645.

[10] Steven R. Ratner and Anne-Marie Slaughter, 'Appraising the methods of international law: a prospectus for readers' (1999) 93 *American Journal of International Law* 291–302 at 292.

[11] Hilary Charlesworth and Christine Chinkin, *The Boundaries of International Law: A Feminist Analysis* (Manchester: Manchester University Press, 2000).

[12] Kerry Rittich, 'Book review: *The Boundaries of International Law: A Feminist Analysis*' (2001) 14 *Leiden Journal of International Law* 935–956.

[13] Andrea Bianchi, *International Law Theories: An Inquiry into Different Ways of Thinking* (Oxford: Oxford University Press, 2016), p. 183.

[14] Charlesworth and Chinkin, *Boundaries of International Law*, p. 50.

Approaching international law holistically, the authors highlighted, as noted by José Alvarez,

> the role that gender and sex play in the international legal system, how feminist conceptions of law relate to well-established theories of international law, how women's participation (or more importantly, their absence) affects international law-making, and how feminist analysis can be used to understand basic doctrinal concepts (including the law of treaties, the idea of the state, human rights, the use of force, and the peaceful settlement of disputes).[15]

This analysis extended through core areas of sovereignty – the traditional cornerstone of the international legal system, which for feminism is 'a reflection of the patriarchal model of social organization'[16] – and through a series of structuring dichotomies, such as legal/political, national/cultural, objective/subjective, public/private spheres, state/international community, questioning the 'autonomy, objectivity, neutrality', and even the 'universality of international law'.[17] Charlesworth and Chinkin also elaborated further on central concepts in international law like *ius cogens*, which, the authors claimed, despite recognizing the fundamental character of the prohibition of racial discrimination does not explicitly comprise gender discrimination or violence against women.[18]

The book's impact furthered the research agenda of a movement committed to overcoming women's invisibility in international law, fostering women's voices and viewpoints through efforts to 'include women in international institutions and extend the protections of international law and human rights to women' and contributing to the reform or dismantling of a male-dominated international law system which, in the feminist analysis, deeply reflects a masculine 'way of thinking'.[19] Indeed, since the early 2000s, feminist contributions to the study of international law and its scholarship have continued expanding, particularly but not uniquely in the English language in the circle of British, North American, and Australian universities.[20]

---

[15] José E. Alvarez, 'Book review: *The Boundaries of International Law: A Feminist Analysis*' (2001) 95 *American Journal of International Law* 459–464.
[16] See Charlesworth and Chinkin, *Boundaries of International Law*.
[17] Bianchi, *International Law Theories*, p. 187.
[18] Hilary Charlesworth and Christine Chinkin, 'The gender of jus cogens' (1993) 15 *Human Rights Quarterly* 63–76.
[19] Bianchi, *International Law Theories*, p. 189.
[20] The reception has been far more diffuse in other places and languages. But see Emmanuelle Tourme-Jouannet et al. (eds.), *Féminisme(s) et droit international: études du réseau Olympe* (Paris: Société de Législation Comparée, 2016).

However, in the wake of this emergence of a feminist 'scientific/intellectual movement'[21] in international legal scholarship has also come much intellectual diversity within it. This in turn has resulted in a pluralistic fragmented and polarized research field where different strands of feminist international legal thought compete to be heard and persuade each other about their respective tenets, analytical tools, and scholarly acumen. Included among these different trends are those labelled 'liberal', 'cultural', 'radical', 'post-colonial', 'post-colonial socialist',[22] 'race-based', and 'postmodern legal' feminism, and also 'queer theory', within which questions of sexuality are an independent concern.[23] This internal plurality and the corresponding division have come to be translated into a very theoretically sophisticated, and also fairly self-contained, internal debate among feminist international law scholars, a state of affairs resignedly captured by Hilary Charlesworth in the expression 'talking to ourselves'.[24]

Commenting further on the argumentative theoretical sophistication of the professionally self-contained subfield of feminist studies which feminist analyses in international law have evolved into (in which there appears to be a position for almost every conceivable feminist idea or angle, together with a never-ending critique and problematization of it),[25] Charlesworth has noted that 'to some extent, the internal debates among feminists map onto a divide between scholars and activists'.[26] Indeed, according to this author 'academics seem much more willing to scrutinize the premises of feminist theory and to attack impurity and inconsistency' while 'people working in NGOs or international institutions with feminist agendas, by contrast, are generally keen to work with

---

[21] Scott Frickel and Neil Gross, 'A general theory of scientific/intellectual movements' (2005) 70 *American Sociological Review* 204–232 at 205.

[22] Bhupinder S. Chimni, *International Law and World Order: A Critique of Contemporary Approaches*, 2nd ed. (Cambridge, UK: Cambridge University Press, 2017), p. 360.

[23] Frédéric Mégret, 'Féminisme et droit international: le "féminisme de gouvernance" à l'épreuve du "féminisme critique"', in Emmanuelle Tourme-Jouannet et al. (eds.), *Féminisme(s) et droit international: études du réseau Olympe* (Paris: Société de Législation Comparée, 2016), pp. 1–30 at 4–5.

[24] Hilary Charlesworth, 'Talking to ourselves? Feminist scholarship in international law', in Sari Kouvo and Zoe Pearson (eds.), *Between Resistance and Compliance? Feminist Perspectives on International Law in Era of Anxiety and Terror* (Oxford: Hart Publishing, 2011), pp. 17–32.

[25] See Chimni, *International Law*, pp. 358–439.

[26] Hilary Charlesworth, 'The women question in international law' (2011) 1 *Asian Journal of International Law* 33–38 at 36.

a big picture, and associate feminism with getting more women involved in decisions, or using international law to help women'.[27] Similar considerations are often voiced by feminist scholars in the nearby field of international relations, an area of studies that also emerged almost contemporarily with feminism in the study of international law in the early 1990s.[28] In this field too, 'the variety of activism associated with feminism is paralleled by the variety of ways feminist theory has evolved and the varieties of 'feminisms that have emerged as a result',[29] and, as in international legal scholarship, the compatibilities between 'feminisms' and 'traditional international relations scholarship' have also proved problematic to navigate. This has, in turn, led to a certain degree of self-perceived academic ghettoization of feminist approaches to international law.

Despite the existence of this double divide, the rise of a diversity of feminisms in international law has not so far been translated into a substantial contribution to the study of the history of international law from a gender and history perspective. Indeed, as Immi Tallgren has remarked, 'the history of international law still appears to a great extent oblivious to women's history or gender studies'.[30] 'Perhaps', she adds, 'we lack the *longue durée* for a paradigm shift: the avant-garde has moved ahead but much of the scholarship still struggles to exit the traditionally received historical studies that excluded women'.[31] This is in contrast to the larger number of contributions by feminist international historians and also feminist international relations scholars.[32] It also sits unevenly with the fact that the feminist critical take on the theoretical and practical 'gendered nature' of international law, which is oriented towards challenging and revising the gendered conventional foundations of the

---

[27] Ibid.

[28] See, e.g., Judith Ann Tickner, *Gender in International Relations: Feminist Perspectives on Achieving Global Security* (Columbia, NY: Columbia University Press, 1992).

[29] Sandra Whitworth, 'Feminism', in Christian Reus-Smit and Duncan Snidal (eds.), *The Oxford Handbook of International Relations* (Oxford: Oxford University Press, 2008), pp. 391–403 at 393.

[30] Immi Tallgren, '*Voglio una donna!*' On rewriting the history of international criminal justice with the help of women who committed international crimes', in Thomas Skouteris and Immi Tallgren (eds.), *The New Histories of International Criminal Law* (Oxford: Oxford University Press, 2019), pp. 110–129 at 111.

[31] Ibid.

[32] See e.g. Lisa Disch and Mary Hawkesworth (eds.) *The Oxford Handbook of Feminist Theory* (Oxford: Oxford University Press, 2016).

field,[33] is foundationally erected on the ultimately 'historical' argument, according to Charlesworth and Chinkin, that they are an offspring of the historical silence and exclusion of women from the realms of international law writing, international law-making fora, and/or international adjudicative positions over time.[34] Moreover, it is argued 'that the absence of women in the development of international law has produced a narrow and inadequate jurisprudence that has, among other things, legitimated the unequal position of women around the world rather than challenged it'.[35]

However, some exceptions notwithstanding, feminist international legal scholars have not been particularly interested in producing a systematic line of studies of earlier female historical episodes and figures in the history of international law.[36] This historiographical state of affairs, characterized by a scarcity of works oriented to unearthing neglected episodes and figures in the history of women in international law, and an almost non-existent feminist historiography of international law, is similar to the state of the art of the emerging field of 'gender and legal history', despite the fact that the latter appears more historiographically evolved.[37] The ultimate outcome of this state of affairs is that historical attention to the works and roles played by individual women, and to women organized as collective social movements, in the history of international law remains, as the following overview shows, very sparse in the writings of international law historians.[38] While this has resulted in the existence of a considerable gap in international legal historical knowledge in this area, to conclude on a positive note, it also allows a bright future for women's histories as a research area in international legal history to be foreseen insofar as it may provide a good scholarly

---

[33] Jacqui True, 'The ethics of feminism', in Christian Reus-Smit and Duncan Snidal (eds.), *The Oxford Handbook of International Relations* (Oxford: Oxford University Press, 2008), pp. 408–420 at 408.

[34] Charlesworth and Chinkin, *Boundaries of International Law*, p. 1.

[35] Ibid.

[36] Ibid., pp. 14–16.

[37] Russell Sandberg, 'Women's legal history: the future of legal history?', presented at the 'Doing Women's Legal History' conference (London, 26 October 2016), p. 9; Mariana Valverde, 'The rescaling of feminist analyses of law and state power: from (domestic) subjectivity to (transnational) governance networks' (2014) 4 *University of California Irvine Law Review* 325–352.

[38] This non-exhaustive overview is largely based on, but far extends beyond, Ignacio de la Rasilla, 'Concepción Arenal and the place of women in modern international law' (2020) 88 *Tijdschrift voor Rechtsgeschiedenis* 1–43.

compass at a time when, according to some, 'juxtaposition of progress, stagnation and regression raises uncertainties about the future directions of feminist engagement with international law'.[39]

6.3 Women in International Law and Their Histories until World War I

From Wilhelm Grewe's monumental *The Epochs of International Law*[40] to Martti Koskenniemi's no less influential *The Gentle Civilizer of Nations*,[41] the most widely used and referential accounts of the history of international law have barely devoted any attention to women as objects of international legal interest, let alone to work produced by individual women on international law in a historical perspective. For authoritative works on the history of international law in Antiquity,[42] throughout the Middle Ages,[43] or in ancient extra-European cultures,[44] the main exceptions are a few scattered passages that refer to the customary treatment received by women during war and conquest. These range from enslavement, in the most ancient references, to women's inclusion in later medieval doctrines, such as the so-called peace of God, to spare them from harm alongside children, clerics, and elderly people.[45]

Chronologically speaking, Christine de Pizan (1365–c. 1430) is the first female author in the history of international law to whom explicit reference may be found in the international legal literature on account of her *Le livre des faits d'armes et de chevalerie* (1410),[46] which is considered one of the first known texts on the law of war in the Western world. De Pizan's book, which was very much influenced by

---

[39] Ogg and Harris Rimmer, 'Introduction to the *Research Handbook*', p. 2.
[40] Wilhelm G. Grewe, *The Epochs of International Law*, trans. Michael Byers (Berlin: De Gruyter, 2000).
[41] Martti Koskenniemi, *The Gentle Civilizer of Nations: The Rise and Fall of International Law 1870–1960* (Cambridge, UK: Cambridge University Press, 2001).
[42] David J. Bederman, *International Law in Antiquity* (Cambridge, UK: Cambridge University Press, 2001).
[43] See Grewe, *The Epochs of International Law*.
[44] Robert Kolb, *Esquisse d'un droit international public des anciennes cultures extra-européennes: Amérique précolombienne, Iles Polynésiennes, Afrique noire, Sous-continent indien, Chine et régions limitrophes* (Paris: Pédone, 2010).
[45] Grewe, *The Epochs of International Law*, p. 213.
[46] Christine de Pizan, *The Book of Deeds of Arms and of Chivalry*, ed. Charity C. Willard, trans. Sumner Willard (University Park, PA: Pennsylvania State University Press, 1999).

Honoré Bonet's better-known *L'arbre des batailles* (1387), was examined as early as the late nineteenth century by Ernest Nys.[47] However, it has remained broadly disregarded, some scattered references notwithstanding,[48] among international law historians ever since. Nonetheless, De Pizan also features in the framework of the history of women's human rights,[49] where the origins of 'feminism', understood 'in its original meaning: the theory of, and the struggle for, equality for women',[50] have also been retraced to the publication of De Pizan's *Le livre de la cité des dames* ('The Book of the City of Ladies') in 1405.[51] Moving on to the eighteenth century, historians of international human rights law have also paid some attention to two paramount pioneers of human rights for women: Olympe de Gouges (1748–93), who drafted the 'Declaration des droits de la femme et de la citoyenne' ('Declaration on the Rights of Women and Female Citizens') in 1791, ending up on the guillotine soon afterwards,[52] and Mary Wollstonecraft (1759–97), the author of *Vindication of the Rights of Women*, published in 1792.[53]

This wanting historiographical state of affairs regarding women's individual contributions to international law in this period parallels the lack of attention to women as subjects of international law norms by the classic writers on international law from the sixteenth to the eighteenth centuries. According to Martin Gallié and Maxine Visotzky-Charlebois, there can be found some gender-related references in the work of the

---

[47] Ernest Nys, 'Honoré Bonet et Christine de Pisan' (1882) 24 *Revue de droit international et de législation comparée* 451–472; Ernest Nys, *Christine de Pisan et ses principales œuvres* (The Hague: M. Nijhoff, 1914), p. 83.

[48] See, recently, Franck Latty, 'Christine de Pizan (vers 1365 – vers 1430): Société française pour le droit international' (2019), www.sfdi.org/internationalistes/pizan/. See also Stephen C. Neff, *Justice among Nations: A History of International Law* (Cambridge, MA: Harvard University Press, 2014), p. 85.

[49] Arvonne S. Fraser, 'Becoming human: the origins and development of women's human rights' (1999) 21 *Human Rights Quarterly* 853–906 at 858–860.

[50] Ibid., p. 859.

[51] Christine de Pizan, *The Book of the City of Ladies*, trans. Earl Jeffrey Richards (New York: Persea Books, 1982).

[52] Dominique Gaurier, 'Quelle place faite aux femmes dans l'ordre international de l'Antiquité et du début de l'époque moderne?', in Emmanuelle Tourme-Jouannet et al. (eds.), *Féminisme(s) et droit international: études du réseau Olympe* (Paris: Société de Législation Comparée, 2016), pp. 225–265.

[53] Dolores Morondo Taramundi, 'Mary Wollstonecraft (1759–1797): the undutiful daughter of the Enlightenment and her loud demands for justice', in Kasey McCall-Smith, Jan Wouters, and Felipe Gómez Isa (eds.), *The Faces of Human Rights* (Oxford: Hart Publishing, 2019), pp. 41–50.

scholastics, ranging from divorce to rape, at a time when the private-public divide was not clearly demarcated.[54] However, regarding the classic domains of international law, their interest was, according to Dominique Gaurier, mainly limited, once again, to knowing the place of women in wartime, with references to the writings of Francisco de Vitoria, who considered them to belong to the category of 'innocents',[55] Alberico Gentili,[56] or Hugo Grotius.[57] Beyond the classic context of customs of warfare, some attention was also given to the question of the capacity of women to serve as ambassadors, and to that of whether a wife could accompany her husband in an ambassadorial post.[58]

Moving on to the study of the contribution of women to international law in the nineteenth century, some historical work has, for instance, been done on women acting in semi-diplomatic capacities at the Congress of Vienna.[59] There are also several works on the history of the human rights movement regarding the role of women in organizing campaign platforms for political purposes on anti-slavery and women's rights, first at the national level and then increasingly on a transnational platform basis throughout the nineteenth century, particularly in the United States and Western and northern Europe.[60] However, in the mainstream international legal historical literature references to women's contribution to international law are still scarce and hard to find with the exception of some references to the late nineteenth-century author Bertha von Suttner (1843–1914).[61] Baroness von Suttner is remembered as the author of the widely read pacifist novel *Lay Down Your Arms* (1899), which came to symbolize the early ideals of the peace movement. She has been recognized as an early 'international norm

---

[54] Martin Gallié and Maxine Visotzky-Charlebois, 'Les droits des femmes tel qu'il a été enseigne par les pères fondateurs du droit international public et leurs héritiers: notes de lecture sur les ouvrages et les manuels du XVIe au XXIe siècle', in Emmanuelle Tourme-Jouannet et al. (eds.), *Féminisme(s) et droit international: études du réseau Olympe* (Paris: Société de Législation Comparée, 2016), pp. 189–224.

[55] Grewe, *The Epochs of International Law*, p. 214.

[56] Ibid., p. 213.

[57] Ibid., p. 215.

[58] Gaurier, 'Quelle place faite aux femmes', pp. 231–242.

[59] Glenda Sluga, 'Madame de Stael and the transformation of European politics 1812–1817' (2015) 37 *International History Review* 142–166; Glenda Sluga, 'On the historical signifi-cance of the presence, and absence, of women at the Congress of Vienna 1814–1815' (2014) 25 *L'homme* 49–62. See, further, Glenda Sluga and Carolyn James, *Women, Diplomacy and International Politics since 1500* (London: Routledge, 2015).

[60] Fraser, 'Becoming human', pp. 853–906.

[61] Peter, 'Bertha von Suttner', pp. 1145–1149.

entrepreneur'[62] on account of her contribution to The Hague Peace Conference in 1899, for which she was awarded the Nobel Peace Prize, which she had herself persuaded Alfred Nobel to establish in 1905.[63]

In the absence, according to Gallié and Visotzky-Charlebois's review of French nineteenth-century textbooks,[64] of women as subjects of international legal interest in the nineteenth century, a few critical feminist historians of international law have focused on late nineteenth-century male writers on international law, 'challenging the recent valorization of some of these figures and the lack of explicit recognition of the misogyny that stands alongside the racism and imperialism in these texts'.[65] Aoife O'Donoghue has, for instance, chartered 'the explicit gendering of the state in 19th century texts', in particular in, but not limited to, the work of Johann Caspar Bluntschli, the author of *Der Stat ist der Mann* ('The State is the Man'), to conclude that, considering that 'it is in the 19th century that international law's contemporary structure and language were established and the authors of this period remain the touchstone figures of today',[66] their derogatory use of 'female imaginary' should influence 'how we perceive the academics of this era and their authoring of the modern discipline'.[67]

Particularly symptomatic of the fairly limited study that the history of women in international law in the nineteenth century has received among international law historians is the long-overlooked *avant la lettre* contribution to the discipline by Concepción Arenal (1820–93), a penologist, social reformer, humanitarian thinker, and early pioneer of women's rights and feminism in Spain, who published *Ensayo sobre el derecho de gentes* ('Essay on the Law of Peoples') in Madrid in 1879.[68] Arenal's work stands out as the first treatise on international law in the modern sense ever published by a woman. Although in 1915 the United States Library of Congress's *Guide to the Law and Legal Literature of*

---

[62] Roger P. Alford, 'The Nobel effect: Nobel Peace Prize laureates as international norm entrepreneurs' (2008–2009) 49 *Virginia Journal of International Law* 61–153.

[63] Peter, 'Bertha von Suttner', pp. 1145–1149.

[64] Gallié and Visotzky-Charlebois, 'Les droits des femmes', pp. 189–224.

[65] Aoife O'Donoghue, 'The admixture of feminine weakness and susceptibility: gendered personifications of the state in international law' (2018) 19 *Melbourne Journal of International law* 227–258 at 229.

[66] Ibid., p. 230.

[67] Ibid., pp. 227–258.

[68] Concepción Arenal, *Ensayo sobre el derecho de gentes* (Madrid: Impr. de la Revista de Legislación, 1879). See De la Rasilla, 'Concepción Arenal'.

Spain appraised Arenal's book as 'the most original Spanish work in the field of international law published during the nineteenth century',[69] *Ensayo sobre el derecho de gentes* has been only marginally studied in Spanish,[70] and has been altogether ignored in other languages ever since. The dearth of attention to Arenal's pioneering opus in the annals of international legal history may be attributed to the absence of foreign translations, to the limited interest of international lawyers in the historical memory of international law in Spain in the nineteenth century,[71] and more specifically to the only nascent state of the field of gender in international legal history.

With its absolute ethical commitment to the abolition of war through law and its characteristic faith in the progress of law through internationalization, Arenal's pioneering book stands out, however, as an under-studied early pinnacle of the ideals of the international peace movement. Moreover, Arenal's treatise, being the work of a self-taught social penitentiary worker and pioneering advocate of women's rights, illustrates a unique humanitarian sensitivity to social and pedagogical concerns which sets it apart from the work of her (male) contemporaries. It inaugurated a distinct sensitivity to the potentialities of international law with social justice and human-centred values (including, but not limited to, gender equality under the law) at its core. This sensitivity was born from Arenal's first-hand experience of the suffering of the most vulnerable, in particular women in situations of social exclusion and imprisoned and wounded soldiers in wartime, and it also had much in common with the humanitarian impulse that led to the establishment in 1863 of the International Committee of the Red Cross (ICRC), with which Arenal actively collaborated in Spain. Many other early female peace and women's rights activists, including those who decisively contributed, as we shall later see, to the influential resolutions of the first International Congress of Women (ICW) held at The Hague in 1915, and later a generation of professional academic female international law scholars, were to step, even if inadvertently, onto the trail that Arenal's book blazed at the modern origins of international law.[72]

---

[69] Edwin M. Borchard and Thomas W. Palmer, *The Guide to the Law and Legal Literature of Spain* (Washington, DC: US Government Publishing Office, 1915), p. 132.

[70] See, early on, Jesús G. Gassis, 'Concepción Arenal y el derecho de gentes' (1920) 3 *Revista de ciencias jurídicas y sociales* 60–72.

[71] See recently Ignacio de la Rasilla, 'El estudio del derecho internacional en el corto siglo XIX español' (2013) 21 *Journal of the Max Planck Institute for European Legal History* 48–65.

[72] For a detailed analysis of Arenal's book in its historical intellectual context, see De la Rasilla, 'Concepción Arenal'.

Indeed, the last part of the nineteenth century and the early twentieth century witnessed a slow emergence of Western women's activism and engagement with international law. Two main drivers can be highlighted as accounting for the international legal sphere becoming an important site of activity for women in the early twentieth century. First, international phenomena affecting women began to (re)appear at the margins of international legal scholarship as topics of interest in international law. This was the case of 'la traite des blanches' (or white slave trading), with an International Agreement and an International Convention for the Suppression of the White Slave Trade signed respectively in 1904 and 1910.[73] Second, the outbreak of World War I galvanized the transnationalization of a series of earlier women's movements such as the International Council of Women, the oldest of them, founded in 1888, and the Congress of the International Woman Suffrage Alliance (IWSA), an international leading banner for the suffragette movement, founded in Stockholm in 1904. These organizations, which partly overlapped with and built on the international peace movement in terms of composition and orientation, went on to lead peace activism campaigns and favour the establishment of the League of Nations and mechanisms for the peaceful settlement of disputes during World War I.[74] They also, as Sluga has highlighted, 'fought for female suffrage in conjunction with the right to determine their own nationality and to exert their 'feminine' influence on international relations'.[75] These early international feminist organizations, along with other social movements and forerunners of modern non-governmental organizations are, as Chapter 8 examines, a little-explored part of the social history of international law.

6.4   Women in International Law and Their Histories in World War I and the Interwar Years

The central galvanizing event in the early history of women in international law in the twentieth century was the ICW.[76] Building on the

[73] See, for a historical account, Jean Allain, 'White slave traffic in international law' (2017) 1 *Journal of Trafficking and Human Exploitation* 1–40.
[74] Lela B. Costin, 'Feminism, pacifism, internationalism and the 1915 International Congress of Women' (1982) 5 *Women's Studies International Forum* 301–315.
[75] Glenda Sluga, 'Female and national self-determination: a gender re-reading of "the apogee of nationalism"' (2000) 6 *Nations and Nationalism* 495–521 at 496.
[76] Gertrude C. Bussey and Margaret Tims, *Pioneers for Peace: Women's International League for Peace and Freedom 1915–1965* (London: WILPF British Section, 1980); Jo

suffragist transnational network, this event gathered 1,136 American and European women among up to 1,500 participants at The Hague between 28 April and 1 May 1915. The ICW's resolutions were influential in shaping the League of Nations during the Peace Paris Conference, and several of them have later been portrayed as antecedents of normative developments that were to occur later throughout the twentieth century.[77]

Women's rights and the war settlement question symbiotically traverse, as may be expected, the resolutions of the ICW. These are dominated by an overreaching conceptual framework clearly inspired by Kant's *Perpetual Peace* (1795)[78] and other influential idealist writings by Kant, such as *Idea for a Universal History with a Cosmopolitan Purpose* (1784).[79] The ICW's resolutions, which spanned various topics, were divided into seven parts: (1) 'Women and war'; (2) 'Actions toward peace'; (3) 'Principles of a permanent peace'; (4) 'International cooperation'; (5) 'The education of children and women'; (6) 'The peace settlement conference'; and (7) 'Actions to be taken'.[80] While these twenty resolutions stand out as a landmark in the early history of women in international law in their own right, many an interesting parallel may be drawn between their contents and Arenal's treatment of similar questions in her *Ensayo*, which had been published almost forty years earlier, in 1879.

The sufferings endured by women, children, and other vulnerable persons, both during wartime and as a direct outcome of war, are ever present throughout Arenal's book. In turn, the ICW's resolutions went a step beyond Arenal's concerns about the welfare of women by 'opposing the assumption that women can be protected under the conditions of modern warfare'.[81] By stressing the insufficiency of the laws of war to

---

Vellacot, 'A place for pacifism and transnationalism in feminist theory: the early work of the Women's International League for Peace and Freedom' (1993) 2 *Women's History Review* 23–56.

[77] Freya Baetens, 'International Congress of Women', in *Max Planck Encyclopedia of Public International Law* (2011), https://opil.ouplaw.com/view/10.1093/law:epil/9780199231690/law-9780199231690-e2102, pp. 1–11.

[78] Immanuel Kant, *Zum ewigen Frieden: Ein philosophischer Entwurf* (Königsberg: Friedrich Nicolovius, 1795).

[79] Immanuel Kant, 'Die Idee zu einer allgemeinen Geschichte in weltbürgerlicher Absicht' (November 1784) 4 *Berlinische Monatsschrift* 385–411.

[80] *Resolutions of the First International Congress of Women* (The Hague, 1915), wilpf.org/wp-content/uploads/2012/08/WILPF_triennial_congress_1915.pdf.

[81] Ibid., Resolution 2.

address the 'odious wrongs of which women are the victims in time of war' and 'especially the horrible violation of women which attends all war',[82] the ICW's resolutions have been seen as anticipating the notion of 'mass rape as a war crime' which the ad hoc criminal tribunals in the 1990s and later the statute of the International Criminal Court (1998) crystallized.[83] Another parallel area of concern in the ICW's resolutions and Arenal's book regards the rights and protection of children. As Baetens has noted, the ICW's resolutions attached 'great importance to the rights of all children, in particular relating to a qualitatively high-standard mandatory education system which had to be freely accessible and, among other issues, had to instruct children on international legal values'.[84] Arenal, whose faith in international law was largely premised on its ability to foster social change, devoted a good part of chapter 14 of her *Ensayo* to advancing ideas on how the law of peoples may contribute to the development of international labour standards through international conventions such as, in particular, an International Convention on Child Labour.[85]

Among its five principles for a permanent peace, the ICW also included the enfranchisement of women.[86] This notion included, above all, the right to vote. Arenal does not refer to voting rights for women in her *Ensayo*, which was published at a time when no country in the world had yet recognized female suffrage, but she defended it (albeit with limitations) in other publications of hers devoted to the subaltern conditions of women in Spanish society.[87] Between the publication of *Ensayo* in 1879 and 1915, when the ICW was held, only six countries in the world (New Zealand, 1893; Australia, 1902; Finland, 1906; Norway, 1913; Denmark, 1915; and Iceland, 1915) granted women suffrage in national elections.[88] Although in some instances it was limited by special qualifications, other Western European countries gradually followed suit during the interwar period, such as the United Kingdom (1918), Germany (1918), and Spain (from 1931 until 1939, the end of the Spanish Civil War).[89] The claim for the political enfranchisement for women in the ICW's

[82] Ibid.
[83] Baetens, 'International Congress', p. 3.
[84] Ibid., p. 5.
[85] Arenal, *Ensayo*, pp. 263–273.
[86] See *Resolutions*, Resolution 9.
[87] See Arenal, *Ensayo*.
[88] Baetens, 'International Congress', p. 4.
[89] Whereas others had to wait to the aftermath of World War II, such as France (1945) or Italy (1945), or much beyond, like Switzerland (1970) or Portugal (1976), to enshrine it.

resolutions also included the recommendation 'both nationally and internationally to put into practice the principle that women should share all civil and political rights and responsibilities on the same terms as men'.[90] As a result of women's activism, the Covenant of the League of Nations declared in its Article 7 that 'all positions under and in connection with the league, including the Secretariat, shall be open to men and women', although in practice 'less than 1% of the top-tier positions were held by women during the life of the League'.[91]

A second theme that pervaded the ICW's resolutions, and which also finds an echo in Arenal's earlier writings, was a stress on democratization. The ICW's declaration 'that it can only recognize as democratic a system which includes the equal representation of men and women'[92] was inserted in a larger Kantian conceptual framework by reference to a series of 'principles for permanent peace' after World War I. These included the prohibition of 'any transference of territory without the consent of the men and women residing therein' and the principle in this context that 'autonomy and a democratic parliament should not be refused to any people'.[93] These demands accompanied an even more forward-looking principle that foreign-policy-making ought to be under democratic control.[94] While Arenal does not refer to the political form of governments in her book, she often makes reference to the link between peace and democratization and the role of public opinion in shaping foreign policy. This is why she explicitly addresses her book to the public: 'We do not intend to discuss a point of law among jurisconsults, but a question of humanity before the public for it to take it as its own, without which we are certain it will not be resolved.'[95] Considering public opinion to be equivalent 'for the present' to 'the Supreme Court to which all peoples are subjected',[96] she wrote that the power of public opinion 'grows' to the extent that the secret 'guesses of the old diplomacy disappear' and 'international questions are given to the public for them to be

---

Karen Garner, *Women and Gender in International History: Theory and Practice* (London: Bloomsbury Academic, 2018), p. 50.

[90] See *Resolutions*, Resolution 15.

[91] Glenda Sluga, *Internationalism in the Age of Nationalism* (Philadelphia: University of Pennsylvania Press, 2013), p. 69.

[92] *Resolutions*, Resolution 8.

[93] Ibid., Resolution 5.

[94] Ibid., Resolution 8.

[95] Arenal, *Ensayo*, p. 2 (my translation).

[96] Ibid., p. xxiv.

discussed instead of dispatching them mysteriously in the ministerial cabinet'.[97] Following the same logic of fostering transparency and parliamentary control over foreign-policy decisions, almost forty years later the ICW also defended the prohibition of any future secret treaties and argued that all existing ones should be made automatically void.[98]

A third theme that Arenal's book and the ICW's resolutions had in common was the importance that they both ascribed to the role of international associations, the forerunners of the functionally specialized NGOs of the present. For Arenal, these played a central role in promoting international 'intellectual exchanges which, by contributing to generalizing knowledge, reduce differences among peoples'[99] and in helping international law to progress in parallel with the progress of national laws.[100] While Arenal did not expressly envisage (or exclude) a role for women in the framework provided by the few international law associations existing at her time, the ICW resolutions suggested that 'national Commissions be created and International Conferences convened for the scientific study and elaboration of the principles and conditions of permanent peace' and that these 'should contain women in their deliberations'.[101] The International Law Commission (ILC), which was established as a subsidiary organ of the General Assembly with the mission of promoting the codification and the progressive development of international law in 1949, is an example of the institutionalization of the early private epistemological initiatives of Arenal's times into organic parts of the UN system. However, the fact that the first female member of the ILC was only appointed in the 1990s reveals that the inclusion of women has been far slower than the ICW had bargained for.

A fourth theme in common between the ICW's resolutions and Arena's book is a radical pacifism. In the resolutions, the defence of the cause of women is embedded in the fundamental purpose of putting an end to World War I and of setting the ground for a post-bellum

---

[97] Ibid.
[98] *Resolutions*, Resolution 14. See Art. 18 in Covenant of the League of Nations (1919). 'Every treaty or international engagement entered into hereafter by any Member of the League shall be forthwith registered with the Secretariat and shall as soon as possible be published by it. No such treaty or international engagement shall be binding until so registered.'
[99] See Arenal, *Ensayo*, p. 248.
[100] Chapter 11 analyses why international law has not progressed in the same measure than domestic law. See Arenal, *Ensayo*, pp. 229–242.
[101] See *Resolutions*, Resolution 14.

settlement that would guarantee a lasting peace. First, the ICW's demand for the immediate cessation of World War I, against the 'madness' and 'horror' of which they protested,[102] was accompanied by the consideration that the war was 'illegal'.[103] This is the same radical pacifism which, like Arenal's approach almost forty years earlier, did not distinguish between just and unjust wars at a time when, following Clausewitz's axiom, war was still considered the 'continuation of politics by other means'. Instead, Arenal considered all wars unjust, and therefore illegal by definition.[104] Second, also inherently related to anti-war inspiration and seen as a means to prevent the outbreak of conflict was the ICW's advancing of the principle of 'mandatory peaceful settlement of inter-State disputes by means of arbitration or conciliation',[105] which was to be combined with the principle that states 'ought to exert social, moral and economic pressure on States that use military force to solve disputes'.[106] Writing a few years after the success of the Alabama Case in 1872, at a time of rising prestige of international arbitration, Arenal was hopeful about the progress of international adjudication although realistic regarding its potential to control the actions of great powers on political questions. Furthermore, she referred several times to the use of public moral condemnation of the use of force as a way to put pressure on warring states. Although her work mirrors similar concerns, Arenal could not anticipate that the Covenant of the League of Nations would provide for a system of 'pooled security', which went on to divide feminist views between those who saw it 'as a continuation and widening of war' and those who looked at it more favourably as 'an extension of the rule of law to the international' plane.[107] Whereas, still during the interwar era, the later Kellogg–Briand Pact of 1928 advanced the cause of renunciation of war,[108] it was only later in Article 2(4) of the UN Charter that the prohibition of the threat and use of force in international

---

[102] Ibid., Resolution 1.
[103] See Baetens, 'International Congress'.
[104] See Arenal, *Ensayo*.
[105] See *Resolutions*, Resolution 6.
[106] Ibid., Resolution 7.
[107] Lucian M. Ashworth, *Women and War: The Women's International League for Peace and Freedom (WILPF) and the Problem of Collective Security*, www.academia.edu/7915388/Women_and_War._The_Women_s_International_League_for_Peace_and_Freedom_WILPF_and_the_Problem_of_Collective_Security, p. 2.
[108] Onna A. Hathaway and Scott J. Shapiro, *The Internationalists: How a Radical Plan to Outlaw War Remade the World* (New York: Simon and Schuster, 2017).

relations crystallized and the principle of peaceful settlement of international disputes became a fundamental purpose of the UN. Third, the ICW also advocated 'universal disarmament', arguing that a step towards that end was that the manufacturing of and trade in weapons ought to be under the exclusive control of national governments.[109] Echoing a similar position, Arenal continually refers in her book to the socially pernicious consequences of war and the related waste of valuable resources on arms and weapons in preparation for it, resources which should instead be invested in social welfare measures across European societies.[110]

Finally, the ICW famously recommended the establishment of a 'Society of Nations',[111] which in its organic structure would include 'a permanent International Conference', a sort of permanent general assembly, and alongside it two courts. The first of these courts was the long-sought goal of the 'peace through law' movement: a permanent international court of justice. More original was the ICW's proposal to establish a 'Council of Conciliation and Investigation for the settlement of international differences arising from economic competition, expanding commerce, increasing population and changes in social and political standards'.[112] This suggestion anticipated by eight decades, as Baetens stresses, the Dispute Settlement mechanism of the World Trade Organization (WTO). Beside this prescient proposal, the ICW also suggested 'the settlement of investment disputes via arbitration outside the diplomatic protection system' which, again, has come to be generally realized only since the 1990s.[113] Writing forty years earlier, Arenal was a staunch supporter of the peaceful settlement of international disputes and echoed the ideas and projects for a supreme court of the law of peoples favourably. She also referred indirectly to the creation of an international organization in the context of her review of the classical arguments against the possibility of a truly positive international law in the light of the non-existence of legislative, judicial, and executive powers on the international plane. She pointed to the horizon of such 'a reflective organization that reason glimpses and will lead to a full development of the positive law of peoples', wondering, furthermore, whether 'it is not true that in contemporary history there are some facts that enable us to

---

[109] See *Resolutions*, Resolution 12.
[110] See Arenal, *Ensayo*.
[111] See *Resolutions*, Resolution 11.
[112] Ibid.
[113] See Baetens, 'International Congress'.

believe that this is not a chimerical illusion, but it is instead advancing more or less quickly to become a real and positive truth'.[114]

The activist galvanizing international moment for women embodied by the ICW was followed with an activist plan of action.[115] This involved the creation of the Women's International Committee for Permanent Peace (WICPP), which through a series of special 'envoys' arranged meetings with heads of state and foreign ministers 'to argue their case for negotiating an end to the war and establishing the international mechanisms that might avoid future wars'.[116] After the war in 1919, this committee became the Women's International League for Peace and Freedom (WILPF).[117] With its headquarters in Geneva, the WILFP became one of the most important NGOs, joining other international women's organizations to work in collaboration with the League of Nations on the promotion of women's causes during the interwar years. While women's collective movements, like the ICW, have often occupied the foreground in the memory of the discipline of international law,[118] leaving individual women's contributions to recede into the background in the work of international law historians, the collective activism that crystallized during World War I came to be translated into a hitherto less noted increase in women's presence in the work of the League of Nations and in female contributions to international law matters in the interwar period.

However, the access of women to publishing their works in specialized academic periodicals on international law, which started to emerge in Europe in the late 1860s,[119] was slow. The American Society of International Law (ASIL, 1906) and the first international law academic journal in English, the *American Journal of International Law* (1907), were established in the United States in the early twentieth century. However, women were not formally accepted for membership in the

---

[114] See Arenal, *Ensayo*, pp. 25–26.

[115] See *Resolutions*, Resolutions 19–20.

[116] See Garner, *Women and Gender*, p. 53.

[117] See Carmen Magallón Portolés and Sandra Blasco Lisa, 'Mujeres contra la Primera Guerra Mundial: el comité internacional de mujeres por una paz permanente', in Yolanda Gamarra Chopo and Carlos R. Femando Liesa (eds.), *Los orígenes del derecho internacional contemporáneo: estudios conmemorativos del centenario de la Primera Guerra Mundial* (Zaragoza: Institución Fernando el Católico, 2015), pp. 157–180.

[118] Beryl Haslam, *From Suffrage to Internationalism: The Political Evolution of Three British Feminists 1908–1939* (New York: P. Lang, 1999).

[119] Ignacio de la Rasilla, 'A very short history of international law journals 1869-2018' (2018) *European Journal of International Law* 137–168.

ASIL, which was, instead, reserved to 'any man of good moral character' until 1921.[120] Although a book review was veiledly published by a woman in the *American Journal of International Law* in 1919,[121] the first international law article by a female writer had to wait until its twentieth volume in 1927.[122] The journal went on to publish eleven articles on international law issues written by women in the 1930s. This figure, which remained unsurpassed in each of the following five decades,[123] signals a peak in women's engagement with international law during this period.

Two of the co-authors of *Women at The Hague: The International Congress of Women and Its Results* (1915),[124] Jane Addams (1860–1935),[125] who presided over the ICW at The Hague, and Emily Greene Balch (1867–1961),[126] went on to become the first female United States Nobel Peace Prize laurates in 1931 and 1946 respectively. Both of them attended the second ICW held in Zurich in 1919, becoming president (Addams) and secretary (Greene Balch) of the WILPF. Addams, an active social reformer in the United States, where inter alia she had co-founded the American Civil Liberties Union (ACLU) and the National Association for the Advancement of Colored People (NAACP),[127] many times met Woodrow Wilson, whose fourteen-point plan brought forward with modifications some of the ideas contained in the ICW's resolutions.[128] However, of the two, it was Greene Balch, appointed professor of economics and sociology at Wellesley College in

---

[120] Editorial comment, 'Admission of women to membership in the American Society of International Law' (1921) 15 *American Journal of International Law* 76.

[121] Hope K. Thompson, 'Book review: *League of Nations*' (1919) 13 *American Journal of International Law* 627–630.

[122] Cora Luella Gettys, 'The effects of changes of sovereignty on nationality' (1927) 21 *American Journal of International Law* 268–278.

[123] Alona E. Evans and Carol Per Lee Plumb, 'Women and the American Society of International Law' (1974) 68 *American Journal of International Law* 290.

[124] Emily Greene Balch, *Women's International League for Peace and Freedom 1915–1938: A Venture in Internationalism* (Geneva: Maison Internationale, 1938).

[125] Emily Greene Balch, 'Biographical: The Nobel Prize' (5 July 2019), www.nobelprize.org/prizes/peace/1946/balch/biographical/.

[126] Harriet H. Alonso, 'Nobel Peace Prize laureates Jane Addams and Emily Greene Balch: two women of the Women's International League for Peace and Freedom' (1995) 7 *Journal of Women's History* 6–26.

[127] She also wrote several books on peace: Jane Addams, *Newer Ideals of Peace* (New York: Macmillan & Co., 1907).

[128] Garner, *Women and Gender*, p. 106.

1913, whose contributions more directly related to international law matters, writing on 'international colonial administration' and on the peace settlement,[129] participating in many League of Nations projects, including 'disarmament, the internationalization of aviation, drug control, the participation of the United States in the affairs of the League',[130] and projecting a constructive vision of the world community mediated by international organizations.[131] Another active suffragist, a Scottish woman who was the first female barrister to ever plead before the House of Lords (1908) and later became a founder of the WILPF, Chrystal MacMillan (1872–1937), became the first woman to address the International Law Association (ILA), arguing for nationality for women independently of the nationality of their husbands.[132]

Another woman from the Anglo-American world with ties with the WILPF who distinguished herself in the field of international law in the interwar period was the American political scientist Sarah Wambaugh (1882–1955), who gave the first course taught by a woman at The Hague Academy of International Law in 1927.[133] Wambaugh's earlier *Monograph* on *Plebiscites: With a Collection of Official Documents* (1920) was first prepared for use at the Versailles Peace Conference of 1919 and granted her the recognition of being the world's leading authority on plebiscites, in which context she argued for universal suffrage for women. Wambaugh went on to publish *Plebiscites since the World War* (1933) and *The Saar Plebiscite* (1940).[134] Commenting on Wambaugh's work, Karen Knop has remarked that 'given that the treaties were negotiated when women's suffrage was still the

---

[129] Emily Greene Balch, *Approaches to the Great Settlement* (New York: B. W. Huebsch, 1918).

[130] She was a member of Neutral Conference for Continuous Mediation, based at Stockholm, for which she drew up a position paper called 'International colonial administration', proposing a system of administration not unlike that of the mandate system later accepted by the League of Nations.

[131] Alford, 'The Nobel effect', p. 99–100.

[132] Karen Knop and Christine Chinkin, 'Remembering Chrystal MacMillan: women's equality and nationality in international law' (2001) 22 *Michigan Journal of International Law* 523–585.

[133] Sarah Wambaugh, *La pratique des plébiscites internationaux* (Paris: Hachette, 1928).

[134] Sarah Wambaugh, *A Monograph on Plebiscites: With a Collection of Official Documents* (Oxford: Oxford University Press, 1920); Sarah Wambaugh, *Plebiscites since the World War: With a Collection of Official Documents* (Washington, DC: Carnegie Endowment for International Peace, 1933); Sarah Wambaugh, *The Saar Plebiscite: With a Collection of Official Documents* (Cambridge, MA: Harvard University Press, 1940).

exception, it is remarkable that women were given the vote in all the plebiscites held'.[135]

While Anglo-American women were important drivers of female engagement in the field of international law in the interwar period, women of other nationalities have individually received attention in the literature on the history of international law, such as Rosa Luxemburg (1871–1919) for her early analysis of the rights of peoples to self-determination.[136] Moreover, other non-Anglo-Saxon women, like Suzanne Basdevant Bastid (1906–95), also played important pioneering roles. The daughter of a distinguished French international jurist and the wife of an interwar French minister and then member of the French resistance, Basdevant Bastid published her PhD dissertation in 1931 and several academic articles in French journals in the interwar period.[137] Furthermore, Basdevant Bastid marked a symbolic turning point in the academic professionalization of women's engagement with international law as a discipline when she became the first woman to join the academic professional international law *establishment*, first as a lecturer at the University of Lyons and then as a chaired professor of international law, again in Lyons (1943) and later in Paris from 1946 onwards.[138]

The outbreak of World War I led to an unprecedented collective mobilization of women in the war effort. Combined with the earlier transnational campaign for female suffrage, the war furthermore stimulated an unprecedented female engagement with international law's role both in fostering international peace and the conditions for its sustainability and in addressing women's concerns. In 1925 twelve international women's associations joined into a 'Joint Standing Committee' to act before the League of Nations in Geneva. Its membership increased to eighteen organizations when it became the 'Liaison Committee of Women's International Organizations' in 1931.[139] The engagement of the committee with the structures of the league influenced a series of

---

[135] Karen Knop, *Diversity and Self-Determination in International Law* (Cambridge, UK: Cambridge University Press, 2004), p. 284.

[136] Deborah Whitehall, 'A rival history of self-determination' (2016) 27 *European Journal of International Law* 719–743; Alexandra Kemmerer, 'Editing Rosa: Luxemburg, the revolution, and the politics of infantilization' (2016) 27 *European Journal of International Law* 853–864.

[137] Suzanne Bastid, *Les fonctionnaires internationaux* (Paris: Recueil Sirey, 1931), p. 335.

[138] Rebecca M. Salokar and Mary L. Volcansek, *Women in Law: A Bio-bibliographical Sourcebook* (Westport, CT: Greenwood Press, 1996), pp. 34–37.

[139] Garner, *Women and Gender*, p. 107. See also a table showing the members, ibid., p. 108.

conventions to establish protective measures in the areas of legal labour standards for women and woman and child trafficking.[140] Most of these issues were channelled through the fifth committee of the Assembly on Social Questions, which was the only one headed by a woman, Lady Rachel Crowdy, from 1919 to 1931.[141] The question of the long-campaigned-for nationality of married women, to which MacMillan had devoted much attention, eventually led to a convention being passed by the league in the framework of The Hague Conference for the Codification of International Law in 1930. Although this convention did not enshrine the goal of protected nationality rights for married women in the sense argued by women's associations,[142] it led to the creation of a 'women's consultative committee on nationality' rights which added itself to an earlier 'women's consultative committee on disarmament' at the League of Nations.[143] The official sanction of women's consultative status on these matters opened the door for the 'question of the status of women' in terms of civil, political and discrim-inatory labour laws to be put on the League of Nations' agenda in 1935, and a committee of experts was appointed to carry out an inquiry into the unequal 'legal status of women' in the various states of the world in 1937, although its work was later discontinued because of World War II.

World War I and the interwar period marked, as we have seen, the first wave of women's engagement as a group and as individuals with inter-national law. Their influence was notable in the peace settlement and the incorporation of women's concerns on the international plane through women's international organizations and the role played by particular women who have for the most part been ignored by historians of international law. Indeed, it has been adequately argued that 'the history of feminist activism in the League of Nations' – and more broadly women's contribution to international law during the interwar

[140] See Christine Chinkin, 'International protection of rights of women', in *Max Planck Encyclopedia of Public International Law* (2010), opil.ouplaw.com/view/10.1093/law:epil/9780199231690/law-9780199231690-e1745, p. 2.
[141] Garner, *Women and Gender*, p. 111.
[142] See Convention on Certain Questions Relating to the Conflict of Nationality Laws (Convention on Certain Questions), reprinted in 'Conference for the codification of international law – final act' (1930) 24 (Supplement) *American Journal of International Law* 192–200 at 193. This goal had to wait several decades until Convention on the Nationality of Married Women (adopted 29 January 1957, entered into force 11 August 1958).
[143] Garner, *Women and Gender*, pp. 114–115.

period – 'is only beginning to be written'.[144] Part of this effort are
some recent scattered works that have attempted to explore further
feminist-driven interwar international and regional legal developments and the histories of the work of female activists and the institutions they created in striving to achieve them. Among these hitherto
neglected regional legal developments are, for instance, two treaties
signed at the 1933 Montevideo Pan-American Conference, the Equal
Nationality Treaty and the Equal Rights Treaty.[145]

6.5   Women in International Law and Their Histories in the Aftermath of World War II and Beyond

While the actual activist achievements during the interwar period in the
pursuit of women's causes were meagre, their work, however, nurtured
the soil for developments that took place in the aftermath of World War
II. It was then that, as Emmanuelle Tourme-Jouannet notes, the
approach to women changed from 'un simple objet particulier de droit,
en tant que mère ou être humain plus faible ou vulnérable que l'homme,
et qui doit donc faire l'objet de protection ou de traitement spécifiques'[146]
('a mere particular object of law as a mother or as a human being, who is
weaker or more vulnerable than man, and who should, therefore, be
protected or treated specially') to a new international legal recognition of
women as legal subjects equal to men. This was included in the Preamble
of the UN Charter and the provisions on safeguarding the principle of
non-discrimination on the ground of sex in Article 1(3) in the Charter
of the UN and later after World War II in the Universal Declaration of
Human Rights.

The groundwork for the shift in the underlying legal paradigm from
being based on protective considerations to being based on legal equality

---

[144] Gülay Caglar, Elisabeth Prügl, and Susanne Zwingel, 'Introducing feminist strategies in international governance', in Gülay Caglar, Elisabeth Prügl, and Susanne Zwingel (eds.), *Feminist Strategies in International Governance* (London: Routledge, 2013), pp. 1–18 at 7.

[145] Paolo Amorosa, 'Pioneering international women's rights? The US National Woman's Party and the 1933 Montevideo Equal Rights Treaties' (2019) 30 *European Journal of International Law* 415–437.

[146] Emmanuelle Tourme-Jouannet, 'Les différentes étapes pour la reconnaissance des droits des femmes: droits des femmes et droit international de la reconnaissance', in Emmanuelle Tourme-Jouannet et al. (eds.), *Féminisme(s) et droit international: études du réseau Olympe* (Paris: Société de Législation Comparée, 2016), pp. 467–482 at 469.

itself, which was reflected in subsequent developments, had been done by the previous interwar women's activism. For instance, despite the fact that World War II had prevented any substantial progress in the work of the committee of experts on the status of women, established in 1937,[147] reports produced during its tenure acted 'as a bridge from the League of Nations to the United Nations'[148] by informing the early work of the UN Commission on the Status of Women.[149] Established in 1946 as a functional commission of the United Nations Economic and Social Council, this commission remains the 'principal global intergovernmental body exclusively dedicated to the promotion of gender equality and the empowerment of women'.[150] Over the next decades, multiple ground-breaking influential UN initiatives, declarations, and conventions, including the 1952 Convention on Women's Political Rights and the General Assembly's Declaration on the Elimination of Discrimination against Women in 1967, sprang up from the work of this commission.[151]

The role played by certain women in these international-institution-based legal processes has fostered retrospective historical attention to their lives, times, and works. More than anyone, Eleanor Roosevelt (1884–1962) has been the focus of historical works on account of her leadership role in the drafting of what, as she announced, 'may well become the international Magna Carta of all men everywhere'[152] at the helm of the Commission on Human Rights. Historical attention in international law works on the work of leading individual women developed further throughout the second half of the twentieth century with the political theorist Hannah Arendt's coverage of the trial and condemnation of the Nazi war criminal Otto Adolf Eichmann in Jerusalem in 1961 in her classic book *Eichmann in Jerusalem: A Report on the Banality of Evil*.[153] Moreover, several other pioneering women also

---

[147] Chinkin, 'International protection', p. 2.
[148] Jaci Eisenberg, 'The status of women: a bridge from the League of Nations to the United Nations' (2013) 4 *Journal of International Organizations Studies* 8–24.
[149] Garner, *Women and Gender*, p. 114.
[150] See UN Women, 'Commission on status of women', www.unwomen.org/en/csw.
[151] UN General Assembly Res. 2263 [XXII], 7 November 1967.
[152] Eleanor Roosevelt, Address to the UN General Assembly, Paris, France, 9 December 1948, www.kentlaw.edu/faculty/bbrown/classes/HumanRightsSP10/CourseDocs/2Eleanor Roosevelt.pdf
[153] Hannah Arendt, *Eichmann in Jerusalem: A Report on the Banality of Evil* (New York: Viking Press, 1963). See, e.g., Seyla Benhabib, 'International law and human plurality in the shadow of totalitarianism: Hannah Arendt and Raphael Lemkin' (2009) 16

played remarkable roles in the 1950s and 1960s in the UN. One of them was Alva Myrdal, who was the first woman to hold a high-ranking position in the UN, serving as chairman of UNESCO's social science section from 1950 to 1955 and as the Swedish delegate to the UN disarmament conference in Geneva from 1962 to 1973. Building on these experiences, in 1977 she published her influential book *The Game of Disarmament*,[154] which included a detailed survey of international law and was later awarded the Nobel Peace Prize in 1982.[155]

The early history of women in international law is characterized by contributions by women who came from the women's suffrage and rights activism movement and the international peace movement. Those who possessed an academic background were not trained in international law but came instead from other disciplines, as Greene Balch and Sarah Wambaugh did. A generation of trained female international law scholars still had to wait, with the exception of a few cases such as that of Suzanne Basdevant Bastid, for several decades. This late arrival at the highest levels of academia accounts for why the first female member to be elected to the Institut de droit international (IDI) was Basdevant Bastid, in 1948, who later became its first, and so far only, female secretary general (1963–69) after having previously presided over the UN Administrative Tribunal between 1953 and 1960. Basdevant Bastid also followed in the footsteps of Wambaugh, in the aftermath of World War I giving a course at The Hague Academy in 1951,[156] which was followed by others in 1957[157] and 1962.[158] Indeed, as Stephen Neff notes, 'women steadily, if slowly, gained a higher prominence within the international legal profession in the years after 1970'.[159]

This development coincided with the UN's designation of 1975 as International Women's Year, and the adoption in 1979 of the

Constellations 331–350; or David Luban, 'Hannah Arendt as a theorist of international criminal law' (2011) 11 *International Criminal Law Review* 621–641.

[154] Alva Myrdal, *The Game of Disarmament: How the United States and Russia Run the Arms Race* (New York: Pantheon Books, 1977).

[155] Alford, 'The Nobel effect', p. 126.

[156] Suzanne Bastid, 'La jurisprudence de la Cour internationale de justice' (1951) 78 *Collected Courses of The Hague Academy of International Law* 575–702.

[157] Suzanne Bastid, 'Les tribunaux administratifs internationaux et leur jurisprudence' (1957) 92 *Collected Courses of The Hague Academy of International Law* 343–489.

[158] Suzanne Bastid, 'Les problèmes territoriaux dans la jurisprudence de la Cour internationale de justice' (1962) 107 *Collected Courses of The Hague Academy of International Law* 361–495.

[159] Neff, *Justice among Nations*, p. 464.

international normative landmark of the Convention on the Elimination of All Forms of Discrimination against Women (CEDAW).[160] This was then accompanied by the organization of four quinquennial UN world conferences in world capital cities in the Americas, Europe, Africa, and Asia from 1975 to 1995, which assembled women from all over the globe increasingly organized at the international civil society level 'in nongovernmental organizations, networks and alliances specifically around the conference objectives of equality, development and peace'.[161] Against this background, the years from the mid-1960s onwards saw the slow consolidation of women in academic international law positions and international institutions opening a period of 'first woman' in multiple different positions in international law circles. This process would be crowned by the gradual occupation, notwithstanding some early exceptional cases, of the first chairs of international law by women in Western universities in the 1970s.

In the United States, the first female member of the *American Journal of International Law*'s board of editors took her seat in 1966 and, after twenty-seven previous male incumbents, the presidency of the society was given to Alona E. Evans in 1980.[162] Evans had also served as the first woman on the journal's board of editors from 1966 and as the ASIL's first woman vice-president from 1976 to 1979. She had also devoted scholarly attention to the history of women at the ASIL.[163] At Harvard Law School, an expert on international tax law, Elisabeth A. Owens, became the first female offered tenure in 1972.[164] It was also in the 1970s that the second and third female members, Denise Bindschedler (1975) and Krystyna Marek (1979), joined the IDI, which had been established more than a century earlier. Rosalyn Higgins, a professor at the London School of Economics, joined the IDI in 1987 and later became the first female to be elected to sit as permanent judge on the bench of the International Court

---

[160] UN General Assembly Res. 34/180, 18 December 1979. See Karen Offen, 'Women's rights or human rights? International feminism between the wars', in Patricia Grimshaw, Katie Holmes, and Marilyn Lake (eds)., *Women's Rights and Human Rights* (London: Palgrave Macmillan, 2001), pp. 243–253 at 250.

[161] Chinkin, 'Feminism', p. 1.

[162] Oscar Schachter, 'Alona Evans' (1980) 74 *American Journal of International Law* 891–892; Alona E. Evans and Carol Per Lee, 'Plumb women and the American Society of International Law' (1974) 68 *American Journal of International Law* 290–299 at 293.

[163] Evans and Plumb, 'Women and the American Society', p. 293.

[164] 'The first tenured women professors at Harvard University', hwpi.harvard.edu/files/faculty-diversity/files/timeline-final_ 32.pdf.

of Justice in 1995. In Spain, Elisa Pérez Vera became appointed the first female chair professor of international law in 1979 (exactly a century since the publication of Concepción Arenal's pioneer *Ensayo sobre el derecho de gentes*) and later became the first Spanish woman to join the IDI in 1993.

Over the subsequent decades, women's access to teaching and research positions in international law, international law-making fora, and international adjudicative positions have increased exponentially, becoming generally normalized in some regions while far from it yet in others. This has largely propitiated the emergence of feminist voices, on occasion gathered in international research groups, and attention to women's concerns in international law, and also the emergence, as previously discussed, of a great variety of 'feminist approaches to international law' since the early 1990s. However, the rise of women in the ranks of international law academia has yet to be substantially translated into more attention to women's histories in international law.

6.6   The Gendering Impact on Knowledge Production Processes

Engaging with the programmatic aim of redressing women's historical invisibility, both as a movement and individually, in diplomacy and international law will contribute to enriching the historical sociological dimension of international law. However, in spite of the pattern of re-inclusion of traditionally excluded groups in the history of international law, as examined in Chapter 4 and as we shall see in more in detail in Chapters 8 and 10, by recourse, inter alia, to international intellectual legal biography over the last decades, the study of the lives, works and times of individual women has largely remained at the margins of international legal scholarship.

The intellectual biographical focus in their historical contexts on women in what has historically been deemed the 'man's world' of international law is therefore part of 'engendering legal history.' Doing this involves integrating, as T. A. Thomas and T. J. Boisseau have noted, 'the stories of women into the dominant history of the law [to] reconstruct the assumed contours of history'[165] in the intellectual and practical development of the discipline over time. This includes developing what

---

[165] Tracy A. Thomas and Tracey J. Boisseau, 'Introduction: law, history, and feminism', in Tracy A. Thomas and Tracey J. Boisseau (eds.), *Feminist Legal History: Essays on Women and Law* (New York: New York University Press, 2011), pp. 1–32 at 1.

feminist historians see as the existing 'one dimensional historical accounts of women's legal rights, adding new events, providing new details and suggesting alternative explanations of the traditional historical narrative'.[166] However, realizing the great potential contribution of women's histories to the study of the historical sociology of international law through exploration of the historical engagements of both individual women and women's social movements with international law involves expanding the scope of these investigations beyond their traditional site in the Western and northern worlds. Indeed, the historiographical soil is already a sufficiently nurtured field for a fruitful collaboration between gender/feminist approaches and both the 'globalist' and 'post-colonial' approaches to the history of international law, which were examined in Chapters 5 and 4 respectively, to continue expanding in the years to come.

Second, in the wake of the much-discussed phenomenon of the fragmentation of international law, which arises from the diversification and expansion experienced by the international legal order in recent decades,[167] the history of international law is also currently experiencing a parallel process of historiographical fragmentation. This process, in which international legal historians retrace the historical genealogies of particular sub-disciplines in international law, provides a new historiographical space for the inclusion of women's histories and their contributions to the intellectual history of each sub-discipline at different moments in its historical development. In fact, it is within the general framework provided by the history of international human rights law that the history of the successes and frustrations in the struggle for gender equality and the recognition and effective implementation of women's rights through international law has traditionally found its place.[168] The history of international criminal law and international humanitarian law are adjacent sub-fields where a woman-centred perspective has also developed over recent years. While international criminal law has attracted historical attention, in particular regarding the efforts addressed to the international criminalizing of conducts

[166] Ibid.
[167] International Law Commission, *Fragmentation of International Law: Difficulties Arising from the Diversification and Expansion of International Law: Report of the International Law Commission* (13 April 2006, finalized by Martti Koskenniemi), legal.un.org/ilc/documentation/english/a_cn4_l682.pdf.
[168] Kasey McCall-Smith, Jan Wouters, and Felipe Gómez Isa (eds.), *The Faces of Human Rights* (Oxford: Hart Publishing, 2019); Fraser, 'Becoming human', pp. 853–906.

particularly affecting women in times of conflict or war,[169] it is in parallel also becoming a site for historiographical experimentation, as is shown by Tallgren's engagement with the histories of women perpetrators of international crimes.[170] The continuing study of women's contributions to shaping internationally typified rights and actions deemed illegal under international law may contribute to further illuminating the normative development of the history of international human rights law, international humanitarian law, and international criminal law. However, while the bulk of feminist international legal historical attention has focused on these areas, the historical normative development of other specialized international legal regimes is similarly open to investigation from a woman-centred perspective.

Third, the conceptual history of international law may also benefit from a deeper understanding of how the intellectual genealogy of the discipline has, arguably, been shaped by the dominance of 'male thought structures' and ways of thinking in the development of its main legal doctrines and fundamental concepts over time.[171] Moreover, the application of a feminist gender-conceptual critique of fundamental concepts in international law in a historical perspective may also in parallel unearth little-known female historical contributions to the intellectual shaping of the discipline and in so doing fill out the incomplete record of international law's conceptual past and normative categories beyond the realm of some maximalist structural tenets.

Fourth, gender and the history of international law also have much to contribute to the renewal of historiographical perspectives, the selection of topics and scales and (owing to the highly self-reflective nature of feminist approaches) the issues of perspective and positionality (such as on geography, social status or race) from a distinct women's perspective. This would find a fertile ground in a time of salutary rejuvenation of the field in which the study of historiographical and methodological issues is becoming increasingly sophisticated in international legal history. Similarly, the larger cultivation of gender and the history of international law may also contribute to a critique of established periodizations in the history of international law. This, as we shall see in more detail in Chapter 11, can lead to the inclusion of gender-based alternative

---

[169] See, e.g., Doris Buss, 'Performing legal order: some feminist thoughts on international criminal law' (2011) 11 *International Criminal Law Review* 409–423.

[170] Tallgren, '*Voglio una donna!*', pp. 110–129.

[171] See Charlesworth and Chinkin, *Boundaries of International Law*.

periodizations of the historical development of international law.[172] An obvious illustration of the potential of women's histories to flesh out the bones of such an alternative periodization as a platform for new research is how Concepcion Arenal's long-neglected *Ensayo sobre el derecho de gentes*, the first treatise on international law in the modern sense published by a woman, offers a hitherto ignored or unknown milestone in a still-missing gender-based historical periodization of international law.[173]

6.7 Historiographical Debates, Confluences, and Critiques

The history of women in international law presents many points of confluence with other 'contributory or compensatory histories' of international law,[174] namely post-colonial history and, to a certain extent, global history. Some of these confluences naturally ensue from the existence of potential points of convergence between feminist approaches to international law (or at least some of them) and other intellectual/ scientific movements in international legal scholarship, namely with the (so-called) Third World Approaches to International Law (TWAIL) some of the main tenets and overall historiographical orientation of which were examined in Chapter 4. Indeed, according to Dianne Otto, 'TWAIL and feminism' have 'much in common' because 'both are bodies of theory about power, and how it works systematically to privilege the interests of some groups over the majority of disadvantaged "others"'. Moreover, she adds that 'both bodies of work are aiming to better understand how hierarchical systems of power reproduce themselves, and thus to find ways to contest and transform them'.[175]

Despite these points in common, the most recurrent academic writers on these trends have also marked distances between their different scholarly persuasions on account of problems of 'essentialism' and the so-called imperialist 'Western feminists' imposition of their conceptual frameworks and reform agendas on non-Western women.[176] Regarding

---

[172] Ignacio de la Rasilla, 'The problem of periodization in the history of international law' (2019) 37 *Law and History Review* 275–308.

[173] For a detailed analysis, on part of which this chapter builds, see de la Rasilla, 'Concepción Arenal'.

[174] Tallgren, '*Voglio una donna!*', p. 115.

[175] Dianne Otto, 'The gastronomics of TWAIL's feminist flavourings: some lunch-time offerings' (2007) 9 *International Community Law Review* 345–352 at 347–348.

[176] See Chimni, *International Law*.

the first of these, the 'contested issue' of feminist 'essentialism' revolves around the fact that, according to Chinkin, 'taking sex or gender as a point of identity and examining the consequences of that identity assumes this to be the key defining characteristic' while 'in reality people have multiple, intersecting identities, for example racial and ethnic identities, nationality, age, religion, disability, sexuality, education and class',[177] which cannot be isolated from one another in holistically approaching any individual. Regarding the second, a concern has also often been voiced regarding the idea of 'feminist imperialism' which revolves around 'the accusation that women from the north are seeking to civilize women from the south without perceiving their own privileged position as closer to the centres of power and influence'. Moreover, as Chinkin argues, 'some women remain even further at the peripheries of the international legal system – migrant women, indigenous women, refugee women'.[178]

On the other hand, from a TWAIL perspective 'the absence of a feminist history of international law', which as Bhupinder S. Chimni has remarked 'is yet to be written',[179] has been regretted; Chimni adds furthermore that 'when this history is written it will allow a complex and integrated narration of the ways in which international law has constituted the categories of gender (and class and race) and legitimized oppression against women over the centuries'.[180] This maximalist charging of international law with nothing less than the responsibility for the oppression of women around the world over the centuries in academic fairness needs to be contrasted with the fact that one of the historiographical critiques often voiced against post-colonial approaches to the history of international law has, as was discussed in Chapter 4, in fact been TWAIL's almost exclusive attention to male historical characters and its extremely limited historical engagement with the subaltern condition of women under both culturally and religiously entrenched social patriarchal structures before and during the Western waves of colonialism and also after these had formally ended. Moreover, TWAIL's historiography is largely inspired, as was previously shown,

---

[177] Chinkin, 'Feminism', p. 5.
[178] Ibid.
[179] Chimni, *International Law*, p. 481.
[180] Bhupinder S. Chimni, 'Concluding response from Professor Chimni: international law and world order', 29 December 2017, www.ejiltalk.org/concluding-response-from-pro fessor-chimni-international-law-and-world-order/.

by a historical presentist orientation which has made its leitmotiv the denunciation of a contemporary form of neo-colonialism channelled through international law and international institutions that under the cloak of democracy and human rights (including women's rights!) has, in the TWAIL view, been 'haunting the Third World'.[181] Once again, certain blind spots and biases in different contemporary historiographical trends of thought which are, almost by definition, prone to exclusionary dynamics regarding issues that do not sit well with their core persuasion become apparent when they are examined through the lenses of multi-perspectivity.

Another divergence between TWAIL and feminist approaches to international law has to do with the historiographical interest they have shown in their intellectual precursors. Recent post-colonial historiographies initially found their precursors, as we saw in Chapter 4, in the age of decolonization of the African and Asian continents in the aftermath of World War II and only later moved back in time to examine earlier experiences of imperialism and other post-colonial contributions, namely from Latin America, to scholarship and the practice of, international law. By contrast, feminist approaches have remained interested in the contemporary and most recent history of the movement within the discipline,[182] rather than in the systematic study of earlier historical episodes and figures involving women in international law. This relative lack of historization of international law from the perspective of women may be due to the relatively late arrival of feminism, in comparison to postcolonial approaches, as a methodologically structured discourse in international legal scholarship. It may also have to do with the 'practical ethics' informing the underlying feminist activism in the present, which in turn also generally informs the persuasions of different feminist strands in international legal scholarship. Moreover, the relative lack of women's histories in international law may also be connected with the fact that, similarly to international relations feminism, feminist approaches to international law have evolved 'in both relation and reaction to mainstream' international law 'and its insistence that feminism

---

[181] Bhupinder S. Chimni, 'Third World Approaches to International Law: a manifesto' (2006) 8 *International Community Law Review* 3–27 at 3. See further Bhupinder S. Chimni, 'International institutions today: an imperial global state in the making' (2004) 15 *European Journal of International Law* 1–37.

[182] See Karen Engle, 'Feminist governance and international law: from liberal to carceral feminism', in Janet Halley et al. (eds.), *Governance Feminism: Notes from the Field* (Minneapolis: University of Minnesota Press, 2018), pp. 3–30.

[should] set out and defend its theoretical approach and research agenda'.[183] This defensively assertive methodological orientation may have led feminist international law scholars to remain too attached to abstract theoretical and methodological tenets and debates that new generations may well now see as already integrated within the discipline and therefore not attentive enough to contribute to new trends within international legal scholarship, including the turn to the history of international law from a woman-centred perspective.

6.8   Conclusion

There is an extraordinary potential for the further development of the field of gender and the history of international law in today's deeply sociologically transformed 'invisible college' of international lawyers, in which the incorporation of women in various leading international law roles that hitherto were the exclusive patrimony of men has been little short of exponential in many regions in the world, albeit far from all.

To develop this field would first be a long-overdue tribute to historically neglected female role models in the long-standing struggle mediated by international law for the peaceful resolution of international disputes and gender equality across the globe. Indeed, fostering a pattern of re-inclusion of women in the history of international law with reference to individual women, or women as a group, in its writing and making, or as influential agents of international legal change, can contribute, as examined earlier, to deepening the historical narrative of international law in several directions and therefore to fostering new knowledge production processes about the multidimensional relationship between history and international law.

Feminist approaches to international law, with their baggage of theoretical sophistication and their continuation of a hard-fought tradition of struggling activism, appear well positioned as analytical lenses to employ in the exploration of women's histories of international law. However, these approaches to international law, which in spite of all their internal variety may all be said to have 'an overtly political agenda for change: the advancement and empowerment of women',[184] are not the only approaches that could, by engaging the history of women in international law, help to provide, as Koskenniemi once suggested (but never followed

---

[183] True, 'The ethics of feminism', p. 417.
[184] Chinkin, 'Feminism', p. 3.

through himself), 'a more complete image of the profession's political heritage'.[185]

Like any other theme in the history of international law, women's histories in international law do not require per se to be written by female authors,[186] and neither do they need to be militant or overtly feminist in orientation, or even particularly influenced by one or other strand of 'feminism', to make good international law histories. In fact, like any other histories in international law, women's histories need first and foremost to exist *more* in international legal scholarship. For this to happen they need, first, to be less generally evoked in their imagined absence as if there were some kind of 'lost' or even suppressed and therefore irretrievable history of women in international law which was worth only talking about in passing. Instead, many untold women's histories which have for long remain hidden in plain sight should first and foremost be properly researched and then effectively written so that they may become better integrated in a more inclusive, more diversified, and less-male-centred history of international law which should be committed, as Michel Foucault put it in regard to his historical genealogical method, to 'relentless erudition'.[187]

---

[185] Martti Koskenniemi, *The Gentle Civilizer of Nations*, p. 9.
[186] Frédéric Mégret, 'The laws of war and the structure of masculine power' (2018) 7 *Melbourne Journal of International Law* 200–226.
[187] Michel Foucault, 'Nietzsche, genealogy, history', in Donald F. Bouchard (ed.), Language, *Counter-memory, Practice: Selected Essays and Interviews* (Ithaca, NY: Cornell University Press, 1977), pp. 139–164 at 140.

7

Normative Approaches to the History
of International Law

7.1 Introduction

International norms, principles, and legal doctrines are always present in all histories of international law. Without them, the histories being narrated would arguably appear to be instead histories of something else. However, the extent to which these juridical identifiers are the central focus of the narrative, or recede instead into the background to different degrees until they occasionally become a silent frame of reference for the historical narrative, varies greatly across different approaches. The category of normative approaches to the history of international law belongs to the history of concepts within the general categorization of the 'modes or forms in which history' and, by extension, the history of international law 'may be written'.[1] As a form of conceptual history, normative approaches are commonly recognized as the prototypical illustration of what passes as international jurists' history. This, according to Valentina Vadi, is a form of history written by international 'lawyers [who] tend to be interested in the past for the light it throws on the present and consider it as "a self-contained universe", tracing the genealogy of given concepts with little if any attention to the context'.[2] This approach is generally distinguished from that of historians whose enquiries are oriented to casting light on the past for its own sake and not for what it allegedly 'brought about'.[3] Being less generally informed by a juridical form of functional presentism, their scholarly work is more receptive to historical professional methods and to the reconstruction of the particular historical context, intellectual, sociological, and

---

[1] Bardo Fassbender and Anne Peters, 'Introduction: towards a global history of international law', in Bardo Fassbender and Anne Peters (eds.), *The Oxford Handbook of the History of International Law* (Oxford: Oxford University Press, 2012), pp. 1–26.

[2] Valentina Vadi, 'International law and its histories: methodological risks and opportunities' (2017) 58 *Harvard International Law Journal* 311–352 at 312.

[3] Ibid., pp. 320–321.

otherwise, relevant to their object of historical research, with acute attention, as was seen in Chapter 2, to avoiding the pitfalls of anachronism and other related historical fallacies.

Since ancient times, history has had pride of place as a 'material source'[4] in the long-lasting historical processes which led to the crystallization of international law as a separate legal discipline. The relative scientific autonomy of international law as a separate legal system from history and a markedly speculative and philosophical tradition whereby natural law was the main source of the *jus naturae et gentium* gained credentials throughout the nineteenth century and was further fostered in the wake of the rise of the codification movement. This gained a new channel of expression and developmental force through the establishment of the first international law associations, inheritors of earlier 'associations for the progress of the social sciences',[5] in the 1870s. This process, which took place under the influence of the rise of positivism and empiricism, mirrored similar processes in domestic legal systems where the rise of the scientific method ran in parallel with the spread of the liberal theory of politics and the principles of the rule of law in the formation of Western liberal and constitutional states in the mid- to late nineteenth century.

The new professional programme channelled the tendency towards juridification of the outer realm in its search for the identification and development of a positive international law corpus. It did so through the recollection and examination of usages, customs, text-writers of authority (in which 'the principle of tradition and authority was predominant'),[6] treaties, and gradually a growing repertoire of both municipal case law on international matters and international arbitration awards, all of which re-conducted in a more systematically normative sense previous studies of diplomatic history. The gradual establishment of university chairs in international law across Europe, the Americas, and, far more limitedly, in Asia, further contributed to the systematic academic configuration of international law as a field of scientific study. A number of early international conventions, namely The Hague Peace Conferences of 1898 and

---

[4] Robert Kolb, 'Legal history as a source: from classical to modern international law', in Jean d'Aspremont and Samantha Besson (eds.), *The Oxford Handbook of the Sources of International Law* (Oxford: Oxford University Press, 2017), pp. 279–300 at 299.

[5] See, e.g., Vincent Genin, *Le laboratoire belge du droit international: une communauté épistémique et internationale de juristes (1869–1914)* (Brussels: Académie Royale de Belgique, 2018).

[6] Kolb, 'Legal history as a source', p. 283.

1907, reflected the international legal codification spirit in a limited set of areas, thus crowning the normative and intellectual evolution that occurred in the 'long nineteenth century',[7] during which discussions on the notion of sources of international law had become firmly rooted in treatises written by publicists.[8] If Jeremy Bentham, the coiner of the term 'international law' in the late eighteenth century, had with the new denomination sought to take a departure from the term 'law of nations', which by then was dominated by a morally based speculative brand of natural law, and to point instead to the existence of a body of positive codified international norms,[9] in 1905 Lassa Oppenheim could assuredly declare that '[o]nly a positive Law of Nations can be a branch of the science of law'.[10]

The systemic approach to norm identification in international law was definitively crystallized in Article 38 of the Statute of the Permanent Court of International Justice (PCIJ) on the 'sources' available to the first international court with a universal vocation. The same international legal history, which as a *material* source of international law had become enlisted to identify the secondary norms of the international legal system, has since then become the handmaiden of an international legal system now provided – at least, unofficially – with a list of *formal* sources as a 'means for the determination of rules of law'.[11] According to some, the establishment of a system of applicable sources by the first international court with general jurisdiction and permanent character represented a paradigm shift,[12] which contributed to consolidating the international

---

[7] Inge Van Hulle and Randall Lesaffer (eds.), *International Law in the Long Nineteenth Century 1776–1914: From the Public Law of Europe to Global International Law?* (Leiden: Brill/Nijhoff, 2019).

[8] Miloš Vec, 'Sources in the 19th century European tradition: the myth of positivism', in Jean d'Aspremont and Samantha Besson (eds.), *The Oxford Handbook of the Sources of International Law* (Oxford: Oxford University Press, 2017), pp. 121–145.

[9] Mark Weston Janis, 'Jeremy Bentham and the fashioning of "international law"' (1984) 78 *American Journal of International Law* 405–418.

[10] Lassa Oppenheim, *International Law: A Treatise*, 2 vols. (London: Longmans, Green and Company, 1905), vol. 1, p. 92.

[11] Ole Spiermann, 'The history of Article 38 of the Statute of the International Court of Justice: "a purely platonic discussion"?', in Jean d'Aspremont and Samantha Besson (eds.), *The Oxford Handbook of the Sources of International Law* (Oxford: Oxford University Press, 2017), pp. 165–178 at 165.

[12] Mark Weston Janis, 'Sources in the meta-history of international law: a little meta-theory – paradigms, Article 38, and the sources of international law', in Jean d'Aspremont and Samantha Besson (eds.), *The Oxford Handbook of the Sources of International Law* (Oxford: Oxford University Press, 2017), pp. 264–278.

legal-positivist method.[13] For classical positivists, very broadly speaking, 'international law is a system of objective principles and neutral rules that emanate principally from States' will, either directly, through treaty, or indirectly through international custom'.[14] A set of general methodological boundaries further derive from this traditional characterization of international law as a 'unitary system' that, because it is scientifically 'autonomous' and theoretically 'gapless', is able to provide a 'correct legal answer' to any international juridical problem.[15] The first boundary derives from the centrality of state sovereignty authoritatively considered as nothing less, as the successor to the PCIJ would years later put it, than 'the fundamental principle … on which the whole of international law rests'.[16] The second general methodological boundary is based on the distinction between 'law' and 'non-law' that ensues from the theory of sources accounting for the existence of 'formal pedigrees for establishing the validity of rules, or for explaining their normative force'.[17] The third methodological boundary that traditional positivist approaches often draw is the distinction between legal and extra-legal considerations, the latter being immaterial to international law.[18]

These generally described methodological boundaries in turn condition the interaction between international law and history. As was briefly seen in Chapter 2, according to the tripartite typology proposed by Matthew Craven and elaborated by Randall Lesaffer, this interaction may be examined using the categories of 'history in international law', the 'history of international law', and 'international law in history', spanning a broad intertwined continuum.[19] The first category is often seen as the preserve of international lawyers, whose purpose in resorting

---

[13] See, distinguishing different strands of positivism, Stephen C. Neff, *Justice among Nations: A History of International Law* (Cambridge, MA: Harvard University Press, 2014), p. 226. See also Monica Garcia-Salmones Rovira, *The Project of Positivism in International Law* (Oxford: Oxford University Press, 2013).

[14] Andrea Bianchi, *International Law Theories: An Inquiry into Different Ways of Thinking* (Oxford: Oxford University Press, 2016), p. 21.

[15] Ibid.

[16] Military and Paramilitary Activities (Nicaragua v. United States of America), Merits [1986] ICJ Rep 14, para. 263.

[17] Bianchi, *International Law Theories*, p. 21.

[18] Ibid.

[19] Randall Lesaffer, 'Law and history: law between past and present', https://lirias.kuleuven .be/1856246, p. 6. This essay also appears in Bart van Klink and Sanne Taekema (eds.), *Law and Method: Interdisciplinary Research into Law* (Tübingen: Mohr Siebeck, 2011), pp. 133–152.

to history is to contribute to a form of argumentative legal closure, whereas the third is the most permeable of all three to engagement by historians in their search for historical disclosure. Between these two, contemporary literature on the normative 'history of international law' has mirrored a move towards a greater socio-contextualization and interdisciplinarization yet without losing its juridical underpinnings and the strong pull they exert on the cultivation of it.

This chapter examines this tripartite typology with attention to its impact on knowledge production processes and the confluences, debates, and critiques generated in the recent historical international legal literature. First, as discussed in Section 7.2, the category of 'history in international law', which generally corresponds to the uses of history in international law and is, as such, largely influenced by a form of juridical functional presentism, can be divided into four levels ranging from the uses of historical materials, normative and otherwise, to interpret, identify, and apply international law. Section 7.3 then examines the category of 'history of international law', which is generally coincidental with the 'internal' normative approach and can be deployed at both the micro and the macro levels to study both the history of specialized international legal regimes and the history of general public international law more broadly. As discussed in Section 7.4, the category of 'international law in history', which broadly coincides in the normative domain with the so-called external normative approach, is more directly concerned with the contextual interaction between society and international law and so is very much open to a diversity of historical methodologies, particularly but not only regarding the history of concepts underlying international legal materials. Section 7.5 considers whether a new form of methodological hybridity attentive to both juridical and historical purposes can encompass this general three-tiered typology of interfaces between history and international law.

7.2   History in International Law: Interpretation, Identification, Application

Nowhere does Benedetto Croce's oft-quoted statement that 'every history is contemporary history'[20] appear truer than in the practice-oriented realm of international legal history, where the past is generally retrieved,

[20] Benedetto Croce, *Theory and History of Historiography*, trans. Douglas Ainslie (London: George G. Harrap & Company, 1921), p. 12.

discussed, and enlisted to serve a particular instrumental juridical purpose in the present. Because of the technical international legal specialization it presupposes, its cultivators consequently for the most part tend
to be international lawyers by training and profession acting in different
capacities, ranging from legal counsels to arbitrators or judges in international adjudicative processes.

Two broad categories of 'history in international law' may initially be
distinguished. One of these concerns the use of historical normative or
legal materials *proprio sensu* – norms, principles or legal doctrines,
typically but not only in the form of invoked precedents – for normative
purposes. However, the uses of history under the gravitational pull of
juridical functional presentism also extend beyond the realm of the
purposes of norm identification and norm interpretation to encompass
the appraisal of factual or historical evidence in specific contemporary
legal categories. This dimension, which is illustrated by the domain of the
application of international law in international adjudicative settings,
may in turn be subdivided into two levels. In the first, the juridical
relevance of the historical or factual context is circumscribed by what is
deemed to be legally relevant in the framework established by certain
legal categories, whether they are specific temporally related or general
ones. The second – although jurisdictionally speaking, preliminary – level
concerns how the outlines of a dispute and its resolution are invariably
conditioned by the 'distinct temporal elements of particular rules'[21] and
the substantive limitations faced by international courts and tribunals in
appraising past facts and conducts in the light of established legal
categories. Finally, a third general category of 'history in international
law' may be identified to account for the influence of international
judicial decisions in shaping the development of historical narratives.
These categories will now be briefly examined.

The first type of 'history in international law' includes the argumentative use of historical legal precedents in order to support the application
of a legal norm, rule, or practice according to the 'fixed meaning that
has been established by past usage'[22] or, in contrast, to suggest that its
interpretation 'must change over time to adapt to changing

---

[21] David J. Bederman, 'Foreign office international legal history', in Matthew Craven,
Malgosia Fitzmaurice, and Maria Vogiatzi (eds.), *Time, History and International Law*
(Leiden: Martinus Nijhoff/Brill, 2007), pp. 43–64 at 43.

[22] Robert W. Gordon, 'The struggle over the past' (1996) 44 *Cleveland State Law Review*
123–143 at 124–126.

conditions'.[23] This approach, which is apparent in the most usual ways in which international legal practitioners tackle history, what David Bederman critically referred to as 'foreign office international legal history',[24] coincides with the 'dynamic' and 'static' attitudes of lawyers to history in Robert Gordon's tripartite ad hoc taxonomy. The 'dynamic attitude' stands alongside the 'static' one in that the 'common denominator of those two attitudes is that they look to the past for authority'. Meanwhile, a third attitude, which Gordon terms the 'critical attitude', aims to 'destroy, or anyway to question, the authority of the past'.[25] This 'critical attitude' in international law underlies reflections such as that of David Kennedy, for whom 'an argument about a rule or principle, or institutional technique in international law is almost always an argument about history – that the particular norm proffered has a provenance as law rather than politics, has become general rather than specific, has come through history to stand outside history'.[26]

Whereas a critical attitude stands somewhat outside the legal box and, as we have seen in Chapter 3, seeks to historicize and socio-contextualize the origins and subsequent historical evolution of a rule, principle, or institutional technique in order to show discontinuities in its strategic and political use over time, there are many echoes of the static and dynamic attitudes in the use of precedents in international judicial legal reasoning. A static attitude may, for instance, be prompted by considerations of judicial economy such as when the International Court of Justice (ICJ) mechanically resorts to its own past jurisprudence in order to buttress the authority of its decisions in both the jurisdictional and merits stages of its proceedings. By contrast, a more dynamic attitude, which stresses the importance of fleshing out the meaning of the provisions of an international treaty to adapt to changing times, is apparent in the case law of the European Court of Human Rights, which regularly re-examines its own jurisprudence in order to interpret the European Convention of Human Rights as a 'living legal instrument'.[27]

---

[23] Ibid.
[24] Bederman, 'Foreign office'.
[25] R. Gordon, 'The struggle', pp. 124–126.
[26] David Kennedy, 'The disciplines of international law and policy' (1999) 12 *Leiden Journal of International Law* 9–133 at 88.
[27] See, e.g., Kanstantsin Dzehtsiarou, 'European consensus and the evolutive interpretation of the European Convention on Human Rights' (2011) 12 *German Law Journal* 1730–1745.

The normative purposes which the past is resorted to as a means of norm interpretation also include examination of the inclusion of a provision in an international treaty in order to identify the original meaning of its composite terms in the light of the *travaux preparatoires* when recourse to them is advised by Article 32 of the 1969 Vienna Convention on the Law of Treaties (VCLT) as a supplementary means of interpretation.[28] Similarly, there are many cases where the normative past is argumentatively enlisted for norm-identification purposes, such as in the determination of the existence and scope of a norm of customary international law on the basis of past state practice and *opinio iuris sive necessitatis*. The purposes to which 'history in international law' may be put also include a doctrinal and international semi-legislative dimension in many a related effort at international norm entrepreneurship, or proposals for *lege ferenda* in international law, and similarly in tasks related to the codification and progressive development of international law that began to become institutionalized in the interwar period with the establishment by the League of Nations of the Committee for the Progressive Codification of International Law in 1924.[29] Although it did not offer much in terms of outcomes, this set the ground for the work on the codification and progressive development of international law mandated to the International Law Commission (ILC) in 1949 under the UN Charter.

As we have seen, the first category of 'history in international law' is characterized by the use of history for normative purposes in the present, and it concerns the interpretation or identification of principles, norms, or legal practices from the past. The second one, in contrast, concerns how the factual or historical past is filtered through present legal categories in the application of international law. The area of international adjudication clearly illustrates the two subsequent levels at which engagement with history is mediated through international law.

The first of these levels includes the reliance, as David Bederman notes, on historical materials by 'arbitrators and judges [who] are increasingly called upon to consider historical evidence, and to render a forensic analysis of its putative weight and significance'[30] in the light of legally established categories. In some of these cases, such as ones involving

[28] Bederman, 'Foreign office', p. 59.
[29] Shabtai Rosenne (ed.), *League of Nations: Committee of Experts for the Progressive Codification of International Law 1925–1928* (New York: Oceana Publications, 1972).
[30] Bederman, 'Foreign office', p. 45.

international boundary dispute settlement,[31] there are a 'series of positive legal institutions, which refer to historical aspects interrelated to the law' such as, for example, the 'legal concepts of "historic rights", "historic waters", or "historic bays"'.[32] However, besides the domain of application of these particular temporal legal institutions, the fact remains that every single application of international law involves reference to a historical or factual past and therefore involves a legal qualification of past – or in some cases even ongoing – events, conducts, and facts. This practice extends through every single international legal regime, be it in the area of international criminal law (e.g. through the legal determination of whether a past factual situation amounts to a war crime, genocide, and so on), international trade law, or any breach of an international obligation established by a treaty or customary international law covered by a system of international adjudication, or even merely compliance mechanisms for the monitoring of international legal obligations. In a nutshell, the application of international legal rules invariably involves a contextual historical investigation mediated by other legal categories, which in providing the criteria for the relevance of legally qualifying the past also automatically bring into play the application of corresponding qualifiers (e.g. the circumstances precluding wrongfulness), means of proof, and relevant fact-finding mechanisms specific to each international legal regime. It is within the boundaries of this legally framed historical context that external context-attentive historiographical methods find a straightforward application in the domain of 'international law in history', and may also come back to the fore in the domain of the 'history in international law', as was seen in Chapter 2 and as we shall examine again below.

The second level in the domain of the application of international law concerns how the outlines of a dispute and its eventual resolution are invariably conditioned by 'distinct temporal elements of particular rules'.[33] These include 'jurisdictional consent and continuing acts under the international law of state responsibility', the retrospective application of international law rules, prescriptive limitations (including

---

[31] Giovanni Stefano, 'Time factor and territorial disputes', in Marcelo Kohen and Mamadou Hébié (eds.), *Research Handbook on Territorial Disputes in International Law* (Cheltenham: Edward Elgar Publishing, 2018), pp. 397–416.

[32] Kolb, 'Legal History as a source', p. 280.

[33] Bederman, 'Foreign office', p. 43.

international statutes of limitations, laches, estoppel,[34] and acquiescence), and the principle of 'intertemporal law'[35] or 'inter-temporal rule', according to which, in Judge Huber's widely discussed formulation, 'a judicial fact must be appreciated in the light of the law contemporary it, and not of the law in force at the time such a dispute in regard falls to be settled'.[36] The ensuing generally ambivalent relationship of history to international courts becomes particularly apparent in the case of international criminal trials, where historical controversial questions are particularly acute. However, courts can, admittedly, have only a limited role in dealing with them because of the tensions they face as they 'seek to address diverging aims':[37] on the one hand to 'tell the whole truth and to create a historical record'[38] and on the other to adhere to jurisdictional and evidentiary rules in order to be able to render justice to the parties in the case while safeguarding the fairness of the judicial process.

Indeed, the procedural and substantive limitations that criminal international courts must confront when seeking to create a complete historical record are manifold. In international criminal procedure, where the jurisdictional and evidentiary rules are commonly regarded as being originally tilted in favour of the 'adversarial model',[39] these limitations include, as Fergal Gaynor notes, those constraints that such courts face determined by the scope of their jurisdiction, whether it be *ratione materiae, ratione temporis,* or *ratione loci.*[40] These limitations also extend to the 'temporal, territorial and substantive extent of the indictment',[41] which furthermore can be affected by the 'workings' of a 'plea agreement'.[42] Other procedural constraints affecting the creation of a 'complete historical record' by international criminal courts flow from the

---

[34] Thomas Cottier and Jörg Paul Müller, 'Estoppel', in *Max Planck Encyclopedia of Public International Law* (2007), opil.ouplaw.com/view/10.1093/law:epil/9780199231690/law-9780199231690-e1401?rskey=k4SaGa&result=13&prd=OPIL.

[35] Markus Kotzur, 'Intertemporal law', in *Max Planck Encyclopedia of Public International Law* (2008), opil.ouplaw.com/view/10.1093/law:epil/9780199231690/law-9780199231690-e1433?rskey=VD6i3z&result=2&prd=OPIL.

[36] Rosalyn Higgins, 'Time and the law: international perspectives on an old problem' (1997) 46 *International and Comparative Law Quarterly* 501–520 at 515–520.

[37] Fergal Gaynor, 'Uneasy partners – evidence, truth and history in international trials' (2012) 10 *Journal of International Criminal Justice* 1257–1275 at 1258.

[38] Ibid.

[39] Kai Ambos, 'International criminal procedure: "adversarial", "inquisitorial" or mixed?' (2003) 5 *International Criminal Law Review* 1–37 at 5.

[40] Gaynor, 'Uneasy partners', p. 1263.

[41] Ibid., p. 1266.

[42] Ibid., pp. 1268–1269.

effects of prosecutorial discretion,[43] confidentiality restrictions, and a range of reasons for the exclusion of evidence rendered by a party.[44] Moreover, the 'historical objectives' pursued through international criminal adjudication can be affected by implementation of a higher burden of proof, the 'beyond reasonable doubt test'[45] and the fact that 'what may be historically relevant may be legally irrelevant'.[46]

The third category of interaction between history and international law in the domain of 'history in international law' concerns the study of the effects that the engagement of international law with history may have on historical research. Indeed, as we have seen, academic work on the relationship between international criminal trials and history has understandably raised doubts as to the extent that 'courts are well equipped to make authoritative findings regarding representation of the past'.[47] To put it differently, while, as Joseph Kunz remarked in assessing the 'judicial cosmopolitan'[48] ambitions of Hans Kelsen's *Peace through Law* in 1944,[49] it might well be 'an illusion to believe that it will ever be possible to transform world history into nothing but a court procedure',[50] an indirect – and often overlooked – legacy of judicial proceedings, both international and domestic alike (e.g. under memory laws)[51] is their impact on the expansion of historical research on the context in which atrocities took place and both the historical patterns that led to them and their aftermaths.[52]

The constructive role that international legal proceedings may have in the advance of historical narratives is, for instance, particularly relevant

---

[43] Ibid., pp. 1264–1265.

[44] Ibid., pp. 1269–1271.

[45] Ibid., p. 1264.

[46] Ibid.

[47] Carsten Stahn, 'Re-constructing history through courts? Legacy in international criminal justice' (9 June 2015), ssrn. com/abstract=2616491, p. 6.

[48] Joseph Kunz, cited in Danilo Zolo, 'Hans Kelsen: international peace through international law' (1998) 9 *European Journal of International Law* 306–324.

[49] Hans Kelsen, *Peace through Law* (Chapel Hill: University of North Carolina Press, 1944).

[50] Joseph L. Kunz, 'Compulsory international adjudication and maintenance of peace' (1944) 38 *American Journal of International Law* 673–678.

[51] See, e.g., Luigi Cajani, 'Criminal laws on history: the case of the European Union' (2011) 11 *Historein* 19–48.

[52] Ignacio de la Rasilla, 'Playing hide and seek with "Vergangenheit, die nicht vergehen will" ("a past that will not pass") in the history of international law', in George Ulrich and Ineta Ziemele (eds.), *How International Law Works in Times of Crisis* (Oxford: Oxford University Press, 2019), pp. 223–239.

in the study of the field of transitional justice, which is understood as 'the collective reckoning with the legacies of human rights abuse after dictatorship or violent conflict',[53] with the central role it ascribes to the 'right to truth'[54] and its corollary the 'duty to remember' on the part of the state. This is due to the importance transitional justice experts ascribe to the 'healing force of remembering' or 'remembrance as justice' and its commitment to establish 'historical truths' through different mechanisms (e.g. truth and reconciliation commissions) for the purpose of 'reconciliation through truth telling'.[55] The constructive role that international legal proceedings may have in the advance of historical narratives is also relevant in all sorts of 'memory studies', in particular branches such as international humanitarian law,[56] and in the construction of 'collective memories'. The latter both influence and are influenced by international tribunals acting as agents of memory, whether they do so by commemorating a historical event for the sake of remembering the suffering of victims of human rights violations,[57] or through constructing or developing historical narratives when they compose judicial-historical pronouncements in rendering their judicial decisions.[58]

7.3 History of International Law: Between Juridical Presentism and Interdisciplinarization

Occupying a middle position on the continuum between the domain of 'history in international law' and that of 'international law in history', the area of the normative 'history of international law' is what legal historians also diversely term 'traditional legal history' and define as 'a historic

---

[53] Berber Bevernage, 'Writing the past out of the present: history and the politics of time in transitional justice' (2010) 69 *History Workshop Journal Issue* 111–131 at 111.
[54] Patricia Naftali, 'The "right to truth" in international law: the "last Utopia"?', in Uladzislau Belavusau and Aleksandra Gliszczyńska-Grabias (eds.), *Law and Memory: Towards Legal Governance of History* (Cambridge, UK: Cambridge University Press, 2017), pp. 70–88.
[55] Berber Bevernage, 'Transitional justice and historiography: challenges, dilemmas and possibilities' (2014) 13 *Macquarie Law Journal* 7–24 at 7.
[56] Vincent Bernard, 'Memory: a new humanitarian frontier' (2019) 101 *International Review of the Red Cross* (special issue on memory and war) 1–9.
[57] For examples drawn for the case law of the Inter-American Court of Human Rights, see Moshe Hirsch, 'The role of international tribunals in the development of historical narratives' (2018) 20 *Journal of the History of International Law* 391–428.
[58] Ibid.

[al] analysis of law rather than a legal history', or 'a historical legal science [that] is written by lawyers for lawyers'.[59]

This approach, which may be equated with 'internal' international legal history or with an internal normative approach to the history of international law, is the domain, according to Robert Gordon, of the internal legal historian as one 'who stays as much as possible within the box of distinctive-appearing legal things; his sources are legal, and so are the basic matters he wants to describe or explain'.[60] This internal normative approach, where law has traditionally been considered 'a self-contained historical phenomenon',[61] may be found practised at both the micro and the macro level. At the micro level, it may be applied, according to Randall Lesaffer, to 'just a particular branch, institution, principle, rule or concept', or a certain legal doctrine: *Dogmengeschichte* (dogmatic history). However, at the macro level, 'the focus is often on jurisprudence'.[62] The latter is admittedly a loose term which in this context may, broadly speaking, be understood to indicate that it is traditionally restricted to discussion either of the field's intellectual history or alternatively of the basic outlines of its legal theory (its system of sources, its law-making institutions, and both its adjudicative and law enforcement-related ones) or a combination thereof.

While both the micro and macro levels are identified with reference to the dominant emphasis put on normative elements and internal perspectives on legal development in the practice of historical legal writing, this characterization may be adapted in its extrapolation from legal history to international legal history in order to consider certain particularities in the practice of historical writing about international law. The first of these relates to the fact that the turn to the history of international law has largely coincided in time with a period in which the academic study of international law has experienced a parallel phenomenon of academic fragmentation into niches of specialized international legal scholarship as a result of the expansion and diversification experienced by international law over recent decades. In the wake of this, there has been a remarkable parallel thematic fragmentation of the history of international law in

---

[59] Dirk Heirbaut, 'A tale of two legal histories: some personal reflections on the methodology of legal history', in Dag Michalsen (ed.), *Reading Past Legal Texts* (Oslo: Unipax, 2006), pp. 91–112 at 92.
[60] Robert W. Gordon, 'Introduction: J. Willard Hurst and the common law tradition' (1975) 10 *American Legal Historiography Law and Society Review* 9–55 at 11.
[61] Lesaffer, 'Law between past and present', p. 7.
[62] Ibid.

which each international legal branch has embarked on the generation of its own sub-disciplinary historical narrative(s).

This intellectual diversification has been particularly translated at the macro level into the production of historicizations of different sub-specialized areas of international law such as international criminal law,[63] international humanitarian law and the laws of war,[64] international investment law,[65] international environmental law,[66] international economic law,[67] international human rights law,[68] and so on. Moreover, since the turn to the history of international law, the history of some transversal international law fields like international dispute settlement and within it international adjudication, as will be seen below, have also grown in autonomy. This expanding thematic fragmentation results in a series of academic sub-disciplinary international legal-historical tributaries generating on occasion their own historiographical debates that flow back into the general stream of the turn to the history of international law.

---

[63] See Mark Lewis, *The Birth of the New Justice: The Internationalization of Crime and Punishment 1919–1950* (Oxford: Oxford University Press, 2014); Frédéric Mégret and Immi Tallgren (eds.), *The Dawn of a Discipline: International Criminal Justice and Its Early Exponents* (Cambridge, UK: Cambridge University Press, 2020); Morten Bergsmo, Cheah Wui Ling, and Yi Ping (eds.), *Historical Origins of International Criminal Law*, vols. 1–2 (Brussels: Torkel Opsahl Academic EPublisher, 2014); Morten Bergsmo et al. (eds.), *Historical Origins of International Criminal Law*, vols. 3–4 (Brussels: Torkel Opsahl Academic EPublisher, 2015); Morten Bergsmo, Klaus Rackwitz, and Song Tianying (eds.), *Historical Origins of International Criminal Law*, vol. 5 (Brussels: Torkel Opsahl Academic EPublisher, 2017).

[64] See Amanda Alexander, 'A short history of international humanitarian law' (2015) 26 *European Journal of International Law* 109–138; Stephen C. Neff, *War and the Law of Nations: A General History* (Cambridge, UK: Cambridge University Press, 2005).

[65] See Kate Miles, *The Origins of International Investment Law: Empire, Environment, and the Safeguarding of Capital* (Cambridge, UK: Cambridge University Press, 2013); Stephan W. Schill, Christian J. Tams, and Rainer Hofmann (eds.), *International Investment Law and History* (Cheltenham: Edward Elgar Publishing, 2018), p. 70.

[66] See Peter H. Sand (ed.), *The History and Origin of International Environmental Law* (Cheltenham: Edward Elgar Publishing, 2015).

[67] See, e.g., Rafael Lima Sakr, 'Beyond history and boundaries: rethinking the past in the present of international economic law' (2019) 22 *Journal of International Economic Law* 57–91; Steve Charnovitz, 'The historical lens in international economic law' (2019) 22 *Journal of International Economic Law* 93–97.

[68] See Paul Gordon Lauren, *The Evolution of International Human Rights: Visions Seen* (Philadelphia: University of Pennsylvania Press, 1998); Micheline Ishay, *The History of Human Rights: From Ancient Times to the Globalization Era* (Berkeley: University of California Press, 2008).

Likewise, at the micro level the international legal historical literature on specialized international legal regimes also shows a considerable historical focus on legal principles, institutions, doctrines and norms, and the legislative history of international treaties. This has expanded into histories of international and transnational crimes, war crimes, crimes against humanity, crimes of aggression, genocide, slave trade, piracy, terrorism, and legal doctrines such as universal jurisdiction.[69] It has also encompassed histories of key universal declarations,[70] particular specialized international conventions,[71] and regional systems,[72] with special attention being paid to the *travaux préparatoires* – official documents recording the negotiations, drafting, and discussions during the process of creating multiple international treaties,[73] such as, to mention but a few, the International Covenant of Economic, Social and Cultural Rights or the Indigenous and Tribal Peoples Convention.[74]

However, the functional fragmentation of the history of international law has not meant that the normative realm of general public international law has not continued to be historicized. On the contrary, recent years have witnessed a remarkable expansion of research at both the micro and macro levels. At the micro level, the literature shows extensive coverage of international legal institutions, norms, and legal concepts which has continued expanding in recent years. This has extended from the sources of international law[75] to the norms of treaty publication,[76]

---

[69] Máximo Langer and Mackenzie Eason, 'The quiet expansion of universal jurisdiction' (2019) 30 *European Journal of International Law* 779–817.

[70] Johannes Morsink, *The Universal Declaration of Human Rights: Origins, Drafting, and Intent* (Philadelphia: University of Pennsylvania Press, 1999).

[71] Ed Bates, *The Evolution of the European Convention on Human Rights: From Its Inception to the Creation of a Permanent Court of Human Rights* (Oxford: Oxford University Press, 2010).

[72] Obiora Okafor, *The African Human Rights System, Activist Forces and International Institutions* (Cambridge, UK: Cambridge University Press, 2010).

[73] See a list of classic and recent publication at Collected Travaux Préparatoires, Yale Law School, library.law.yale.edu/collected-travaux-preparatoires.

[74] Ben Saul (ed.), *The International Covenant on Economic, Social and Cultural Rights: Travaux Preparatoires* (Oxford: Oxford University Press, 2016); Lee Swepston, *The Foundations of Modern International Law on Indigenous and Tribal Peoples: The Preparatory Documents of the Indigenous and Tribal Peoples Convention, and Its Development through Supervision* (Leiden and Boston: Brill/Nijhoff, 2015).

[75] See Jean d'Aspremont and Samantha Besson (eds.), *The Oxford Handbook of the Sources of International Law* (Oxford: Oxford University Press, 2017), with over a dozen contributions to the history of the sources of international law.

[76] Megan Donaldson, 'The survival of the secret treaty: publicity, secrecy, and legality in the international order' (2017) 111 *American Journal of International Law* 575–627.

territorial sovereignty by treaty,[77] general principles of law,[78] *ius cogens*,[79] peace treaties,[80] the principle of self-determination of peoples,[81] the principle of *uti possidetis iuris*,[82] the doctrine of state recognition,[83] the law on immunity,[84] the prohibition of slavery,[85] prescription,[86] condominium,[87] international legal personality,[88] the fundamental principles of international law,[89] unilateral

---

[77] Mamadou Hébié, *Souveraineté territoriale par traité: une étude des accords entre puissances coloniales et entités politiques locales* (Paris: Presses Universitaires de France and the Graduate Institute, 2015).

[78] Marija Đorđeska, *General Principles of Law Recognized by Civilized Nations (1922–2018): The Evolution of the Third Source of International Law through the Jurisprudence of the Permanent Court of International Justice and the International Court of Justice* (Leiden: Brill/Nijhoff, 2020).

[79] Felix Lange, 'Challenging the Paris Peace Treaties, state sovereignty, and Western-dominated international law – the multifaceted genesis of the *jus cogens* doctrine' (2018) 31 *Leiden Journal of International Law* 821–839.

[80] Randall Lesaffer (ed.), *Peace Treaties and International Law in European History: From the Late Middle Ages to World War One* (Cambridge, UK: Cambridge University Press, 2004).

[81] Arnulf Becker Lorca, 'Petitioning the international: a "pre-history" of self-determination' (2014) 25 *European Journal of International Law* 497–523.

[82] Marta Lorente Sariñena, 'Uti possidetis, ita domini eritis: international law and the historiography of the territory', in Massimo Meccarelli and María Julia Solla Sastre (eds.), *Spatial and Temporal Dimensions for Legal History Research Experiences and Itineraries* (Frankfurt: Max Planck Institute for European Legal History, 2016), pp. 131–172.

[83] Martti Clark, 'British contributions to the concept of recognition during the interwar period: Williams, Baty and Lauterpacht', in Robert McCorquodale and Jean-Pierre Gauci (eds.), *British Influences on International Law 1915–2015* (Leiden: Brill/Nijhoff, 2016), pp. 110–144.

[84] Philippa Webb, 'British contribution to the law on immunity', in Robert McCorquodale and Jean-Pierre Gauci (eds.), *British Influences on International Law 1915– 2015* (Leiden: Brill/Nijhoff, 2016), pp. 145–166.

[85] Michel Erpelding, *Le droit international antiesclavagiste des 'nations civilisées' 1815–1945* (Paris: Institut Universitaire Varenne, 2017).

[86] Edward Cavanagh, 'Prescription and empire from Justinian to Grotius' (2016) 60 *The Historical Journal* 1–27.

[87] Christopher Rossi, 'The Gulf of Fonseca and international law: condominium or anti-colonial imperialism?' (2018) 3 *Jus Gentium: Journal of International Legal History* 115–153.

[88] Janne E. Nijman, *The Concept of International Legal Personality: An Inquiry into the History and Theory of International Law* (The Hague: T. M. C. Asser Press, 2004).

[89] Jorge E. Viñuales (ed.), *The UN Friendly Relations Declaration at 50: An Assessment of the Fundamental Principles of International Law* (Cambridge, UK: Cambridge University Press, in press).

acts,[90] the prohibition of the use and threat of force,[91] humanitarian intervention,[92] and so on.

In comparison with earlier normatively solipsistic historical treatments of different subjects, the newer contributions tend to be more thoroughly based on archival research and to pay more attention to the external context relevant to the historical investigation, and are also more attentive to providing alternative political and intellectual trajectories. There is also a greater emphasis on the study of historical international legal practice as a questioning counterpoint to a more doctrinaire emphasis on normative landmarks as marking temporal *caesurae*. As we shall later see, this, which is a reaction to the criticized traditional genealogical approach to normative history from the present to the past, has included on some remarkably interesting occasions explicitly departing from 'one-sided stories' and trying instead a 'mediating' approach to 'different historical perspectives'[93] oriented to better engaging and more faithfully depicting the 'complexity and multicausality of historical developments'[94] as they have impacted the formation and uses of international law norms and concepts in international law over time. Dislodging historical approaches from one-sided perspectives and instead assimilating multicausality in their study is indeed one of the promising historiographical venues that lie, as Chapter 11 examines, on the horizon of a more attentive embracing of multi-perspectivity in the service of the history of international law.

At the macro level, the expansion of general histories of international law has encompassed many languages extending, besides English, to German,[95] French,[96]

---

[90] Betina Kuzmarov, *Unilateral Acts: A History of a Legal Doctrine* (London: Routledge, 2018).

[91] Randall Lesaffer, 'Too much history: from war as sanction to the sanctioning of war', in Marc Weller (ed.), *The Oxford Handbook of the Use of Force in International Law* (Oxford: Oxford University Press, 2015), pp. 35–55; Agatha Verdebout, 'The contemporary discourse on the use of force in the nineteenth century: a diachronic and critical analysis' (2014) 1 *Journal on the Use of Force and International Law* 223–246.

[92] Mark Swatek-Evenstein, *A History of Humanitarian Intervention* (Cambridge, UK: Cambridge University Press, 2020).

[93] Lange, 'Challenging the Paris Peace Treaties', p. 824.

[94] Ibid., p. 839.

[95] Karl Heinz Ziegler, *Volkerrechtsgeschichte: Ein Studienbuch* (Munich: C. H. Beck, 2007).

[96] Dominique Gaurier, *Histoire du droit international: de l'Antiquité à la création de l'ONU* (Rennes: Presses Universitaires de Rennes, 2014); Slim Laghmani, *Histoire du droit des gens, du jus gentium impérial au jus publicum europæum* (Paris: Pédone, 2004).

Italian,[97] or Portuguese,[98] to mention but a few. Traditionally, this genre has been written in the mode of 'intellectual history' within an idealist tradition or one of doctrinal history which analyses the teachings of important theorists of international law, their development, and their inter-action,[99] or in a realist mode with greater emphasis on legal practice, historical landmark events, wars, and power, with many historical accounts putting emphasis on one or the other while combining the two to different degrees in their narratives. No more cultivated at the macro level today is the macro-doctrinal type of normative history such as attempted by Jan H. W. Verzjil extending from international persons to the law of maritime prize in eleven volumes from 1968 to 1979.[100] However, recollections of treaty practice are still published,[101] as are surveys of particularly notable works.[102] Moreover, adding itself to classic works on the historical sources of international law,[103] a new bibliographical sub-genre has emerged which can be general in orientation,[104] or may be annotated and divided into topics or specific periods.[105] One may add that the macro level has seen a larger number

[97] Carlo Focarelli, *Introduzione storica al diritto internazionale* (Milan: Giuffre, 2012); Gustavo Gozzi, *Diritti e civilta: storia e filosofia del diritto internazionale* (Bologna: Il Mulino, 2010)

[98] Pedro Caridade de Freitas, *História do direito internacional público da antiguidade à II Guerra Mundial* (Lisbon: Principia, 2015).

[99] Antonio Truyol y Serra, *Historia del derecho internacional público* (Madrid: Tecnos, 1998).

[100] Jan Hendrik Willem Verzijl, *International Law in Historical Perspective*, 11 vols. (Leiden: Martinus Nijhoff, 1968–79).

[101] Peter Macalister-Smith and Joachim Schwietzke (eds.), *Treaties and Other Acts in Multilateral Conference Diplomacy: A Brief Calendar of State Practice 1641 to 1924* (Vienna: Neugebauer Verlag, 2019).

[102] Robert Kolb, *Les cours généraux de droit international public de La Haye* (Brussels: Bruylant/Éditions de l'Université de Bruxelles, 2003).

[103] Wilhem G. Grewe (ed.), *Fontes historiae iuris gentium* (Berlin: De Gruyter, 1988–95).

[104] Peter Macalister-Smith and Joachim Schwietzke, 'Literature and documentary sources relating to the history of international law' (1999) 1 *Journal of the History of International Law* 136–212; Peter Macalister-Smith and Joachim Schwietzke, 'Bibliography of the textbooks and comprehensive treatise on positive international law of the 19th century' (2001) 3 *Journal of the History of International Law* 75–142; Randall Lesaffer (ed.), *Bibliography on the History of International Law*, www .tilburguniversity.edu/research/institutes-and-research-groups/i-hilt/i-hilt-bibliography.

[105] Rose Parfitt, 'The League of Nations', in *Oxford Bibliographies in International Law* (2017), www.oxfordbibliographies.com/view/document/obo-9780199796953/obo-9780199796953-0151.xml; and see, e.g., Ignacio de la Rasilla, 'Medieval international law', in *Oxford Bibliographies in International Law* (2014), www.oxfordbibliographies .com/view/document/obo-9780199796953/obo-9780199796953-0112.xml, pp. 1–25.

of works defined by a specific temporal coverage, whether this corresponds to antiquity,[106] the Carolingian period,[107] the Middle Ages, or other periods including modern ones such as the Cold War,[108] and that a particular emphasis on the nineteenth century has also developed.[109] Finally, in comparison to the synoptic holistic coverage of earlier works, the new literature has also shown more attention to specific geographical coverage, in particular regarding nation-specific histories of international law, as we shall see in Chapter 8.

The history of international adjudication is a particular genre within the 'history of international law'.[110] The constitutively ambivalent relationship that, as we saw in exploring the domain of 'history in international law', international legal practice and international legal history entertain accounts for why the history of international adjudication brings to the international lawyer's mind an almost automatic association with the 'juridical afterglow' of such a history, i.e. with the history of international case law. This association, in its turn, goes a long way to account for the international lawyer's traditional penchant for approaching the history of international adjudication as a sort of *aide de camp* for international adjudicative processes in international legal scholarship.

The historical focus on analytical exegeses of international case law, or aspects thereof, is widely illustrated in innumerable pages of international legal literature. From the late nineteenth century and early twentieth century, when the first collections were assembled of international law cases decided by domestic courts and international arbitral tribunals,[111] to the first digests emerging in parallel with the establishment of the first

---

[106] See, e.g., Amnon Altman, *Tracing the Earliest Recorded Concepts of International Law: The Ancient Near East (2500–330 BCE)* (Leiden: Martinus Nijhoff, 2012).

[107] Heinhard Steiger, *Die Ordnung der Welt: Eine Völkerrechtsgeschichte des Karolingischen Zeitalters (741 bis 840)* (Cologne: Böhlau Verlag, 2010).

[108] Matthew Craven et al. (eds.), *Cold War and International Law* (Cambridge, UK: Cambridge University Press, 2019).

[109] Luigi Nuzzo, *Origini di una scienza: diritto internazionale e colonialismo nel XIX secolo* (Frankfurt am Main: Klostermann, 2012).

[110] Ignacio de la Rasilla and Jorge Viñuales, *Experiments in International Adjudication: Historical Accounts* (Cambridge, UK: Cambridge University Press, 2019).

[111] See John Bassett Moore, *A Digest of International Law*, 8 vols. (Washington, DC: Government Printing Office, 1906); William E. Darby, *International Arbitration, International Tribunals: A Collection of the Various Schemes Which Have Been Propounded; and of Instances in the Nineteenth Century*, 4th ed. (London: J. M. Dent and Co., 1904).

permanent international courts,[112] the history of international case law has been patiently recollected and commented on,[113] in some instances with reference to its engagement by national supreme courts.[114] Over time, these collections and the myriad punctual international case-law commentaries scattered through international legal scholarship have become the fabric of a systematic scholarly historical endeavour, or the basis for modern theorizations like the notion of 'comparative international law'.[115] In the meantime certain cases have consolidated their status as 'classics' of the discipline, while others, judging by how international lawyers continue to repetitively scrutinize them, are on their way to becoming so.[116]

On the other hand, the study of international legal cases as teaching material is still very much the bedrock of classical international legal education.[117] Even when this is not provided by reference to primary sources but in the standard manufactured form of textbooks, the key areas into which the discipline is generally divided, and the key concepts within each of these areas, are illustrated in snippet-like form with reference to cases adjudicated many decades ago. This traditional understanding of the history of international adjudication as somewhat equivalent to the history of international case law is part and parcel of the traditional internal normative approach to the history of international law under the pull of a juridical form of functional presentism. However, over recent years, the history of international adjudication has itself also been impacted by the turn to the external context, in particular, as we shall see below, regarding the historicization of certain landmark

[112] Hersch Lauterpacht, *Annual Digest of Public International Law Cases: 1919-1922* (London: Longmans, Green and Company, 1932).
[113] Christopher Greenwood and Karen Lee (eds.), *International Law Reports*, vol. 169 (Cambridge, UK: Cambridge University Press, 2017).
[114] David L. Sloss, Michael D. Ramsey, and William S. Dodge (eds.), *International Law in the U.S. Supreme Court: Continuity and Change* (Cambridge, UK: Cambridge University Press, 2011).
[115] Anthea Roberts, 'Comparative international law? The role of national courts in creating and enforcing international law' (2011) 60 *International and Comparative Law Quarterly* 57-92.
[116] See Laurence Boisson de Chazournes and Philippe Sands (eds.), *International Law, the International Court of Justice and Nuclear Weapons* (Cambridge, UK: Cambridge University Press, 1999); Edgardo Sobenes Obregon and Benjamin Samson, *Nicaragua before the International Court of Justice: Impacts on International Law* (Cham: Springer, 2018).
[117] Christian J. Tams and Malgosia Fitzmaurice, *Legacies of the Permanent Court of International Justice* (Leiden: Martinus Nijhoff/Brill, 2013).

international adjudicative events. Moreover, when the focus shifts from case law as outputs of functionally oriented international adjudicative processes to institutional appraisals of international courts and tribunals, the history of international adjudication can also be approached, as Chapter 9 examines in certain detail, from other perspectives, including in particular that provided by 'historical institutionalism'.[118]

A general particularity of the traditional or internal approach to the 'history of international law' for which it has been criticized is that at both levels it has often been, as Craven notes, reconstructed backwards in terms of its evolutionary history from legal categories in the present, with the consequence that 'the primary concern, in such cases, is not to understand the past in its own terms with all its complexities, ambivalence or ambiguity, but rather to identify within it a thin tradition of thought and practice that is in some way normative'.[119] This does not mean that 'history of international law' may not also be approached in internal normative terms synchronically so as to allow for the precise identification of the state of the *lege data* in a particular time and place in the past. In the latter case, the 'history of international law' generally converges with 'history *in* international law' insofar as it may perform juridical functions in the present such as in the previously mentioned application of the 'inter-temporal rule'. However, the synchronic study of the 'history of international law' is generally carried out in conjunction with the study of 'international law in history'. This, as was seen in Chapter 2 and as we shall examine again below, means that synchronic approaches tend to be receptive to considering the broader sociohistorical context that affected the formation and/or development of a norm, rule, legal doctrine, or principle or aim to illuminate the role of particular norms, principles, or legal institutions (e.g. slavery) in the society of their time.

Against this background, the most common diachronic and genealogical study of the normative historical realm presents two faces or dimensions. The first mirrors the factual normative evolution experienced by international law as a legal system reflected in the growing extension and diversification of the international *corpus iuris* over time –

---

[118] Orfeo Fioretos, Tulia G. Falleti, and Adam Sheingate (eds.), *The Oxford Handbook of Historical Institutionalism* (Oxford: Oxford University Press, 2016).

[119] Matthew Craven, 'Introduction: international law and its histories', in Matthew Craven, Malgosia Fitzmaurice, and Maria Vogiatzi (eds.), *Time, History and International Law* (Leiden: Martinus Nijhoff/Brill, 2006), pp. 1–25 at 16.

taking account of the international normative evolution which is the result of the evolving and constantly updating programming of the international legal system, for which the strictly normative study of the past offers useful material. This is not less so because of the historical influence of norm-entrepreneurship or advocacy in special particular areas such as typically international human rights law, where, as Philip Alston notes, there is 'a strong genealogical or ancestral component in the sense that one generation has provided the foundation or the impetus for the emergence and shaping of the next generation's usage'.[120] Alongside this objective dimension, there is a second one that refers to an embedded axiologically driven component that sees this process as teleologically progressing in a beneficial cosmopolitan direction and consequently further pushes international law towards a continual juridification of international relations in the image of domestic settings.

As the mainstream perspective, this general orientation has been historiographically criticized on many accounts for its conclusions, blinds spots, exclusions, and biases. From a contextualist perspective, the anachronistic nature of a teleologically inspired normative approach is often highlighted, and, because of it, some may not even consider this to be legal history in the sense of being historical.[121] In a depiction provided by a classical postmodernist critique, as we shall see in more detail in Chapter 11, the traditional approach is represented as fostering a grand narrative of normative progress which in turn becomes crystallized in fixed historical normative periodizations that gloss over structural continuities across different periods. Critical and post-colonial international legal historians in their turn have made much, as was seen in Chapters 3 and 4, of the critique of the grand narrative of international law.

While traditionally the normative focus tends to confine the study of the historical contextual frame to what is essential for the functional purpose of illuminating its normative research object, the 'history of international law', as seen before in both the micro and the macro dimensions, has notably gained in contextual depth and in methodological hybridity because of the more thematically extensive and methodologically interdisciplinary cultivation that the field of research as a whole has experienced since the early 2000s. However, this does not

---

[120] Philip Alston, 'Does the past matter? On the origins of human rights' (2012–13) 126 *Harvard Law Review* 2043–2081 at 2052.
[121] Lesaffer, 'Law between past and present'.

imply that the traditional internal normative approach to international legal history has been debunked. Historiographically, the internal normative approach underlies a relevant normative approach to the periodization of the history of international law. As we shall see in more detail in Chapter 11, this can be described as an approach that uses an 'analytical prism' that is 'less concerned with contextual features of an "order" and more with the lineage of individual rules, systemic perceptions of those rules by the subjects of the system, and doctrines'.[122]

Moreover, when examined from a purely intradisciplinary angle, the relative autonomy that international legal historical research has gained as a result of the decrease in doctrinalism and pragmatism in international legal scholarship should not lead to a minimization of the strong pull of the mainstream orthodoxy in contemporarily relevant research in international law. After all, this is a juridical discipline and as such is one largely politically driven, functionally oriented to problem-solving and with much potential to have social effects on a worldwide scale, including those regarding its essential task of maintaining international peace and security, which should never, ever be taken for granted. When compared with other disciplines that value more speculative, contemplative, or knowledge-for-its-own sake-based historical enquiries, which on occasion have even been decried as 'antiquarian' because of their lack of connection to any discernible social effects, international lawyers' engagement with their normative past is largely influenced by the state of positive law, or *lex lata*, and with the functional purposes that historical research may produce, such as international legal reform with the potential to save lives. As was seen with regard to 'history in international law', the professional consensus on the methodology to discern or distil from historical knowledge what may be provided with the weight of legal authority and, as such, be potentially susceptible to having immediate legal effects, differs from the equally loose professional methodological consensus emerging among historians on what makes historical knowledge professionally acceptable. Underlying this consensus lies what Samuel Moyn has termed 'enduring features of professional difference' between communities of historians and international lawyers, each

---

[122] William E. Butler, 'Periodization and international law', in Alexander Orakhelashvili (ed.), *Research Handbook on the Theory and History of International Law* (Cheltenham: Edward Elgar Publishing, 2011), pp. 379–393 at 391.

provided with their 'own powerful professional norms guiding and controlling interpretation'.[123]

7.4 International Law in History: Opening Up to External Contexts

At the most distant point from juridical functional presentism on the continuum on which the three dimensions of the interaction between history and international law are situated, completing Craven and Lesaffer's tripartite typology there is the domain of 'international law in history'. This domain, which generally coincides with an 'external' normative approach to the history of international law, is one that focuses on international norms, principles, and doctrines embedded in their historical contexts, typically international political, social, intellectual, cultural, and economic ones. According to Robert Gordon, with reference to the domain of domestic legal history, 'an external legal historian writes about the interaction between the boxful of legal things and the wider society of which they are a part, in particular to explore the social context of law and its social effects, and he is usually looking for conclusions about those effects'.[124] Or, as put by Dirk Heirbaut, 'for contextual legal historians, the autonomy of law is anathema: law is anything but an isolated phenomenon, it is a product of a society that in its turn influences that same society'.[125]

As thus generally delimited, the research domain of 'international law in history' is more permeable to historiographical methods and politico-epistemological perspectives, and therefore more prone, notwithstanding the mentioned methodological turn experienced in the domain of the 'history of international law', to integrate other historical methods. It is also a domain generally more receptive to the influence of critical approaches to the history of international law, including those that purport to channel emancipatory, social-conflict-oriented, disruptive, or dissident discourses, than those usually employed within the other broadly characterized categories. Indeed, the study of 'international law in history' is generally more receptive to interdisciplinarity – the effort at

[123] Samuel Moyn, 'Legal history as a source of international law: the politics of knowledge', in Jean d'Aspremont and Samantha Besson (eds.), *The Oxford Handbook of the Sources of International Law* (Oxford: Oxford University Press, 2017), pp. 301–322 at 308.
[124] R. Gordon, 'Introduction', p. 11.
[125] Heirbaut, 'A tale of two legal histories', p. 93.

'knowledge production that cross[es] or bridge[s] disciplinary boundaries'.[126] This factor puts these approaches in a better position to produce 'innovation in knowledge production – making knowledge more relevant, balancing incommensurable claims and perspectives, and raising questions concerning the nature and viability of expertise'[127] with regard to traditional historical knowledge. Moreover, the fact that this domain is more detached from juridical functional presentism does not imply that works aimed at exploring 'international law in history' are devoid, as was seen in Chapter 2, of any presentist purpose, understood as the ambition to have a transformative effect in the present because it still partakes of the performative function of all international legal history writing.

A particularity of the practice of historical writing about international law regarding its normative dimension in connection with both the study of the 'history of international law' and 'international law in history' lies in its increasing interdisciplinary cultivation. This has come to be translated in the latter domain into a less attentive research focus on the 'legal' aspects of norms, principles, and institutions and a more accentuated research focus instead on a series of fundamental interdisciplinary common notions or concepts,[128] which either underlie or provide them with a politico-historical framing context within which to be subsumed. These concepts include sovereignty,[129] war,[130] diplomacy,[131] humanitarianism, cosmopolitanism,[132] international society or international community, civilization,[133]

[126] Robert Frodeman, 'Introduction', in Robert Frodeman, Julie Thompson Klein, and Carl Mitcham (eds.), *The Oxford Handbook of Interdisciplinarity* (Oxford: Oxford University Press, 2010), pp. xxix–xl at xxix.
[127] Ibid.
[128] There have also been attempts to elaborate a list of partially overlapping but also disciplinarily distinct concepts for international law, see Jean d'Aspremont and Sahib Singh (eds.), *Concepts for International Law – Contributions to Disciplinary Thought* (Northampton, MA: Edward Elgar Publishing, 2019).
[129] Antony Anghie, *Imperialism, Sovereignty and the Making of International Law* (Cambridge, UK: Cambridge University Press, 2005).
[130] Neff, *War and the Law of Nations.*
[131] David Atkinson, 'History of diplomacy', in David Armstrong et al. (eds.), *Oxford Bibliographies in International Relations* (2014), www.oxfordbibliographies.com/view/document/obo-9780199743292/obo-9780199743292-0013.xml.
[132] Mónica García-Salmones Rovira and Pamela Slotte (eds.). *Cosmopolitanisms in Enlightenment Europe and Beyond* (Brussels: P. I. E. Peter Lang S.A., 2013).
[133] Liliana Obregon, 'Civilized, uncivilized', in Bardo Fassbender and Anne Peters (eds.), *The Oxford Handbook of the History of International Law* (Oxford: Oxford University Press, 2012), pp. 917–943.

7.4 INTERNATIONAL LAW IN HISTORY 245

inequality,[134] progress,[135] decolonization,[136] colonialism, Eurocentrism,[137] empire,[138] property,[139] gender, statelessness,[140] and so on. The treatment of the common concepts which 'legal rules consist of, and are based on'[141] diverges across disciplines as methodologically diverse as international relations, political thought, philosophy, and history.

As was seen in Chapter 2, historical methodological treatments of certain concepts that international law shares with other disciplines bring, for instance, greater emphasis, following the tenets of historical methodological contextualization including those of the type preconized by the Cambridge School of intellectual history, on 'the social and political context of the concept, and the political agenda behind it, about the 'speakers; and the 'addressees', and about the shifting meaning of a concept in the course of time'.[142] This contributes to dislodging the traditional approach to the 'history of international law' from its attachment to a conception of law as a separate entity or as a self-contained phenomenon and to instead opening to the external social context. However, in a field of international legal history which has been traditionally attached, as was seen regarding the domain of 'history of international law', to evolving historical genealogical diachronic perspectives, the move to the external context has itself generated debates, as was seen in Chapter 2, between contextualist historians and critical international legal ones when moved onto the diachronic axis. This is due to

---

[134] Rose Parfitt, *The Process of International Legal Reproduction: Inequality, Historiography, Resistance* (Cambridge, UK: Cambridge University Press, 2019).

[135] Thomas Skouteris, *The Notion of Progress in International Law Discourse* (The Hague: T. M. C. Asser Press, 2010); see also Tilmann Altwicker and Oliver Diggelmann, 'How is progress constructed in international legal scholarship?' (2014) 25 *European Journal of International Law* 425–444 at 437.

[136] Sundhya Pahuja, *Decolonising International Law: Development, Economic Growth and the Politics of Universality* (Cambridge, UK: Cambridge University Press, 2011).

[137] Arnulf Becker Lorca, 'Eurocentrism in the history of international law', in Bardo Fassbender and Anne Peters (eds.), *The Oxford Handbook of the History of International Law* (Oxford: Oxford University Press, 2012), pp. 1034–1057.

[138] Jennifer Pitts, *Boundaries of the International: Law and Empire* (Cambridge, MA: Harvard University Press, 2018); Martti Koskenniemi, Walter Rech, and Manuel Jiménez Fonseca (eds.), *International Law and Empire – Historical Explorations* (Oxford: Oxford University Press, 2017).

[139] Andrew Fitzmaurice, *Sovereignty, Property and Empire 1500–2000* (Cambridge, UK: Cambridge University Press, 2014).

[140] Mira L. Siegelberg, *Statelessness: A Modern History* (Cambridge, MA: Harvard University Press, 2020).

[141] Fassbender and Peters, 'Introduction', pp. 11–14.

[142] Ibid.

the fact that some of these 'concepts' are themselves central, as was seen in Chapter 4 regarding TWAIL/post-colonial approaches and also in Chapter 6 concerning feminist and gender-centred approaches to the construction of 'counter-history' narratives, understood in Foucauldian terms as ones aimed at deploying a disruptive narrative in favour of 'subjugated groups'.[143]

An interesting illustration of this type of conceptual history is provided by the concept of the 'international community', which, according to Koskenniemi, is the 'present-day rhetorical equivalent' of earlier idealist manifestations of the 'expression of, or perhaps a metaphor for, the ideals of universalism, community, and solidarity beyond political divisions, the ideal of humanity united into one'.[144] Indeed, its different historical distillations range from *ius gentium*[145] or Dante's reflections on universal monarchy in his *De monarchia*[146] to Vitoria's equation of the 'whole world' with a 'commonwealth' with its 'power to enact laws which are just and convenient to all men',[147] Christian Wolff's *civitas maxima*,[148] and Immanuel Kant's principle that 'the law of nations shall be founded on a federation of free states'[149] up to the interwar conceptual treatments of *ius gentium* as opposed to *ius inter gentes* by Georges Scelle,[150] and to Hersch's Lauterpacht's juridical perspective on the 'international community'[151]

---

[143] Michel Foucault, *Society Must Be Defended: Lectures at the Collège de France 1975–1976*, ed. Mauro Bertani and Alessandro Fontana (London: Penguin Books, 2003), pp. 70–72.

[144] Martti Koskenniemi, '"International community" from Dante to Vattel', in Vincent Chetail and Peter Haggenmacher (eds.), *Vattel's International Law from a XXIst Century Perspective* (Leiden: Brill, 2011), pp. 49–74 at 50.

[145] Randall Lesaffer, 'Roman law and the intellectual history of international law', in Anne Orford and Florian Hoffmann with Martin Clark (eds.), *The Oxford Handbook of the Theory of International Law* (Oxford: Oxford University Press, 2016), pp. 38–58.

[146] Dante Alighieri, *Monarchy*, trans. Prue Shaw (Cambridge, UK: Cambridge University Press, 1996); Oliver Lepsius, 'Hans Kelsen on Dante Alighieri's political philosophy' (2016) 27 *European Journal of International Law* 1153–1167.

[147] Francisco de Vitoria, 'On civil power', in *Vitoria: Political Writings*, ed. and trans. Anthony Pagden and Jeremy Lawrance (Cambridge, UK: Cambridge University Press, 1991), pp. 1–44 at 40.

[148] Christian Wolff, *Ius gentium methodo scientifi ca pertractatum*, trans. Joseph H. Drake (Washington, DC: Carnegie Institution of Washington, 1934), para. 12 (Prolegomena).

[149] Immanuel Kant, *Perpetual Peace: A Philosophical Sketch*, trans. and ed. M. Campbell Smith (London: George Allen & Unwin, 1903), p. 68.).

[150] Georges Scelle, 'Règles générales du droit de la paix' (1934) 46 *Recueil des cours de l'Académie de La Haye* 331–703.

[151] Hersch Lauterpacht, *The Function of Law in the International Community* (Oxford: Clarendon Press, 1933); Emmanuelle Jouannet, 'La communauté internationale vue par les juristes' (2005) 6 *Annuaire français de relations internationales* 3–26.

over time. This conceptual history has included multiple contributions from different disciplines, including, as particularly influential among international lawyers, the English School of international relations, for which, according to Martin Wight's influential tripartite classification, the Grotian tradition stands as a middle-of-the-road position between the extremes of the Machiavellian and Hobbesian traditions of realism in an anarchical international society, and the Kantian tradition of revolutionism or utopianism advocating the progress of the world community toward a *civitas maxima* or global federation.[152]

In the traditional normative-oriented rendering of the historical evolution of the concept of 'international community', these ideational and intellectual precedents used to be placed in a synoptic narrative of its historical conceptual evolution and eventual evolution as a 'legal concept' accruing its pedigree over time so as to naturally lead, against conceptions of national sovereignty, to the establishment and legitimation of certain categories of international legal norms designed to protect 'community interests' such as *ius cogens*, obligations *erga omnes*, etc.[153] However, in more interdisciplinary and contextualized contemporary historical treatments of the concept, the historical evolution of the notion of international community appears in constant tension with the concept of empire or the hegemony of great powers. This, in turn, approaches the resulting type of contextualized conceptual history, as Chapter 8 shows, to the historical sociology of international law and the contextualized historical study of its different 'social actors' over time.

Another interesting development in the conceptual history of international law is the historicization of the theory of international law with reference to particular schools of international legal thought and their associated tenets, methods, diversity, and influence. This particular type of conceptual intellectual history further overlaps with the sociological domain of international legal history and international legal biographical approaches insofar as it is often narrated with reference to the intellectual contributions of leading international law scholars and thinkers.[154]

---

[152] Martin Wight, *Four Seminal Thinkers in International Theory: Machiavelli, Grotius, Kant, and Mazzini*, ed. Gabriele Wight and Brian Porter (Oxford: Oxford University Press, 2005).

[153] Christian J. Tams, 'The "international community" as a legal concept', in Jean d'Aspremont and Sahib Singh (eds.), *Concepts for International Law – Contributions to Disciplinary Thought* (Northampton, MA: Edward Elgar Publishing, 2019), pp. 505–523.

[154] Jochen von Bernstorff, *The Public International Law Theory of Hans Kelsen: Believing in Universal Law* (Cambridge, UK: Cambridge University Press, 2010).

This historical study of international legal theory has extended to naturalism,[155] positivism,[156] functionalism,[157] sociological theories, and policy-oriented jurisprudence and also more recently, as was seen in Chapters 3 and 4, to post-colonial theory and critical/postmodern international law schools of thought with reference to the historical and intellectual context from which different theories emanated and the biographical features and professional careers of their leading exponents.

Beyond the conceptual realm, another area that attracts external contextual methodologies is the history of events (*Ereignisgeschichte*) with significance for international law,[158] or ones directly associated with international normative outputs. Influential declarations have attracted this type of contextualization as has external history, starting, as was seen in Chapter 2, with the Peace of Westphalia but extending to many other conceptually context-breaking and historically normative-related episodes such as the American Declaration of Independence,[159] the French Revolution,[160] and the Russian Revolution,[161] and including some of particular relevance to alternative periodizations of the history of international law such as the Berlin Conference,[162] the International Congress of Women, or the Bandung Conference. An illustration of this tendency is how the history of international adjudication has also been impacted by the turn to the external context, in particular regarding the historicization of certain landmark international adjudicative events. This has occurred in particular in certain international legal regimes such as international criminal law, where, for instance, significant events

---

[155] Geoff Gordon, 'Natural law in international legal theory: linear and dialectical presentations', in Anne Orford and Florian Hoffmann with Martin Clark (eds.), *The Oxford Handbook of the Theory of International Law* (Oxford: Oxford University Press, 2016), pp. 279–305.

[156] Garcia-Salmones Rovira, *The Project of Positivism*.

[157] See Jan Klabbers, 'The emergence of functionalism in international institutional law: colonial inspirations' (2014) 25 *European Journal of International Law* 645–675.

[158] Fleur Johns, Richard Joyce, and Sandhya Pahuja (eds.), *Events: The Force of International Law* (New York: Routledge, 2011).

[159] David Armitage, 'The Declaration of Independence and international law' (2002) 59 *William and Mary Quarterly* 39–64.

[160] Marc Belissa, 'French Revolution', in *Oxford Bibliographies in International Law* (2017), www.oxfordbibliographies.com/view/document/obo-9780199796953/obo-9780199796953-0111.xml.

[161] Anne Peters, 'A century after the Russian Revolution: its legacy in international law' (2017) 19 *Journal of the History of International Law* 133–146.

[162] Matthew Craven, 'Between law and history: the Berlin Conference of 1884–1885 and the logic of free trade' (2015) 3 *London Review of International Law* 31–59.

such as the trial of the Kaiser,[163] the Nuremberg Trials,[164] or the Tokyo Trials[165] have received new detailed historical attention.

7.5 Conclusion

Despite the emergence of an increasingly interdisciplinary and relatively semi-autonomous area of international legal history writing with the corresponding emergence of a diversity of historiographical trends and an ample thematic expansion that includes, as Chapters 8, 9, and 10 show, a far larger attention to social actors, when international lawyers engage in historical enquiries they still put considerable stress on normative approaches understood in the light of their object as a focus on international norms, fundamental principles, legal institutions, case law, and also underlying interrelated concepts, historically situated conceptual frameworks, and events with a normative significance in the field.

There is not a magical one-size-fits-all methodology that historians, legal historians, and international lawyers can apply equally to the different dimensions of interaction between the normative realm of international law and history across the continuum represented by the tripartite typology briefly mapped out above. However, better syntheses and tailored uses may be expected from a more acute awareness of the possibilities that each domain offers for renewed cultivation. This, in the light of the present state of the art in the field, is not addressed to making the study of history more juridical or *jus*-internationalist but to making instead the study of international law more historical. When seen in this light, the methodological progress experienced by international legal history since the turn to the history of international law may have a corrective role to play even in the most juridicized of these domains of interaction, that of 'history in international law'. Being directly influenced by a juridical form of juridical presentism, this has a strong formalist anti-disciplinary bias that isolates the internal normative approach from other approaches that bring into consideration methods and perspectives from other disciplines. One can agree in this sense with

---

[163] William A. Schabas, *The Trial of the Kaiser* (Oxford: Oxford University Press, 2018).

[164] Kevin J. Heller and Catherine E. Gascoigne, 'Nuremberg Trials', in *Oxford Bibliographies in International Law* (2017), www.oxfordbibliographies.com/view/document/obo-9780199796953/obo-9780199796953-0126.xml.

[165] Kirsten Sellars, 'Tokyo Trials', in *Oxford Bibliographies in International Law* (2019), www.oxfordbibliographies.com/view/document/obo-9780199796953/obo-9780199796953-0182.xml.

Thomas Skouteris that 'understanding the precise role of the past, of history, of historiography, and of historical narrative in the structure and authority of legal argument would cast light on the practices of international law'.[166] Indeed, engagement with history for practice-oriented uses in international law may benefit from greater awareness of historiographical methods, reliance on primary sources, and deeper engagement with secondary historical sources together with historiographical reflections on 'standards and best practices' by providing more 'analytic rigour in historical investigations', by making more apparent 'selectivity in the use of historical materials', by disqualifying instrumentalism in the 'conclusions drawn from historical data', and overall by being more attentive to the pitfalls and fallacies of what Bederman called 'law office international legal history'.[167] Similarly, in the domain of the 'history of international law', recent years have witnessed a greater cultivation of archival research and more integration of methodologies traditionally applied in the domain of 'international law in history' and with it the access to a greater incorporation of insights and historical texture has been unlocked.

However, the move away from 'self-contained' international legal history should also be wary of some of the possible downsides of historicism in the history of international law such as those noted by Valentina Vadi, which include a 'possible lack of focus and/or expertise on issues that are perceived as crucial by international lawyers ... , painstaking attention to historical details and data that may seem irrelevant to international lawyers; and ... little to no attention to the current relevance of international legal history'.[168] Dirk Heirbaut has also pointed out the limitations of a purely historical external approach to the study of law by noting 'while the traditional legal historian is not worth much without the context, the contextual historian is worth nothing at all without a traditional knowledge of law'.[169] These highlighted downsides are remindful of the understanding of 'international law as a discipline and as a profession'. This, according to James

---

[166] Thomas Skouteris, 'The turn to history in international law', in *Oxford Bibliographies in International Law* (2017), www.oxfordbibliographies.com/view/document/obo-9780199796953/obo-9780199796953-0154.xml, p. 5.

[167] Bederman, 'Foreign office', p. 46.

[168] Vadi, 'International law and its histories', p. 321.

[169] Dirk Heirbaut, 'Some reflexions on the methodologies of legal history', in Martin Löhnig (ed.), *Zeitschrift für europäische Rechtskultur*, 2 vols. (Regensburg: Edition Rechtskultur in der H. Gietl Verlag & Publikationsservice, 2013), vol. 1, pp. 89–92 at 90.

Crawford, means that 'we need to be, in a measure, interdisciplinary. But we can only be usefully interdisciplinary if we are first capable of being disciplinary: we have to have a home base, so to speak, somewhere to be interdisciplinary from. We are lawyers first and last.'[170]

In conclusion, although one can agree with Lauren Benton, according to whom historians and lawyers can find a settled foundation by committing to both the 'pursuit of evidence-based history' and 'to analytical coherence',[171] it is safe to conclude that the houses of Clio and Themis will never merge with each other. However, while Clio's and Themis's temples will remain separate, the common premises they share in international legal history still present a good margin for refurbishing, and this is a task that primarily falls on the shoulders of the priestess of Themis.

---

[170] James Crawford, 'International law as discipline and profession' (2012) 106 *Proceedings of the Annual Meeting of the American Society of International Law* 471–486 at 473.

[171] Lauren Benton, 'Beyond anachronism: histories of international law and global legal politics' (2019) 21 *Journal of the History of International Law* 7–40 at 33.

8

Sociological Approaches to the History
of International Law

8.1 Introduction

Writing some years ago, in an early phase in the so-called turn to the history of international law, Martti Koskenniemi noted that 'there has been virtually no attempt to study international law from the perspective of the sociology of the international system' and that the 'possibilities for a historical sociology of international law are, in fact, almost limitless'.[1] Since then, the history of international law has become more inclusive in its narratives of the multiplicity of social contexts and the social actors that have been shaping international law as a historical social product and of the moulding effects of the latter on the global society following Clifford Geertz, for whom all law is 'constructive of social realities rather than merely reflective of them'.[2] In good proportion, this historiographical development mirrors the extent to which state-centrism has lost some of its traditional paradigmatic position in international legal scholarship as a result of the relative decline or demise of the sovereign state as the main actor – and, classically, also the sole legal subject – of the international legal order.

The parallel growth of the descriptive and analytical relevance of the tropes of global governance,[3] post-national law,[4] and multilevel governance,[5] which have been marching in the wake of the proliferation of international institutions, regional integration processes, and the increase

[1] Martti Koskenniemi, 'Why history of international law today?' (2004) 4 *Rechtsgeschichte* 61–66 at 65–66.
[2] Clifford Geertz, *Local Knowledge: Further Essays in Interpretive Anthropology* (New York: Basic Books, 1983), p. 232.
[3] David Kennedy, 'The mystery of global governance' (2008) 34 *Ohio Northern University Law Review* 827–860.
[4] Nico Krisch, *Beyond Constitutionalism: The Pluralist Structure of Postnational Law* (Oxford: Oxford University Press, 2010).
[5] Christian Joerges and Ernest-Ulrich Petersmann (eds.), *Constitutionalism, Multilevel Trade Governance and International Economic Law* (Oxford: Hart Publishing, 2011).

in influence of non-state actors worldwide, are testimony to the intellectual leverage of a remarkable post-state-centric pull in the field in the aftermath of the Cold War.[6] This has furthermore been reflected in a reconceptualization of traditional notions of state sovereignty as is shown, for instance, by the notions of 'disaggregated sovereignty',[7] 'late sovereignty',[8] and 'post-sovereignty'[9] and the consequent application of new interdisciplinary methods and lenses to the study of sovereignty and the Westphalian paradigm. Moreover, globalization, the materialization of new trans-boundary threats and global challenges, the emergence of functionally distinct specialized technical international legal regimes,[10] and the recognition of the growing international importance of non-state actors as subjects of international law and bearers of international rights and obligations have all contributed to the development of a large international legal literature on the role of global, transnational, and non-state law in the international sphere.[11] They have also prompted a rethinking of the descriptive and predictive inaccuracy of a 'state-dominated understanding of global society'.[12]

The post-state-centric pull in the post-Cold War era, with its paradigmatic shift from archetypal notions of sovereignty towards a more plural and socially inclusive conception of the international legal order,[13] has largely been filtered in and mutually reinforced by the research agenda of the turn to the history of international law since the early

---

[6] Christoph Schreuer, 'The waning of the sovereign state: towards a new paradigm for international law' (1993) 4 *European Journal of International Law* 447–471.

[7] Anne-Marie Slaughter, *A New World Order* (Princeton, NJ: Princeton University Press, 2004).

[8] See, e.g., Neil Walker, 'Late sovereignty in the European Union', in Neil Walker (ed.), *Sovereignty in Transition* (London: Bloomsbury Publishing, 2003), pp. 3–32.

[9] Neil MacCormick, 'Sovereignty and after', in Hent Kalmo and Quentin Skinner (eds.), *Sovereignty in Fragments: The Past, Present and Future of a Contested Concept* (Cambridge, UK: Cambridge University Press, 2010), pp. 151–168 at 151.

[10] Daniel Bethlehem, 'The end of geography: the changing nature of the international system and the challenge to international law' (2014) 25 *European Journal of International Law* 9–24 at 15.

[11] Andrew Clapham, *Human Rights Obligations of Non-state Actors* (Cheltenham: Edward Elgar Publishing, 2013); Peer Zumbansen, 'Transnational law, evolving', in Jan M. Smits (ed.), *Encyclopedia of Comparative Law*, 2nd ed. (Cheltenham: Edward Elgar Publishing, 2012), pp. 899–925.

[12] Joel P. Trachtman, *The Future of International Law: Global Government* (Cambridge, UK: Cambridge University Press, 2013), p. 18.

[13] Tilmann Altwicker and Oliver Diggelmann, 'How is progress constructed in international legal scholarship?' (2014) 25 *European Journal of International Law* 425–444 at 437.

2000s. The long-in-the-making move from the practice-oriented normativist positivist conception of international law, according to which the
domain of study of international law should be mainly concerned with
the normative emanations of the sovereign will of nation-states and so
must be its history, has broadly crystallized into a particular international
socio-'legal consciousness' among international lawyers. This may be
understood, following Duncan Kennedy, as 'a set of concepts and intellectual operations that evolves according to a pattern of its own, and
exercises an influence on results distinguishable from those of power and
economic interests'.[14] Among international legal historians, this particular socio-'legal consciousness' is largely confluent, as we have seen in
previous chapters, with several historiographical trends. Among these are
global and contextualist approaches and also post-colonial and critical
ones, all of which underscore the background 'social' milieu and conditions from which international law has historically sprung up and
evolved.

   Against this background, sociological approaches to the history of
international law can be broadly understood with reference to either
their main research object and/or the method(s) employed when carrying
out a historical investigation into international law's pasts. Regarding the
method, these approaches may resort to an array of sociological, socio-
legal, and historical methodologies and to the use of corresponding
sources of reference. On the other hand, while it is axiomatic in sociological studies, following Émile Durkheim, that society is more than the
actors which compose it, and that it has, therefore, a life of its own that
stretches beyond any of its singular actor's own experiences,[15] the application of a socio-historical methodology to international legal phenomena in different times and places has run in parallel with a renewed
study of its social actors in a historical perspective. It is in this second
sense that the term 'sociological approaches' may be broadly used with
reference to the main objects of historical investigation to encompass the
history of the different 'social actors' of international law, independently
of the method employed to do so.

   The general category of social actors of international law may in turn
be approached either as an all-encompassing and holistic one or in a

---

[14] Duncan Kennedy, 'Toward an historical understanding of legal consciousness: the case of
   classical legal thought in America, 1850–1940' (1980) 3 *Research in Law & Society* 3–24
   at 4.
[15] Émile Durkheim, *Sociology and Philosophy* (Glencoe: Free Press, 1953), pp. 54–55.

more limited way with reference to a criterion of relevance regarding the impact, influence, or contributions of these same social actors, whether as subjects and/or objects, in the making, interpretation, and application of international law in history. In this latter understanding, which loosely coincides with that of 'subjects of international law' as applied to 'those entities which are capable of holding rights or of being made subject to obligations created by international law',[16] the study of the social history of international law primarily encompasses the history of sovereign national states. It secondly includes the history of international institutions or organizations and, by extension, international courts and tribunals, which will be examined specifically in Chapter 9, and finally it includes the historical study of an array of other non-state actors.

Among the latter are included individuals in their different international legal capacities, such as foreign-policy-makers, legal advisors, diplomats, international legal servants, international law scholars and scholars, judges, international norm-entrepreneurs, and advocates, all of whom are broadly included in the scope of studying the rise of contextualized historical biographical accounts of international law's professionals and intellectuals over time, as will be examined in Chapter 10. Directly concerned with the 'sociology of the field', the 'sociology of the discipline', and the 'sociology of the profession' is also the study of the role of women as individuals and as a group in the history of international law, as was seen in Chapter 6. Finally, a residual general category in a non-exhaustive list would also include non-governmental organizations (NGOs) of different sorts (including but not limited to faith-based institutionalized religious communities, scientific and epistemological associations, international advocacy groups of all stripes, and, underlying them, a variety of social movements), non-autonomous and indigenous peoples, non-state armed groups, criminal networks and terrorist groups, multinational or transnational corporations, and others. The aggregate of the histories of all these social actors of international law, which in turn is ultimately defined by their mutual interactions over time, is what one may generally speaking call the social history of international law.

Against this background, Section 8.2 below reviews the impact of the turn to the history of international law on the new development of

---

[16] Christian Walter, 'Subjects of international law', in *Max Planck Encyclopedia of Public International Law* (2007), opil.ouplaw.com/view/10.1093/law:epil/9780199231690/law-9780199231690-e1476, p. 10.

national histories of international law and on the histories of an array of non-state actors. Section 8.3 provides a brief overview of sociological approaches to international law over time. Section 8.4 examines the potential impact of sociological and socio-historical approaches on knowledge production processes regarding the relationship between international law and history, and Section 8.5 revisits the historiographical confluences, debates, and critiques associated with the application of sociological historical lenses to international legal history. Section 8.6 recaps some insights from previous sections and points to some of the risks of heeding the mermaid's song of the 'global' without keeping a strong footing in historical social reality.

8.2   Actors in the Social History of International Law

Historical writing about international law has traditionally been markedly characterized by the twin features of Eurocentrism and state-centrism. Thematically, the double temporal and spatial bias bequeathed to the study of the history of international law by the gravitational pull of this orientation has been partly assuaged by the rise of post-colonial approaches and world-history and then global historical lenses, as was seen in Chapters 4 and 5. However, a good measure of what the study of international legal history typically consists of still revolves around international legal practice, both theoretical and normative intellectual constructs and also non-state actors, including but not limited to individuals historically associated with European states and in particular with the great European imperial states.

Admittedly, the turn to the history of international law has contributed by extending the gaze of international legal history both temporally and spatially through different periods, and by bringing about the application of different historical methodologies to the study of its potential objects of historical investigation far beyond the traditional normative realm of international legal history. It has also both prompted a critical revision of earlier historical legal literature and entailed a historical re-contextualization of both past and new events, theories, concepts, framing historical constructs, norms, and social actors. By fostering greater inclusion and pushing for different units of historical analysis, the turn has largely contributed to the epistemic pluralization and intellectual democratization of the history of international law as a global research field.

However, less often remarked is the parallel thickening of the already existing large body of disciplinary knowledge associated with great

Western powers that the turn to the history of international law has also brought about. Indeed, the production of multiple histories touching on the colonial history of great powers or animated by the application of global lenses to myriad Western 'encounters' with non-Western peoples and transnational networks across vast spaces or specific to certain areas – but, as was seen in Chapter 5, still dealing fairly little with encounters and networks connecting the 'rest' among themselves – has indirectly fostered a deepening of the historiography of international law regarding great Western powers over recent years. In fact, it may be argued that to a certain extent the overt Eurocentrism of the early days has been super-seded by new variants of historiographical and epistemological 'hidden eurocentrism' even when European histories are re-examined from non-European perspectives today.[17]

Modern historical writing about international law has also shown increasing attention to specific Western national histories of inter-national law during the nineteenth and twentieth centuries. This return to the study of the 'local, the national and international together' springs from a realization, as Anthony Pagden notes, that 'the "national" origin of all things international is undeniable and inescapable'.[18] According to Pagden, from this acknowledgment it follows that 'the recognition and analysis of the contexts, practices, idioms, traditions and discourses etc', which helped shape the evolution of the discipline might help us to see, in Martti Koskenniemi's words, that 'all players are both universal and particular at the same time, speaking a shared language but doing that from their own, localisable standpoint'.[19] Moreover, investigating the relationship of mutually shaping influence between the local and national contexts and the emergence of international legal rules, institutions, principles, and legal doctrines over time is particularly relevant in the light of the aspiration to, or drive towards, universality that is often embedded in these international norms and principles.[20]

---

[17] Martti Koskenniemi, 'The case for comparative international law' (2011) 20 *Finnish Yearbook of International Law* 1–8.
[18] Anthony Pagden, 'Series Editor's preface', in Giulio Bartolini (ed.), *A History of International Law in Italy* (Oxford: Oxford University Press, 2020), pp. v–vii at v.
[19] Ibid., citing Koskenniemi, 'The case', p. 4.
[20] Giulio Bartolini, 'Introduction: what is a history of international law in Italy for? International law through the prism of national perspectives', in Giulio Bartolini (ed.), *A History of International Law in Italy* (Oxford: Oxford University Press, 2020), pp. 3–18 at 3.

Some new national histories have sought to re-investigate the local and national contexts – political, economic, social, intellectual, cultural, religious, and also in terms of legal culture – of great Western powers like the United States,[21] Germany,[22] and the United Kingdom.[23] However, several others have focused their attention on semi-peripheral national histories of international law such as those regarding Spain,[24] Belgium,[25] Italy,[26] Russia,[27] and the Nordic countries.[28] This emerging trend channels an effort to cast light on the margins of Western dominant traditions and therefore beyond the homogenizing perspective of a totalizing 'Western' tradition of international law that had often been constructed around a limited set of historical events, particular international law writers, and the specific experiences and circumstances of Western great powers, with an underestimation or mere exclusion of the rest. Beyond the West, the rise of the historiographical sub-genre of national histories of international law can also be identified regarding non-Western countries including China,[29] the Ottoman Empire,[30] and

[21] Mark Weston Janis, *The American Tradition of International Law: Great Expectations 1789–1914* (Oxford: Oxford University Press, 2004); Mark Weston Janis, *America and the Law of Nations 1776–1939* (Oxford: Oxford University Press, 2010).

[22] Thomas Giegerich and Andreas Zimmermann, 'Introduction' (2007) 50 *German Yearbook of International Law* 16–29 at 16, introducing a symposium with seventeen other contributions. See also Felix Lange, 'Between systematization and expertise for foreign policy – the practice-oriented approach in Germany's international legal scholarship 1920–1980' (2017) 28 *European Journal of International Law* 535–558.

[23] Robert McCorquodale and Jean-Pierre Gauci (eds.), *British Influences on International Law 1915–2015* (Leiden: Brill/Nijhoff, 2016), pp. 110–144.

[24] Ignacio de la Rasilla, *In the Shadow of Vitoria: A History of International Law in Spain 1770–1953* (Leiden: Brill/Nijhoff, 2017).

[25] Vincent Genin, *Le laboratoire belge du droit international: une communauté épistémique et internationale de juristes (1869–1914)* (Brussels: Académie Royale de Belgique, 2018); and Vincent Genin, *La Belgique et ses juristes: du mythe juridique au déclassement international 1914–1940* (Brussels: Peter Lang, 2018).

[26] Giulio Bartolini (ed.), *A History of International Law in Italy* (Oxford: Oxford University Press, 2020).

[27] Lauri Mälksoo, *Russian Approaches to International Law* (Oxford: Oxford University Press, 2017).

[28] Astrid Kjeldgaard-Pedersen, *Nordic Approaches to International Law* (Leiden: Brill/ Nijhoff, 2017).

[29] Maria Adele, *Carrai Sovereignty in China: A Genealogy of a Concept since 1840* (Cambridge, UK: Cambridge University Press, 2019); Anthony Carty and Janne Nijman (eds.), *Morality and Responsibility of Rulers: European and Chinese Origins of a Rule of Law as Justice for World Order* (Oxford: Oxford University Press, 2018).

[30] Umut Özsu and Thomas Skouteris (eds.), 'International legal histories of the Ottoman Empire: an introduction to the symposium' (2016) 19 *Journal of the History of*

India,[31] and there have also been new historical works, often adopting a more traditional normative 'contributionist' approach, from regions such as Latin America,[32] the East Asian region,[33] Eastern Europe,[34] and Africa.[35]

These new national historically based contributions find parallels in, and serve as a basis for, analyses of contemporary national or regional approaches and perspectives, including those with a prognostic angle in contemporary literature.[36] This use goes some way to showing the important role historical writing has in shaping our perspectives on both the present and the future of international law. Critical well-contextualized documented accounts of the genre of national histories of international law, which in the past have too often been prone to nationalist overtones, have much to reveal about aspirations and achievements, but also about the blind spots and dark sides, in different international law epistemological communities in different places in Europe and elsewhere in different periods in international legal history. However, for all the efforts at socio-historical contextualization underlying many of these new national histories, the fact remains that the (re)turn to the national history of international law may also be dubbed a double-edged sword, in particular when it is oriented to identifying a particular unitary 'national' conception – or reconstructing an identitarian socio-historical embedded way – of engaging in international law.

International Law 1–4; Berdal Aral, 'The Ottoman "school" of international law as featured in textbooks' (2016) 18 *Journal of the History of International Law* 70–97.

[31] Fleur Johns, Thomas Skouteris, and Wounter Werner, 'The Periphery Series: India and international law' (2010) 23 *Leiden Journal of International Law* 1–3.

[32] Antônio A. C. Trindade, *The Contribution of Latin American Legal Doctrine to the Progressive Development of International Law* (Leiden: Brill, 2016).

[33] Masaharu Yanagihara, 'Significance of the history of the law of nations in Europe and East Asia' (2014) *Recueil des cours de l'Académie de droit international de La Haye* 273–435.

[34] Stefan Troebst, 'Eastern Europe's imprint on modern international law', in Annalisa Ciampi (ed.), *History and International Law: An Intertwined Relationship* (Cheltenham: Edward Elgar Publishing, 2019), pp. 22–43.

[35] Adetola Onayemi and Olufemi Elias, 'Aspects of Africa's contribution to the development of international law', in Charles Chernor Jalloh and Olufemi Elias (eds.), *Shielding Humanity: Essays in International Law in Honour of Judge Abdul G. Koroma* (Leiden: Brill, 2015), pp. 591–613.

[36] Simon Chesterman, 'Asian ambivalence about international law and institutions: past, present and future' (2016) 27 *European Journal of International Law* 945–978.

This consideration has gained new credentials in the light of new scholarship on 'comparative international law'.[37] This has reopened a debate on whether or not international law is truly 'international' in the light of the fact that many national epistemic communities and networks of international lawyers still remain attached to particular 'national' visions of international law as a means to foster narrowly conceived national interests on the global stage – which on occasion may make international legal scholarship itself appear as a strategic intellectual extension of 'international lawfare'.[38] This revolves around a suspicion that not so much instead of but perhaps alongside the much vaunted like-minded international 'college of international lawyers',[39] one may also speak of the existence of a 'divisible college of international lawyers'[40] working strictly along 'national' lines in the international legal arena. This suspicion goes beyond the general understanding that 'the international legal scholarship in a certain country might be more likely to possess certain characteristics, depending on its specific philosophical, political and legal traditions and the way international law is taught at its universities'.[41] Instead, the sociologically inspired concept of a 'divisible college' of 'separate, though sometimes overlapping, communities with their own understandings and approaches'[42] may be usefully reminiscent of the influence that scientifically directed expertise on foreign policy may have on the shaping of international legal scholarship under specific political conditions both present and past. This not only concerns specific national differences in approaches to contemporary themes or the allocation of resources to some of them rather than others but also draws attention to how different national epistemic communities of international legal historians may appropriate the past with a view to rewriting it in the present and influencing the future in the service of narrow foreign-policy designs.

Indeed, it is an interesting paradox that while the historical discipline has for some time now been turning away from 'methodological

---

[37] Anthea Roberts, *Is International Law International?* (Oxford: Oxford University Press, 2017).

[38] Congyan Cai, *The Rise of China and International Law: Taking Chinese Exceptionalism Seriously* (Oxford: Oxford University Press, 2019).

[39] Oscar Schachter, 'The invisible college of international lawyers' (1977) 72 *Northwestern University School of Law Review* 217–226.

[40] Roberts, *Is International Law International?*

[41] Giegerich and Zimmermann, 'Introduction', pp. 15 and 19.

[42] See Roberts, *Is International Law International?*, p. 2.

nationalism' and towards global history, international legal history may, in responding to very similar methodological shifts of perspective, including a turn to the local and a renewed focus on global interactions, be instead turning back to writing histories for a re-nationalized future. This consideration, which should be read in the light of the different stages in the nation-state-building processes reached by different states, and in particular, as was mentioned in Chapter 4, by those new nation-states which emerged from the decolonization process, may also go some way towards suggesting in the context of the contemporary decline of liberal internationalism the merit of further delving into the study of national and/or regional historiographies of international law over time.[43]

However, although the nation-state remains either directly or indirectly central in the new histories of international law, non-state actors have gained centre stage in international law during the twentieth century. This rise took place incipiently during the interwar period, coinciding with the move towards the institutionalization of international society embodied by the League of Nations, where discussions on new legal topics in international law began to develop,[44] and consolidated in the shadow of the establishment of the UN. Their ascendancy was definitively crystallized in the new global post-Cold War period, which witnessed a growing role for non-state actors in international-law entrepreneurship, law-making, law-interpretation, monitoring, adjudication, and enforcement processes and in its wake a greater interest on their international rights and also the obligations to which they can be held accountable under international law.[45]

Sharing in the tendency to look trans-historically inside, across, and beyond the porous borders of the nation-state as an abstract entity of analysis, the globalist move to venture beyond national enclosures has furthered historical interest in the different historical embodiments of non-state actors and their roles in shaping the workings of international law in different historical periods. Besides the new attention that international legal historians have devoted to international organizations and individuals, which are treated separately in Chapters 6, 9, and 10, other

---

[43] Randall Lesaffer and Anne Peters (eds.), *The Cambridge History of International Law*, vol. 1: *Historiography* (in press).
[44] Natasha Wheatley, 'Spectral legal personality in interwar international law: on new ways of not being a state' (2017) 35 *Law and History Review* 753–787.
[45] See Clapham, *Human Rights Obligations*.

non-state actors have also received much more attention than hitherto.[46] Indeed, the history of many international legal regimes, such as for example international humanitarian law, international environmental law, international economic law, and international human rights law in all its many sub-variants (ranging from the advocacy of women's rights to freedom of expression and religion, disability laws and so on), cannot be comprehensively grasped without reference to the historical influence of many such non-state actors.[47]

Partly as an offspring of the diversification and expansion of international law, just as contemporary international legal regimes are highly influenced by a variety of non-state actors and so was their history, interest in them extends beyond their direct participation in historical international legal processes to further encompass attention to them as objects of international regulation. This is diversely shown by the historical role of non-state armed groups, transnational criminal networks, terrorist groups, and pirates as *hostis humani generis* (enemies of all mankind) in the history of the laws of war and international criminal law.[48] Likewise, the contemporary importance of multinational and transnational corporations in the world economy and their influence on international law regimes have also spurred investigation of the historical role of private mercantile entities from the perspective of the international legal history. One of the diverse lines of historical exploration that has gained momentum in this area follows in the wake of the search for precedents of a 'third legal order' between municipal and international law for the transnational business community and the subsequent tracing of parallelisms between the post-state-centric hybrid legal world of the present and the 'a-national' web of legal rules and principles of the medieval *lex mercatoria* which arose from the customary practices of merchants in the area of maritime trade and other trading

---

[46] Not included in the category of non-state actors for the present purposes are 'international organizations or formations of states (e.g. the Group of Eight [G8]) as well as sub-State actors (Federal States)' which 'retain statal or governmental characteristics'. See Markus Wagner, 'Non-state actors', in *Max Planck Encyclopedia of Public International Law* (2013), opil.ouplaw.com/view/10.1093/law:epil/9780199231690/law-9780199231690-e1445.

[47] Jean d'Aspremont (ed.), *Participants in the International Legal System Multiple Perspectives on Non-state Actors in International Law* (New York: Routledge, 2011).

[48] Stephen C. Neff, *War and the Law of Nations: A General History* (Cambridge, UK: Cambridge University Press, 2005); Morten Bergsmo, Cheah Wui Ling, and Yi Ping (eds.), *Historical Origins of International Criminal Law*, vols. 1–2 (Brussels: Torkel Opsahl Academic EPublisher, 2014).

and commercial dealings in the pre-modern-state sovereign space.[49] Another driver that has stimulated the historical study of commercial non-state actors in international legal history is the role of trade, chartered companies, and mercantile associations in colonial empires and their responsibility for colonial exploitation,[50] starting with what is deemed the world's first international corporation, the Dutch East India Company (Vereenigde Oostindische Compagnie; VOC) established in 1602, in particular, as was seen in Chapter 4, under the influence of post-colonial approaches. Investigation of the connection between chartered companies and particular commercial pursuits such as the slave trade has furthermore led to an unearthing of obscure episodes in the genealogy of contemporary international legal institutions.[51]

Moreover, one of the most remarkable features of the post-Cold War era in international law has been the further development of a broad galaxy of international NGOs operating across a broad area of sectors from sports and religion to medical science and human rights so as to encompass 'virtually all areas of social life'.[52] Their great number,[53] in addition to their broad thematic reach, means that almost every single international legal regime is contemporarily affected and influenced by the workings of NGOs,[54] whether through their participation in international conferences, treaty-making processes, the development of

---

[49] Nikitas Hatzimihail, 'The many lives and faces of *lex mercatoria*: an essay on the genealogy of international business law' (2008) 71 *Law & Contemporary Problems* 169–190.

[50] Koen Stapelbroek, 'Trade, chartered companies, and mercantile associations', in Bardo Fassbender and Anne Peters (eds.), *The Oxford Handbook of the History of International Law* (Oxford: Oxford University Press, 2012), pp. 338–358; Phillip J. Stern, '"Bundles of hyphens": corporations as legal communities in the early modern British Empire', in Lauren Benton and Richard J. Ross (eds.), *Legal Pluralism and Empires 1500–1800* (New York: New York University Press, 2013), pp. 21–47.

[51] Anne-Charlotte Martineau, 'A forgotten chapter in the history of international commercial arbitration: the slave trade's dispute settlement system' (2018) 31 *Leiden Journal of International Law* 219–241.

[52] Stephan Hobe, 'Non-governmental organizations', in *Max Planck Encyclopedia of Public International Law* (2010), opil.ouplaw.com/view/10.1093/law:epil/9780199231690/law-9780199231690-e968, p. 3.

[53] The Union of International Associations, which lists both intergovernmental organizations (IGOs) and international non-governmental organizations (INGOs), included information on circa 73,000 international organizations from 300 countries and territories in 2020. See Union of International Associations (ed.), *Yearbook of International Organizations* (Leiden: Brill, 2020), also available at uia.org/ybio/.

[54] Steve Charnovitz, 'Non-governmental organizations and international law' (2006) 100 *American Journal of International Law* 348–372.

regulations and standards often regarded as soft law (and/or, occasionally, as norms of customary international law *in nuce*) or in a panoply of verification and monitoring functions as they operate as watchdogs on compliance with international legal norms and obligations, including at the national, regional, and international adjudicative levels.[55] This has in turn led to a revamped socio-historical investigation into the impulses and contributions of different embodiments of the international associational movement such as professional international law societies, churches, faith-based groups, missions, and a diversity of social movements stretching back for more than 200 years,[56] with the British and Foreign Anti-Slavery Society, established in 1839, usually being identified as the 'first modern NGO of an international reach'.[57]

According to Steve Charnovitz, from the late eighteenth century the main initiatives to 'inspire globalizing NGOs' were the fight against the slave trade, the pursuit of peace, the struggle for national and then transnational worker solidarity, free trade, and the promotion of international law,[58] with the main growth of international NGOs taking flight in the second part of the nineteenth century and becoming further consolidated in the wake of the establishment of the League of Nations. As has already been seen, they would further increase their number in the aftermath of World War II and quantitatively explode in the 1990s. Against this background, one prominent focus of international legal historians' interest in NGOs has been the study of different professional associations in the development and promotion of international law.

Indeed, in the wake of Martti Koskenniemi's seminal treatment of 'the men of 1873',[59] and in extending the turn to international legal biography, examined in Chapter 10, earlier centennial commemorative works on the 'first NGOs particularly concerned with the development of international law'[60] have been largely complemented with new works

[55] Hobe, 'Non-governmental organizations', pp. 3–5.
[56] Steve Charnovitz, 'Two centuries of participation: NGOs and international governance' (1997) 18 *Michigan Journal of International Law* 183–286.
[57] Hobe, 'Non-governmental organizations', p. 3.
[58] Charnovitz, 'Two centuries of participation', pp. 191–195.
[59] See further Martti Koskenniemi, *The Gentle Civilizer of Nations: The Rise and Fall of International Law 1870–1960* (Cambridge, UK: Cambridge University Press, 2001).
[60] Gerald Fitzmaurice, *The Contribution of the Institute of International Law to the Development of International Law* (Leiden: Martinus Nijhoff, 1973). See, further, Peter Macalister-Smith, 'Institut de Droit international', in *Max Planck Encyclopedia of Public International Law* (2011), opil.ouplaw.com/view/10.1093/law:epil/9780199231690/law-9780199231690-e947?prd=EPIL.

on the International Law Association or the Institut de droit international.[61] New historical research has also sought to revisit national associations, like the American Society of International Law,[62] on their anniversaries or has been produced on regional associations like the American Institute of International Law.[63] Furthermore, following in the wake of the fragmentation of the history of international law, new historical research has been produced in '"people with projects" mode'[64] on the members of disciplinarily adjacent professional associations, like the Association internationale de droit pénale, which was founded at the dawn of the discipline of international criminal justice in the early interwar period.[65] One of the characteristics of the new wave of historical research which opens up to the social context of the development of international law in history is the sociological stress on network theory in unpacking the role that professional interrelations and intertwined interests has played in the shaping of the pasts of international law.

In contrast to the great attention international legal historians have paid to epistemological associations of international law professionals, which historically emerged at the time when the international lawyer was still pictured, in an Austinian vein in the London *Times*, as 'that amphibious being who works mid-way between law and morality',[66] other NGOs, the history of which has been investigated in adjacent disciplinary traditions, have still to receive more attention from international lawyers. Despite the fact that there has been attention to them as part of the retracing of the origins of different international law regimes, more socio-legal historical attention from the perspective of international law can be devoted to the establishment of the International Committee for the Relief of Wounded in the Event of War (1862), today the International Committee of the Red Cross (ICRC), a 'sui generis entity

---

[61] See Genin, *Le laboratoire belge du droit international*.

[62] Frederic L. Kirgis, *The American Society of International Law's First Century 1906–2006* (Leiden: Brill/Nijhoff, 2006).

[63] Juan Pablo Scarfi, *The Hidden History of International Law in the Americas: Empire and Legal Networks* (Oxford: Oxford University Press, 2017).

[64] Martti Koskenniemi, 'Foreword', in Frédéric Mégret and Immi Tallgren (eds.), *The Dawn of a Discipline: International Criminal Justice and Its Early Exponents* (Cambridge, UK: Cambridge University Press, 2020), pp. xiii–xix.

[65] See Frédéric Mégret and Immi Tallgren (eds.), *The Dawn of a Discipline: International Criminal Justice and Its Early Exponents* (Cambridge, UK: Cambridge University Press, 2020).

[66] Cited in Irwin Abrams, 'The emergence of international law societies' (1957) 19 *The Review of Politics* 361–380 at 362.

in the international legal process' with the status of a private association that 'makes it akin to an NGO',[67] and the workings of the International Workers Association (1864), the Inter-Parliamentary Union (1889),[68] the Permanent International Peace Bureau (1891), and, moving into the twentieth century, the International Federation of Trade Unions (1919), the International Chamber of Commerce (1919), and some of the most famous NGOs born in the years and decades following World War II such as the International Commission of Jurists (1952),[69] Amnesty International (1961),[70] Greenpeace (1971),[71] and Human Rights Watch (1978).[72]

In fact, besides the institutional history of these NGOs as 'products of a forward-moving current of ideas',[73] their histories are also entry-points for international law to be brought from its elite cosmopolitan configuration towards grass-roots social movements and thus to progress towards the history of the local in international law. This can be carried forward through a greater engagement with the role of social movements in international law as expressions of impulses from civil society in response to major economic developments and social transformations across time and space,[74] from the local – even the rural – level, as, among others, explorations of resistance and radical contestation in the name of race, indigeneity, social conditions, labour, gender, environment, sexual orientation, development, and other concerns.

Moving further into the socio-cultural historical substratum of international law, one encounters the long-standing influence of churches, faith-based groups, and missions on its development. The complex and multifaceted relationship between religion and international law has long

[67] Steven R. Ratner, 'Law promotion beyond law talk: the Red Cross, persuasion, and the laws of war' (2011) 22 *European Journal of International Law* 459–506 at 464.
[68] Yéfime Zarjevski, *The People Have the Floor: A History of the Inter-Parliamentary Union* (Aldershot: Dartmouth, 1989).
[69] Howard B. Tolley, *The International Commission of Jurists: Global Advocates for Human Rights* (Philadelphia: University of Pennsylvania Press, 1994).
[70] Anne Marie Clark, *Diplomacy of Conscience: Amnesty International and Changing Human Rights Norms* (Princeton, NJ: Princeton University Press, 2001).
[71] Frank Zelko, *Make It a Green Peace! The Rise of a Countercultural Environmentalism* (Oxford: Oxford University Press, 2013).
[72] Jeri Laber, *The Courage of Strangers: Coming of Age with the Human Rights Movement* (New York: Public Affairs, 2002).
[73] Abrams, 'The emergence', pp. 362 and 380.
[74] Balakrishnan Rajagopal, *International Law from Below: Development, Social Movements and Third World Resistance* (Cambridge, UK: Cambridge University Press, 2003).

attracted the attention of international law scholars.[75] This is so because faith-based institutionalized communities have been important actors, with the Roman Catholic Church being considered probably the 'earliest internationally active NGO',[76] in the prescriptive shaping of international norms, both directly as proponents of international treaties in different normative areas, and in particular in the realm of international human rights, and more broadly as sources of support for a greater role for an axiologically inspired or value-ridden international legal order inspired by religious and moral considerations both in general terms (e.g. the peace movement) and regarding particular causes (e.g. anti-slavery) or circumstances (e.g. the humanitarianization of war) historically.[77] Moreover, while the twentieth century largely contributed to the secularization of international law, historical studies of the intellectual evolution of international law theories and concepts in the Western world cannot ignore the inextricably embedded cultural influence of Christianity, in particular during what Auguste Comte theorized as 'theological' and 'metaphysical' stages in the progress of domestic societies in their historical evolution,[78] and by extension in their outer-realm.[79] In addition, well beyond Christianity,[80] the decisive influence of religions and moral

[75] Mark Weston Janis et al., 'Religion and international law' (1988) 82 *Proceedings of the Annual Meeting (American Society of International Law)* 195–220; George Goyau, 'L'église catholique et le droit des gens' (1925) 6 *Recueil des cours de l'Académie de droit international de La Haye* 123–240; Marc Boegner, 'L'influence de la Réforme sur le développement du droit international' (1925) 6 *Recueil des cours de l'Académie de droit international de La Haye* 241–324; Ahmed Rechid, 'L'Islam et le droit des gens' (1937) 60 *Recueil des cours de l'Académie de droit international de La Haye* 371–506 at 385; Kulatissa N. Jayatilleke, 'The principles of international law in Buddhist doctrine' (1967) 120 *Recueil des cours de l'Académie de droit international de La Haye* 441–568.

[76] See Charnovitz, 'Two centuries of participation', p. 190. See also Christian J. Tams, 'World peace through international adjudication?', in Heinz-Gerhard Justenhoven and Mary E. O'Connell (eds.), *Peace through Law: Reflections on* Pacem in Terris *from Philosophy, Law, Theology, and Political Science* (Baden-Baden: Nomos, 2016), pp. 215–254.

[77] Emmanuel Decaux, 'Les influences réciproques entre religion(s) et droit international', in Robert Uerpmann-Wittzack, Evelyne Lagrange, and Stefan Oeter (eds.), *Religion and International Law: Living Together* (Leiden: Brill/Nijhoff, 2018), pp. 353–373.

[78] Auguste Comte, *Cours de philosophie positive*, 6 vols. (Paris: Édition Rouen Frères, 1830–42).

[79] Martti Koskenniemi, Mónica García-Salmones Rovira, and Paolo Amorosa (eds.), *International Law and Religion: Historical and Contemporary Perspectives* (Oxford: Oxford University Press, 2017).

[80] Leonard Francis Taylor, *Catholic Cosmopolitanism and Human Rights* (Cambridge, UK: Cambridge University Press, 2020).

traditions on local and national cultures, and more specifically on different legal cultural traditions – both municipal and by extension international – encompasses their major historical traditional exponents such
as Confucianism,[81] Hinduism,[82] Judaism,[83] and Islam[84] across vast geographical spaces both past and also present.

8.3   Sociological Approaches to International Law

The turn to the history of international law has, as we have seen,
prompted a revamped sociological thickening of the study of national
histories of international law and more – albeit still limited – attention
among international law historians to the histories of non-state actors
and to the social, cultural, ethical, religious, and commercial stimuli and
forces underlying them. Moreover, as Thomas Skouteris and Immi
Tallgren note, the turn has also stimulated a 'move towards sociological
accounts of the international system, the profession, and its professional
practices, as well as biographical accounts of its professionals or intellectuals'.[85] While the biographical socio-historical focus on international
law's professionals has grown exponentially and, as Chapter 10 examines,
presents   new   interesting   methodological   features,   sociological
approaches to the study of the international legal system have a long
pedigree in international legal scholarship too. These emerged to serve in
contradistinction to the focus on nation-states and the ensuing methodological dominance of voluntarist positivism in international law. They
did so by stressing the broader international social milieu within which
states operate and the particular social forces within them and, gradually,
the many levels of existing interactions among the different social actors
of which states are made, and of those which were destined to

---

[81] Yang Zewei, 'Western international law and China's Confucianism in the 19th century:
      collision and integration' (2011) 13 *Journal of the History of International Law* 285–306.
[82] K. R. R. Sastry, 'Hinduism and international law' (1966) 117 *Collected Courses of the
      Hague Academy of International Law* 507–614.
[83] James Loeffler and Moria Paz (eds.), *The Law of Strangers: Jewish Lawyers and
      International Law in the Twentieth Century* (Cambridge, UK: Cambridge University
      Press, 2019).
[84] Ignacio de la Rasilla and Ayesha Shahid (eds.), *International Law and Islam: Historical
      Explorations* (Leiden and Boston: Brill/Nijhoff, 2019).
[85] Thomas Skouteris and Immi Tallgren, 'Editors' introduction', in Thomas Skouteris and
      Immi Tallgren (eds.), *New Histories of International Criminal Law* (Oxford: Oxford
      University Press, 2019), pp. 1–15 at 2.

increasingly gain different levels of autonomy from them on the international plane.

Arising at the beginning of the twentieth century, sociological theories of, or approaches to, international law are often retraced back to Max Huber's *Beiträge zur Kenntnis dersoziologischen Grundlagen des Völkerrechts und der Staatengesellschaft* (1910)[86] and his 'analytical breakdown' of the elements that influence international society's inclination towards integration or disintegration,[87] along with his notion of 'collective interest' of states as one from which Huber believed that the general binding force of international law derives.[88] However, it was in the interwar period that sociological perspectives joined up in the critique of state sovereignty so as to prioritize the normative force of the 'international community' as epitome of a common social reality marked by interdependence and the exigence of cooperation among its members over that of the individual state-consent-based paradigm.[89] This sociological strand in international law, which as Robert Kolb notes was 'a means of fighting against state-centred and will-oriented positivism without giving up the anti-speculative and anti-metaphysical tradition',[90] was particularly influential in France.[91] There, several authors including Nicolas Politis[92] and more famously Georges Scelle fostered a particular socio-international legal consciousness by transposing to the international realm the writings of Émile Durkheim and Leon Duguit's *droit*

---

[86] First published as Max Huber, 'Beiträge zur Kenntnis der soziologischen Grundlagen des Völkerrechts und der Staatengesellschaft' (1910) 4 Jahrbuch des öffentlichen Rechts 56–134.

[87] Anthony Carty, 'Sociological theories of international law', in *Max Planck Encyclopedia of Public International Law* (2008), opil.ouplaw.com/view/10.1093/law:epil/9780199231690/law-9780199231690-e735?prd=EPIL.

[88] Jost Delbrück, 'Max Huber's sociological approach to international law' (2007) 18 *European Journal of International Law* 97–113 at 110.

[89] See, e.g., Dietrich Schlinder, 'Contribution à l'étude des facteurs sociologiques et psychologiques du droit international' (1933) 46 *Recueil des cours de l'Académie de droit international de La Haye* 229–326; Théodore Ruyssen, 'Les caractères sociologiques de la communauté humaine' (1939) 67 *Recueil des cours de l'Académie de droit international de La Haye* 121–232.

[90] Robert Kolb, 'Politis and sociological jurisprudence of inter-war international law' (2012) 23 *European Journal of International Law* 233–241 at 236.

[91] On interwar French sociological approaches to international law, see Koskenniemi, *The Gentle Civilizer of Nations*, pp. 266–352.

[92] Linos-Alexander Sicilianos and Thomas Skouteris (eds.), 'Symposium – the European tradition in international law: Nicolas Politis' (2012) 23 *European Journal of International Law* 215–273.

naturel biologique,[93] for which 'the basis of the law is the fact of 'solidarity' or of 'interdependence' between human beings'.[94] This led to what is perhaps the most representative interwar variant of 'progressive sociological approaches' in the so-called solidarist (or sociological) school of international law, epitomized by Scelle's consciously anti-positivist monism premised on the lodestar of the 'objective law' of the international community.[95]

Another parallel sociological strand was to emerge under the influence of American legal realism and sociological jurisprudence,[96] on the anti-formalist grounds of 'the sociological school of law's insistence on scientific fact-finding as a precondition for rational legal problem-solving',[97] calling for a study of a 'science of international relations' in the understanding that the combination of the study of law and international politics would further the practical realization of the social ends of the international system.[98] One of the most idiosyncratic crystallizations of this tradition was the policy-oriented methodology of the New Haven School in the aftermath of World War II.[99] Indeed, the theorizing architects of policy-oriented jurisprudence developed a distinctive approach that stressed the continual anti-formal policy-process relationship between law – which they defined as the interlocking of authority with power[100] – and politics. Their perspective, moreover, was informed by an underlying call for ethical responsibility in upholding a number of goals and values in the pursuit of context-dependent 'comprehensive global processes of authoritative decision'.[101] This policy-oriented jurisprudence's commitment to the realization of a

---

[93] Antonio Truyol y Serra, *Histoire du droit international public* (Paris: Economica, 1998), p. 145.

[94] Kolb, 'Politis and sociological jurisprudence', p. 237.

[95] Georges Scelle, *Précis de droit des gens: principes et systematique* (Paris: Librairie du Recueil Sirey, 1932).

[96] Samuel J. Astorino, 'The impact of sociological jurisprudence on international law in the inter-war-period: the American experience' (1995–96) 34 *Dusquene Law Review* 277–298.

[97] Edward McWhinney, 'Julius Stone and the sociological approach to international law' (1986) 9 *The University of New South Wales Law Journal* 14–25 at 23.

[98] Antony Anghie, *Imperialism, Sovereignty and the Making of International Law* (Cambridge, UK: Cambridge University Press, 2005), p. 131.

[99] Günter Frankenberg, 'Critical theory', in *Max Planck Encyclopedia of Public International* Law (2010), opil.ouplaw.com/view/10.1093/law:epil/9780199231690/law-9780199231690-e693?prd=EPIL, p. 6.

[100] Rosalyn Higgins, *Problems and Process: International Law and How We Use It* (Oxford: Clarendon Press, 1994).

[101] Harold D. Lasswell and Myres S. McDougal, *Jurisprudence for a Free Society: Studies in Law, Science and Policy* (New Haven, CT: New Haven Press, 1992).

set of 'goal values of international human dignity' is one that the New
Haven School's approach justifies by developing a systematic and open
training method for the scientific interpretation of policy factors so as to
ensure adequate performance of the decision-making function.[102]
Throughout the 1950s, several courses at The Hague Academy
revolved around sociological theories and approaches to international
law,[103] including one by Julius Stone,[104] a disciple of Roscoe Pound and
considered after him 'perhaps the key theorist of the US-based sociological approach to law'.[105] These sociological perspectives developed 'at
the extremes of the sociology of international law and theory of international relations' in efforts, against the systematic Kelsenian attempt to
eliminate extra-juridical elements from legal theory, to cut short 'the
progressive distancing of the theory of law from social reality'.[106] They
were further spurred, and also complicated, by international law's need to
adapt the macro-sociological transition from, as Edward McWhinney
notes, the 'essentially European and European-by-extension (North
American and Latin American) international special legal community
of yesterday to the plural multicultural multi-systemic (legal, and
ideological-legal) world community'[107] that was by then emerging in
the wake of decolonization processes in Africa and Asia.

This post-colonial new multipolar scenario, which crystallized in the
post-Cold War era, has prompted, as noted in the introduction to this
chapter, a decrease in the epistemological purchase of the nation-state as
the exclusively dominant unit of international legal analysis in a new
golden age of liberal internationalism. The subsequent certain decline in
the epistemological grip of 'realist' theories of international relations (IR)
that had dominated Cold War thinking was further accompanied by the

---

[102] Ibid.
[103] Bartholomeus Landheer, 'Contemporary sociological theories and international law'
(1957) 91 *Recueil des cours de l'Académie de droit international de La Haye* 1–104;
Antonio Truyol y Serra, 'Genèse et structure de la société internationale' (1959) 96
Recueil des cours de l'Académie de droit international de La Haye 553–642.
[104] Julius Stone, 'Problems confronting sociological enquiries concerning international law'
(1956) 89 *Recueil des cours de l'Académie de droit international de La Haye* 61–180;
Julius Stone, 'A sociological perspective on international law', in Ronald St J. Macdonald
and Douglas M. Johnston (eds.), *The Structure and Process of International Law: Essays
in Legal Philosophy, Doctrine, and Theory* (The Hague: Martinus Nijhoff, 1983),
pp. 263–304 at 284.
[105] McWhinney, 'Julius Stone and the sociological approach', p. 15.
[106] Truyol y Serra, 'Genèse et structure', pp. 558–559.
[107] McWhinney, 'Julius Stone and the sociological approach', p. 20.

rise of constructivism with its original insight that meaning is socially constructed and therefore 'people act toward objects, including other actors, on the basis of the meanings that the objects have for them',[108] which in the case of the states implies that their 'social relationships' define the scope of their interests, expectations, and motivations.

In this intellectually transformed scenario, sociological lenses have had many theoretical applications in international law. These include, to mention but a few, the application of the framework of 'autopoiesis' from a functionalist sociology of law to the phenomenon of the fragmentation of international law,[109] or the emphasis by sociological studies of international law on the fact 'that socio-cultural factors are involved in two primary (and inter-related) dimensions of international law: behavior and knowledge' – but also at the level of the 'cognitive dimension' of the actors in the international legal system.[110] They also have included the application of a sociological scientific fields perspective to map out and make better sense of the sheer methodological and theoretical diversity experienced by international law as an academic field over recent decades.[111]

8.4   The Socio-historical Impact on Knowledge Production Processes

There is some truth in Koskenniemi's statement that 'although social history has now entered the world of international relations, no comparable turn has appeared yet in international law'.[112] Indeed, socio-legal historical methods have been sparsely applied to the study of international legal history, in particular by international lawyers moonlighting as historians. However, it is also true that the influence of historical contextualist approaches, as was seen in Chapter 2, a greater cultivation

---

[108] See e.g. Alexander Wendt, 'Anarchy is what states make of it: the social construction of power politics' (1992) 46 *International Organization* 391–342.

[109] Gunther Teubner, *Law As an Autopoietic System* (Oxford: Blackwell, 1989).

[110] Moshe Hirsch, *The Sociological Perspective on International Law in International Legal Theory: Foundations and Frontiers*, ed. Jeffrey L. Dunoff and Mark A. Pollack (in press), p. 12 (in draft).

[111] Andrea Bianchi, *International Law Theories: An Inquiry into Different Ways of Thinking* (Oxford: Oxford University Press, 2016), pp. 9–13.

[112] Martti Koskenniemi, 'Histories of international law: significance and problems for a critical view' (2013) 27 *Temple International Law and Comparative Law Journal* 215–240 at 238.

of the study of 'international law in history', and also, inter alia, of global approaches together with more attention devoted to individual professionals and to different non-state actors, as seen in other chapters, have also marked a shift of historiographical tendency.

While socio-historical lenses in international legal history may still have a long way to go, there has already clearly been a historiographical departure from some of the more normative-oriented state-centric approaches to international legal history of before and from understandings of international legal history as concerned with describing the internal 'evolution (or stasis) of legal doctrine or legal institutions over time' rather than being attentive to the central idea of law- and society-oriented legal historians that 'the meaning and function of law cannot be understood without close attention to social, economic and political context'.[113] Having noted this, there is still a very ample margin for the application of sociological theories to the historical study of international law's 'formation, evolution and implementation', which is, according to Moshe Hirsch, influenced by 'sociological factors and processes' that in turn are influenced by international law understood as a mechanism of social control and socialization. Indeed, the application of the lenses provided by what Hirsch terms the tripartite typology of dominant sociological perspectives – the 'structural-functional perspective', the 'symbolic-interactionist approach', and the 'social conflict perspective'[114] – can retrospectively illuminate the controlling mechanisms of historical international legal processes in multiple historical episodes, in particular in the domains of the 'history of international law' and 'international law in history', as was seen in Chapter 7. Such exploration can inter alia make more apparent the 'contingency' of the historical development of the discipline for what regards the reconstruction of decision-making mechanisms and complex chains of historical causation by putting the stress on competition among social interests and the societal groups sponsoring them in the exploration of different historical episodes in international law. This opening up to context, albeit within the porous limits marked by the still strong pull of a juridical form of presentism in the disciplinary international normative historical realm, is already well under way.

---

[113] Catherine L. Fisk, '&: law society in historical legal research', in Markus Dirk Dubber and Christopher L. Tomlins (eds.), *The Oxford Handbook of Legal History* (Oxford: Oxford University Press, 2018) pp. 479–496 at 481.

[114] Hirsch, *The Sociological Perspective*, pp. 3–9.

On the other hand, the rising of consciousness about the social dimension of the history of international law promotes a less hierarchically organized and therefore a more horizontal history of the individual dramatis personae of the history of international law. Indeed, while the turn to the sociology of the profession has prompted an increased cultivation, as will be seen in Chapter 10, of the intellectual biography of international law in context, this can still be largely criticized for its tendency to continue producing an overlapping series of historical studies on the intellectual elite of 'great men' or 'heroic' figures à la Carlyle in the historical canon of the discipline of international law. By contrast, the larger the sociological inclination of the approach, the more encompassing the history of international law becomes so as to include the study of the historical role of lesser well-known international law scholars, lawyers, and other players who may have been obscurely influential within larger transnational professional networks.

Moreover, the intellectual and practical influence of individuals is not restricted to those working within the academic domain, even when their traditional professional ramifications in other areas of international legal practice are considered. In fact, the application of sociological lenses naturally extends the gaze beyond the individual to the realm of prosopography and the history of social groups around each of the main social actors of international law so as to include many other individual agents working within different types of organizations and social movements. They are responsible for setting up standards, and also for the daily application and enforcement of international law as interpretive and management communities within specific international organizations, whether governmental, as Chapter 9 examines, or non-governmental ones. But if, as Hirsch notes, 'casting light on the social factors and processes taking place in the context of – and within – international legal decision-makers' social environments, as well as the social interactions between such social groups, is often vital for understanding the formation, interpretation and implementation of international law',[115] the potential of studying the intellectual contribution implied in the tailoring of the international *corpus iuris* to the practice in the field equally extends to the role of bureaucrats, minor state civil servants, and different groups involved in legal processes with an element of internationality.

---

[115] Ibid.

At the opposite extreme of micro-socio-historical enquiries revolving around historically socio-contextualized accounts of the lives and works of different international law professionals in their social milieu lies the study of the macro-social historical dimension of international law. This, as Koskenniemi suggests, may involve studying the interplay between 'the development of normative systems' and 'macro-level economic and social developments' so as to unearth the levers of mutual interaction between international law and such developments.[116] These generally evoked 'economic and social developments' may include phenomena as broad as the industrial revolution, or the most recent digital one, the generalization of women entering the labour force, transitions to new energy models, the establishment of public policies of compulsory schooling, and the enabling of citizen's access to higher education, all of which can be variously socio-historically retraced at different junctures to the evolving course of the international legal system.

On the other hand, any international lawyer possesses a good intuitional understanding that myriad background social conditions and political forces of diverse persuasion have largely conditioned the development of international law through, albeit among others, the operation of the foreign-policy apparatuses at both the regional and global levels. However, much archival work – including some in many still temporally sealed national archives – is needed to unearth the actual levers behind decision-making and their connection to larger national, regional, and international societal contexts, societal changes, and social forces, and also to lobby national commercial groups and multinational private interests representing industrial and productive sectors. In this sense, having adopted, as was seen in Chapter 3, a more marked political economy perspective of late in his historical work, Koskenniemi has suggested the need to gaze beyond what one may call the historiographical bottleneck of the 'vocabularies of political causation' that have traditionally 'dominated diplomatic history and the associated realisms'.[117] Instead, he suggests engaging more deeply the 'social or economic forces that seem to account for such important aspects of the way the world has come about'[118] and in particular 'the global network of property relations', itself an offspring of how the 'notions of property and

---

[116] Koskenniemi, 'Why history of international law today?', pp. 65–66.
[117] Koskenniemi, 'Histories of international law: significance and problems', p. 237.
[118] Ibid.

contract, the structures of family law, inheritance and succession, as well as the corporate form have developed over time'.[119]

Koskenniemi suggests that historians of international law should, to use a geological metaphor, dig deeper in the social strata which form the various layers of sediments from which both the domestic and the international legal order have emanated over time. However, this does not automatically imply, as highlighted by Joseph Weiler, that these different historical layers have superseded each other in their international legal emanations.[120] Koskenniemi's call for *mutatis mutandi* a *histoire totale* of international law must also consider that the history of the different international legal regimes that form it cannot be grasped solely as the history of specialized international branches of law in the wake of the progressive specialization of public international law in response to shifting international societal background conditions. Instead, their historical development should also be examined with an attentive eye to the theoretical and practical legislative development of functionally specialized trends of legal thought in domestic settings and both the social forces and the phenomena that brought them about.

However, besides this, which one may term the vertical dimension of the socio-legal historical approach to international law, there is also an international horizontal dimension of sorts to account for. This may be equated with the study of the connection 'between different historical types of international society and the types of normative system connected with them' or in other words 'attempts to study international law from the perspective of the international system', of which according to Koskenniemi there have been 'virtually none'.[121] The convenience of such a study taking 'international society as a historiographical subject, that is to say as a useful conceptual category',[122] ensues naturally from one of the axioms of legal sociology, whose adherents have 'long emphasized that law is rooted in communities, and laws are expressive types of those communities'.[123] However, unless the geographical scale chosen is

[119] Ibid.
[120] Joseph H. H. Weiler, 'The geology of international law – governance, democracy and legitimacy' (2004) 64 *Zeitschrift für ausländisches öffentliches Recht und Völkerrecht* 547–562.
[121] Koskenniemi, 'Why history of international law today?', pp. 65–66.
[122] Erez Manela, 'International society as a historical subject' (2020) 44 *Diplomatic History* 184–209 at 184.
[123] Moshe Hirsch, *Invitation to the Sociology of International Law* (Oxford: Oxford University Press, 2005), p. 9.

regional rather than global, it remains less straightforwardly evident how to sociologically categorize the different historical types of 'international society' that may have actually existed on the global plane in the light of the asymmetrical relations in which its main actors have traditionally been formally placed in regard to each other.

It should be apparent in the light of the aforementioned that the historiographical implications of sociological approaches to international legal history are manifold. One particularly obvious example involves the study of its periodization, which can be broken down anew in the light of social phenomena hitherto largely unexplored by international law scholars. Another methodological offspring includes a certain departure from the intellectual history of international law as embodied in canonical texts so as to delve deeper into international socio-legal practices, including, as Lauren Benton notes, through the 'recognition of 'legal politics' as a broad object of analysis encompassing discourse, legal strategies, and institutional arrangements'[124] in the fashion of E. P. Thompson.[125] This in turn has inter alia 'also suggested new ways of understanding the relation of municipal law and international law through analysis of processes shaping and spanning both'.[126] To the still little-explored historical sources brought to bear by a finely targeted socio-legal historical methodological focus, one can also add other sociological sources rarely explored by international lawyers such as 'public records and statistics, surveys, interviews, content analysis (e.g. of visual or digital media) and secondary data analysis',[127] or more broadly, any empirically based method allowing for the study of the social effects of international legal norms in historical terms and, moving forward in the arrow of time, across contemporary historical processes too.

8.5   Historiographical Debates, Confluences, and Critiques

In parallel with the move already evoked among international lawyers to devoting far more attention to the role of non-state actors both in present and past analyses of international law, history as a discipline has in good

---

[124] Lauren Benton, 'Beyond anachronism: histories of international law and global legal politics' (2019) 21 *Journal of the History of International Law* 7–40 at 20.
[125] Edward P. Thompson, *The Making of the English Working Class* (New York: Pantheon Books, 1963).
[126] Ibid.
[127] Hirsch, *Invitation to the Sociology of International Law*, p. 32.

proportion also turned away, as was seen in Chapter 5, from 'methodological nationalism'. This term, which originated in the sociological field,
is understood by global historians as 'the still-powerful nineteenth-
century assumption that nations were the logical containers of meaningful history, serving as the most important point of reference even for
research and teaching conducted on different scales'.[128] As global historians engage in the need to produce, as Kenneth Pomeranz notes,
'histories for a less national age'[129] and open up their discipline to
'international, transnational and global circuits and connections'[130]
among a large array of non-state actors, they contribute to the thickening
of the social historical context of international law. This in turn both
encourages and facilitates the socio-historical exploration of the history
of international law. Indeed, the success of global history has prompted it
to take a methodological sociological turn in the hands of IR theorists, for
whom the new field of 'global historical sociology' means 'the study of
two interrelated dynamics: first, the transnational and global dynamics
that enable the emergence, reproduction and breakdown of social orders
whether these orders are situated at the subnational, national, or global
scales; and second, the historical emergence, reproduction and breakdown of transnational and global social forms'.[131]

The development of these confluent research agendas, through among
others a number of strands of socio-legal study of global legal history
which have situated the 'history of international law as an inquiry related
to the historical study of global order'[132] in adjacent disciplines at a time
of interdisciplinarization of international legal history, may offer fruitful
synergies to international legal historians interested in empowering different sets of historical narratives. Included among these are ones that
focus on histories which assert a transnational social-identity basis –
whether according to ethnicity, class, gender, religion, sexuality, geographical origin, or political ideology – as a meaningful reference point
across national boundaries in the remaking from below of a Western-
centric elite historiography which has traditionally been constructed

---

[128] Kenneth Pomeranz, 'Histories for a less national age' (2014) 119 *American Historical Review* 1–22 at 2.
[129] Ibid.
[130] Ibid.
[131] Julian Go and George Lawson, 'Introduction: for a global historical sociology', in Julian Go and George Lawson (eds.), *Global Historical Sociology* (Cambridge, UK: Cambridge University Press, 2017), pp. 1–34 at 2.
[132] Benton, 'Beyond anachronism', p. 17.

from above. In this context of increasing methodological pollination, it is unsurprising that critical international legal historiography, which has long been influenced, as was seen in Chapter 3, by the socio-legal strand of the 'Law & Society' movement, in particular but not only via Critical Legal Studies,[133] has favoured the transposition of the lenses of the historical sociology of IR to the field of international law as a potentially fruitful one in the light of the historiographical commonalities involving a 'number of features that stem from their shared nineteenth- and early twentieth-century history'.[134]

Moreover, just as sociological approaches to international law emerged as an alternative to a legalistic state-centric rule-oriented positivist focus among international lawyers and in doing so went on to prepare the ground for the emergence of IR as a separate discipline, historical sociological perspectives in IR are in turn largely a reaction to a state-centric neo-realist orientation among IR theorists. In this sense, the transposition of some of the methodological insights of historical sociology into IR, with their approach to the state as a 'historically contingent mode of socio-political organization as opposed to a temporally stable 'unit of analysis',[135] may contribute to dispelling what John M. Hobson terms the two main modes of 'a-historicism' and 'a-sociologism': 'cronofetishism' and 'tempocentrism' in the history of international law too.

The first of these, cronofetishism, understood as 'the assumption that the present can adequately be explained only by examining the present (thereby bracketing or ignoring the past)',[136] results, according to Hobson, in three types of illusion: the 'reification illusion', the 'natural-ization illusion', and the 'immutability illusion'. It is argued that in each case, historical sociology may provide a 'remedy' to these illusions by respectively revealing the present as a 'malleable construct embedded in a

---

[133] Fisk, '&: law society in historical legal research', pp. 479–496.

[134] Jennifer Pitts, 'International relations and the critical history of international law' (2017) 31 *International Relations* 282–298 at 283.

[135] Eric Daniel Loefflad, 'Popular will and international law: the expansion of capitalism, the question of legitimate authority, and the universalisation of the nation–state' (PhD thesis, University of Kent, 2019), kar.kent.ac.uk/80677/1/169_E_Loefflad_Ph D_Thesis. pdf, p. 45.

[136] John M. Hobson, 'What's at stake in "bringing historical sociology back into international relations"? Transcending "chronofetishism" and "tempocentrism" in international relations', in Stephen Hobden and John M. Hobson (eds.), *Historical Sociology of International Relations* (Cambridge, UK: Cambridge University Press, 2002), pp. 3–41 at 6.

social context', by showing that it emerged 'through processes of power, identity/social exclusion and norms', and by exposing it as 'constituted by transformative (morphogenetic) processes that continually reconstitute present institutions and practices'.[137] On the other hand, tempocentrism, the second mode of a-historicism, is defined as an inverted form of path-dependency insofar as it leads to the 'isomorphic illusion' in which the 'naturalized and reified present is extrapolated backwards in time to present all historical systems as isomorphic or homologous' (e.g. the axiom that history takes the form of repetitive and isomorphic 'great power/hegemonic' cycles).[138] In this context, the application of historical sociology conceived as a remedy to tempocentrism allows the scholar to retrace the fundamental differences between historical systems 'to thereby reveal the unique constitutive features of the present'.[139]

8.6   Conclusion

As in Paul Valéry's evocation of the sea as 'la mer, la mer, toujours renouvelée' ('the sea, the sea, always recommenced'),[140] history is the chief developmental force behind the large reservoir of rules, principles, doctrines, legal institutions, and practices existing across the large number of functionally specialized contemporary international legal regimes. These have not appeared as a *deus ex machina* on the international stage and then evolved as semi-self-contained abstract entities, as a-historicist and a-sociological formalist normative approaches catering for the functional needs of legal operators are often content to describe them in terms of internal evolution. Instead, while one should not minimize the ample influence of these legal operators in moulding and fleshing out the international norms and rules in situations in which they have performed political and juridical tasks, they remain offsprings of evolving background social contexts and of the interaction of different types of local, national, regional, and global social actors involved in processes of constant accommodation of their respective interests, concerns, and aspirations through international law. Included among the latter are also nation-states, which remain central actors in any historization of modern international law owing to both their past and

---

[137] Ibid., p. 9.
[138] Ibid.
[139] Ibid., p. 7.
[140] Paul Valéry, *Le cimetière marin* (Paris: Émile-Paul Frères, 1920), p. 1.

contemporary influence in shaping through their respective foreign policies, each of which has at present, as it also had in the past, a 'different weight in the end result', a 'law that is deemed to be common to all'.[141] Moreover, there is a cyclical recurrence of state-centred and sovereigntist phases in world politics which is in turn refracted or mirrored in both the shaping of and attitudes towards international law.[142]

If it still holds true, as Louis Henkin famously noted, that 'it is probably the case that almost all nations observe almost all principles of international law and almost all of their obligations almost all of the time',[143] this is largely due to the common attitudes of different past and present social actors to the functional utility served by the international socialization of the nation-state alongside the macro ideal of the international rule of law. Similarly, as we persevere in living the dream of the present while dreaming of fragments of the past, sociological approaches to the history of international law have a socializing effect on their addressees insofar as they increase their awareness of the dynamics of 'temporality, which requires close attention to processes of change, sequence and the unfolding of action over time'.[144] Moreover, sociological approaches may contribute to moving the history of international law in many directions, including towards the empirical study of the social effects of international law norms as a vector of what Saskia Sassen calls 'the global inside the national'[145] in the devising of empirically based better-tailored solutions to international legal problems and as a stimulus for domestic legal reform.

However, it is less clear whether the declared motivation lying behind attempts to advance global historical sociological lenses and frames of analyses in order 'to keep up with the world'[146] may risk overemphasizing, in its eagerness to apply new methodologies and select hitherto unexplored historical topics, certain features of 'the global' in international legal history. In this sense, an acute awareness of an array of

---

[141] Carlo Focarelli, *International Law as Social Construct: The Struggle for Global Justice* (Oxford: Oxford University Press, 2012), p. 136.

[142] John G. Ikenberry, 'The end of liberal international order?' (2018) 94 *International Affairs* 7–23.

[143] Louis Henkin, *How Nations Behave: Law and Foreign Policy*, 2nd ed. (New York: Columbia University Press, 1979), pp. 45–46.

[144] Go and Lawson, 'Introduction', p. 2.

[145] Saskia Sassen, 'The global inside the national: a research agenda for sociology', www .saskiasassen.com/pdfs/publications/ the-global-inside-the-national.pd.

[146] Go and Lawson, 'Introduction', p. 2.

background societal historical conditions, beginning with global illiteracy levels and ranging from labour conditions to inter alia the place of women in both Western and non-Western societies across time, may, following Kenneth Pomeranz, help remind international legal historians that in the same way as previously historians 'needed to remain wary of how nationalism made use of' their work, they also 'need to think today both about how we use the global and about how various versions of the global may use us'.[147] It is in this latter sense that the 'social' is the ultimate reference measure in any scale of international legal history.

---

[147] Pomeranz, 'Histories for a less national age', p. 10.

9

Institutional Approaches to the History
of International Law

9.1 Introduction

Whether it is in terms of standard-setting, international law-making, international adjudication, or international enforcement of international norms, global, regional, and operationally conceived international institutions and organizations have become fundamental actors in the great contemporary world theatre where the drama of international law is constantly being re-staged. International institutions and organizations (IOs) are 'frequently, if not exclusively' terminologically equated with 'intergovernmental organizations',[1] which are defined as 'organization[s] established by a treaty or other instrument governed by international law and possessing [their] own international legal personality' that 'may include as members, in addition to states, other entities'.[2] Although IOs have had a number of both practical and intellectual historical forerunners since the Central Commission for Navigation on the Rhine, which is usually considered the first IO, was set up in 1815, the reach of IOs has expanded exponentially through multiple functional international areas to reach an estimated number of over 350 worldwide today.

It is hard to imagine any piece of contemporary international legal scholarship that does not refer directly or indirectly to one or more of the ubiquitous IOs and their principal and/or subsidiary organs. It is likewise hard to imagine writing about twentieth-century or late nineteenth-century international legal history without making reference to IOs in some of their different embodiments and/or in connection with their related normative outputs. Indeed, the establishment of IOs as central poles for the development of international law across manifold legal

---

[1] Kirsten Schmalenbach, 'International organizations or institutions, general aspects', in *Max Planck Encyclopedia of Public International Law* (2014), opil.ouplaw.com/view/10.1093/law:epil/9780199231690/law-9780199231690-e499, p. 2.
[2] Art. 2 lit. (a) of the draft articles on the responsibility of international organizations, in *Yearbook of the International Law Commission* (2011), vol. 2, part 2.

regimes, and in particular of those universal in scope like the UN, has exerted an almost irresistible historiographical gravitational pull on the work of international law historians. Moreover, the fact that the institutional structures and constitutive charters of some IOs were set up in the aftermath of major international military conflicts has further contributed to the establishments of some of them being commonly depicted as fundamental landmarks and even as context-breaking events marking a before and an after in the historical periodization of the discipline, and also in twentieth-century international history writ large. And, even for some IOs whose foundation took place under less dramatic circumstances, their association with the crystallization or coming of age of particular international legal regimes assures them a significant place in multiple chronologies of international normative development.

By the loose category of institutional approaches to the history of international law we may refer to an approach defined by its main research theme or object of investigation: the study of the history of universal, regional, or otherwise differently circumscribed IOs, whether particular or general, and/or their specific organs in a historical perspective. Thus, narrowly characterized by their objects, many historiographical approaches and methods inspired by different *animus historiandi*, including all those seen in previous chapters including, in particular, those in Chapter 4 or a combination thereof, can be found in historical works about IOs and the functional activities of their organs. In particular, because IOs are important social actors in the history of international law, as was seen in Chapter 8, and their rise crystallized in the institutionalization of the international society in the twentieth century, they have gained centre stage, both in their own right and also by framing and providing a context for the actions and intellectual and normative constructions of other participants in the historical sociology of international law.

However, besides the many approaches and methods with which, and multiple interactive social contexts in which, IOs may be found historically tackled in international legal history, IOs have also generated their own particular historical methodologies. It is in this sense that 'historical institutionalism' (HI), understood as a 'research tradition that examines how temporal processes and events influence the origin and transformation of institutions that govern political and economic traditions'[3] and

---

[3] Orfeo Fioretos, Tulia G. Falleti, and Adam Sheingate, 'Historical institutionalism in political science', in Orfeo Fioretos, Tulia G. Falleti, and Adam Sheingate (eds.), *The*

the effects of these institutions across time and space, is an institutional approach to the history of international law defined by the 'method' with which it examines IOs as its main object of historical investigation. Having emerged in the area of sociology and political science, where, according to Orfeo Fioretos et al., it has consolidated its position along with 'rational choice and sociological varieties' among the modern 'traditions of institutional analysis',[4] historical institutionalism has empirically extended its reach over the last twenty-five years, along the way perfecting its analytical toolbox in its systematic study of all types of institutions, including IOs. It has also extended its analytical reach to consider international courts and tribunals (ICTs) whether they are conceived of as a subcategory of IOs or as their judicial or semi-judicial organs.

Section 9.2 below provides a bird's-eye view of the practice and idea of IOs with reference to the recent surge of historical writing on IOs in international legal history. Section 9.3 provides an overview of the historical institutionalism research tradition before examining how it opens up a more nuanced perspective on the history of international adjudication and surveying the expansion this field has experienced in the light of its four main areas of topical development. Section 9.4 examines the impact of new histories of IOs and approaches used to write them on knowledge creation processes and points to the potential impact of historical research on the future of international adjudication. Section 9.5 reviews some of the historiographical confluences and debates that have emerged around the study of IOs in international legal history, including the long-standing divide between the identification of structural patterns of causation and the unpredictable role of happenstance and contingency in historical processes. Finally, Section 9.6 revisits the correlation between the teleology of progress in pursuit of a cosmopolitan ideal into which international lawyers are disciplinarily socialized and their general appraisal of the historic role of IOs and their histories.[5]

Oxford Handbook of Historical Institutionalism (Oxford: Oxford University Press, 2016), pp. 3–30 at 3.

[4] Ibid.

[5] Jean d'Aspremont, 'The professionalization of international law', in Jean d'Aspremont, et al. (eds.), *International Law As a Profession* (Cambridge, UK: Cambridge University, 2017), pp. 19–37 at 19–17, 33–36.

9.2 Histories of International Organizations

Different criteria in terms of the functions IOs perform, their predominant powers, and the functional scope of their activities or, more broadly, their membership, which is namely open to states, serve to classify IOs into different and partially overlapping categories. For instance, the membership of 'closed' organizations 'may depend on geographical factors (e.g. the EU, NATO, ASEAN)', on a 'common cultural or historical background' of their members (e.g. the Commonwealth, the League of Arab States)[6] or on some of the core functions IOs perform in a particular domain (the Organization of Petroleum Exporting Countries, or OPEC; the Danube Commission), whereas the potentially worldwide membership under certain conditions of certain IOs (e.g. the UN) makes them potentially global or universal in reach and scope.[7]

Robert Kolb has usefully divided the forerunners of IO into 'forerunners *in re* and *in spe*'.[8] The forebears of IOs *in re* are then divided into the categories of 'international federations' and 'international conferences'. The first type, which closely or loosely linked together under different forms of organization a number of polities, existed, according to Kolb, both in the European world (with historical examples ranging from the Greek Amphictyonies in Antiquity to the German Hanse in the Middle Ages) and in the non-European world (e.g. the Triple Alliance of the Aztecs with other pre-Colombian peoples and the confederation of Iroquois nations in North America from the fifteenth to the eighteenth centuries).[9] Similarly, international regional conferences, which were convened to 'coordinate public policies and to seek political or technical cooperation',[10] have also existed for long both in Europe (e.g. the Concert of Europe) and beyond the European world, such as in China preceding the Warring States period (481–221 BC). Although these forerunners are the objects of a long-standing literature on occasion going back to efforts to find traces of international law in ancient non-European settings,[11] the international legal historical literature touching on these and other

[6] Schmalenbach, 'International organizations or institutions', p. 5.
[7] Ibid.
[8] Robert Kolb, 'International organizations or institutions, history of', in *Max Planck Encyclopedia of Public International Law* (2011), opil.ouplaw.com/view/10.1093/law:epil/9780199231690/law-9780199231690-e501, p. 2.
[9] Ibid., pp. 5–6.
[10] Ibid., p. 6.
[11] William Alexander and Parsons Martin, 'Traces of international law in ancient China' (1883) 14 *International Review* 63–77.

historical antecedents of IOs has also developed under the impulse of world and global history,[12] as was seen in Chapter 5.

On the other hand, the category of forerunners of OIs *in spe* encompasses a large variety of intellectual projects for international organization aimed at assuring, or at least projecting the hope of the possibility of, a long-lasting or permanent peace among states. These proposals were generally based on the idea of some institutionally structured 'federation of states', including permanent organs provided on different scales and to different degrees with legislative, executive, and judicial powers to resolve disputes, and were on occasion further accompanied, as in Immanuel Kant's archetypical project for perpetual peace,[13] by the commendation of a common republican political form of domestic government within their members as the bedrock of their success.[14] Contributions to the intellectual history of international law have revolved extensively around Kant's writings and the presentist significance that under the label of so-called Kantian peace, or democratic peace theory in its monadic, dyadic, and systemic versions, has been accorded to them in the aftermath of the Cold War.[15] Less massive, but also significant, has been the attention devoted to other historical peace projects by the likes of Emeric de Crucé, the Duke of Sully, William Penn, Abbé de St-Pierre, Jean-Jacques Rousseau, Jeremy Bentham, Johann Caspar Bluntschli, James Lorimer, and Pasquale Fiore, to mention but a few.[16] Moreover, for long there have also been studies of non-European precursors of the idea of IOs.[17]

Besides the study of their predecessors, it is standard practice to divide the modern history of international organizations, a term which was 'probably first used' by James Lorimer in the late nineteenth century,[18]

[12] David J. Bederman, *International Law in Antiquity* (Cambridge, UK: Cambridge University Press, 2001).

[13] Immanuel Kant, *Zum ewigen Frieden: Ein philosophischer Entwurf* (Königsberg: Friedrich Nicolovius, 1795).

[14] Kolb, 'International organizations or institutions', p. 6.

[15] Dan Reiter, 'Democratic peace theory', in *Oxford Bibliographies in Political Science* (2017), www.oxfordbibliographies.com/view/document/obo-9780199756223/obo-978019 9756223-0014.xml.

[16] Dominique Gaurier, 'Cosmopolis and Utopia', in Bardo Fassbender and Anne Peters (eds.), *The Oxford Handbook of the History of International Law* (Oxford: Oxford University Press, 2012), pp. 250–271.

[17] Boutros Boutros-Ghali, 'Un précurseur de l'organisation internationale: Al Kawakibi' (1960) 16 *Revue égyptienne de droit international* 15–22.

[18] James Lorimer, *The Institutes of the Law of Nations: A Treatise of the Jural Relations of Separate Political Communities*, 2 vols. (London and Edinburgh: W. Blackwood & Sons,

into different stages or waves of international institutional building processes, with the first of these being that comprising the so-called 'technical' IOs of the nineteenth century. These early IOs were mainly of two types: first, 'fluvial commissions', which managed several major river courses across Europe, including, representatively, the European Commission for the Danube set up in 1856 but also others gradually elsewhere. Second, there were the so-called international 'administrative unions' such as the International Telegraphic Union (1865), which was the first technical IO that was universal in scope, followed by the Universal Postal Union (1874), the International Copyright Union (1886), and other IOs variously concerned with international trade, communications, the standardization of measures and weights, meteorology, health issues, and so on.[19]

A second wave or stage in the history of IOs corresponds to the process of institutionalization of the international sphere in a universalizing direction that took place in the aftermaths of World War I and World War II, with the former also corresponding with a parallel deepening of institution-building processes at the regional level. The second wave is traditionally described as having been followed by a third stage of international institutional proliferation in both universal and regional directions in the post-Cold War era, with IOs mushrooming in parallel with the extension and diversification of international law into functionally specialized regimes and the multiplication of ICTs and other international adjudicatory and quasi-adjudicatory bodies. The bulk of the international legal historical literature on IOs revolves around the foundation and development of the major experiments in international institution building in the twentieth century: the League of Nations[20] and the United Nations Organization.[21] These histories, which are written from different perspectives stressing in their narratives certain factors over others, extend furthermore to multiple specific aspects falling within

---

1883–84), vol. 2, pp. 186 and 216ff., cited in Kolb, 'International organizations or institutions', p. 2.

[19] Rüdiger Wolfrum, 'International administrative unions', in *Max Planck Encyclopedia of Public International Law* (2006), opil.ouplaw.com/view/10.1093/law:epil/9780199231690/law-9780199231690-e471.

[20] Rose Sydney Parfitt, 'The League of Nations', in *Oxford Bibliographies in International Law*(2017), www.oxfordbibliographies.com/view/document/obo-9780199796953/obo-9780199796953-0151.xml.

[21] Mark Mazower, *No Enchanted Palace: The End of Empire and the Ideological Origins of the United Nations* (Princeton, NJ: Princeton University Press, 2013).

the functional and operational remits of the League and the UN, from the mandates system[22] to peace-keeping operations. Historical writing has equally extended to each and every of their principal organs, and further to include the history of projects to reform some of them.[23] It also includes histories of their subsidiary organs and programmes across their organigrams or within their frameworks, from the International Labour Organization to the World Bank[24] and the UN Human Rights Programme and Secretariat,[25] retracing their intellectual history, practical operations,[26] and legacy across different historical episodes. Whether as a background or foreground, temporal ordering factors drawing a temporal boundary between the two periods, both the League and even to a larger extent the UN, now tripling the former in age, are omnipresent in every work of twentieth-century international legal history whatever its focus, from the specifically normative and all its sociological and intellectual dimensions to others inherently linked to them such as the theory of functionalism in international institutional law.[27] Besides the multiple histories generated by and around the two historically largest universal organizations, there is also a large literature on the history of specific international organizations, both universal and regional in scope.[28] These extend to their organs and the many mutual

[22] Susan Pedersen, *The Guardians: The League of Nations and the Crisis of Empire* (Oxford: Oxford University Press, 2015).

[23] Dimitris Bourantonis, *The History and Politics of UN Security Council Reform* (London: Routledge, 2005).

[24] Guy Fiti Sinclair, *To Reform the World: International Organizations and the Making of Modern States* (Oxford: Oxford University Press, 2017).

[25] Bertrand G. Ramcharan, *A History of the UN Human Rights Programme and Secretariat* (Leiden: Brill/Nijhoff, 2020).

[26] Umut Özsu, 'Organizing internationally: Georges Abi-Saab, the Congo crisis, and the decolonization of the United Nations' (2021) *European Journal of International Law* (in press), revisiting Georges Abi-Saab, *The United Nations Operation in the Congo 1960-1964* (Oxford: Oxford University Press, 1978).

[27] Jan Klabbers, 'The emergence of functionalism in international institutional law: colonial inspirations' (2014) 25 *European Journal of International Law* 645–675.

[28] The literature is very vast. See e.g. the book series 'Global Institutions' (edited by Thomas G. Weiss and Rorden Wilkinson) at Routledge, which comprises a stream dedicated to providing 'accessible guides to the history, structure, and activities of key international organizations' including titles on the International Organization for Migration; the Organization of Islamic Cooperation; the UN High Commissioner for Refugees; the UN Security Council; the UN General Assembly; the Arab League, the Gulf Cooperation Council, and the Arab–Maghreb Union; the UN Environment Programme; the World Bank; the International Monetary Fund, the World Intellectual

influences they have entertained with each other, and also in particular with the UN since its establishment seventy-five years ago.

9.3   Historical Institutionalism and the History of International Adjudication

The turn to the history of international law has prompted the emergence of an interdisciplinarily revamped historiographical common ground which has spread its effects by inspiring new historical writing in international legal scholarship. One of the defining features of the turn has been, as we have seen in different chapters, the extent to which the methodological toolkit of the history of international law has gone through a process of adaptation to the historical discourses and research methods employed in adjacent disciplines. In some of them, like international relations (IR), the study of IOs and of their histories is itself a vehicular or a central research topic with the ability to enhance the approaches and methodologies employed to study IOs from the perspective of international legal history.

One of the relevant best-established research traditions in IR is 'historical institutionalism'. According to Robert Keohane, when historical institutionalism is compared with other 'established analytical frameworks in the study of world politics' (such as realism), the distinctive feature of which is to 'emphasise specific insights' that are generated by 'anomalies' (such as in the case of realism the 'anomaly of war'), the 'comparable anomaly identified by historical institutionalism' is 'the anomaly of institutional persistence' and therefore its ability to 'account for the fact that institutions often persist well after the distinctive conditions that generate them have disappeared'.[29] Indeed, it is unsurprising that the persistence of earlier IOs, accrued through the exponential proliferation of IOs and the multiplication of international regimes, and also international adjudicative bodies and international dispute settlement mechanisms, at the regional and global levels during the 1990s and early stages of the twenty-first century, has further fostered the development of the conceptual toolbox of HI in, inter alia, research

Property Organization; the North Atlantic Treaty Organization; the UN Children's Fund; and so on: https://www.routledge.com/Global-Institutions/book-series/GI.
[29] Robert O. Keohane, 'Observations on the promise and pitfalls of historical institutionalism in international relations', in Orfeo Fioretos (ed.), *International Politics and Institutions in Time* (Oxford: Oxford University Press, 2017), pp. 321–336 at 322.

areas related to regional integration processes, international security, international political economy, and global governance institutions.[30] With its focus on 'temporal phenomena, timing and variation to gain insight into institutional change',[31] HI has developed a clearly demarcated series of research themes, techniques, topoi, foci, and historiographical modes of enquiry which are applicable to the history of IOs and by extension to the history of international adjudication.

Central temporal concepts in the analytical toolbox of HI are 'critical junctures', understood as 'relatively short periods of time during which structural economic, political and cultural conditions are in flux so that the choices available to powerful actors expand'.[32] According to historical institutionalists, 'focusing on temporal phenomena, like critical junctures' and the path-dependent trajectories that result from them helps to 'reveal the far-reaching consequences that institutions may have in terms of the nature of political power and the strategies, preferences and identities of actors over time'.[33] Another key concept in the analytical toolkit of HI is 'path-dependence', with its focus on factors that generate 'self-reinforcing feedback effects' in international institutions and the roles of 'intercurrence' and 'incremental change' as occasional bases for 'radical change'.[34] Along with path-dependence (understood as a descriptor for a 'situation in which reversing a trend, or path, becomes more difficult over time', thus causing institutions to 'persist, even after they are no longer efficient'),[35] other key concepts of historical institutionalism may provide a common analytical grid for the study of the origins and evolution of international organizations and international adjudicative mechanisms over time, including those concerning questions of regional matter variation and subject matter variation. Among these are the study of 'antecedent conditions' and 'permissive factors', which in enabling action are defined as 'factors or conditions preceding a critical juncture that combine with causal forces during a critical juncture to produce long-term divergence in outcomes'.[36]

---

[30] Fioretos, Falleti, and Sheingate, 'Historical institutionalism', p. 4.
[31] Ibid.
[32] Giovanni Capoccia, 'Critical junctures', in Orfeo Fioretos, Tulia G. Falleti, and Adam Sheingate (eds), *The Oxford Handbook of Historical Institutionalism* (Oxford: Oxford University Press, 2016), pp. 89–106 at 89.
[33] Fioretos, Falleti, and Sheingate, 'Historical institutionalism', p. 4.
[34] Ibid., pp. 11 and 14.
[35] Ibid., p. 11.
[36] Capoccia, 'Critical junctures', p. 96.

International lawyers and historians have long learned to remain guarded against the programmatic modelling and absolutist projection of IR theories onto world politics and overall remain sceptical about the narrow-tailored puzzle questions which political science-inspired analytical tools in IR are carefully designed to provide answers to. However, the fact remains that there is a margin for the integration within the history of IOs as traditionally carried forward by international lawyers of some of the analytical tools of HI. In this sense, an interesting case in point for interdisciplinary analytical experimentation is provided by the history of international adjudication, an area where, as Karen Alter notes, 'historical institutional approaches provide insight into international systemic change'.[37]

Indeed, the traditional understanding of the history of international adjudication as somewhat equivalent to the history of international case law was previously examined in Chapter 7 as part and parcel of a doctrinally internal normative approach to the history of international law characterized by reference to its main research object as mainly focused on tracing the genealogy of international norms, principles, and legal doctrines understood as 'a self- contained universe . . . with little if any attention to the context'.[38] The history of ICTs, besides being influenced by a normative approach to the study of the history of international case law, which, as we have also seen, is being partially corrected by greater attention to the external sociological context in international legal history, has also been conventionally examined with reference to the gradual rise of adjudicative bodies on the international plane. This institution-based approach to the history of international adjudication often adopts the form, as Cesare Romano notes, of a 'standard narrative of international judicialization, a mostly linear story of successes from nineteenth-century arbitration to the current constellation of adjudicative bodies'.[39] Such an institution-based history of international adjudication overlaps with

---

[37] Karen J. Alter, 'The evolution of international law and courts', in Orfeo Fioretos (ed.), *International Politics and Institutions in Time* (Oxford: Oxford University Press, 2017), pp. 251–273 at 251.

[38] Valentina Vadi, 'International law and its histories: methodological risks and opportunities' (2017) 58 *Harvard International Law Journal* 311–352 at 312–313. Parts of the following analysis build on Ignacio de la Rasilla, 'The turn to the history of international adjudication', in Ignacio de la Rasilla and Jorge E. Viñuales (eds.), *Experiments in International Adjudication: Historical Accounts* (Cambridge, UK: Cambridge University Press, 2019), pp. 33–51.

[39] Cesare P. R. Romano, 'Trial and error in international adjudication', in Cesare P. R. Romano, Karen J. Alter, and Yuval Shany (eds.), *The Oxford Handbook of International Adjudication* (Oxford: Oxford University Press, 2014), pp. 111–134 at 112.

historical accounts of international law as a long and hard-fought history of international normative and institutional progress that tends to validate the contemporary status quo as the best of all possible outcomes resulting from the constant balancing of political and other forces through an admittedly often cataclysmic historical process. This perspective, which rather than examining experiments in international adjudication on their own merits and in their own context tends to chronologize them as stepladders towards the triumph of 'international adjudication as a means to develop the law and the idea of the international rule of law',[40] is one that is historically supported by international lawyers' advocacy for the establishment of ICTs increasingly provided with a compulsory jurisdiction and supplemented with a binding and enforceable nature of their decisions.

The double historical narrative track of normative and international adjudicative institutional progress is often described with reference to a periodized series of stages of combined normative and institutional evolution.[41] Like the previous overview of the historical evolution of IOs, in very broad terms this evolving paradigmatic narrative of progress can generally be found divided into several stages. The first of these is a pre-modern history of international adjudication, where earlier antecedents are identified, evolving towards the rise of international arbitration in the nineteenth century. The second major stage in this narrative is a shift from arbitration to the establishment of the first permanent international courts in the early twentieth century, a move gradually crystallizing since The Hague Peace Conferences and culminating under the umbrella of the move to institutions in the interwar period. After surveying the fleeting contribution of the League of Nations system to the international institutionalization of the nineteenth century project of 'peace through law', the third stage usually focuses on the UN system, which comprises a court of general jurisdiction and the gradual enshrinement of the cardinal principle of 'peaceful settlement of disputes', prompting the establishment of the first regional international human rights courts. Finally, the latest stage in this narrative coincides with the post-Cold War era, characterized by institutional proliferation, an

---

[40] Philippe Sands, 'Reflections on international judicialization' (2017) 27 *European Journal of International Law* 885–900 at 890.
[41] See, e.g., Tilmann Altwicker and Oliver Diggelmann, 'How is progress constructed in international legal scholarship?' (2014) 25 *European Journal of International Law* 425–444 at 425.

extraordinary rise in all forms of international litigation, the 'move from general toward specialized compulsory jurisdiction',[42] and the emergence of a new generation of ICTs presenting new features, including in some cases *ius standi* for individuals and non-state actors. This evolutionary description is punctuated by a series of temporal boundaries or dividing lines between a series of 'before and after' in the history of international adjudication. Nowhere is this more apparent than in the decreeing that the history of international courts 'can be divided into two main phases, with the end of the Cold War, in 1990, being year zero'.[43]

However, neither an internal normative historical approach to international case law nor a forward-looking evolutionary approach to the institutional history of international adjudication – which tends to gloss over its failures, its uncomfortable memories, and also its darker legacies – exhausts the potential of the research scope of the history of international adjudication. Instead, by focusing on the background conditions and levers informing the triggering, development, and gradual change over time of institutional processes, HI may provide, as in the case of IOs more generally, a useful analytical toolkit with the potential to open new perspectives and to illuminate neglected aspects in the study of the evolution of the international judiciary and the history of international adjudication over time.[44]

With its focus on 'causality, time and attention to historical contingency',[45] when brought on board by international legal historians, some of the concepts of HI can help to deepen the historical sociology of ICTs by bringing into relief the roles of myriad different stakeholders including state and non-state actors and networks present at the creation of adjudicative institutions, and also the mutually shaping role of those actors who have engaged with them over time, and in addition, by ricochet, of those institutions over them. Indeed, application of path-dependence allows examination of the effects of judgements delivered

---

[42] Mary Ellen O'Connell and Lenore Vander Zee, 'The history of international adjudication', in Cesare P. R. Romano, Karen J. Alter, and Yuval Shany (eds.), *The Oxford Handbook of International Adjudication* (Oxford: Oxford University Press, 2014), pp. 40–62.

[43] Cesare P. R. Romano, 'International courts', in *Oxford Bibliographies in International Law* (2012), www.oxfordbibliographies.com/view/document/obo-9780199796953/obo-9780199796953-0046.xml.

[44] Suzanne Katzenstein, 'In the shadow of crisis: the creation of international courts in the twentieth century' (2014) 55 *Harvard International Law Journal* 151–209.

[45] Fioretos, Falleti, and Sheingate, 'Historical institutionalism', p. 11.

over time in 'generating positive (or self-reinforcing) feedback effects to political actors embedded within them'.[46] Alternatively, its use can help to locate the source of 'departures or deviations' that certain decisions (e.g. the Nicaragua case for the United States or the South West Africa cases for African states during the decolonization era) or prosecutorial patterns (e.g. in the case of African states' attitudes regarding the ICC) may have had regarding the punctual disengagement, or variation in the terms of engagement, shown by certain states regarding ICTs. This dimension of the history of international case law is also worth exploring from the perspective of constructivism, with its attention to the power of institutions to form identities and shape interests imprinting and constituting agents' beliefs and identities.[47] However, attention should also be given to the role of culture, including legal culture, and the role of collective memories emerging from previous historical episodes of exposure to Western international legal constructs to account for substantial patterns of deviations across non-Western states and actors regarding ICTs.[48]

It has been pointed out that, while 'rational design scholarship expects design choices to be shaped by the functional needs of member states', other 'strong influences shaping the design of ICs' that are better captured under HI lenses are 'mimesis and diffusion'.[49] Moreover, the role of the internal evolution of international legal doctrine and scholarship which in turn nurtures a particular international 'legal consciousness' among elite international lawyers – including government advisors and also judges – should also be considered to account for the role of experts in shaping foreign-policy decisions involving changes in legal practice – what HI terms 'institutional change' – involving both IOs and ICTs. Similarly, with its focus on the role of 'incremental change' and 'intercurrence', which, rather than 'singular historical break points', may on occasion be the 'source of radical change'[50] within international institutions, HI may likewise offer interesting insights into other areas, which

---

[46] Ibid.
[47] Ian Hurd, 'Constructivism', in Christian Reus-Smit and Duncan Snidal (eds.), *The Oxford Handbook of International Relations* (Oxford: Oxford University Press, 2008), pp. 298–316.
[48] Hisashi Owada, 'The experience of Asia with international adjudication' (2005) 9 *Singapore Year Book of International Law* 9–18.
[49] Alter, 'The evolution', p. 252.
[50] Fioretos, Falleti, and Sheingate, 'Historical institutionalism', p. 14.

also fall under the purview of the history of international adjudication such as the study of the history of international procedural law.[51]

In a nutshell, the combined effect of the turn to international legal history – and of the background factors underlying and accompanying it – and the potential of the analytical toolkit of HI are important drivers for a revamped re-turn to the history of IO and international adjudication. Against the background of the mainstream depiction of a linear and periodized history of normative and institutional progress in the discipline of international law, a turn to the history of international adjudication contributes to a more contextualized historical perspective on the ebbs and flows of international adjudication and its contribution to the legalization of world politics over time. The topical expansion that the field of the history of international adjudication is currently undergoing can be surveyed in connection with four main areas. First, the new literature has shown, as in the case of the general turn itself, a renewed treatment of 'traditional' research subjects within the history of international adjudication. These historical re-readings have included a new treatment of the intellectual origins and the history of some of the most emblematic twentieth-century ICTs,[52] including the first one.[53] The intellectual biographical genre, inspired by a historiographical shift towards the sociology of the profession, as Chapter 10 examines, has also been renewed to include the lives and work of international judges in leading Western countries,[54] and of those in peripheral and semi-peripheral ones.[55] The background influence of the contextualist approach to the history of ideas following the Cambridge School, as was seen in Chapter 2, can be equally observed in the new and more

---

[51] See the *Max Planck Encyclopedia of International Procedural Law*, https://www.mpi.lu/mpeipro/.

[52] See Angelo Golia Jr and Ludovic Hennebel, 'The intellectual foundations of the European Court of Human Rights', in Ignacio de la Rasilla and Jorge E. Viñuales (eds.), *Experiments in International Adjudication. Historical Accounts* (Cambridge, UK: Cambridge University Press, 2019), pp. 263–286.

[53] See Freya Baetens, 'First to rise and first to fall: the Court of Cartago (1907–1918)', in Ignacio de la Rasilla and Jorge E. Viñuales (eds.), *Experiments in International Adjudication: Historical Accounts* (Cambridge, UK: Cambridge University Press, 2019), pp. 211–239.

[54] See Elihu Lauterpacht, *The Life of Hersch Lauterpacht* (Cambridge, UK: Cambridge University Press, 2010).

[55] See Fleur Johns, Thomas Skouteris, and Wouter Werner, 'Editors' introduction: Alejandro Álvarez and the launch of the Periphery Series' (2006) 19 *Leiden Journal of International Law* 875–1040.

nuanced view of the historicity of intellectual movements and trends in legal thought that offer a better glimpse of the historical contextual situationality and legal consciousness of those who were present at the creation of certain international courts,[56] or who were involved in significant experiments in international adjudication.[57]

Second, the field of the history of international adjudication has also experienced the remarkable deepening of the temporal and geographical dimensions of the history of international law that has been common to other areas. Whereas the temporal focus on the twentieth century has deepened, following the general move in the new historiography it has also shifted towards earlier instances of intellectual projects and antecedents of significant international adjudicative processes.[58] Moreover, the geographical scope of the research has also been affected by the general historiographical 'move away from grand Eurocentric narratives and toward global, micro and subaltern histories'.[59] This expansion has provided a more nuanced and detailed perspective on the relationship of international adjudication with the colonial experience,[60] unearthing in the process new archival materials,[61] and on the evolution of international adjudication in different regions.[62]

Third, new research on the history of international adjudication has also brought into relief topics and areas of historical research little

---

[56] Francis A. Boyle, *Foundations of World Order: The Legalist Approach to International Relations (1898–1922)* (Durham, NC: Duke University Press, 1999).

[57] See Andrei Mamolea, 'Saving face: the political work of the Permanent Court of Arbitration (1902–1914)', in Ignacio de la Rasilla and Jorge E. Viñuales (eds.), *Experiments in International Adjudication: Historical Accounts* (Cambridge, UK: Cambridge University Press, 2019), pp. 193–210.

[58] Ziv Bohrer, 'International criminal law's millennium of forgotten history' (2006) 34 *Law and History Review* 393–485.

[59] Thomas Skouteris, 'The turn to history in international law', in *Oxford Bibliographies in International Law* (2017), www.oxfordbibliographies.com/view/document/obo-97801997 96953/obo-9780199796953-0154.xml, p. 16.

[60] Inge van Hulle, 'Imperial consolidation through arbitration: territorial and boundary disputes in Africa (1870–1914)', in Ignacio de la Rasilla and Jorge E. Viñuales (eds.), *Experiments in International Adjudication: Historical Accounts* (Cambridge, UK: Cambridge University Press, 2019), pp. 55–75.

[61] See Mamadou Hebié, *Souveraineté territoriale par traité: une étude des accords entre puissances coloniales et entités politiques locales* (Paris: Presses Universitaires de France and the Graduate Institute, 2015).

[62] Cesare P. R. Romano, 'Mirage in the desert: regional judicialization in the Arab world', in Ignacio de la Rasilla and Jorge E. Viñuales (eds.), *Experiments in International Adjudication: Historical Accounts* (Cambridge, UK: Cambridge University Press, 2019), pp. 169–190.

explored until now. One of the most remarkable developments – insofar as it provides a counterpart to the blind spots generated by the pull of the mainstream linear narrative of institutional progress – is the history of short-lived, failed, or aborted ICTs,[63] and other historical experiments in international adjudication. Developed according to some of the methodological parameters of HI, this new research has included works on the role of international legal 'crises' as factors in the historical emergence of ICTs,[64] and on the history of projects for international courts *in nuce*.[65] These can be understood as providing a reservoir of 'antecedent conditions' that interact with critical junctures in prompting the setting up of ICTs in a discipline which conceives of its historical course as a great inter-generational evolutionary process in which even the failures of each generation set the ground for the works of the incoming one. Indeed, an inner understanding of the role of ideas and inter-generational dynamics fostered by normative and institutional projects emerging within international legal scholarship over time is central for 'global historical institutionalism' to methodologically overcome what has been defined as 'the most glaring conceptual challenge for historical institutionalism as it investigates global institutions': 'the lack of any international equivalent of the hierarchical state'.[66]

Fourth, a remarkable thematic expansion of the research scope of the history of international law has also sprung up following the coincidence of the turn to international legal history with the expansion and diversification of international law in recent decades. In particular, the development of the history of international adjudication has exponentially increased in those fields which have experienced a recent institutionalization of specialized international courts and other adjudicative bodies since the 1990s. Although this constitutes a general tendency common to several specialized areas, ranging from the field of international trade

---

[63] Donal K. Coffey, 'The failure of the 1930 tribunal of the British Commonwealth of Nations: a conflict between international and constitutional law', in Ignacio de la Rasilla and Jorge E. Viñuales (eds.), *Experiments in International Adjudication: Historical Accounts* (Cambridge, UK: Cambridge University Press, 2019), pp. 240–260.

[64] Katzenstein, 'In the shadow of crisis', p. 151.

[65] See Ben Saul, 'The legal response of the League of Nations to terrorism' (2006) 4 *Journal of International Criminal Justice* 78–102 at 81.

[66] Henry Farrell and Martha Finnemore, 'Global institutions without a global state', in Orfeo Fioretos, Tulia G. Falleti, and Adam Sheingate (eds.), *The Oxford Handbook of Historical Institutionalism* (Oxford: Oxford University Press, 2016), pp. 572–589 at 574.

law[67] to international investment law,[68] the history of international criminal law is one of the fields deeply engaged in a process of self-historicization which has attracted the greatest number of contributions related to its historical adjudicative dimension. Along with a general reassessment of classic themes and their legacies,[69] renewed attention has been devoted to the search for precedents of international criminal adjudicative processes,[70] and to the intellectual genealogy of the work of its precursors as early advocates of an international criminal code and international criminal courts.[71] Similarly, this interest has also extended more broadly to the history of war crimes trials,[72] and more recently to truth commissions and other forms of international transitional justice. The history of international human rights has also attracted extensive historical attention and historiographical debates. This has extended temporally back to historical precedents in connection with its adjudicative historical dimension,[73] and now includes a more nuanced perspective on the contexts and intellectual processes leading to the establishment of certain regional courts,[74] mechanisms for the protection

[67] Gabrielle Marceau (ed.), *A History of Law and Lawyers in the GATT/WTO: The Development of the Rule of Law in the Multilateral Trading System* (Cambridge, UK: Cambridge University Press, 2015).

[68] Antonio R. Parra, *A History of ICSID* (Oxford: Oxford University Press, 2012) (narrating the origins and evolution of the International Centre for Settlement of Investment Disputes).

[69] See Yuki Tanaka, Timothy L. H. McCormack, and Gerry Simpson (eds.), *Beyond Victor's Justice? The Tokyo War Crimes Trials Revisited* (Leiden: Martinus Nijhoff, 2011).

[70] Morten Bergsmo et al., (eds.), *Historical Origins of International Criminal Law*, vols. 1–4 (Brussels: Torkel Opsahl Academic EPublisher, 2014–15). See also Jan Martin Lemnitzer, 'How to prevent a war and alienate lawyers – the peculiar case of the 1905 North Sea Incident Commission', in Ignacio de la Rasilla and Jorge E. Viñuales (eds.), *Experiments in International Adjudication: Historical Accounts* (Cambridge, UK: Cambridge University Press, 2019), pp. 76–97.

[71] Mark Lewis, *The Birth of the New Justice: The Internationalization of Crime and Punishment 1919–1950* (Oxford: Oxford University Press, 2014).

[72] See Kevin J. Heller and Gerald Simpson (eds.), *The Hidden Histories of War Crimes Trials* (Oxford: Oxford University Press, 2013).

[73] See Jenny S. Martinez, *The Slave Trade and the Origins of International Human Rights Law* (Oxford: Oxford University Press, 2012).

[74] See Morten Rasmussen, 'From international law to a constitutionalist dream? The history of European law and the European Court of Justice (1950 to 1993)', in Ignacio de la Rasilla and Jorge E. Viñuales (eds.), *Experiments in International Adjudication: Historical Accounts* (Cambridge, UK: Cambridge University Press, 2019), pp. 287–312.

of human rights,[75] and even universalistic adjudicative projects such as a world court of human rights.[76]

The ongoing turn to the history of international adjudication is remarkable for the breadth of renewal of classic topics and the cultivation of new subjects pertaining to it, including ones spurred by a rise in the 'historical consciousness' in some of its subfields. The outcome is the production of more socio-historically contextualized accounts of the events, forces, and actors surrounding the origins and development of particular ICTs. This tendency has extended to historical research on international case law, which, as was seen in Chapter 7, is opening up towards an 'external' normative approach to the history of international norms, principles, and doctrines embedded in their contexts, typically their international political, social, or economic ones. The cultivation of the external variant of the history of international law, which is one that examines the dynamics of mutual influence that international judicial decisions have entertained with different national and international societal, ideological, intellectual, and professional historical contexts over time, can also be fruitfully integrated within an analytical framework that considers its impact on ICTs with reference to instances of 'backlash' by states against their authority, and even more frequently instances of 'pushback' in which states challenge 'the directions of their case law and jurisprudence'[77] in both contemporary and historical terms. In a nutshell, the application of the framework of analysis of HI in combination with other historiographical forces spurred by the turn to the study of the history of international adjudication, with which the history of IOs presents many parallels, provides a cognitively healthy counterpoint to an earlier historical normative focus on the history of international case law and to the pull of the mainstream's narrative of normative and institutional progress that had hitherto dominated the field.[78]

---

[75] See Alexandra V. Huneeus and Mikael R. Madsen, 'Between universalism and regional law and politics: a comparative history of the American, European and African human rights systems' (2018) 16 *International Journal of Constitutional Law* 136–160.

[76] Ignacio de la Rasilla, 'The World Court of Human Rights: rise, fall and revival?' (2019) 19 *Human Rights Law Review* 585–603.

[77] Mikael R. Madsen, Pola Cebulak, and Micha Wiebusch, 'Special issue – resistance to international courts: introduction and conclusion' (2018) 14 *International Journal of Law in Context* 193–196 at 195.

[78] Thomas Skouteris, 'The idea of progress', in Anne Orford and Florian Hoffmann with Martin Clark (eds.), *The Oxford Handbook of the Theory of International Law* (Oxford: Oxford University Press, 2016), pp. 939–953.

9.4   Impact on Knowledge Production Processes

The revamped historical study of IOs and also, under the influence of different methodologies, the new historical attention from which ICTs are benefiting contributes to providing a thicker historical texture to their evolution and therefore contributes to illuminating and unearthing the role that a series of particularly inspirational social movements, international advocacy groups, scholarly figures, and others have had on their historical development at specific times, as was seen in Chapter 8. Likewise, historical research contributes to providing a more nuanced perspective on the role of underlying conflicts and historical political processes, the contextual-historical relevance of different international legal philosophies, certain international legal traditions, and the weight of the presence (or absence) of precedents in fostering historical developments. Knowledge of the roles played by the contextual relative power of certain actors and economic driving forces, of the impacts of context-breaking events, and of international legal crises in the history of IOs and also of international adjudication equally benefits from more detailed and finely grained historical research and the application of different analytical frameworks to these interconnected areas.

Knowledge of the past – and of the interpretations the past has received – greatly shapes, moreover, contemporary perceptions of the present and future of international organizations and also of international adjudication. For what regards more specifically ICTs, the enabling potential of more and more refined historical knowledge to better make sense of what Cesare Romano has called the 'shadow zones of international adjudication'[79] allows us to better appreciate the features of existing contemporary courts and tribunals and other adjudicative and dispute-settlement bodies which did not surge *ex nihilo* but were instead built on earlier precedents. On the other hand, while admittedly many international adjudicative building processes have occurred since the 1990s, many of the new ICTs created in the post-Cold War era are still in very early stages of development, and several of them, despite being formally constituted, remain either dormant or barely active nowadays. Study of these contemporary ICTs 'on standby' can therefore benefit from more detailed historical research on, among other things, the

---

[79] Cesare P. R. Romano, 'The shadow zones of international adjudication', in Cesare P. R. Romano, Karen J. Alter, and Yuval Shany (eds.), *The Oxford Handbook of International Adjudication* (Oxford: Oxford University Press, 2014), pp. 90–110 at 90.

various failed, aborted, and short-lived precedents of international judicial bodies and experiments in international adjudication from earlier times.

The study of precedents – including failed ones – can also offer insights into contemporary international courts *in nuce*, thus allowing a better appraisal of the merits, and perhaps risks, involved in contemporary proposals. If, on the other hand, as Romano has noted 'the future of international adjudication depends on learning and internalizing what are the factors that stymie international judicialization',[80] this needs to be done on the basis provided by a historical docket of a rich and yet often cast-aside history of experiments in international adjudication. In fact, early attempts to establish international adjudicative mechanisms and institutions show, moreover, that it was not only successful international courts which generated a domino-like effect on the establishment of other ICTS. In fact, it is often failed and aborted experiments in international court creation, and in dead-letter international courts and tribunals, that we find playing the role of institution-building lodestars in the historical genealogy of international adjudication. These earlier projects also played a role as critical antecedents of contemporary proposals and on occasion influenced them verbatim. Finally, looking forward through the history of international adjudication can inform more refined theories of institutional change through the distillation of a more precise empirically based description of historical patterns regarding both failures and successes of international adjudication from which strategic advocacy lessons and better-tailored design choices for international adjudicative bodies may be extracted.

For what regards the historiographical dimension, new works on the history of IOs and international adjudication in integrating methodological and analytical interdisciplinary toolkits contribute to rethinking their traditional periodized stages of combined normative and institutional evolution of both IOs and ICTs. In particular, the framework of 'critical junctures', which 'yields valuable insights into trajectories of political change in which major episodes of innovation are followed by the emergence of enduring institutions'[81] and which, moreover, 'in international relations, are likely to last longer than in domestic politics,

---

[80] Romano, 'Trial and error', p. 112.

[81] David Collier and Gerardo L. Munck, 'Building blocks and methodological challenges: a framework for studying critical junctures' (2017) 15 *Qualitative & Multi-method Research* 2–9 at 2.

since institutions require agreement among many states',[82] can be identified in many of the traditional landmarks in international legal history
alongside the 'antecedent conditions and the cleavage or shock that
precede' them.[83]

9.5 Historiographical Debates, Confluences, and Critiques

Many explanatory theories have been constructed to account for the establishment and development of IOs, examining factors that favour their
creation, permanence, and extension of the original scope of their activities,
including their contribution to the solution of collective action, coordin-
ation, and collaboration problems; a reduction of the transition costs
involved in decision-making; influential transformations of the behaviour
of great power; and path-dependence and so on.[84] Similarly, the array of
'functional benefits' from states agreeing to regularly submit their international disputes to ICTs for resolution, to accept judicial mechanisms of
oversight of their internationally contracted legal obligations, has also generated a large literature.[85] These benefits range from fostering increased
credibility or avoiding the risk of escalation inherent in international disputes to the consideration of international adjudication as a 'global public
good'.[86] On the other hand, however, many analytical frameworks have
been employed to examine the factors weighing against IOs, which are
usually interpreted as reasons behind the decay of IOs over time. These
include relative gains concerns, which are typical of zero-sum-game
approaches; coercive cooperation concerns; institutional failure; disrupting
great-power transition dynamics; the appraisal of IOs as hegemonic status-
quo platforms under the 'lock-in' effect on their scope of operation of
embedded unchangeable normative arrangements; their perceived or
existing 'democratic deficits' and related charges of illegitimacy; and so on.[87]
    Against this background, and in the light of IOs' direct intervening
capacities under certain circumstances, their shaping influence on the

---

[82] Keohane, 'Observations', pp. 326–327.
[83] Collier and Munck, 'Building blocks', pp. 4–5.
[84] Arthur A. Stein, 'Neoliberal institutionalism', in Christian Reus-Smit and Duncan Snidal
    (eds.), *The Oxford Handbook of International Relations* (Oxford: Oxford University Press,
    2008), pp. 201–221 at 208–211.
[85] Alter, 'The evolution', p. 252.
[86] Joshua Paine, 'International adjudication as global public good' (2018) 29 *European
    Journal of International Law* 1223–1249.
[87] Stein, 'Neoliberal institutionalism', pp. 208–211.

behaviour of states across all areas under modern conditions of supra-national multilevel governance, their effective impingement on both the constitutive form and internal affairs of states, and, therefore, on the daily lives of multitudes around the globe, there are multiple politically, economically, or geo-strategically informed assessments of the effects IOs contribute to incite, nurture, develop, and ultimately implement partly through the means of international law. These assessments are in turn informed by the relative positions of different social actors of inter-national law asymmetrically positioned with regard to IOs within the contemporary framework of global institutions without a global state, and also, inter alia, the relative stage in which they are placed with regard to their respective modern nation-state-building processes. These present-day considerations invariably influence how different trends and historiographical traditions, inspired by a considerably diverse set of *animus historiandi* like, for instance, a critical post-colonial orienta-tion, may go about offering contrasting perspectives under different interpretative keys of the history of IOs on historical attempts to reform them or set a different course for them.

The history of IOs and ICTs is also a site for a classical rift between the analytical frameworks of social science, including those focused on con-tinuity and discontinuity across temporal processes, and historical meth-odologies, in particular for what regards risks of prognosis. Historians informed by social-science methodologies and political scientists with expertise in the history of international relations examine the history of international organizations and also international adjudication *ex post facto*. This allows them to retrospectively select from myriad variables those causal factors fitting explanatory theories that can offer useful hindsight on patterns of continuity and change in international institution-building processes. However, whereas HI can skim through the history of international organizations and ICTs and distil a retro-spective interpretative framework that accounts for their historical suc-cesses and failures, one should be wary of relying too much on them as bases for prognoses about the future. This is partly because of the certain liberality with which deterministic, structural, and contingent or prob-abilistic causal patterns can often be found intermingled in the explana-tory 'critical juncture framework'[88] that is retrospectively cast on historical processes. Indeed, while the study of earlier international

---

[88] Thad Dunning, 'Contingency and determinism in research on critical junctures: avoiding the "inevitability framework"' (2017) 15 *Qualitative & multi-Method Research* 41–47.

institutional developments and experiments in international adjudication can offer valuable insights into the history of IOs and ICTs through a distillation of structural patterns and parameters regarding their creation and evolution over time, historians themselves, as Quincy Wright wrote back in 1955, 'in their emphasis on contingency provide a healthy antidote to the overenthusiastic social scientist'.[89] Indeed, as Wright recalled, history contributes to a better realization of 'the complexity and uncertainty of human affairs, the many factors to be considered in making judgments, the dangers of abstraction, of dogmatism, of prediction, of action, and of inaction' and to a better understanding of 'the abundance and variability of human values and the opportunities as well as the insecurities of any situation'.[90]

9.6 Conclusion

International lawyers have been historically inclined to favour IOs if only because they are the linchpins of the time-honoured international legal project of enhancing the rule of law beyond domestic settings in pursuit of a cosmopolitan telos embedded in the chromosome of the Kantian Enlightenment.[91] This sees in the replication of something akin to the domestic structures of the Western liberal state on the international plane the first remedy to the social anarchy that only a fair and effective legal system anchored in solid institutions can ultimately aspire to tame and reconvert into a society that enables the human flourishing of its members in fulfilment of their innate capacities for good. If international law has been described as a gentle civilizer of nations, IOs have very much become the strongest foothold on which international law's promised contribution to eradicate violence, fear, injustice, and all sort of threats and dangers associated with lawlessness for a better world and a better life for both present and future human beings (and for all other creatures we share this planet with too) can be accomplished over time.

An illustration of how these broadly evoked elevated or lofty ideals, which are embedded in the transition from a breakable 'state-contract' approach to an 'international rule of law' orientation in which IOs are

---

[89] Quincy Wright, *A Study of War*, 2 vols. (Chicago: University of Chicago Press, 1955), vol. 1, p. 87.
[90] Ibid., p. 89.
[91] See Kant, *Zum ewigen Frieden*.

pivotal,[92] operate in practice through adjudicative mechanisms established in the context of IOs is how the pull exerted by regional processes of integration, especially at the European Union level, has fostered a global 'internationalization of constitutional law'.[93] This operates by incorporating international human rights standards into domestic constitutions, and by establishing supra-national mechanisms of judicial review of domestic decisions regarding fundamental freedoms. The gradual consolidation of what Anne-Marie Slaughter called a 'global community of courts'[94] has greatly benefited from the standard model that the European Court of Human Rights and the European Union judicial mechanisms in Europe have offered to other regions. In providing a foundation for a new *jus publicum europaeum*,[95] these European judicial bodies have extended their appeal in what Jürgen Habermas calls 'an important step on the path towards a politically constituted world society'[96] to other supra-national processes of ongoing political and economic regional integration around the globe.

Against this background, the study of the history of IOs and international adjudication can contribute to the international lawyer's principled liberal international institutionalist commitment by providing inspiration in the light of what its course has already accomplished in a relatively very short span of time in terms of human history. It can also teach international lawyers a lesson or two about the price to be paid for compromising or settling their ideals and about how the original aspiration needs to be wisely navigated through the tempestuous waters of domestic and international politics generation after generation. Likewise, the study of the history of IOs and international adjudication can instil the necessary perspective and, in its wake, the patience to witness incremental change and perhaps also the self-effacing wisdom in those who study it to set the right courses in motion today in keen awareness of the ineffable but certain impact of the past on the future. However, the

[92] Alter, 'The evolution', p. 252.
[93] Wen-Chen Chang and Jiunn-Rong Yeh, 'Internationalization of constitutional law', in Michel Rosenfeld and András Sajó (eds.), *The Oxford Handbook of Comparative Constitutional Law* (Oxford: Oxford University Press, 2012), pp. 1165–1184.
[94] Anne-Marie Slaughter, 'A global community of courts' (2003) 44 *Harvard International Law Journal* 191–219.
[95] Armin von Bogdandy et al., *Handbuch ius publicum europaeum*, 6 vols. (Heidelberg: C. F. Muller, 2007–16).
[96] Jürgen Habermas, 'The crisis of the European Union in the light of a constitutionalization of international law' (2012) 23 *European Journal of International Law* 335–348 at 336.

history of IOs and international adjudication can equally illustrate other ways of thinking, seeing, and interpreting historical events, ideas, and concepts in the light of the troubled 'civilizing' genealogy of IOs and their legacy of operationally 'locked-in' institutional capacities catering for the long-term preservation of current power asymmetries. Other concerns that can also go a long way to questioning and relativizing the 'narrative of normative progress'[97] and the teleological ethics of institutional internationalism in which international lawyers are intellectually socialized include the inherent association of IOs with an international technocratic ruling culture that may repress legal and political imagination; the relatively limited ability IOs have demonstrated beyond the technical and the humanitarian dimensions to tackle matters with high political stakes such as denuclearization despite the 'positive feedback effects' that facilitating 'repeated interaction among political actors'[98] is supposed to engender; and the extent to which the universal promise of IOs may well embody culturally specific West-centric understandings of historical progress or perhaps even channel looming dangers of long-standing subjugation on a worldwide scale.[99] It is against this background that the arresting value of the history of international law and, by extension, the history of IOs and international adjudication lies in its both uplifting and critical potential to nurture a well-calibrated intellectual standpoint on this world among those who study it reflectively.

---

[97] See Altwicker and Diggelmann, 'How is progress constructed?', p. 425.

[98] Orfeo Fioretos, 'Institutions and time in international relations', in Orfeo Fioretos (ed.), *International Politics and Institutions in Time* (Oxford: Oxford University Press, 2017), pp. 3–38 at 14.

[99] Martti Koskenniemi, 'What use for sovereignty today?' (2011) 1 *Asian Journal of International Law* 61–70.

10

Biographical Approaches to the History
of International Law

10.1 Introduction

The lives, works, and times of international lawyers, thinkers, and scholars, who during their careers may often interchangeably play the roles of international judges, diplomats, or legal advisors to states, international institutions, transnational corporations, or non-governmental organizations, broadly constitute the scope of biographical approaches to the history of international law. A methodologically revamped turn to the cultivation of international 'legal biography' has been one of the characteristic features of the turn to the history of international law. Although reconstruction of the lives, works, and times of prominent international lawyers has long been a sub-genre in international legal scholarship, such lawyers and scholars have never been the object, apart from a very few limited exceptions, of professional historical biographical studies in the guise of those devoted to great statesmen or famous artists.[1] The new wave of biographical approaches to the history of international law is thus characterized by a greater stress on the use of a 'biographical tone'[2] and by more detailed attention to the political, intellectual, and professional contexts within which intellectually biographed international lawyers have contributed to the discipline over time. The turn to international legal biography has also encompassed a far greater coverage of the dramatis personae of the history of international law than was provided by earlier biographical accounts. The treatment they are currently receiving is, furthermore, more clearly influenced by the far larger diversity of *animus historiandi* underlying contemporary developments in historiography than hitherto in international legal history.

---

[1] Philippe Sands, *East West Street: On the Origins of 'Genocide' and 'Crimes against Humanity'* (New York: Alfred A. Knopf, 2016).
[2] George R. B. Galindo, 'Martti Koskenniemi and the historiographical turn in international law' (2005) 16 *European Journal of International Law* 539–559.

The modern biographical contextualist move in international legal history owes volumes to Martti Koskenniemi's attempt in his influential *The Gentle Civilizer of Nations* to depart 'from the constraints of the structural method in order to infuse the study of international law with a sense of historical motion and political, even personal, struggle'.[3] Koskenniemi's method of looking 'at people with projects framing individuals in their context'[4] was influenced by the methodological insights of the Cambridge School of intellectual history, with its emphasis, as we saw in Chapter 2, on 'context' as the ultimate provider of meaning for speech-acts or utterances. It was also influenced by critical historiographical tenets and by postmodernism in history, as examined in Chapter 3, insofar as biography is 'an element of the individualistic or individualizing zeitgeist following the demise of the Grand Narrative',[5] which in turn ushered in a retreat from social science history and a return to the narrative mode of history.[6] Koskenniemi's efforts at showing through semi-biographical studies that 'international law is made by individuals with their projects, interests and ambitions, rather than by abstract temporal concepts or ideas'[7] contributed to revamping and de-mystifying the traditional historiographic sub-genre of 'synoptic histories of thought',[8] where biographical attention had been given to only a limited number of mostly European writers.

However, other than to a turn to the historical 'sociology of the profession' which, as was seen in Chapter 8, is partly built on the assumption that 'the behaviour of, and choices made by legal professionals are influenced by their social context, including their particular professional role',[9] the increasing cultivation of biographical approaches in international law also owes much to the rise of post-colonial attitudes

---

[3] Martti Koskenniemi, *The Gentle Civilizer of Nations: The Rise and Fall of International Law 1870–1960* (Cambridge, UK: Cambridge University Press, 2001), p. 2.
[4] Ibid.
[5] Birgitte Possing, 'Biography: historical', possing.dk/pdf/historicalbio.pdf. See also Birgitte Possing, *Understanding Biographies: On Biographies in History & Stories in Biography*, trans. Gaye Kynoch (Odense: University Press of Southern Denmark, 2017).
[6] Daniel R. Meister, 'The biographical turn and the case for historical biography' (2018)16 *History Compass* 1–10 at 6.
[7] Andrea Bianchi, *International Law Theories: An Inquiry into Different Ways of Thinking* (Oxford: Oxford University Press, 2016), p. 180.
[8] See seminally Lawrence Stone, 'The return of the narrative: reflections on a new old history' (1979) 85 *Past and Present* 3–24.
[9] Jean d'Aspremont et al., 'Introduction', in Jean d'Aspremont et al. (eds.), *International Law As a Profession* (Cambridge, UK: Cambridge University Press, 2007), pp. 1–15 at 2.

in international legal history. This is shown by the efforts of scholars affiliated to Third World Approaches to International Law (TWAIL) at retrieving historically representative scholars, as we saw in Chapter 4, beyond the confines of the European and Western canon of international law. Similarly influential in fostering the cultivation of international law biographical studies has been the 'global turn' in history. This has contributed to the expansion, as we saw in Chapter 5, of both the temporal and geographical scope of international legal history and with it to its extension to other previously little-studied historical figures. Albeit influential to a lesser degree, as examined in Chapter 6, the efforts of feminist approaches at retrieving the 'lost' or forgotten history of women in international law should also be accounted for. Finally, the development known by the history of non-state actors, including international organizations, as was seen in Chapters 8 and 9, and the current fragmentation of the history of international law into specialized international legal regimes have nurtured a more specific attention to the lives, works, and times of their intellectual historical precursors and of those who contributed to the practical and theoretical development of different international organizations and their related specialized fields over time.

Against this background, Section 10.2 below examines the evolution of biography as a branch of historiography and some of the main features of its earlier limited cultivation among international law scholars. Section 10.3 reviews six main areas of thematic expansion of the new biographical trend in international legal scholarship and considers how it has profoundly impacted the 'who's who' in the new history of international law. Section 10.4 looks into the influence of the biographical turn in international legal history on knowledge creation processes regarding different dimensions of the relationship between international law and history, whereas Section 10.5 analyses some historiographical debates connected to the revamped cultivation of biography in international legal history. Finally, Section 10.6 reflects on the individualist zeitgeist underlying the return to historical biographizing in international law and offers some reflections on the potential of the biographical sub-genre as a site for experimentation and innovation in international legal scholarship.

10.2   Biography As a Branch of Historiography

Historical biography is a branch of historiography characterized by variety and diversity. In the West it is a genre often traced back to

Plutarch's *Parallel Lives*, which set up the classical Roman-Hellenistic biography of great statesmen on an ethical basis in the first century CE, while two centuries earlier in the East, Sima Qian in his *Shiji* developed a biographical form with a far more diverse set of biographed characters.[10] From there, the historical biographical genre traversed through the stages of the Christian hagiographical approach to the lives and deeds of saints and martyrs, through early forms of secular biography beginning in the Italian Renaissance at the hands of Giovanni Boccaccio and Francesco Petrarca in the fourteenth century and later James Boswell's empirically based and highly influential *Life of Samuel Johnson* in the late eighteenth century, to the innovations of members of the Bloomsbury group as 'pioneers in the 20th century paradigm of *literary* historical biography'.[11]

During the twentieth century, the genre of historical biography progressed enormously as a hybrid genus incorporating new historiographical innovations and narrative styles. However, despite its wide cultivation and popularity, historical biography was generally considered 'a lesser form of history',[12] with some academic historians still characterizing 'biography as a degraded form of historical writing',[13] until the turn of the twenty-first century. Since then, historical biography has changed from being a historical approach the capacity of which 'to convey the kind of analytically sophisticated interpretation of the past that academics expected'[14] many professional historians were sceptical about, to being 'an inherently inter-disciplinary and self-assertive genre'[15] that is 'inextricably linked to Western democratic societies' increasing focus on concepts such as the freedom, integrity and complexity of the individual' according to Birgitte Possing.[16] New debates have, consequently, arisen about the 'biographical turn in the humanities and the social sciences',[17] with specialists signalling the rise of the branch of 'Biography Studies', which 'combines both the practice of writing biography as well as the study of biography as a genre'.[18]

---

[10] Possing, 'Biography: historical', p. 4.
[11] Ibid.
[12] David Nasaw, 'AHR roundtable – historians and biography: introduction' (2009) 114 *American Historical Review* 573–578.
[13] Possing, 'Biography: historical', p. 6.
[14] Nasaw, 'AHR roundtable', p. 574.
[15] Possing, 'Biography: historical', p. 7.
[16] Possing, *Understanding Biographies*, p. 30.
[17] Meister, 'The biographical turn', p. 2.
[18] Ibid., p. 4.

According to Daniel Meister, one can speak of 'two opposing approaches to biography among historians'.[19] In the first of these, biography 'is a way of addressing a larger historical question or theme using individual lives as 'lenses' to look at events and processes'.[20] According to this approach, which foregrounds 'the times', biographers should generally focus on historical figures who 'manifest ... historical forces'.[21] By contrast, in a second approach championed by historical biographers in the field of 'microhistory', understood as a 'subfield of history that starts from the premise that studying objects on a smaller scale will reveal phenomena, or aspects of them, that would otherwise evade historians',[22] historical 'biography should focus on the life itself, with the larger context discussed only in a limited way'.[23] Finally, an intermediate perspective suggests that historical biography 'should chart a middle course', alternating 'its gaze between the subject and the context, exploring the ways in which they interact. In this way, such works can examine both the life and the historical events and processes, and detail how their stories are interwoven'.[24] Indeed, contemporary definitions of historical biography generally put the accent on the space where the individual and the society interrelate by stressing 'the study of the life of an individual, based on the methods of historical scholarship, with the goal of illuminating what is public, explained and interpreted in part from the perspective of the personal';[25] or, more specifically, as noted by Handlin, by stressing that the focus of the biography 'is not the complete person or the complete society, but the point at which the two interact'.[26]

In international legal scholarship, where, as Peter Macalister-Smith notes, 'the biography of public international law in general is a neglected field, not only from the standpoint of history',[27] the international legal biographical genre traditionally developed with its own particular characteristics within the frame provided by the first type of biographical

---

[19] Ibid.
[20] Ibid.
[21] Ibid.
[22] Ibid., p. 5.
[23] Ibid.
[24] Ibid.
[25] Hans Renders and Binne de Haan (eds.), *Theoretical Discussions of Biography: Approaches from History, Microhistory, and Lifewriting* (Leiden: Brill, 2014), p. 2.
[26] Oscar Handlin, *Truth in History* (Cambridge, MA: Belknap, 1979), p. 276.
[27] Peter Macalister-Smith, 'Bio-bibliographical key to the membership of the Institut de droit international 1873–2001' (2003) 5 *Journal of the History of International Law* 77–159 at 78.

approach referred to above. The public life or professional career of, usually, a distinguished international law thinker and/or scholar, who on occasion also performed other roles in the making and application of international law, was commonly used to address a larger topic or series of topics of theoretical or normative relevance in the field. This traditional approach to international legal biography, with its stress on the intellectual and/or professional dimension of the life of a historically semi-biographed character, generally appeared in three main guises. The first variant mostly took the form of a praiseful intellectual biographical depiction, often bordering on hagiography, frequently composed by a former academic mentee or disciple, through recollections of the life and deeds of his 'master' in the opening chapter of a *Festschrift*, *liber amicorum*, or *liber discipulorum* written in his honour, often on the occasion of his retirement from his academic position. This genre occasionally contains a valuable wealth of otherwise almost irretrievable information,[28] often punctuated by the personal and sentimental recollections of the writer and supplemented with a complete academic bibliography of the retiree. Very similar in orientation is the 'obituary', or *in memoriam*. This minor genre, often adopting a much shorter format, was often found in international law journals.[29] It has now, some exceptions notwithstanding,[30] broadly fallen into disuse or migrated to blogs.[31] Both these ways of tackling the biographical in international law are not particularly characterized by being dispassionate objective accounts of the lights and shadows of the lives and careers of the international law characters depicted but instead are often highly hagiographical and occasionally also emotional testimonies.

The third traditional type of biographical excursus or bio-intellectual portraits in international legal scholarship consisted in snippet-like intellectual biographies of great thinkers and scholars fitted into a diachronic

---

[28] Lilly Melchior Roberts (ed.), *A Bibliography of Legal Festschriften* (The Hague: Martinus Nijhoff, 1972). See as a good exponent e.g. Antonio Truyol y Serra, 'Don Antonio de Luna García (1901–1967)', in A. Truyol y Serra et al., *Estudios de derecho internacional: homenaje a D. Antonio de Luna* (Madrid: C.S.I.C., Instituto Francisco de Vitoria, 1968), pp. 9–31.

[29] See, e.g., Gerald G. Fitzmaurice, 'Arnold Duncan Lord McNair of Gleniffer 1885–1975' (1975) 47 *British Yearbook of International Law* xi–xix.

[30] Iain Scobbie, 'Out of the shadows: an appreciation of Sir Elihu Lauterpacht's contribution to the doctrine of international law' (2017) 87 *British Yearbook of International Law* 1–17.

[31] Iain Scobbie, 'Sir Elihu Lauterpacht: a celebration of his life and work' (2017), ejiltalk.org/sir-elihu-lauterpacht-a-celebration-of-his-life-and-work/.

perspective on the evolution of the discipline through different periods. This special genre of, in Quentin Skinner's words, 'synoptic histories of thought, in which the focus is on the individual thinkers (or the procession of them)'[32] was often, and still remains to this day, cultivated in an encyclopaedia-like style and semi-decontextualized form. Although more historically detached than the versions contained in the *liber amicorum* or *in memoriam*, it also often contains broadly encomiastic and semi-heroic depictions of the characters biographed. These excursuses on the life and times of certain historical figures are often an impressionistic prologue to the study of their intellectual opuses within the background framework provided by particular typologies, such as those of natural lawyers vs positivists. These were later extended to account for a more pluralist and less dichotomist methodological scientific diversity in international legal scholarship.

These three traditional forms of biographical production on 'lives, works, and times' have in common that they are merely descriptive and are generally written by fellow international law scholars. Although they are often highly useful as historical materials, in particular on twentieth-century international lawyers, for the most part they constitute instances of 'amateurish' historical biography that do not apply the methods of historical scholarship or the standards of professional historical biographical work. In fact, Valentina Vadi has suggested that 'there was an anti-biographical tradition in international law', and international legal biography was indeed 'obscured' in favour of 'an examination of trends, events and concepts' in international legal history.[33] By transposing the 'triple obstacles' in the making of legal biographies identified by Susan Tridgell to the area of historical writing about international law, she identifies three main sets of reasons behind the scarce cultivation of international legal biographical work among international lawyers. The three 'obstacles' Vadi borrows from Tridgell to account for the relative neglect of the life of the individual in international legal history are 'irrelevance of the topic', a 'scarcity of evidence', and an 'absence of stylish models'.[34] While these three hindrances are probably relevant

---

[32] Quentin Skinner, 'Meaning and understanding in the history of ideas' (1969) 8 *History and Theory* 3–53 at 7.

[33] Valentina Vadi, 'International law and its histories: methodological risks and opportunities' (2017) 58 *Harvard Journal of International Law* 311–352 at 342.

[34] Susan Tridgell, *Understanding Ourselves: The Dangerous Art of Biography* (Oxford: Peter Lang, 2004), p. 25. See also Vadi, 'International law and its histories', p. 343.

regarding the biographical lacunae affecting everyday legal scholars or lawyers specializing in domestic law matters, they may appear slightly over-rated as a complete explanation of the scarcity of international legal biographical cultivation given the often far more colourful biographies of some cosmopolitan international law thinkers or lawyers in a historical perspective. The increasingly obvious global repercussions of international law in an interconnected world and the large availability of materials made easily accessible by new technology have meant that these obstacles, if they ever were such, can now be largely brushed aside. Moreover, despite the fact that far more attentive engagement with historical biography as a historiographical genre and the large diversity of perspectives from which it may be approached is still needed,[35] a new wave of international legal scholarship is also gradually dispelling the 'obstacle' of an 'absence of stylish models'.

One may, nonetheless, agree with Vadi that international legal historical biography still remains a genre *in nuce* in methodological terms. This is because most of those who engage in biography in international law focus their attention on the 'professional dimension' of the life of the person biographed and so disregard, comparatively speaking, the historical context and purely biographical or even bio-psychological dimensions of the protagonist's contributions to international law. If historical biography is understood as a genre that is both 'a branch of historiography as well as literary portraiture'[36] and also 'a story about and an interpretation of a life',[37] international law biographers' attention has for the most part remained confined to the public life of their biographed characters and exegetic commentaries of their writings. However, thanks to the great expansion of the newly diverse selection of historical characters as objects of revamped biographical attention, a new wave of literature is enriching the historical sociology of the international legal profession. It does so by bringing more clearly to the foreground the connections between the national and international historical, intellectual, and political contexts and the academic, advisory, or even adjudicative functions, along with some hitherto unknown or unexplored biographical facets of its greatest, and also now increasingly minor or forgotten, protagonists.

---

[35] Possing, *Understanding Biographies*, pp. 69–84.
[36] Ibid., p. 68.
[37] Ibid., p. 22.

10.3   The Biographical Turn in the History of International Law

The growth in attention to the international legal biographical genre of what Oscar Schachter referred to as 'a kind of invisible college dedicated to a common intellectual enterprise'[38] in a historical perspective has contributed to revamping the traditionally Eurocentric canon of the history of international law by making it far more critical and interdisciplinary, and also more geographically and racially inclusive, than hitherto. This historiographical development, which is slowly but steadily correcting the 'who's who' of the history of international law, has been developing in several academic directions.

First, the new intellectual biographical historiographical trend has included a move towards revisiting European writers who have for long been household names in the history of international law, along with an extension of international law's classical canon so as to include writers from other adjacent disciplines. Second, it has also comprised an extension of intellectual biographical work on celebrated European scholars, in particular from the late nineteenth century and the first half of the twentieth century. This development has been accompanied by far greater attention to figures and groups of historically and geographically situated international lawyers traditionally considered minor within Europe. Third, it has also involved an extension of the solely 'European' traditional canon towards a 'Western' canon, thus extending its coverage of historical figures throughout North America and Latin America from the early to mid-nineteenth century to the aftermath of World War II. Fourth, it has also channelled a pattern of (re-)inclusion of traditionally excluded or historically deemed subaltern groups from non-Western countries in Asia,[39] Africa,[40] and the Middle East[41] in particular, though not only since the decolonization decades, back into the writing of the history of international law. Fifth, largely fostered by the academic fragmentation of the study of international law, and in its wake the fragmentation of the study of the history of international law itself into

---

[38] Oscar Schachter, 'The invisible college of international lawyers' (1977) 72 *Northwestern University School of Law Review* 217–226 at 217.

[39] Bhupinder S. Chimni, 'International law scholarship in post-colonial India: coping with dualism' (2010) 23 *Leiden Journal of International Law* 23–51.

[40] See Fleur Johns, Thomas Skouteris, and Wouter Werner, 'Editors' introduction: Taslim Olawale Elias in the Periphery Series' (2008) 21 *Leiden Journal of International Law* 289–290.

[41] See Khaled R. Bashir, *Islamic International Law: Historical Foundations and Al-Shaybani's Siyar* (Cheltenham: Edward Elgar, 2018).

different international legal regimes catering for the functional needs of their associated institutions, it has also included a renewed attention to their individual precursors in each case. Sixth, the bio-intellectual historiographical move has furthermore expanded, albeit only to a very limited extent, to include women, who have traditionally been considered marginal characters in the history of international law. Each of these six categories has in turn both been part and parcel of, and been impacted to a lesser or greater degree by, the new historiographical trends and developments in the historiography of international law examined in earlier chapters. These six general areas will now be examined in turn.

First, the lives, works, and intellectual legacies of classic European writers on international law, including some who took part in the long-standing contest to be considered the 'founding father' of international law and have come to incarnate distinct traditions of international legal thought, have been largely revisited in recent years. In particular, as already discussed in Chapters 2 and 5, some of the most notable recent contextualist re-readings of lives and works have been carried out on, for instance, Francisco de Vitoria[42] and Hugo Grotius[43] in both a critical post-colonial revisionist light and a historical contextualist one, while other recent works have delved in more depth into biographical details.[44] With a greater or lesser stress on the colonial or imperial dimension of the work of these historical European writers, or as a refutation of post-colonialist readings, this revisionist trend has extended to other European writers from the sixteenth and seventeenth centuries, including Bartolomé de las Casas,[45] Alberico Gentili,[46]

---

[42] Francisco de Vitoria, *Vitoria: Political Writings*, ed. Anthony Pagden and Jeremy Lawrance (Cambridge, UK: Cambridge University Press, 1992).

[43] See e.g. Martine Julia van Ittersum, *Profit and Principle: Hugo Grotius, Natural Rights Theories and the Rise of Dutch Power in the East Indies 1595–1615* (Leiden: Brill, 2006); David Armitage, *Hugo Grotius, The Free Sea* (Indianapolis, IN: Liberty Fund, 2004).

[44] Henk Nellen, *Hugo Grotius: A Lifelong Struggle for Peace in Church and State, 1583–1645* (Leiden: Brill, 2014).

[45] Lawrence A. Clayton, *Bartolomé de las Casas and the Conquest of the Americas* (Hoboken, NJ: John Wiley & Sons, 2011). See, e.g., Ignacio de la Rasilla, 'Bartolomé de las Casas: a radical humanitarian in the age of the great encounter', in Kasey McCall-Smith, Jan Wouters, and Felipe Gómez Isa (eds.), *The Faces of Human Rights* (Oxford: Hart Publishing, 2019), pp. 13–21.

[46] See, e.g., Benedict Kingsbury and Benjamin Straumann (eds.), *The Roman Foundations of the Law of Nations: Alberico Gentili and the Justice of Empire* (Oxford: Oxford University Press, 2010); Valentina Vadi, *War and Peace: Alberico Gentili and the Early Modern Law of Nations* (Leiden: Brill/Nijhoff, 2020).

Serafim de Freitas,[47] Richard Zouche,[48] Samuel Pufendorf,[49] and
Samuel Rachel,[50] eighteenth-century ones like Christian Wolff,[51]
Emerde Vattel,[52] and Georg Friedrich von Martens,[53] and nineteenth-
century ones such as Johann Caspar Bluntschli,[54] James Lorimer,[55] and
Gustave Rolin-Jaequemyns,[56] to mention just a few of the most
widely discussed.

Likewise, attention to classic European writers has also extended to the
lives and works of others who contributed to the history of the formation
of knowledge about the law of nations from adjacent disciplines and who
have now been brought more squarely under the lens of international

[47] Serafim de Freitas, *De iusto imperio Lusitanorum Asiatico* (Vallisoleti: Ex Officina Hieronymi Morillo, 1625). See, e.g., Monica Brito Vieira, 'Mare liberum vs. mare clausum: Grotius, Freitas and Selden's debate on dominion over the sea' (2003) 64 *Journal of the History of Ideas* 361–377.

[48] Richard Zouche, Thomas Erskine Holland, and J. L. Brierly, *Iuris et judicii fecialis, sive juris inter gentes, et quaestionum de eodem explication: qua quae ad pacem et bellum inter diversos principes, aut populos spectant, ex praecipuis historico-jure-peritis, exhibentur* (Washington, DC: Carnegie Institute of Washington, 1911).

[49] Samuel Pufendorf, *De jure naturae et gentium libri octo* (Londini Scanorum: Sumtibus Adami Junghans oprimebat Vitus Haberegger, 1672). See, e.g., Martti Koskenniemi, 'Miserable comforters: international relations as new natural law' (2009) 15 *European Journal of International Relations* 395–422.

[50] Samuel Rachel, *De jure naturae et gentium dissertationes* (Kiloni: Literis Joachimi Reumani. Acad. Typogr., 1676).

[51] Christian Wolff, *Jus institutiones juris naturae et gentium* (Halle: Prostat in Officina Rengeriana, 1750; reprinted Hildesheim, 1972). See, e.g., Matthew Craven, 'On Foucault and Wolff or from law to political economy' (2012) 25 *Leiden Journal of International Law* 627–645.

[52] Emer de Vattel, *Le droit des gens, ou principes de la loi naturelle, appliqués à la conduite et aux affaires des nations et des souverains* (London: Neuchâtel, 1758). See, e.g., Emmanuelle Jouannet, *The Liberal-Welfarist Law of Nations: A History of International Law*, trans. Christopher Sutcliffe (Cambridge, UK: Cambridge University Press, 2012); Walter Rech, *Enemies of Mankind: Vattel's Theory of Collective Security* (Leiden: Martinus Nijhoff, 2013).

[53] George Friedrich von Martens, *Précis du droit des gens moderne de l'Europe, fondé sur les traités et l'usage* (Göttingen: Chés Jean Chret. Dieterich, 1789).

[54] Johann Caspar Bluntschli, *Das moderne Völkerrecht der civilisirten Staten als Rechtsbuch dargestellt* (Nördlingen: Beck, 1868).

[55] James Lorimer, *The Institutes of the Law of Nations: A Treatise of the Jural Relations of Separate Political Communities*, 2 vols. (Edinburgh: W. Blackwood & Sons, 1883–84); Martti Koskenniemi, 'Race, hierarchy and international law: Lorimer's legal science' (2016) 27 *European Journal of International Law* 415–429.

[56] Gustave Rolin-Jaequemyns, 'De l'étude de la législation comparée et du droit international' (1869) 1 *Revue de droit international et de la législation comparée* 1–17 at 1; Vincent Genin, *Le laboratoire belge du droit international: une communauté épistémique et internationale de juristes (1869–1914)* (Brussels: Académie Royale de Belgique, 2018).

legal history.[57] This move has extended to authors like Thomas Hobbes, Niccolò Machiavelli, Jean Bodin, Johannes Althusius, Baruch Spinoza, the Baron de Montesquieu, Gottfried Wilhelm Leibniz,[58] Jean-Jacques Rousseau, John Locke, Immanuel Kant, and Friedrich Hegel, and in the twentieth century, Carl Schmitt[59] and Hans Morgenthau, to mention but a few. This interdisciplinary extension of the classics of the discipline is a consequence of the larger interdisciplinary porosity of contemporary international law as a field of studies, which finds an echo chamber in the renewed study of its intellectual history.

Second, there has also been a steady growth in intellectual bio-graphical work, occasionally presented in the form of 'intellectual portraits', on influential European international law scholars from the 'long nineteenth century' and the first half of the twentieth cen-tury. This contextualized attention to the modern European 'greats' of the discipline such as Tobias Asser,[60] Dionisio Anzilotti,[61] Hans Kelsen,[62] Hersch Lauterpacht,[63] Max Huber,[64] Alfred Verdross,[65]

---

[57] See, e.g., Martti Koskenniemi, 'The law of nations and the "conflict of faculties"' (2018) 8 *History of the Present* 4–28.

[58] See, e.g., Tilmann Altwicker, 'International law in the best of all possible worlds: an introduction to G. W. Leibniz's theory of international law' (2019) 30 *European Journal of International Law* 137–158.

[59] See, e.g., Martti Koskenniemi, 'Carl Schmitt and international law', in Jens Meierhenrich and Oliver Simons (eds.), *The Oxford Handbook of Carl Schmitt* (New York: Oxford University Press), pp. 592–611.

[60] Arthur Eyffinger, *T. M. C. Asser (1838–1913): 'In Quest of Liberty, Justice, and Peace'*, 2 vols. (Leiden: Brill/Nijhoff, 2019).

[61] Roberto Ago et al., 'The European tradition in international law: Dionisio Anzilotti' (1992) 3 *European Journal of International Law* 92–172.

[62] Charles Leben et al., 'The European tradition in international law: Hans Kelsen' (1998) 9 *European Journal of International Law* 287–400.

[63] Hersch Lauterpacht, *The Function of Law in the International Community* (Oxford: Oxford University Press, 1933). The new literature is particularly extensive. See Martti Koskenniemi et al., 'The European tradition in international law: Hersch Lauterpacht' (1997) 8 *European Journal of International Law* 215–320.

[64] Max Huber, 'Beiträge zur Kenntnis der soziologischen Grundlagen des Völkerrechts und der Staatengesellschaft' (1910) 4 *Jahrbuch des öffentlichen Rechts* 56–134. See the issue of the symposium series 'The European tradition in international law' of the *European Journal of International Law* devoted to Max Huber ('Symposium: the European tradition in international law – Max Huber' (2007) 18 *European Journal of International Law* 69–197).

[65] B. Simma et al., 'The European tradition in international law: Alfred Verdross' (1995) 6 *European Journal of International Law* 32–115.

and Georges Scelle,[66] to mention but a few, may often be found
studied under the heading 'the European tradition of international
law'.[67] The renewed historical attention to renowned European international law scholars, often themselves representatives of new theoretical developments and paradigmatic conceptions fostered by the
great international transformations brought about by the move to
international institutions in the aftermath of World War I, has been
supplemented by a greater focus on authors traditionally considered
minor or lesser scholarly figures in the European tradition. The effort
to retrieve relevant figures who have remained outside the spotlight in
different parts of Europe, including Eastern Europe, has expanded
through new publications in international law journals and edited
collections and, on occasion, even monographs.[68]

Alongside this greater attention to individual scholars, there has also
been a move to pay more historical attention to specific groups of
international lawyers historically and geographically situated in
Europe.[69] This has fostered the study of groups of international lawyers
in particular turning-point-like moments or longer periods, such as the
study of Nazi international lawyers during the Third Reich,[70] fascist
international lawyers in Italy, Francoist international lawyers during
and after the Spanish Civil War,[71] and, at the other end of the political
spectrum, communist international law scholars during the so-called
period of 'real communism'.[72] On occasion, the new attention has
equally revolved around the role of particular groups of international
lawyers in particular episodes in the history of international law, such as
the role of British international lawyers in the face of the Spanish Civil

[66] Georges Scelle, *Précis de droit des gens: principes et systematique* (Paris: Librairie du
Recueil Sirey, 1932). See, e.g., Hubert Thierry et al., 'The European tradition in international law: Georges Scelle' (1990) 1 *European Journal of International Law* 193–249.
[67] There are more than two dozen instalments of this series. See recently, e.g., Altwicker,
'International law in the best of all possible worlds', pp. 137–158.
[68] Antonio Blanc Altemir, *El Marqués de Olivart y el derecho internacional (1861-1928):
sociedad internacional y aportación científica* (Lleida: Edicions de la Universitat de
Lleida, 1999).
[69] See Genin, *Le laboratoire belge du droit international*.
[70] Christian Joerges and Navraj Singh Ghaleigh (eds.), *Darker Legacies of Law in Europe:
The Shadow of National Socialism and Fascism over Europe and Its Legal Traditions*
(Oxford: Hart, 2003).
[71] Ignacio de la Rasilla, *In the Shadow of Vitoria: A History of International Law in Spain
1770-1953* (Leiden: Brill/Nijhoff, 2017).
[72] Emmanuelle Jouannet and Iulia Motoc (eds.), *Les doctrines internationalistes durant les
années du communisme réel en Europe* (Paris: Société de Législation Comparée, 2012).

War,[73] United States international lawyers during the Vietnam War, and, more recently, during the Iraq War and its aftermath.[74] There has also been a parallel increase in the historization of certain professional international legal roles, such as that of foreign office legal advisor, a position often occupied by international law professors, with reference to specific individuals or groups thereof. This has occasionally extended to a semi-prosopographical orientation, understood as a research-method that aimed at learning about patterns of relationships and activities through the study of collective biography, otherwise the 'investigation of the common background characteristics of a group of actors in history by means of a collective study of their lives'.[75] Of all those occupying international legal roles, it is, however, international judges of Western origin and, as we shall later see, also of non-Western origin, who have been more often the subjects of biographical excursuses.

Other criteria adopted to bring a number of bio-intellectual portraits of international lawyers together include cultural and linguistic factors, such as *francophonie*,[76] or their common conditions as *émigré* (international) legal scholars,[77] or even, with a considerable degree of overlapping with the latter group, as Jewish international lawyers.[78] Of note is also the historical work produced on Western national epistemological communities of international lawyers over a longer span of time. This has included work on Belgian international lawyers, through the application of historical methods including network theories,[79] from the 1860s to the aftermath of World War II, on Spanish international lawyers from the late eighteenth century to the mid-twentieth century,[80] on North Americans from the Declaration of Independence to the interwar

---

[73] See also, e.g., Ignacio de la Rasilla, 'In the general interest of peace – British international lawyers and the Spanish Civil War' (2015) 17 *Journal of the History of International Law* 197–238.

[74] Philippe Sands, *Torture Team: Rumsfeld's Memo and the Betrayal of American Values* (London: St Martin's Press, 2008).

[75] Lawrence Stone, 'Prosopography' (1971) 100 *Daedalus* 46–79 at 46.

[76] 'Galerie des internationalistes francophones', Société française de droit international, sfdi. org/ internationalistes/.

[77] Jack Beatson and Reinhard Zimmermann (eds.), *Jurists Uprooted: German-Speaking Émigré Lawyers in Twentieth-Century Britain* (Oxford: Oxford University Press, 2004).

[78] See, e.g., James Loeffler and Moria Paz (eds.), *The Law of Strangers: Jewish Lawyers and International Law in the Twentieth Century* (Cambridge, UK: Cambridge University Press, 2019).

[79] Genin, *Le laboratoire belge du droit international*.

[80] De la Rasilla, *In the Shadow of Vitoria*.

period,[81] and on Russian[82] and Italian[83] generations of international lawyers. These emerging national histories of international law, which are, as we saw in Chapters 5 and 8, a welcome complementary counterpart to global histories, lay the foundations for future historiographical developments in the comparative historiography of international law in different regions.[84]

Third, international legal historians have greatly contributed to an expansion of the traditionally Eurocentric historiographical international legal canon to include a larger representation of international jurists from the United States and Latin America.[85] Regarding the first group, attention has extended to the American precursors of the 'peace movement' and to the author of the first English-language treatise on international law, Henry Wheaton,[86] followed by Francis Lieber,[87] Francis Wharton, and, already in the twentieth century, James Brown Scott, the ubiquitous founder of the American Society of International Law and long-standing editor-in-chief of its journal.[88] Regarding Latin American international lawyers and scholars, the stress has often been put on their semi-peripheral 'strategies of appropriation' of international law and their roles as pace-setters of regionalism in the history of international law in the nineteenth and early twentieth centuries.[89] The impact of postcolonial attitudes in overcoming what George Galindo called 'the traditional reluctance of many scholars to examine international law's

---

[81] Mark Weston Janis, *The American Tradition of International Law: Great Expectations 1789–1914* (Oxford: Oxford University Press, 2004); Mark Weston Janis, *America and the Law of Nations 1776–1939* (Oxford: Oxford University Press, 2010).

[82] Lauri Mälksoo, *Russian Approaches to International Law* (Oxford: Oxford University Press, 2015).

[83] Giulio Bartolini (ed.), *A History of International Law in Italy* (Oxford: Oxford University Press, 2020).

[84] Randall Lesaffer and Anne Peters, *The Cambridge History of International Law*, vol. 1: *Historiography* (in press).

[85] See, e.g., Liliana Obregón Tarazona, 'Construyendo la región Americana: Andrés Bello y el derecho internacional' (2010) 24 *Revista de derecho público* 65–86.

[86] Henry Wheaton, *Elements of International Law: With a Sketch of the History of the Science* (Philadelphia: Carey, Lea & Blanchard, 1836); Liliana Obregón Tarazona, 'Writing international legal history: an overview' (2015) 7 *Monde(s)* 95–112.

[87] Francis Lieber, *Instructions for the Government of Armies of the United States in the Field* (Washington, DC: Adjutant General's Office, 1863).

[88] See, e.g., Paolo Amorosa, *Rewriting the History of the Law of Nations: How James Brown Scott Made Francisco de Vitoria the Founder of International Law*, with prologue by Anthony Pagden (Oxford: Oxford University Press, 2019).

[89] Arnulf Becker Lorca, *Mestizo International Law: A Global Intellectual History 1842–1933* (Cambridge, UK: Cambridge University Press, 2015).

reception by and transformation in the extra-European world'[90] has, in particular, attracted a larger literature on scholarly representatives from post-independence Latin America, where the first university chairs were devoted *eo nomine* to international law (*derecho internacional*), including on Andrés Bello,[91] Carlos Calvo,[92] Ruy Barbosa,[93] and Alejandro Alvarez.[94]

Fourth, the intellectual biographical historiographical trend has also channelled a strategic pattern of re-including traditionally excluded or historically deemed subaltern groups in the writing of the history of international law. This move is consonant with the modern tendency to address one 'of the problems in studying the history of international law from a biographical point of view', which was, as Galindo notes, 'that, in doing so, attention is paid only to what the great masters of the discipline thought and did'.[95] As in the field of history writ large, where according to Possing, 'historical biography became part of the democratic project in an increasingly globalised community',[96] the effort to dispel Eurocentrism from the history of international law[97] has led to efforts to write back these traditionally under-represented groups into the intellectual history of international law.

This re-inclusive move extends from late nineteenth-century figures up to a new generation of TWAIL post-colonial writers who have portrayed themselves as inheritors, despite their differences, of a first

---

[90] ˙See Umut Özsu and Thomas Skouteris, 'International legal histories of the Ottoman Empire: an introduction to the symposium' (2016) 19 *Journal of the History of International Law* 1–4 at 1.

[91] Andrés Bello, *Principios de derecho de jentes* (Santiago de Chile: Imprenta de la Opinión, 1832). See Nina Keller-Kemmerer, *Die Mimikry des Völkerrechts: Andrés Bello 'Principios de derecho internacional'* (Baden-Baden: Nomos, 2018).

[92] Carlos Calvo, *Derecho internacional teórico y practico de Europa y América* (Paris: D'Amyot, 1868).

[93] Ruy Barbosa, *The Equality of Sovereign States* (The Hague: The Hague Peace Conference, 1907).

[94] Alejandro Álvarez, *Le droit international américain: son fondement, – sa nature: d'après l'histoire diplomatique des états du nouveau monde et leur vie politique et économique* (Paris: A. Pédone, 1910). See the Periphery Series symposium of *the Leiden Journal of International Law* devoted to Alejandro Álvarez (vol. 19, no. 4, 2006).

[95] George R. B. Galindo, 'Martti Koskenniemi and the historiographical turn in international law' (2005) 16 *European Journal of International Law* 539–559 at 541.

[96] Possing, 'Biography: historical', p. 9.

[97] See, e.g., Martti Koskenniemi, 'Histories of international law: dealing with Eurocentrism' (2011) 19 *Rechtsgeschichte* 152–176.

generation of post-colonial Asian and African authors.[98] Among them are, as we saw in Chapter 4, African international lawyers like Taslim Olawale Elias[99] and Mohammed Bedjaoui[100] and Asian post-colonial international law scholars such as the Indian R. P. Anand[101] and even the Polish-British-nationalized Charles H. Alexandrowicz,[102] who developed the bulk of his career in Madras. Also indirectly enhanced by post-colonial approaches to international legal history on the basis of common historical experiences, including their common peripheral situationality in engaging with 'Western' international law, is an emerging literature on Asian international lawyers coming from Japan and, in particular, China.[103] More directly attributable to the historio-graphical influence of 'global history' on the history of international law, there has been a remarkable extension towards the study of the Islamic tradition of international law or 'As-Siyar', dating back to treatises written in the eighth and ninth centuries,[104] with several studies devoted to Al-Shaybani, the so-called Islamic Grotius.[105]

A fifth emerging source of development of biographical interest leading to the inclusion of hitherto neglected or ignored international lawyers in the annals of the discipline is the fragmentation of the history of international law. This biographical trend possesses a longer tradition in the field of international human rights law, where it has often been accompanied by rivets of hagiography. In this context, some modern historical figures have already become household names, such as René

---

[98] See, e.g., Martti Koskenniemi, 'Expanding histories of international law' (2016) 56 *American Journal of Legal History* 104–112.

[99] Johns, Skouteris, and Werner, 'Editors' introduction', pp. 289–290.

[100] Umut Özsu, 'Determining new selves: Mohammed Bedjaoui on Algeria, western Sahara, and post-classical international law', in Jochen von Bernstorff and Philipp Dann (eds.), *The Battle for International Law in the Decolonization Era* (Oxford: Oxford University Press, 2019), pp. 341–357.

[101] Prabhakar Singh, 'Reading R. P. Anand in the post-colony: between resistance and appropiation', in Jochen von Bernstorff and Philipp Dann (eds.), *The Battle for International Law in the Decolonization Era* (Oxford: Oxford University Press, 2019), pp. 297–318.

[102] Charles H. Alexandrowicz, *An Introduction to the History of the Law of Nations in the East Indies* (Oxford: Clarendon Press, 1967).

[103] Pasha L. Hsieh, 'Wellington Koo, international law and modern China' (2016) 56 *Indian Journal of International Law* 307–323.

[104] Ignacio de la Rasilla and Ayesha Shahid (eds.), *International Law and Islam: Historical Explorations* (Leiden and Boston: Brill/Nijhoff, 2019).

[105] Bashir, *Islamic International Law*.

Cassin[106] and Eleanor Roosevelt.[107] It has extended to different areas, whether in the name of racial equality or, as we shall see below, women's rights, and across other specialized international legal regimes such as what can be regarded its intellectual precursor, the field of international criminal law and justice,[108] in particular in the interwar period,[109] with detailed biographies of some its main characters, such as Raphael Lemkin.[110] Similarly to the growing focus on individual actors in adjacent disciplines such as the history of European Union Law, the development of the history of different international legal regimes, ranging from international investment law to international environmental law and international trade law, has also been fostering attention to the lives and deeds of some of their intellectual figures and practitioners.[111]

The biographical move through compartmentalization of disciplinary expertise not only affects historical figures but also encompasses contemporary international lawyers, who are often polyglot and cosmopolitan professionals who in their careers may become strategic key players in global legal policy-making processes and international adjudicative settings. The same tendency towards specialization underlies the development of a new biographical attention to earlier generations of international law historians. In this context, particularly indicative of how the history of international law's own research dynamics foster new historiographical agendas is the new biographical focus on those who contributed to the modern fame of classic international thinkers over time such as James Brown Scott[112] and Camilo

---

[106] See, e.g., Anya Luscombe and Barbara Oomen, 'René Cassin (1887–1976): the foot soldier of human rights', in Kasey McCall-Smith, Jan Wouters, and Felipe Gómez Isa (eds.), *The Faces of Human Rights* (Oxford: Hart Publishing, 2019), pp. 105–114.

[107] See, e.g., Mitchell Glen Johnson, 'The contributions of Eleanor and Franklin Roosevelt to the development of international protection for human rights' (1987) 9 *Human Rights Quarterly* 19–48.

[108] Morten Bergsmo and Emiliano J. Buis (eds.), *Philosophical Foundations of International Criminal Law: Correlating Thinkers* (Brussels: Torkel Opsahl Academic EPublisher, 2018).

[109] Frédéric Mégret and Immi Tallgren (eds.), *The Dawn of a Discipline: International Criminal Justice and Its Early Exponents* (Cambridge, UK: Cambridge University Press, 2020).

[110] Douglas Irvin-Erickson, *Raphael Lemkin and the Concept of Genocide* (Philadelphia: University of Pennsylvania Press, 2016).

[111] Gabrielle Marceau (ed.), *A History of Law and Lawyers in the GATT/WTO: The Development of the Rule of Law in the Multilateral Trading System* (Cambridge, UK: Cambridge University Press, 2015).

[112] Amorosa, *Rewriting the History of the Law of Nations*.

Barcia Trelles[113] regarding Francisco de Vitoria and Cornelis Van Vollenhoven[114] and Hersch Lauterpacht regarding Grotius.[115] Similarly, Charles H. Alexandrowicz has recently received international legal biographical attention as a precursor of post-colonial historiography in international law.[116]

Sixth, in contrast to the historiographical developments mentioned, which go a long way towards showing that in effect 'international lawyers are gradually becoming more interested in their predecessors',[117] when it comes to works on gender and the history of international law written by international lawyers, despite some exceptions its development has been, as we saw in Chapter 6, fairly scarce. The biographical study of the contribution of female international law scholars to the discipline, or more broadly of women acting in other influential capacities, before the mid-twentieth century has remained the object of a still very limited level of attention.[118] Nonetheless, partaking in the general historiographical trend, new works are emerging beyond the 'collective contours' of women's movement rights towards a more specific attention to particular women such as Olympe de Gouges[119] and Mary Wollstonecraft[120] in the context of the history of international human rights law, and to

---

[113] Ignacio de la Rasilla, 'Camilo Barcia Trelles in and beyond Vitoria's shadow (1888–1977)' (2021) 32 *European Journal of International Law* (in press).

[114] Johann K. Oudendijk, 'Van Vollenhoven's "The three stages in the evolution of the law of nations": a case of wishful thinking' (1980) 48 *Tidschrift voor Rechtsgeschiedenis* 3–27.

[115] Hersch Lauterpacht, 'The Grotian tradition in international law' (1946) 23 *British Yearbook of International Law* 1–53.

[116] David Armitage and Jennifer Pitts, '"This modern Grotius": an introduction to the life and thought of C. H. Alexandrowicz', in Charles H. Alexandrowicz, *The Law of Nations in Global History* (Oxford: Oxford University Press, 2017), pp. 1–34.

[117] Vadi, 'International law and its histories', p. 342.

[118] Dominique Gaurier, 'Quelle place faite aux femmes dans l'ordre international de l'Antiquité et du début de l'époque moderne?', in Emmanuelle Tourme-Jouannet et al. (eds.), *Féminisme(s) et droit international: études du réseau Olympe* (Paris: Société de Législation Comparée, 2016), pp. 248–255.

[119] Teresa Pizarro Beleza and Helena Pereira de Melo, 'Olympe de Gouges (1748–1793) impressively ahead of her time: a visionary, daring activist and martyr', in Kasey McCall-Smith, Jan Wouters, and Felipe Gómez Isa (eds.), *The Faces of Human Rights* (Oxford: Hart Publishing, 2019), pp. 33–39.

[120] Dolores Morondo Taramundi, 'Mary Wollstonecraft (1759–1797): the undutiful daughter of the Enlightenment and her loud demands for justice', in Kasey McCall-Smith, Jan Wouters, and Felipe Gómez Isa (eds.), *The Faces of Human Rights* (Oxford: Hart Publishing, 2019), pp. 41–50.

precursors, such as Concepción Arenal,[121] the author of *Ensayo sobre el derecho de gentes*, the first treatise on international law in a modern sense written by a female author, which dates back to 1879.

10.4 The Biographical Impact on Knowledge Production Processes

Historical international biography contributes in different ways and degrees to knowledge creation processes on the multifaceted relationship between international law and history. Even when the interrelation of international law and history is broadly considered a purely legal-technical affair – otherwise, as explained in Chapters 2 and 7, within the framework of the 'history in international law' – biographical details can illuminate background circumstances regarding the professional training, cultural upbringing, or sociological and historical perspectives of its practitioners. For instance, international legal biography can serve as useful guidance for making better retrospective sense of particular solutions provided for dispute resolution in international adjudicative fora. In particular, since decolonization, many concurring and dissenting opinions written by international judges at the International Court of Justice show a particular leaning towards some doctrinal solutions over others which, in turn, can be retraced to their personal biographies, including geographical factors and a larger diversity of legal cultural traditions present on the bench.[122] Moreover, on occasion, international judges leave 'memoirs' that may help to illuminate the influence of their personal upbringing and life experiences in the exercise of their international judicial functions.[123]

More broadly, biographical approaches to international law also make it possible to unearth a wealth of information on particular historical characters, which enriches our retrospective understanding of the 'his-

---

[121] Ignacio de la Rasilla, 'Concepción Arenal and the place of women in modern international law' (2020) 88 *Tijdschrift voor Rechtsgeschiedenis* 1–43.

[122] Hisashi Owada, 'The experience of Asia with international adjudication' (2005) 9 *Singapore Yearbook of International Law* 9–18.

[123] Thomas Buergenthal, *A Lucky Child: A Memoir of Surviving Auschwitz as a Young Boy* (New York: Little, Brown and Company, 2009). See also, e.g., Christopher G. Weeramantry, *Towards One World: The Memoirs of Judge C. G. Weeramantry*, 3 vols. (Colombo: Weeramantry International Centre for Peace Education and Research, 2010–14).

torical dimension of international legal theory'[124] by making more explicit how abstract concepts and ideas have crystallized into international
law norms and principles and how they have been shaped by the
purposes for which different actors have deployed them over time.
Indeed, biographically contextualized intellectual accounts of the lives,
deeds, and times of international thinkers and lawyers allow us to
contextualize the cultural, religious, intellectual, and/or, inter alia, sociological influences underlying their intellectual production. The latter does
not only allow for a more precise bio-conjectural guessing of the illocutionary purpose of their work in their own times, but allows, furthermore, a better understanding of the 'presentist' recreation of historical
figures and the reading, inspired by 'precursiorism', of their doctrines as
either prefiguring modern ones or, ultimately, as suited to contemporary
circumstances or both. On others, it allows retracing to the biographical
domain the coinage of legal concepts (e.g. genocide) or the gradual
normative fleshing out and uses of certain legal concepts (e.g. the
principle of self-determination of peoples) by different authors, thus
unveiling the 'personal' behind the historically contextualized intellectual
genealogy of concepts produced by the great variety of interpretations
and intentions they carry inserted in them. This is of crucial importance
from the perspective of contextualism, as we saw in Chapter 2, pursuant
to the Cambridge School following the influence of John L. Austin's
speech-act theory on Quentin Skinner's approach to the importance in
grasping the meaning of the intended illocutionary force of any speech-
act. Without situating the author in different contexts, including the
primary context of his or her own life and circumstances, such illocutionary intention would remain forever shrouded in mystery.

Unveiling biographical details of certain international lawyers,
thinkers, and scholars may also allow better comprehension of the
ultimate levers that in terms of personal agency underlie the relationship
of mutual influence that international law and/or parts thereof have
entertained with different national and international societal, ideological,
intellectual, and professional historical contexts, and also particularly
significant international 'events'. Multiple examples may illustrate how
the study of 'international law in history' can be largely substantiated
with well-contextualized professional biographical accounts of its main

---

[124] Anne Orford and Florian Hoffmann, 'Introduction: theorizing international law', in
Anne Orford and Florian Hoffmann with Martin Clark (eds.), *The Oxford Handbook of
the Theory of International Law* (Oxford: Oxford University Press, 2016), pp. 1–20 at 10.

protagonists, be it as a result of their political (statesmen, foreign affairs ministers, diplomats) or intellectual (judges, scholars) influence. In fact, it was not rare, especially in the early to mid-twentieth century, to find professors of international law holding roles as international public officials.

International legal biography may also contribute to knowledge creation processes regarding, in particular, the production of normative perspectives at the micro level within the domain of the 'history of international law' examined in Chapter 7. It does so by fleshing out with biographical colour the bones of historical-normative studies of particular international doctrines, international legal principles, and norms in one sub-discipline or across different sub-disciplines of international law, both in a diachronic and in a synchronic historical perspective. When it is applied to historians of international law, it may offer insights about the conceptions underlining the reconstruction of the historical evolution of international law in a macro perspective too. International legal biography contributes, furthermore, to knowledge creation processes regarding the 'historical sociology of international law' in all its dimensions, starting with the academic dimension, but also extending to individuals variously involved in transnational movements or other non-state actors, including international organizations and international civil servants – what Frédéric Mégret represented as 'international man'[125] – and, of course, to other state servants performing international roles in the service of their respective nation-states.

Last but not least, biographical approaches to historical writing about international law contribute to knowledge creation processes regarding the study of the historiography of international law. This is first and foremost because as a historiographical genre historical biography in international law contributes, as the next section briefly illustrates, to the methodological toolkit and related debates in the broader field of international legal history itself. Second, biographical approaches also contribute to the questioning of received periodizations and to the carving-out of new alternative periodizations in the history of international law, with the question of periodization playing a central role in structuring international legal historiography.

---

[125] Frédéric Mégret, 'The rise and fall of "international man"', in Prabhakar Singh and Benoît Mayer (eds.), *Critical International Law: Postrealism, Postcolonialism and Transnationalism* (Oxford: Oxford University Press, 2014), pp. 223–233.

10.5   Historiographical Debates, Confluences, and Critiques

One may well agree with Meister 'that biography, like history, is essentially revisionist (rewritten by each generation)'.[126] Indeed, over recent years the history of international law has been informed by a critical drive towards the debunking of past established figures in the discipline. This has been accompanied by their parallel, and perhaps too hasty, ideational replacement by others whom contemporary 'intellectual/scientific movements' identify as people whose intellectual legacy they may associate themselves with.

However, as the review of the debate between contextualist, critical/postmodern, and post-colonial historiographies in international law strove to illustrate in Chapters 2, 3, and 4, it may indeed turn out to be 'anachronistic' to pass judgement on historical characters using contemporary social and cultural standards, with the modern commentator assuming the unjustified role of morally or ethically superior judge of attitudes that could be fully appraised and understood only in the context of the intellectual and social conditions prevailing at the time.[127] This attention to context does not entail condoning historical abuses, contradictions, bad faith, or hidden agendas in historical works. However, any critical stance should nonetheless be well premised by carefully distinguishing historical figures and their works from the hagiographical and partly invented, or imagined, historiographical characterization which they may have been given by ulterior generations of international law scholars. In other words, it is essential to distinguish the historical character and her or his contribution to international law or, depending on the epoch, the law of nations or *ius gentium*, as they stood in the context of contemporary times, from the 'myth' later constructed by successive historiographical portrayals built around her or his figure and works.

To be able to do so may well require engaging with the classic author (be it Francisco de Vitoria,[128] Bartolomé de las Casas,[129] Hugo

---

[126] Meister, 'The biographical turn', p. 3.

[127] Lynn Hunt, 'Against presentism' (2002) 40 *Perspectives on History* 1, www.historians.org/publications-and-directories/perspectives-on-history/may-2002/against-presentism.

[128] Ignacio de la Rasilla, 'The three revivals of Francisco de Vitoria in the theory and history of international law', in José Maria Beneyto (ed.), *Peace or Just War? The Influence of Erasmus and Vitoria on the Monarchia Universalis of Charles V and the Law of Nations* (in press).

[129] De la Rasilla, 'Bartolomé de las Casas'.

Grotius,[130] Emerich de Vattel,[131] or any other classic of international law) not only at the contextual historical level but also, importantly, at a meta-historical level. Paying attention to the meta-historical context implies first and foremost being fully aware of the protean nature of the classics of international law. That is, the single most defining characteristic of a classic is that his or her figure and works have already become the objects of different interpretations and reinterpretations in the light of different historical circumstances, the rise and fall of diverse ideologies, and trends in international legal thought over time. This is why, instead of endeavouring to add yet another overlapping reading of an already highly scrutinized historical work and its author in the context of his or her times, a meta-intellectual historical approach to context strives instead to offer a fuller historically contextualized and genealogical picture of the transformations, interpretations, and reinterpretations received by the classic (or even 'classic-to-be') of international law against different historical backgrounds over time. The ultimate purpose of this methodological approach involving a degree of 'serial contextualization' is to unravel what each of the transformations, interpretations, or appropriations of a classic's work and figure can tell us about the different authors who made his or her modern fame, and the background trends in international legal thought and episodes in the history of international law that provided a context for those appropriations and reinterpretations with, moreover, due acknowledgement of the intellectual synergies that were set in course in each case. This is how what began as a biographical intellectual enquiry into a classic (or 'classic-to-be') in the history of international law may well end up involving the author in the study of the lives, times, and works of those who contributed to one or other of the classic's intellectual revivals against completely different background contexts in the history of international law centuries later.[132]

On the other hand, as the previous overview of different areas of international legal biography has illustrated, multiple international lawyers and thinkers are currently objects of bio-intellectual historical attention for a different set of motivations under the influence of

---

[130] Ignacio de la Rasilla, 'Grotian revivals in the theory and history of international law', in Randall Lesaffer and Janne Nijman (eds.), *The Cambridge Companion to Hugo Grotius* (in press).

[131] Emmanuelle Jouannet, *Emer de Vattel et l'émergence doctrinale du droit international classique* (Paris: Pédone, 1998).

[132] As a recent example, see Amorosa, *Rewriting the History of the Law of Nations*.

different historiographical trends, including post-colonialism, feminism, globalism, and their sub-variants. However, debunking a historical myth may often be just a pretext for laying the foundations on which to erect a new 'totemic' historical figure in international legal history. As revisionism is almost consubstantial to biographizing in international legal history, one should be wary when new classics-to-be are treated in a relatively uncritical manner by contemporary historiographers in order to carve out for themselves a reconstructed tradition fitting their own contemporary agenda. This is why some degree of caution should also be exercised with regard to historical figures who may be prey to a form of historiographically biased 'militantism'. In the same manner as the term *droit-de-l'hommisme*'('human rightism') describes an excess of tolerance of, or an emotionally driven and unreflective ultra-positive attitude to, human rights which blurs the distinction between the rights themselves and the ideological uses or invocations of rights in domestic and international settings,[133] the *animus historiandi* underlying some of the most militant trends in international legal historical thought may also foster the creation of biographical blind spots through an unreflective or selective embellishing or whitewashing of the life and deeds of the modern 'classic to be'.

Indeed, behind every international legal biography lies a previous choice of a specific international legal 'life' to be chronicled.[134] Awareness of what motivates the choice of one historical character (or characters) over another (or others) may well require first becoming familiar with ongoing developments in the historiography of international law in this rapidly developing area, such as those broadly sketched in the six-tiered typology previously presented. This should go hand in hand with due attention to criteria for maximizing feasibility and the potential contribution of the international legal biography. Among these criteria are personal features pertaining to the international legal biographer herself or himself, such as an in-depth familiarity with the working language (or languages), national history, and culture of the figure biographed. Attention to the latter is often relatively glossed over in favour of a more broadly recognizable international dimension, in particular of the conceptual and normative development of the discipline

[133] Chloé Leprince, '"Droit-de-l'hommisme": histoire d'un néologisme péjoratif' (2018), franceculture.fr/histoire/droit-de-lhommisme-histoire-dun-neologisme-pejoratif.
[134] James Loeffler, 'Reflections on Jewish international legal biography', in Annette Weinke and Leora Bilsky (eds.), *Émigré Lawyers and International Law* (in press).

of international law and related events and processes. However, stress on the 'international' without careful consideration of the 'national' framework is more likely than not to produce a distorted intellectual portrait of the figure biographed than what a balanced consideration of both facets may achieve.

Against this background, certain caution should nonetheless also be exercised when selecting a historical figure who has already been variously scrutinized by multiple other authors. Indeed, certain 'great figures' in the history of international law have attracted overlapping attention from successive generations of scholars to the extent that they have eventually become objects of an industry of scholarly commentary in themselves. This is the case for the classics, who are born as much as they are made, and are later continually reinterpreted and appropriated to the extent that even attempts at demystifying them only contribute to further consolidating their status within the discipline. This pattern of cyclical attention to the classics is, nonetheless, largely unavoidable insofar as the passing of time has crystallized them into didactic archetypes handed on to incoming generations so that they can become socialized within the intellectual traditions of the field. However, this latter consideration does not alter the fact that while the classics – ancient, modern, or even 'in the making' – come in different shapes and shades, all of them share the ability to displace to the margins the stories of many other dramatis personae which have been left untold and forgotten in their overgrown shadows.

This is why the potential historical and scholarly value of devoting a study to one of these almost unknown or forgotten historical characters – including but not limited to the many neglected women existing in the history of international law because, as Possing notes, 'the biography is an ancient genre with a gender imbalance'[135] – may be vastly superior to that of adding yet another essay – if not absolutely seminal in character – to the well-stocked shelves on the most well-trodden historical figures, or even on those who are on their way to becoming so. Admittedly, the ready availability of archival textual research materials, including private correspondence, unpublished diaries, and memoirs, remains a criterion in a decision to engage with the life, deeds, and times of an international lawyer in a historical perspective. This presupposes, in most cases, a successful career path that has facilitated the recording of additional

---

[135] Possing, *Understanding Biographies*, p. 8.

materials on the subject's life and deeds. By contrast, the archival materials on historically neglected characters may be far scarcer and hard to find. Against this background, it may be pondered that pursuing the 'original' path is, of course, always easier said than done, and even when it is effectively done the paradox remains that it is, indeed, often done in pursuance of everything except originality per se.

Beyond the crucial choice of the 'biographed-to-be', international legal biography is also a fertile ground for experimenting with different historiographical methodologies. Four areas of development stand out. First, the very centrality of the life experiences of specific historical characters in international law calls for a greater use of the narrative form in approaching international legal biography. This in itself calls for a potentially creative, even if difficult, balancing exercise when it is, for instance, combined with the most familiar modes of conceptual analysis among international law scholars. While, as Vadi notes, 'so far, international legal historians have maintained an essentially academic approach, avoiding too much narrative, and prioritizing evaluation and historical insight',[136] it is worth pondering on what particular historical methodologies may foster a greater engagement with non-specialist audiences regarding particularly appealing characters in the history of international law for broader scientific dissemination purposes and awareness-raising, including among young students contemplating career-path decisions. The successful release of some intimate international legal biographies aimed at the general public[137] – including one doubly devoted to Hersch Lauterpacht and Raphael Lemkin which also includes components of autobiography and family biography of its own author, a celebrated contemporary international lawyer – seems to point to a new direction for international legal biography beyond specialist audiences.[138]

Second, international legal biography allows for greater experimentation with the application of network theory or with a collective or relational biographical approach showing the connections between the lives, career paths, and different network relations of elite academic groups. Thirdly, international legal biography may be an area conducive to coupling textual research with 'visual and ethnographical

---

[136] Vadi, 'International law and its histories', p. 347.
[137] Elihu Lauterpacht, *The Life of Hersch Lauterpacht* (Cambridge, UK: Cambridge University Press, 2010). See also Christine Jennings, *Robbie: The Life of Sir Robert Jennings* (Kibworth: Troubador Publishing, 2019).
[138] Sands, *East West Street*.

research',[139] in particular on the international legal lives of those who lived and worked in a too far distant past. Despite the perils of excessive reliance on anecdotal aestheticism rather than in-depth intellectual reflection that the application of such a methodology may entail, the methodology may also prove to be useful in breaking new ground for historical pursuits in the history of international law. Finally, international legal historians should engage far more with the theorization of historical biography as a historiographical genre because, as Possing notes, 'there is not just the one, but many ways in which to approach it – and these approaches can be mapped out'.[140] A good starting point is, precisely, Possing's characterization of eight 'archetypes' that 'characterize different approaches to biography', ranging from 'mirror' biography to 'interpretive biography', 'life-and-times' biography, and, interestingly, 'polyphonic biography' that 'deliberately proposes conflicting interpretations of its protagonist'.[141]

10.6 Conclusion

It may be seen as totally reductionist and, needless to say, merely circular to claim that international law is just what international lawyers do, write, say, or think,[142] or that international law is but the 'law of international lawyers'.[143] While, as we saw in Chapter 2, this characterization is in part born out of a historically contextualized reassessment of the argumentative use of international law made by members of the international legal profession over time, an echo of this self-aggrandized conception of the international lawyer resounds in the (re)turn to international legal biography among international lawyers.[144] This is so because conceiving international law from the perspective of an individualistic or individualizing zeitgeist evokes the power of individual agency in the making and shaping of international law, and thus invites

---

[139] Vadi, 'International law and its histories', p. 347.
[140] Possing, *Understanding Biographies*, p. 9.
[141] Ibid., pp. 69–84.
[142] Koskenniemi, *The Gentle Civilizer of Nations*, p. 8.
[143] Wouter Werner, Marieke de Hoon, and Alexis Galán (eds.), *The Law of International Lawyers: Reading Martti Koskenniemi* (Cambridge, UK: Cambridge University Press, 2017).
[144] Andrew Lang and Susan Marks, 'People with projects: writing the lives of international lawyers' (2013) 27 *Temple International and Comparative Law Journal* 437–453.

a sense of self-empowerment for the international lawyer as an architect of sorts of the international *ars aequi et boni*.

This image of the international lawyer as a vector of change and political, intellectual, and normative reform, which, as Chapter 3 examines, is largely cherished by scholars subscribing to critical and social-conflict approaches, is a conscious departure from the grand narrative and related social science history conceptions stressing material considerations and technological progress as the dominating framework within which multiple individualities are almost powerlessly immersed. As such, it is inherently in tension with an opposite conception that stresses the power-based and interest-driven sociological realities of international law-making in present times. According to this opposite view, the former perspective would not even chime with the less than negligible potential intellectual influence of any particular international lawyer in each and every one of the large variety of existing specialized international law regimes that, despite their points of intersection and overlap, are contemporarily organized as clusters of highly specialized knowledge. It would not faithfully correspondto the very small individual international lawyerly influence on any of those particular international law regimes either, and even less so when it comes to appraising any international lawyer's individual influence on the practical application of international law for the resolution of international disputes.

However, despite the risk of assuming an emulating dynamic of emancipatory potential at the individual level with regard to international law which may not correspond to the current state of the discipline – or probably to its past, which all historization tends to romanticize to different degrees, despite the fact that the international legal system is now far more developed than hitherto – and its future prospects, the collective ethos of the discipline can still find inspiration in the retrospective historizing of well-contextualized personal narratives from its hectic and colourful past. It is in this sense that biographical work in the history of international law may be seen as partly performing the historiographical function of being a collective repertoire of intertwined personal and international normative stories that as a whole project an inspiring and moralizing ethos into the present. These histories reinforce the professional identity of contemporary international lawyers and become empathetic short cuts for the cyclical socialization of incoming generations to the long-standing cosmopolitan aspirations of the discipline. Moreover, recourse to this form of semi-biographical international legal history also contributes to insufflating a sense of collective responsibility to pursue aspirations transcending the mere individual through, paradoxically, the narrative recourse to individual historical role models, or alternatively to the less than edifying examples provided by other murkier historical characters in the context of their times.

These considerations combine well with the contemporary appeal that international legal biography exercises for international law scholars, who are now provided with far more stylish models for international legal biography and more venues for the publication of this type of work. Moreover, beyond its contribution to the 'emancipatory function of historiography'[145] insofar as this invariably contributes to the de-reification of present concepts and current arrangements, international legal biography in a historical perspective also responds to the occasional desire that scholars experience to distance themselves momentarily from conceptual and juridical-technical analyses of contemporary develop-ments and from the complexity of contemporary 'great theory'. Cultivating international legal biography allows international law scholars, instead, to carve out for themselves a longer-term perspective on current events or retrace the genealogy of essential concepts, and thus become more aware of the uses – including contradictory uses – to which they have been put in different historical contexts. Moreover, writing in the style of the international law biography almost unavoidably triggers an emphatic affinity and sense of moral responsibility towards the character biographed on the part of the author. While the latter causes biography to more easily fall into the trap of hagiographical and eulogiz-ing depictions, this larger involvement of the subjectivity of the author, in turn, translates into making the writing of international law (and its histories) more of a 'personal affair' than just a legal-technical or purely theoretical endeavour.

These are some of the reasons why the new scholarly engagement of international lawyers and historians with the lives and works of their predecessors appears more than a passing fad in international legal scholarship. For all its still germinal state of development and diversity, international legal biography is becoming an increasingly significant sub-genre of the history of international law. In addition to helping to bridge multiple historical lacunae, it also fosters knowledge production pro-cesses on the relationship between international law and history and

---

[145] Georg G. Iggers, *Historiography in the Twentieth Century: From Scientific Objectivity to the Post-Modern Challenge* (Middletown, CT: Wesleyan University Press, 2013), p. 99.

performs, as we have seen, a series of relevant historiographical functions, including that of being a new site for methodological experimentation in the field of the history of international law. Last but not least, the rejuvenation of international legal biography also works as a latent reminder to contemporary international lawyers that they themselves may be called to answer for their actions and their omissions, for the causes they support, for those they ignore, for the paymasters they choose to serve, and for their 'betrayals (and self-betrayals)'[146] before the capricious tribunal of history . . . one day.

---

[146] Koskenniemi, *The Gentle Civilizer of Nations*, p. 7.

11

Multi-perspectivity and Periodization in the History of International Law

11.1 Introduction

The thematic expansion and methodological sophistication experienced by historical writing about international law has greatly enriched contemporary international legal scholarship. Up to a point it has also prompted the intellectual emancipation of international legal history, which until not long ago was considered to be 'a singularly underprivileged field of studies'[1] as a semi-autonomous and relatively self-contained research area. This is not a minor intellectual development in itself and neither one without significance for the discipline as a whole to continue evolving, as Jürgen Habermas would put it, from 'a flexible medium for shifting constellations of power' towards 'a crucible in which quasi-natural power relations could be dissolved.[2]

Previous chapters have illustrated what Valentina Vadi calls 'the battle of ideas about the proper methodology of the history of international law'[3] with reference to some of international legal history's dominant historiographical trends, themes, and contemporary debates. Furthermore, they have shown that there are, indeed, many channels one can choose to sail up the river of the history of international law. However, despite the great epistemological progress that the field has experienced, multi-perspectivity in its study has much to offer to free international legal history from polarizing and stagnating debates so that it may continue opening itself up to new vistas of knowledge for historiographical creativity and innovation in both methodological and thematic

---

[1] Upendra Baxi, 'New approaches to the history of international law' (2006) 19 *Leiden Journal of International Law* 555–566 at 555.
[2] Jürgen Habermas, 'Does the constitutionalization of international law still have a chance?', in Jürgen Habermas (ed.), *The Divided West*, trans. Ciaran Cronin (Oxford: Wiley, 2006), pp. 115–193 at 116.
[3] Valentina Vadi, 'International law and its histories: methodological risks and opportunities' (2017) 58 *Harvard International Law Journal* 311–352.

terms. Just as in literary theory, where 'the most prototypical cases of multiperspectivity can be found in repeated, successive renderings of one and the same event from different character's points of view',[4] in international legal history, too, multi-perspectivity 'characteristically foregrounds some form of "tension" or "dissonance" that emerges from the clash of the staged perspectives'.[5] In this sense, multi-perspectivity may help international legal historians to appreciate limitations and pitfalls, including the more common biases, blind spots, omissions, limitations, and exclusionary dynamics associated with different historiographical methodologies together with the existing points of confluence and friction among them and/or between the 'epistemic communities' that resort to them. Moreover, methodological comparison may foster creative forms of hybrid cultivation better tailored to the objects of historical investigation and also contribute to 'plant the seeds for new methodological projects that can invigorate [the] field'.[6]

Multi-perspectivity does not entail replacing one's own particular positionality and subjectivism with that of others. According to Friedrich W. Nietzsche, 'there is only a perspective "seeing", only a perspective "knowing"; the more affects we allow to speak about a thing, the more eyes, various eyes we are able to use for the same thing, the more complete will be our "concept" of the thing, our "objectivity"'.[7] Indeed, through the acknowledgement of the existence of other multiple subjectivisms, multi-perspectivity enables the reader to access a companion form of objectivity in approaching the study of the history of international law. By contributing to liberating the perpetual student of the history of international law from one-sided perspectives, the principled assimilation of multi-perspectivity makes us more attuned to the historiographical potential of considering the diversity of factors and causes at play in the study of historical processes so as to better engage

---

[4] Marcus Hatner, 'Narrative theory meets blending: multiperspectivism', in Jürgen Schlaeger and Gesa Stedman (eds.), *The Literary Mind* (Tübingen: Narr, 2008), pp. 181–194 at 182.
[5] Ibid.
[6] Steven R. Ratner and Anne-Marie Slaughter, 'Appraising the methods of international law: a prospectus for readers' (1999) 93 *American Journal of International Law* 291–302 at 301.
[7] Friedrich W. Nietzsche, 'Zur Genealogie der Moral', in *Sämtliche Werke: Kritische Studienausgabe in 15 Einzelbänden*, 5 vols., ed. Giorgo Colli and Mazzino Montinari (Berlin: Walter de Gruyter, 1988), vol. 1, p. 365, cited in Alexander Nehamas, *Nietzsche: Life As Literature* (Cambridge, MA: Harvard University Press, 1987), p. 50.

and more faithfully depict the 'complexity and multicausality of historical developments'[8] involved in the formation and development of the norms and concepts of international law over time.

Multi-perspectivity is not a substitute for passion in putting forward the causes the historian of international law may wish to herald through his or her writings. If, indeed, we agree with Robert Kolb, for whom 'the proper genius of the lawyer is to be able to think a case from different perspectives and to imagine uncommon legal arguments, i.e. arguments which others do not see. The study of legal history considerably sharpens that ability',[9] then a multi-perspectival study of the history of international law should bring the refinement of these skills into a new dimension. Multi-perspectivity is, moreover, and even more importantly, a recipe, first and foremost, against any form of exclusionary inclination with regard to the history of international law. For good reason, the Council of Europe has long been implementing a training methodology based on multi-perspectivity for history teaching at all levels of the education cycle so as to be able to better 'contribute to a spirit of tolerance with respect to promoting different points of view, respect for the other and developing the critical and autonomous judgement of future active citizens within democratic societies'.[10] Multi-perspectivity, which in history education 'refers to the epistemological idea that history is interpretational and subjective, with multiple coexisting narratives about particular historical events, rather than history being objectively represented by one "closed" narrative',[11] is by now an empirically well-tested and broadly adopted healthy antidote against any form of zealotry. This, in its academic variant, may present itself cloaked under different robes, including that of a promised form of emancipation.

---

[8] For a promising example, see Felix Lange, 'Challenging the Paris Peace Treaties, state sovereignty, and Western-dominated international law – the multifaceted genesis of the *jus cogens* doctrine' (2008) 31 *Leiden Journal of International Law* 821–839 at 839.

[9] Robert Kolb, 'Legal history as a source: from classical to modern international law', in Jean d'Aspremont and Samantha Besson (eds.), *The Oxford Handbook of the Sources of International Law* (Oxford: Oxford University Press, 2017), pp. 279–300.

[10] Robert Stradling, *Multiperspectivity in History Teaching: A Guide for Teachers* (Strasbourg: Council of Europe Press, 2003); see also Council of Europe, *Crossroads of European Histories: Multiple Outlooks on Five Key Moments in the History of Europe* (Strasbourg: Council of Europe Press, 2009).

[11] Bjorn Wansink et al., 'Where does teaching multiperspectivity in history education begin and end? An analysis of the uses of temporality' (2018) 46 *Theory & Research in Social Education* 495–527.

Multi-perspectivity may equally also contribute to problematizing 'epistemic nationalism', by which in the international legal context Anne Peters means 'the twofold phenomenon that international legal scholars often espouse positions which can be linked to their prior education in their domestic legal system and/or which serve the national interest'.[12] It can do this by making 'epistemic nationalism' more apparent not just to others, but also to those who espouse it without, perhaps, a full awareness of it when writing about the history of international law. Moreover, it is through the shifting lenses of multi-perspectivity which are aligned, as Anne Peters notes, with 'universal intersubjective comprehensibility, allowing scholars with diverging geographical, educational or theoretical backgrounds to understand an argument or a research finding',[13] that international law can be seen in its innate historical contingency as an ever-evolving yet common intellectual platform, where an interest, whether common or particular, is never absolute but always relative to others, as are all perspectives.

This is why, by exercising the willingness to put ourselves in as many others' shoes as possible, by making the effort to understand others more deeply with regard to their viewpoints on the history of international law, we not only greatly refine our historical and international lawyerly skills and contribute to facilitating a more effective communication among different epistemic communities but, more importantly, become *more plural ourselves* and so better equipped to reaffirm with Lucien Febvre our 'foi dans les destins du libre esprit'.[14]

In an effort to uphold the value of multi-perspectivity, each of the different chapters in this book has paid attention to how both different historiographical approaches and new historical scholarship on particular themes have contributed to knowledge production processes on the relationship between international law and history. One of the dimensions more directly impacted, as we have seen, by the turn to the history of international law has been that of the historiography of international law, of which a central element, as in any historiography, is the question of periodization. This question, which has been rightly described as 'the more elusive task of historical scholarship' and 'as an analytical issue,

---

[12] Anne Peters, 'Multiperspectivism in and on international law', in *Völkerrechtsblog* (15 January 2019), voelkerrechtsblog.org/multiperspectivism-in-and-on-international-law/.
[13] Ibid.
[14] Lucien Febvre, *Le problème de l'incroyance au XVIe siècle: la religion de Rabelais* (Paris: Albin Michel, 1942), p. 36.

perhaps the fundamental intellectual issue in historical thinking',[15] is an apposite illustration of the role of multi-perspectivity in the history of international law. Indeed, one may agree with William A. Green, who noted, 'periodisation is both the product and the begetter of theory. The organising principles upon which we write history, the priorities we assign to various aspects of human endeavour and the theories of change we adopt to explain the historical process – all are represented in periodisation. Once firmly established, periodisation exerts a formidable, often subliminal, influence on the refinement and elaboration of theory.'[16]

To illustrate the central if often overlooked role that periodization plays in the history of international law and how the traditional periodizing of the field has been impacted by the new wave of literature, this chapter proceeds as follows.[17] After briefly introducing in Section 11.2 the concept of periodization and the relative neglect of its study in international legal history, Sections 11.3 and 11.4 critically discuss six approaches to periodization in the history of international law: the hegemonic, the Eurocentric universalist, the state-centric, the doctrinal, the institutional and the normative. Section 11.5 then studies how postmodern critical historiography, of which notice was given in Chapter 3, has problematized the question of periodization because of the homogenizing effect and the 'teleology of progress' which periodization is interpreted as contributing to. This section also shows that even despite a radical postmodern critique of periodization which distrusts 'great meta-narratives', alternative meta-narratives and ideological frameworks nonetheless structure other periodizations for contemporary historians of

---

[15] Jerry H. Bentley, 'Cross-cultural interaction and periodization in world history' (1996) 101 *American Historical Review* 749–770 at 749; Peter N. Stearns, 'Periodization in world history teaching: identifying the big changes' (1987) 20 *The History Teacher* 561–580 at 562.

[16] William A. Green, 'Periodizing world history' (1995) 34 *History and Theory* 99–111 at 99.

[17] To the best of the author's knowledge, only two specific works have been solely devoted to the study of periodization in the international legal literature: Oliver Digglemann, 'The periodization of the history of international law', in Bardo Fassbender and Anne Peters (eds.), *The Oxford Handbook of the History of International Law* (Oxford: Oxford University Press, 2012), pp. 997–1011; and William Butler, 'Periodization and international law', in Alexander Orakhelashvili (ed.), *Research Handbook on the Theory and History of International Law* (Cheltenham: Edward Elgar, 2011), pp. 379–393. This chapter partially builds on the first journal article specifically devoted to periodization in international legal history, Ignacio de la Rasilla, 'The problem of periodization in the history of international law' (2019) 37 *Law and History Review* 275–308.

international law. Section 11.6 elaborates on the heuristic potential of a multi-perspective approach to the question of periodization and addresses the notion of 'alternative periodizations'. With examples from a new wave of literature on the history of international law, Section 11.7 illustrates the value of four such alternative periodizations as a launch pad for the 'formation of new formerly unknown periods', a task that can be considered 'an essential part of historiographical innovation'.[18] To conclude, Section 11.8 brings us back to the relevance of multi-perspectivity as a frame that opens to multiple lenses through which to approach the study of the history of international law.

11.2   A Typology of Periodization in the History of International Law

In his essay 'Über die Theoriebedürftigkeit der Geschichtswissenschaft' ('On the Need for Theory in the Discipline of History'), Reinhart Koselleck points out that history can exist as a discipline only if it is capable of developing 'eine Theorie der geschichtlichen Zeiten' ('a theory of historical time').[19] Periodization, which is understood as the act of compartmentalizing the past into blocks of time for purposes of studying and analysing it, is used to cut up history's 'seamless web'.[20] Historians use historical periods as metaphorical moving buoys in the marshlands of historical research to diachronically or synchronically set out the confines of significant historical investigations. This is a task that involves taking decisions of exclusion and inclusion regarding scale, time, space, and the planning of the use of archival, bibliographical, and other relevant historical sources.

Every field of historical research has a well-established catalogue of standard historical periodizations relevant to its objects of study. The history of international law is no exception. Traditionally, scholars have broken down this history into historical periods built around

---

[18] Stearns, 'Periodization', pp. 561 and 562.
[19] Reinhart Koselleck, 'Über die Theoriebedürftigkeit der Geschichtswissenschaft', in Reinhart Koselleck (ed.), *Zeitschichten: Studien zur Historik* (Berlin: Suhrkamp, 2000), pp. 298–316 at 302.
[20] The 'seamless web' reference is drawn from Sir Frederick Pollock and Frederic William Maitland, *The History of English Law* (Carmel: Liberty Fund, 1898), p. 1.

conventional landmarks, turning points, or 'stereotypical context-breaking events'.[21] These conventional periods are temporal porticos through which international law scholars contemplate different historically and normatively intertwined international contexts. Arguably, without this ready-to-use historical menu of 'before' and 'after', it would not be possible to grasp the dynamics of continuity and change, repetition, and renewal, or to locate the sources of transformation or stagnation in the history of international law. Neither would it be possible to penetrate the shifting international 'legal consciousness' of the 'invisible college' of international lawyers, or to assess the effects of their influence on international law-making and international institution-making processes, including, as was seen in Chapter 9, on the establishment of international courts and tribunals, over time.[22]

However, despite the analytical centrality of periodization in historical research, Oliver Diggelmann has rightly argued that periodization is one of 'the most fundamental and most underestimated questions in the historiography of international law'.[23] As international legal history continues to undergo a period of rejuvenation, the relatively understudied issue of periodization provides a valuable heuristic tool with which to reappraise contemporary historical research methodologies in the light of multi-perspectivity. To provide a balanced multi-perspective on periodization in international legal history, Section 11.3 discusses Randall Lesaffer's survey of the 'hegemonic approach', the 'Eurocentric approach', and the 'state-centric' type of periodisation with reference to contemporary literature. Lesaffer identified these approaches to periodization as the 'three main types of periodisation in the historiography of international law since the late Middle Ages', further noting that they are 'not mutually exclusive and can be combined into a single narrative'.[24] Section 11.4 will furthermore identify the existence of three other conventional approaches to periodization which are widely influential in the modern historiography of international law and which can also be found

---

[21] Martti Koskenniemi, 'Vitoria and us: thoughts on critical histories of international law' (2014) 22 *Rechtsgeschichte* 119–138 at 119.

[22] Duncan Kennedy, 'Toward an historical understanding of legal consciousness: the case of classical legal thought in America 1850–1940' (1980) 3 *Research in Law & Society* 3–24 at 3.

[23] Diggelmann, 'The periodization', p. 998.

[24] Randall Lesaffer, 'The end of the Cold War: an epochal event in the history of international law?' (2010) 10 *Tilburg Working Paper Series on Jurisprudence and Legal History* 1–25 at 1 and 5.

combined and recombined to different degrees with both each other and
Lesaffer's three approaches into multiple narratives. This complementary
three-tiered typology consists of what one may call 'intellectual idealist',
'institutionalist', and 'normative' approaches to periodization in the
history of international law.

11.3   Empire, Western Universalism, and the Sovereign State

The first type of periodization surveyed by Lesaffer is the 'epochal realist'
approach. This approach was proposed by Wilhelm Grewe in his *The
Epochs of International Law* to overcome the biases of an 'idealist intellectual' historiography of international law. This, in Grewe's view, had
become lost in 'an abstract history of the theory' because it did not take
enough account of the 'close connection between legal theory and state
practice'.[25] Instead, Grewe opted to divide the history of international law
into epochs characterized by the dominance of particular hegemonic
powers. According to Grewe's reading of the historical evolution of international law as epiphenomenal to major power structures, the history of
international law should be divided into the Spanish Age (1494–1648), the
French Age (1648–1815), the British Age (1815–1919), the Age of the
Anglo-American Condominium (1919–44), and the Age of American–
Soviet Rivalry (1945–89).[26] To this sequence of shifting major imperial
constellations since the end of the Middle Ages, one could add the
contemporary post-Cold War period (1989–2020) of North American
hegemony, which has been punctuated by the enlargement of the
European Union and, for the first time going beyond the Western-centric
framework proposed by Grewe, the rise of China as a major global power
in the twenty-first century.

Grewe's 'hegemonic epochal' periodization of the historical development of international law was methodologically ingrained in a hyper-
realist characterization of the intertwined development of international
relations and international law in which the latter plays the instrumental
role of an 'ideological façade' to facilitate power-aggrandisement and
hegemonic domination.[27] Recent years have witnessed a revamping of

---

[25] Wilhelm Grewe, *The Epochs of International Law*, trans. Michael Byers (Berlin: De
Gruyter, 2000), p. 6.

[26] Lesaffer, 'The end of the Cold War', pp. 16 and 23.

[27] Martti Koskenniemi, 'Review of the epochs of international law' (2002) 51 *International
and Comparative Law Quarterly* 746–751 at 747.

the classical view of international law as a 'superstructure' in the form of a post-colonial historical meta-narrative that, as was seen in Chapter 4, has portrayed the 'historical role of international law as an instrument of (Western) expansion and hegemony'.[28] This reinterpretation in a Marxist vein of international law as a mere epiphenomenon of Western imperialism has proceeded by challenging the received interpretation of central historical episodes in the discipline, including, as was seen inter alia in Chapter 2, the significance of Francisco de Vitoria's work at the time of the Spanish discovery and conquest of America.[29] However, the post-colonial reinterpretation has expanded, as has been seen in previous chapters and, in particular, in Chapter 10, to include other classic Western thinkers and episodes in the history of international law from the sixteenth century to the post-World War II decolonization decades. It has also reached the contemporary period, in which post-colonial approaches to international law have described international institutions as a 'global imperial state in the making' dominated by Western powers and managed by 'transnational capitalist classes'.[30] With its interpretation of the past in the light of Western hegemonic relations with other peoples as the determining factor in the historical progress of international law, this counter-imperial historical narrative has also forged new historical periods. In each of them, different 'colonial encounters' are interpreted as stages in a Western-led imperial genealogy of international law and, alternatively, as sites of resistance to it.

Both the Western hegemonic epochal approach to periodization (in which a sequence of historical events is condensed into a discernible hegemonic age) and its most recent 'shadow' counter-imperial periodization (with its focus on 'the great shifting currents of global imperialism')[31] can be questioned, as we saw in earlier chapters, for their historical reductionism and their either explicit or 'hidden' Eurocentrism. However, these criticisms do not diminish the pervasive influence of the

---

[28] Martti Koskenniemi, 'Introduction: international law and empire – aspects and approaches', in Martti Koskenniemi, Walter Rech, and Manuel J. Fonseca (eds.), *International Law and Empire – Historical Explorations* (Oxford: Oxford University Press, 2017), pp. 1–20 at 4.

[29] See Antony Anghie, *Imperialism, Sovereignty and the Making of International Law* (Cambridge, UK: Cambridge University Press, 2005).

[30] Bhupinder S. Chimni, 'International institutions today: an imperial global state in the making' (2004) 15 *European Journal of International Law* 1–37 at 1.

[31] Anne Orford, *Reading Humanitarian Intervention: Human Rights and the Use of Force in International Law* (Cambridge, UK: Cambridge University Press, 2003), p. 39.

Western-centric epochal approach to periodization or of its counterpart in the construction of historical international legal narratives. Neither should the practical influence that these have had, and continue to have, as means of instrumentally contesting contemporary aspects of the international legal order in the discourses of non-Western countries be underestimated. This is a reminder of the illocutionary or performative narrative force of all historical writing about international law, which, however, as it was pointed out in Chapter 2, cannot be automatically equated to its eventual 'perlocutionary effect'.

Alongside these two conceptually intertwined periodizations of international legal history, there is another 'Eurocentric and universalist' approach.[32] Lesaffer exemplified this approach with reference to the work of Heinhard Steiger,[33] who subdivided the history of international law since the late Middle Ages into the 'Age of Christianity' (1300–1800), the 'Age of the Civilized Nations' (from the nineteenth century to 1918), and the 'Age of Mankind' (since 1919). Steiger also considered that the pattern of gradual universalization of the *jus publicum europaeum* had accelerated towards an 'age of the global citizen'[34] since 1945. Contrasting with the realist underpinnings of the 'hegemonic epochal' approach and its post-colonial reinterpretation, Steiger's 'Eurocentric universalist' periodization is aligned with a Western-led narrative of human-centred progress. In this perspective, the Western political model is the linchpin of the evolving path of the international legal order. It axiologically portrays the role of international law and, by extension, international institutions as a force for good in the inexorable progress of world history towards a global realization of the ideals of the Enlightenment.[35]

The key landmarks of this periodization underpin multiple accounts of the historical evolution of the discipline from an international liberal perspective. These can variously be found based on, for instance, the comparative liberal constitutional evolution of different states by making

---

[32] Lesaffer, 'The end of the Cold War', p. 6.
[33] Heinhard Steiger, 'From the international law of Christianity to the international law of the world citizen – reflections on the formation of the epochs of the history of international law' (2001) 3 *Journal of the History of International Law* 180–193.
[34] Ibid.
[35] Martti Koskenniemi, 'On the idea and practice for universal history with a cosmopolitan purpose', in Bindu Puri and Heiko Sievers (eds.), *Terror, Peace and Universalism: Essays on the Philosophy of Immanuel Kant* (Oxford: Oxford University Press, 2007), pp. 122–148.

reference to their joining international institutions; their domestic application of the liberal principles of the rule of law and the separation of
powers; their introduction of constitutional arrangements concerning
international human rights; or their ratification and implementation of
international treaties in different areas. However, this liberal forward-
looking approach to the historical periodization of international law has
been criticized as a form of 'Whig history'. This is a term which, as it was
seen in Chapter 2 in the context of a discussion of the role for anachronism in international legal history, has often been pejoratively applied by
international legal historians to histories of the discipline based on a
reading of its past as a 'progress narrative' that conceals, embellishes, or
altogether ignores the sheer inequalities underlying both past and present
international legal arrangements.[36] The charge that international lawyers
often rely on a common type of historical 'ascending periodization'
which entrenches a correlation between the progress of international
law and its role as a global agent of social progress underlies the critical
problematizing of periodization in particular with regard to traditional
internal normative approaches in the domain of the 'history of international law'[37] as was seen in Chapter 7.

Completing the foundational triad of the conventional historiographical paradigm in the history of international law is what Lesaffer termed
the 'state-centric' approach to periodization. According to Lesaffer, this
approach is the 'most foundational one' as 'it underlies the vast majority
of grand narratives of the history of international law, because it is
consciously used, because it is implicit or because it is contested'.[38] The
historical depiction of an international legal order in which 'state
sovereignty' is foundational remains a *locus classicus* in the historical
ordering of the evolving path of the discipline. The centrality of the
sovereign state in a *longue durée* perspective on the evolution of international law is traced back to the origins of classical international law at a
time when an early form of *jus publicum europaeum* emerged from the
collapse of the medieval *Respublica Christiana*. The first stage in the
classical periodization of international law is, consequently, often

---

[36] See also Thomas Skouteris, 'Engaging history in international law', in David Kennedy and
José M. Beneyto (eds.), *New Approaches to International Law: The European and
American Experiences* (The Hague: T. M. C. Asser Press, 2011), pp. 99–121.
[37] Tilmann Altwicker and Oliver Diggelmann, 'How is progress constructed in international
legal scholarship?' (2014) 25 *European Journal of International Law* 425–444.
[38] Lesaffer, 'The end of the Cold War', p. 7.

identified as beginning in 1648, the date of the Peace of Westphalia, which put an end to the Thirty Years War. Westphalia constitutes the most representative illustration in the history of international law of what Stéphane Beaulac has termed an 'etiological myth', that is, a myth about the origins of things.[39] Since then, international lawyers have variously interpreted Westphalia as a converging point of the principles of equal sovereignty of European states in both their internal and external facets.[40]

However, the importance of Westphalia as a departure point for the history of international law in the state-centric approach, other than being questioned in historically contextualist terms, as was seen in Chapter 2, has also been both temporally and geographically contested in the literature.[41] This contestation has revolved around the definition of international law that underpins each chronological periodization. Influenced by the tenets of world-history, Wolgang Preiser relied on a socio-legal understanding based on the axiom *ubi societas inter potestates, ibi ius gentium* to define international law as the law of 'several independent political entities that had relations with each other on an equal footing and acknowledged that their relations were governed by legal norms'.[42] From this definition a shift in the temporal and geographical localization of the historical origins of international law logically ensues. Since these earlier works, which adopted an universal perspective on the historical evolution of international law, new scholarship has investigated, as was seen in Chapter 5, the history of international law in the Middle Ages and ancient civilizations both within Europe and in extra-European geographical spaces.[43] This new literature has also touched on the myth-constructing role of the Western historiographical

---

[39] Stéphane Beaulac, *The Power of Language in the Making of International Law: The Word Sovereignty in Bodin and Vattel and the Myth of Westphalia* (Leiden: Martinus Nijhoff, 2004).

[40] See Ignacio de la Rasilla, 'History of international law – 1550–1700', in *Oxford Bibliographies in International Law* (2017), www.oxfordbibliographies.com/view/docu ment/obo-9780199796953/obo-9780199796953-0036.xml, pp. 1–20.

[41] Robert Kolb, *Esquisse d'un droit international public des anciennes cultures extra-européennes: Amérique precolombienne, Iles Polynésiennes, Afrique Noire, Sous-continent indien, Chine et régions limitrophes* (Paris: Pédone, 2010).

[42] Wolfgang Preiser, 'Die Epochen der antiken Volkerrechtsgeschichte' (1956) 11 *Juristenzeitung* 737–744 at 737 (my translation).

[43] Ignacio de la Rasilla, 'Medieval international law', in *Oxford Bibliographies in International Law* (2014), www.oxfordbibliographies.com/view/document/obo-9780199796953/obo-9780199796953-0112.xml, pp. 1–25.

reconstruction of the 'origins' of international law.[44] This began to take place in the mid- to late nineteenth century during a period when the professional study of both history and law at the national level, and alongside them the study of international law and the history of international law themselves, emerged as intellectually linked to 'methodological nationalism' in the Western world.[45]

New literature has also been particularly critical of the archetypal Eurocentrism of Westphalia. This perspective, which equates the beginning of the 'classical' period of international legal history with the advent of the principle of sovereign equality among secular states, makes it the leitmotiv of the ulterior historical development of the discipline. However, this is an overstatement for Europe itself and, arguably, merely false for non-European states.[46] As Lauren Benton and Lisa Ford argue, for many non-European states the origins of international law may be found in empires.[47] Besides being historically distrusted, the absolute centrality of the state-centric periodization of the history of international law becomes further undermined when it is examined from the perspective of the much-debated decline in state sovereignty. Furthermore, this questioning of the centrality of state sovereignty, which has been brought about by globalization and the increasingly important role of international organizations and supra-national regional institutions together with non-state actors in the shaping of contemporary international law,[48] has prompted a larger attention, as was seen in Chapter 8, to socio-legal approaches to the history of international law and the rise of an array of new histories of non-state actors.

Shifting constellations of imperial power, liberal Western universalism, and the centrality of the sovereign nation-state are the respective foundations of the 'epochal hegemonic', the 'Eurocentric universalist', and the 'state-centric' approaches to the periodization of the history of international law. They are the three symbiotic pillars of the conventional historiographical paradigm implicitly underlying most conventional

---

[44] See Ignacio de la Rasilla, 'The shifting origins of international law' (2015) 28 *Leiden Journal of International Law* 419–440 at 419 and 424.

[45] Daniel Chernilo, 'The critique of methodological nationalism: theory and history' (2011) 106 *Thesis Eleven* 98–117.

[46] Teemu Ruskola, 'Raping like a state' (2010) 57 *UCLA Law Review* 1477–1536 at 1485.

[47] Lauren Benton and Lisa Ford, *Rage for Order: The British Empire and the Origins of International Law 1800–1850* (Cambridge, MA: Harvard University Press, 2016).

[48] Martti Koskenniemi, 'What use for sovereignty today?' (2011) 1 *Asian Journal of International Law* 61–70 at 61.

international legal periodizations.[49] However, alongside this foundational triad one can identify at least three other equally widely influential types of periodization. These are also often used as the square and triangle of historical time in the international legal historian's toolkit. The writings of the most highly qualified academics in different schools of international legal thought, the historical development of international institutions or organizations, and the historical evolution of international legal norms and principles are also widely used as ordering factors to categorize the history of international law into discrete named blocks of time.

11.4   International Theories, Institutions, and Norms

A fourth type of widely used periodization is the 'idealist intellectual' approach. This approach divides the past into a succession of intellectual frameworks and theories proposed in canonical texts by philosophers, political thinkers, and international lawyers, and it relies on a Western canon of intellectual landmarks in the history of the discipline.[50] In the Western tradition, the intellectual periodization of the history of international law usually originates with the *Seconda Scholastica*, represented by the School of Salamanca, over which Francisco de Vitoria presided. Broadly speaking, it later extends through Alberico Gentili, Hugo Grotius – whose *De iure belli ac pacis* (1625) served to attribute to him the 'fatherhood' of international law – and later still to Protestant thinkers such as Samuel Pufendorf or Christian Wolff with his influential concept of *civitas maxima* as the foundation of the law of nations. During the Enlightenment, some of Immanuel Kant's essays, including *The Idea of a Universal History with a Cosmopolitan Purpose* (1784), established, following in the wake of earlier peace projects, the basis for what would become a cosmopolitan teleology of progress in international legal thought that extends to the present and, as was seen in Chapter 9, largely influences how international lawyers appraise the role of international organizations in world politics.[51] Another common eighteenth-century

---

[49] See Lesaffer, 'The end of the Cold War', p. 5.

[50] Martti Koskenniemi, 'Histories of international law: significance and problems for a critical view' (2013) 27 *Temple International and Comparative Law Journal* 215–240 at 215.

[51] Martti Koskenniemi, 'Constitutionalism as mindset: reflections on Kantian themes about international law and globalization' (2007) 8 *Theoretical Inquiries in Law* 9–36 at 1 and 12.

landmark in this type of intellectual periodization of the history of international law is Emer de Vattel's *Le droit des gens*. Following its publication in 1758, de Vattel's work was widely circulated in both Europe and the United States in various translations and subsequent editions.[52] This classic Western intellectual genealogy continues through the rise of positivism and the first efforts to systematically codify the law of nations in the mid- to late nineteenth century, where one meets the founders of the Institut de droit international, a landmark in what in time would become, as was seen in Chapter 8, the highly diverse and influential contemporary NGO movement. It further progressed through the twentieth century with 'the greats' of the discipline in the interwar period, including, as was seen in Chapters 10 and others, towering intellectual international legal figures such as Hans Kelsen, Alfred Verdross, Georges Scelle, and Hersch Lauterpacht with their respective great theoretical frameworks, and even seminal international relations theorists, such as Hans Morgenthau and others.[53]

In a snapshot perspective, this intellectual idealist approach to periodization, which periodizes the history of international law in terms of a succession of intellectual and theoretical frameworks put forward in canonical texts by representatives of international legal schools of thought, continued developing during the Cold War. This witnessed inter alia the emergence of the ideologically opposite configurative jurisprudence of the New Haven School and the Soviet-Marxist theory of international law punctuated by the emergence of post-colonial voices during the decolonization era.[54] The post-Cold War period is, in turn, one characterized by the central doctrinal pre-eminence of liberal internationalism and its different institutionalist exponents. However, as was seen in Chapter 3, the golden age of international liberalism, which seems now to be heading to its end, has been compounded by the unparalleled rise of critical and alternative approaches to international law, methodological pluralization, and inter-disciplinarization

[52] Emmanuelle Jouannet, *Emmer de Vattel et l'émergence doctrinale du droit international classique* (Paris: Pédone, 1998).
[53] Martti Koskenniemi, *The Gentle Civilizer of Nations: The Rise and Fall of International Law 1870–1960* (Cambridge, UK: Cambridge University Press, 2001).
[54] See as representative of the New Haven School, Harold Dwight Lasswell and Myress McDougal, *Jurisprudence for a Free Society: Studies in Law, Science and Policy* (New Haven, CT: New Haven Press, 1992). See as an early representative of post-colonial voices, Georges Abi-Saab, 'The newly independent states and the rules of international law: an outline' (1962) 8 *Howard Law Journal* 95–121 at 95.

of the academic study of international law, and also the study of its history.[55]

Revitalization of the doctrinal approach to periodization is one of the defining characteristics of the recent wave of historical scholarship in international law. Indeed, contemporary literature has expanded in the direction of contextualist re-readings of intellectual classics of the discipline from different periods by often adopting, as we saw in Chapter 10, contextualist methods to carve out a revamped genre of international legal 'biography'. This move has also fostered the addition of authors such as Niccolò Machiavelli, Johannes Althusius, Baruch Spinoza, the Baron de Montesquieu, Jean-Jacques Rousseau, Friedrich Hegel, Karl Marx, and others who were not usually regarded as central in the traditional historical intellectual canon of international law.[56] Indeed, according to Martti Koskenniemi, the canon of the disciplinary history of international law should be extended further to include within its boundaries other excluded voices which in his view contributed to the history of the formation of knowledge about the law of nations from different disciplines.[57] Under the influence of post-colonial approaches, this revisionist trend has already impacted the modern understanding of classic figures.[58] Furthermore, the intellectual history of international law has extended into examination of work by previously neglected less prominent figures in international law, including for the first time a group of international legal historians.[59] As was seen in Chapter 10, the renewed cultivation of the historical biographical genre has brought the connection between the personal and the academic more acutely to the foreground, and on occasion also the advisory and adjudicative facets of the work of highly qualified writers in different socio-historical

---

[55] See Anne Orford and Florian Hoffmann with Martin Clark (eds.), *The Oxford Handbook of the Theory of International Law* (Oxford: Oxford University Press, 2016).

[56] See Stefan Kadelbach, Thomas Kleinlein, and David Roth-Isigkeit (eds.), *System, Order, and International Law: The Early History of International Legal Thought from Machiavelli to Hegel* (Oxford: Oxford University Press, 2017).

[57] Martti Koskenniemi, 'The law of nations and the "conflict of faculties"' (2018) 8 *History of the Present* 4–28.

[58] Georg Cavallar, 'Vitoria, Grotius, Pufendorf, Wolff and Vattel: accomplices of European colonialism and exploitation or true cosmopolitans?' (2008) 10 *Journal of the History of International Law* 181–209.

[59] See David Armitage and Jennifer Pitts, 'This modern Grotius: an introduction to the life and thought of C. H. Alexandrowicz', in Charles H. Alexandrowicz, *The Law of Nations in Global History*, ed. David Armitage and Jennifer Pitts (Oxford: Oxford University Press, 2017), pp. 1–34.

contexts. This contemporary literature, which delves into the lives, works, and times of international thinkers, scholars, legal advisors, judges, and lawyers, is also adding new landmarks to the mainly Western intellectual periodization of international law by gradually encompassing the contribution of international law scholars from non-Western traditions.[60]

Historians of international political thought and international intellectual historians, often informed by the Cambridge School, the main historiographical tenets of which Chapter 2 examined, have long cultivated the contextual intellectual biographical genre.[61] These include works on Hugo Grotius, who, from being traditionally celebrated as the founding father of international law, has, according to Arthur Weststeijn, 'turned into a founding father of a Dutch empire by law'.[62] The list extends to include many other classic Western authors such as Francisco de Vitoria.[63] Some of their works have tackled traditional figures in the canon of the history of international law, like Thomas Hobbes, Jean Bodin, and the Spanish scholastics.[64] The historically nuanced work of these contextualist intellectual historians is often used by international legal historians to question the international jurist's received interpretation of the significance of classical figures and their relative positions in doctrinal intellectual periodizations. However, while the work of historians of political thought has greatly contributed to thickening the contextualization of historical figures in their own time, the treatment of the question of periodization remains first and foremost

---

[60] See Fleur Johns, Thomas Skouteris, and Wouter Werner, 'Editors' introduction: Alejandro Álvarez and the launch of the Periphery Series' (2006) 19 *Leiden Journal of International Law* 875–1040; Fleur Johns, Thomas Skouteris, and Wouter Werner, 'Editors' introduction: Taslim Olawale Elias in the Periphery Series' (2008) 21 *Leiden Journal of International Law* 289–290.

[61] Skinner, 'Meaning and understanding', pp. 3–53.

[62] Arthur Weststeijn, 'Provincializing Grotius: international law and empire in a seventeenth-century Malay mirror', in Martti Koskenniemi, Walter Rech, and Manuel Jiménez Fonseca (eds.), *International Law and Empire: Historical Explorations* (Cambridge, UK: Cambridge University Press, 2017), pp. 21–38 at 21–22.

[63] Andrew Fitzmaurice, 'The problem of Eurocentrism in the thought of Francisco de Vitoria', in José M. Beneyto and Justo Corti Varela (eds.), *At the Origins of Modernity: Francisco de Vitoria and the Discovery of International Law* (Cham: Springer, 2017), pp. 77–93.

[64] Richard Tuck, *The Rights of War and Peace: Political Thought and the International Order from Grotius and Kant* (Oxford: Oxford University Press, 1999); Martine Julia van Ittersum, *Profit and Principle: Hugo Grotius, Natural Rights Theories and the Rise of Dutch Power in the East Indies 1595–1605* (The Hague: Brill, 2006).

defined by traditional periodization schemes in the field of the history of political thought.

The fourth main type of 'master periodization' in the historiography of international law, and the most influential in coverage of the twentieth century, is the 'international institutionalist' approach. This approach identifies major 'historical moments' in which there is a transformative impact of the creation of international institutions. The three main waves of establishment of international institutions in the twentieth century have indeed much influenced the historiographical splitting up of inter- national legal history since the establishment of the League of Nations roughly a hundred years ago. As we saw in Chapter 9, major inter- national institution-building processes have taken place during what historical institutionalism terms 'critical junctures' – 'relatively short periods of time during which structural economic, political and cultural conditions are in flux, so that the choices available to powerful actors expand'.[65] The setting up of major international institutions, the quint- essence of context-breaking events from a normative perspective, often marks a 'before' and an 'after' in the historical study of international law in the twentieth century. Indeed, only with the utmost difficulty could one find any historical account of the historical evolution of international law in the twentieth and twenty-first centuries which is not informed by major international institution-building processes structuring broad his- torical *caesurae*.

The three major instances of what David Kennedy, referring to the establishment of the League of Nations, calls the 'move to institutions' correspond to the ends of World War I, World War II, and the Cold War.[66] Indeed, the significance in the contemporary periodization of the history of international law of the historically unprecedented character of the 'new world order' ushered in by the Covenant of the League of Nations is matched only by that of the establishment of the UN system, which was inaugurated by the Charter of the UN in 1945.[67] Likewise, the relevance of these two major international institutional efforts in enab- ling historians to contemplate different normatively and historically

---

[65] Giovanni Capoccia, 'Critical junctures', in Orfeo Fioretos, Tulia G. Falleti, and Adam Sheingate (eds.), *The Oxford Handbook of Historical Institutionalism* (Oxford: Oxford University Press, 2016), pp. 89–106 at 89.

[66] David Kennedy, 'The move to institutions' (1987) 8 *Cardozo Law Review* 841–988 at 841.

[67] See Robert Kolb (ed.), *Commentaire sur le Pacte de la Société des Nations* (Brussels: Bruylant, 2015).

intertwined international contexts is equalled in the literature only by the contemporary proliferation of international institutions and the multiplication of international courts and tribunals, which have continued at both the regional and global levels, since the end of the Cold War.[68] Completing the standard periodization of the history of international law in the twentieth century, the international institution-building effort that characterized the 1990s and the early 2000s is indeed today often referred to as having given birth to a new 'age of global governance' in the twenty-first century.

Last, but not least, in this brief appraisal of periodization in the history of international law is the 'international normative' approach to periodization. This can be described as an approach that uses an 'analytical prism' that is 'less concerned with contextual features of an "order" and more with the lineage of individual rules, systemic perceptions of these rules by the subjects of the system, and doctrines'.[69] This perspective, which involves a periodical 'concentration upon intrinsic rather than extrinsic approaches to the history of international law', is one that stresses the diachronical aspect of the normative evolution of international law. As we saw in Chapter 7, it concerns itself with the internal evolution and change over time of international legal norms, principles, and doctrines.[70] The international normative approach to periodization is, needless to say, the most juridical – and therefore the most intrinsic to the strictly normative legal history of the discipline – of the six conventional approaches to the periodization of the history of international law. Therefore, it represents the clearest exponent of what has been defined as international 'jurists' history'.[71]

At least as far as the study of twentieth-century international legal history is concerned, the normative approach to periodization is closely related to the institutional approach to periodization, with which it can often be found either explicitly or implicitly combined. The prohibition of the 'threat or use of force' in international relations (as established by Art. 2.4 of the constitutive treaty of the Organization of the United Nations, founded to 'save succeeding generations from the scourge of war, which twice in our lifetime has brought untold sorrow to mankind'),

---

[68] Yuval Shany, 'No longer a weak department of power? Reflection on the emergence of a new international judiciary' (2009) 20 *European Journal of International Law* 73–91 at 73.
[69] Butler, 'Periodization and International Law', p. 391.
[70] Ibid.
[71] See Vadi, 'International law and its histories', p. 312.

provides a paradigmatic example of a watershed normative event marking a 'before' and an 'after' in the periodization of the history of the legal discourse on *ius ad bellum* which is itself inter alia retraceable to moral theological writings on the just war doctrine in the Middle Ages and early modernity.[72] The normative approach to periodization is also central to the periodization of particular branches of international law, each of which presents a series of normative turning points (e.g. typically the 'International Bill of Human Rights', made up of the Universal Declaration of Human Rights (1948) together with the International Covenant on Civil and Political Rights and the International Covenant on Economic, Social and Cultural Rights in 1966) which are retrospectively deemed to have crystallized an earlier historical and normative progression marked by a previous series of other normative landmarks towards the present.

The presence to a lesser or greater degree of a juridical prism in a historical narrative is ultimately the differentiating factor between an enquiry into international legal history and other types of historical analysis. However, the promise of the purely internal international normative approach to allow international legal history to develop its own periodizations distinctly and independently of periodizations based on other criteria can be questioned from a historical point of view. As was seen in Chapter 7, this is inter alia because in its concentration on 'intrinsic' approaches to the history of international law, this perspective exhibits a marked anti-disciplinary ethos in studying the past. The legalistic exclusion of other approaches to the history of international law generates a doctrinarian a-historical normatization of the past of international law as a solipsistic discipline completely separated from sociology, economics, and politics. Moreover, the isolation of international law from other disciplines is often accompanied by 'the tendency to underestimate structural continuities' such as the previously mentioned landmark in the history of the prohibition of the use of force shows in the form of 'power asymmetries in decisions over war and peace in the UN Security Council'. This, in turn, results in the 'entrenching or "freezing" [of] political and economic practices, which are already

---

[72] Randall Lesaffer, 'Too much history: from war as sanction to the sanctioning of war', in Marc Weller (ed.), *The Oxford Handbook of the Use of Force in International Law* (Oxford: Oxford University Press, 2015), pp. 35–55.

prevalent at the inception of a legal norm'.[73] Moreover, the use of such an intradisciplinary methodology brings the approach closer to what Quentin Skinner would call the 'mythology of doctrines',[74] which in turn makes this approach to periodization more susceptible to falling prey to a normative type of reductive 'precursorism'. This is the consequence of a tendency to constantly identify normative antecedents of present-day institutions or ideas in earlier historical periods with little or no regard to the unique societal historical contexts from which international legal norms emerge and the shifting background against which they have evolved and which they continually impact on and are impacted by. It is, nonetheless, worthwhile to highlight that the study of earlier efforts at international norm entrepreneurship and institutional building projects, including those regarding the history of international adjudication, can offer interesting insights as 'antecedent conditions' from the perspective of historical institutionalism into the evolution of international normative developments and institutions.

11.5 The Postmodern Critique of the Periodization of International Law

The above six approaches to periodization in the history of international law (generally based on hegemonic power, Western liberal universalism, state sovereignty, intellectual or jurisprudential history, international institutions, and international legal norms and principles) can be found constantly combined and recombined to different degrees as functional reference points in the narratives of those who investigate the intertwined dimensions of interaction and interfaces existing between history and international law. However, in the wake of the turn to the history of international law, as is 'typical of times of cognitive dissonance when new forms of thought are challenging traditional horizons',[75] the practice of

---

[73] For a critique, see Jochen von Bernstorff, 'International legal history and its methodologies: how (not) to tell the story of the many lives and deaths of the *ius ad bellum*', in Andreas von Arnauld (ed.), *Völkerrechtsgeschichte(n): Historische Narrative und Konzepte im Wandel* (Berlin: Duncker & Humblot, 2017), pp. 39–52 at 43.

[74] Quentin Skinner, 'Meaning and understanding in the history of ideas' (1969) 8 *History and Theory* 3–53 at 3.

[75] Beverley Southgate, 'Postmodernism', in Aviezer Tucker (ed.), *A Companion to the Philosophy of History and Historiography* (Hoboken, NJ: Wiley-Blackwell, 2009), pp. 540–549.

periodization itself has been made the object of a powerful critical problematization.

Lurking behind this critical questioning of the concept of periodization, which revolves around the idea, as Diggelmann notes, that 'any periodisation is inherently problematic as any period is an abstraction from the historical process',[76] is the influence of the methodological toolkit of 'critical technologies' more directly associated, as was seen in Chapter 3, with critical/postmodern approaches.[77] Critical/postmodern historians, who are often overtly militant in their wish to stress recourse to history as a means of intervening politically in contemporary international legal debates, have endeavoured to set themselves at the avant-garde of the historiographical rejuvenation of the hitherto dormant field of international legal history.[78] Critical contributors to the field have also variously reflected on historiographical matters, by, among other means, defending the legitimate role of 'anachronism' in international legal methodology, as was examined in Chapter 2.[79] The critical problematization of the study of periodization is part and parcel of a broader critical historiographical re-reading of the role of international law in shaping the contemporary world. It is also a transmission belt fostering greater doses of reflexivity and awareness of 'false necessity' in international legal scholarship.[80]

In this revisionist context, periodization has first been foundationally attacked for reinforcing the 'commonplace view that there are single homogeneous periods when international law has been either this or that'.[81] Against the reductionism involved in splitting historical time into different periods, critical historiography has instead taken on the mission of stressing the value of focusing on the tension between discontinuity and continuity and on the roles of contingency and agency as critical

---

[76] Diggelmann, 'The periodization', p. 1002.
[77] For a selected bibliography, see Thomas Skouteris, 'New Approaches to International Law', in Oxford Bibliographies in International Law (2011), www.oxfordbibliographies .com/view/document/obo-9780199796953/obo-9780199796953-0012.xml, p. 1.
[78] Thomas Skouteris, 'The turn to history in international law', in Oxford Bibliographies in International Law (2017), oxfordbibliographies.com/view/document/obo-9780199796953/ obo-9780199796953-0154.xml.
[79] Anne Orford, 'On international legal method' (2013) 1 London Review of International Law 166–197 at 171.
[80] Henry Jones, 'The radical use of history in the study of international law' (2012–13) 23 Finnish Yearbook of International Law 309–350.
[81] Koskenniemi, The Gentle Civilizer of Nations, p. 7.

historiographical topoi.[82] This is very much in syntony with the militant interpretation of the history of international law made by Marxist post-colonial international law scholars like Bhupinder S. Chimni.[83] Second, the study of periodization in the history of international law has also been impacted by the postmodernist trashing of the *grand* historical narrative of international law.[84] Critical perspectives are ontologically pitched to invariably politicize and critically antagonize historical accounts that project a narrative of progress and normative accomplishment in international law, and to instead highlight the permanence of unequal background factors in world society. In particular, they have stressed how certain types of conventional periodization contribute to an axiologically driven narrative of disciplinary progress in which international lawyers become the handmaidens of 'humanity's telos'.[85] Other authors, like Nathaniel Berman, have built on Michel Foucault's significant impact on the social sciences and humanities in making space for new paths of critical enquiry to argue, as we saw in Chapter 3, in favour of a 'genealogical approach' to the history of international law.[86]

However, critical international law historians have not limited themselves to challenging established periods in order to 'challenge established interpretations of history'[87] in the name of a purist conception of the development of historical time. It is important to realize that their ontological and deconstructive critique of historical periodization is, more often than not, a backdoor used to nurture the ground for the advancement of alternative forms of periodization of the history of international law. Critical international law scholars consider that all history writing constitutes a 'political intervention in the present' and

[82] Aeyal Gross, 'After the falls: international law between post-modernity and anti-modernity', in Emmanuelle Jouannet, Helene Ruiz-Fabri, and Jean Marc Sorel (eds.), *Regards d'une génération de juristes sur le droit international* (Paris: Pédone, 2008), pp. 183–208 at 207.
[83] Bhupinder S. Chimni, 'The past, present and future of international law: a critical Third World approach' (2007) 8 *Melbourne Journal of International Law* 499–515 at 513.
[84] Jean-François Lyotard, *The Postmodern Condition: A Report on Knowledge* (Manchester: Manchester University Press, 1984).
[85] Martti Koskenniemi, 'Between context and telos: reviewing the structures of international law', in Henning Trüper, Dipesh Chakrabarty, and Sanjay Subrahmanyam (eds.), *Historical Teleologies in the Modern World* (London: Bloomsbury, 2015), p. 216.
[86] See Michel Foucault, 'Nietzsche, genealogy, history', in Donald F. Bouchard (ed.), *Language, Counter-memory, Practice: Selected Essays and Interviews*, ed. Donald F. Bouchard (Ithaca, NY: Cornell University Press, 1980), pp. 139–164 at 139.
[87] Diggelmann, 'The periodization', p. 999.

that, paraphrasing Benedetto Croce, the 'periodization of the past is always also contemporary history'.[88] In practice, this understanding is translated into an effort to make space for the production of new critical historical meta-narratives which in turn end up fostering alternative periodizations in the history of international law. For instance, as Oliver Diggelmann highlights, a 'socialist theory of international law' would look to 'history through the lens of class struggles and expected gradual progress for the working class'.[89] Inspired by a Marxist historiography, this approach tends to identify particular events (such as the Bolshevik Revolution) as the most influential turning points or critical junctures in a socialist periodization paradigm of the history of international law.[90]

A similar case of emergence of a critical periodization has followed from the attention accorded by critical approaches to the so-called others of international law.[91] Indeed, a post-colonial periodization of the history of international law has emerged as a counterpoint to the historical narrative of international law punctuated by a Western periodization in the twentieth century gravitating for what regards the twentieth century around the watershed dates of 1919, 1945, and 1990. According to its critics, this periodization serves an ideological purpose by contributing to universalizing and legitimizing the Western historical perspective.[92] By contrast, the key historical turning points in such a new post-colonial periodization may include events, or sequences of events, oriented to flesh out the bones of an alternative 1880s–1970s periodization which moves Western imperial schemes and their colonial architecture into the foreground. As was seen in Chapter 4, a look into the contribution of recent literature to an expansion of the available histories of international law indeed shows semi-concerted efforts in the direction of this

---

[88] Ibid., p. 1010.
[89] Ibid., p. 1000.
[90] Luigi Cajani, 'Periodization', in Jerry H. Bentley (ed.), *The Oxford Handbook of World History* (Oxford: Oxford University Press, 2012), pp. 54–71; Anne Peters, 'A century after the Russian Revolution: its legacy in international law' (2017) 19 *Journal of the History of International Law* 133–146.
[91] Anne Orford (ed.), *International Law and Its Others* (Cambridge, UK: Cambridge University Press, 2006).
[92] Arnulf Becker Lorca, 'Eurocentrism in the history of international law', in Bardo Fassbender and Anne Peters (eds.), *The Oxford Handbook of the History of International Law* (Oxford: Oxford University Press, 2012), pp. 1034–1057 at 1035.

meta-re-periodization in a post-colonial vein.[93] This post-colonial periodization is built on events, or sequences thereof, such as the regimes of
colonial unequal treaties;[94] the Berlin Conference;[95] the mandate system
in the Covenant of the League of Nations;[96] the struggle for the principle
of sovereignty over natural resources;[97] the gradual emergence of the
principle of self-determination of peoples during the decolonization era;
the conference of non-aligned countries in Bandung;[98]and the proclam-
ation of a New International Economic Order (NIEO) in the early
1970s.[99]

11.6 A Multi-perspective Approach to Periodization

The challenging theoretical contributions of critical historians to the
elusive question of periodization in the history of international law have
drawn attention to an under-studied area in the historiography of international law. However, somewhat muffled by the maximalist tenets of
critical and postmodernist historiography is the fact that both international lawyers and historians of all persuasions are continually making
use of multiple periodizations of the history of international law in
developing their historical crafts. This is because, ultimately, every historian feels obliged to explain her or his methodological choice regarding
the 'time and scale' of any historical research undertaken, and to present
the selection of the resulting 'temporal canvas' as meaningfully propor-
tionate and objective to her or his academic peers. The practical unavoidability of resorting to periodization in international legal history was
highlighted by Wolfgang Preiser, who years ago noted that

---

[93] See Makau Mutua, 'What is TWAIL?' (2000) 94 *Proceedings of the American Society of International Law* 31–38; Martti Koskenniemi, 'Expanding histories of international law' (2016) 56 *American Journal of Legal History* 104–112.

[94] Anghie, *Imperialism*.

[95] Matthew Craven, 'Between law and history: the Berlin Conference of 1884–1885 and the logic of free trade' (2015) 23 *London Review of International Law* 31–59 at 31.

[96] Antony Anghie, 'Nationalism, development and the postcolonial state: the legacies of the League of Nations' (2016) 41 *Texas Journal of International Law* 447–463.

[97] Sundhya Pahuja, *Decolonising International Law: Development, Economic Growth and the Politics of Universality* (Cambridge, UK: Cambridge University Press, 2011).

[98] Luis Eslava, Michael Fakhri, and Vasuki Nesiah (eds.), *Bandung, Global History and International Law: Critical Pasts and Pending Futures* (Cambridge, UK: Cambridge University Press, 2016).

[99] Mohammed Bedjaoui, *Towards a New International Economic Order* (New York: Holmes & Meier, 1979), p. 123.

we accept that writers of the history of international law must also be allowed to apply the intellectual principle of order called categorisation by period which is utilized by all historians, irrespective of specialisation, when they perceive their task to be the comprehension retrospectively of an uninterrupted flow of events. It is regrettable that a living process should be thus divided into chronological and locational sections; yet, taking our limited powers of absorption into consideration, it cannot be avoided.[100]

As a heuristic device enabling international legal historians to make more conscious periodization decisions in today's highly polarized field of the history of international law, a multi-perspective approach steers a middle course between its critical and its descriptive analytical historio-graphical functions. On the one hand, a multi-perspective approach allows us to point to the blind spots and biases of the different approaches to periodization that it encounters; on the other hand, it allows us to clarify the typical assumptions and drivers behind the interpretative historical frameworks underlying them. It is also an approach that acknowledges that in historical writing in international law, rather than being mutually exclusive, periodizations are useful prisms that overlap in their historiographical utility. This approach to the question of periodization is one that emerges from the practice of historical writing itself and also from an analytical reading of how different periodizations are combined and recombined in the contem-porary literature. Multi-perspectivity has the potential to result in a gradual healthy juxtaposition of new periodizations alongside conven-tional ones as part of the toolkit available to international legal historians for a more conscious construction of new historical narratives. If, as Charles Renouvier wrote, 'La formule de la science, faire. Non pas devenir, mais faire, et en faisant se faire' ('the formula of science is to make; not to become, but to make, and in making to make itself')[101] as the field of international law extends into new areas of specialization, and historical research expands into new topics and engages with more diverse standpoints, so does the catalogue of periodizations that can be added to the functional toolkit of the international legal historian. A multi-perspective approach to periodization in the history of

---

[100] Wolfgang Preiser, 'History of the law of nations: basic questions and principles', in *Max Planck Encyclopedia of Public International Law* (2007), opil.ouplaw.com/view/10.1093/law:epil/9780199231690/law-9780199231690-e717.

[101] Gabriel Séailles, *La philosophie de Charles Renouvier: introduction à l'étude du néo-criticisme* (Paris: Felix Alcan, 1905), p. 228.

international law cherishes this development and does historiographical stocktaking of it with a view to nurturing further innovation in historiographical writing on international law.

In 1975, one of the founders of the Critical Legal Studies movement, Duncan Kennedy, provided an example of an influential alternative periodization of the history of legal thought in the United States.[102] Kennedy used the metaphor of 'the rise and fall' of what he termed 'classical legal thought' in the United States by placing it between the dates 1850 and 1940.[103] Twenty-five years later, building on exactly the same metaphor, in his *The Gentle Civilizer of Nations*, which is referred to in detail in Chapters 2 and 3 above, Martti Koskenniemi produced a highly influential periodization of the intellectual and sociological history of international law. He selected the date 1870, the prelude to the foundation of the Institut de droit international in 1873, to mark what he referred to as the beginning of the 'rise of international law', and 1960 for its 'fall', interpreting this as coinciding with the 'emergence of a depoliticised legal pragmatism on the one hand, and ... the colonisation of the profession by imperial policy agendas on the other'.[104]

In what follows, I present five different typologies of alternative periodization. These are, first, derived from the effects of the contemporary phenomenon of diversification and expansion of international law in the history of international law. At a time of revitalization of historical writing on international law,[105] a second source is the greater attention that international legal historians now pay to geographical factors in developing their histories of international law. The third novel and related alternative approach to periodization mirrors how research on international legal history has expanded in scope towards global and cross-cultural studies. The fourth approach builds on the historically neglected study of women's histories in international law. Finally,

---

[102] Duncan Kennedy, 'The rise and fall of classical legal thought', unpublished manuscript, 1975; reformatted 1998; published with a new preface by the author, 'Thirty years later', as *The Rise and Fall of Classical Legal Thought* (Washington, DC: Beard Books, 2006).
[103] Duncan Kennedy built on this earlier periodization of American legal thought to frame what he called the three globalizations of law and legal thought years later. Duncan Kennedy, 'Three globalizations of law and legal thought: 1850–2000', in David Trubek and Alvaro Santos (eds.), *The New Law and Economic Development: A Critical Appraisal* (Cambridge, UK: Cambridge University Press, 2006), pp. 19–73.
[104] Koskenniemi, *The Gentle Civilizer of Nations*, p. 4.
[105] Emmanuelle Tourme-Jouannet and Anne Peters, 'The *Journal of the History of International Law*: a forum for new research' (2014) 16 *Journal of the History of International Law* 1–8 at 2.

attention is paid to the role that traditionally neglected research subject matters in the history of international law can play in fostering new periodizations as prisms that intersect in their historiographical utility.

11.7 Fragmentation, Geography, Global Cross-Cultural Interactions, Gender, and Other Unexplored Themes

The question of the fragmentation of international law, prompted by the diversification and expansion of international law, by the 'emergence of specialised and (relatively) autonomous rules or rule-complexes, legal institutions and spheres of legal practice',[106] has attracted enormous attention among international law scholars in the last two decades.[107] From an academic viewpoint, its outcome has been an increasing fragmentation of the study of international law into niches of specialized international legal scholarship. This tendency mirrors but in turn also influences the progress of specialized branches within domestic legal orders across multiple jurisdictions. This diversification and specialization of international legal scholarship itself has in turn resulted in a more pronounced diversification and expansion of the study of different branches of the history of international law itself. The ensuing fragmentation of the history of international law as an academic discipline can be observed insofar as each sub-discipline tends to generate its own sub-disciplinary historical narrative. Indeed, as Chapter 7 examined, the effects of fragmentation on the history of international law can be observed in the emergence of histories that have examined the normative and intellectual development of different branches of international law and institutions thereof. The new efforts to document the history of these sub-disciplines within international law have resulted in a constant search for precedents and landmarks corresponding to genealogies of normative, sociological, and intellectual sub-disciplinary development. As a result, each sub-discipline or specialized branch of international law is increasingly being studied with reference to its own historical expansion in an independent fragmented manner. However, much more

---

[106] 'Fragmentation of international law: difficulties arising from the diversification and expansion of international law', in 58th session of the International Law Commission, *Report of the Study Group on the Fragmentation of International Law*, finalized by Martti Koskenniemi, UN Doc A/CN.4/L.682, Commission (2006).

[107] Pierre-Marie Dupuy, 'Un débat doctrinal à l'ère de la globalisation: sur la fragmentation du droit international' (2007) 1 *European Journal of Legal Studies* 1–19.

work is still needed on the historical synergies and mutual interactions of specialized sectors of international law and on the comparative legal history of different legal branches in domestic settings across both time and space.

The overall result of this sub-disciplinary fragmentation of the history of international law is an emergence of new sub-disciplinary period-izations. Each of these, which are based on their own sub-disciplinary landmarks and corresponding sub-periodizations, tends to reflect a chronology different from the traditional general periodization of the discipline as a whole. The history of international human rights law, the modern origins of which are conventionally retraced to the Universal Declaration of Human Rights (UDHR) in 1948, is one of the subfields that more clearly exemplifies this latest trend in contemporary litera-ture.[108] However, examples could be extracted from any other inter-national legal regime too, such as the history of international environmental law. This has been traditionally divided into three or four major periods or phases, according to Peter H. Sand: the 'traditional era' until about 1970 (i.e. preceding the 1972 UN Stockholm Conference on the Human Environment, UNCHE), which is sometimes sub-divided into pre-1945 and post-1945 periods, followed by a 'modern era' from Stockholm to the 1992 UN Conference on Environment and Development (UNCED) in Rio de Janeiro and completed by 'the "post-modern era" from Rio onwards'.[109] This shows that the usefulness of periodizations of the history of international law is to a large extent sub-disciplinarily specific.

Second, as in other fields of historical research, periodization tends to be geographically specific. Spatial considerations, or more simply geo-graphical factors, have played an integral part in the study of inter-national law since the inception of modern study of it. As we saw in Chapter 5, the study of the history of international law developed from an almost strictly Eurocentric basis, gradually expanding in the wake of decolonization to extend its coverage in terms of the world or global history of international law. Influenced by the infusion of the strong identities of emerging nations in the decolonization era, and partly as a

---

[108] Philip Alston, 'Does the past matter? On the origins of human rights' (2012–13) 126 *Harvard Law Review* 2043–2081.

[109] Peter H. Sand, 'Introduction', in Peter H. Sand (ed.), *The History and Origin of International Environmental Law* (Cheltenham: Edward Elgar Publishing, 2015), pp. xiii–xxv at xiii.

reaction to globalization, contemporary post-colonial authors investigating regionalism in the history of international law follow in the footsteps of earlier pace-setters.[110] This underlying influence can be observed in new semi-peripheral and alternative periodizations in the history of international law from geographically distinct viewpoints.[111] The stress on the role of geographical factors in shifting the perspective from which the history of international law is written, and in questioning the standing of Western events as gravitational centres of the standard periodizations in the history of international law, has been one of the preferred topoi of recent post-colonial contributions.

A recent example is provided by Arnulf Becker Lorca, who proposes one of these semi-peripheral historical periodizations of international law. Becker Lorca frames a period between 1842 (when Britain and China signed the Treaty of Nanjing, which put an end to the First Opium War) and 1933, the date of the adoption of the Montevideo Convention on the Rights and Duties of States. In proposing this alternative periodization, Becker puts emphasis on what he terms the 'universal particularism' and the 'strategies of appropriation' of international law developed mainly by semi-peripheral nations, and in particular by Latin American scholars.[112] Also revolving around the history of international law in Latin America is another recent work which explores the 'emergence and development of a distinctive hemispheric discourse and practice of American international law in the Western hemisphere between 1890 and 1943', mainly with reference to the American Institute of International Law (1912–43). This was a pan-American legal organization established with the aim of advancing a distinct United States-led conception of international law for the Americas.[113]

Similar semi-peripheral regional periodizations of the history of international law could be developed for other regional or continental geographical settings. For instance, Oliver Diggelmann has highlighted how a history of international law 'from an African perspective' could develop

[110] Antony Anghie, 'Identifying regions and sub-regions in the history of international law', in Bardo Fassbender and Anne Peters (eds.), *The Oxford Handbook of the History of International Law* (Oxford: Oxford University Press, 2012), pp. 1058–1080.

[111] Stephan Verosta, 'Regionen und Perioden der Geschichte des Völkerrechts' (1979) 30 *Österreichische Zeitschrift für öffentliches Recht und Volkerrecht* 1–21.

[112] Arnulf Becker Lorca, *Mestizo International Law: A Global Intellectual History 1842–1933* (Cambridge, UK: Cambridge University Press, 2015).

[113] Juan Pablo Scarfi, *The Hidden History of International Law in the Americas: Empire and Legal Networks* (Oxford: Oxford University Press, 2017), p. xvii.

by 'distinguish[ing], for example, the periods of "ancient and pre-Medieval Africa", "indigenous African states", the "beginnings of European trade" and the "period of colonial rule"'.[114] Likewise, analogous alternative periodizations could be developed for Asia, and subregional and national units within it, such as China, where the dates of 1842, the end of the First Opium War,[115] and 1971, the time when the People's Republic of China replaced the Taiwan-based government of the Republic of China as the 'sole and legitimate representative Government of China'[116] in the UN, indicate a particularly relevant nation-specific periodization for China in the history of international law. This shows that the usefulness of generally accepted periodizations of the history of international law is to a large extent geographically specific.

However, alternative regional or sub-regional periodizations in the history of international law,[117] developed under the infusion of global and post-colonial history from ancient to modern times, do not need to account only for historical outer-European or extra-Western experiences. There is also ample scope for possible alternative European periodizations beyond the homogenizing perspective of a 'European tradition' of international law, often constructed around the history of a limited number of Western European powers to the exclusion of many others.[118] If certain myths regarding the history of international law in Europe are to be dispelled, it seems that a far more complete history of international law within European states themselves will be required, from which new relevant geographically and culturally specific national periodizations may also emerge. A recent history of international law in Spain from 1770 ('when the study of public law, natural law and the law of peoples was included for the first time in a Spanish curriculum') to the year 1953 (which 'marked the beginning of the end of the post-war period of international ostracism of Spain as a relic of the interwar rise of fascist ideologies across Europe') offers an example of such a 'national' periodization for a former great imperial power which then became a

---

[114] Diggelmann, 'The periodization', p. 1001.
[115] Phil C. W. Chan, 'China's approaches to international law since the Opium War' (2014) 27 *Leiden Journal of International Law* 859–892.
[116] See UN General Assembly, Res. A/RES/2758 (XXVI), 25 October 1971.
[117] Anghie, 'Identifying regions'.
[118] Iain Scobbie, 'Redefining European tradition' (2013) 107 *Proceedings of the American Society of International Law* 382–385.

semi-peripheral European country.[119] The latter is part of a recent historiographical trend that, as was seen in Chapter 8, is contributing to revamping the study of semi-peripheral national histories of international law in Europe.[120]

Third, closely connected by the spatial factors brought into sharp relief by decolonization and globalization, the history of international law is also a research area well positioned for historians wishing to investigate the extent to which it is 'possible to identify periods that are both meaningful and coherent across the boundary lines of societies and cultural regions'.[121] The development of international law, being a truly global process transcending individual societies and cultural regions, is no stranger to multiple and significant political, social, economic, and cultural ramifications for all peoples and cross-cultural interactions. Processes of cross-cultural interaction affecting international law, as with any other cross-cultural process,[122] can thus also contribute to 'identifying historical periods from a global point of view'.[123] The hitherto neglected history of the contribution to different peoples in different regions of the world through cross-cultural interaction with the history of international law helps to show how by using 'cross-cultural interactions as their criteria, historians might better avoid ethnocentric periodisations that structure the world's past', including international law's past, 'according to the experiences of some particular privileged people'.[124]

This world-history-inspired perspective has been methodologically further developed under the lenses of global history and in particular, as was seen in Chapter 5, of what Richard Drayton and David Motadel call the 'connective approach', which seeks to elucidate 'how history is made through the interactions of geographically (or temporally) separate historical communities'.[125] However, a fruitful extension of such a

[119] See, e.g., Ignacio de la Rasilla, *In the Shadow of Vitoria: A History of International Law in Spain 1770–1953* (The Hague: Brill/Nijhoff, 2017).
[120] See e.g. Giulio Bartolini (ed.) *A History of International Law in Italy* (Oxford: Oxford University Press, 2020).
[121] Bentley, 'Cross-cultural interaction', p. 750.
[122] See UNESCO's efforts to promote world peace through a new non-nationalistic world history: Paulo Estêvão de Berrêdo Carneiro (ed.), *The History of Mankind: Cultural and Scientific Development (UNESCO 1963–1969)* (London: Allen & Unwin, 1969).
[123] Bentley, 'Cross-cultural interaction', p. 750.
[124] Ibid.
[125] Richard Drayton and David Motadel, 'Discussion: the futures of global history' (2018) 13 *Journal of Global History* 1–21 at 3.

connective approach may well rely on other non-Eurocentric period-izations of the history of international law so as to transcend the hidden Eurocentrism which still remains the gravitational core of most of the new narratives of historical encounters with Western international law's others. Ideally, these non-Eurocentric periodizations would be able to fruitfully combine the current temporal and spatial expansion of the research scope of the history of international law to investigate inter-actions between non-Western peoples over time. These developments could further contribute to meeting the goals that, according to Thomas Duve, global legal history should set for itself.[126] These, according to Duve, include 'a critical, sometimes even deconstructive function' because a 'fundamental aspect of historical research involves the disclos-ure, examination, and, when necessary, revision' of both explicit and implicit understandings and conceptions of the past.[127] Further develop-ment of historiographical awareness in the most inherently relational of all legal fields is, therefore, part and parcel of the fulfilment of such a global legal-methodological promise, the relevance of which increases the more one gazes at the timeline of the history of international law beyond the historical hiatus of Western formal imperialism.

Fourth, as was seen in Chapter 6, the cultivation of gender in the history of international law may also contribute to critiquing established periodizations in the history of international law by promoting the inclusion of gender-centred alternative periodizations in the temporal ordering of the historical development of the discipline. Despite the inherent historical limitations that this historiographical re-inclusive move may encounter, such a gender-centred alternative re-periodization of international legal history would then be continually fleshed out by new historical international legal scholarship. This revealing of different episodes and female dramatis personae who have so far remained hidden or invisible in the history of international law would further illustrate the perspectival value of gender in the history of international law as a launch pad for the 'formation of new formerly unknown periods'.[128] Concepción Arenal's long historiographically neglected *Ensayo sobre el derecho de*

---

[126] Thomas Duve, 'Global legal history: a methodological approach', Max Planck Institute for European Legal History, Research Paper Series, No. 2016–04, ssrn.com/abstract=2781104.
[127] Ibid., p. 11.
[128] Stearns, 'Periodization', pp. 561–562.

gentes (1879),[129] the first treatise on international law in the modern
sense published by a woman, offers a hitherto neglected milestone in
such a still-missing gender-based historical periodization of international
law. Set in this context, Arenal's pioneering book is a timeless reminder
that faith in international law was not only born out of the pragmatic and
rational calculations of late nineteenth-century diplomats, statesmen, and
armchair legal scholars, nor just as a tool for colonial domination
and exploitation of non-Western peoples, as the leitmotiv of a recent
strand of post-colonial international legal scholarship stresses for almost
every period in international law.[130] Instead, despite having been written
in the age of Western 'imperialism', her book is a representative reminder
that the professional study of international law was in no lesser measure
born out of the compassionate hope that it may contribute to alleviating
the sufferings of those most vulnerable in all societies. Other important
landmarks in such as feminist or gender-centred periodization of international legal history are, as it was seen in Chapter 6, the influential
resolutions of the first International Congress of Women held at The
Hague in 1915.[131] However, many other relevant landmarks in terms of
intellectual history and international normative development may be
equally pointed out in the attentive assembly of such a women-centred
periodization in international legal history.

Finally, a traditionally little-studied area or neglected topic of study in
the history of international law can provide new historical reference
points which may in turn serve as the basis for deeper and more nuanced
historical narratives. One original historiographical example of this type
is provided by Martti Koskenniemi in his 'history of international law
histories'.[132] Koskenniemi's presentation of a 'sketch of forms of historical consciousness'[133] within the discipline from early Christianity up to
some of the most recent historiographical approaches in the twenty-first
century provides a basis for an original intra-historiographical

---

[129] Concepción Arenal, *Ensayo sobre el derecho de gentes* (Madrid: Impr. de la Revista de Legislación, 1879). See Ignacio de la Rasilla, 'Concepción Arenal and the place of women in modern international law' (2020) 88 *Tijdschrift voor Rechtsgeschiedenis* 1–43.
[130] Anghie, *Imperialism*.
[131] *Resolutions of the First International Congress of Women* (The Hague, 1915), wilpf.org/wp-content/uploads/2012/08/WILPF_triennial_congress_1915.pdf.
[132] Martti Koskenniemi, 'A history of international law histories', in Bardo Fassbender and Anne Peters (eds.), *The Oxford Handbook of the History of International Law* (Oxford: Oxford University Press, 2012), pp. 943–971.
[133] Ibid.

periodization of the history of international law. Another example of such a research topic is a global history of international law journals that allows for a mapping of their patterns of global geographical diffusion since the launch in 1869 of the first one, *La révue de droit international et de la législation comparée*.[134] These and other examples that could be provided from recent literature show that the present enlargement of the history of international law as a field of research also offers great potential for the development of alternative periodizations in the history of international law based on hitherto neglected areas of study in the discipline.

11.8 Conclusion

Starting from a conventional three-tiered typology of approaches to periodization in the historiography of international law premised on the cornerstones of imperial hegemonic power, Western liberal universalism, and the centrality of the sovereign state, this final chapter has illustrated the utility of a multi-perspective approach to periodization by identifying several types of conventional and alternative periodizations in the thriving field of the history of international law. As in the ancient classic Indian parable of the blind men and the elephant, multi-perspectivity helps us to better come to terms with the underlying rationale, political-ideological uses (descriptive analytical functions), and relative limitations (the critical function) of different approaches to the history of international law and by extension to different approaches to its periodization.

Multi-perspectivity further shows that while different approaches to periodization can be found combined and recombined in different historical narratives, the attitude to periodization itself and reliance on the particular dates and factors underlying a certain type of periodization of the history of international law are generally indicative of the methodological preferences and ideological significance an author attributes to some factors over others.[135] This conveys useful information to the reader about the projection of each author's own personal circumstances and ideological preferences, of the author's world view of the history of

---

[134] Ignacio de la Rasilla, 'A very short history of international law journals 1869–2018' (2018) 29 *European Journal of International Law* 137–168.
[135] Gary Y. Okihiro, *The Columbia Guide to Asian American History* (New York: Columbia University Press, 2001), p. 34.

international law.[136] In the discipline of international law, which is contemporarily characterized by unprecedented levels of methodological diversity in its study,[137] any periodization decisions regarding its history invariably appear permeated by each interpreter's own reading of an irreducibly diverse present.[138] If one agrees with Martti Koskenniemi that 'a clear separation between the object of historical research and the researcher's own context cannot be sustained',[139] such a reading of the history of international law would in turn be variously influenced by the interpreter's nationality, religion, geographical location, race, class, values, ideological preferences, aspirations, and fears and, perhaps no less decisively, by his or her 'cognitive interests' or his or her legal and/or historical training. This stress on identity and positionality needs to be particularly acute in international law and its histories because, far more than in domestic settings, it incorporates a globally diverse and diversely socialized authorship.

A multi-perspective approach to periodization in the history of international law takes stock of the promise held by this new interpretative diversity in the history of international law to open new vistas of knowledge. This is so because different approaches to, and objects of, the history of international law become the source of different periodization decisions. These in turn contribute to providing the historical fabric of international law with a deeper texture and granularity in nurturing knowledge production processes on the relationship between international law and history, and in doing so foster the development of more nuanced historical investigations over time. However, it is mainly through the practice of historical writing that new narratives should build their perspectives and stimulate new periodizations. These, in juxtaposing themselves to earlier temporal *caesurae*, contribute to the development of innovative historical narratives in which are embedded the seeds of a transformative intervention in the present and future unfolding of international law that, like history and truth, is also *filia temporis*.

---

[136] Diggelmann, 'The periodization', p. 1001.
[137] See Robert Cryer, Tamara Hervey, and Bal Sokhi-Bulley (eds.), *Research Methodologies in EU and International Law* (Oxford: Hart Publishing, 2011), p. 5.
[138] See, e.g., Ruskola, 'Raping like a state', p. 1485, noting that 'in historical analysis, periodization is inevitable, but never innocent'.
[139] Koskenniemi, 'Histories of international law: significance and problems', p. 226.

BIBLIOGRAPHY

Abi-Saab, Georges, Foreword', in Luis Eslava, Michael Fakhri, and Vasuki Nesiah (eds.), *Bandung, Global History, and International Law: Critical Pasts and Pending Futures* (Cambridge, UK: Cambridge University Press, 2017), pp. xxix–xxx
'The newly independent states and the rules of international law: an outline' (1926) 8 *Howard Law Journal* 95–121
'The Third World intellectual in praxis: confrontation, participation, or operation behind enemy lines?' (2016) 37 *Third World Quarterly* 1957–1971
Abrams, Irwin, 'The emergence of international law societies' (1957) 19 *The Review of Politics* 361–380
Addams, Jane, *Newer Ideals of Peace* (New York: Macmillan & Co., 1907)
Ago, Roberto, et al., 'The European tradition in international law: Dionisio Anzilotti' (1992) 3 *European Journal of International Law* 92–172
Alexander, Amanda, 'A short history of international humanitarian law' (2015) 26 *European Journal of International Law* 109–138
Alexander, William, and Martin, Parsons, 'Traces of international law in ancient China' (1883) 14 *International Review* 63–77
Alexandrowicz, Charles H., 'The Afro-Asian world and the law of nations (historical approach)' (1968) 123 *Recueil des cours de l'Académie de droit international de La Haye* 117–214
  'The Grotian Society' (1967) 61 *American Journal of International Law* 1058–1058
  An Introduction to the Law of Nations in the East Indies (Oxford: Clarendon Press, 1967)
  The Law of Nations in Global History, ed. David Armitage and Jennifer Pitts (Oxford: Oxford University Press, 2017)
Alford, Roger P., 'The Nobel effect: Nobel Peace Prize laureates as international norm entrepreneurs' (2008) 49 *Virginia Journal of International Law* 61–153
Allain, Jean, 'White slave traffic in international law' (2017) 1 *Journal of Trafficking and Human Exploitation* 1–40

Allott, Philip, 'International law and the idea of history' (1999) 1 *Journal of the History of International Law* 1–21

Alonso, Harriet H., 'Nobel Peace Prize laureates Jane Addams and Emily Greene Balch: two women of the Women's International League for Peace and Freedom' (1995) 7 *Journal of Women's History* 6–26

Alston, Philip, 'Does the past matter? On the origins of human rights' (2012–13) 126 *Harvard Law Review* 2043–2081

'Remarks on Professor B. S. Chimni's *A Just World under Law: A View From the South*' (2007) 22 *American University International Law Review* 221–236

Altemir, Antonio Blanc, *El Marqués de Olivart y el derecho internacional (1861–1928): sociedad internacional y aportación científica* (Lleida: Edicions de la Universitat de Lleida, 1999)

Alter, Karen J., 'The evolution of international law and courts', in Orfeo Fioretos (ed.), *International Politics and Institutions in Time* (Oxford: Oxford University Press, 2017), pp. 251–273

Altman, Amnon, *Tracing the Earliest Recorded Concepts of International Law: The Ancient Near East (2500–330 BCE)* (Leiden: Martinus Nijhoff, 2012)

Altwicker, Tilmann, 'International law in the best of all possible worlds: an introduction to G. W. Leibniz's theory of international law' (2019) 30 *European Journal of International Law* 137–158

Altwicker, Tilmann, and Diggelmann, Oliver, 'How is progress constructed in international legal scholarship?' (2014) 25 *European Journal of International Law* 425–444

Álvarez, Alejandro, 'Latin America and international law' (1909) 3 *American Journal of International Law* 269–353

Le droit international américain: son fondement, sa nature; d'après l'histoire diplomatique des états du nouveau monde et leur vie politique et économique (Paris: A. Pédone, 1910)

Álvarez, José E., 'Book review: *The Boundaries of International Law: A Feminist Analysis*' (2001) 95 *American Journal of International Law* 459–464

Ambos, Kai, 'International criminal procedure: "adversarial", "inquisitorial" or mixed?' (2003) 5 *International Criminal Law Review* 1–37

Amorosa, Paolo, 'Pioneering international women's rights? The US National Woman's Party and the 1933 Montevideo equal rights treaties' (2019) 30 *European Journal of International Law* 415–437

Rewriting the History of the Law of Nations: How James Brown Scott Made Francisco de Vitoria the Founder of International Law (Oxford: Oxford University Press, 2019)

Anand, Ram P., *New States and International Law* (Delhi: Vikas Publishing House, 1972)

Origin and Development of the Law of the Sea: History of International Law Revisited (Leiden: Martinus Nijhoff, 1983)

Studies in International Law and History: An Asian Perspective (Leiden: Martinus Nijhoff, 2004)

Anghie, Antony, 'Colonialism and the birth of international institutions: sovereignty, economy, and the mandate system of the League of Nations' (2002) 34 *New York University Journal of International Law and Politics* 513–563

'The evolution of international law: colonial and postcolonial realities' (2006) 27 *Third World Quarterly* 739–753

'Francisco de Vitoria and the colonial origins of international law' (1996) 5 *Social and Legal Studies* 321–336

'Identifying regions and sub-regions in the history of international law', in Bardo Fassbender and Anne Peters (eds.), *The Oxford Handbook of the History of International Law* (Oxford: Oxford University Press, 2012), pp. 1058–1080

Imperialism, Sovereignty and the Making of International Law (Cambridge, UK: Cambridge University Press, 2005)

'Nationalism, development and the postcolonial state: the legacies of the League of Nations' (2016) 41 *Texas Journal of International Law* 447–463

Anghie, Antony, and Chimni, Bhupinder S., 'Third World Approaches to International Law and individual responsibility in internal conflicts' (2003) 2 *Chinese Journal of International Law* 77–103

Antonio, Robert J., 'Immanent critique as the core of critical theory: its origins and developments in Hegel, Marx and contemporary thought' (1981) 32 *The British Journal of Sociology* 330–345

Aral, Berdal, 'The Ottoman "school" of international law as featured in textbooks' (2016) 18 *Journal of the History of International Law* 70–97

Arenal, Concepción, *Ensayo sobre el derecho de gentes* (Madrid: Impr. de la Revista de Legislación, 1879)

Arendt, Hannah, *Eichmann in Jerusalem: A Report on the Banality of Evil* (New York: Viking Press, 1963)

Armitage, David, 'The Declaration of Independence and international law' (2002) 59 *William and Mary Quarterly* 39–64

Foundations of Modern International Thought (Cambridge, UK: Cambridge University Press, 2013)

Hugo Grotius, The Free Sea (Indianapolis, IN: Liberty Fund, 2004)

'In defense of presentism', in Darrin M. McMahon (ed.), *History and Human Flourishing* (in press), https://scholar.harvard.edu/armitage/publications/defense-presentism

Armitage, David, and De la Rasilla, Ignacio, 'The most neglected province: historiography of international law in the British Empire and the Commonwealth', in Anne Peters and Randall Lesaffer (eds.), *The Cambridge History of International Law*, vol. 1: *Historiography* (in press)

Armitage, David, and Guldi, Jo, *A History Manifesto* (Cambridge, UK: Cambridge University Press, 2014)

Armitage, David, and Pitts, Jennifer,' "This modern Grotius": an introduction to the life and thought of C. H. Alexandrowicz', in Charles Alexandrowicz, *The Law of Nations in Global History*, ed. David Armitage and Jennifer Pitts (Oxford: Oxford University Press, 2017), pp. 1–34

Astorino, Samuel J., 'The impact of sociological jurisprudence on international law in the inter-war-period: the American experience' (1995–96) 34 *Dusquene Law Review* 277–298

Atkinson, David, 'History of diplomacy', in David Armstrong et al. (eds.), *Oxford Bibliographies in International Relations*, www.oxfordbibliographies.com/view/document/obo-9780199743292/obo-9780199743292-0013.xml

Bachand, Rémi, 'Le droit international et l'idéologie "droits-de-l'hommiste" au fondement de l'hégémonie occidentale' (special issue, 2014) *Revue Québécoise de droit international* 70–97

Badaru, Opeoluwa Adetoro, 'Examining the utility of Third World Approaches to International Law for international human rights law' (2008) 10 *International Community Law Review* 379–387

Baetens, Freya, 'Decolonization: Belgian territories', in *Max Planck Encyclopedia of Public International Law* (2017), opil.ouplaw.com/view/10.1093/law:epil/9780199231690/law-9780199231690-e923

'First to rise and first to fall: the Court of Cartago (1907–1918)', in Ignacio de la Rasilla and Jorge E. Viñuales (eds.), *Experiments in International Adjudication: Historical Accounts* (Cambridge, UK: Cambridge University Press, 2019), pp. 211–239

'International Congress of Women', in *Max Planck Encyclopedia of Public International Law* (2011), opil.ouplaw.com/view/10.1093/law:epil/9780199231690/law-9780199231690-e2102, pp. 1–11

Balch, Emily Greene, *Approaches to the Great Settlement* (New York: B. W. Huebsch, 1918)

'Biographical: The Nobel Prize' (5 July 2019), www.nobelprize.org/prizes/peace/1946/balch/biographical/

Women's International League for Peace and Freedom 1915–1938: A Venture in Internationalism (Geneva: Maison Internationale, 1938)

Ball, Terence, 'The value of the history of political philosophy', in George Klosko (ed.), *The Oxford Handbook of the History of Political Philosophy* (Oxford: Oxford University Press, 2011), pp. 47–59

Bandyopadhyay, Pramathanath, *International Law and Custom in Ancient India* (Calcutta: University of Calcutta Press, 1920)

Barbosa, Ruy, *The Equality of Sovereign States* (The Hague: Hague Peace Conference, 1907)

Bartolini, Giulio, 'Introduction: what is a history of international law in Italy for? International law through the prism of national perspectives', in Giulio

Bartolini (ed.), *A History of International Law in Italy* (Oxford: Oxford University Press, 2020), pp. 3–18

(ed.), *A History of International Law in Italy* (Oxford: Oxford University Press, 2020)

Bashir, Khaled R., *Islamic International Law: Historical Foundations and Al-Shaybani's Siyar* (Cheltenham: Edgar Elgar, 2018)

Bastid, Suzanne, 'La jurisprudence de la Cour internationale de justice' (1951) 78 *Collected Courses of The Hague Academy of International Law* 575–702

Les fonctionnaires internationaux (Paris: Recueil Sirey, 1931)

'Les problèmes territoriaux dans la jurisprudence de la Cour internationale de justice' (1962) 107 *Collected Courses of The Hague Academy of International Law* 361–495

'Les tribunaux administratifs internationaux et leur jurisprudence' (1957) 92 *Collected Courses of The Hague Academy of International Law* 343–489

Bates, Ed, *The Evolution of the European Convention on Human Rights: From Its Inception to the Creation of a Permanent Court of Human Rights* (Oxford: Oxford University Press, 2010)

Bauman, Richard W., *Critical Legal Studies: A Guide to the Literature* (Boulder, CO: Westview, 1996)

Baxi, Upendra, 'New approaches to the history of international law' (2006) 19 *Leiden Journal of International Law* 555–566

Bayly, Christopher A., *The Birth of the Modern World 1780–1914: Global Connections and Comparisons* (Malden, MA: Blackwell, 2004)

Beatson, Jack, and Zimmermann, Reinhard (eds.), *Jurist Uprooted: German-Speaking Émigré Lawyers in Twentieth-Century Britain* (Oxford: Oxford University Press, 2004)

Beaulac, Stéphane, *The Power of Language in the Making of International Law: The Word Sovereignty in Bodin and Vattel and the Myth of Westphalia* (Leiden: Martinus Nijhoff, 2004)

'The Westphalian legal orthodoxy – myth or reality?' (2000) 2 *Journal of the History of International Law* 148–177

Becker Lorca, Arnulf, 'Eurocentrism in the history of international law', in Bardo Fassbender and Anne Peters (eds.), *The Oxford Handbook of the History of International Law* (Oxford: Oxford University Press, 2012), pp. 1034–1057

Mestizo International Law: A Global Intellectual History 1842–1933 (Cambridge, UK: Cambridge University Press, 2015)

'Petitioning the international: a "pre-history" of self-determination' (2014) 25 *European Journal of International Law* 497–523

'Universal international law: nineteenth-century histories of imposition and appropriation' (2010) 51 *Harvard Journal of International Law* 475–552

Becket, Jason, 'Critical international legal theory', in *Oxford Bibliographies in International Law* (2012, rev. 2017), www.oxfordbibliographies.com/view/document/obo-9780199796953/obo-9780199796953-0007.xml

Bederman, David J., 'Foreign office international legal history', in Matthew Craven, Malgosia Fitzmaurice, and Maria Vogiatzi (eds.), *Time, History and International Law* (Leiden: Martinus Nijhoff/Brill, 2007), pp. 43–64

International Law in Antiquity (Cambridge, UK: Cambridge University Press, 2001)

Bedjaoui, Mohammed, 'Non-alignement et droit international' (1976) 151 *Collected Courses of The Hague Academy of International Law* 337–456

'Observations sur le texte d'Antony Anghie', in Mark Toufayan, Emmanuelle Jouannet, and Hélène Ruiz-Fabri (eds.), *Droit international et nouvelles approches sur le tiers-monde: entre répétition et renouveau* (Paris: Société de Législation de Comparée, 2013), pp. 81–92

'Problèmes récents de succession d'états dans les états nouveaux' (1970) 130 *Collected Courses of The Hague Academy of International Law* 455–586

Towards a New International Economic Order (New York: Holmes & Maier, 1979)

Beleza, Teresa Pizarro, and Melo, Helena Pereira de, 'Olympe de Gouges (1748–1793) impressively ahead of her time: a visionary, daring activist and martyr', in Kasey McCall-Smith, Jan Wouters, and Felipe Gómez Isa (eds.), *The Faces of Human Rights* (Oxford: Hart Publishing, 2019), pp. 33–39

Belissa, Marc, 'French Revolution', in *Oxford Bibliographies in International Law* (2017), www.oxfordbibliographies.com/view/document/obo-9780199796953/obo-9780199796953-0111.xml

Bello, Andrés, *Principios de derecho de jentes* (Santiago de Chile: Imprenta de la Opinión, 1832)

Benhabib, Seyla, 'International law and human plurality in the shadow of totalitarianism: Hannah Arendt and Raphael Lemkin' (2009) 16 *Constellations* 331–350

Benoist, Charles, 'L'influence des idées de Machiavel' (1925) 9 *Recueil des cours de l'Académie de droit international de La Haye* 127–306

Bentley, Jerry H., 'Cross-cultural interaction and periodization in world history' (1996) 101 *American Historical Review* 749–770

'A new forum for global history' (1990) 1 *Journal of World History* iii–v

'The task of world history', in Jerry H. Bentley (ed.), *The Oxford Handbook of World History* (New York: Oxford University Press, 2013), pp. 1–22

Bentley, Michael (ed.), *Companion to Historiography* (New York: Routledge, 1997)

Benton, Lauren, 'Beyond anachronism: histories of international law and global legal politics' (2019) 21 *Journal of the History of International Law* 7–40

Benton, Lauren, and Ford, Lisa, *Rage for Order: The British Empire and the Origins of International Law 1800–1850* (Cambridge, MA: Harvard University Press, 2016)

Bergsmo, Morten, and Buis, Emiliano J. (eds.), *Philosophical Foundations of International Criminal Law: Correlating Thinkers* (Brussels: Torkel Opsahl Academic EPublisher, 2018)

Bergsmo, Morten, Ling, Cheah Wui, and Ping, Yi (eds.), *Historical Origins of International Criminal Law*, vols. 1–2 (Brussels: Torkel Opsahl Academic EPublisher, 2014)

Bergsmo, Morten, Rackwitz, Klaus, and Tianying, Song (eds.), *Historical Origins of International Criminal Law*, vol. 5 (Brussels: Torkel Opsahl Academic EPublisher, 2017)

Bergsmo, Morten, et al. (eds.), *Historical Origins of International Criminal Law*, vols. 3–4 (Brussels: Torkel Opsahl Academic EPublisher, 2015)

Berman, Nathaniel, '"But the alternative is despair": European nationalism and the modernist renewal of international law' (1993) 106 *Harvard Law Review* 1792–1903

Passion and Ambivalence: Nationalism, Colonialism and International Law (Leiden and Boston: Martinus Nijhoff, 2012)

'A perilous ambivalence: nationalist desire, legal autonomy, and the limits of the interwar framework' (1992) 33 *Harvard International Law Journal* 353–380

Bernard, Vincent, 'Memory: a new humanitarian frontier' (2019) 101 *International Review of the Red Cross* 1–9

Bethlehem, Daniel, 'The end of geography: the changing nature of the international system and the challenge to international law' (2014) 25 *European Journal of International Law* 9–24

Bevernage, Berber, 'Transitional justice and historiography: challenges, dilemmas and possibilities' (2014) 13 *Macquarie Law Journal* 7–24

'Writing the past out of the present: history and the politics of time in transitional justice' (2010) 69 *History Workshop Journal* Issue 111–131

Bevir, Mark, 'The contextual approach', in George Klosko (ed.), *The Oxford Handbook of the History of Political Philosophy* (Oxford: Oxford University Press, 2011), pp. 11–23

Bianchi, Andrea, 'Epistemic communities', in Jean d'Aspremont and Sahib Singh (eds.), *Concepts for International Law: Contributions to Disciplinary Thought* (Northampton, MA: Edward Elgar Publishing, 2019), pp. 251–266

International Law Theories: An Inquiry into Different Ways of Thinking (Oxford: Oxford University Press, 2016)

Bluntschli, Johann Caspar, *Das moderne Völkerrecht der zivilisierten Staaten, als Rechtsbuch dargestellt* (Nördlingen: Beck, 1868)

Boegner, Marc, 'L'influence de la Réforme sur le développement du droit international' (1925) 6 *Recueil des cours de l'Académie de droit international de La Haye* 241–324

Bohrer, Ziv, 'International criminal law's millennium of forgotten history' (2016) 34 *Law and History Review* 393–485

Boisson de Chazournes, Laurence, and Sands, Philippe (eds.), *International Law, the International Court of Justice and Nuclear Weapons* (Cambridge, UK: Cambridge University Press, 1999)

Borchard, Edwin M., and Palmer, Thomas W., *The Guide to the Law and Legal Literature of Spain* (Washington, DC: US Government Publishing Office, 1915)

Bourantonis, Dimitris, *The History and Politics of UN Security Council Reform* (London: Routledge, 2005)

Bourdieu, Pierre, *Outline of a Theory of Practice*, trans. Richard Nice (Cambridge, UK: Cambridge University Press, 1977)

Bourke, Richard, 'The Cambridge School', www.qmul.ac.uk/history/media/ph/news/The-Cambridge-School.pdf

Boutros-Ghali, Boutros, 'Un précurseur de l'organisation internationale: Al Kawakibi' (1960) 16 *Revue égyptienne de droit international* 15–22

Boyle, Francis A., *Foundations of World Order: The Legalist Approach to International Relations (1898–1922)* (Durham, NC: Duke University Press, 1999)

Boyle, James, 'Ideals and things: international legal scholarship and the prison-house of language' (1985) 26 *Harvard International Law Journal* 327–359

Braudel, Fernand, *The Mediterranean and the Mediterranean World in the Age of Philip II* (New York: Harper & Row, 1972; first published 1949)

Buergenthal, Thomas, *A Lucky Child: A Memoir of Surviving Auschwitz as a Young Boy* (New York: Little Brown and Company, 2009)

Burchill, Scott, and Linklater, Andrew (eds.), *Theories of International Relations*, 5th ed. (London: Macmillan, 2013)

Buss, Doris, 'Performing legal order: some feminist thoughts on international criminal law' (2011) 11 *International Criminal Law Review* 409–423

Bussey, Gertrude C., and Tims, Margaret, *Pioneers for Peace: Women's International League for Peace and Freedom 1915–1965* (London: WILPF British Section, 1980)

Butler, William E., 'On teaching the history of international law' (2013) 53 *American Journal of Legal History* 457–461

    'Periodization and international law', in Alexander Orakhelashvili (ed.), *Research Handbook on the Theory and History of International Law* (Cheltenham: Edward Elgar, 2011), pp. 379–393

Butterfield, Herbert, *The Whig Interpretation of History* (Kensington: University of New South Wales Library, 1981; first published 1931)

Caglar, Gülay, Prügl, Elisabeth, and Zwingel, Susanne, 'Introducing feminist strat-
egies in international governance', in Gülay Caglar, Elisabeth Prügl, and
Sussnne Zwingel (eds.), *Feminist Strategies in International Governance*
(London: Routledge, 2013), pp. 1–18

Cai, Congyan, *The Rise of China and International Law: Taking Chinese
Exceptionalism Seriously* (Oxford: Oxford University Press, 2019)

Cajani, Luigi, 'Criminal laws on history: the case of the European Union' (2011) 11
Historein 19–48

'Periodization', in Jerry H. Bentley (ed.), *The Oxford Handbook of World
History* (Oxford: Oxford University Press, 2012), pp. 54–71

Calvo, Carlos, *Derecho internacional teórico y practico de Europa y América* (Paris:
D'Amyot, 1868)

*Le droit international théorique et pratique précédé d'un exposé historique
des progrès de la science du droit des gens*, 6 vols. (Paris: A. Rousseau,
1887–96)

*Una página de derecho internacional: o la América del Sur ante la ciencia del
derecho de gentes moderno* (Paris: A. Durand, 1864)

Capoccia, Giovanni, 'Critical junctures', in Orfeo Fioretos, Tulia G. Falleti,
and Adam Sheingate (eds.), *The Oxford Handbook of Historical
Institutionalism* (Oxford: Oxford University Press, 2016), pp. 89–106

Cardahi, Choucri, 'La conception et la pratique du droit international privé dans
l'Islam (étude juridique et historique)' (1937) 60 *Recueil des cours de
l'Académie de droit international de La Haye* 507–650

Cardinal, Pierre-Alexandre, and Mégret, Frederic, 'The other "other": moors,
international law and the origin of the colonial matrix', in Ignacio de la
Rasilla and Ayesha Shahid (eds.), *International Law and Islam: Historical
Explorations* (The Hague: Martinus Nijhoff, 2018), pp. 165–197

Caridade de Freitas, Pedro, *História do direito internacional público da antiguidade
à II Guerra Mundial* (Lisbon: Principia, 2015)

Carr, Edward Hallet, *What Is History?* (Cambridge, UK: Cambridge University
Press, 1961), 2nd ed. (1987)

Carrai, Maria Adele, 'Admission of women to membership in the American Society
of International Law' (1921) 15 *American Journal of International Law* 76.

Sovereignty in China: A Genealogy of a Concept since 1840 (Cambridge, UK:
Cambridge University Press, 2019)

Carty, Anthony, 'Critical international law: recent trends in the theory of international law' (1991) 2 *European Journal of International Law* 1–26

*The Decay of International Law: A Reappraisal of the Limits of Legal Imagination
in International Affairs* (Manchester: Manchester University Press, 1986)

'Doctrine versus state practice', in Bardo Fassbender and Anne Peters (eds.),
The Oxford Handbook of the History of International Law (Oxford: Oxford
University, 2012), pp. 972–997

'International legal personality and the end of the subject: natural law and phenomenological responses to New Approaches to International Law' (2005) 6 *Melbourne Journal of International Law* 534–552

'Sociological theories of international law', in *Max Planck Encyclopedia of Public International Law* (2008), opil.ouplaw.com/view/10.1093/law:epil/9780199231690/law-9780199231690- e735?prd=EPIL

Carty, Anthony, and Nijman, Janne (eds.), *Morality and Responsibility of Rulers: European and Chinese Origins of a Rule of Law as Justice for World Order* (Oxford: Oxford University Press, 2018)

Cass, Deborah, 'Navigating the newstream: recent critical scholarship in international law' (1996) 65 *Nordic Journal of International Law* 341–383

Catellani, Enrico, 'Les maîtres de l'école italienne du droit international au XIXe siècle' (1933) 46 *Recueil des cours de l'Académie de droit international de La Haye* 705–826

Cavallar, Georg, *Imperfect Cosmopolis: Studies in the History of International Legal Theory and Cosmopolitan Ideas* (Chicago: University of Chicago Press, 2011)

'Vitoria, Grotius, Pufendorf, Wolff and Vattel: accomplices of European colonialism and exploitation or true cosmopolitans?' (2008) 10 *Journal of the History of International Law* 181–209

Cavanagh, Edward, 'Prescription and empire from Justinian to Grotius' (2016) 60 *The Historical Journal* 1–27

Chacko, Chirakaikaran Joseph, 'India's contribution to the field of international law concepts' (1958) 93 *Recueil des cours de l'Académie de droit international de La Haye* 121–221

Chakrabarty, Dipesh, *Provincializing Europe: Postcolonial Thought and Historical Difference* (Princeton, NJ: Princeton University Press, 2000); 2nd ed. (2007)

Chan, Phil C. W., 'China's approaches to international law since the Opium War' (2014) 27 *Leiden Journal of International Law* 859–892

Chang, Wen-Chen, and Yeh, Jiunn-Rong, 'Internationalization of constitutional law', in Michel Rosenfeld and András Sajó (eds.), *The Oxford Handbook of Comparative Constitutional Law* (Oxford: Oxford University Press, 2012), pp. 1165–1184

Charlesworth, Hilary, 'Talking to ourselves? Feminist scholarship in international law', in Sari Kouvo and Zoe Pearson (eds.), *Between Resistance and Compliance? Feminist Perspectives on International Law in Era of Anxiety and Terror* (Oxford: Hart Publishing, 2011), pp. 17–32

'The women question in international law' (2011) 1 *Asian Journal of International Law* 33–38

Charlesworth, Hilary, and Chinkin, Christine, *The Boundaries of International Law: A Feminist Analysis* (Manchester: Manchester University Press, 2000)

'The gender of jus cogens' (1993) 15 *Human Rights Quarterly* 63–76

Charlesworth, Hilary, Chinkin, Christine, and Wright, Shelley, 'Feminist approaches to international law' (1991) 85 *American Journal of International Law* 613–645

Charnovitz, Steve, 'The historical lens in international economic law' (2019) 22 *Journal of International Economic Law* 93–97

'Non-governmental organizations and international law' (2006) 100 *American Journal of International Law* 348–372

'Two centuries of participation: NGOs and international governance' (1997) 18 *Michigan Journal of International Law* 183–286

Chatterjee, Hiralal, *International Law and Inter-state Relations in Ancient India* (Calcutta: Mukhopadhyay, 1958)

Chatterjee, Partha, 'The legacy of Bandung', in Luis Eslava, Michael Fakhri, and Vasuki Nesiah (eds.), *Bandung, Global History, and International Law: Critical Pasts and Pending Futures* (Cambridge, UK: Cambridge University Press, 2017), pp. 657–674

Chernilo, Daniel, 'The critique of methodological nationalism: theory and history' (2011) 106 *Thesis Eleven* 98–117

Chesterman, Simon, 'Asian ambivalence about international law and institutions: past, present and future' (2016) 27 *European Journal of International Law* 945–978

Chetail, Vincent, 'Sovereignty and migration in the doctrine of the law of nations: an intellectual history of hospitality from Vitoria to Vattel' (2016) 27 *European Journal of International Law* 901–922

Chimni, Bhupinder S., 'Anti-imperialism then and now', in Luis Eslava, Michael Fakhri, and Vasuki Nesiah (eds.), *Bandung, Global History, and International Law: Critical Pasts and Pending Futures* (Cambridge, UK: Cambridge University Press, 2017), pp. 35–48

'Concluding Response from Professor Chimni: international law and world order', 29 December 2017, www.ejiltalk.org/concluding-response-from-pro fessor-chimni-international-law-and-world-order/

'International institutions today: an imperial global state in the making' (2004) 15 *European Journal of International Law* 1–37

International Law and World Order: A Critique of Contemporary Approaches (2nd edn, Cambridge, UK: Cambridge University Press, 2017)

'International law scholarship in post-colonial India: coping with dualism' (2010) 23 *Leiden Journal of International Law* 23–51

'An outline for a Marxist course on public international law' (2004) 17 *Leiden Journal of International Law* 1–30

'The past, present and future of international law: a critical Third World approach' (2007) 8 *Melbourne Journal of International Law* 499–515

'Third World Approaches to International Law: a manifesto' (2006) 8 *International Community Law Review* 3–27

Chinkin, Christine, 'Feminism, approach to international law', in *Max Planck Encyclopedia of Public International Law* (2010), opil.ouplaw.com/view/10 .1093/law:epil/9780199231690/law-9780199231690-e701

'International protection of rights of women', in *Max Planck Encyclopedia of Public International Law* (2010), opil.ouplaw.com/view/10.1093/law:epil/ 9780199231690/law-9780199231690-e1745

Clapham, Andrew, *Human Rights Obligations of Non-state Actors* (Cheltenham: Edward Elgar Publishing, 2013)

Clarence-Smith, William Gervase, Pomeranz, Kenneth, and Vries, Peer, 'Editorial' (2006) 1 *Journal of Global History* 1–2

Clark, Anne Marie, *Diplomacy of Conscience: Amnesty International and Changing Human Rights Norms* (Princeton, NJ: Princeton University Press, 2001)

Clark, Martti, 'British contributions to the concept of recognition during the inter-war period: Williams, Baty and Lauterpacht', in Robert McCorquodale and Jean-Pierre Gauci (eds.), *British Influences on International Law 1915–2015* (Leiden: Brill/Nijhoff, 2016), pp. 110–144

Clayton, Lawrence A., *Bartolomé de las Casas and the Conquest of the Americas* (Hoboken, NJ: John Wiley & Sons, 2011)

Coffey, Donal K., 'The failure of the 1930 tribunal of the British Commonwealth of Nations: a conflict between international and constitutional law', in Ignacio de la Rasilla and Jorge E. Viñuales (eds.), *Experiments in International Adjudication: Historical Accounts* (Cambridge, UK: Cambridge University Press, 2019), pp. 240–260

Collier, David, and Munck, Gerardo L., 'Building blocks and methodological challenges: a framework for studying critical junctures' (2017) 15 *Qualitative & Multi-method Research* 2–9

Collins, Harold M., 'The TEA-set: tacit knowledge and scientific networks' (1974) 4 *Social Studies of Science* 165–184

Comte, Auguste, *Cours de philosophie positive*, 6 vols. (Paris: Édition Rouen Frères, 1830–42)

'Conference for the codification of international law – final act' (1930) 24 (Supplement) *American Journal of International Law* 192–200

Conrad, Sebastian, *What Is Global History?* (Princeton, NJ: Princeton University Press, 2007)

Corten, Olivier, 'Les TWAIL: approche scientifique originale ou nouveau label fédérateur?', in Mark Toufayan, Emmanuelle Tourme-Jouannet, and Hélène Ruiz-Fabri (eds.), *Droit international et nouvelles approches sur le tiers-monde: entre répétition et renouveau (International Law and New Approaches to the Third World: Between Repetition and Renewal)* (Paris: Société de Législation de Droit Comparée, 2013), pp. 359–366

Costin, Lela B., 'Feminism, pacifism, internationalism and the 1915 International Congress of Women' (1982) 5 *Women's Studies International Forum* 301–315

Cottier, Thomas, and Müller, Jörg Paul, 'Estoppel', in *Max Planck Encyclopedia of Public International Law* (2007), opil.ouplaw.com/view/10.1093/law:epil/9780199231690/law-9780199231690-e1401?rskey=k4SaGa&result=13&prd=OPIL

Council of Europe, *Crossroads of European Histories: Multiple Outlooks on Five Key Moments in the History of Europe* (Strasbourg: Council of Europe Press, 2009)

Cox, Robert, 'Social forces, states and world orders: beyond international relations theory' (1981) 10 *Millennium: A Journal of International Studies* 126–155

Craven, Matthew, 'Between law and history: the Berlin Conference of 1884–85 and the logic of free trade' (2015) 1 *London Review of International Law* 31–59

'Colonialism and domination', in Bardo Fassbender and Anne Peters (eds.), *The Oxford Handbook of the History of International Law* (Oxford: Oxford University Press, 2012), pp. 862–889

'Introduction: international law and its histories', in Matthew Craven, Malgosia Fitzmaurice, and Maria Vogiatzi (eds.), *Time, History and International Law* (Leiden: Martinus Nijhoff/Brill, 2006), pp. 1–25

'On Foucault and Wolff or from law to political economy' (2012) 25 *Leiden Journal of International Law* 627–645

'Theorizing the turn to history in international law', in Anne Orford and Florian Hoffmann with Martin Clark (eds.), *The Oxford Handbook of the Theory of International Law* (Oxford: Oxford University Press, 2016), pp. 21–37

et al. (eds.), *Cold War and International Law* (Cambridge, UK: Cambridge University Press, 2019)

Crawford, James, 'International law as discipline and profession' (2012) 106 *Proceedings of the Annual Meeting (American Society of International Law)* 471–486

'Public international law in 20th century England', in Jack Beatson and Reinhard Zimmermann (eds.), *Jurists Uprooted: German-Speaking Emigré Layers in Twentieth Century Britain* (Oxford: Oxford University Press, 2004), pp. 681–693

Croce, Benedetto, 'Il concetto della filosofia come storicismo assoluto' (1939) 37 *La critica: rivista di letteratura, storia e filosofia diretta da B. Croce* 253–268

Theory and History of Historiography, trans. Douglas Ainslie (London: George G. Harrap & Company, 1921)

Cryer, Robert, Hervey, Tamara, and Sokhi-Bulley, Bal, *Research Methodologies in EU and International Law* (Oxford: Hart Publishing, 2011)

Currie, Mark, *About Time: Narrative Fiction and the Philosophy of Time* (Edinburgh: Edinburgh University Press, 2006)

Dante, Alighieri, *Monarchy*, trans. Prue Shaw (Cambridge, UK: Cambridge University Press, 1996)

Darby, William E., *International Arbitration, International Tribunals: A Collection of the Various Schemes Which Have Been Propounded; and of Instances in the Nineteenth Century*, 4th ed. (London: J. M. Dent and Co., 1904)

D'Aspremont, Jean, 'The critical attitude and the history of international law' (2018) 1 *International Legal Theory and Practice* 1–60

'Critical histories of international law and the repression of disciplinary imagination' (2019) 7 *London Review of International Law* 89–115

'The professionalization of international law', in Jean d'Aspremont et al. (eds.), *International Law As a Profession* (Cambridge, UK: Cambridge University, 2017), pp. 19–37.

(ed.), *Participants in the International Legal System Multiple Perspectives on Non-state Actors in International Law* (New York: Routledge, 2011)

et al., 'Introduction', in Jean d'Aspremont et al. (eds.), *International Law As a Profession* (Cambridge, UK: Cambridge University Press, 2017), pp. 1–15

D'Aspremont, Jean, and Besson, Samantha (eds.), *The Oxford Handbook of the Sources of International Law* (Oxford: Oxford University Press, 2017)

D'Aspremont, Jean, and Singh, Sahib (eds.), *Concepts for International Law: Contributions to Disciplinary Thought* (Northampton, MA: Edward Elgar Publishing, 2019)

De Berredo Carneiro, Paulo Estavao (ed.), *The History of Mankind: Cultural and Scientific Development (UNESCO 1963-1969)* (London: Allen & Unwin, 1969)

Decaux, Emmanuel, 'Les influences réciproques entre religion(s) et droit international', in Robert Uerpmann-Wittzack, Evelyne Lagrange, and Stefan Oeter (eds.), *Religion and International Law: Living Together* (Leiden: Brill/Nijhoff, 2018), pp. 353–371

De Geouffre de la Pradelle, Albert, *Maîtres et doctrines du droit des gens*, 2nd ed. (Paris: Les Éditions Internationales, 1950)

De la Rasilla, Ignacio, 'Bartolomé de las Casas: a radical humanitarian in the age of the great encounter', in Kasey McCall-Smith, Jan Wouters, and Felipe Gómez Isa (eds.), *The Faces of Human Rights* (Oxford: Hart Publishing, 2019), pp. 13–21

Camilo Barcia Trelles in and beyond Vitoria's shadow 1888-1977' (2021) 32 *European Journal of International Law* (in press)

'Concepción Arenal and the place of women in modern international law' (2020) 88 *Tijdschrift voor Rechtsgeschiedenis* 1–43

'El estudio del derecho internacional en el corto siglo XIX español' (2013) 21 *Journal of the Max Planck Institute for European Legal History* 48–65

'In the general interest of peace – British international lawyers and the Spanish Civil War' (2015) 17 *Journal of the History of International Law* 197–238

'Grotian revivals in the history and theory of international law', in Randall Lesaffer and Janne Nijman (eds.), *The Cambridge Companion to Hugo Grotius* (in press)

'History of international law – 1550–1700', in *Oxford Bibliographies in International Law* (2017), www.oxfordbibliographies.com/view/document/obo-9780199796953/obo-9780199796953-0036.xml, pp. 1–20

'International law in the historical present tense' (2009) 22 *Leiden Journal of International Law* 629–649

'Martti Koskenniemi and the spirit of the beehive in international law' (2010) 10 *Global Jurist* 1–53

'Medieval international law', in *Oxford Bibliographies in International Law* (2014), www.oxfordbibliographies.com/view/document/obo-9780199796953/obo-9780199796953-0112.xml, pp. 1–25

'Notes for the history of new approaches to international legal studies: not a map but perhaps a compass', in José Maria Beneyto and David Kennedy (eds.), *New Approaches to International Law: The European and the American Experiences* (Hague: T. M. C. Asser Press, 2011), pp. 225–248

'Playing hide and seek with "Vergangenheit, die nicht vergehen will" ("a past that will not pass") in the history of international law', in George Ulrich and Ineta Ziemele (eds.), *How International Law Works in Times of Crisis* (Oxford: Oxford University Press, 2019), pp. 223–239

'The problem of periodization in the history of international law' (2019) 37 *Law and History Review* 275–308

In the Shadow of Vitoria: A History of International Law in Spain 1770–1953 (Leiden: Brill/Nihjoff, 2017)

'The shifting origins of international law' (2015) 28 *Leiden Journal of International Law* 419–440

'The three revivals of Francisco de Vitoria in the history of international law', in José Maria Beneyto (ed.), *Peace or Just War? The Influence of Francisco de Vitoria and Erasmus on Charles V and the Law of Nations* (in press)

'The turn to the history of international adjudication', in Ignacio de la Rasilla and Jorge E. Viñuales (eds.), *Experiments in International Adjudication: Historical Accounts* (Cambridge, UK: Cambridge University Press, 2019), pp. 33–51

'A very short history of international law journals 1869–2018' (2018) 29 *European Journal of International Law* 137–168

'The World Court of Human Rights: rise, fall and revival? (2019) *19 Human Rights Law Review* 585–603

De la Rasilla del Moral, Ignacio, and Shahid, Ayesha (eds.), *International Law and Islam: Historical Explorations* (Leiden and Boston: Brill/Nijhoff, 2019)

De la Rasilla, Ignacio, and Viñuales, Jorge (eds.), *Experiments in International Adjudication: Historical Accounts* (Cambridge, UK: Cambridge University Press, 2019)

De las Casas, Bartolomé, *Brevísima relación de la destrucción de las Indias* (Seville, 1552)

Delbrück, Jost, 'Max Huber's sociological approach to international law' (2007) 18 *European Journal of International Law* 97–113

De Pizan, Christine, *The Book of Deeds of Arms and of Chivalry*, ed. Charity C. Willard, trans. Sumner Willard (University Park, PA: Pennsylvania State University Press, 1999)

    The Book of the City of Ladies (New York: Persea Books, 1982)

Depuis, René, 'Aperçu des relations internationales en Europe de Charlemagne à nos jours' (1939) 68 *Recueil des cours de l'Académie de droit international de La Haye* 1–94

Dienstag, Joshua Foa, 'Postmodern approaches to the history of political thought', in George Klosko (ed.), *The Oxford Handbook of the History of Political Philosophy* (Oxford: Oxford University Press, 2013), pp. 36–46

Diggelmann, Oliver, 'The periodization of the history of international law', in Bardo Fassbender and Anne Peters (eds.), *The Oxford Handbook of the History of International Law* (Oxford: Oxford University Press, 2012), pp. 997–1011

Disch, Lisa, and Hawkesworth, Mary (eds.), *The Oxford Handbook of Feminist Theory* (Oxford: Oxford University Press, 2016)

Donaldson, Megan, 'The survival of the secret treaty: publicity, secrecy, and legality in the international order' (2017) 111 *American Journal of International Law* 575–627

Đorđeska, Marija, *General Principles of Law Recognized by Civilized Nations (1922–2018): The Evolution of the Third Source of International Law through the Jurisprudence of the Permanent Court of International Justice and the International Court of Justice* (Leiden: Brill/Nijhoff, 2020)

Douzinas, Costas, 'History trials: can law decide history?' (2012) 8 *Annual Review of Law and Social Science* 273–289

Drayton, Richard, and Motadel, David, 'Discussion: the futures of global history' (2018) 13 *Journal of Global History* 1–21

Dubber, Markus Dirk, and Tomlins, Christopher L. (eds.), *The Oxford Handbook of Legal History* (Oxford: Oxford University Press, 2018).

Dumont, Jean, Rousset de Missy, Jean, and Barbeyrac, Jean, *Corps universel diplomatique du droit des gens: contenant un recueil des traitez d'alliance, de paix, de treve, de neutralité, de commerce, d'échange de neutralité, de commerce, d'échange, de protection & de garantie, de toutes les conventions, transactions, pactes, concordats & autres contrats, qui ont été faits en Europe, depuis le regne de l'empereur Charlemagne jusques à present* (Amsterdam: Brunel, 1726–39)

Dunning, Thad, 'Contingency and determinism in research on critical junctures: avoiding the "inevitability framework"' (2017) 15 *Qualitative & Multimethod Research* 41–47

Dupuis, Charles, 'Les antécédents de la Société des Nations' (1937) 60 *Recueil des cours de l'Académie de droit international de La Haye* 1–110

Dupuy, Pierre-Marie, 'A doctrinal debate in the globalization era: on the fragmentation of international law' (2007) 1 *European Journal of Legal Studies* 1–19 'Un débat doctrinal à l'ère de la globalisation: sur la fragmentation du droit international' (2007) 1 *European Journal of Legal Studies* 1–19

Durkheim, Émile, *Sociology and Philosophy* (Glencoe: Free Press, 1953)

Duve, Thomas, Thomas Duve, 'European legal history – global perspectives', working paper for the colloquium 'European normativity – global historical perspectives' (Max Planck Institute for European Legal History, Frankfurt, 2–4 September 2013), ssrn.com/abstract =2292666 'Global legal history: a methodological approach', Max Planck Institute for European Legal History, Research Paper Series, No. 2016–04, ssrn.com/abstract=2781104

Dzehtsiarou, Kanstantsin, 'European consensus and the evolutive interpretation of the European Convention on Human Rights' (2011) 12 *German Law Journal* 1730–1745

Eisenberg, Jaci, 'The status of women: a bridge from the League of Nations to the United Nations' (2013) 4 *Journal of International Organizations Studies* 8–24

Elias, Taslim Olawale, *Africa and the Development of International Law* (Leiden: A. W. Sijthoff, and Dobbs Ferry, NY: Oceana, 1972)

Elton, Geoffrey, *The Practice of History*, The Fontana Library (London: Collins, 1969)

Engle, Karen, 'Feminist governance and international law: from liberal to carceral feminism', in Janet Halley et al. (eds.), *Governance Feminism: Notes from the Field* (Minneapolis: University of Minnesota Press, 2018), pp. 3–30

Erpelding, Michel, *Le droit international antiesclavagiste des 'nations civilisées' 1815–1945* (Paris: Institut Universitaire Varenne, 2017)

Eslava, Luis, 'TWAIL coordinates', in *Critical Legal Thinking* (2019), criticallegalthinking.com/2019/04/02/twail-coordina tes/#fn-27281-3

Eslava, Luis, Fakhri, Michael, and Nesiah, Vasuki (eds.), *Bandung, Global History, and International Law: Critical Pasts and Pending Futures* (Cambridge, UK: Cambridge University Press, 2017) 'The spirit of Bandung', in Luis Eslava, Michael Fakhri, and Vasuki Nesiah (eds.), *Bandung, Global History, and International Law: Critical Pasts and*

Pending Futures (Cambridge, UK: Cambridge University Press, 2017), pp. 3–32

Eslava, Luis, and Pahuja, Sundhya, 'Between resistance and reform: TWAIL and the universality of international law' (2011) 3 *Trade Law and Development* 103–130

Evans, Alona E., and Plumb, Carol Per Lee, 'Women and the American Society of International Law' (1974) 68 *American Journal of International Law* 290–299

Eyffinger, Arthur, *T. M. C. Asser (1838–1913): 'In Quest of Liberty, Justice, and Peace'*, 2 vols. (Leiden: Brill/Nijhoff, 2019)

Fakhri, Michael, and Reynolds, Kelly, 'The Bandung Conference', in *Oxford Bibliographies in International Law* (2017), www.oxfordbibliographies .com/view/document/obo-9780199796953/obo-9780199796953-0150.xml

Falk, Richard A., 'New approaches to the study of international law' (1967) 61 *American Journal of International Law* 477–495

Farrell, Henry, and Finnemore, Martha, 'Global institutions without a global state', in Orfeo Fioretos, Tulia G. Falleti, and Adam Sheingate (eds.), *The Oxford Handbook of Historical Institutionalism* (Oxford: Oxford University Press, 2016), pp. 572–589

Fasolt, Constantin, *The Limits of History* (Chicago: University of Chicago Press, 2004)

Fassbender, Bardo, and Peters, Anne, 'Introduction: towards a global history of international law', in Bardo Fassbender and Anne Peters (eds.), *The Oxford Handbook of the History of International Law* (Oxford: Oxford University Press, 2012), pp. 1–26

(eds.), *The Oxford Handbook of the History of International Law* (Oxford: Oxford University Press, 2012)

Febvre, Lucien, *Combats pour l'histoire* (Paris: Librairie Armand Colin, 1992)

Le problème de l'incroyance au XVIe siècle: la religion de Rabelais (Paris: Albin Michel, 1942)

Fish, Jörg, *Die europäische Expansion und das Völkerrecht* (Stuttgart: Steiner, 1984)

Fisk, Catherine L., '&: law _ society in historical legal research', in Markus Dirk Dubber and Christopher L. Tomlins (eds.), *The Oxford Handbook of Legal History* (Oxford: Oxford University Press 2018), pp. 479–496

Fitzmaurice, Andrew, 'Context in the history of international law' (2018) 20 *Journal of the History of International Law* 5–30

'The problem of Eurocentrism in the thought of Francisco de Vitoria', in José Maria Beneyto and Justo Corti Varela (eds.), *At the Origins of Modernity: Francisco de Victoria and the Discovery of International Law* (Cham: Springer, 2017), pp. 77–93

Sovereignty, Property and Empire 1500–2000 (Cambridge, UK: Cambridge University Press, 2014)

Fitzmaurice, Gerald, *The Contribution of the Institute of International Law to the Development of International Law* (Leiden: Martinus Nijhoff, 1973)

Fioretos, Orfeo, 'Institutions and time in international relations', in Orfeo Fioretos (ed.), *International Politics and Institutions in Time* (Oxford: Oxford University Press, 2017), pp. 3–38

Fioretos, Orfeo, Falleti, Tulia G., and Sheingate, Adam, 'Historical institutionalism in political science', in Orfeo Fioretos, Tulia G. Falleti, and Adam Sheingate (eds.), *The Oxford Handbook of Historical Institutionalism* (Oxford: Oxford University Press, 2016), pp. 3–30

Fioretos, Orfeo, Falleti, Tulia G., and Sheingate, Adam (eds.), *The Oxford Handbook of Historical Institutionalism* (Oxford: Oxford University Press, 2016)

Fitzmaurice, Gerald G., 'Arnold Duncan Lord McNair of Gleniffer 1885–1975' (1975) 47 *British Yearbook of International Law* xi–xix

Focarelli, Carlo, *International Law as Social Construct: The Struggle for Global Justice* (Oxford: Oxford University Press, 2012)

Introduzione storica al diritto internazionale (Milan: Giuffre, 2012)

Foucault, Michel, 'Nietzsche, genealogy, history', in *Language, Counter-memory, Practice: Selected Essays and Interviews*, ed. Donald F. Bouchard (Ithaca, NY: Cornell University Press, 1977), pp. 139–164

Society Must Be Defended: Lectures at the Collège de France 1975–1976, ed. Mauro Bertani and Alessandro Fontana (London: Penguin Books, 2003)

Franck, Thomas M., 'The emerging right to democratic governance' (1992) 86 *American Journal of International Law* 46–91

Frankenberg, Günter, 'Critical theory', in *Max Planck Encyclopedia of Public International Law* (2010), opil.ouplaw.com/view/10.1093/law:epil/9780199231690/law-9780199231690-e693?prd=EPIL

Fraser, Arvonne S., 'Becoming human: the origins and development of women's human rights' (1999) 21 *Human Rights Quarterly* 853–906

Freitas, Serafim de, *De iusto imperio Lusitanorum Asiatico* (Vallisoleti: Ex Officina Hieronymi Morillo, 1625)

Frickel, Scott, and Gross, Neil, 'A general theory of scientific/intellectual movements' (2005) 70 *American Sociological Review* 204–232

Frodeman, Robert, 'Introduction', in Robert Frodeman, Julie Thompson Klein, and Carl Mitcham (eds.), *The Oxford Handbook of Interdisciplinarity* (Oxford: Oxford University Press, 2010), pp. xxix–xl

Fuller, Steve, 'Deviant interdisciplinarity', in Robert Froedman (ed.), *The Oxford Handbook of Interdisciplinarity* (2010), pp. 51–64

Gadamer, Hans-Georg, *Truth and Method* (London: Bloomsbury Academic, 2014)

Galindo, George Rodrigo Bandeira, 'Africa', in Bardo Fassbender and Anne Peters (eds.), *The Oxford Handbook of the History of International Law* (Oxford: Oxford University Press, 2012), pp. 407–428

'Force field: on history and theory of international law' (2012) 20 *Rechtsgeschichte - Legal History* 86–103

'Martti Koskenniemi and the historiographical turn in international law' (2005) 16 *European Journal of International Law* 539–559

'Splitting TWAIL?' (2016) 33 *Windsor Yearbook of Access to Justice* 37–56

Gallié, Martin, and Visotzky-Charlebois, Maxine, 'Les droits des femmes tel qu'il a été enseigne par les pères fondateurs du droit international public et leurs héritiers: notes de lecture sur les ouvrages et les manuels du XVIe au XXIe siècle', in *Féminisme(s) et droit international: études du réseau Olympe* (Paris: Société de Législation Comparée, 2016), pp. 189–224

García-Salmones Rovira, Mónica, *The Project of Positivism in International Law* (Oxford: Oxford University Press, 2013)

García-Salmones Rovira, Mónica, and Slotte, Pamela (eds.). *Cosmopolitanisms in Enlightenment Europe and Beyond* (Brussels: P.I.E. Peter Lang S.A., 2013)

Gardot, André, 'Jean Bodin: sa place parmi les fondateurs du droit international' (1934) 50 *Recueil des cours de l'Académie de droit international de La Haye* 545–748

Garner, Karen, *Women and Gender in International History: Theory and Practice* (London: Bloomsbury Academic, 2018)

Gassis, Jesús G., 'Concepción Arenal y el derecho de gentes' (1920) 3 *Revista de ciencias juridicas y sociales* 60–72

Gathii, James T., 'Africa', in Bardo Fassbender and Anne Peters (eds.), *The Oxford Handbook of the History of International Law* (Oxford: Oxford University Press, 2012), pp. 407–429

'Neoliberalism, colonialism and international governance: decentering the international law of governmental legitimacy' (2000) 98 *Michigan Law Review* 1996–2020

'TWAIL: a brief history of its origins, its decentralized network, and a tentative bibliography' (2011) 3 *Trade Law and Development* 26–32

Gaurier, Dominique, 'Cosmopolis and Utopia', in Bardo Fassbender and Anne Peters (eds.), *The Oxford Handbook of the History of International Law* (Oxford: Oxford University Press, 2012), pp. 250–271

Histoire du droit international: de l'Antiquité à la création de l'ONU (Rennes: Presses Universitaires de Rennes, 2014)

'Quelle place faite aux femmes dans l'ordre international de l'Antiquité et du début de l'époque moderne?', in Emmanuelle Tourme-Jouannet et al. (eds.), *Féminisme(s) et droit international: études du réseau Olympe* (Paris: Société de Législation Comparée, 2016), pp. 225–265

Gaynor, Fergal, 'Uneasy partners – evidence, truth and history in international trials' (2012) 10 *Journal of International Criminal Justice* 1257–1275

Geertz, Clifford, *Local Knowledge: Further Essays in Interpretive Anthropology* (New York: Basic Books, 1983)

Genin, Vincent, *La Belgique et ses juristes: du mythe juridique au déclassement international 1914–1940* (Brussels: Peter Lang, 2018)

Le laboratoire belge du droit international: Une communauté épistémique et internationale de juristes (1869–1914) (Brussels: Académie Royale de Belgique, 2018)

Gentili, Alberico, *De jure belli libri tres* (Hanau, 1598)

Gettys, Cora Luella, 'The effects of changes of sovereignty on nationality' (1927) 21 *American Journal of International Law* 268–278

Gibbons, Michael, et al., *The New Production of Knowledge: The Dynamics of Science and Research* (London: Sage Publications Ltd, 1994)

Giegerich, Thomas, and Zimmermann, Andreas, 'Introduction' (2007) 50 *German Yearbook of International Law* 16–29

Gilman, Nils, 'The new international economic order: a reintroduction' (2015) 6 *Humanity: An International Journal of Human Rights, Humanitarianism, and Development* 1–16

Ginsburg, Tom, 'Authoritarian international law?' (2020) 114 *American Journal of International Law* 221–260

Go, Julian, and Lawson, George, 'Introduction: for a global historical sociology', in Julian Go and George Lawson (eds.), *Global Historical Sociology* (Cambridge, UK: Cambridge University Press, 2017), pp. 1–34

Golia, Angelo, Jr, and Hennebel, Ludovic, 'The intellectual foundations of the European Court of Human Rights', in Ignacio de la Rasilla and Jorge E. Viñuales (eds.), *Experiments in International Adjudication: Historical Accounts* (Cambridge, UK: Cambridge University Press, 2019), pp. 263–286

Gong, Gerrit W., *The Standard of 'Civilization' in International Society* (Oxford: Clarendon Press, 1984)

Golder, Ben, 'Foucault and the incompletion of law' (2008) 21 *Leiden Journal of International Law* 747–763

Goody, Jack, *The Theft of History* (Cambridge, UK: Cambridge University Press, 2006)

Gordon, Geoff, 'Natural law in international legal theory: linear and dialectical presentations', in Anne Orford and Florian Hoffmann with Martin Clark (eds.), *The Oxford Handbook of the Theory of International Law* (Oxford: Oxford University Press, 2016), pp. 279–305

Gordon, Robert W., 'The arrival of critical historicism' (1997) 49 *Stanford Law Review* 1023–1030

'Critical legal histories' (1984) 36 *Stanford Law Review* 57–125

'Introduction: J. Willard Hurst and the common law tradition' (1975) 10 *American Legal Historiography Law and Society Review* 9–55

'The struggle over the past' (1996) 44 *Cleveland State Law Review* 123–143

Taming the Past: Essays on Law in History and History in Law (Cambridge, UK: Cambridge University Press, 2017)

Goyau, George, 'L'église catholique et le droit des gens' (1925) 6 *Recueil des cours de l'Académie de droit international de La Haye* 123–240

Gozzi, Gustavo, *Diritti e civilta: storia e filosofia del diritto internazionale* (Bologna: Il Mulino, 2010)

Green, Anna, and Troup, Kathleen, *The Houses of History: A Critical Reader in Twentieth-Century History and Theory* (Manchester: Manchester University Press, 1999); 2nd ed. (2016)

Green, William A., 'History and theory' (1995) 34 *World Historians and Their Critics* 99–111

  'Periodizing world history' (1995) 34 *History and Theory* 99–111

Greenwood, Christopher, and Lee, Karen (eds.), *International Law Reports*, vol 169 (Cambridge, UK: Cambridge University Press, 2017)

Grewe, Wilhelm G., *The Epochs of International Law*, trans. Michael Byers (Berlin: De Gruyter, 2000)

  Fontes historiae iuris gentium (Berlin: De Gruyter, 1988–95)

Gross, Aeyal, 'After the falls: international law between post-modernity and anti-modernity', in Emmanuelle Jouannet, Helene Ruiz-Fabri, and Jean Marc Sorel (eds.), *Regards d'une génération de juristes sur le droit international* (Paris: Pédone, 2008), pp. 183–208

Grotius, Hugo, *De jure belli ac pacis* (Paris, 1625)

Gunnell, John G., 'History of political philosophy as a discipline', in George Klosko (ed.), *The Oxford Handbook of the History of Political Philosophy* (Oxford: Oxford University Press, 2011), pp. 60–74

Gutzwiller, Max, 'Le développement historique du droit international privé' (1929) 29 *Recueil des cours de l'Académie de droit international de La Haye* 291–400

Habermas, Jürgen, The crisis of the European Union in the light of a constitutionalization of international law' (2012) 23 *European Journal of International Law* 335–348

  'Does the constitutionalization of international law still have a chance?', in Jürgen Habermas (ed.), *The Divided West*, trans. Ciaran Cronin (Oxford: Wiley, 2006), pp. 115–193

Haggenmacher, Peter, 'La place de Francisco de Vitoria parmi les fondateurs du droit international', in Antonio Truyol Serra et al. (eds.), *Actualité de la pensée juridique de Francisco de Vitoria* (Brussels: Bruylant, 1988), pp. 27–80

Handlin, Oscar, *Truth in History* (Cambridge, MA: Belknap, 1979)

Haslam, Beryl, *From Suffrage to Internationalism: The Political Evolution of Three British Feminists 1908–1939* (New York: P. Lang, 1999)

Hathaway, Onna A., and Shapiro, Scott J., *The Internationalists: How a Radical Plan to Outlaw War Remade the World* (New York: Simon and Schuster, 2017)

Hatner, Marcus, 'Narrative theory meets blending: multiperspectivism', in Jürgen Schlaeger and Gesa Stedman (eds.), *The Literary Mind* (Tübingen: Narr, 2008), pp. 181–194

Hatzimihail, Nikitas, 'The many lives and faces of *lex mercatoria*: an essay on the genealogy of international business law' (2008) 71 *Law & Contemporary Problems* 169–190

Hebié, Mamadou, *Souveraineté territoriale par traité: une étude des accords entre puissances coloniales et entités politiques locales* (Paris: Presses Universitaires de France and the Graduate Institute, 2015)

Heilbron, Johan, 'A regime of disciplines: toward a historical sociology of disciplinary knowledge', in Charles Camic and Hans Joas (eds.), *The Dialogical Turn* (Lanham, MD: Rowman & Littlefield, 2004), pp. 23–42

Heirbaut, Dirk, 'Some reflexions on the methodologies of legal history', in Martin Löhnig (ed.), *Zeitschrift für europäische Rechtskultur*, 2 vols. (Regensburg: Edition Rechtskultur in der H. Gietl Verlag & Publikationsservice, 2013), vol. 1, pp. 89–92
'A tale of two legal histories: some personal reflections on the methodology of legal history', in Dag Michalsen (ed.), *Reading Past Legal Texts* (Oslo: Unipax, 2006), pp. 91–112

Heller, Kevin J., *The Nuremberg Military Tribunals and the Origins of International Criminal Law* (Oxford: Oxford University Press, 2011)

Heller, Kevin J., and Gascoigne, Catherine E., 'Nuremberg Trials', in *Oxford Bibliographies in International Law* (2017), www.oxfordbibliographies .com/view/document/obo-9780199796953/obo-9780199796953-0126.xml

Heller, Kevin J., and Simpson, Gerald (eds.), *The Hidden Histories of War Crimes Trials* (Oxford: Oxford University Press, 2013)

Henkin, Louis, *How Nations Behave: Law and Foreign Policy*, 2nd ed. (New York: Columbia University Press, 1979), pp. 45–46

Hershey, Amos S., 'History of international law since the peace of Westphalia' (1912) 6 *The American Journal of International Law* 30–69

Heyking, Alphonse, 'L'exterritorialité et ses applications en Extrême-Orient' (1925) 7 *Recueil des cours de l'Académie de droit international de La Haye* 241–335

Higgins, Alexander Pearce, 'La contribution de quatre grands juristes britanniques au droit international (Lorimer, Westlake, Hall et Holland)' (1932) 40 *Recueil des cours de l'Académie de droit international de La Haye* 1–86

Higgins, Rosalyn, *Problems and Process: International Law and How We Use It* (Oxford: Clarendon Press, 1994)
'Time and the law: international perspectives on an old problem' (1997) 46 *International and Comparative Law Quarterly* 501–520

Hirsch, Moshe, *Invitation to the Sociology of International Law* (Oxford: Oxford University Press, 2005)
'The role of international tribunals in the development of historical narratives' (2018) 20 *Journal of the History of International Law* 391–428
The Sociological Perspective on International Law in International Legal Theory: Foundations and Frontiers, ed. Jeffrey L. Dunoff and Mark A. Pollack (in press)

Hobe, Stephan, 'Non-governmental organizations', in *Max Planck Encyclopedia of Public International Law* (2010), opil.ouplaw.com/view/10.1093/law:epil/ 9780199231690/law-9780199231690-e968

Hobson, John M., 'What's at stake in "bringing historical sociology back into international relations"? Transcending "chronofetishism" and "tempocentrism" in international relations', in Stephen Hobden and John M. Hobson (eds.), *History Sociology of International Relations* (Cambridge, UK: Cambridge University Press, 2002), pp. 3–41

Holland, Thomas Erskine, 'Alberico Gentili', in *Studies in International Law* (Oxford: Clarendon Press, 1898), pp. 1–39

Hsieh, Pasha L., 'Wellington Koo, international law and modern China' (2016) 56 *Indian Journal of International Law* 307–323

Huber, Max, 'Beiträge zur Kenntnis der soziologischen Grundlagen des Völkerrechts und der Staatengesellschaft' (1910) 4 *Jahrbuch des öffentlichen Rechts* 56–134

Hueck, Ingo J., 'The discipline of the history of international law: new trends and methods on the history of international law' (2001) 3 *Journal of the History of International Law* 194–217

Huneeus, Alexandra V., and Madsen, Mikael R., 'Between universalism and regional law and politics: a comparative history of the American, European and African human rights systems' (2018) 16 *International Journal of Constitutional Law* 136–160

Hunt, Lynn, 'Against presentism' (2002) 40 *Perspectives on History* 1, www .historians.org/publications-and-directories/perspectives-on-history/may-2002/against-presentism

Hunter, Ian, 'The figure of man and the territorialisation of justice in "enlightenment" natural law: Pufendorf and Vattel' (2013) 23 *Intellectual History Review* 289–307

Hurd, Ian, 'Constructivism', in Christian Reus-Smit and Duncan Snidal (eds.), *The Oxford Handbook of International Relations* (Oxford: Oxford University Press, 2008), pp. 298–316

Iggers, Georg G., 'Historicism: the history and meaning of the term' (1995) 56 *Journal of the History of Ideas* 129–152

   Historiography in the Twentieth Century: From Scientific Objectivity to the Post-Modern Challenge (Middletown, CT: Wesleyan University Press, 2013)

Iggers, Georg G., and Wang, Q. Edward, with Mukherjee, Supriya, *A Global History of Modern Historiography* (New York: Routledge, 2013)

Ikenberry, John G., 'The end of liberal international order?' (2018) 94 *International Affairs* 7–23

Irvin-Erickson, Douglas, *Raphael Lemkin and the Concept of Genocide* (Philadelphia: University of Pennsylvania Press, 2016)

Ishay, Micheline, *The History of Human Rights: From Ancient Times to the Globalization Era* (Berkeley: University of California Press, 2008)

Janis, Mark Weston, *America and the Law of Nations 1776-1939* (Oxford: Oxford University Press, 2010)

The American Tradition of International Law: Great Expectations 1789-1914 (Oxford: Oxford University Press, 2004)

'Jeremy Bentham and the fashioning of "international law"' (1984) 78 *American Journal of International Law* 405-418

'Sources in the meta-history of international law: a little meta-theory— paradigms, Article 38, and the sources of international law', in Jean d'Aspremont and Samantha Besson (eds.), *The Oxford Handbook of the Sources of International Law* (Oxford: Oxford University Press, 2017), pp. 264-278

Janis, Mark Weston, et al., 'Religion and international law' (1988) 82 *Proceedings of the Annual Meeting (American Society of International Law)* 195-220

Jay, Martin, 'Historical explanation and the event: reflections on the limits of contextualization' (2011) 42 *New Literary History* 557-571

'Intention and irony: the missed encounter of Hayden White and Quentin Skinner' (2013) 52 *History and Theory* 323-348

Jayatilleke, Kulatissa N., 'The principles of international law in Buddhist doctrine' (1967) 120 *Recueil des cours de l'Académie de droit international de La Haye* 441-568

Jennings, Christine, *Robbie: The Life of Sir Robert Jennings* (Kibworth: Troubador Publishing, 2019)

Joerges, Christian, and Ghaleigh, Navraj Singh (eds.), *Darker Legacies of Law in Europe: The Shadow of National Socialism and Fascism over Europe and Its Legal Traditions* (Oxford: Hart, 2003)

Joerges, Christian, and Petersmann, Ernest-Ulrich (eds.), *Constitutionalism, Multilevel Trade Governance and International Economic Law* (Oxford: Hart Publishing, 2011)

Johns, Fleur, Joyce, Richard, and Pahuja, Sundhya (eds.), *Events: The Force of International Law* (New York: Routledge, 2011)

Johns, Fleur, Skouteris, Thomas, and Werner, Wouter, 'Editors' introduction: Alejandro Álvarez and the launch of the Periphery Series' (2006) 19 *Leiden Journal of International Law* 875-1040

'Editors' introduction: Taslim Olawale Elias in the Periphery Series' (2008) 21 *Leiden Journal of International Law* 289-290

'The Periphery Series: India and international law' (2010) 23 *Leiden Journal of International Law* 1-3

Jones, Henry, 'The radical use of history in the study of international law' (2012-13) 23 *Finnish Yearbook of International Law* 309-350

Johnson, Mitchell Glen, 'The contributions of Eleanor and Franklin Roosevelt to the development of international protection for human rights' (1987) 9 *Human Rights Quarterly* 19–48

Johnston, Douglas M., *The Historical Foundations of World Order: The Tower and the Arena* (Leiden: Martinus Nijjhoff, 2008)

Jouannet, Emmanuelle, 'A critical introduction', trans. Euan Macdonald, in Nathaniel Berman, *Passion and Ambivalence: Nationalism, Colonialism and International Law* (Leiden and Boston: Martinus Njihoff, 2012), pp. 1–38

   Emer de Vattel et l'émergence doctrinale du droit international classique (Paris: Pédone, 1998)

   'La communauté internationale vue par les juristes' (2005) 6 *Annuaire français de relations internationales* 3–26

   The Liberal-Welfarist Law of Nations: A History of International Law, trans. Christopher Sutcliffe (Cambridge, UK: Cambridge University Press, 2012)

Jouannet, Emmanuelle, and Motoc, Iulia (eds.), *Les doctrines internationalistes durant les années du communisme réel en Europe* (Paris: Société de Législation Comparée, 2012)

Kadelbach, Stefan, Kleinlein, Thomas, and Roth-Isigkeit, David (eds.), *System, Order, and International Law: The Early History of International Legal Thought from Machiavelli to Hegel* (Oxford: Oxford University Press, 2017)

Kaltenborn von Stachau, Carl, *Vorläufer des Hugo Grotius auf dem Gebiete des ius naturae et gentium* (Leipzig: G. Mayer, 1848)

Kant, Immanuel, 'Die Idee zu einer allgemeinen Geschichte in weltbürgerlicher Absicht' (November 1784) 4 *Berlinische Monatsschrift* 385–411

   Perpetual Peace: A Philosophical Sketch trans. and ed. M. Campbell Smith (London: George Allen & Unwin, 1903)

   Zum ewigen Frieden: Ein philosophischer Entwurf (Königsberg: Friedrich Nicolovius, 1795)

Katzenstein, Suzanne, 'In the shadow of crisis: the creation of international courts in the twentieth century' (2014) 55 *Harvard International Law Journal* 151–209

Keohane, Robert O., 'Observations on the promise and pitfalls of historical institutionalism in international relations', in Orfeo Fioretos (ed.), *International Politics and Institutions in Time* (Oxford: Oxford University Press, 2017) pp. 321–336

Keller-Kemmerer, Nina, *Die Mimikry des Völkerrechts: Andres Bello 'Principios de derecho internacional'* (Baden-Baden: Nomos, 2018)

Kelsen, Hans, *Peace through Law* (Chapel Hill: University of North Carolina Press, 1944)

Kemmerer, Alexandra, 'Editing Rosa: Luxemburg, the revolution, and the politics of infantilization' (2016) 27 *European Journal of International Law* 853–864

'Towards a global history of international law? Editor's note' (2014) 25 *European Journal of International Law* 287–295

'"We do not need to always look to Westphalia . . ." A conversation with Martti Koskenniemi and Anne Orford' (2015) 17 *Journal of the History of International Law* 1–14

Kennedy, David, 'Critical theory, structuralism and contemporary legal scholarship' (1985–1986) 21 *New England Law Review* 209–289

The Dark Sides of Virtue: Reassessing International Humanitarism (Princeton, NJ: Princeton University Press, 2004)

'The disciplines of international law and policy' (1999) 12 *Leiden Journal of International Law* 9–133

'The international human rights movement: part of the problem?' (2002) 14 *Harvard Human Rights Journal* 101–126

'The international human rights regime: still part of the problem?', in Rob Dickenson et al. (eds.), *Examining Critical Perspectives on Human Rights* (Cambridge, UK: Cambridge University Press, 2012), pp. 19–34

'International law and the nineteenth century: history of an illusion' (1997) 17 *Quinnipiac Law Review* 99–136

International Legal Structures (Baden-Baden: Nomos Verlagsgesellschaft, 1987)

'The international style in postwar law and policy' (1994) 1 *Utah Law Review* 7–103

'The last treatise: project and person (reflections on Martti Koskenniemi's *From Apology to Utopia*)' (2006) 7 *German Law Journal* 982–992

'The move to institutions' (1987) 8 *Cardozo Law Review* 841–988

'The mystery of global governance' (2008) 34 *Ohio Northern University Law Review* 827–860

'A new stream of international law scholarship' (1988) 7 *Wisconsin International Law Journal* 1–49

'The political economy of centers and peripheries' (2012) 25 *Leiden Journal of International Law* 7–48

'Primitive legal scholarship' (1986) 27 *Harvard International Law Journal* 1–98

'My talk at the ASIL: what is new thinking in international law?' (2000) 94 *Proceedings of the American Society of International Law* 104–125

'Theses about international law discourse' (1980) 23 *German Yearbook of International Law* 353–391

'The TWAIL Conference: keynote address, Albany, New York, April 2007' (2007) 9 *International Community Law Review* 333–344

'When renewal repeats: thinking against the box' (2000) 32 *New York Journal of International Law and Politics* 335–500

Kennedy, David, and Beneyto, José Maria (eds.), *New Approaches to International Law: The European and American Experiences* (The Hague: T. M. C. Asser Press, 2013)

Kennedy, David, and Tennant, Christopher, 'New Approaches to International Law: a bibliography' (1944) 35 *Harvard International Law Journal* 417–460

Kennedy, Duncan, *A Critique of Adjudication: Fin de Siècle* (Cambridge, MA: Harvard University Press, 1997)

'The critique of rights in Critical Legal Studies', in Wendy Brown and Janet E. Halley (eds.), *Left Legalism/Left Critique* (Durham, NC: Duke University Press, 2002), pp. 178–228

'Form and substance in private law adjudication' (1976) 89 *Harvard Law Review* 1685–1778

'Nota sobre la historia de CLS en los Estados Unidos' (1992) 11 *Doxa* 283–293

'The paradox of American legal realism' (1997) 3 *European Law Journal* 359–377

The Rise and Fall of Classical Legal Thought (Washington, DC: Beard Books, 2006)

'The structure of Blackstone's commentaries' (1979) 28 *Buffalo Law Review* 205–382

'Three globalizations of law and legal thought: 1850–2000', in David Trubek and Alvaro Santos (eds.), *The New Law and Economic Development: A Critical Appraisal* (Cambridge, UK: Cambridge University Press, 2006), pp. 19–73

'Toward an historical understanding of legal consciousness: the case of classical legal thought in America 1850–1940' (1980) 3 *Research in Law & Society* 3–24

Kingsbury, Benedict, and Straumann, Benjamin (eds.), *The Roman Foundations of the Law of Nations: Alberico Gentili and the Justice of Empire* (Oxford: Oxford University Press, 2010)

Kirgis, Frederic L., *The American Society of International Law's First Century 1906–2006* (Leiden: Brill/Nijhoff, 2006)

Kjeldgaard-Pedersen, Astrid, *Nordic Approaches to International Law* (Leiden: Brill/Nijhoff, 2017)

Klabbers, Jan, 'The emergence of functionalism in international institutional law: colonial inspirations' (2014) 25 *European Journal of International Law* 645–675

Knop, Karen, *Diversity and Self-Determination in International Law* (Cambridge, UK: Cambridge University Press, 2004)

Knop, Karen, and Chinkin, Christine, 'Remembering Chrystal MacMillan: women's equality and nationality in international law, (2001) 22 *Michigan Journal of International Law* 523–585

Kolb, Robert (ed.), *Commentaire sur le Pacte de la Société des Nations* (Brussels: Bruylant, 2015)

Esquisse d'un droit international public des anciennes cultures extra-européennes: Amérique precolombienne, Iles Polynésiennes, Afrique Noire, Sous-continent indien, Chine et régions limitrophes (Paris: Pédone, 2010)

'International organizations or institutions, history of', in *Max Planck Encyclopedia of Public International Law* (2011), opil.ouplaw.com/view/10 .1093/law:epil/9780199231690/law-9780199231690-e501

'Legal history as a source: from classical to modern international law' in Jean d'Aspremont and Samantha Besson (eds.), *The Oxford Handbook of the Sources of International Law* (Oxford: Oxford University Press, 2017), pp. 279–300

Les cours généraux de droit international public de La Haye (Brussels: Bruylant/ Éditions de l'Université de Bruxelles, 2003)

'Politis and sociological jurisprudence of inter-war international law' (2012) 23 *European Journal of International Law* 233–241

Korff, Serge A., 'Introduction à l'histoire du droit international' (1923) 1 *Recueil des cours de l'Académie de droit international de La Haye* 1–23

Korhonen, Outi, 'New international law: silence, defence of deliverance?' (1996) 7 *European Journal of International Law* 1–28

'The role of history in international law' (2000) 94 *Proceedings of the Annual Meeting (American Society of International Law)* 45–46

Koselleck, Reinhart, 'Über die Theoriebedürftigkeit der Geschichtswissenschaft', in Reinhart Koselleck (ed.), *Zeitschichten: Studien zur Historik* (Berlin: Suhrkamp, 2000), pp. 298–316

Koskenniemi, Martti, 'Between context and telos: reviewing the structures of international law', in Henning Trüper, Dipesh Chakrabarty, and Sanjay Subrahmanyam (eds.), *Historical Teleologies in the Modern World* (London: Bloomsbury, 2015)

'Carl Schmitt and international law', in Jens Meierhenrich and Oliver Simons (eds.), *The Oxford Handbook of Carl Schmitt* (New York: Oxford University Press, 2016), pp. 592–611

'The case for comparative international law' (2011) 20 *Finnish Yearbook of International Law* 1–8

'Constitutionalism as mindset: reflections on Kantian themes about international law and globalization' (2007) 8 *Theoretical Inquiries in Law* 9–36

'Empire and international law: the real Spanish contribution' (2011) 61 *University of Toronto Law Journal* 1–36

'Enchanted by the tools? An enlightenment perspective' (2019) 113 *Proceedings of the ASIL's Annual Meeting* 3–19

'Expanding histories of international law' (2016) 56 *American Journal of Legal History* 104–112

'The fate of public international law: between technique and politics' (2007) 70 *The Modern Law Review* 1–30

'Foreword: history of human rights as political intervention in the present', in
  Pamela Slotte and Miia Halme Tuomisaari (eds.), *Revisiting the Origins of
  Human Rights* (Cambridge, UK: Cambridge University Press, 2015),
  pp. ix–xx

From Apology to Utopia: The Structure of the International Legal Argument
  (Helsinki: Lakimiesliiton Kustannus, 1989); reissued with a new epilogue
  (Cambridge, UK: Cambridge University Press, 2005)

'The function of law in the international community: 75 years after' (2008) 79
  British Yearbook of International Law 353–366

*The Gentle Civilizer of Nations: The Rise and Fall of International Law
  1870–1960* (Cambridge, UK: Cambridge University Press, 2001)

'Georg Friedrich von Martens (1756–1821) and the origins of modern international law', in Christian Calliess, Georg Nolte and Peter-Tobias Stoll
  (eds.), *Von der Diplomatie zum kodifizierten Völkerrecht: 75 Jahre Institut
  für Völkerrecht der Universität Göttingen (1930–2005)* (Cologne: Heymanns,
  2006), pp. 13–30

'Hersch Lauterpacht 1897–1960', in Jack Beatson and Reihard Zimmermann
  (eds.), *Jurists Uprooted: German-Speaking Emigré Lawyers in Twentieth-
  Century Britain* (Oxford: Oxford University Press, 2004), pp. 601–662

'Hersch Lauterpacht and the development of international criminal law' (2004)
  2 *Journal of International Criminal Justice* 810–825

'Histories of international law: dealing with Eurocentrism' (2011) 19
  Rechtsgeschichte 152–176

'Histories of international law: significance and problems for a critical view'
  (2013) 27 *Temple International Law and Comparative Law Journal* 215–240

'A history of international law histories' in Bardo Fassbender and Anne Peters
  (eds.), *The Oxford Handbook of the History of International Law* (Oxford:
  Oxford University Press, 2012), pp. 943–971

'Human rights mainstreaming as a strategy for institutional power' (2010) 1
  *Humanity: An International Journal of Human Rights, Humanitarianism,
  and Development* 47–58

'Imagining the rule of law: rereading the Grotian "tradition"' (2019) 30
  European Journal of International Law 17–52

'"International community" from Dante to Vattel', in Vincent Chetail and
  PeterHaggenmacher (eds.), *Vattel's International Law from a XXIst
  Century Perspective* (Leiden: Brill, 2011), pp. 49–74

'International law and the emergence of mercantile capitalism: Grotius to
  Smith', in Pierre-Marie Dupuy and Vincent Chetail (eds.), *The Roots of
  International Law/Les fondements du droit international: Liber Amicorum
  Peter Haggenmacher* (Leiden: Martinus Nijhoff, 2013), pp. 3–37

International Law and the Far Right: Reflections on Law and Cynicism (The
  Hague: T. M. C. Asser Press, 2019)

'International law as political theology: how to read the *Nomos der Erde*' (2004) 11 *Constellations* 492–511

'Introduction: international law and empire – aspects and approaches', in Martti Koskenniemi, Walter Rech, and Manuel J. Fonseca (eds.), *International Law and Empire: Historical Explorations* (Oxford: Oxford University Press, 2017), pp. 1–20

'Lauterpacht: the Victorian tradition in international law' (1997) 8 *European Journal of International Law* 215–263

'The law of nations and the "conflict of faculties"' (2018) 8 *History of the Present* 4–28

'Legal history as begriffsgeschichte?', in Claudia Wiesner (ed.), *In Debate with Karl Palonen: Concepts, Politics, Histories* (Baden-Baden: Nomos, 2015), pp. 63–68

'Le style comme méthode: lettres aux organisateurs du symposium', in *La politique du droit international* (Paris: Pédone, 2007), pp. 391–408

'Methodology of international law', in *Max Planck Encyclopedia of Public International Law* (2007), opil.ouplaw.com/view/10.1093/law:epil/9780199231690/law-9780199231690-e1440, pp. 2–9.

'Miserable comforters: international relations as new natural law' (2009) 15 *European Journal of International Relations* 395–422

'On the idea and practice for universal history with a cosmopolitan purpose', in Bindu Puri and Heiko Sievers (eds.), *Terror, Peace and Universalism: Essays on the Philosophy of Immanuel Kant* (Oxford: Oxford University Press, 2007), pp. 122–148

'The politics of international law' (1990) 1 *European Journal of International Law* 4–32

'The politics of international law – 20 years later' (2009) 20 *European Journal of International Law* 7–19

'Preface' (1996) 65 *Nordic Journal of International Law* 337–340

'Race, hierarchy and international law: Lorimer's legal science' (2016) 27 *European Journal of International Law* 415–429

'A response' (2006) 7 *German Law Journal* 1103–1108

'Review of the epochs of international law' (2002) 51 *International and Comparative Law Quarterly* 746–751

'Sovereignty, property and empire: early modern English contexts' (2017) 18 *Theoretical Inquiries in Law* 357–389

'The style as method: letter to the editors of the symposium' (1999) 93 *American Journal of International Law* 351–361

To the Uttermost Parts of the World: Legal Imagination and International Power c. 1300–1800 (Cambridge: Cambridge University Press, 2021)

'Vitoria and us: thoughts on critical histories of international law' (2014) 22 *Rechtsgeschichte* 119–138

'What is critical research in international law? Celebrating structuralism' (2016) 29 *Leiden Journal of International Law* 727–735

'What should international lawyers learn from Karl Marx?' (2004) 17 *Leiden Journal of International Law* 229–246

'What should international legal history become?', in Stefan Kadelbach, Thomas Kleinlein and David Roth-Isigkeit (eds.), *System, Order and International Law: The Early History of International Legal Thought from Machiavelli to Hegel* (Oxford: Oxford University Press, 2017), pp. 381–397

'What use for sovereignty today?' (2011) 1 *Asian Journal of International Law* 61–70

'Why history of international law today?' (2004) 4 *Rechtsgeschichte* 61–66

Koskenniemi, Martti, et al., 'The European tradition in international law: Hersch Lauterpacht' (1997) 8 *European Journal of International Law* 215–320

Koskenniemi, Martti, Rech, Walter, and Fonseca, Manuel Jiménez (eds.), *International Law and Empire* (Oxford: Oxford University Press, 2017)

Koskenniemi, Martti, Rovira, Mónica García-Salmones, and Amorosa, Paolo (eds.), *International Law and Religion: Historical and Contemporary Perspectives* (Oxford: Oxford University Press, 2017)

Kotzur, Markus, 'Intertemporal law', in *Max Planck Encyclopedia of Public International Law* (2008), opil.ouplaw.com/view/10.1093/law:epil/ 9780199231690/law-9780199231690-e1433?rskey=VD6i3z&result=2&prd=OPIL

Krisch, Nico, *Beyond Constitutionalism: The Pluralist Structure of Postnational Law* (Oxford: Oxford University Press, 2010)

Kroll, Stefan, *Normgenese durch Re-Interpretation: China und das europäische Völkerrecht im 19. und 20. Jahrhundert* (Baden-Baden: Nomos, 2012)

Kunz, Joseph L., 'Compulsory international adjudication and maintenance of peace' (1944) 38 *American Journal of International Law* 673–678

Kuzmarov, Betina, *Unilateral Acts: A History of a Legal Doctrine* (London: Routledge, 2018)

Laber, Jeri, *The Courage of Strangers: Coming of Age with the Human Rights Movement* (New York: Public Affairs, 2002)

Laghmani, Slim, *Histoire du droit des gens, du jus gentium impérial au jus publicum europæum* (Paris: Pédone, 2004)

Landauer, Carl, 'J. L. Brierly and the modernization of the law' (1992–93) 5 *Vanderbilt Journal of Transnational Law* 881–917

'Passage from India: Nagendra Singh's India and international law' (2016) 56 *India Journal of International Law* 265–305

'Taslim Olawale Elias: from British colonial law to modern international law', in Jochen von Bernstorff and Philipp Dann (eds.), *The Battle for International Law in the Era of Decolonization* (Oxford: Oxford University Press, 2019), pp. 318–340

Landheer, Bartholomeus, 'Contemporary sociological theories and international law' (1957) 91 *Recueil des cours de l'Académie de droit international de La Haye* 1–104

Lang, Andrew, and Marks, Susan, 'People with projects: writing the lives of international lawyers' (2013) 27 *Temple International and Comparative Law Journal* 437–53

Lange, Christian L., 'Histoire de la doctrine pacifique et de son influence sur le développement du droit international' (1927) 13 *Recueil des cours de l'Académie de droit international de La Haye* 171–426

Lange, Felix, 'Between systematization and expertise for foreign policy – the practice-oriented approach in Germany's international legal scholarship 1920–1980' (2017) 28 *European Journal of International Law* 535–558

'Challenging the Paris Peace Treaties, state sovereignty, and Western-dominated international law – the multifaceted genesis of the *jus cogens* doctrine' (2018) 31 *Leiden Journal of International Law* 821–839

Langella, Simona, 'The sovereignty of law in the works of Francisco de Vitoria', in José Maria Beneyto and Justo Corti Varela (eds.), *At the Origins of Modernity: Francisco de Vitoria and the Discovery of International Law* (Cham: Springer, 2017), pp. 45–61

Langer, Máximo, and Eason, Mackenzie, 'The quiet expansion of universal jurisdiction' (2019) 30 *European Journal of International Law* 779–817

Lasswell, Harold D., and McDougal, Myres S., *Jurisprudence for a Free Society: Studies in Law, Science and Policy* (New Haven, CT: New Haven Press, 1992)

Latty, Franck, 'Christine de Pizan (vers 1365 – vers 1430): Société française pour le droit international' (2019), www.sfdi.org/internationalistes/pizan/

Lauren, Paul Gordon, *The Evolution of International Human Rights: Visions Seen* (Philadelphia: University of Pennsylvania Press, 1998)

Laurent, François, *Histoire des droits des gens et relations internationales*, 18 vols. (Paris: Durand, 1951)

Lauterpacht, Elihu, *The Life of Hersch Lauterpacht* (Cambridge, UK: Cambridge University Press, 2010)

Lauterpacht, Hersch, *Annual Digest of Public International Law Cases: 1919–1922* (London: Longmans, Green and Company, 1932)

The Function of Law in the International Community (Oxford: Oxford University Press, 1933)

'The Grotian tradition in international law' (1946) 23 *British Yearbook of International Law* 1–53

Leben, Charles, et al., 'The European tradition in international law: Hans Kelsen' (1998) 9 *European Journal of International Law* 287–400

Le Fur, Louis-Erasme, 'La théorie du droit naturel depuis le XVII siècle et la doctrine moderne' (1927) 18 *Recueil des cours de l'Académie de droit international de La Haye* 259–442

'Le développement historique du droit international: de l'anarchie internationale à une communauté internationale organisée' (1932) 41 *Recueil des cours de l'Académie de droit international de La Haye* 501–601

Lemnitzer, Jan Martin, 'How to prevent a war and alienate lawyers – the peculiar case of the 1905 North Sea Incident Commission', in Ignacio de la Rasilla and Jorge E. Viñuales (eds.), *Experiments in International Adjudication: Historical Accounts* (Cambridge, UK: Cambridge University Press, 2019), pp. 76–97

Leprince, Chloé, '"Droit-de-l'hommisme": histoire d'un néologisme péjoratif' (2018), franceculture.fr/histoire/droit-de-lhommisme-histoire-dun-neolo gisme-pejoratif

Lepsius, Oliver, 'Hans Kelsen on Dante Alighieri's political philosophy' (2016) 27 *European Journal of International Law* 1153–1167

Lerner, Gerda, *The Creation of Feminist Consciousness: From the Middle Ages to Eighteen-Seventy* (Oxford: Oxford University Press, 1993)

Lesaffer, Randall (ed.), *Bibliography on the History of International Law*, www.tilburguniversity.edu/research/institutes-and-research-groups/i-hilt/i-hilt-bibliography

'The classical Law of Nations (1500–1800)', in Alexander Orakhelashvili (ed.), *Research Handbook on the Theory and History of International Law* (Cheltenham: Edward Elgar Publishing, 2011), pp. 408–440

'The cradle of international law: Camilo Barcia Trelles on Francisco de Vitoria at the Hague in 1927' (2021) 32 *European Journal of International Law* (forthcoming)

'The end of the Cold War: an epochal event in the history of international law?' (2010) 10 *Tilburg Working Paper Series on Jurisprudence and Legal History* 1–25

'International law and its history: the story of an unrequited love', in Matthew Craven et al. (eds.), *Time, History and International Law* (Leiden: Martinus Nijhoff, 2007), pp. 27–41

'Law and history: law between past and present', https://lirias.kuleuven.be/ 1856246; also published in Bart van Klink and Sanne Taekema (eds.), *Law and Method: Interdisciplinary Research into Law* (Tübingen: Mohr Siebeck, 2011), pp. 133–152

'Peace treaties from Lodi to Westphalia', in Randall Lesaffer (ed.), *Peace Treaties and International Law in European History: From the Late Middle Ages to World War One* (Cambridge, UK: Cambridge University Press, 2004), pp. 9–44

'Roman law and the intellectual history of international law', in Anne Orford and Florian Hoffmann with Martin Clark (eds.), *The Oxford Handbook of the Theory of International Law* (Oxford: Oxford University Press, 2016), pp. 38–58

'Too much history: from war as sanction to the sanctioning of war', in Marc Weller (ed.), *The Oxford Handbook of the Use of Force in International Law* (Oxford: Oxford University Press, 2015), pp. 35–55

Lesaffer, Randall *Peace Treaties and International Law in European History: From the Late Middle Ages to World War One* (Cambridge, UK: Cambridge University Press, 2004)

Lewis, Mark, *The Birth of the New Justice: The Internationalization of Crime and Punishment 1919-1950* (Oxford: Oxford University Press, 2014)

Lieber, Francis, *Instructions for the Government of Armies of the United States in the Field* (Washington, DC: Adjutant General's Office, 1863)

Liu, Cixin, *The Remembrance of Earth's Past*, trans. Ken Liu and Joel Martinsen (London: Head of Zeus, 2017)

Loefflad, Eric Daniel, 'Popular will and international law: the expansion of capitalism, the question of legitimate authority, and the universalisation of the nation state' (PhD thesis, University of Kent, 2019), kar.kent.ac.uk/80677/1/169_E_Loefflad_PhD_Thesis.pdf

Loeffler, James, 'Reflections on Jewish international legal biography', in Annette Weinke and Leora Bilsky (eds.), *Émigré Lawyers and International Law* (in press), papers. ssrn.com/sol3/papers.cfm?abstract_id=3454558

Loeffler, James, and Paz, Moria (eds.), *The Law of Strangers: Jewish Lawyers and International Law in the Twentieth Century* (Cambridge, UK: Cambridge University Press, 2019)

Llorente Sariñena, Marta, 'Uti possidetis, ita domini eritis: international law and the historiography of the territory', in Massimo Meccarelli and María Julia Solla Sastre (eds.), *Spatial and Temporal Dimensions for Legal History Research Experiences and Itineraries* (Frankfurt: Max Planck Institute for European Legal History, 2016), pp. 131–172

Lorimer, James, *The Institutes of the Law of Nations: A Treatise of the Jural Relations of Separate Political Communities*, 2 vols. (London and Edinburgh: W. Blackwood & Sons, 1883–84)

Luban, David, 'Hannah Arendt as a theorist of international criminal law' (2011) 11 *International Criminal Law Review* 621–641

Luscombe, Anya, and Oomen, Barbara, 'René Cassin (1887-1976): the foot soldier of human rights', in Kasey McCall-Smith, Jan Wouters, and Felipe Gómez Isa (eds.), *The Faces of Human Rights* (Oxford: Hart Publishing, 2019), pp. 105–114

Lyotard, Jean-François, *The Postmodern Condition: A Report on Knowledge* (Manchester: Manchester University Press, 1984)

Lysen, Arnoldus (ed.), *Hugo Grotius: Essays on His Life and Works Selected for the Occasion of the Tercentenary of His* De jure belli ac pacis *1625–1925* (Leiden: A. W. Sythoff's Publishing Co.,1925)

Macalister-Smith, Peter, 'Bio-bibliographical key to the membership of the Institut de droit international 1873–2001' (2003) 5 *Journal of the History of International Law* 77–159

'Institut de droit international', in *Max Planck Encyclopedia of Public International Law* (2011), opil.ouplaw.com/view/10.1093/law:epil/9780199231690/law-9780199231690-e947?prd=EPIL

Macalister-Smith, Peter, and Schwietzke, Joachim, 'Bibliography of the textbooks and comprehensive treatise on positive international law of the 19th century' (2001) 3 *Journal of the History of International Law* 75–142

'Literature and documentary sources relating to the history of international law' (1999) 1 *Journal of the History of International Law* 136–212

(eds.), *Treaties and Other Acts in Multilateral Conference Diplomacy: A Brief Calendar of State Practice 1641 to 1924* (Vienna: Neugebauer Verlag, 2019)

MacCormick, Neil, 'Sovereignty and after', in Hent Kalmo and Quentin Skinner (eds.), *Sovereignty in Fragments: The Past, Present and Future of a Contested Concept* (Cambridge, UK: Cambridge University Press, 2010), pp. 151–168

MacDonald, Euan, *International Law and Ethics after the Critical Challenge: Framing the Legal within the Post-foundational* (Leiden: Brill/Nijhoff, 2011)

Madsen, Mikael R., Cebulak, Pola, and Wiebusch, Micha, 'Special issue – resistance to international courts: introduction and conclusion' (2018) 14 *International Journal of Law in Context* 193–196

Mälksoo, Lauri, *Russian Approaches to International Law* (Oxford: Oxford University Press, 2015)

Mamolea, Andrei, 'Saving face: the political work of the Permanent Court of Arbitration (1902–1914)', in Ignacio de la Rasilla and Jorge E. Viñuales (eds.), *Experiments in International Adjudication: Historical Accounts* (Cambridge, UK: Cambridge University Press, 2019), pp. 193–210

Manela, Erez, 'International society as a historical subject' (2020) 44 *Diplomatic History* 184–209

Manning, Patrick, 'William H. McNeill: Lucretius and Moses in world history' (2007) 46 *History and Theory* 428–445

Marceau, Gabrielle (ed.), *A History of Law and Lawyers in the GATT/WTO: The Development of the Rule of Law in the Multilateral Trading System* (Cambridge, UK: Cambridge University Press, 2015)

Marín y Mendoza, Joaquín, *Historia del derecho natural y de gentes* (Madrid: Impr. Manuel Martín, 1776)

Marks, Susan, 'Introduction', in Susan Marks (ed.), *International Law on the Left: Re-examining Marxist Legacies* (Cambridge, UK: Cambridge University Press, 2008), pp. 1–29

The Riddle of All Constitutions, International Law, Democracy, and the Critique of Ideology (Oxford: Oxford University Press, 2000)

Martens, Georg Friedrich von, *Précis du droit des gens moderne de l'Europe, fondé sur les traités et l'usage* (Göttingen: Chés Jean Chret. Dieterich, 1789) *Summary of the Law of Nations*, trans. William Cobbett (Philadelphia: Thomas Bradford, 1795)

Martineau, Anne-Charlotte, 'A forgotten chapter in the history of international commercial arbitration: the slave trade's dispute settlement system' (2018) 31 *Leiden Journal of International Law* 219–241

'Overcoming Eurocentrism? Global history and *The Oxford Handbook of the History of International Law*' (2014) 25 *European Journal of International Law* 329–336

Martinez, Jenny S., *The Slave Trade and the Origins of International Human Rights Law* (Oxford: Oxford University Press, 2012)

Marx, Karl, 'Preface to a contribution to the critique of political economy', reprinted in *Karl Marx: Selected Writings*, ed. D. McLellan, 2nd ed. (Oxford: Oxford University Press, 2000), pp. 209–213

Mazower, Mark, *No Enchanted Palace: The End of Empire and the Ideological Origins of the United Nations* (Princeton, NJ: Princeton University Press, 2013)

McCall-Smith, Kasey, Wouters, Jan, and Isa, Felipe Gómez (eds.), *The Faces of Human Rights* (Oxford: Hart Publishing, 2019)

McCorquodale, Robert, and Gauci, Jean-Pierre (eds.), *British Influences on International Law 1915–2015* (Leiden: Brill/Nijhoff, 2016)

Mcneill, William H., *The Rise of the West: A History of the Human Community* (Chicago: University of Chicago Press, 1963)

McWhinney, Edward, 'Julius Stone and the sociological approach to international law' (1986) 9 *The University of New South Wales Law Journal* 14–25

Megill, Alan, '"Grand narrative" and the discipline of history', in F. Ankersmit and H. Kellner (eds.), *A New Philosophy of History* (Chicago: University of Chicago Press, 1995), pp. 151–173

Mégret, Frédéric, 'Droit international et esclavage: pour une réévaluation' (2013) 18 *African Yearbook of International Law* 121–183

'Féminisme et droit international: le "féminisme de gouvernance" à l'épreuve du "féminisme critique"', in Emmanuelle Tourme-Jouannet et al. (eds.), *Féminisme(s) et droit international: études du réseau Olympe* (Paris: Société de Législation Comparée, 2016), pp. 1–30

'The laws of war and the structure of masculine power' (2018) 7 *Melbourne Journal of International Law* 200–226

'The rise and fall of "international man"', in Prabhakar Singh and Benoît Mayer (eds.), *Critical International Law: Postrealism, Postcolonialism and Transnationalism* (Oxford: Oxford University Press, 2014), pp. 223–233

'Where does the critique of international human rights stand? An exploration in 18 vignettes', in David Kennedy and José Maria Beneyto (eds.), *New Approaches to International Law: The European and American Experiences* (The Hague: T. M. C. Asser Press, 2013), pp. 3–40

Mégret, Frédéric, and Tallgren, Immi (eds.), *The Dawn of a Discipline: International Criminal Justice and Its Early Exponents* (Cambridge, UK: Cambridge University Press, 2020)

Meijers, Eduard-Maurits, 'L'histoire des principes fondamentaux du droit international privé à partir du Moyen Âge spécialement dans l'Europe occidentale' (1934) 49 *Recueil des cours de l'Académie de droit international de La Haye* 543–686

Meister, Daniel R., 'The biographical turn and the case for historical biography' (2018)16 *History Compass* 1–10

Mickelson, Karin, 'Taking stock of TWAIL histories' (2008) 10 *International Community Law Review* 355–362

Miguel, Pablo Zapatero, 'Francisco de Vitoria and the postmodern grand critique of international law', in José Maria Beneyto and Justo Corti Varela (eds.), *At the Origins of Modernity: Francisco de Vitoria and the Discovery of International Law* (Cham: Springer, 2017), pp. 177–196

Miles, Kate, *The Origins of International Investment Law: Empire, Environment, and the Safeguarding of Capital* (Cambridge, UK: Cambridge University Press, 2013)

Milliot, Louis, 'La conception de l'état et de l'ordre légal dans l'Islam' (1949) 75 *Recueil des cours de l'Académie de droit international de La Haye* 591–688

Mirkine-Guetzêvitch, Boris, 'L'influence de la Révolution française sur le développement du droit international dans l'Europe orientale' (1928) 22 *Recueil des cours de l'Académie de droit international de La Haye* 295–458

Moore, John Bassett, *A Digest of International Law*, 8 vols. (Washington, DC: Government Printing Office, 1906)

Morgenthau, Hans J., *Politics among Nations: The Struggle for Power and Peace* (New York: Alfred A. Knopf, 1948)

Morsink, Johannes, *The Universal Declaration of Human Rights: Origins, Drafting, and Intent* (Philadelphia: University of Pennsylvania Press, 1999)

Moyn, Samuel, *Human Rights and the Uses of History* (London: Verso, 2017)

The Last Utopia: Human Rights in History (Cambridge, MA: Harvard University Press, 2012)

'Legal history as a source of international law: the politics of knowledge', in Samantha Besson and Jean d'Aspremont (eds.), *The Oxford Handbook of the Sources of International Law* (Oxford: Oxford University Press, 2017), pp. 301–322

Moyn, Samuel, and Özsu, Umut, 'The historical origins and setting of the Friendly Relations Declaration', in Jorge E. Viñuales (ed.), *The UN Friendly Relations*

Declaration at 50: An Assessment of the Fundamental Principles of International Law (Cambridge, UK: Cambridge University Press, 2021), pp. 23–48

Müller-Jochmus, Mauritius, *Geschichte des Völkerrechts im Altertum* (Leipzig, 1848; reprint Berlin: Kessinger, 2010)

Mutua, Makua, 'The ideology of human rights' (1995) 36 *Virginia Journal of International Law* 589–657

'What is TWAIL?' (2000) 94 *American Society of International Law Proceedings* 31–38

Myrdal, Alva, *The Game of Disarmament: How the United States and Russia Run the Arms Race* (New York: Pantheon Books, 1977)

Naftali, Patricia, 'The "right to truth" in international law: the "last Utopia"?', in Uladzislau Belavusau and Aleksandra Gliszczyńska-Grabias (eds.), *Law and Memory: Towards Legal Governance of History* (Cambridge, UK: Cambridge University Press, 2017), pp. 70–88

Nasaw, David, 'AHR roundtable – Historians and biography: Introduction' (2009) 114 *American Historical Review* 573–578

Naumann, Katja, 'Long-term and decentred trajectories of doing history from a global perspective: institutionalization, postcolonial critique, and empiricist approaches, before and after the 1970s' (2019) 14 *Journal of Global History* 335–354

Nawaz, M. K., 'The law of nations in ancient India' (1957) 6 *Indian Yearbook of International Affairs* 172–188

Neff, Stephen C., *Justice among Nations: A History of International Law* (Cambridge, MA: Harvard University Press, 2014)

War and the Law of Nations: A General History (Cambridge, UK: Cambridge University Press, 2005)

Nehamas, Alexander, *Nietzsche: Life As Literature* (Cambridge, MA: Harvard University Press, 1987)

Nellen, Henk, *Hugo Grotius: A Lifelong Struggle for Peace in Church and State, 1583–1645* (Leiden: Brill, 2014)

Nesiah, Vauki, 'The ground beneath her feet: Third World "feminisms"' (2003) 4 *Journal of International Women's Studies* 30–38

Nietzsche, Friedrich W., *Beyond Good and Evil*, trans. Helen Zimmern (Miami: Oregan France, 2020)

'Zur Genealogie der Moral', in *Sämtliche Werke: Kritische Studienausgabe in 15 Einzelbänden*, ed. Giorgo Colli and Mazzino Montinari, 5 vols. (Berlin: Walter de Gruyter, 1988)

Nijman, Janne E., *The Concept of International Legal Personality: An Inquiry into the History and Theory of International Law* (The Hague: T. M. C. Asser Press, 2004)

Seeking Change by Doing History (Amsterdam: Universiteit van Amsterdam, 2017)

Nippold, Otfried, 'Le développement historique du droit international depuis le
    Congrès de Vienne' (1924) 2 *Recueil des cours de l'Académie de l'Académie
    de droit international de La Haye* 5–124
Nussbaum, Arthur, *A Concise History of the Law of Nations* (New York:
    Macmillan, 1947)
Nuzzo, Luigi, *Origini di una scienza: diritto internazionale e colonialismo nel XIX
    secolo* (Frankfurt am Main: Klostermann, 2012)
Nys, Ernest, *Christine de Pisan et ses principales œuvres* (The Hague: M. Nijhoff,
    1914)
    'The codification of international law' (1911) 5 *American Journal of
        International Law* 871–900
    'Honoré Bonet et Christine de Pisan' (1882) 24 *Revue de droit international et
        de législation comparée* 451–472
    Les origines de droit international (Brussels: A. Castaigne, 1894)
    'Les publicistes espagnols du XVI siècle et les droits des indiens' (1889) 21
        Révue de droit international et de législation comparée 532–560
Obregon, Edgardo Sobenes, and Samson, Benjamin, *Nicaragua before the
    International Court of Justice: Impacts on International Law* (Cham:
    Springer, 2018)
Obregón Tarazona, Liliana, 'The civilized and the uncivilized', in Bardo Fassbender
    and Anne Peters (eds.), *The Oxford Handbook of the History of International
    Law* (Oxford: Oxford University Press, 2012), pp. 917–943
    'Construyendo la región Americana: Andrés Bello y el derecho internacional'
        (2010) 24 *Revista de derecho público* 65–86
    'Martti Koskenniemi´s critique of Eurocentrism in International Law', in
        Wouter Werner, Marieke de Hoon, and Alexis Galan (eds.), *The Law of
        International Lawyers: Reading Martti Koskenniemi* (Cambridge, UK:
        Cambridge University Press, 2017), pp. 360–392
    'Noted for dissent: the international life of Alejandro Álvarez' (2006) 19 *Leiden
        Journal of International Law* 983–1016
    'Peripheral histories of international law' (2019) 15 *Annual Review of Law and
        Social Science* 437–451
    'Writing international legal history: an overview' (2015) 7 *Monde(s)* 95–112
O'Connell, Mary Ellen, and Zee, Lenore Vander, 'The history of international
    adjudication', in Cesare P. R. Romano, Karen J. Alter, and Yuval Shany
    (eds.), *The Oxford Handbook of International Adjudication* (Oxford: Oxford
    University Press, 2014), pp. 40–62
O'Donoghue, Aoife, 'The admixture of feminine weakness and susceptibility:
    gendered personifications of the state in international law' (2018) 19
    Melbourne Journal of International Law 227–258
Offen, Karen, 'Women's rights or human rights? International feminism between
    the wars', in Patricia Grimshaw, Katie Holmes, and Marilyn Lake (eds.),

Women's Rights and Human Rights (London: Palgrave Macmillan, 2001), pp. 243–253

Ogg, Kate, and Harris Rimmer, Susan, 'Introduction to the *Research Handbook on Feminist Engagement with International Law*', in Kate Ogg and Susan Harris Rimmer (eds.) *Research Handbook on Feminist Engagement with International Law* (Cheltenham: Edward Elgar Publishing, 2019), pp. 1–16

Okafor, Obiora, *The African Human Rights System, Activist Forces and International Institutions* (Cambridge, UK: Cambridge University Press, 2010)

Okihiro, Gary Y., *The Columbia Guide to Asian American History* (New York: Columbia University Press, 2001)

Ompteda, Dietrich Heinrich Ludwig von, *Literatur des gesammten sowol naturlichen als positive Volkerrechts*, 2 vols. (Regensburg: Montags Regensburg, 1785)

Onayemi, Adetola, and Elias, Olufemi, 'Aspects of Africa's contribution to the development of international law', in Charles Chernor Jalloh and Olufemi Elias (eds.), *Shielding Humanity: Essays in International Law in Honour of Judge Abdul G. Koroma* (Leiden: Brill, 2015), pp. 591–613

Onuma, Yasuaki, '"Japanese international law" in the postwar period: perspectives on the teaching and research of international law in postwar Japan' (1990) 33 *Japanese Annual of International Law* 25–53

'"Japanese international law" in the prewar period: perspectives on the teaching and research of international law in prewar Japan' (1986) 29 *Japanese Annual of International Law* 23–47

A Transcivilizational Perspective on International Law: Questioning Prevalent Cognitive Frameworks in the Emerging Multi-polar and Multi-civilizational World of the Twenty-First Century (Leiden and Boston: Martinus Nijhoff, 2010)

'When was the law of international society born?' (2000) 2 *Journal of the History of International Law* 1–64

Oppenheim, Lassa, *International Law: A Treatise*, 2 vols. (London: Longmans, Green and Company, 1905)

Orakhelashvili, Alexander (ed.), *Research Handbook of the Theory and History of International Law* (Cheltenham: Edward Elgar Publishing, 2011)

Oreskes, Naomi, 'Why I am a presentist' (2013) 26 *Science in Context* 595–609

Orford, Anne, 'International law and the limits of history', in Wouter Werner, Marieke de Hoon, and Alexis Galan (eds.), *The Law of International Lawyers: Reading Martti Koskenniemi* (Cambridge, UK: Cambridge University Press, 2017), pp. 297–320

'On international legal method' (2013) 1 *London Review of International Law* 166–197

'The past as law or history? The relevance of imperialism for modern international law', in Mark Toufayan, Emmanuelle Tourme-Jouannet, and

Hélène Ruiz Fabri (eds.), *Droit international et nouvelles approches sur le tiers-monde: entre répétition et renouveau (International Law and New Approaches to the Third World: Between Repetition and Renewal)* (Paris: Société de Législation Comparée, 2013), pp. 97–118

Reading Humanitarian Intervention: Human Rights and the Use of Force in International Law (Cambridge, UK: Cambridge University Press, 2003)

Orford, Anne, and Hoffmann, Florian, 'Introduction', in Anne Orford and Florian Hoffmann with Martin Clark (eds.), *The Oxford Handbook of the Theory of International Law* (Oxford: Oxford University Press, 2016)pp. 1–20

Orford, Anne (ed.), *International Law and Its Others* (Cambridge, UK: Cambridge University Press, 2006)

Orford, Anne, and Hoffmann, Florian, with Clark, Martin (eds.), *The Oxford Handbook of the Theory of International Law* (Oxford: Oxford University Press, 2016)

Osterhammel, Jürgen, *The Transformation of the World: A Global History of the Nineteenth Century* (Princeton, NJ: Princeton University Press, 2014)

Otto, Dianne, 'The gastronomics of TWAIL's feminist flavourings: some lunch-time offerings' (2007) 9 *International Community Law Review* 345–352

Oudendijk, Johanna K., 'Van Vollenhoven's "The three stages in the evolution of the law of nations": a case of wishful thinking' (1980) 48 *Tidschrift voor Rechtsgeschiedenis* 3–27

Owada, Hisashi, 'The experience Of Asia with international adjudication' (2005) 9 *Singapore Year Book of International Law* 9–18

Özsu, Umut, 'Determining new selves: Mohammed Bedjaoui on Algeria, western Sahara, and post-classical international law', in Jochen von Bernstorff and Philipp Dann (eds.), *The Battle for International Law in the Decolonization Era* (Oxford: Oxford University Press, 2019), pp. 341–357

'"In the interests of mankind as a whole": Mohammed Bedjaoui's new international economic order' (2015) 6 *Humanity: An International Journal of Human Rights, Humanitarianism, and Development* 129–143

Özsu, Umut, and Skouteris, Thomas, 'International legal histories of the Ottoman Empire: an introduction to the symposium' (2016) 19 *Journal of the History of International Law* 1–4

Pagden, Anthony, 'Legislating for the "whole world that is, in a sense, a commonwealth": conquest, occupation, and "the defence of the innocent"', in Anthony Carty and Janne Elisabeth Nijman (eds.), *Morality and Responsibility of Rulers: European and Chinese Origins of a Rule of Law as Justice for World Order* (Oxford: Oxford University Press, 2018), pp. 132–148

'Series Editor's preface', in Giulio Bartolini (ed.), *A History of International Law in Italy* (Oxford: Oxford University Press, 2020), pp. v–vii

Pahuja, Sundhya, *Decolonising International Law: Development, Economic Growth and the Politics of Universality* (Cambridge, UK: Cambridge University Press, 2011)

'Technologies of empire: IMF conditionality and the reinscription of the north/ south divide' (2000) 13 *Leiden Journal of International Law* 749–813

Paine, Joshua, 'International adjudication as global public good' (2018) 29 *European Journal of International Law* 1223–1249

Parfitt, Rose S., 'The League of Nations', in *Oxford Bibliographies in International Law* (2017), www.oxfordbibliographies.com/view/document/obo-9780199796953/obo-9780199796953-0151.xml

The Process of International Legal Reproduction: Inequality, Historiography, Resistance (Cambridge, UK: Cambridge University Press, 2019)

Parra, Antonio R., *A History of ICSID* (Oxford: Oxford University Press, 2012)

Parry, John T., 'What is the Grotian tradition in international law?' (2014) 35 *University of Pennsylvania Journal of International Law* 299–377

Paulus, Andreas L., 'International law after postmodernism: towards renewal or decline of international law?' (2001) 14 *Leiden Journal of International Law* 727–755

Pedersen, Susan, *The Guardians: The League of Nations and the Crisis of Empire* (Oxford: Oxford University Press, 2015)

Peter, Simone, 'Bertha von Suttner (1843–1914)', in Bardo Fassbender and Anne Peters (eds.), *The Oxford Handbook of the History of International Law* (Oxford: Oxford University Press, 2012), pp. 1145–1149

Peters, Anne, 'A century after the Russian Revolution: its legacy in international law' (2017) 19 *Journal of the History of International Law* 133–146

'Multiperspectivism in and on international law', in *Völkerrechtsblog* (15 January 2019), voelkerrenchtsblog.org/multiperspectivism-in-and-on-international-law/

'Treaties, unequal', in *Max Planck Encyclopedia of Public International Law* (2018), opil.ouplaw.com/view/ 10.1093/law:epil/9780199231690/law-9780199231690-e1495?rskey=jQDTL7&result=1&prd=OPIL, pp. 1–14

Pierre-Cot, Jean, 'Tableau de la pensée juridique américaine' (2006) 110 *Révue generale de droit international public* 537–596

Pillet, Antoine (ed.), *Les fondateurs du droit international* (Paris: V. Giard et E. Briere, 1904)

Pitts, Jennifer, *Boundaries of the International: Law and Empire* (Cambridge, MA: Harvard University Press, 2018)

'International relations and the critical history of international law' (2017) 31 *International Relations* 282–298

Pocock, John G. A., 'Languages and their implications: the transformation of the study of political thought', in *Politics, Language, and Time: Essays on Political Thoughts and History* (New York: Atheneum, 1973), pp. 3–41

Pollock, Frederick, and Maitland, Frederic William, *The History of English Law* (Carmel: Liberty Fund, 1898)

Pomeranz, Kenneth, *The Great Divergence* (Princeton, NJ: Princeton University Press, 2000)

'Histories for a less national age' (2014) 119 *American Historical Review* 1–22

Portolés, Carmen Magallón, and Lisa, Sandra Blasco, 'Mujeres contra la Primera Guerra Mundial: el comité internacional de mujeres por una paz permanente', in Yolanda Gamarra Chopo and Carlos R. Fernando Liesa (eds.), *Los orígenes del derecho internacional contemporáneo: Estudios conmemorativos del centenario de la Primera Guerra Mundial* (Zaragoza: Institución Fermando el Católico, 2015), pp. 157–180

Possing, Birgitte, 'Biography: gistorical', possing.dk/pdf/historicalbio.pdf

Understanding Biographies: On Biographies in History & Stories in Biography, trans. Gaye Kynoch Odense: University Press of Southern Denmark, 2017)

Preiser, Wolfgang, 'Die Epochen der antiken Volkerrechtsgeschichte' (1956) 11 *Juristenzeitung* 737–744

Frühe völkerrechtliche Ordnungen der aussereuropäischen Welt: Ein Beitrag zur Geschichte des Völkerrechts (Wiesbaden: Steiner, 1976)

'History of international law: basic questions and principles', in *Max Planck Encyclopedia of Public International Law* (2007), opil.ouplaw.com/view/10.1093/law:epil/9780199231690/law-9780199231690-e717

'Über die Ursprünge des modernen Völkerrechts', in Erich Bruel (ed.), *Internationalrechtliche und staatsrechtliche Abhandlungen: Festschrift für Walter Schatzel zum 70. Geburtstag* (Düsseldorf: Hermes, 1960), pp. 373–387

Pufendorf, Samuel, *De jure naturae et gentium libri octo* (Londini Scanorum: Sumtibus Adami Junghans oprimebat Vitus Haberegger, 1672)

Purvis, Nigel, 'Critical Legal Studies in public international law' (1991) 32 *Harvard International Law Journal* 81–127

Quidde, Ludwig, 'Histoire de la paix publique en Allemagne au Moyen Âge' (1929) 28 *Recueil des cours de l'Académie de droit international de La Haye* 449–598

Rachel, Samuel, *De jure naturae et gentium dissertationes* (Kiloni, Literis Joachimi Reumani. Acad. Typogr., 1676)

Rajagopal, Balakrishnan, 'Counter-hegemonic international law: rethinking human rights and development as a Third World strategy' (2006) 27 *Third World Quarterly* 767–783

'International law and its discontents: rethinking the global south' (2012) 106 *Proceedings of the Annual Meeting of the American Society of International Law* 176–181

International Law from Below: Development, Social Movements and Third World Resistance (Cambridge, UK: Cambridge University Press, 2003)

'Locating the Third World in cultural geography' (1998–99) 98 *Third World Legal Studies* 1–20

Ramcharan, Bertrand G., *A History of the UN Human Rights Programme and Secretariat* (Leiden: Brill/Nijhoff, 2020)

Ranke, Leopold von, 'Introduction', in *Histories of Latin and Germanic Nations 1494–1514* (London: G. Bell & Sons, 1887; first published 1824)

Rasmussen, Morten, 'From international law to a constitutionalist dream? The history of European law and the European Court of Justice (1950 to 1993)', in Ignacio de la Rasilla and Jorge E. Viñuales (eds.), *Experiments in International Adjudication: Historical Accounts* (Cambridge, UK: Cambridge University Press, 2019), pp. 287–312

Rasulov, Akbar, 'International law and the poststructuralist challenge' (2000) 19 *Leiden Journal of International Law* 799–827

'New Approaches to International Law: images of a genealogy', in José Maria Beneyto and David Kennedy (eds.), *New Approaches to International Law: The European and the American Experiences* (The Hague: T. M. C. Asser Press, 2013), pp. 151–191

Ratner, Steven R., 'Law promotion beyond law talk: the Red Cross, persuasion, and the laws of war' (2011) 22 *European Journal of International Law* 459–506

Ratner, Steven R., and Slaughter, Anne-Marie, 'Appraising the methods of international law: a prospectus for readers' (1999) 93 *American Journal of International Law* 291–302

(eds.), *The Methods of International Law: A Prospectus for Readers* (Washington, DC: American Society of International Law, 2004)

Rech, Walter, *Enemies of Mankind: Vattel's Theory of Collective Security* (Leiden: Martinus Nijhoff, 2013)

Rechid, Ahmed, 'L'Islam et le droit des gens' (1937) 60 *Recueil des cours de l'Académie de droit international de La Haye* 371–506

Redslob, Robert, *Histoire des grands principes du droit des gens depuis l'Antiquité jusqu'à la veille de la grande guerre* (Paris: Rousseau, 1923)

Le principe des nationalités les origines, les fondements psychologiques, les forces adverses, les solutions possibles (Paris: Recueil Sirey, 1930)

Reeves, Jesse S., 'First edition of Grotius' De jure belli ac pacis 1625' (1925) 19 *American Journal of International Law* 12–22

'Grotius De jure belli ac pacis: a bibliographical account' (1925) 19 *American Journal of International Law* 251–262

Reiter, Dan, 'Democratic peace theory', in *Oxford Bibliographies in Political Science* (2017), www.oxfordbibliographies.com/view/document/obo-9780199756223/obo-9780199756223-0014.xml

Renders, Hans, and de Haan, Binne (eds.), *Theoretical Discussions of Biography: Approaches from History, Microhistory, and Lifewriting* (Leiden: Brill, 2014)

Resolutions of the First International Congress of Women (The Hague, 1915), wilpf. org/wp-content/uploads/2012/08/WILPF_triennial_congress_1915.pdf

Reynolds, John, and Xavier, Sujith, "'The dark corners of the world": TWAIL and international criminal justice' (2016) 14 *International Criminal Justice* 959–983

Rittich, Kerry, 'Book review: *The Boundaries of International Law: A Feminist Analysis*' (2001) 14 *Leiden Journal of International Law* 935–956

Roberts, Anthea, 'Comparative international law? The role of national courts in creating and enforcing international law' (2011) 60 *International and Comparative Law Quarterly* 57–92

Is International Law International? (Oxford: Oxford University Press, 2017)

Roberts, Lilly Melchior (ed.), *A Bibliography of Legal Festschriften* (The Hague: Martinus Nijhoff, 1972)

Rolin-Jaequemyns, Gustave, 'De l'étude de la législation comparée et du droit international' (1869) 1 *Revue de droit international et de la législation comparée* 1–17

Romano, Cesare P. R., 'International courts', in *Oxford Bibliographies in International Law* (2012), www.oxfordbibliographies.com/view/document/ obo-9780199796953/obo-9780199796953-0046.xml

'Mirage in the desert: regional judicialization in the Arab world', in Ignacio de la Rasilla and Jorge E. Viñuales (eds.), *Experiments in International Adjudication: Historical Accounts* (Cambridge, UK: Cambridge University Press, 2019), pp. 169–190

'The shadow zones of international adjudication', in Cesare P. R. Romano, Karen J. Alter, and Yuval Shany (eds.), *The Oxford Handbook of International Adjudication* (Oxford: Oxford University Press, 2014), pp. 90–110

'Trial and error in international adjudication', in Cesare P. R. Romano, Karen J. Alter, and Yuval Shany (eds.), *The Oxford Handbook of International Adjudication* (Oxford: Oxford University Press, 2014), pp. 111–134

Rosenne, Shabtai (ed.), *League of Nations: Committee of Experts for the Progressive Codification of International Law 1925–1928* (New York: Oceana Publications, 1972)

Roshchin, Eugeny, 'The challenges of "contextualism"', in Andreas Gofas, Inanna Hamati-Ataya, and Nicholas Onuf (eds.), *The SAGE Handbook of the History, Philosophy and Sociology of International Relations* (Los Angeles: SAGE Reference, 2018), pp. 162–175

Rossi, Christopher R., 'The Gulf of Fonseca and international law: condominium or anti-colonial imperialism?' (2018) 3 *Jus Gentium: Journal of International Legal History* 115–153

Whiggish International Law: Elihu Root, the Monroe Doctrine, and International Law in the Americas (Leiden: Brill/Nijhoff, 2019)

Ruskola, Teemu, 'Raping like a state' (2010) 57 *UCLA Law Review* 1477–1536

Ruyssen, Théodore, 'Les caractères sociologiques de la communauté humaine' (1939) 67 *Recueil des cours de l'Académie de droit international de La Haye* 121–232

Sakr, Rafael Lima, 'Beyond history and boundaries: rethinking the past in the present of international economic law' (2019) 22 *Journal of International Economic Law* 57–91

Salokar, Rebecca M., and Volcansek, Mary L., *Women in Law: A Bio-bibliographical Sourcebook* (Westport, CT: Greenwood Press, 1996), pp. 34–37

Sand, Peter H., 'Introduction', in Peter H. Sand, (ed.), *The History and Origin of International Environmental Law* (Cheltenham: Edward Elgar Publishing, 2015)

(ed.), *The History and Origin of International Environmental Law* (Cheltenham: Edward Elgar Publishing, 2015), pp. xiii–xxv

Sands, Philippe, *East West Street: On the Origins of 'Genocide' and 'Crimes against Humanity'* (New York: Alfred A. Knopf, 2016)

'Reflections on international judicialization' (2017) 27 *European Journal of International Law* 885–900

Torture Team: Rumsfeld's Memo and the Betrayal of American Values (London: St. Martin's Press, 2008)

Sastry, K. R. R., 'Hinduism and international law' (1966) 117 *Collected Courses of The Hague Academy of International Law* 507–614.

Saul, Ben (ed.), *The International Covenant on Economic, Social and Cultural Rights: Travaux Preparatoires* (Oxford: Oxford University Press, 2016)

'The legal response of the League of Nations to terrorism' (2006) 4 *Journal of International Criminal Justice* 78–102

Scarfi, Juan Pablo, *The Hidden History of International Law in the Americas: Empire and Legal Networks* (Oxford: Oxford University Press, 2017)

Scelle, Georges, *Précis de droit des gens : principes et systematique* (Paris: Librairie du Recueil Sirey, 1932)

'Règles générales du droit de la paix' (1934) 46 *Recueil des cours de l'Académie de La Haye* 331–703

Schabas, William A., *The Trial of the Kaiser* (Oxford: Oxford University Press, 2018)

Schachter, Oscar, 'Alona Evans' (1980) 74 *American Journal of International Law* 891–892

'The invisible college of international lawyers' (1977) 72 *Northwestern University School of Law Review* 217–226

Schill, Stephan W., Tams, Christian J., and Hofmann, Rainer (eds.), *International Investment Law and History* (Cheltenham: Edward Elgar Publishing, 2018)

Schlinder, Dietrich, 'Contribution à l'étude des facteurs sociologiques et psychologiques du droit international (1933) 46 *Recueil des cours de l'Académie de
droit international de La Haye* 229–326

Schmalenbach, Kirsten, 'International organizations or institutions, general
aspects', in *Max Planck Encyclopedia of Public International Law* (2014),
opil.ouplaw.com/view/10.1093/law:epil/9780199231690/law-
9780199231690-e499

Schmitt, Carl, *The Nomos of the Earth in the International Law of the* Jus Publicum
Europaeum trans. G. L. Ulmen (New York: Telos Press, 2003)

Schonberger, Howard, 'Purposes and ends in history: presentism and the new left'
(1974) 7 *The History Teacher* 448–458

Schreuer, Christoph, 'The waning of the sovereign state: towards a new paradigm
for international law' (1993) 4 *European Journal of International Law*
447–471

Schwarzenberger, George, 'The standard of civilization in international law' (1955)
8 *Current Legal Problems* 212–234

Scobbie, Iain, 'Out of the shadows: an appreciation of Sir Elihu Lauterpacht's
contribution to the doctrine of international law' (2017) 87 *British
Yearbook of International Law* 1–17

'Redefining European tradition' (2013) 107 *Proceedings of the American Society
of International Law* 382–385

'Sir Elihu Lauterpacht: a celebration of his life and work' (2017), ejiltalk.org/sir-
elihu-lauterpacht-a-celebration-of-his-life-and-work/

Scott, James Brown, *The Catholic Conception of International Law: Francisco de
Vitoria, Founder of the Law of Nations; Francisco Suárez, Founder of the
Modern Philosophy of Law in General and in Particular of the Law of
Nations* (Washington, DC: Georgetown University Press, 1934)

'The classics of international law' (1909) 3 *American Journal of International
Law* 701–707

(ed.), *The Classics of International Law*, 22 vols. (Washington, DC: Carnegie
Endowment for International Peace, 1911–50)

'Preface', in Richard Zouche, *Iuris et iudicii fecialis, sive, iuris inter gentes, et
quaestionum de eodem explicatio*, ed. Thomas Erskine Holland, Classics of
International Law 1 (Washington, DC: Carnegie Institution, 1911)

Séailles, Gabriel, *La philosophie de Charles Renouvier: introduction à l'étude du
néo-criticisme* (Paris: Felix Alcan, 1905)

Sellars, Kirsten, 'Tokyo Trials', in *Oxford Bibliographies in International Law*
(2019), www.oxfordbibliographies.com/view/document/obo-9780199796953/
obo-9780199796953-0182.xml

Shany, Yuval, 'No longer a weak department of power? Reflection on the emergence of a new international judiciary' (2009) 20 *European Journal of
International Law* 73–91

Sicilianos, Linos-Alexander, and Skouteris, Thomas (eds.), 'Symposium – the European tradition in international law: Nicolas Politis' (2012) 23 *European Journal of International Law* 215–273

Siegelberg, Mira L., *Statelessness: A Modern History* (Cambridge, MA: Harvard University Press, 2020)

Simma, Bruno, 'Editorial' (1992) 3 *European Journal of International Law* 215–218

Simma, Bruno, et al., 'The European tradition in international law: Alfred Verdross' (1995) 6 *European Journal of International Law* 32–115

Simpson, Gerry, *Great Powers and Outlaw States: Unequal Sovereigns in the International Legal Order* (Cambridge, UK: Cambridge University Press, 2004)

Sinclair, Guy Fiti, *To Reform the World: International Organizations and the Making of Modern States* (Oxford: Oxford University Press, 2017)

Singer, Joseph W., 'Legal realism now' (1988) 76 *California Law Review* 465–544

Singh, Nagendra, *India and International Law* (Delhi: S. Chand, 1969)

Singh, Prabhakar, 'Reading RP Anand in the post-colony: between resistance and appropiation', in Jochen von Bernstorff and Philipp Dann (eds.), *The Battle for International Law in the Decolonization Era* (Oxford: Oxford University Press, 2019), pp. 297–318

Singh, Sahib, 'The critic(al subject)', in Wouter Werner, Marieke de Hoon, and Alexis Galán (eds.), *The Law of International Layers: Reading Martti Koskenniemi* (Cambridge, UK: Cambridge University Press, 2017), pp. 197–224

Sinha, Prakash S., 'Perspective of the newly independent states on the binding quality of international law' (1965) 14 *International and Comparative Law Quarterly* 121–131

Skinner, Quentin, *Hobbes and the Republican Liberty* (Cambridge, UK: Cambridge University Press, 2008)

'Meaning and understanding in the history of ideas' (1969) 8 *History and Theory* 3–53

'Motives, intentions and the interpretations of texts', in James Tully (ed.), *Meaning and Context: Quentin Skinner and His Critics* (Princeton, NJ: Princeton University Press, 1988), pp. 68–78

'Sir Geoffrey Elton and the practice of history' (1997) 7 *Transactions of the Royal Historical Society* 301–316

Visions of Politics: Regarding Method (Cambridge, UK: Cambridge University Press, 2002)

Skouteris, Thomas, 'Engaging history in international law', in David Kennedy and José M. Beneyto (eds.), *New Approaches to International Law: The European and American Experiences* (The Hague: T. M. C. Asser Press, 2011), pp. 99–121

'FIN de NAIL: New Approaches to International Law and its impact on contemporary international legal scholarship' (1997) 10 *Leiden Journal of International Law* 415–420

'The idea of progress', in Anne Orford and Florian Hoffmann with Martin Clark (eds.), *The Oxford Handbook of the Theory of International Law* (Oxford: Oxford University Press, 2016), pp. 939–953

'New Approaches to International Law', in *Oxford Bibliographies in International Law* (2011), www.oxfordbibliographies.com/view/document/obo-9780199796953/obo-9780199796953-0012.xml

The Notion of Progress in International Law Discourse (The Hague: T. M. C. Asser Press, 2010)

'The turn to history in international law', in *Oxford Bibliographies in International Law* (2017), www.oxfordbibliographies.com/view/document/obo-9780199796953/obo-9780199796953-0154.xml

'What is progress in international law?', in Anne Orford and Florian Hoffmann with Martin Clark (eds.), *The Oxford Handbook of the Theory of International Law* (Oxford: Oxford University Press, 2016), pp. 939–953

Skouteris, Thomas, and Tallgren, Immi, 'Editors' introduction', in Thomas Skouteris and Immi Tallgren (eds.), *New Histories of International Criminal Law* (Oxford: Oxford University Press, 2019), pp. 1–15

Slaughter, Anne-Marie, 'A global community of courts' (2003) 44 *Harvard International Law Journal* 191–219

A New World Order (Princeton, NJ: Princeton University Press, 2004)

Sloss, David L., Ramsey, Michael D., and Dodge, William S. (eds.), *International Law in the U.S. Supreme Court: Continuity and Change* (Cambridge, UK: Cambridge University Press, 2011)

Sluga, Glenda, 'Female and national self-determination: a gender re-reading of "the apogee of nationalism"' (2000) 6 *Nations and Nationalism* 495–521

Internationalism in the Age of Nationalism (Philadelphia: University of Pennsylvania Press, 2013)

'Madame de Stael and the transformation of European politics 1812–1817' (2015) 37 *International History Review* 142–166

'On the historical significance of the presence, and absence, of women at the Congress of Vienna 1814–1815' (2014) 25 *L'homme* 49–62.

Sluga, Glenda, and James, Carolyn, *Women, Diplomacy and International Politics since 1500* (London: Routledge, 2015)

Smeltzer, Joshua, 'On the use and abuse of Francisco de Vitoria: James Brown Scott and Carl Schmitt' (2018) 20 *Journal of the History of International Law* 345–372

Sornarajah, Muthucumaraswamy, 'On fighting for global justice: the role of a Third World international lawyer' (2016) 37 *Third World Quarterly* 1972–1989

Southgate, Beverley, 'Postmodernism', in Aviezer Tucker (ed.), *A Companion to the Philosophy of History and Historiography* (Hoboken, NJ: Wiley-Blackwell, 2009), pp. 540–549

Spengler, Oswald, *Der Untergang des Abendlandes: Umrisse einer Morphologie der Weltgeschichte* (Munich: H. Beck, 1923)

Spiermann, Ole, 'The history of Article 38 of the Statute of the International Court of Justice: "a purely platonic discussion"?', in Jean d'Aspremont and Samantha Besson (eds.), *The Oxford Handbook of the Sources of International Law* (Oxford: Oxford University Press, 2017), pp. 165–178

Spoerhase, Carlos, and King, Colin G., 'Historical fallacies of historians', in Aviezer Tucker (ed.), *A Companion to the Philosophy of History and Historiography* (London: Blackwell, 2009), pp. 274–284

Stahn, Carsten, 'Re-constructing history through courts? Legacy in international criminal justice' (9 June 2015), ssrn.com/abstract=2616491

Stapelbroek, Koen, 'Trade, chartered companies, and mercantile associations', in Bardo Fassbender and Anne Peters (eds.), *The Oxford Handbook of the History of International Law* (Oxford: Oxford University Press, 2012), pp. 338–358

Stearns, Peter N., 'Periodization in world history teaching: identifying the big changes' (1987) 20 *The History Teacher* 561–580

Stefano, Giovanni, 'Time factor and territorial disputes', in Marcelo Kohen and Mamadou Hébié (eds.), *Research Handbook on Territorial Disputes in international Law* (Cheltenham: Edward Elgar Publishing, 2018), pp. 397–416

Steiger, Heinhard, *Die Ordnung der Welt: Eine Völkerrechtsgeschichte des Karolingischen Zeitalters (741 bis 840)* (Cologne: Böhlau Verlag, 2010)

'From the international law of Christianity to the international law of the world citizen – reflections on the formation of the epochs of the history of international law' (2001) 3 *Journal of the History of International Law* 180–193

'Universality and continuity in international public law', in Thilo Marauhn and Heinhard Steiger (eds.), *Universality and Continuity in International Law* (The Hague: Eleven International Publishing, 2011), pp. 13–43

Stein, Arthur A., 'Neoliberal institutionalism', in Christian Reus-Smit and Duncan Snidal (eds.), *The Oxford Handbook of International Relations* (Oxford: Oxford University Press, 2008), pp. 201–221

Stern, Phillip J., '"Bundles of hyphens": corporations as legal communities in the early modern British Empire', in Lauren Benton and Richard J. Ross (eds.), *Legal Pluralism and Empires 1500–1800* (New York: New York University Press, 2013), pp. 21–47

Stone, Julius, 'Problems confronting sociological enquiries concerning international law' (1956) 89 *Recueil des cours de l'Académie de droit international de La Haye* 61–180

'A sociological perspective on international law', in Ronald St J. Macdonald and Douglas M. Johnston (eds.), *The Structure and Process of International Law: Essays in Legal Philosophy, Doctrine, and Theory* (The Hague: Martinus Nijhoff, 1983), pp. 263–304

Stone, Lawrence, 'Prosopography' (1971) 100 *Daedalus* 46–79

'The return of the narrative: reflections on a new old history' (1979) 85 *Past and Present* 3–24

Stradling, Robert, *Multiperspectivity in History Teaching: A Guide for Teachers* (Strasbourg: Council of Europe Press, 2003)

Sunter, Andrew F. 'TWAIL as naturalized epistemological inquiry' (2007) 20 *Canadian Journal of Law & Jurisprudence* 475–507.

Swatek-Evenstein, Mark, *A History of Humanitarian Intervention* (Cambridge, UK: Cambridge University Press, 2020)

Swepston, Lee, *The Foundations of Modern International Law on Indigenous and Tribal Peoples: The Preparatory Documents of the Indigenous and Tribal Peoples Convention, and Its Development through Supervision* (Leiden and Boston: Brill/Nijhoff, 2015)

Syatauw, J. J. G., *Some Newly Established Asian States and the Development of International Law* (The Hague: Martinus Nijhoff, 1961)

Taha, Mia, 'Decolonization in international law', in *Oxford Bibliographies in International Law* (2019), www.oxfordbibliographies.com/view/document/obo-9780199796953/obo-9780199796953-0195.xml.

Takahashi, Susumu, 'Le droit international dans l'histoire du Japon' (1901) 3 *Revue de droit international et de la législation comparée* 188–201

Tallgren, Immi, '*Voglio una donna!* On rewriting the history of international criminal justice with the help of women who committed international crimes', in Immi Tallgren and Thomas Skouteris (eds.), *The New Histories of International Criminal Law* (Oxford: Oxford University Press, 2019), pp. 110–129

Tallgren, Immi, and Skouteris, Thomas (eds.), *The New Histories of International Criminal Law: Retrials* (Oxford: Oxford University Press, 2017)

Tams, Christian J., 'The "international community" as a legal concept', in Jean d'Aspremont and Sahib Singh (eds.), *Concepts for International Law – Contributions to Disciplinary Thought* (Northampton, MA: Edward Elgar Publishing, 2019), pp. 505–523

'World peace through international adjudication?', in Heinz-Gerhard Justenhoven and Mary E. O'Connell (eds.), *Peace through Law: Reflections on* Pacem in Terris *from Philosophy, Law, Theology, and Political Science* (Baden-Baden: Nomos, 2016), pp. 215–254

Tams, Christian J., and Fitzmaurice, Malgosia, *Legacies of the Permanent Court of International Justice* (Leiden: Martinus Nijhoff/Brill, 2013)

Tanaka, Yuki, McCormack, Timothy L. H., and Simpson, Gerry (eds.), *Beyond Victor's Justice? The Tokyo War Crimes Trials Revisited* (Leiden: Martinus Nijhoff, 2011)

Taramundi, Dolores Morondo, 'Mary Wollstonecraft (1759–1797): the undutiful daughter of the Enlightenment and her loud demands for justice', in Kasey McCall-Smith, Jan Wouters, and Felipe Gómez Isa (eds.), *The Faces of Human Rights* (Oxford: Hart Publishing, 2019), pp. 41–50

Taube, Michel de, 'Études sur le développement historique du droit international dans l'Europe orientale' (1926) 11 *Recueil des cours de l'Académie de droit international de La Haye* 341–536

'L'apport de Byzance au développement du droit international occidental' (1939) 67 *Recueil des cours de l'Académie de droit international de La Haye* 233–340

'Les origines de l'arbitrage international: Antiquité et Moyen Âge' (1932) 42 *Recueil des cours de l'Académie de droit international de La Haye* 1–116

Taylor, Leonard Francis, *Catholic Cosmopolitanism and Human Rights* (Cambridge, UK: Cambridge University Press, 2020)

Teubner, Gunther, *Law As an Autopoietic System* (Oxford:Blackwell, 1989)

Thierry, Hubert, et al., 'The European tradition in international law: Georges Scelle' (1990) 1 *European Journal of International Law* 193–249

Thomas, Tracy A., and Boisseau, Tracey J., 'Introduction: law, history, and feminism', in Tracy A. Thomas and Tracey J. Boisseau (eds.), *Feminist Legal History: Essays on Women and Law* (New York: New York University Press, 2011), pp. 1–32

Thompson, Edward P., *The Making of the English Working Class* (New York: Pantheon Books, 1963)

Thompson, Hope K., 'Book review: *League of Nations*' (1919) 13 *American Journal of International Law* 627–630

Tickner, Judith Ann, *Gender in International Relations: Feminist Perspectives on Achieving Global Security* (Columbia, NY: Columbia University Press, 1992)

Todorov, Tzvetan, *La conquête de l'Amérique: la question de l'autre* (Paris: Seuil, 1982)

Tolley, Howard B., *The International Commission of Jurists: Global Advocates for Human Rights* (Philadelphia: University of Pennsylvania Press, 1994)

Toufayan, Mark, 'When British justice (in African colonies) points two ways: on dualism, hybridity, and the genealogy of juridical negritude in Taslim Olawale Elias', in Oche Onazi (ed.), *African Legal Theory and Contemporary Problems* (Dordrecht: Springer, 2014), pp. 31–70

Toufayan, Mark, Tourme-Jouannet, Emmanuelle, and Ruiz-Fabri, Hélène (eds.), *Droit international et nouvelles approches sur le tiers-monde: entre répétition et renouveau (International Law and New Approaches to the Third World:*

Between Repetition and Renewal) (Paris: Société de Législation Comparée, 2013)

Tourme-Jouannet, Emmanuelle, 'Les différentes étapes pour la reconnaissance des droits des femmes: droits des femmes et droit international de la reconnaissance', in Emmanuelle Tourme-Jouannet et al. (eds.), *Féminisme(s) et droit international: études du réseau Olympe* (Paris: Société de Législation Comparée, 2016), pp. 467–482

Tourme-Jouannet, Emmanuelle, Gaurier, Dominique, and Toublanc, Alix (eds.), *Histoire globale des idées internationalists: recueil de textes* (2017), globalhistoryof internationallaw.wordpress.com

Tourme-Jouannet, Emmanuelle, and Peters, Anne, 'The Journal of the History of International Law: a forum for new research' (2014) 16 *Journal of the History of International Law* 1–8

Emmanuelle, Jouannet, et al. (eds.), *Féminisme(s) et droit international: études du réseau Olympe* (Paris: Société de Législation Comparée, 2016)

Toynbee, Arnold, *A Study of History*, 12 vols. (Oxford: Oxford University Press, 1934–61)

Trachtman, Joel P., *The Future of International Law: Global Government* (Cambridge, UK: Cambridge University Press, 2013)

Trelles, Camilo Barcia, 'Fernando Vazquez de Menchaca (1512–1569): l'école espagnole du droit international du XVIe siècle' (1939) 67 *Recueil des cours de l'Académie de droit international de La Haye* 429–534

'Francisco de Vitoria et l'école moderne du droit international' (1927) 17 *Recueil des cours de l'Académie de droit international de La Haye* 109–342

'Francisco Suarez (1548–1617): les théologiens espagnols du XVIe siècle et l'école moderne du droit international' (1933) 43 *Recueil des cours de l'Académie de droit international de La Haye* 385–554

'La doctrine de Monroe dans son développement historique particulièrement en ce qui concerne les relations interamericaines' (1930) 32 *Recueil des cours de l'Académie de droit international de La Haye* 391–606

Tridgell, Susan, *Understanding Ourselves: The Dangerous Art of Biography* (Oxford: Peter Lang, 2004)

Trindade, Antônio A. C., *The Contribution of Latin American Legal Doctrine to the Progressive Development of International Law* (Leiden: Brill, 2016)

Troebst, Stefan, 'Eastern Europe's imprint on modern international law', in Annalisa Ciampi (ed.), *History and International Law: An Intertwined Relationship* (Cheltenham: Edward Elgar Publishing, 2019), pp. 22–43

True, Jacqui, 'The ethics of feminism', in Christian Reus-Smit and Duncan Snidal (eds.), *The Oxford Handbook of International Relations* (Oxford: Oxford University Press, 2008), pp. 408–420

Truyol y Serra, Antonio, 'Don Antonio de Luna García (1901–1967)', in *Estudios de derecho internacional: homenaje a D. Antonio de Luna* (Madrid: C.S.I.C., Instituto Francisco de Vitoria, 1968), pp. 9–31

'Genèse et structure de la société international' (1959) 96 *Recueil des cours de l'Académie de droit international de La Haye* 553–642

Histoire du droit international public (Paris: Economica, 1998)

Historia del derecho internacional público (Madrid: Tecnos, 1998)

Tuck, Richard, *The Rights of War and Peace: Political Thought and the International Order from Grotius and Kant* (Oxford: Oxford University Press, 1999)

Tully, James (ed.), *Meaning and Context: Quentin Skinner and His Critics* (Princeton, NJ: Princeton University Press, 1988)

Unger, Roberto M., *The Critical Legal Studies Movement: Another Time, a Greater Task* (London: Verso, 2015)

Knowledge and Politics (New York: Free Press, 1976)

Union of International Associations (ed.), *Yearbook of International Organizations* (Leiden: Brill, 2020), also available at uia.org/ybio/

Vadi, Valentina, 'International law and its histories: methodological risks and opportunities' (2017) 58 *Harvard International Law Journal* 311–352

'Perspective and scale in the architecture of international legal history' (2019) 30 *European Journal of International Law* 53–72

War and Peace: Alberico Gentili and the Early Modern Law of Nations (Leiden: Brill/Nijhoff, 2020)

Valverde, Mariana, 'The rescaling of feminist analyses of law and state power: from (domestic) subjectivity to (transnational) governance networks' (2014) 4 *University of California Irvine Law Review* 325–352

Van der Linden, Mieke, *The Acquisition of Africa (1870–1914): The Nature of Nineteenth-Century International Law* (Leiden: Brill/Nijhoff, 2017)

Van Hulle, Inge, 'Imperial consolidation through arbitration: territorial and boundary disputes in Africa (1870–1914)', in Ignacio de la Rasilla and Jorge E. Viñuales (eds.), *Experiments in International Adjudication: Historical Accounts* (Cambridge, UK: Cambridge University Press, 2019), pp. 55–75

Van Hulle, Inge, and Lesaffer, Randall (eds.), *International Law in the Long Nineteenth Century 1776–1914: From the Public Law of Europe to Global International Law?* (Leiden: Brill/Nijhoff, 2019)

Van Ittersum, Martine Julia, *Profit and Principle: Hugo Grotius, Natural Rights Theories and the Rise of Dutch Power in the East Indies 1595–1605* (Leiden: Brill, 2006)

Vattel, Emer de, *Le droit des gens, ou principes de la loi naturelle, appliqués à la conduite et aux affaires des nations et des souverains* (London: Neuchâtel, 1758)

Vec, Miloš, 'National and transnational legal evolutions – teaching history of international law', in Kjell Å. Modéer and Per Nilsén (eds.), *How to Teach Comparative European History* (Lund: Jurisförlaget, 2011), pp. 25–38

'Sources in the 19th century European tradition: the myth of positivism', in Jean d'Aspremont and Samantha Besson (eds.), *The Oxford Handbook of the Sources of International Law* (Oxford: Oxford University Press, 2017), pp. 121–145

Vellacot, Jo, 'A place for pacifism and transnationalism in feminist theory: the early work of the Women's International League for Peace and Freedom' (1993) 2 *Women's History Review* 23–56

Venzke, Ingo 'Possibilities of the past: histories of the NIEO and the travails of critique' (2018) 20 *Journal of the History of International Law* 263–302.

Verdebout, Agatha, 'The contemporary discourse on the use of force in the nineteenth century: a diachronic and critical analysis' (2014) 1 *Journal on the Use of Force and International Law* 223–246

Verosta, Stephan, 'International law in Europe and western Asia between 100 and 650 A.D.' (1964) 113 *Recueil des cours de l'Académie de droit international de La Haye* 485–620

'Regionen und Perioden der Geschichte des Volkerrechts' (1979) 30 *Österreichische Zeitschrift für öffentliches Recht und Volkerrecht* 1–21

Verzijl, Jan Hendrik Willem, *International Law in Historical Perspective*, 11 vols. (Leiden: Martinus Nijhoff, 1968–79)

'Western European influence on the foundations of international law', in Jan Hendrik Willem Verzijl (ed.), *International law in Historical Perspective* (Leiden: A. W. Sijthoff, 1968)

Vieira, Monica Brito, 'Mare liberum vs. mare clausum: Grotius, Freitas and Selden's debate on dominion over the sea' (2003) 64 *Journal of the History of Ideas* 361–377

Vinogradoff, Paul, 'Historical types of international law' (1923) 1 *Bibliotheca Visseriana* 1–70

Viñuales, Jorge E. (ed.), *The UN Friendly Relations Declaration at 50: An Assessment of the Fundamental Principles of International Law* (Cambridge, UK: Cambridge University Press, 2021)

Vitoria, Francisco de, *De Indis et de Iure Belli Relectiones* (Washington, DC: The Carnegie Institution of Washington, 1917)

Vitoria: Political Writings, ed. and trans. Anthony Pagden and Jeremy Lawrance (Cambridge, UK: Cambridge University Press, 1992)

Vlugt, Willem van der, 'L'œuvre de Grotius et son influence sur le développement du droit international' (1925) 7 *Recueil des cours de l'Académie de droit international de La Haye* 395–510

Vollenhoven, Cornelis Van, *The Three Stages in the Evolution of the Law of Nations* (The Hague: Martinus Nijhoff, 1919)

Vollerthun, Ursula, *The Idea of International Society: Erasmus, Vitoria, Gentili and Grotius*, ed. James L. Richardson (Cambridge, UK: Cambridge University Press, 2017)

Von Bernstorff, Jochen, 'International legal history and its methodologies: how (not) to tell the story of the many lives and deaths of the *ius ad* bellum', in Andreas von Arnauld (ed.), *Völkerrechtsgeschichte(n): Historische Narrative und Konzepte im Wandel* (Berlin: Duncker & Humblot, 2017), pp. 39–52

  The Public International Law Theory of Hans Kelsen: Believing in Universal Law (Cambridge, UK: Cambridge University Press, 2010)

Von Bernstorff, Jochen, and Dann, Philipp (eds.), *The Battle for International Law: South–North Perspectives on the Decolonization Era* (Oxford: Oxford University Press, 2019)

Von Bogdandy, Armin, et al., *Handbuch ius publicum europaeum*, 6 vols. (Heidelberg: C. F. Muller, 2007–16)

Wagner, Markus, 'Non-state actors', in *Max Planck Encyclopedia of Public International Law* (2013), opil.ouplaw.com/view/10.1093/law:epil/9780199231690/law-9780199231690-e1445

Walker, Neil, 'Late sovereignty in the European Union', in Neil Walker (ed.), *Sovereignty in Transition* (London: Bloomsbury Publishing, 2003), pp. 3–32

Wallerstein, Immanuel, *The Modern World-System: Capitalist Agriculture and the Origins of the European World-Economy in the Sixteenth Century* (New York: Academic Press, 1976)

Walsh, Edmund A., 'L'évolution de la diplomatie aux États-Unis' (1939) 69 *Recueil des cours de l'Académie de droit international de La Haye* 149–236

Walter, Christian, 'Subjects of international law', in *Max Planck Encyclopedia of Public International Law* (2007), opil.ouplaw.com/view/10.1093/law:epil/9780199231690/law-9780199231690-e1476

Wambaugh, Sarah, *A Monograph on Plebiscites: With a Collection of Official Documents* (Oxford : Oxford University Press, 1920)

  La pratique des plébiscites internationaux (Paris: Hachette, 1928)

  Plebiscites since the World War: With a Collection of Official Documents (Washington, DC: Carnegie Endowment for International Peace, 1933)

  The Saar Plebiscite: With a Collection of Official Documents (Cambridge, MA: Harvard University Press, 1940)

Wansink, Bjorn, et al., 'Where does teaching multiperspectivity in history education begin and end? An analysis of the uses of temporality' (2018) 46 *Theory & Research in Social Education* 495–527

Ward, Robert P., *An Inquiry into the Foundations and Origins of the Law of Nations from the Times of the Greeks and the Romans to the Age of Grotius*, 2 vols. (London: Butterworth, 1795)

Warren, Christopher N., 'Henry V, Anachronism, and the history of international law', in Lorna Hutson (ed.), *The Oxford Handbook of English Law and Literature 1500–1700* (Oxford: Oxford University Press, 2017), pp. 709–727
  'History, literature, and authority in international law', in Maksymilian Del Mar, Bernadette Meyler and Simon Stern (eds.), *The Oxford Handbook of Law and Humanities* (Oxford: Oxford University Press, 2020), pp. 565–582
Webb, Philippa, 'British contribution to the law on immunity', in Robert McCorquodale and Jean-Pierre Gauci (eds.), *British Influences on International Law 1915–2015* (Leiden: Brill/Nijhoff, 2016), pp. 145–166
Weeramantry, Christopher Gregory, *Islamic Jurisprudence: An International Perspective* (London: Macmillan, 1988)
  Towards One World: The Memoirs of Judge C. G. Weeramantry, 3 vols. (Colombo: Weeramantry International Centre for Peace Education and Research, 2010–14)
Weil Afonso, Henrique, and Quadros de Magalhães, José Luiz, 'The Third World, history and international law' (2013) 8 *Anuário brasileiro de direito internacional* 107–125
Weiler, Joseph H. H., 'The geology of international law – governance, democracy and legitimacy' (2004) 64 *Zeitschrift für ausländisches öffentliches Recht und Völkerrecht* 547–562
Wendt, Alexander, 'Anarchy is what states make of it: the social construction of power politics' (1992) 46 *International Organization* 391–425
Werner, Wouter, de Hoon, Marieke, and Galán, Alexis (eds.), *The Law of International Lawyers: Reading Martti Koskenniemi* (Cambridge, UK: Cambridge University Press, 2017)
Weststeijn, Arthur, 'Provincializing Grotius: international law and empire in a seventeenth-century Malay mirror', in Martti Koskenniemi, Walter Rech, and Manuel Jiménez Fonseca (eds.), *International Law and Empire: Historical Explorations* (Cambridge, UK: Cambridge University Press, 2017), pp. 21–38
Wheatley, Natasha, 'Spectral legal personality in interwar international law: on new ways of not being a state' (2017) 35 *Law and History Review* 753–787
Wheaton, Henry, *Elements of International Law: With a Sketch of the History of the Science* (Philadelphia: Carey, Lea & Blanchard, 1836)
  Histoire du progrès des droits de gens depuis la Paix de Westphalie jusqu'au Congrès de Vienne (Leipzig: Brokhaus, 1841)
  History of the Law of Nations in Europe and America: From the Earliest Times to the Treaty of Washington (New York: Gould, Banks & Co., 1842)
White, G. Edward, 'Round and round the bramble bush: from legal realism to critical legal scholarship' (1984) 95 *Harvard Law Review* 1669–1690

White, Hayden, 'The question of narrative in contemporary historical theory' (1984) 23 *History and Theory* 1–33
  Tropics of Discourse: Essays in Cultural Criticism (Baltimore: Johns Hopkins University Press, 1982)
Whitehall, Deborah, 'A rival history of self-determination' (2016) 27 *European Journal of International Law* 719–743
Whitworth, Sandra, 'Feminism', in Christian Reus-Smit and Duncan Snidal (eds.), *The Oxford Handbook of International Relations* (Oxford: Oxford University Press, 2008), pp. 391–403
Wight, Martin, *Four Seminal Thinkers in International Theory: Machiavelli, Grotius, Kant, and Mazzini*, ed.Gabriele Wight and Brian Porter (Oxford: Oxford University Press, 2005)
Williams, Robert A., Jr, *The American Indian in Western Legal Thought: The Discourse of Conquest* (New York: Oxford University Press, 1990)
Wolf, Eric R., *Europe and the People without History* (Los Angeles and Berkeley: University of California Press, 1982)
Wolff, Christian, *Ius gentium methodo scientifi ca pertractatum*, trans. Joseph H. Drake (Washington, DC: Carnegie Institution of Washington, 1934)
  Jus institutiones juris naturae et gentium (Halle: Prostat in Officina Rengeriana, 1750; reprinted Hildesheim, 1972)
Wolfrum, Rüdiger, 'International administrative unions', in *Max Planck Encyclopedia of Public International Law* (2006), opil.ouplaw.com/view/ 10.1093/law:epil/97801992 31690/law-9780199231690-e471
Wood, Gordon S., *The Purpose of the Past: Reflections on the Use of History* (New York: Penguin Press, 2008)
Wright, Quincy, *A Study of War*, 2 vols. (Chicago: University of Chicago Press, 1955)
Yanagihara, Masaharu, 'Significance of the history of the law of nations in Europe and East Asia' (2014) *Recueil des cours de l'Académie de droit international de La Haye* 273–435
Yepes, Jesus Maria, 'La contribution de l'Amérique latine au développement du droit international public et privé' (1928) 32 *Recueil des cours de l'Académie de droit international de La Haye* 691–800
Zapatero, Pablo, 'Legal imagination in Vitoria: the power of ideas' (2009) 11 *Journal of the History of International Law* 221–271
Zarbiyev, Fouad, *Le discours interprétatif en droit international contemporain: un essai critique* (Brussels: Bruylant, 2015)
Zarjevski, Yéfime, *The People Have the Floor: A History of the Inter-Parliamentary Union* (Aldershot: Dartmouth, 1989)
Zelko, Frank, *Make It a Green Peace! The Rise of a Countercultural Environmentalism* (Oxford: Oxford University Press, 2013)

Zewei, Yang, 'Western international law and China's confucianism in the 19th century: collision and integration' (2011) 13 *Journal of the History of International Law* 285–306

Ziegler, Karl Heinz, *Volkerrechtsgeschichte: Ein Studienbuch* (Munich: C. H. Beck, 2007)

Zimmermann, Michel, 'La crise de l'organisation internationale à la fin du Moyen Âge' (1933) 44 *Recueil des cours de l'Académie de droit international de La Haye* 315–438

Zollmann, Jakob, 'African international legal histories—international law in Africa: perspectives and possibilities' (2018) 31 *Leiden Journal of International Law* 897–914

Zolo, Danilo, 'Hans Kelsen: international peace through international law' (1998) 9 *European Journal of International Law* 306–324

Zouche, Richard, Holland, Thomas Erskine, and Brierly, James L., *Iuris et judicii fecialis, sive juris inter gentes, et quaestionum de eodem explication: qua quae ad pacem et bellum inter diversos principes, aut populos spectant, ex praecipuis historico-jure-peritis, exhibentur* (Washington, DC: Carnegie Institute of Washington, 1911)

Zumbansen, Peer, 'Transnational law, evolving', in Jan M. Smits (ed.), *Encyclopedia of Comparative Law*, 2nd ed. (Cheltenham: Edward Elgar Publishing, 2012), pp. 899–925

INDEX

CAMBRIDGE STUDIES IN INTERNATIONAL AND COMPARATIVE LAW

Books in the Series

For EU product safety concerns, contact us at Calle de José Abascal, 56–1°, 28003 Madrid, Spain or eugpsr@cambridge.org.

www.ingramcontent.com/pod-product-compliance
Ingram Content Group UK Ltd.
Pitfield, Milton Keynes, MK11 3LW, UK
UKHW020404140625
459647UK00020B/2630